Cases and Materials in Company Law

Fifth edition

L S Sealy

S J Berwin Professor of Corporate Law,
University of Cambridge;
Barrister and Solicitor (New Zealand)

Butterworths
London, Dublin, Edinburgh
1992

United Kingdom	Butterworth & Co (Publishers) Ltd, 88 Kingsway, LONDON WC2B 6AB and 4 Hill Street, EDINBURGH EH2 3JZ
Australia	Butterworths, SYDNEY, MELBOURNE, BRISBANE, ADELAIDE, PERTH, CANBERRA and HOBART
Belgium	Butterworth & Co (Publishers) Ltd, BRUSSELS
Canada	Butterworths Canada Ltd, TORONTO and VANCOUVER
Ireland	Butterworth (Ireland) Ltd, DUBLIN
Malaysia	Malayan Law Journal Sdn Bhd, KUALA LUMPUR
New Zealand	Butterworths of New Zealand Ltd, WELLINGTON and AUCKLAND
Puerto Rico	Equity de Puerto Rico, Inc, HATO REY
Singapore	Butterworths Asia, SINGAPORE
USA	Butterworth Legal Publishers, AUSTIN, Texas; BOSTON, Massachusetts; CLEARWATER, Florida (D & S Publishers); ORFORD, New Hampshire (Equity Publishing); ST PAUL, Minnesota; and SEATTLE, Washington

A CIP Catalogue record for this book is available from the British Library.

ISBN 0 406 60985 3

Printed by Butler & Tanner Ltd, Frome and London

Preface to the First Edition

Although there have been Companies Acts in regular succession from 1844 to the present day, these enactments have never contained more than a partial statement of the law governing the limited liability company. Company law is uncodified, and a student needs to look far beyond the statute for his material. Many traditional principles have roots which go back into the distant past; their origin can sometimes be found in the old law of corporations or of partnership, and sometimes in wider doctrines of equity and contract. Other rules, newer in point of time but quite as fundamental in importance, have been developed on the basis of the Companies Acts, but are not so much an interpretation of specific provisions of the statutes as a revelation of the underlying spirit or genius of the institution whose creation the Acts have made possible. The ultra vires doctrine is one example; and the various rules designed to ensure the maintenance of capital are others; the code of fiduciary duties of promoters and directors, the constitutional rights of members, indeed, the very concept of the company's own personality—all owe their existence to the pioneering decisions of the courts in another age, but find no statement in the Act itself. The first aim of this book is to provide students with a ready means of access to the leading cases in which these principles have been established and developed. Other cases have been included which throw light on more detailed provisions of the Companies Acts presently in force, or on formulae which have by hallowed usage become more or less standard in the modern company's constitutional documents.

A second need of the student which it is hoped that this work will go some way to meet is that of seeing for himself what these documents look like. For a study of the subject which is based only on the statute-book and the law reports is bound to emphasis those things which a company may *not* do on the one hand and things which a company has done badly on the other. It is salutary for the student to be reminded that there is more to company law than its pathology, and that the great majority of companies are well conducted, healthy and prosperous. I have been indeed fortunate in securing the goodwill and ready co-operation of a number of such companies, who have generously allowed me to include the specimen documents from their files which make up the larger part of the Appendix. I am sorry that considerations of space have prevented some of them from being reproduced in full, and that for practical reasons their coloured illustrations and typographical embellishments have had to be sacrificed.

It has been assumed that the reader will have guidance from a text book or course of lectures on company law; for this book is intended to provide supplementary materials for study and illustration rather than to stand on its own. Again, it would have been pointless to endeavour to reproduce the whole text of the Companies Act: this is readily available and it is expected that the student will have his own copy.

LSS

Preface to the Fifth Edition

When the fourth edition of this book was going to press, the Companies Bill 1988 (destined to become the Companies Act 1989) was in the middle of its passage through Parliament. This was the latest in a steady succession of legislative amendments to company law which have seen the subject in a state of continuous flux for over three decades, gradually losing whatever claims it may once have had to shape or focus. This unhappy state of affairs has generally been received by practitioners with resignation and by students with understandable bewilderment. Against such a background, it is vital that every effort should be made to identify the underlying principles which are fundamental to the subject and, perhaps more interestingly, to differentiate between those which seem to be unshakeable and timeless and those which are yielding to change.

In the cases and materials collected in this book I believe that it is possible to see basic principles which fall into each of these categories. Judicial respect for the concepts of corporate personality and limited liability – immortalised by the case of Mr Aron Salomon whose company might, but for a twist of fate, have been celebrating its centenary this year – appears, if anything, to have grown in strength and solidarity over the last two or three decades. But the Companies Act 1989 has dealt a body blow to two other principles of equally ancient respectability – the doctrines of ultra vires and constructive notice – whose demise is bound to have repercussions in large areas of the rest of company law. These innovations and their consequences, about which we can at present only speculate, are discussed at appropriate places in the commentary to the selected materials.

This new edition takes full account of all the statutory changes and new case material published up to the end of February 1992. Among the new decisions that are discussed are some which show the radical new provisions of the Insolvency Acts of 1985–86 and the Company Directors Disqualification Act 1986 in operation: *Re Harris Simons Construction Ltd* (1989), on the administration regime; *Re Produce Marketing Consortium Ltd* (1989), on wrongful trading; *Re Sevenoaks Stationers (Retail) Ltd* (1990), on director disqualification; and *Re MC Bacon Ltd* (1991), on preferences and transactions at an undervalue. In the mainstream of company law, the new cases include *Adams v Cape Industries plc* (1990), *Byng v London Life Association Ltd* (1990), *Caparo Industries plc v Dickman* (1990), *Guinness plc v Saunders* (1990) and *Kuwait Asia Bank EC v National Mutual Life Nominees Ltd* (1991). And, of course, full account is taken of the Companies Act 1989, which implemented the Seventh and Eighth EC Company Law Directives and made many other changes to the law.

Once again, it is a pleasure to acknowledge the help which I have had from Butterworths and their expert staff at all stages of production.

May 1992

LSS

Contents

Acknowledgments

I am grateful to the following for kindly allowing the reproduction of copyright material and commercial documents: Her Majesty's Stationery Office for the statutes, the Rules of the Supreme Court, the Report of the Jenkins Committee on Company Law, the Report of the Cork Committee on Insolvency and the statistical tables; the Registrar of Companies for the certificate of incorporation; the Incorporated Council of Law Reporting for England and Wales for the *Law Reports* and *Weekly Law Reports*; Butterworth & Co (Publishers) Ltd for the *All England Law Reports, Law Journal Reports, Law Times Reports* and *Butterworths Company Law Cases*: the Scottish Council of Law Reporting and Messrs T & T Clark for the *Session Cases*; Lloyd's of London Press Ltd for *Lloyd's Reports*; CCH Editions Ltd for *British Company Cases*; Canada Law Book Ltd for the *Dominion Law Reports*; the Law Book Company Ltd for the *Commonwealth Law Reports* and *Australian Law Journal Reports*; Butterworths Pty Ltd for the *Australian Company Law Reports*; Butterworths of New Zealand for the *New Zealand Law Reports*; the Panel on Take-overs and Mergers for the City Code; Varsity Publications Ltd; Micro Scope plc; the General Electric Company plc; Tricentrol plc; Dunlop Holdings plc; 3i plc; the former NMA Company of New Zealand Ltd; Kleinwort, Benson Ltd; Grant Thornton (formerly Thornton Baker); de Zoete & Bevan Ltd; and the various officers of these companies and firms. De Zoete & Bevan Ltd is part of the Barclays de Zoete Wedd Group, the Barclays Group Investment Bank.

I am particularly grateful to my cousin, Chris Sealy, and his fellow enterpreneurs for allowing me to use the various documents illustrating the remarkable rise to success of their company, Micro Scope. It cannot often have happened that a business should go from a standing start to a full official listing in less than six years, and shortly thereafter be sold on in an agreed bid, at a still further enhanced price, to take its place in the complex network of a major manufacturing enterprise. It gives me great pleasure to demonstrate to my student readers that not all members of the family have chosen a risk-averse way of life (such as legal authorship!).

The case on p 250 is reproduced from *The Times* by permission. The consent of the Controller of Her Majesty's Stationery Office has been obtained for the reproduction of the Tables in Appendix C and the other materials mentioned above.

I wish also to thank my publishers for their help in preparing the tables and index.

The abbreviation 'CA 1985' has been used throughout to refer to the Companies Act 1985, and the letters 'CA' with appropriate dates stand for the earlier and later Companies Acts. 'IA 1985' and 'IA 1986' refer to the Insolvency Acts of 1985 and 1986, respectively, and 'FSA 1986' to the Financial Services Act 1986.

All references to the Companies Act 1985 are to that Act as amended by the Companies Act 1989, even though some of these amendments were not in force at the time of going to press.

LSS

Table of Statutes

Page references printed in **bold** type indicate where a section of an Act is set out in part or in full.

List of Cases

Numbers printed in **bold** type are references to the serial number of cases; page references printed in *italic* type indicate where the case extracts are set out.

xxi

CHAPTER 1

The Company and its Incorporation

A. Introduction

Definition

A company for our purposes is very easily defined.[1] It is the kind of legal entity or corporate body which is brought into being by the registration procedures laid down by the Companies Act 1985 and its predecessors.[2] Its creation is evidenced by the issue of a certificate of incorporation by the Registrar of Companies. Except in a few, rare, cases the last word of its name will be 'Limited' (Ltd) or, in the case of a public company, the unpronounceable abbreviation 'plc' (public limited company).[3] In the United States, the word corresponding to company is 'corporation', and the name normally terminates in that word or 'Incorporated' (Inc), although 'Limited' is sometimes used there, too.

Sources of company law

The first Companies Act was passed in 1844. But it was not concerned with the *creation* of companies: the 'joint stock companies' for whose benefit and regulation it was enacted already existed in considerable numbers, and had been known for over a century. This Act provided for the registration of the 'deed of settlement' of such companies—their principal constitutional document; and in return for registration, they were accorded corporate status, that is, were recognised by the law as entities in their own right. 'Joint stock' companies formed on the basis of a deed of settlement were different from the chartered corporations like the Hudson's Bay Company and the Bank of England, and different again from the statutory companies which sprang up in great numbers early in the nineteenth century to build the nation's railways

---

1 Of course, the word 'company' has other meanings in everyday speech; and we should note in particular the abbreviation 'Co' (and especially '& Co'), which is very commonly used as part of the name of an unincorporated partnership that is not a 'company' in any strict legal sense, and sometimes used even by an individual trader.
2 A company may also be created by Royal Charter and by special Act of Parliament. Most of these companies are a century or more old. A student should note that a few such companies still exist, and bear in mind that the rules of 'company law' which he studies may not always apply to them, e g neither the ultra vires doctrine (below, p 125) nor the winding up procedure (below, p 551) has ever applied to chartered companies. Beyond this, these types of company are mainly of interest in helping to explain some of the more arcane rules of the subject which evolved long ago and have been allowed to survive into modern times.
3 CA 1985, s 25. Exceptions are unlimited companies (s 1(2)(c)) and charitable and similar companies granted a dispensation under s 30. There are Welsh equivalents for 'Limited' and 'plc'—but these alternatives, if used, must be accompanied by a warning for the benefit of the uninitiated of their significance in English (s 351(3) and (4)). The word 'limited' is also used by co-operatives and similar bodies registered under the Industrial and Provident Societies Act 1965.

and canals and docks.[4] They were outsized, unincorporated partnerships, running sometimes into hundreds of members, carefully set up with the aid of clever equity draftsmen so that large-scale ventures could be organised on the basis of a joint or common 'stock' pooled by the participants, and run by directors and managers for the benefit of all concerned. By 1844, they were too important to be ignored or outlawed and too unwieldy to fit at all easily into such everyday legal procedures as litigation; and so the 1844 Act was the first step in giving these companies legal recognition. A decade later, in 1855, a further Act was passed which allowed the shareholders who invested in a company to limit their liability; and a year later a revised statute, the Joint Stock Companies Act 1856, established the framework for the modern-style company, incorporated by the process of registration and enjoying limited liability. The old deed of settlement gave way to the memorandum and articles of association; the constitutional documents which are still the basis of today's companies; and there have been no really major changes either in the institution of 'the company' or in the legislation dealing with it from 1856 to the present day. Of course Parliament has been busy in company affairs from time to time, passing amending and consolidating Acts, each bigger than the last one. But our last fundamental reassessment of the subject took place at the time of the Crimean War.

The companies legislation currently in force dates from 1985, when Parliament made a fresh start by consolidating all the statutory provisions that were then operative into one major Act, the Companies Act 1985, and three minor ones, the Company Securities (Insider Dealing) Act 1985, the Company Directors Disqualification Act 1986 and the Companies Consolidation (Consequential Provisions) Act 1985. But this tidying up exercise achieved very little. The Companies Act 1985—a 'jumbo' enactment of 747 sections and 25 schedules—did not survive long intact: the Insolvency Act 1985 (now almost entirely repealed and replaced by the Insolvency Act 1986) superseded nearly a third of it with sweeping new provisions. Further changes were made by the Financial Services Act 1986, discussed in Chapter 12, below, and the Companies Act 1989—again, a substantial piece of legislation containing 216 sections and 24 schedules. It is an unhappy fact that the volume of companies legislation almost quadrupled in the course of the 1980s.

No Companies Act, however, has ever been a complete code. Much of company law goes back to the days of the deed of settlement companies and the chartered and statutory corporations which flourished in earlier centuries: our textbooks solemnly cite decisions of the courts as old as the *Sutton's Hospital* case of 1612 (10 Co Rep 1a, 23a)! A great deal of the essence and spirit of our company law is derived from this old case-law rather than from anything in the Companies Acts themselves, for the very good reason that those Acts have always assumed the existence of companies, and have taken for granted matters of everyday practice in company affairs and the body of judicial precedent which has grown up over the years. The influence of these background factors has been remarkably persistent; even, sometimes, on matters where business circumstances today are quite different.

In addition to these principles of common law and equity which have evolved independently of statute, there are of course many other rulings of

---

4 The Companies Clauses Consolidation Act 1845, which is still in force, applies to these 'statutory' companies. This Act contains standard provisions which may be incorporated by reference into the particular incorporating Act, so making the procedure shorter and cheaper. For examples of statutory companies, see below, pp 134, 189.

the courts based on the Companies Acts themselves—sometimes on the literal wording of particular sections and sometimes broader interpretations of the general institutional framework which the Acts have established—for instance, and the 'maintenance of capital' rules (below, p 341). And there are also decisions concerned with the interpretation of memoranda and articles of association and other documents and shareholders' resolutions of individual companies. Many of these are of a common or standard type—e g provisions in articles defining the functions of the board of directors, or the terms on which preference shares are issued—and so have significance for company law generally as well as for the parties in the case in question.

In some areas, practice is virtually as important as the law itself. A student of English company law who did not know something of 'the City' and its self-regulating bodies such as The Stock Exchange would gain only an imperfect impression of such matters as public issues of shares and take-over bids. Changes have recently been made, partly through the influence of the EEC and partly as a result of the Financial Services legislation of 1986,[5] which give some legal backing to the bodies which have hitherto regulated affairs in the City without recourse to the law; but their essentially self-regulating character is enshrined in the new legislation and has been acknowledged and endorsed by the courts. And so, even though they may not be in a full sense 'law', reference will be made at appropriate points in this book to the rules and practice of these agencies.

Currently, we must bear in mind the many ways in which the United Kingdom's membership of the EEC is influencing its company law.[6] The objectives of the Treaty of Rome include the facilitating of trade and the removal of barriers to people's freedom to establish their businesses and invest their capital on a basis of equality throughout the Community. To this end, a programme for the 'harmonisation' of the domestic company laws of the member states has been instituted, which seeks to remove the differences of detail between those local laws which might act as impediments to such equality. The Treaty expressly authorises and empowers its organs—the Council and the Commission—to issue 'directives' for this purpose.

In principle, a directive is binding only on the member state, which must implement it by its own legislation; it does not immediately or directly affect individual companies or citizens as a 'source' of law. But directives, even when only in draft stage, cannot be neglected, for they do indicate the lines along which tomorrow's law is likely to develop. And when they have been implemented by domestic legislation, they are sometimes used by the judges as an aid to resolve questions of statutory interpretation.

The directives that have already been implemented by Parliament are listed in the Table below. In addition to these, the latest publication of the Department of Trade and Industry (February 1992) lists eight measures which have either been adopted by the Council or upon which a common position has been agreed, and a further nine which are at various stages of proposal, discussion or draft.

---

5 See below, p 538.
6 The January 1992 issue (vol 13) of *The Company Lawyer* contains a series of articles on the effect of EEC membership on UK company law.

Table of EEC directives which have been implemented by UK legislation

NO	SUBJECT	ENACTED BY	CURRENT REFERENCE
First 68/151	Corporate powers and representation	European Communities Act 1972, s 9	CA 1985, ss 35-35B, 36C, 42
Second 77/91	Capital requirements	CA 1980	CA 1985, passim
Third 78/855	Mergers	SI 1987/1991	CA 1985, Sch 15
Fourth 78/660	Accounts	CA 1981	CA 1985, Pt VII, Schs 4, 5
Sixth 82/891	Demergers	SI 1987/1991	CA 1985, Sch 15
— 79/279	Admission to listing	SI 1984/716	FSA 1986, Pt IV
— 80/390	Listing particulars	SI 1984/716	FSA 1986, Pt IV
— 82/121	Continuing disclosure	SI 1984/716	FSA 1986, Pt IV
UCITS 85/611	Collective investment schemes	FSA 1986	FSA 1986, s 86
Seventh 83/349	Consolidated accounts	CA 1989	CA 1985, Pt VII, Sch 4A
Eighth 84/253	Qualification of auditors	CA 1989	CA 1989, Pt II, Schs 11-14
— 87/345	Mutual recognition of listing particulars	FSA 1986 amendments	FSA 1986 and the 'Yellow Book'
— 89/298	Directive on prospectuses	SI 1981/823 and FSA 1986, Pt V	FSA 1986, Pt V[7]
— 90/211	Mutual recognition of prospectuses	Amendments to Yellow Book	Yellow Book

Community law may also be made by regulations. A regulation, in contrast with a directive, has direct effect as part of the domestic law of each member state, although local legislation may be necessary to supplement a regulation by, for instance, providing administrative facilities. To date, only one regulation has been enacted in the area of company law, Council Regulation No 2137/85 on the European Economic Interest Grouping (EEIG).[8] The EEIG is intended to be used for non-profit-making cross-border ventures for purposes such as joint research and development. The Commission also has plans for a European Company Statute, to be established partly by regulation and partly by directive, which would enable the formation of supra-national companies governed in important respects by EEC rather than local law.

Lastly, reference should be made to the reports of a number of government-appointed committees which have discussed matters relating to company law. Of course, these reports are not 'sources' of law, but the material which they contain is of great interest. Many of the major reforming Companies

---

7 FSA 1986, Pt V is not yet in force.
8 Supplemented by the EEIG Regulations (SI 1989/638), which set out in Sch 1 the full text of the EEC regulation.

Acts in the past were based on such reports, as the Table below shows. But much learning is buried in those other reports which made proposals for change that governments have declined or neglected to implement: the Gedge Report (1954), Jenkins Report (1962) and Bullock Report (1977). No account of the subject of company law would be complete without some mention of this background material.

Law reform committees

Loreburn Committee, reported 1906, leading to Companies Acts of 1907–08
Wrenbury Committee, reported 1918
Greene Committee, reported 1926, leading to Companies Acts of 1928–29
Bodkin Committee, reported 1937 (sharepushing), leading to Prevention of Fraud (Investments) Act 1939
Anderson Committee, reported 1936 (unit trusts)
Cohen Committee, reported 1945, leading to Companies Acts of 1947–48
Gedge Committee, reported 1954 (no par value shares)
Jenkins Committee, reported 1962
Bullock Committee, reported 1977 (employee representation)
Wilson Committee, reported 1980 (financial institutions)
Cork Committee, reported 1982 (insolvency), leading to Insolvency Acts of 1985 and 1986
Gower, *Review of Investor Protection*, reported 1984
Prentice, *Reform of the Ultra Vires Rule*, reported 1986
Dearing, *The Making of Accounting Standards,* reported 1988
Diamond, *A Review of Security Interests in Property,* reported 1989 (company charges).

B. Types of company

The Companies Acts recognise a number of types and classifications of company, which are defined in CA 1985, s 1(2),(3).

1 *Limited and unlimited companies*

An *unlimited company* has no limit on the liability of its members. In other words, they can be called on to satisfy personally the whole of its liabilities to its creditors. In a *limited company*, this liability is restricted by law to an amount fixed by the terms of issue of the shares or by the company's constitutional documents. Unlimited companies are exempt from the statutory obligation to publish their accounts and reports (s 254).

2 *Companies limited by shares and companies limited by guarantee*

There are two types of limited company. In a company *limited by shares* a member is not liable for the company's debts beyond the amount remaining unpaid on his shares. This is, of course, in addition to what he (or a previous owner of the shares) has already paid on those shares. Thus, if a company allots to Smith a share of nominal value £1 'at par' (ie for a price of £1), and 60p is paid to the company by Smith on the issue of that share to him, the maximum potential liability of Smith or any later holder of that share to meet the company's debts is the outstanding balance of 40p. In a company *limited by guarantee* a member is only liable to make a contribution to the assets of the company in the event of its being wound up, and the amount of this contribution (very commonly a nominal sum such as £5) is fixed at the outset by the company's constitution.

3 Public and private companies

A *public company* must state in its memorandum of association that it is a public company and must be formally registered as such (s 1(3)). Only a company limited by shares or by guarantee may be a public company. Public companies have the advantage of being able to offer their shares by advertisement to the public for investment; but they are subject to a greater degree of regulation by the law. A *private company* is any company that is not a public company. The legislation makes a number of concessions for private companies—e g a private company may have only one director while a public company must have at least two (s 282), and a public company is subject to minimum capital requirements (ss 11, 117–118). Only private companies may take advantage of the 'deregulatory' provisions introduced by CA 1989 for the 'elective regime' (CA 1985, s 379A) and unanimous written resolutions (ss 381A–381C). The name of a public company terminates with the designation 'plc', and that of a private company with the word 'Limited'.

There is provision in the Act, Part II, for a company to alter its status (e g from limited to unlimited, or from private to public) by re-registration.

The above are classifications formally made by the Act. In addition, a de facto division of private companies and groups is made on the basis of *size* by ss 246 ff, which give dispensations from certain of the accounting requirements to 'small' and 'medium-sized' companies and groups.

C. Registration and the role of the registrar

To incorporate a company, it is necessary to draw up the two basic constitutional documents, the *memorandum of association* and *articles of association*, have them signed by the first members ('subscribers'), and deliver them to the office of the Registrar of Companies, together with the prescribed fee (at present £50) and certain supporting documents.[9] Since the documents have to include the company's name, it is prudent to check in advance that a proposed name is likely to be available; but there is nowadays no procedure (as there once was, and plainly still should be) for securing provisional approval of a proposed name in advance of registration.

If the documents are in order, the registrar issues a *certificate of incorporation* (for an example, see below, p 593) and the company thereupon comes into existence.

A private company may commence business straight away; but a public company is subject to the limitations of s 117. Some of these limitations may

---

9 A statement giving particulars of the first directors and secretary and notice of the intended situation of the company's registered office (s 10(2)–(6)) and a declaration that the statutory requirements regarding incorporation have been complied with (s 12(3)).

be circumvented by the device of forming the company in the first instance as a private company and later converting it to a public company under s 43.

Companies Act 1985

1 *Mode of forming incorporated company*

(1) Any two or more persons associated for a lawful purpose may, by subscribing their names to a memorandum of association and otherwise complying with the requirements of this Act in respect of registration, form an incorporated company, with or without limited liability.

13 *Effect of registration*

(1) On the registration of a company's memorandum, the registrar of companies shall give a certificate that the company is incorporated and, in the case of a limited company, that it is limited.

(2) The certificate may be signed by the registrar, or authenticated by his official seal.

(3) From the date of incorporation mentioned in the certificate, the subscribers of the memorandum, together with such other persons as may from time to time become members of the company, shall be a body corporate by the name contained in the memorandum.

(4) That body corporate is then capable forthwith of exercising all the functions of an incorporated company, but with such liability on the part of its members to contribute to its assets in the event of its being wound up as is provided by this Act and the Insolvency Act.

...

(7) A certificate of incorporation given in respect of an association is conclusive evidence—

(a) that the requirements of this Act in respect of registration and of matters precedent and incidental to it have been complied with, and that the association is a company authorised to be registered, and is duly registered, under this Act, and

(b) if the certificate contains a statement that the company is a public company, that the company is such a company.

The registrar cannot refuse registration if the objects of the company are lawful and the documents are in order.

1 R v Registrar of Companies, ex p Bowen [1914] 3 KB 1161 (King's Bench Divisional Court)

Application was made to register a proposed company named The United Dental Service Ltd. The subscribers to the memorandum were seven unregistered dental practitioners. The registrar refused to register the company unless either the memorandum was altered so as to provide that the work of the company should be undertaken only by registered dentists, or the name of the company was amended so as not to include the word 'dental' or 'dentist'. The applicants sought a writ of mandamus to compel the registrar to register the company. It was held that the registrar's refusal was unjustified, and mandamus was granted.

LORD READING CJ: In my opinion the question turns in the main ... upon whether the use of these words, 'The United Dental Service', would amount to an offence under the Dentists Act 1878 ... I think these words, 'United Dental Service', imply a description of the acts to be performed, and do not imply that the persons who will perform them are persons specially qualified under the statute of 1878. The Registrar of Companies would be entitled, if the use of the proposed name would be an offence under the statute (either under this or any other statute), to refuse to register the company with that name; but, having arrived at the conclusion that that would not be the effect of the use of the words 'United Dental Service', I hold that the registrar was wrong in refusing registration upon that ground. . . .

AVORY J delivered a concurring judgment.

BANKS J concurred.

NOTE

The registrar's powers in relation to company names have varied under successive Companies Acts. For the present law, see ss 25–34 of CA 1985. The use of the word 'Dental' is now restricted by regulations made under s 29 and requires the consent of the General Dental Council.

The registrar may refuse to register a company whose objects are unlawful.

2 R v Registrar of Companies, ex p More [1931] 2 KB 197 (Court of Appeal)

The registrar refused to register a company formed to sell tickets in an Irish lottery. It was held that the lottery was illegal in England and that his refusal was right.

SCRUTTON LJ: This is a short point involving the construction of s 41 of the Lotteries Act 1823. Two gentlemen proposed to sell tickets in England in connection with an Irish lottery. For some reason they did not propose to do this themselves; they proposed to form a private company to do it. It is merely conjecture on my part that this may be due to the fact that the provisions in the Act of 1823 making offenders liable to be punished as rogues and vagabonds do not apply to a company, and so the two gentlemen intending to form this company wished in this way to avoid the risk of being prosecuted under the Act. They accordingly lodged the memorandum and articles of association of the proposed company with the Registrar of Companies, who, when he saw that the object of the company was to sell tickets in a lottery known as the Irish Free State Hospitals Sweepstake, refused to register the company. Thereupon an application was made to the court for a writ of mandamus directing the registrar to register the company. To succeed in that application the applicant must show that it is legal to sell in England tickets for the Irish Free State Hospital Sweepstake authorised by an Act of the Irish Free State. The only Act which can be supposed to authorise the selling in England is an Irish Act, but the Irish Parliament has no jurisdiction in England, and that being so, the Irish Parliament cannot authorise lottery tickets to be sold in England. The authority to sell in any place must be given by the Parliament having jurisdiction in that place, and the Imperial Parliament has given no authority to sell lottery tickets in England ... The appeal must be dismissed.

GREER and SLESSER LJJ delivered concurring judgments.

Registration does not establish conclusively that the objects of a company are lawful; but after the issue of a certificate of incorporation the regularity of the incorporation cannot be challenged on the grounds of illegality except in proceedings especially brought in the name of the Crown to have the registration cancelled.

3 Bowman v Secular Society Ltd [1917] AC 406 (House of Lords)

The main object of the society, which was registered as a company limited by guarantee, was 'to promote ... the principle that human conduct should be based upon natural knowledge, and not upon super-natural belief, and that human welfare in this world is the proper end of all thought and action ...'. It was alleged that this object, involving a denial of christianity,was against public policy, so that a bequest to the society was invalid. The House of Lords (Lord Finlay LC dissenting) upheld the view of the courts below that this object was not unlawful. This extract from the speech of Lord Parker of Waddington is concerned with the incidental point of the conclusiveness of the certificate of incorporation. His views were supported by Lords Dunedin and Buckmaster.

LORD PARKER OF WADDINGTON: My Lords, in the present case ... the testator has given his residuary estate through the medium of trustees for sale and conversion to the Secular Society Limited, and the question is as to the validity of this gift. There is no doubt as to the certainty of the subject-matter, or as to the testator's disposing power, or as to the validity of his will. So far as the conditions essential to the validity of the gift are concerned, the only doubt is as to the capacity of the donee.

The Secular Society Limited was incorporated as a company limited by guarantee under the Companies Acts 1862 to 1893, and a company so incorporated is by s[18] of the Act of 1862 [CA 1985, s 13(4)] capable of exercising all the functions of an incorporated company. Prima facie, there-fore, the society is a corporate body created by virtue of a statute of the realm, with statutory power to acquire property by gift, whether inter vivos or by will. The appellants endeavour to displace this prima facie effect of the Companies Acts in the following manner. If, they say, you look at the objects for which the society was incorporated, as expressed in its memorandum of association, you will find that they are either actually illegal or, at any rate, in conflict with the policy of the law. This being so, the society was not an association capable of incorporation under the Acts. It was and is an illegal association, and as such incapable of acquiring property by gift. I do not think this argument is open to the appellants, even if their major premise be correct. By the first section of the Companies Act 1900 [CA 1985, s 13 (7)] the society's certificate of registration is made conclusive evidence that the society was an association authorised to be registered—that is, an association of not less than seven persons associated together for a lawful purpose. The section does not mean that all or any of the objects specified in the memorandum, if otherwise illegal, would be rendered legal by the certificate. On the contrary, if the directors of the society applied its funds for an illegal object, they would be guilty of misfeasance and liable to replace the money, even if the object for which the money had been applied were expressly authorised by the memorandum. In like manner a contract entered into by the company for an unlawful object, whether authorised by the memorandum or otherwise, could not be enforced either in law or in equity. The section does, however, preclude all His Majesty's lieges from going behind the certificate or from alleging that the society is not a corporate body with the status and capacity conferred by the Acts. Even if all the objects specified in the memorandum were illegal, it does not follow that the company cannot on that account apply its funds or enter into a contract for a lawful purpose. Every company has power to wind up voluntarily, and moneys paid or contracts entered into with that object are in every respect lawfully paid or entered into. Further, the disposition provided by the company's memorandum for its surplus assets in case of a winding-up may be lawful though all the objects as a going concern are unlawful. If there be no lawful manner of applying such surplus assets they would on the dissolution of the company belong to the Crown as bona vacantia: *Cunnack v Edwards*.[10]

My Lords, some stress was laid on the public danger, or at any rate the anomaly, of the courts recognising the corporate existence of a company all of whose objects, as specified in its memorandum of association, are transparently illegal. Such a case is not likely to occur, for the registrar fulfils a quasi-judicial function,[11] and his duty is to determine whether an association applying for registration is authorised to be registered under the Acts. Only by misconduct or great carelessness on the part of the registrar could a company with objects wholly illegal obtain registration. If such a case did occur it would be open to the court to stay its hand until an opportunity had been given for taking the appropriate steps for the cancellation of the certificate of registration. It should be observed that neither s 1 of the Companies Act 1900, nor the corresponding section of the Companies (Consolidation) Act 1908, is so expressed as to bind the Crown, and the Attorney-General, on behalf of the Crown, could institute proceedings by way of certiorari to cancel a registration which the registrar in affected discharge of his quasi-judicial duties had improperly or erroneously allowed. But ... I do not think that the present is a case requiring such action on the part of your Lordships' House.

My Lords, it follows from what I have already said that the capacity of the Secular Society Limited to acquire property by gift must be taken as established, and, all the conditions essential to the validity of the gift being thus fulfilled, the donee is entitled to receive and dispose of the subject-matter thereof...

LORDS DUNEDIN, SUMNER and BUCKMASTER delivered concurring opinions.

LORD FINLAY LC dissented.

---

10 [1896] 2 Ch 679.
11 [The use of the term 'quasi-judicial' is misleading. This function of the registrar can only be described as 'ministerial': as we have seen above, in the matter of registration, he exercises no discretionary powers, still less is he concerned to adjudicate any dispute.]

4 HA Stephenson & Son Ltd v Gillanders, Arbuthnot & Co (1⌐
476 (High Court of Australia)

[For the facts and the main part of the decision, see below, (65⌐

EVATT J: [The] effect of formal incorporation is not regarded by the ⌐ᴇgᵢₛₗₐₜᵤᵣᵉ as empowering the registrar to ignore compliance with the Act; but the legislature wishes to ensure that after the new legal entity has been brought into existence by the formal act of a state functionary, it will not be necessary for persons dealing with the company to ascertain at their peril whether the various statutory requirements have been complied with . . . It is not so much a power given to the registrar by the legislature, as a protection given to the public who may be dealing with the company because of the assumption that the registrar will be careful in the matter . . .

[See also *Salomon v Salomon & Co Ltd* (**12**) and *Scott v Frank F Scott* (*London*) *Ltd* (**45**).]

NOTES

(1) Section 13(7) fortunately makes it unnecessary in English company law to consider the topics of defective incorporation and declarations of nullity which have traditionally occupied a substantial amount of space in the textbooks in other European countries and in parts of the United States. It was not therefore considered necessary for the UK to take any steps to implement arts 11 and 12 of the First EEC Directive on Company Law, which deal with those questions.

(2) The Companies Act and many textbooks encourage the belief that companies are formed by a genuine 'association' of people with a real business that they wish to incorporate, who have constitutional documents drawn up for that specific purpose, subscribe to them and send them off to the registrar for registration. But this is to turn a blind eye to the facts. In the case of something like half of the companies formed in the United Kingdom today, the incorporation procedure is a charade: it is purely a paper exercise carried out by people who have no intention of using the company themselves for any business whatsoever. These incorporations are undertaken to meet the very considerable demand for 'ready-made' or 'shelf' companies; and (as a glance at the advertisements in any solicitors' professional journal will show) many firms exist which specialise in supplying such companies to buyers, and hold extensive stockpiles of dormant companies of every type and kind ready to be 'delivered' to customer's order. The initial subscribers and officers will be clerks in the firm's employment, and the company's name a figment of someone's imagination.

(3) Until quite recently, there was no recorded case in which the Attorney-General had brought proceedings to have a company's registration cancelled in the manner suggested in *Bowman v Secular Society Ltd* (**3**). This gap has now been filled by the case next cited.

The registrar's decision to incorporate a company is subject to judicial review at the suit of the Crown.

5 R v Registrar of Companies, ex p A-G (1980), reported [1991] BCLC 476 (Queen's Bench Divisional Court)

[The facts appear from the judgment.]

ACKNER LJ: This application has many of the indicia that one might expect to find in a students' end of term moot. It appears indirectly to have been stimulated by the action of the Policy Division of the Inland Revenue.

The Attorney-General applies to quash the incorporation and registration by the Registrar of Companies nearly a year ago, that is on 18 December 1979, of Lindi St Claire (Personal Services) Ltd as a limited company under the provisions of the Companies Act 1948 to 1976.

The grounds of the application, to state them quite briefly, are these. In certifying the incorporation of a company and in registering the same the Registrar of Companies acted ultra vires or misdirected himself or otherwise erred in law, in particular as to the proper construction and application of s 1(1) of the Companies Act 1948 in that the company was not formed for any lawful purpose but, on the contrary, was formed expressly with the primary object of carrying on the business of prostitution, such being an unlawful purpose involving the commission of acts which are immoral and contrary to public policy.

The first point to consider is the validity of the procedure which has been adopted in this case, that is by way of application for judicial review, such application being made by the Attorney-General.

[His Lordship referred to *Bowman v Secular Society Ltd* (3) and continued:] So clearly the Attorney-General is entitled to bring these proceedings.

Now as to the facts, these come within a very short compass and they amount to the following. A firm of certified accountants, Gilson Clipp & Co, on 16 August 1979 wrote to the Registrar of Companies at Companies House, Crown Way, Maindy, Cardiff pointing out that they had received a letter from the Inland Revenue Policy Division, who stated that they considered prostitution to be a trade which is fully taxable, and that they, the certified accountants, saw no reason why their client should not be able to organise her business by way of a limited company. They asked whether the name 'Prostitute Ltd' was available for registration as a limited company, pointing out the main object of the company would be that of organising the services of a prostitute.

The registrar did not like that name and did not accept it, nor did he accept another name 'Hookers Ltd' which was offered. But subsequently two further names were offered, 'Lindi St Claire (Personal Services) Ltd' and 'Lindi St Claire (French Lessons) Ltd', and it was the former which he registered.

The memorandum of association said in terms that the first of the objects of the company was 'To carry on the business of prostitution'.

The only director of the company is Lindi St Claire, Miss St Claire describing herself specifically as 'Prostitute'. The other person who owns also one share is a Miss Duggan, who is referred to as 'the cashier'.

Leave having been obtained to apply for judicial review, Miss St Claire wrote in these terms:

> I would like to say that prostitution is not at all unlawful, as you have stated, and I feel it is most unfair of you to take this view, especially when I am paying income tax on my earnings from prostitution to the government Inland Revenue.
>
> Furthermore, I feel it is most unfair of you to imply that I have acted wrongly, as I was most explicit to all concerned about the sole trade of the company to be that of prostitution and nothing more. If my company should not be deemed valid, then it should have not been granted in the first place by the Board of Trade. It is most unfair of the government

to allow me to go ahead with my company one moment, then quash it the next. ...

It is well settled that a contract which is made upon a sexually immoral consideration or for a sexually immoral purpose is against public policy and is illegal and unenforceable. The fact that it does not involve or may not involve the commission of a criminal offence in no way prevents the contract being illegal, being against public policy and therefore being unenforceable. Here, as the documents clearly indicate, the association is for the purpose of carrying on a trade which involves illegal contracts because the purpose is a sexually immoral purpose and as such against public policy.

Mr Simon Brown submits that if that is the position, as indeed it clearly is on the authorities, then the association of the two or more persons cannot be for 'any lawful purpose'.

To my mind this must follow. It is implicit in the speeches in the *Bowman* case to which I have just made reference. In my judgment, the contention of the Attorney-General is a valid one and I would order that the registration be therefore quashed.

SKINNER J concurred.

QUESTIONS

(1) Tom, Dick and Harry wish to incorporate the plumbing business which they have carried on in partnership for some years. What would you say might be (i) the advantages and (ii) the disadvantages for them of buying a ready-made company rather than having one incorporated by their own solicitor?
(2) If they do decide to use a ready-made company, what steps may have to be taken in order to transfer the company to them and to make it fit their needs?
(3) What might be the consequences of the court's order in Miss St Claire's case, so far as concerns acts done in the year that the company was on the register?

D. Preliminary contracts

It is very common for negotiations about a contract to take place, and for a contract (or what purports to be a contract) to be made, when one of the parties to this 'contract' is a company which has not yet been formed. Sometimes, the fact that the company has not been incorporated may be known to all concerned and may even be stated in the contract; on the other hand, there may have been some misunderstanding or even a misrepresentation about its existence. Such situations can give rise to all sorts of legal problems at common law, as the next few cases show, for a 'non-entity' cannot have legal rights or duties ascribed to it. Article 7 of the First EEC Company Law Directive, cited below, required the member states to take steps which would have eliminated many of these problems, but the United Kingdom's response (CA 1985, s 36C, cited below) has tackled only some of the issues.

QUESTIONS

(1) What business reasons might cause people to wish to make a pre-incorporation contract, rather than form the company first and then conclude the deal?

(2) How far would it help solve the problems to use a ready-made company (above, p 11)?

A company has no legal existence before it is incorporated. It is incapable of entering into a contract itself, and equally incapable of acting through an agent. A person who purports to make a contract on behalf of a proposed company may do so in a way which renders him personally liable at common law. [12]

6 Kelner v Baxter (1866) LR 2 CP 174 (Court of Common Pleas)

Kelner agreed with the promoters of an unformed company to sell wine in the terms of the following letter:

January 27th, 1866.

To John Dacier Baxter, Nathan Jacob Calisher, and John Dales, on behalf of the proposed Gravesend Royal Alexandra Hotel Company, Limited.

Gentlemen,—I hereby propose to sell the extra stock now at the Assembly Rooms, Gravesend, as per schedule hereto, for the sum of £900, payable on the 28th of February, 1866.

(Signed) John Kelner.

Then followed a schedule of the stock of wines, etc to be purchased, and at the end was written as follows:

To Mr John Kelner.
Sir,—We have received your offer to sell the extra stock as above, and hereby agree to and accept the terms proposed.

(Signed) JD Baxter,
NJ Calisher,
J Dales,

On behalf of the [13] Gravesend Royal Alexandra
Hotel Company, Limited.

The hotel business was already being carried on, and the wine was delivered and in due course consumed. On 1 February 1866 the proposed directors held a meeting at which they purported to ratify the purchase. The incorporation of the company was completed on 20 February 1866. The company failed before Kelner had been paid and so he brought this action against the promoters personally. They were held liable on the contract.

ERLE CJ: I agree that if the Gravesend Royal Alexandra Hotel Company had been an existing company at this time, the persons who signed the agreement would have signed as agents of the company. But, as there was no company in existence at the time, the agreement would be wholly inoperative unless it were held to be binding on the defendants personally. The cases referred to in the course of the argument fully bear out the proposition that,

12 See also the statutory provision in CA 1985, s 36C (below, p 18).
13 [The report in (1866) 36 LJCP 94 inserts here the word 'proposed'.]

where a contract is signed by one who professes to be signing 'as agent', but who has no principal existing at the time, and the contract would be altogether inoperative unless binding upon the person who signed it, he is bound thereby: and a stranger cannot by a subsequent ratification relieve him from that responsibility. When the company came afterwards into existence it was a totally new creature, having rights and obligations from that time, but no rights or obligations by reason of anything which might have been done before. It was once, indeed, thought that an inchoate liability might be incurred on behalf of a proposed company, which would become binding on it when subsequently formed: but that notion was manifestly contrary to the principles upon which the law of contract is founded. There must be two parties to a contract; and the rights and obligations which it creates cannot be transferred by one of them to a third person who was not in a condition to be bound by it at the time it was made. The history of this company makes this construction to my mind perfectly clear. It was no doubt the notion of all the parties that success was certain: but the plaintiff parted with his stock upon the faith of the defendants' engagement that the price agreed on should be paid on the day named. It cannot be supposed that he for a moment contemplated that the payment was to be contingent on the formation of the company by 28 February. The paper expresses in terms a contract to buy. And it is a cardinal rule that no oral evidence shall be admitted to show an intention different from that which appears on the face of the writing. I come, therefore, to the conclusion that the defendants, having no principal who was bound originally, or who could become so by a subsequent ratification, were themselves bound, and that the oral evidence offered is not admissible to contradict the written contract.

WILLES, BYLES and KEATING JJ delivered concurring judgments.

NOTE

In the Australian case of *Summergreene v Parker* (1950) 80 CLR 304 at 323, Fullagar J said:

> ... I do not myself think that *Kelner v Baxter* (**6**) or any of the cases cited affords any assistance in the present case. Where *A*, purporting to act as agent for a non-existent principal, purports to make a binding contract with *B*, and the circumstances are such that *B* would suppose that a binding contract had been made, there must be a strong presumption that *A* has meant to bind himself personally. Where, as in *Kelner v Baxter*, the consideration on *B*'s part has been fully executed in reliance on the existence of a contract binding on somebody, the presumption could, I should imagine, only be rebutted in very exceptional circumstances. But the fundamental question in every case must be what the parties intended or must be fairly understood to have intended.

To be liable under, or entitled to sue on, the purported contract of an unformed company at common law, a person must have held himself out either as agent or as principal.

7 Newborne v Sensolid (Great Britain) Ltd [1954] 1 QB 45, [1953] 1 All ER 708 (Court of Appeal)

The contract in this case was for the sale to Sensolid of 200 cases of tinned ham. It was written on a printed form headed 'Leopold Newborne (London)

Ltd', which ended with the typewritten words: 'Yours faithfully, Leopold Newborne (London) Ltd', followed by 'a hieroglyphic, which is interpreted in type as being Leopold Newborne'.[14] The market fell, and Sensolid refused to take delivery. When sued on the contract, Sensolid pleaded that on the date when the contract was made, Leopold Newborne (London) Ltd had not been incorporated, and that neither the company nor Newborne personally could enforce it. The Court of Appeal, affirming Parker J, upheld this plea.

LORD GODDARD CJ: Mr Diplock, who has argued the case for the plaintiff, bringing to our attention every point which could possibly be taken, has contended that it is governed by the well-known series of cases of which *Kelner v Baxter* (**6**) is one of the earliest and perhaps the best known. That was a case in which one Kelner sold wine intending to sell it to a company which was to be formed. The contract showed that it was agreed to be sold to certain men who were the proposed directors of a company which was coming into existence. They agreed to buy. The potential directors intended to buy the wine on behalf of the company, but the company was not in existence at the time the contract was made or at the time when the goods were delivered. They took delivery of the goods and, therefore, it was held that as they had contracted on behalf of a principal who did not exist they must, having received the wine, pay for it. That decision seems to me to stop far short of holding that every time an alleged company purports to contract—when there is no company in existence—everybody who is signing for the company is making himself personally liable.

Mr Diplock has also relied strongly on *Schmaltz v Avery*,[15] which lays down a principle, which has been acted on in other cases, notably in *Harper & Co v Vigers Bros*,[16] that where a person purports to contract as agent he may nevertheless disclose himself as being in truth a principal. If he entered into a contract as agent he can bring an action in his own name and show that he was in fact the principal. All those cases are well established and we are not departing in any way from those decisions any more than did Parker J. What we cannot find in this case is that Mr Newborne ever purported to contract to sell as agent or as principal. The contract was one which he was making for the company, and although Mr Diplock has argued that in signing as he did Mr Newborne must have signed as agent, since the company could only contract through agents, that was not really the true position.

The company makes the contract. No doubt the company must do its physical acts, and so forth, through the directors, but it is not the ordinary case of principal and agent. It is a case in which the company is contracting and the company's contract is authenticated by the signature of one of the directors. This contract purports to be a contract by the company; it does not purport to be a contract by Mr Newborne. He does not purport to be selling his goods but to be selling the company's goods. The only person who had any contract here was the company, and Mr Newborne's signature merely confirmed the company's signature. The document is signed 'Yours faithfully, Leopold Newborne (London) Ltd', and then the signature

---

14 Per Lord Goddard CJ, as reported in [1953] 1 All ER 708 at 709.
15 (1851) 16 QB 655.
16 [1909] 2 KB 549.

underneath is the signature of the person authorised to sign on behalf of the company.

In my opinion, unfortunate though it may be, as the company was not in existence when the contract was signed there never was a contract, and Mr Newborne cannot come forward and say: 'Well, it was my contract.' The fact is, he made a contract for a company which did not exist. It seems to me, therefore, that the defendants can avail themselves of the defence which they pleaded and the appeal must be dismissed.

MORRIS LJ delivered a concurring judgment.

ROMER LJ concurred.

NOTES

In *Kelner v Baxter* (**6**), the defendants were held liable *on the contract*, that is, as parties to it. In *Newborne*'s case (**7**), the question was, similarly, whether Newborne personally was a party to the contract, and it was held that he was not. These cases do not decide the alternative question whether an agent who has *not* contracted personally might be liable to the opposite party in damages for breach of warranty of authority on the principle of *Collen v Wright*.[17]

Parker J at first instance in *Newborne*'s case[18] appears to have doubted this 'because the principal is not in existence', but this is to beg the question: there are strong dicta to the contrary in the Australian case of *Black v Smallwood*;[19] and the well-known case of *McRae v Commonwealth Disposals Commission*[20] plainly establishes that a person may impliedly warrant that what is non-existent exists.

The contrasting conclusions reached in *Kelner v Baxter* and *Newborne*'s case led to some fine distinctions being made by commentators, and to arguments whether the issue was one of form or of substance. Fortunately, we can now consider this debate settled, for all practical purposes, by the interpretation put on s 36C of CA 1985 by the Court of Appeal in *Phonogram Ltd v Lane* (**8**). Section 36C was first introduced (as s 9(2) of the European Communities Act 1972) to implement Article 7 of the First EEC Directive on Company Law.

First EEC Council Directive 68/151 (9 March 1968)

ARTICLE 7

If, before a company being formed has acquired legal personality, action has been carried out in its name and the company does not assume the obligations arising from such action, the persons who acted shall, without limit, be jointly and severally liable therefor, unless otherwise agreed.

17 (1857) 8 E & B 647.
18 [1954] 1 QB 45 at 47.
19 [1966] ALR 744.
20 (1950) 84 CLR 377.

Companies Act 1985

36C *Pre-incorporation contracts*

(1) A contract which purports to be made by or on behalf of a company when the company has not been formed has effect, subject to any agreement to the contrary, as one made with the person purporting to act for the company or as agent for it, and he is personally liable on the contract accordingly.

8 Phonogram Ltd v Lane [1982] QB 938, [1981] 3 All ER 182 (Court of Appeal)

[The facts appear from the judgment of Lord Denning.]

LORD DENNING MR: In 1973 there was a group of 'pop' artists. They included two gentlemen called Brian Chatton and John McBurnie. The suggestion was that they should perform under the name 'Cheap Mean and Nasty'. A company was going to be formed to run the group. It was to be called 'Fragile Management Ltd'.

Before the company was formed, negotiations took place for the financing of the group ... It was eventually arranged that money should be provided by Phonogram Ltd. The agreed amount was £12,000, and the first instalment was to be £6,000. The first instalment of £6,000 was paid.

But the new company was never formed. The group never performed under it. And the £6,000 was due to be repaid. But it was never repaid. Phonogram Ltd then tried to discover who was liable to repay the money. Mr Roland Rennie was the man who had negotiated on behalf of Phonogram. Mr Brian Lane was the man who had negotiated on behalf of the new company which was to be formed. I will read the letter from Mr Rennie to Mr Lane of 4 July 1973. It is the subject matter of this action. [Lord Denning read the letter, which contained an undertaking to repay the £6,000 if the deal was not completed. The undertaking was signed by Mr Lane, 'for and on behalf of Fragile Management Ltd'. He continued:]

... Phonogram Ltd say that the law of England has been much altered by s 9(2) of the European Communities Act 1972 [CA 1985, s 36C]. [His Lordship read the section and continued:] That seems to me to cover this very case. The contract purports to be made on behalf of Fragile Management Ltd, at a time when the company had not been formed. It purports to be made by Mr Lane on behalf of the company. So he is to be personally liable for it.

Mr Thompson, on behalf of Mr Lane, argued very skilfully that s 9(2) did not apply. First, he said: 'Look at the directive under the European Community law which led to this section being introduced.' It is Council Directive of 9 March 1968 (68/151/EEC). In 1968 English was not one of the official languages of the European Community. So Mr Thompson referred us to the French text of art 7 of the Directive:

> Si des actes ont été accomplis au nom d'une société en formation, avant l'acquisition par celle-ci de la personnalité morale, et si la société ne reprend pas les engagements résultant de ces actes, les personnes qui les ont accomplis en sont solidairement et indéfiniment responsables, sauf convention contraire.

Mr Thompson says that, according to the French text, that Directive is limited to companies which are 'en formation', that is, companies which have already started to be formed.

Mr Thompson's submission is reinforced by passages from a French textbook—Ripert *Traité Elémentaire de Droit Commercial* (7th edn, 1972). As I read the passage at pp 601 and 604 of that treatise—interpreting the French as best I can—in the case of a French company or société there may be, recognised by law, a period of time while a company is in the course of formation when people have put their signatures to what I may call 'the articles of association'. That period is called the period when the société is 'en formation'. At p 604 a parallel is drawn with a baby at the time of gestation—between the time of conception and the time of birth—and a company when it is 'en formation'.

I reject Mr Thompson's submission. I do not think we should go by the French text of the Directive. It was drafted with regard to a different system of company law from that in this country. We should go by s 9(2) of our own statute, the European Communities Act 1972 . . .

That brings me to the second point. What does 'purports' mean in this context? Mr Thompson suggests that there must be a representation that the company is already in existence. I do not agree. A contract can purport to be made on behalf of a company, or by a company, even though that company is known by both parties not to be formed and that it is only about to be formed.

[Lord Denning dealt with another point and continued:]

But I would not leave the matter there. This is the first time the section has come before us. It will have much impact on the common law. I am afraid that before 1972 the common law had adopted some fine distinctions. As I understand *Kelner v Baxter* (**6**) it decided that if a person contracted on behalf of a company which was nonexistent, he himself would be liable on the contract. Just as, if a man signs a contract for and on behalf 'of his horses', he is personally liable. But, since that case was decided, a number of distinctions have been introduced by *Hollman v Pullin*;[1] *Newborne v Sensolid (Great Britain) Ltd* (**7**) and *Black v Smallwood*[2] in the High Court of Australia. Those three cases seem to suggest that there is a distinction to be drawn according to the way in which an agent signs a contract. If he signs it as 'agent for "X" company'—or 'for and on behalf of "X" company'—and there is no such body as 'X' company, then he himself can be sued upon it. On the other hand, if he signs it as 'X' company per pro himself the managing director, then the position may be different: because he is not contracting personally as an agent. It is the company which is contracting.

That distinction was disliked by Windeyer J in *Black v Smallwood*. It has been criticised by Professor Treitel in *The Law of Contract* (5th edn, 1979), p 559. In my opinion, the distinction has been obliterated by s 9(2) of the European Communities Act 1972. We now have the clear words, 'Where a contract purports to be made by a company, or by a person as agent for a company, at a time when the company has not been formed . . .' That applies whatever formula is adopted. The person who purports to contract for the company is personally liable.

There is one further point on s 9(2) which I must mention. In the latest

1 (1884) Cab & El 254.
2 [1966] ALR 744.

edition of *Cheshire and Fifoot's Law of Contract* (9th edn, 1976), after reciting s 9(2), it says, at p 462:

> How far it in fact does so will depend on the meaning given to the words 'subject to any agreement to the contrary' since it could be argued that words showing that A signs as agent express an agreement that he is not to be personally liable. If this were correct *Newborne v Sensolid* (*Great Britain*) *Ltd* would still be decided the same way. But it may be suspected that the courts will try to give more content to the subsection.

We certainly will. The words 'subject to any agreement to the contrary' mean—as Shaw LJ suggested in the course of the argument—'unless otherwise agreed'. If there was an express agreement that the man who was signing was not to be liable, the section would not apply. But, unless there is a clear exclusion of personal liability, s 9(2) should be given its full effect. It means that in all cases such as the present, where a person purports to contract on behalf of a company not yet formed, then however he expresses his signature he himself is personally liable on the contract.

SHAW and OLIVER LJJ delivered concurring judgments.

A company cannot by adoption or ratification obtain the benefit of a contract purportedly made on its behalf before it came into existence. A new contract must be made after its incorporation in the same terms as the old one.

9 Natal Land Co Ltd v Pauline Colliery Syndicate Ltd [1904] AC 120 (Privy Council)

The respondent company claimed specific performance of an agreement to lease certain coal-mining rights, initially made on 9 December 1897 by the appellants' agent, Rycroft, with a Mrs de Carrey. It was understood by Rycroft that Mrs de Carrey was acting on behalf of a syndicate (then unincorporated) which was incorporated as the respondent company on 22 January 1898. On 31 January, Rycroft's authority to deal further with the land in question was stopped by a telegram from the appellant company's head office in London, and he communicated this fact to the syndicate's solicitors. In September 1898 the respondent company, which had been prospecting the land in pursuance of other terms of the agreement, discovered a seam of coal and claimed its right to the lease. The Privy Council, reversing the court below, held that there was no contract to which the respondent company was a party, and refused to decree specific performance.

The opinion of the Judicial Committee was delivered by LORD DAVEY: The court, consisting of Finnemore J and Mr Acting Justice Beaumont, decided in favour of the respondents ... and by their judgment of 29 May 1902 decreed specific performance of the agreement with costs. On the question of privity of contract, they seem to have held that a new contract on the terms of the old one had been made between the appellants and the respondent. The acts of part performance which were relied on by the learned judges as evidence of such new contract were the occupation and working of the land in question by the respondents, the expenditure of money on the faith of the agreement, and the acceptance by the appellants of the payment of £100 as a guarantee for prospecting operations. This sum, however (as already stated), was in fact paid before the incorporation of the respondents.

Their Lordships do not think it necessary to say whether the agreement was or was not voidable on the grounds alleged, or on other grounds appearing in the correspondence, because they are clearly of opinion that there was no contract between the appellants and the respondents. The contract was made with Mrs de Carrey, and even if she can be treated as having made it on behalf either of the unincorporated syndicate, who were the promoters of the respondent company, or on behalf of the company itself when incorporated, it is clear that a company cannot by adoption or ratification obtain the benefit of a contract purporting to have been made on its behalf before the company came into existence. It is unnecessary to cite all the cases in which this has been decided from *Kelner v Baxter* (**6**) downwards. But the facts may show that a new contract was made with the company after its incorporation on the terms of the old contract. The circumstances relied on for that purpose in the present case are not, in the opinion of their Lordships, necessarily referable to, and do not necessarily imply, a new contract with the respondents. But a conclusive reason which negatives any new contract is that Rycroft, by whose agency the new contract must be supposed to have been made, had no power or authority after 31 January 1898 to make such a contract on behalf of the appellants, and his want of authority was known to the solicitors acting for the respondents. He was not either the actual or the ostensible agent for that purpose of the appellants.

NOTES

(1) The Jenkins Committee in its Report (Cmnd 1749, 1962, paras 44, 54(b)) considered the law unsatisfactory and anomalous, and recommended that 'a company should be enabled unilaterally to adopt contracts which purport to be made on its behalf or in its name prior to incorporation, and thereby become a party thereto to the same extent as if the contract had been made after incorporation...'
Many Commonwealth countries have enacted provisions which follow the lines of this recommendation, and a similar reform was projected for the United Kingdom in the abortive Companies Bill of 1973, but we did not take the opportunity to revive this proposal when the First EEC Directive was implemented; and so the *Natal Land* case is still good law.

(2) As has been mentioned above, it is very common for those wishing to incorporate a business to acquire a ready-made company for the purpose, possibly changing its name if the existing name is not thought suitable. In *Oshkosh B'Gosh Inc v Dan Marbell Inc Ltd* [1989] BCLC 507, CA, Mr Craze bought a company named E Ltd off the shelf and later changed its name to DM Ltd. Before the change of name was registered the company, acting through Craze, bought goods from the plaintiff. In an action to make Craze personally liable it was held that s 9(2) of the European Communities Act 1972 [CA 1985, s 36C] could not be applied because the company had been formed (albeit under another name) at the time when the contract was made: the issue of an amended certificate of incorporation under CA 1985, s 28(6) did not imply that the company had been re-formed or re-incorporated. In contrast, in *Cotronic (UK) Ltd v Dezonie* [1991] BCC 200, CA, a defendant escaped personal liability under s 36C for a different reason. He made a contract in 1986 in the name of W Ltd in ignorance of the fact that W Ltd had been struck off the register under CA 1985, s 652, in 1981 and had ceased to exist. A new company, also named W Ltd, was incorporated in 1989 to continue the business. The court held that he could not be made liable under s 36C because he had purported to make the company on behalf of the

old company and not the new one, which no-one had thought about forming in 1986.

QUESTIONS

(1) Could any or all of the difficulties revealed by the *Natal Land* case have been met by Mrs de Carrey *assigning* her right to the lease to the company after it had been formed?

(2) It is possible to create a valid trust for the benefit of an unborn child. Could the problems revealed by the *Natal Land* case have been surmounted by having someone enter into an agreement as trustee, rather than as agent, for the unformed company?

(3) The facts of *Newborne v Sensolid* (**7**) recur today. Could Mr Newborne enforce the contract in the light of s 36C? What remedy could the court give?

(4) Suppose that in *Phonogram Ltd v Lane* (**8**) there was a second pre-incorporation contract concluded by Mr Lane with the group for the making of the recording and that the group, in breach of this contract, refused to perform. What remedy, if any, would (i) the company, and (ii) Mr Lane, have?

(5) Was Lord Denning in *Phonogram Ltd v Lane* right to disregard the French text? (Contrast *International Sales and Agencies Ltd v Marcus* (**72**), *Official Custodian for Charities v Parway Estates Ltd* (**118**) and *Barclays Bank Ltd v TOSG Trust Fund Ltd* (below, p 231).)

E. Promoters

The term 'promoter' is not defined in the Companies Act; and such attempts at definition as have been made by the courts (mainly in the nineteenth century) seem to have been concerned only to ensure that enough flexibility was retained to catch the next ingenious rogue which that fertile period might produce. There is an enormous body of old case-law concerned with the obligations of a promoter towards the company which he forms and the investing public whose capital he seeks to attract; but to all intents and purposes this law has become obsolete. This is due partly to changes in the practice of securities marketing—it is unusual for a newly formed company to make an immediate public issue, and not normally possible to obtain a market listing without an established trading record. It is also due to the stringent control of such activities now imposed by statute[3] and by The Stock Exchange's rules and the professional codes of issuing houses and others whose services are nowadays essential. The cases which now follow are therefore of mainly historical interest.

Private companies, too, must, of course, be promoted; but as such promotions rarely involve outsiders there is little occasion for abuse.

A promoter stands in a fiduciary relationship towards his company. A contract made between him and the company is voidable at the company's option unless he has disclosed all material facts relating to the contract to an independent board, and the company has freely agreed to the terms.

---

3 Below, chapter 6.

10 Erlanger v New Sombrero Phosphate Co (1878) 3 App Cas 1218 (House of Lords)

A syndicate headed by Erlanger, a Paris banker, acquired for £55,000 the lease of an island in the West Indies with the right to work its phosphate deposits. The syndicate through Erlanger then formed the respondent company and named its first directors. Of these, one, the Lord Mayor of London, was independent of the syndicate, two were abroad, and the remainder were mere puppets of Erlanger. The lease was then sold through a nominee to the company for £110,000, the purchase being 'ratified' without inquiry at a meeting of directors eight days after the incorporation of the company. Many members of the public subscribed for shares, but the real circumstances of the sale and purchase were not disclosed to them and were not discovered until eight months later, after the first phosphate shipments had proved a failure. The shareholders then removed the original directors and elected a new board, which brought these proceedings to have the sale rescinded.

LORD CAIRNS LC: In the whole of this proceeding ... the syndicate, or the house of Erlanger as representing the syndicate, were the promoters of the company, and it is now necessary that I should state to your Lordships in what position I understand the promoters to be placed with reference to the company which they proposed to form. They stand, in my opinion, undoubtedly in a fiduciary position. They have in their hands the creation and moulding of the company; they have the power of defining how, and when, and in what shape, and under what supervision, it shall start into existence and begin to act as a trading corporation. If they are doing all this in order that the company may, as soon as it starts into life, become, through its managing directors, the purchaser of the property of themselves, the promoters, it is, in my opinion, incumbent upon the promoters to take care that in forming the company they provide it with an executive, that is to say, with a board of directors, who shall both be aware that the property which they are asked to buy is the property of the promoters, and who shall be competent and impartial judges as to whether the purchase ought or ought not to be made. I do not say that the owner of the property may not promote and form a joint stock company, and then sell his property to it, but I do say that if he does he is bound to take care that he sells it to the company through the medium of a board of directors who can and do exercise an independent and intelligent judgment on the transaction, and who are not left under the belief that the property belongs, not to the promoter, but to some other person ...

LORD O'HAGAN: The original purchase of the island of Sombrero was perfectly legitimate—and it was not less so because the object of the purchasers was to sell it again, and to sell it by forming a company which might afford them a profit on the transaction. The law permitted them to take that course, and provided the machinery by which the transfer of their interest might be equitably and beneficially effected for themselves and those with whom they meant to deal. But the privilege given them for promoting such a company for such an object, involved obligations of a very serious kind. It required, in its exercise, the utmost good faith, the completest truthfulness, and a careful regard to the protection of the future shareholders. The power to nominate a directorate is manifestly capable of great abuse, and may involve, in the misuse of it, very evil consequences to multitudes of people who have little capacity to guard themselves. Such a power may or may not have been wisely permitted to exist. I venture to have doubts upon the point. It tempts too much to fraudulent contrivance and mischievous deception; and, at least, it should be watched with jealousy and restrained from employment in such a way as to mislead the ignorant and the unwary. In all such cases the directorate nominated by the promoters should stand between them and the public, with such independence and intelligence, that they may be expected to deal fairly, impartially and with adequate knowledge in the affairs submitted to their control. If they have not those qualities, they are unworthy of trust. They are the betrayers and not the guardians of the company they govern, and their acts should not receive the sanction of a court of justice.

Now, my Lords, for reasons repeatedly given by my noble and learned friends, which I shall not detail again, I think that the promoters in this case failed to remember the exigencies of their fiduciary position, when they appointed directors who were in no way independent of themselves, and who did not sustain the interests of the company with ordinary care and intelligence . . .

Apparently, there was no inquiry as to the enormous advance in the price . . ., no consideration of the state of the property—and no intelligent estimate of its capabilities and prospects. If the directors had been nominated merely to ratify any terms the promoters might dictate, they discharged their function; if it was their duty, as it certainly was, to protect the shareholders, they never seem to have thought of doing it. Their conduct was precisely that which might have been anticipated from the character of their selection, and taking that conduct and character together, I concur in, I believe, the unanimous opinion of your Lordships that such a transaction ought not to be allowed to stand.

The promoters, who so forgot their duty to the company they formed, as to give it a directorate without independence of position or vigilance and caution in caring for its interests, must take the consequences. And this without the necessary imputation of evil purpose or conscious fraud. The fiduciary obligation may be violated though there may be no intention to do injustice. If the protection, proper and needful for a person standing at disadvantage in relation to his guardian or his solicitor, or to the promoters of a company, be withheld, the guardian, the solicitor or the promoters cannot sustain a contract equitably invalidated by the want of it, merely because it may be impossible to prove that he is impeachable with indirect or improper motives . . .

LORDS PENZANCE, HATHERLEY, SELBORNE, BLACKBURN and GORDON delivered concurring opinions.

NOTE

It has been accepted at least since *Salomon v Salomon & Co Ltd* (**12**) that, if there is no independent board of directors, the company may be bound by the consent of all the original *shareholders*, provided that a full disclosure is made to them of all material facts. But, as is shown by *Gluckstein v Barnes* (**11**), even this will not protect a promoter if the original shareholders themselves are not independent and the scheme as a whole is designed to attract and deceive the investing public at large.

A promoter may not make a secret profit while acting in that capacity. If he has received it, he may be compelled to account for it to the company.

11 Gluckstein v Barnes [1900] AC 240 (House of Lords)

Gluckstein and three others bought the Olympia exhibition premises in liquidation proceedings for £140,000 and then promoted a company, Olympia Ltd, to which they sold the property for £180,000. There were no independent directors. In a prospectus inviting applications for shares and debentures the £40,000 profit was disclosed, but not a further profit of some £20,000 which they had made by buying securities on the property at a discount and then enforcing them at their face value (though there was a vague reference to 'interim investments'). The company went into liquidation within four years, and the liquidator claimed in this action £6,341, part of the £20,000 received by Gluckstein.

EARL OF HALSBURY LC: My Lords, I am wholly unable to understand any claim that these directors, vendors, syndicate, associates, have to retain this money. I entirely agree with the Master of the Rolls that the essence of this scheme was to form a company. It was essential that this should be done, and that they should be directors of it, who would purchase. The company should have been informed of what was being done and consulted whether they would have allowed this profit. I think the Master of the Rolls is absolutely right in saying that the duty to disclose is imposed by the plainest dictates of common honesty as well as by well-settled principles of common law.

Of the facts there cannot be the least doubt; they are proved by the agreement, now that we know the subject-matter with which that agreement is intended to deal, although the agreement would not disclose what the nature of the transaction was to those who were not acquainted with the ingenious arrangements which were prepared for entrapping the intended victim of these arrangements.

In order to protect themselves, as they supposed, they inserted in the prospectus, qualifying the statement that they had bought the property for £140,000, payable in cash, that they did not sell to the company, and did not intend to sell, any other profits made by the syndicate from interim investments.

Then it is said there is the alternative suggested upon the agreement that the syndicate might sell to a company or to some other purchaser. In the first place, I do not believe they ever intended to sell to anybody else other than a company. An individual purchaser might ask inconvenient questions, and if they or any one of them had stated as an inducement to an individual purchaser that £140,000 was given for the property, when in fact £20,000 less had been given, it is a great error to suppose that the law is not strong enough to reach such a statement; but as I say, I do not believe it was ever intended to get an individual purchaser, even if such an intention would have had any operation. When they did afterwards sell to a company, they took very good care there should be no one who could ask questions. They were to be sellers to themselves as buyers, and it was a necessary provision to the plan that they were to be both sellers and buyers, and as buyers to get the money to pay for the purchase from the pockets of deluded shareholders.

My Lords, I decline to discuss the question of disclosure to the company.

It is too absurd to suggest that a disclosure to the parties to this transaction is a disclosure to the company of which these directors were the proper guardians and trustees. They were there by the terms of the agreement to do the work of the syndicate, that is to say, to cheat the shareholders; and this, forsooth, is to be treated as a disclosure to the company, when they were really there to hoodwink the shareholders, and so far from protecting them, were to obtain from them the money, the produce of their nefarious plans.

I do not discuss either the sum sued for, or why Gluckstein alone is sued. The whole sum has been obtained by a very gross fraud, and all who were parties to it are responsible to make good what they have obtained and withheld from the shareholders.

I move your Lordships that the appeal be dismissed with costs.

LORD MACNAGHTEN: My Lords, Mr Swinfen Eady argued this appeal with his usual ability, but the case is far too clear for argument ... For my part, I cannot see any ingenuity or any novelty in the trick which Mr Gluckstein and his associates practised on the persons whom they invited to take shares in Olympia Limited. It is the old story. It has been done over and over again.

These gentlemen set about forming a company to pay them a handsome sum for taking off their hands a property which they had contracted to buy with that end in view. They bring the company into existence by means of the usual machinery. They appoint themselves sole guardians and protectors of this creature of theirs, half-fledged and just struggling into life, bound hand and foot while yet unborn by contracts tending to their private advantage, and so fashioned by its makers that it could only act by their hands and only see through their eyes. They issue a prospectus representing that they had agreed to purchase the property for a sum largely in excess of the amount which they had, in fact, to pay. On the faith of this prospectus they collect sub-scriptions from a confiding and credulous public. And then comes the last act. Secretly, and therefore dishonestly, they put into their own pockets the difference between the real and the pretended price. After a brief career the company is ordered to be wound up. In the course of the liquidation the trick is discovered. Mr Gluckstein is called upon to make good a portion of the sum which he and his associates had misappropriated. Why Mr Gluckstein alone was selected for attack I do not know any more than I know why he was only asked to pay back a fraction of the money improperly withdrawn from the coffers of the company.

However that may be, Mr Gluckstein defends his conduct or, rather I should say, resists the demand, on four grounds, which have been gravely argued at the bar. In the first place, he says that he was not in a fiduciary position towards Olympia Limited, before the company was formed. Well, for some purposes he was not. For others he was. A good deal might be said on the point. But to my mind the point is immaterial, for it is not necessary to go back beyond the formation of the company.

In the second place, he says that if he was in a fiduciary position he did in fact make a proper disclosure. With all deference to the learned counsel for the appellant, that seems to me to be absurd. 'Disclosure' is not the most appropriate word to use when a person who plays many parts announces to himself in one character what he has done and is doing in another. To talk of disclosure to the thing called the company, when as yet there were no shareholders, is a mere farce. To the intended shareholders there was no disclosure at all. On them was practised an elaborate system of deception.

The third ground of defence was that the only remedy was rescission. That defence, in the circumstances of the present case, seems to me to be as contrary to common sense as it is to authority. The point was settled more than sixty years ago by the decision in *Hichens v Congreve*,[4] and so far as I know, that case has never been questioned.

The last defence of all was that, however much the shareholders may have been wronged, they have bound themselves by a special bargain, sacred under the provisions of the Companies Act 1862,[5] to bear their wrongs in silence. In other words, Mr Gluckstein boldly asserts that he is entitled to use the provisions of an Act of Parliament, which are directed to a very different purpose, as a shield and shelter against the just consequences of his fraud . . .

There are two things in this case which puzzle me much, and I do not suppose that I shall ever understand them. I mention them merely because I should be very sorry if it were thought that in those two matters the House unanimously approved of what has been done. I do not understand why Mr Gluckstein and his associates were not called upon to refund the whole of the money which they misappropriated. What they did with it, whether they put it in their own pockets or distributed it among their confederates, or spent it in charity, seems to me absolutely immaterial. In the next place, I do not understand why Mr Gluckstein was only charged with interest at the rate of 3%. I should have thought it was a case for penal interest.

In these two matters Mr Gluckstein has been in my opinion extremely fortunate. But he complains that he may have a difficulty in recovering from his co-directors their share of the spoil, and he asks that the official liquidator may proceed against his associates before calling upon him to make good the whole amount with which he has been charged. My Lords, there may be occasions in which that would be a proper course to take. But I cannot think that this is a case in which any indulgence ought to be shown to Mr Gluckstein. He may or may not be able to recover a contribution from those who joined with him in defrauding the company. He can bring an action at law if he likes. If he hesitates to take that course or takes it and fails, then his only remedy lies in an appeal to that sense of honour which is popularly supposed to exist among robbers of a humbler type.

I agree that the appeal must be dismissed with costs.

LORD ROBERTSON delivered a concurring opinion.

[See also *Re Darby* (**23**).]

NOTE

There is a wide choice of remedies available against a promoter who has acted in breach of duty. The company may bring proceedings for the restitution of a benefit which the promoter has received, either in equity on the basis of a constructive trust, or at law as a claim for money had and received. The parties to a secret bargain may also be sued in an action of deceit. Where a promoter has been promised, but has not received, a profit, bribe or other benefit, the company may itself enforce his claim for payment against the promisor, on the ground that he holds the claim as trustee for it: *Whaley Bridge Calico Printing Co v Green* (1879) 5 QBD 109.

4 (1831) 4 Sim 420.
5 [Lord Macnaghten is referring to the fact that the contract to purchase the premises was expressly mentioned in the company's memorandum and articles; the 'bargain' was the 'statutory contract' created by the equivalent of CA 1985, s 14 (below, p 89).]

There is some authority which suggests that a company may also have a remedy in *damages* against its promoter for breach of his fiduciary duty: see, e g *Re Leeds & Hanley Theatres of Varieties Ltd* [1902] 2 Ch 809, CA; *Jacobus Marler Estates Ltd v Marler* (1913) 85 LJPC 167n, PC. It would be unusual to award damages for the breach of a purely equitable obligation: Meagher, Gummow and Lehane, *Equity* (2nd edn, 1984) §534, say that these decisions are 'clearly wrong'.[6] (The *Marler* case may, however, be explained on the basis that the defendants were directors as well as promoters, and were held liable for their negligence in that capacity.)

Where a promoter has sold to his company property which he did not acquire as a promoter or with a view to launching the promotion—e g property which he inherited some years before—the remedy of rescission of the contract of sale is of course available to the company if he did not make a proper disclosure of his interest at the time of the sale; but if rescission is no longer possible (e g because of supervening third party rights), or if the company elects to affirm the contract, an alternative remedy by way of an account of profits does not lie: *Re Cape Breton Co* (1885) 29 Ch D 795, CA; *Ladywell Mining Co v Brookes* (1887) 35 Ch D 400, CA. This seemingly anomalous rule is commonly explained by saying that the promoter's alleged 'profit' is unquantifiable, and that by giving such a remedy the court would in effect be fixing a new price for the parties.

These old rulings on the liability of promoters have significance for the student of today because there is a close parallel between the fiduciary obligations of promoters and the fiduciary obligations of directors (below, chapter 5), and decisions like *Re Cape Breton Co* may be relevant in the latter context.

A promoter may also be liable to pay compensation to persons who subscribe for shares or other securities on the faith of listing particulars or a prospectus for which he is responsible: see below, pp 330 ff.

---

6 See, however, I E Davidson, 'The Equitable Remedy of Compensation' (1982) 13 Melb ULR 349.

CHAPTER 2

Corporate Personality[1]

A. The company as a separate legal person

In ordinary speech, we use the word 'person' to refer to an individual human being: a man, woman or child. But the word has in law a more technical meaning: 'a subject of rights and duties'—it can, for instance, include such inanimate entities as a fund (*Arab Monetary Fund v Hashim* [1991] BCC 180, HL), or a Hindu temple (*Bumper Development Corpn Ltd v Metropolitan Police Comr* [1991] 4 All ER 638, [1991] 1 WLR 1362, CA); and it is in this sense that we speak of a corporation as a 'person' and recognise its separate 'personality'.

A company is regarded in law as a person separate and distinct from its members. It makes no difference to this rule that one member owns all[2] or substantially all of the shares.

12 Salomon v A Salomon & Co Ltd [1897] AC 22 (House of Lords)

[The facts and arguments appear from the speech of Lord Macnaghten. Some extracts from the judgments of the trial judge and the Court of Appeal are given below (13).]

LORD MACNAGHTEN: Mr Salomon, who is now suing as a pauper, was a wealthy man in July 1892. He was a boot and shoe manufacturer trading on his own sole account under the firm of 'A Salomon & Co', in High Street, Whitechapel, where he had extensive warehouses and a large establishment. He had been in the trade over thirty years. He had lived in the same

---

1 There is a considerable body of writing on the theory, or theories, of corporate personality. No attempt has been made to select material representing the various schools of thought for inclusion in this volume. For the interested reader, the following are among the best-known writings in English on the subject: F W Maitland, Introduction to Gierke's *Political Theories of the Middle Ages* (London, 1900); F Hallis, *Corporate Personality* (London, 1930); Nekam, *The Personality Conception of the Legal Entity* (Harvard, 1938); L C Webb (ed), *Legal Personality and Political Pluralism* (Melbourne, 1958); S J Stoljar, *Groups and Entities* (Canberra, 1973); W M Geldart, 'Legal Personality' (1911) 27 LQR 90; H J Laski, 'The Personality of Associations' (1916) 29 Harv LR 404; M Radin, 'The Endless Problem of Corporate Personality' (1932) 32 Col LR 643, and 'A Restatement of Hohfeld' (1938) 51 Harv LR 1141; M Wolff, 'On the Nature of Legal Persons' (1938) 54 LQR 494; H L A Hart, 'Definition and Theory in Jurisprudence' (1954) 70 LQR 37, 45 ff. There is also a discussion of the topic in most general textbooks of jurisprudence.

2 A company must have at least two members (CA 1985, s 1(1)). (The number was originally seven, as appears from *Salomon*'s case.) But one person may own all the shares *beneficially* and at the same time comply with the Act by the simple expedient of vesting one or more shares in nominees who hold them on his behalf and act at his direction: the company is then commonly termed a 'one-man' company. Many other jurisdictions allow a company to have only one shareholder, and this will be the case also in this country when the Twelfth EEC Directive on Single-Member Companies (EEC 89/667) is implemented.

neighbourhood all along, and for many years past he had occupied the same premises. So far things had gone very well with him. Beginning with little or no capital, he had gradually built up a thriving business, and he was undoubtedly in good credit and repute.

It is impossible to say exactly what the value of the business was. But there was a substantial surplus of assets over liabilities. And it seems to me to be pretty clear that if Mr Salomon had been minded to dispose of his business in the market as a going concern he might fairly have counted upon retiring with at least £10,000 in his pocket.

Mr Salomon, however, did not want to part with the business. He had a wife and a family consisting of five sons and a daughter. Four of the sons were working with their father. The eldest, who was about thirty years of age, was practically the manager. But the sons were not partners: they were only servants. Not unnaturally, perhaps, they were dissatisfied with their position. They kept pressing their father to give them a share in the concern. 'They troubled me,' says Mr Salomon, 'all the while.' So at length Mr Salomon did what hundreds of others have done under similar circumstances. He turned his business into a limited company. He wanted, he says, to extend the business and make provision for his family. In those words, I think, he fairly describes the principal motives which influenced his action.

All the usual formalities were gone through; all the requirements of the Companies Act 1862 were duly observed. There was a contract with a trustee in the usual form for the sale of the business to a company about to be formed. There was a memorandum of association duly signed and registered, stating that the company was formed to carry that contract into effect, and fixing the capital of £40,000 in 40,000 shares of £1 each. There were articles of association providing the usual machinery for conducting the business. The first directors were to be nominated by the majority of the subscribers to the memorandum of association. The directors, when appointed, were authorised to exercise all such powers of the company as were not by statute or by the articles required to be exercised in general meeting; and there was express power to borrow on debentures, with the limitation that the borrowing was not to exceed £10,000 without the sanction of a general meeting.

The company was intended from the first to be a private company;[3] it remained a private company to the end. No prospectus was issued; no invitation to take shares was ever addressed to the public.

The subscribers to the memorandum were Mr Salomon, his wife, and five of his children who were grown up. The subscribers met and appointed Mr Salomon and his two elder sons directors. The directors then proceeded to carry out the proposed transfer. By an agreement dated 2 August 1892 the company adopted the preliminary contract, and in accordance with it the business was taken over by the company as from 1 June 1892. The price fixed by the contract was duly paid. The price on paper was extravagant. It amounted to over £39,000—a sum which represented the sanguine expectations of a fond owner rather than anything that can be called a businesslike or reasonable estimate of value. That, no doubt, is a circumstance which at first sight calls for observation; but when the facts of the case and the position of the parties are considered, it is difficult to see what bearing it has on the question before your Lordships. The purchase-money was paid in this way:

3 [This expression is used descriptively. The 'private company' was first made the subject of separate statutory provision in CA 1907.]

as money came in, sums amounting in all to [£20,000][4] were paid to Mr Salomon, and then immediately returned to the company in exchange for fully paid shares. The sum of £10,000 was paid in debentures[5] for the like amount. The balance, with the exception of about £1,000 which Mr Salomon seems to have received and retained, went in discharge of the debts and liabilities of the business at the time of the transfer, which were thus entirely wiped off. In the result, therefore, Mr Salomon received for his business about £1,000 in cash, £10,000 in debentures, and half the nominal capital of the company in fully paid shares for what they were worth. No other shares were issued except the seven shares taken by the subscribers to the memorandum, who, of course, knew all the circumstances, and had therefore no ground for complaint on the score of overvaluation.

The company had a brief career: it fell upon evil days. Shortly after it started there seems to have come a period of great depression in the boot and shoe trade. There were strikes of workmen too; and in view of that danger contracts with public bodies, which were the principal source of Mr Salomon's profit, were split up and divided between different firms. The attempts made to push the business on behalf of the new company crammed its warehouses with unsaleable stock. Mr Salomon seems to have done what he could: both he and his wife lent the company money; and then he got his debentures cancelled and reissued to a Mr Broderip, who advanced him £5,000, which he immediately handed over to the company on loan. The temporary relief only hastened ruin. Mr Broderip's interest was not paid when it became due. He took proceedings at once and got a receiver appointed. Then, of course, came liquidation and a forced sale of the company's assets. They realised enough to pay Mr Broderip, but not enough to pay the debentures in full: and the unsecured creditors were consequently left out in the cold.

In this state of things the liquidator met Mr Broderip's claim by a counter-claim, to which he made Mr Salomon a defendant. He disputed the validity of the debentures on the ground of fraud. On the same ground he claimed rescission of the agreement for the transfer of the business, cancellation of the debentures, and repayment by Mr Salomon of the balance of the purchase-money. In the alternative, he claimed payment of £20,000 on Mr Salomon's shares, alleging that nothing had been paid on them.

When the trial came on before Vaughan Williams J,[6] the validity of Mr Broderip's claim was admitted, and it was not disputed that the 20,000 shares were fully paid up. The case presented by the liquidator broke down completely; but the learned judge suggested that the company had a right of indemnity against Mr Salomon. The signatories of the memorandum of association were, he said, mere nominees of Mr Salomon—mere dummies. The company was Mr Salomon in another form. He used the name of the company as an alias. He employed the company as his agent; so the company, he thought, was entitled to indemnity against its principal. The counter-claim was accordingly amended to raise this point; and on the amendment being made the learned judge pronounced an order in accordance with the view he had expressed.

4 [The report reads '£30,000', but this is plainly an error. The figure of £20,000 appears in other reports of the case, e g 66 LJ Ch 35 at 49.]
5 [This means that the sum of £10,000 was advanced by Salomon to the company as a loan, secured by a charge over the assets of the company.]
6 [Part of the judgment of Vaughan Williams J is cited below, (13).]

The order of the learned judge appears to me to be founded on a mis-conception of the scope and effect of the Companies Act 1862. In order to form a company limited by shares, the Act requires that a memorandum of association should be signed by seven persons, who are each to take one share at least. If those conditions are complied with, what can it matter whether the signatories are relations or strangers? There is nothing in the Act requiring that the subscribers to the memorandum should be independent or unconnected, or that they or any one of them should take a substantial interest in the undertaking, or that they should have a mind and will of their own, as one of the learned Lords Justices seems to think, or that there should be anything like a balance of power in the constitution of the company. In almost every company that is formed the statutory number is eked out by clerks or friends, who sign their names at the request of the promoter or promoters without intending to take any further part or interest in the matter.

When the memorandum is duly signed and registered, though there be only seven shares taken, the subscribers are a body corporate 'capable forth-with', to use the words of the enactment, 'of exercising all the functions of an incorporated company'. Those are strong words. The company attains maturity on its birth. There is no period of minority—no interval of inca-pacity. I cannot understand how a body corporate thus made 'capable' by statute can lose its individuality by issuing the bulk of its capital to one person, whether he be a subscriber to the memorandum or not. The company is at law a different person altogether from the subscribers to the mem-orandum; and, though it may be that after incorporation the business is precisely the same as it was before, and the same persons are managers, and the same hands receive the profits, the company is not in law the agent of the subscribers or trustee for them. Nor are the subscribers as members liable, in any shape or form, except to the extent and in the manner provided by the Act. That is, I think, the declared intention of the enactment. If the view of the learned judge were sound, it would follow that no common law partnership could register as a company limited by shares without remaining subject to unlimited liability.

Mr Salomon appealed; but his appeal was dismissed with costs, though the appellate court did not entirely accept the view of the court below[7] ...

Among the principal reasons which induce persons to form private com-panies, as stated very clearly by Mr Palmer in his treatise on the subject, are the desire to avoid the risk of bankruptcy, and the increased facility afforded for borrowing money. By means of a private company, as Mr Palmer observes, a trade can be carried on with limited liability, and without exposing the persons interested in it in the event of failure to the harsh provisions of the bankruptcy law. A company, too, can raise money on debentures, which an ordinary trader cannot do. Any member of a company, acting in good faith, is as much entitled to take and hold the company's debentures as any outside creditor. Every creditor is entitled to get and to hold the best security the law allows him to take.

If, however, the declaration of the Court of Appeal means that Mr Salomon acted fraudulently or dishonestly, I must say I can find nothing in the evidence to support such an imputation. The purpose for which Mr Salomon and the other subscribers to the memorandum were associated was 'lawful'. The fact that Mr Salomon raised £5,000 for the company on debentures that belonged

---

7 [Parts of the judgments given in the Court of Appeal are cited below, (13).]

to him seems to me strong evidence of his good faith and of his confidence in the company. The unsecured creditors of A Salomon and Co Ltd may be entitled to sympathy, but they have only themselves to blame for their misfortunes. They trusted the company, I suppose, because they had long dealt with Mr Salomon, and he had always paid his way; but they had full notice that they were no longer dealing with an individual ...

It has become the fashion to call companies of this class 'one man companies'. That is a taking nickname, but it does not help one much in the way of argument. If it is intended to convey the meaning that a company which is under the absolute control of one person is not a company legally incorporated, although the requirements of the Act of 1862 may have been complied with, it is inaccurate and misleading: if it merely means that there is a predominant partner possessing an overwhelming influence and entitled practically to the whole of the profits, there is nothing in that that I can see contrary to the true intention of the Act of 1862, or against public policy, or detrimental to the interests of creditors. If the shares are fully paid up, it cannot matter whether they are in the hands of one or many. If the shares are not fully paid, it is as easy to gauge the solvency of an individual as to estimate the financial ability of a crowd.

One argument was addressed to your Lordships which ought perhaps to be noticed, although it was not the ground of decision in either of the courts below. It was argued that the agreement for the transfer of the business to the company ought to be set aside, because there was no independent board of directors, and the property was transferred at an overvalue. There are, it seems to me, two answers to that argument. In the first place, the directors did just what they were authorised to do by the memorandum of association. There was no fraud or misrepresentation, and there was nobody deceived. In the second place, the company have put it in their power to restore the property which was transferred to them ...

I am of opinion that the appeal ought to be allowed, and the counter-claim of the company dismissed with costs, both here and below.

LORD HALSBURY LC: My Lords, the important question in this case, I am not certain it is not the only question, is whether the respondent company was a company at all—whether in truth that artificial creation of the legislature had been validly constituted in this instance; and in order to determine that question it is necessary to look at what the statute itself has determined in that respect. I have no right to add to the requirements of the statute, nor to take from the requirements thus enacted. The sole guide must be the statute itself.

Now, that there were seven actual living persons who held shares in the company has not been doubted. As to the proportionate amounts held by each I will deal presently; but it is important to observe that this first condition of the statute is satisfied, and it follows as a consequence that it would not be competent to any one—and certainly not to these persons themselves—to deny that they were shareholders.

I must pause here to point out that the statute enacts nothing as to the extent or degree of interest which may be held by each of the seven, or as to the proportion of interest or influence possessed by one or the majority of the shareholders over the others. One share is enough. Still less is it possible to contend that the motive of becoming shareholders or of making them shareholders is a field of inquiry which the statute itself recognises as legitimate. If they are shareholders, they are shareholders for all purposes; and even if the statute was silent as to the recognition of trusts, I should be prepared to hold that if six of them were [trustees for] the seventh, whatever might be their rights inter se, the statute would have made them shareholders to all intents and purposes with their respective rights and liabilities, and, dealing with them in their relation to the company, the only relations which I believe the law would sanction would be that they were corporators of the corporate body.

I am simply here dealing with the provisions of the statute, and it seems to me to be essential to the artificial creation that the law should recognise only that artificial existence—quite apart from the motives or conduct of individual corporators. In saying this, I do not at all mean to suggest that if it could be established that this provision of the statute to which I am adverting had not been complied with, you could not go behind the certificate of incorporation to show that a fraud had been committed upon the officer entrusted with the duty of giving the certificate, and that by some proceeding in the nature of scire facias you could not prove the fact that the company had no real legal existence. But short of such proof it seems to me impossible to dispute that once the company is legally incorporated it must be treated like any other independent person with its rights and liabilities appropriate to itself, and that the motives of those who took part in the promotion of the company are absolutely irrelevant in discussing what those rights and liabilities are.

I will for the sake of argument assume the proposition that the Court of Appeal lays down—that the formation of the company was a mere scheme to enable Aron Salomon to carry on business in the name of the company. I am wholly unable to follow the proposition that this was contrary to the true intent and meaning of the Companies Act. I can only find the true intent and meaning of the Act from the Act itself; and the Act appears to me to give a company a legal existence with, as I have said, rights and liabilities of its own, whatever may have been the ideas or schemes of those who brought it into existence.

I observe that the learned judge (Vaughan Williams J) held that the business was Mr Salomon's business, and no one else's, and that he chose to employ as agent a limited company; and he proceeded to argue that he was employing that limited company as agent, and that he was bound to indemnify that agent (the company). I confess it seems to me that that very learned judge becomes involved by this argument in a very singular contradiction. Either the limited company was a legal entity or it was not. If it was, the business belonged to it and not to Mr Salomon. If it was not, there was no person and no thing to be an agent at all; and it is impossible to say at the same time that there is a company and there is not.

Lindley LJ, on the other hand, affirms that there were seven members of the company; but he says it is manifest that six of them were members simply in order to enable the seventh himself to carry on business with limited liability. The object of the whole arrangement is to do the very thing which the legislature intended not to be done.

It is obvious to inquire where is that intention of the legislature manifested in the statute. Even if we were at liberty to insert words to manifest that intention, I should have great difficulty in ascertaining what the exact intention thus imputed to the legislature is, or was. In this particular case it is the members of one family that represent all the shares; but if the supposed intention is not limited to so narrow a proposition as this, that the seven shareholders must not be members of one family, to what extent may influence or authority or intentional purchase of a majority among the shareholders be carried so as to bring it within the supposed prohibition? It is, of course, easy to say that it was contrary to the intention of the legislature—a proposition which, by reason of its generality, it is difficult to bring to the test; but when one seeks to put as an affirmative proposition what the thing is which the legislature has prohibited, there is, as it appears to me, an insuperable difficulty in the way of those who seek to insert by construction such a prohibition into the statute.

As one mode of testing the proposition, it would be pertinent to ask whether two or three, or indeed all seven, may constitute the whole of the shareholders? Whether they must be all independent of each other in the sense of each having an independent beneficial interest? And this is a question that cannot be answered by the reply that it is a matter of degree. If the legislature intended to prohibit something, you ought to know what that something is. All it has said is that one share is sufficient to constitute a shareholder, though the shares may be 100,000 in number. Where am I to get from the statute itself a limitation of that provision that that shareholder must be an independent and beneficially interested person?

My Lords, I find all through the judgment of the Court of Appeal a repetition of the same proposition to which I have already adverted—that the business was the business of Aron Salomon, and that the company is variously described as a myth and a fiction. Lopes LJ says: 'The Act contemplated the incorporation of seven independent bona fide members, who had a mind and a will of their own, and were not the mere puppets of an individual who, adopting the machinery of the Act, carried on his old business in the same way as before, when he was a sole trader.' The words 'seven independent bona fide members with a mind and will of their own, and not the puppets of an individual', are by construction to be read into the Act. Lopes LJ also said that the company was a mere nominis umbra. Kay LJ says: 'The statutes were intended to allow seven or more persons, bona fide associated for the purpose of trade, to limit their liability under certain conditions and to become a corporation. But they were not intended to legalise a pretended association for the purpose of enabling an individual to carry on his own business with limited liability in the name of a joint stock company.'

My Lords, the learned judges appear to me not to have been absolutely certain in their own minds whether to treat the company as a real thing or not. If it was a real thing; if it had a legal existence, and if consequently the law attributed to it certain rights and liabilities in its constitution as a company, it appears to me to follow as a consequence that it is impossible to deny the validity of the transactions into which it has entered ...

LORDS WATSON and DAVEY delivered concurring opinions.

LORD MORRIS concurred.

QUESTIONS

(1) To what do you think Lord Macnaghten was alluding when he said that the unsecured creditors of the company 'had full notice that they were no longer

dealing with an individual'? Was it fair to say that 'they have only themselves to blame for their misfortunes'?

(2) *Salomon*'s case has been described as a 'calamitous decision' (O Kahn-Freund, (1944) 7 MLR 54). Would you agree?

(3) Was there a 'very singular contradiction' in the reasoning of Vaughan Williams J, as Lord Halsbury said? (Compare *Re FG Films Ltd* (21), in which the company *was* held to be carrying on business as the agent of its principal shareholder.)

NOTE

The judgments in the lower courts in *Salomon*'s case (reported as *Broderip v Salomon*) deserve study in their own right as examples of 'lifting the veil'. (For this topic, see below, p 46.)

13 Broderip v Salomon [1895] 2 Ch 323 (Chancery Division and Court of Appeal)

VAUGHAN WILLIAMS J: No charge of fraud ... is involved in the amended claim; but to allow a man who carries on business under another name to set up a debenture in priority to the claims of the creditors of the company would have the effect of defeating and delaying his creditors. There must be an implied agreement by him to indemnify the company. Under the Companies Act of 1862 a man may become what is called a private company so as to obtain the benefits of limited liability. I have already held, in a case where the founder of such a company had become bankrupt and the company claimed his assets, that the company was a mere fraud, and the Court of Appeal supported that decision. In this case I propose to hold the same thing—that this business was Mr Salomon's business and no one else's; that he chose to employ as agent a limited company; that he is bound to indemnify that agent, the company; and that his agent, the company, has a lien on the assets which overrides his claims. The creditors of the company could, in my opinion, have sued Mr Salomon. Their right to do so would depend on the circumstances of the case, whether the company was a mere alias of the founder or not. In this case it is clear that the relationship of principal and agent existed between Mr Salomon and the company ...

[His Lordship accordingly ordered that Salomon was bound to indemnify the company for the debts which, as his agent, it had incurred.

Salomon appealed to the Court of Appeal, which affirmed this decision on different grounds:]

LINDLEY LJ: The incorporation of the company cannot be disputed. (See s 18 of the Companies Act 1862 [CA 1985, s 13].) Whether by any proceedings in the nature of a scire facias the court could set aside the certificate of incorporation is a question which has never been considered, and on which I express no opinion;[8] but, be that as it may, in such an action as this the validity of the certificate cannot be impeached. The company must, therefore, be regarded as a corporation, but as a corporation created for an illegitimate purpose. Moreover, there having always been seven members, although six of them hold only one £1 share each, Mr Aron Salomon cannot be reached under s 48 [CA 1985, s 24] to which I have already alluded. As the company must be recognised as a corporation, I feel a difficulty in saying that the

---

8 [See now *R v Registrar of Companies, ex p A-G* (5).]

company did not carry on business as a principal, and that the debts and liabilities contracted in its name are not enforceable against it in its corporate capacity. But it does not follow that the order made by Vaughan Williams J is wrong. A person may carry on business as a principal and incur debts and liabilities as such, and yet be entitled to be indemnified against those debts and liabilities by the person for whose benefit he carries on the business. The company in this case has been regarded by Vaughan Williams J as the agent of Aron Salomon. I should rather liken the company to a trustee for him— a trustee improperly brought into existence by him to enable him to do what the statute prohibits. It is manifest that the other members of the company have practically no interest in it, and their names have merely been used by Mr Aron Salomon to enable him to form a company, and to use its name in order to screen himself from liability ... In a strict legal sense the business may have to be regarded as the business of the company; but if any jury were asked, Whose business was it? they would say Aron Salomon's, and they would be right, if they meant that the beneficial interest in the business was his. I do not go so far as to say that the creditors of the company could sue him. In my opinion, they can only reach him through the company. Moreover, Mr Aron Salomon's liability to indemnify the company in this case is, in my view, the legal consequence of the formation of the company in order to attain a result not permitted by law. The liability does not arise simply from the fact that he holds nearly all the shares in the company. A man may do that and yet be under no such liability as Mr Aron Salomon has come under. His liability rests on the purpose for which he formed the company, on the way he formed it, and on the use which he made of it. There are many small companies which will be quite unaffected by this decision. But there may possibly be some which, like this, are mere devices to enable a man to carry on trade with limited liability, to incur debts in the name of a registered company, and to sweep off the company's assets by means of debentures which he has caused to be issued to himself in order to defeat the claims of those who have been incautious enough to trade with the company without perceiving the trap which he has laid for them ...

LOPES LJ: It would be lamentable if a scheme like this could not be defeated. If we were to permit it to succeed, we should be authorising a perversion of the Joint Stock Companies Acts. We should be giving vitality to that which is a myth and a fiction. The transaction is a device to apply the machinery of the Joint Stock Companies Act to a state of things never contemplated by that Act—an ingenious device to obtain the protection of that Act in a way and for objects not authorised by that Act, and in my judgment in a way inconsistent with and opposed to its policy and provisions. It never was intended that the company to be constituted should consist of one substantial person and six mere dummies, the nominees of that person, without any real interest in the company. The Act contemplated the incorporation of seven independent bona fide members, who had a mind and a will of their own, and were not the mere puppets of an individual who, adopting the machinery of the Act, carried on his old business in the same way as before, when he was a sole trader. To legalise such a transaction would be a scandal.

But to what relief is the liquidator entitled? In the circumstances of this case it is, in my opinion, competent for the court to set aside the sale as being a sale from Aron Salomon to himself—a sale which had none of the incidents of a sale, was a fiction, and therefore invalid; or to declare the company to be a trustee for Aron Salomon, whom Aron Salomon, the cestui que trust, was bound to indemnify; or to declare the formation of the company, the agreement of August 1892, and the issue of the debentures to Aron Salomon pursuant to such agreement, to be merely devices to enable him to carry on business in the name of the company with limited liability, contrary to the true intent and meaning of the Companies Act 1862, and further, to enable him to obtain a preference over other creditors of the company by obtaining a first charge on the assets of the company by means of such debentures ...

KAY LJ delivered a concurring judgment.

A company may make a valid and effective contract with one of its members. It is possible for a person to be at the same time wholly in control of a company (as its principal shareholder and sole director) and a servant employed by that company.

14 Lee v Lee's Air Farming Ltd [1961] AC 12, [1960] 3 All ER 420 (Privy Council)

Lee, the appellant's late husband, had formed the respondent company to carry on his business of spreading fertilisers from the air. He held 2,999 of its 3,000 shares, and was by its articles of association appointed sole governing director and (also pursuant to the articles) employed at a salary as its chief pilot. He was killed in an aircraft crash while flying for the company. If he was a 'worker' (defined as 'any person who has entered into or works under a contract of service ... with an employer ... whether remunerated by wages, salary, or otherwise') then his widow was entitled to be paid compensation by his employer under the Workers' Compensation Act 1922 (NZ). The company, as required by statute, was insured against liability to pay its workers such compensation. Mrs Lee appealed successfully against the ruling of the Court of Appeal of New Zealand that Lee could not be a 'worker' when he was in effect also the employer.

  The opinion of their Lordships was delivered by LORD MORRIS OF BORTH-Y-GEST: The Court of Appeal recognised that a director of a company may properly enter into a service agreement with his company, but they considered that, in the present case, inasmuch as the deceased was the governing director in whom was vested the full government and control of the company he could not also be a servant of the company. After referring in his judgment to the delegation to the deceased of substantially all the powers of the company, North J said:[9] 'These powers were moreover delegated to him for life and there remained with the company no power of management whatsoever. One of his first acts was to appoint himself the only pilot of the company, for, although art 33 foreshadowed this appointment, yet a contract could only spring into existence after the company had been incorporated. Therefore, he became in effect both employer and worker. True, the contract of employment was between himself and the company ... but on him lay the duty both of giving orders and obeying them. In our view, the two offices are clearly incompatible. There would exist no power of control and therefore the relationship of master-servant was not created.'

9 [1959] NZLR 393 at 399.

The substantial question which arises is, as their Lordships think, whether the deceased was a 'worker' within the meaning of the Workers' Compensation Act 1922 and its amendments. Was he a person who had entered into or worked under a contract of service with an employer? The Court of Appeal thought that his special position as governing director precluded him from being a servant of the company. On this view it is difficult to know what his status and position was when he was performing the arduous and skilful duties of piloting an aeroplane which belonged to the company and when he was carrying out the operation of top-dressing farm lands from the air. He was paid wages for so doing. The company kept a wages book in which these were recorded. The work that was being done was being done at the request of farmers whose contractual rights and obligations were with the company alone. It cannot be suggested that when engaged in the activities above referred to the deceased was discharging his duties as governing director. Their Lordships find it impossible to resist the conclusion that the active aerial operations were performed because the deceased was in some contractual relationship with the company. That relationship came about because the deceased as one legal person was willing to work for and to make a contract with the company which was another legal entity. A contractual relationship could only exist on the basis that there was consensus between two contracting parties. It was never suggested (nor in their Lordships' view could it reasonably have been suggested) that the company was a sham or a mere simulacrum. It is well established that the mere fact that someone is a director of a company is no impediment to his entering into a contract to serve the company. If, then, it be accepted that the respondent company was a legal entity their Lordships see no reason to challenge the validity of any contractual obligations which were created between the company and the deceased . . .

Nor in their Lordships' view were any contractual obligations invalidated by the circumstance that the deceased was sole governing director in whom was vested the full government and control of the company. Always assuming that the company was not a sham then the capacity of the company to make a contract with the deceased could not be impugned merely because the deceased was the agent of the company in its negotiation. The deceased might have made a firm contract to serve the company for a fixed period of years. If within such period he had retired from the office of governing director and other directors had been appointed his contract would not have been affected. The circumstance that in his capacity as a shareholder he could control the course of events would not in itself affect the validity of his contractual relationship with the company. When, therefore, it is said that 'one of his first acts was to appoint himself the only pilot of the company', it must be recognised that the appointment was made by the company, and that it was none the less a valid appointment because it was the deceased himself who acted as the agent of the company in arranging it. In their Lordships' view it is a logical consequence of the decision in *Salomon*'s case (**12**) that one person may function in dual capacities. There is no reason, therefore, to deny the possibility of a contractual relationship being created as between the deceased and the company. If this stage is reached then their Lordships see no reason why the range of possible contractual relationships should not include a contract for services, and if the deceased as agent for the company could negotiate a contract for services as between the company and himself there is no reason why a contract of service could not also be negotiated. It is said that therein lies the difficulty, because it is said that the deceased could not both be under the duty of giving orders and also be under the duty of obeying them. But this approach does not give effect to the circumstance that it would be the company and not the deceased that would be giving the orders. Control would remain with the company whoever might be the agent of the company to exercise it. The fact that so long as the deceased continued to be governing director, with amplitude of powers, it would be for him to act as the agent of the company to give the orders does not alter the fact that the company and the deceased were two separate and distinct legal persons. If the deceased had a contract of service with the company then the company had a right of control. The manner of its exercise would not affect or diminish the right to its exercise. But the existence of a right to control cannot be denied if once the reality of the legal existence of the company is recognised. Just as the company and the deceased were separate legal entities so as to permit of contractual relations being established between them, so also were they separate legal entities so as to enable the company to give an order to the deceased ...

Ex facie there was a contract of service. Their Lordships conclude, therefore, that the real issue in the case is whether the position of the deceased as sole governing director made it impossible for him to be the servant of the company in the capacity of chief pilot of the company. In their Lordships' view, for the reasons which have been indicated, there was no such impossibility. There appears to be no greater difficulty in holding that a man acting in one capacity can give orders to himself in another capacity than there is in holding that a man acting in one capacity can make a contract with himself in another capacity. The company and the deceased were separate legal entities. The company had the right to decide what contracts for aerial top-dressing it would enter into. The deceased was the agent of the company in making the necessary decisions. Any profits earned would belong to the company and not to the deceased. If the company entered into a contract with a farmer, then it lay within its right and power to direct its chief pilot to perform certain operations. The right to control existed even though it would be for the deceased in his capacity as agent for the company to decide what orders to give. The right to control existed in the company, and an application of the principles of *Salomon*'s case demonstrates that the company was distinct from the deceased. As pointed out above, there might have come a time when the deceased would remain bound contractually to serve the company as chief pilot though he had retired from the office of sole governing director. Their Lordships consider, therefore, that the deceased was a worker and that the question posed in the case stated should be answered in the affirmative ...

The property of a company belongs to it and not to its members. Neither a shareholder nor a creditor of a company (unless a secured creditor) has an insurable interest in the assets of the company.

15 Macaura v Northern Assurance Co [1925] AC 619 (House of Lords)

Macaura, the owner of the Killymoon estate in county Tyrone, sold the whole of the timber on the estate to a company, Irish Canadian Sawmills Ltd, in consideration of the allotment to him of 42,000 fully paid £1 shares.

All the company's shares were held by Macaura and his nominees, and he was also an unsecured creditor of the company for an amount of £19,000. Subsequently to the sale, he effected insurance policies in his own name with the respondent company and others, covering the timber against fire. Two weeks later, almost all of the timber was destroyed in a fire. A claim brought by Macaura on the policies was disallowed on the ground that he had no insurable interest in the timber.

LORD SUMNER: My Lords, this appeal relates to an insurance on goods against loss by fire. It is clear that the appellant had no insurable interest in the timber described. It was not his. It belonged to the Irish Canadian Sawmills Ltd, of Skibbereen, co Cork. He had no lien or security over it and, though it lay on his land by his permission, he had no responsibility to its owner for its safety, nor was it there under any contract that enabled him to hold it for his debt. He owned almost all the shares in the company, and the company owed him a good deal of money, but, neither as creditor nor as shareholder, could he insure the company's assets. The debt was not exposed to fire nor were the shares, and the fact that he was virtually the company's only creditor, while the timber was its only asset, seems to me to make no difference. He stood in no 'legal or equitable relation to' the timber at all. He had no 'concern in' the subject insured. His relation was to the company, not to its goods, and after the fire he was directly prejudiced by the paucity of the company's assets, not by the fire ...

My Lords, I think this appeal fails.

LORDS BUCKMASTER and WRENBURY delivered concurring opinions.

LORDS ATKINSON and PHILLIMORE concurred.

The fact that one person holds all, or substantially all, of the shares in a company does not *without more make the company's business that person's business in the eyes of the law.*

16 Gramophone and Typewriter Co Ltd v Stanley [1908] 2 KB 89 (Court of Appeal)

All the shares in a German company (Deutsche Grammophon Aktiengesellschaft) were held by the appellant company, which was resident for tax purposes in England. The appellant was assessed for income tax not only upon the profits of the German company actually remitted to it, but also on a sum of £15,000 retained by the German company and transferred by it to a depreciation fund. The unremitted profits were taxable in England only if (as the Commissioners of Inland Revenue had held) they were the profits or gains of a business 'carried on' by the *English* company. The Court of Appeal rejected this view.

BUCKLEY LJ: The question is, I think, one of fact ... The question of fact is whether the business in Germany is carried on by the appellant company. If it is, the [appellants] do not dispute that the Attorney-General is right. If, on the contrary, the German business is not carried on by the English company, then equally the Attorney-General cannot dispute but that the English company is assessable only upon the dividends which it may receive upon its shares in the German company.

In order to succeed the Attorney-General must, I think, make out either, first, that the German company is a fiction, a sham, a simulacrum, and that in reality the English company, and not the German company, is carrying on the business; or, secondly, that the German company, if it is a real thing, is the agent of the English company. As regards the former of these, there are no facts at all to show that the German company is a pretence. It was formed in January 1900 by the union of three other companies, each of which brought in substantial properties, and of two individuals. It is duly constituted and governed according to German law, and there is no ground whatever for saying that it is other than a real German corporation carrying on business in Germany under circumstances in which the company and its officers are amenable to German law and with a view to the acquisition of profit. The only remaining question, therefore, is whether the German company is agent of the English company, whether the English company is really carrying on the business and is employing the German company to do so on its behalf. Upon this point the Attorney-General relies principally upon the fact that, as stated in para 17 of the case, the appellant company now holds all the shares of the German company. In my opinion this fact does not establish the relation of principal and agent between the English company and the German company. It is so familiar that it would be a waste of time to dwell upon the difference between the corporation and the aggregate of all the corporators. But I may point out the following considerations as bearing upon the question whether the possession of all the shares is evidence of agency. Suppose that during the year whose accounts are under review the appellant company had held no shares at all in the first six months and had held all the shares in the last six months, or suppose that, having held all the shares but ten today, it became the holder of all tomorrow and again parted with ten the next day, it cannot seriously be suggested that each time one person becomes the holder of all the shares an agency comes into existence which dies again when he parts with some of them.

Further it is urged that the English company, as owning all the shares, can control the German company in the sense that the German company must do all that the English company directs. In my opinion this again is a misapprehension. This court decided not long since, in *Automatic Self-Cleansing Filter Syndicate Co Ltd v Cuninghame* (**94**) that even a resolution of a numerical majority at a general meeting of the company cannot impose its will upon the directors when the articles have confided to them the control of the company's affairs. The directors are not servants to obey directions given by the shareholders as individuals; they are not agents appointed by and bound to serve the shareholders as their principals. They are persons who may by the regulations be entrusted with the control of the business, and if so entrusted they can be dispossessed from that control only by the statutory majority which can alter the articles. Directors are not, I think, bound to comply with the directions even of all the corporators acting as individuals. Of course the corporators have it in their power by proper resolutions, which would generally be special resolutions,[10] to remove directors who do not act as they desire, but this in no way answers the question here to be considered, which is whether the corporators are engaged in carrying on the business of the corporation. In my opinion they are not. To say that they are involves a complete confusion of ideas ...

10 [An ordinary resolution is now sufficient in all cases: CA 1985, s 303.]

COZENS-HARDY MR and FLETCHER MOULTON LJ delivered concurring judgments.

17 Lonrho Ltd v Shell Petroleum Co Ltd [1980] QB 358 (Court of Appeal); affd [1980] 1 WLR 627 (House of Lords)

Lonrho sought an order for discovery of certain documents which it claimed were in the 'power' of two multinational oil companies, Shell and BP. These documents were held in Rhodesia (now Zimbabwe) and South Africa by local subsidiaries of Shell and BP, the subsidiaries being in each case wholly owned and controlled by those companies between them. The application was refused.

SHAW LJ: This appeal poses as its principal issue a compact question as to the application and scope of RSC, Ord 24. When is a document in the power (as distinct from the possession or control) of a party to litigation so as to require him to disclose it if it relates to matters in question in that litigation?

The question seems elementary, but it poses for me at any rate a difficult philosophical problem as to what constitutes power, and I must confess to some vacillation as the arguments on either side proceeded. In the end I have come to the view that a document can be said to be in the power of a party for the purpose of disclosure only if, at the time and in the situation which obtains at the date of discovery, that party is, on the factual realities of the case virtually in possession (as with a one-man company in relation to documents of the company) or otherwise has a present indefeasible legal right to demand possession from the person in whose possession or control it is at that time.

In the present case no such sure or direct route to acquiring possession existed or exists. The relationship between Shell and BP, on the one hand, and, on the other hand, the various subsidiaries, including those which are wholly owned by the two parent companies, may afford an ultimate but not an immediate or certain prospect of acquiring possession of documents which belong to and are in the possession and control for the time being of a subsidiary. The realisation of that prospect might involve the alteration of the articles of an unwilling or recalcitrant subsidiary followed by the removal of its then directors and their substitution by others more compliant. This would involve a radical transformation of the local scene within the subsidiary company. It would involve not merely raising the corporate veil, but committing an affront on the persona of the company itself. Even then, the directors who are substituted for the recalcitrant ones may find that there exists a conflict of duty so that they have no right to comply with the requirement. It would follow that the outcome of such a procedure would be at the best dubious ...

There are no doubt situations, such as existed in *B v B* (*Matrimonial Proceedings: Discovery*)[11] where on the established facts a company is so utterly subservient or subordinated to the will and the wishes of some other person (whether an individual or a parent company) that compliance with that other person's demands can be regarded as assured. Each case must depend upon its own facts and also upon the nature, degree and context of the control it is sought to exercise ...

11 [1978] Fam 181, [1978] 1 All ER 801.

LORD DENNING MR and BRANDON LJ delivered concurring judgments.
    An appeal to the House of Lords was dismissed: [1980] 1 WLR 627.

18 Tunstall v Steigmann [1962] 2 QB 593, [1962] 2 All ER 417 (Court of Appeal)

Mrs Tunstall ('the tenant') carried on business as a wardrobe dealer in shop premises leased from Mrs Steigmann ('the landlord'). Mrs Steigmann also owned the next-door shop, where she carried on the business of a pork-butcher. In April 1961 the landlord gave the tenant six months' notice to quit, and resisted the latter's application for a new tenancy, made under the Landlord and Tenant Act 1954, on ground (g) of s 30(1) of that Act, which reads as follows: '. . . that on the termination of the current tenancy the landlord intends to occupy the holding for the purposes, or partly for the purposes, of a business to be carried on by him therein'. Before the matter came on for hearing, Mrs Steigmann had formed a company, in which she held all but two of the shares (and held the two also through nominees), to take over her business. The county court judge held that she might still intend to carry on the business notwithstanding that it was owned by the company, and he refused to grant the tenant a new lease. The tenant's appeal was allowed by the Court of Appeal.

WILLMER LJ: The judge decided that the landlord was entitled to suceed. He took the view that in common sense where an individual is in such complete control of the company it can truthfully be said that the intention is to occupy for the purposes of his or her business, such business being the running of the company. In reaching this conclusion he was clearly influenced by some observations made obiter by members of this court in *Pegler v Craven*.[12] The actual question at issue in that case was not quite the same as here. The matter arose under the Leasehold Property (Temporary Provisions) Act 1951 and it was the occupation of the tenant, and not that of the landlord, that was in question. These differences, however, do not affect the question how far, if at all, occupation by a company can be equated with occupation by the individual who controls the company. The significant difference between *Pegler v Craven* and the present case is that in the former case the tenant who was claiming had no more than a majority shareholding, and had not the same measure of control over the company as the landlord in the present case. This court held that in the circumstances of that case the occupation by the company could not be said to be occupation by the tenant so as to bring the tenant within the Act. But the members of the court expressly reserved for future consideration what would be the right of a tenant (and equally, it would seem, of a landlord) who was in fact beneficial owner of all or substantially all the issued shares of such a company. It was suggested by Lord Evershed MR that there might be some circumstances in which it could be said that the company in occupation would be but the alter ego of the individual concerned. The judge here has based his decision on the view that the present is just such a case, that the company is but the alter ego of the landlord and that, accordingly, occupation by the company for the purpose of its business would amount to the same as occupation by the landlord for the purposes of her business.

12 [1952] 2 QB 69, [1952] 1 All ER 685.

Mr Bramall, in an attractive and forceful argument, has sought to support the judge's view on a number of grounds. First, he says that construing the language of the sub-section in accordance with the ordinary meaning of the words used, the landlord here did intend to occupy the holding for the purposes of a business to be carried on by her. The business was in substance her business, the company being a mere piece of mechanism to enable the landlord's business to be carried on. This, it is said, was the reality; and we were invited to look at the reality and substance of the proposed occupation rather than at its form . . .

I have certainly felt the force of the argument on behalf of the landlord; but in the end I am satisfied that it cannot prevail. There is no escape from the fact that a company is a legal entity entirely separate from its corporators—see *Salomon v Salomon & Co* (**12**). Here the landlord and her company are entirely separate entities. This is no matter of form; it is a matter of substance and reality. Each can sue and be sued in its own right; indeed, there is nothing to prevent the one from suing the other. Even the holder of 100 per cent of the shares in a company does not by such holding become so identified with the company that he or she can be said to carry on the business of the company. This clearly appears from *Gramophone and Typewriter Co Ltd v Stanley* (**16**), a decision of this court which seems to me, on due consideration, to be destructive of the argument for the landlord. As was pointed out by Fletcher Moulton LJ, control of a company by a corporator is wholly different in fact and law from carrying on the business himself. 'The individual corporator does not carry on the business of the corporation.' This being so, I do not see how it is possible for the landlord in the present case to assert that she intends to occupy the holding for the purpose of a business to be carried on by her. Her intention, as has been made plain, is that the company which she controls shall carry on its business on the holding. But that, unfortunately for her, is something for which the Act makes no provision . . . She cannot, therefore, successfully oppose the grant of a new tenancy.

I have reached this conclusion with some reluctance, for it seems to me that the construction of s 30(1)(g), which I have felt compelled to adopt, may well lead to some very bizarre results. Thus it will be possible for an absentee landlord, living in idleness away from the holding, to resist the grant of a new tenancy upon proof of an intention to occupy, through his agent or manager, for the purpose of carrying on his business through such agent or manager. On the other hand, a hard-working landlord, who has transferred his business to a company of which he retains complete control, and who genuinely needs to obtain possession of the holding so that his company's business may be carried on there with the aid of his own labour, will nevertheless apparently be without any right to oppose an application for a new tenancy by a tenant however undeserving. It seems, however, impossible to escape the conclusion that this is the effect of what Parliament has enacted. If the results are thought undesirable, only Parliament can put that right . . .

ORMEROD and DANCKWERTS LJJ delivered concurring judgments.

NOTE

The legislation has since been amended. It is now provided by s 6 of the Law of Property Act 1969 that where a landlord has a controlling interest in a company, any business to be carried on by the company shall be treated for the purpose of s 30 of the Landlord and Tenant Act 1954 as a business to be carried on by him.

Tunstall v Steigmann may be contrasted with *Willis v Association of Universities of the British Commonwealth* [1965] 1 QB 140, [1964] 2 All ER 39, where the Court of Appeal allowed the landlord association (a limited company) to resist an application by its tenant Willis for a new tenancy on very similar facts, notwithstanding that the company was about to be superseded by a new corporation (the Association of Commonwealth Universities) incorporated by royal charter, and it was this new corporation that required the premises. The court on this occasion was also undeterred by the fact that the association really wished to use the space to accommodate an autonomous body, the Universities Central Council on Admission ('UCCA'), which the association had set up to discharge functions quite distinct from its own.

B. 'Lifting the veil'

The principle of separate corporate personality as established[13] by *Salomon*'s case and emphatically reasserted in later cases, some of which are cited above, forms the corner-stone of company law. The authority of these cases is unshakeable; and yet exceptionally in some instances the law *is* prepared to disregard or look behind the corporate personality and have regard to the 'realities'[14] of the situation. This approach, which has come to be known as 'lifting the veil' of incorporation, is sometimes expressly authorised by statute, and sometimes adopted by the court of its own accord. It would, perhaps, give a better perspective to the discussion if *Salomon*'s case and the other cases quoted above were regarded not simply as restatements of an elementary and obvious principle, but as instances when a plea that the veil should be lifted, though perhaps initially successful, ultimately failed. (It is particularly instructive to re-examine, *as* examples of 'lifting the veil', the judgments of the lower courts in *Salomon*'s case itself (**13**), bearing in mind that the judges concerned were outstanding company lawyers of considerable experience. The judgments and speeches in this case may be contrasted with those in the *Daimler* case (**20**), where a greatly enlarged Court of Appeal was almost unanimous in adhering to the orthodox line, which the Lords this time rejected.)

Some examples of 'lifting the veil' follow. But the topic cannot really be considered on its own as a phenomenon separable from the rest of company law. Again and again in the succeeding chapters we shall encounter situations in which the issue before the court—or the problem faced by the legislature—has been, in essence, whether the separate personality of the company is to be respected or disregarded. Many of the *statutory* directions to 'lift the veil' occur in revenue law; s 6 of the Law of Property Act 1969, which has been mentioned above, p 45, is another example. The Companies Act 1985 itself allows the 'veil' to be penetrated in certain circumstances: e g where a company's membership falls below the prescribed minimum;[15] where a public company commences business in breach of s 117;[16] and in relation to the

13 Of course, the doctrine was recognised much earlier—see, for instance, *Edmunds v Brown and Tillard* (1668) 1 Lev 237, where members were held not liable on the bond of a corporation after its dissolution, and *Foss v Harbottle* (**232**).

14 It is noteworthy that an appeal to the 'realities' of the situation is often made both in the argument *for* lifting the veil and in the argument *against* it (see, e g *Tunstall v Steigmann* (**18**)).

15 Section 24.

16 Section 117(8).

accounts of holding and subsidiary companies.[17] The insolvency legislation contains a number of sections providing for directors and others to be personally liable for the debts of a limited company, or to make a contribution to its assets in a liquidation, e g where there has been fraudulent or wrongful trading (IA 1986, ss 213–5) or the improper re-use of an insolvent company's name (ss 216–7); and the Company Directors Disqualification Act 1986, s 15 similarly penalises a person who acts as a director in breach of a disqualification order. Provisions to similar effect in other statutes will occasionally be noticed.[18]

Judicial inroads into the principle of separate personality are numerous, and quite often made unconsciously. Commentators[19] have on the whole discerned no set pattern in the decided cases—indeed, in many instances they seem to contradict each other in the most baffling way. The plea is sometimes heard for 'some principles to be injected into this area of the law' from which 'litigants can predict when the courts will, and will not, lift the veil of the corporate entity',[20] but there is much to be said for retaining some flexibility, especially where it enables the court to counter fraud, oppression or sharp practice[1] or to condone informality in the affairs of small companies.[2]

On the other hand, in matters of property and contract, the courts should surely be most hesitant to lift the veil in response to superficial considerations of 'common sense' or 'reality' or 'fairness'. There is much wisdom in the observations of Hughes J in the Canadian case *Hunt v T W Johnstone Co Ltd* (1976) 69 DLR (3d) 639 at 661, where the facts were similar to those of *Macaura v Northern Assurance Co* (**15**). He said:

> Whatever was the purpose behind the incorporation of these two companies—and no doubt relief from taxation was one of them—I can infer that it was of advantage to the prime owner. He cannot be allowed to raise the corporate shield against an assault from one quarter and lower it to get help from another.

The court may go behind the veil of incorporation in order to determine whether a company is to be characterised as an 'enemy' in time of war.

---

17 Sections 227–230 and Sch 4, Pt IV.
18 See, e g Trading with the Enemy Act 1939, s 2 (below, p 52).
19 For further reading, see L C B Gower, *Modern Company Law,* 4th ed (London, 1979), chapter 10; W G Friedmann, *Legal Theory,* 5th ed (London, 1967), pp 556–72; O Kahn-Freund, 'Some Reflections on Company Law Reform' (1944) 7 MLR 54; A K R Kiralfy, 'Some Unforeseen Consequences of Private Incorporation' (1944) 65 LQR 231; A Samuels, 'Lifting the Veil' [1964] JBL 107; M A Pickering, 'The Company as a Separate Legal Entity' (1968) 31 MLR 481; C M Schmitthoff, '*Salomon* in the Shadow' [1976] JBL 305; Whincup, 'Inequitable Incorporation' (1981) 2 Co Law 158; A Beck, 'The Two Sides of the Corporate Veil' in J H Farrar (ed), *Contemporary Issues in Company Law* (1987); F G Rixon, 'Lifting the Veil Between Holding and Subsidiary Companies' (1986) 102 LQR 415; S Ottolenghi 'From Peeping behind the Corporate Veil to Ignoring it Completely' (1990) 53 MLR 338; S Griffin, 'Holding Companies and Subsidiaries—the Corporate Veil' (1991) 12 Co Law 16.
20 See the notes by Lord Wedderburn [1958] CLJ 152 at 155, (1960) 23 MLR 663 at 666.
1 See, e g *Re Darby* (**23**); *Re Bugle Press Ltd* (**260**); *Gilford Motor Co Ltd v Horne* (**24**). There is, of course, an element of question-begging in determining whether there *has* been such misuse of the privilege of incorporation, as is revealed in the attitudes of the different courts in *Salomon*'s case itself.
2 See below, pp 166–171, and compare the cases in which a small company has been treated as a quasi-partnership for the purpose of winding up (below, pp 561 ff).

19 Daimler Co Ltd v Continental Tyre and Rubber Co (Great Britain) Ltd.
[1916] 2 AC 307 (House of Lords)

The Continental Tyre company was incorporated in England, but all except
one of its shares were held by persons resident in Germany, and all the
directors resided in Germany. The secretary, who held the remaining share,
resided in England and was a British subject. The issue was whether the
company had standing in an English court to sue and recover a debt when a
state of war existed between England and Germany. The company was
allowed by the Master to sign summary judgment without proceeding to
trial, under RSC, Ord 14. His decision was affirmed by Scrutton J in chambers
and by a greatly enlarged Court of Appeal (Buckley LJ dissenting). [Extracts
from the judgments delivered in the Court of Appeal are cited below, (**20**).]
The House of Lords unanimously reversed the order of the Court of Appeal,
and directed that the action be struck out as irregular, on the ground that
the secretary was not authorised to commence the action; and it held further
(by a majority, Lords Shaw of Dunfermline and Parmoor dissenting) that
the company, though incorporated in England, was capable of acquiring an
enemy character, so that leave to sign summary judgment under Ord 14
should not have been given.

LORD PARKER OF WADDINGTON: No one can question that a corporation is
a legal person distinct from its corporators; that the relation of a shareholder
to a company, which is limited by shares, is not in itself the relation of
principal and agent or the reverse; that the assets of the company belong to
it and the acts of its servants and agents are its acts, while its shareholders,
as such, have no property in the assets and no personal responsibility for
those acts. The law on the subject is clearly laid down in ... *Salomon v
Salomon & Co* (**12**) ... I do not think, however, that it is a necessary corollary
of this reasoning to say that the character of its corporators must be irrelevant
to the character of the company; and this is crucial, for the rule against
trading with the enemy depends upon enemy character.

A natural person, though an English-born subject of His Majesty, may
bear an enemy character and be under liability and disability as such by
adhering to His Majesty's enemies. If he gives them active aid, he is a traitor;
but he may fall far short of that and still be invested with enemy character.
If he has what is known in prize law as a commercial domicil among the
King's enemies, his merchandise is good prize at sea, just as if it belonged to
a subject of the enemy power. Not only actively, but passively, he may bring
himself under the same disability. Voluntary residence among the enemy,
however passive or pacific he may be, identifies an English subject with His
Majesty's foes. I do not think it necessary to cite authority for these well-
known propositions, nor do I doubt that, if they had seemed material to the
Court of Appeal, they would have been accepted.

How are such rules to be applied to an artificial person, incorporated by
forms of law? As far as active adherence to the enemy goes, there can be no
difference, except such as arises from the fact that a company's acts are those
of its servants and agents acting within the scope of their authority ...

In the case of an artificial person what is the analogue to voluntary
residence among the King's enemies? Its impersonality can hardly put it in
a better position than a natural person and lead to its being unaffected by
anything equivalent to residence. It is only by a figure of speech that a

company can be said to have a nationality or residence at all. If the place of its incorporation under municipal law fixes its residence, then its residence cannot be changed, which is almost a contradiction in terms, and in the case of a company residence must correspond to the birthplace and country of natural allegiance in the case of a living person, and not to residence or commercial domicil. Nevertheless, enemy character depends on these last. It would seem, therefore, logically to follow that, in transferring the application of the rule against trading with the enemy from natural to artificial persons, something more than the mere place or country of registration or incorporation must be looked at.

My Lords, I think that the analogy is to be found in control, an idea which, if not very familiar in law, is of capital importance and is very well understood in commerce and finance. The acts of a company's organs, its directors, managers, secretary, and so forth, functioning within the scope of their authority, are the company's acts and may invest it definitively with enemy character. It seems to me that similarly the character of those who can make and unmake those officers, dictate their conduct mediately or immediately, prescribe their duties and call them to account, may also be material in a question of the enemy character of the company. If not definite and conclusive, it must at least be prima facie relevant, as raising a presumption that those who are purporting to act in the name of the company are, in fact, under the control of those whom it is their interest to satisfy. Certainly I have found no authority to the contrary. Such a view reconciles the positions of natural and artificial persons in this regard, and the opposite view leads to the paradoxical result that the King's enemies, who chance during war to constitute the entire body of corporators in a company registered in England, thereby pass out of the range of legal vision, and, instead, the corporation, which in itself is incapable of loyalty, or enmity, or residence, or of anything but bare existence in contemplation of law and registration under some system of law, takes their place for almost the most important of all purposes, that of being classed among the King's friends or among his foes in time of war.

What is involved in the decision of the Court of Appeal is that, for all purposes to which the character and not merely the rights and powers of an artificial person are material, the personalities of the natural persons, who are its corporators, are to be ignored. An impassable line is drawn between the one person and the others. When the law is concerned with the artificial person, it is to know nothing of the natural persons who constitute and control it. In questions of property and capacity, of acts done and rights acquired or liabilities assumed thereby, this may be always true. Certainly it is so for the most part. But the character in which property is held, and the character in which the capacity to act is enjoyed and acts are done, are not in pari materia. The latter character is a quality of the company itself, and conditions its capacities and its acts. It is not a mere part of its energies or acquisitions, and if that character must be derivable not from the circumstances of its incorporation, which arises once for all, but from qualities of enmity and amity, which are dependent on the chances of peace or war and are attributable only to human beings, I know not from what human beings that character should be derived, in cases where the active conduct of the company's officers has not already decided the matter, if resort is not to be had to the predominant character of its shareholders and corporators . . .

My Lords, having regard to the foregoing considerations, I think the law on the subject may be summarised in the following propositions:

(1) A company incorporated in the United Kingdom is a legal entity, a creation of law with the status and capacity which the law confers. It is not a natural person with mind or conscience. To use the language of Buckley LJ, 'it can be neither loyal nor disloyal. It can be neither friend nor enemy'.

(2) Such a company can only act through agents properly authorised, and so long as it is carrying on business in this country through agents so authorised and residing in this or a friendly country it is prima facie to be regarded as a friend, and all His Majesty's lieges may deal with it as such.

(3) Such a company may, however, assume an enemy character. This will be the case if its agents or the persons in de facto control of its affairs, whether authorised or not, are resident in an enemy country, or, wherever resident, are adhering to the enemy or taking instructions from or acting under the control of enemies. A person knowingly dealing with the company in such a case is trading with the enemy.

(4) The character of individal shareholders cannot of itself affect the character of the company. This is admittedly so in times of peace, during which every shareholder is at liberty to exercise and enjoy such rights as are by law incident to his status as shareholder. It would be anomalous if it were not so also in a time of war, during which all such rights and privileges are in abeyance. The enemy character of individual shareholders and their conduct may, however, be very material on the question whether the company's agents, or the persons in de facto control of its affairs, are in fact adhering to, taking instructions from, or acting under the control of enemies. This materiality will vary with the number of shareholders who are enemies and the value of their holdings. The fact, if it be the fact, that after eliminating the enemy shareholders the number of shareholders remaining is insufficient for the purpose of holding meetings of the company or appointing directors or other officers, may well raise a presumption in this respect. For example, in the present case, even if the secretary had been fully authorised to manage the affairs of the company and to institute legal proceedings on its behalf, the fact that he held one share only out of 25,000 shares, and was the only shareholder who was not an enemy, might well throw on the company the onus of proving that he was not acting under the control of, taking his instructions from, or adhering to the King's enemies in such manner as to impose an enemy character on the company itself. It is an a fortiori case when the secretary is without authority and necessarily depends for the validity of all he does on the subsequent ratification of enemy shareholders. The circumstances of the present case were, therefore, such as to require close investigation and preclude the propriety of giving leave to sign judgment under Order 14, rule 1.

(5) In a similar way a company registered in the United Kingdom, but carrying on business in a neutral country through agents properly authorised and resident here or in the neutral country, is prima facie to be regarded as a friend, but may, through its agents or persons in de facto control of its affairs, assume an enemy character.

(6) A company registered in the United Kingdom but carrying on business in an enemy country is to be regarded as an enemy ...

THE EARL OF HALSBURY LC and LORD ATKINSON delivered concurring opinions. VISCOUNT MERSEY and LORDS KINNEAR and SUMNER concurred. LORDS SHAW OF DUNFERMLINE and PARMOOR delivered opinions concurring in the result, but dissenting on this point.

[Part of the majority judgment in the Court of Appeal is set out below. The arguments in favour of recognising and of disregarding the corporate entity could hardly be contrasted more sharply. No doubt the factor which most influenced the House of Lords was the paramountcy of the public interest in wartime.]

20 Continental Tyre and Rubber Co (Great Britain) Ltd v Daimler Co Ltd
[1915] 1 KB 893 (Court of Appeal)

LORD READING CJ read the judgment of the majority of the court (LORD READING CJ, LORD COZENS-HARDY MR, KENNEDY, PHILLIMORE and PICKFORD LJJ): It cannot be disputed that the plaintiff company is an entity created by statute. It is a company incorporated under the Companies Acts and therefore is a thing brought into existence by virtue of statutory enactment. At the outbreak of war it was carrying on business in the United Kingdom; it had contracted to supply goods, it delivered them, and until the outbreak of the war it was admittedly entitled to receive payment at the due dates. Has the character of the company changed because on the outbreak of war all the shareholders and directors resided in an enemy country and therefore became alien enemies? Admittedly it was an English company before the war. An English company cannot by reason of these facts cease to be an English company. It remains an English company regardless of the residence of its shareholders or directors either before or after the declaration of war. Indeed it was not argued by Mr Gore-Browne that the company ceased to be an entity created under English law, but it was argued that the law in time of war and in reference to trading with the enemy should sweep aside this 'technicality' as the entity was described and should treat the company not as an English company but as a German company and therefore as an alien enemy. If the creation and existence of the company could be treated as a mere technicality, there would be considerable force in this argument. It is undoubtedly the policy of the law as administered in our courts of justice to regard substance and to disregard form. Justice should not be hindered by mere technicality, but substance must not be treated as form or swept aside as technicality because that course might appear convenient in a particular case. The fallacy of the appellants' contention lies in the suggestion that the entity created by statute is or can be treated during the war as a mere form or technicality by reason of the enemy character of its shareholders and directors. A company formed and registered under the Companies Acts has a real existence with rights and liabilities as a separate legal entity. It is a different person altogether from the subscribers to the memorandum or the shareholders on the register (per Lord Macnaghten in *Salomon v Salomon & Co* (12)). It cannot be technically an English company and substantially a German company except by the use of inaccurate and misleading language. Once it is validly constituted as an English company it is an artificial creation of the legislature and it retains its existence for all intents and purposes. It is a living thing with a separate existence which cannot be swept aside as a technicality. It is not a mere name or mask or cloak or device to conceal the identity of persons and it is not suggested that the company was formed for any dishonest or fraudulent purpose. It is a legal body clothed with the form prescribed by the legislature.

In determining whether a company is an English or foreign corporation no inquiry is made into the share register for the purpose of ascertaining whether the members of the company are English or foreign. Once a corporation has been created in accordance with the requirements of the law it is an English company notwithstanding that all its shareholders may be foreign. Just as a foreign corporation does not become British and cease to be foreign if all its members are subjects of the British Crown (per Lord Macnaghten, Lord Brampton and Lord Lindley in *Janson v Driefontein Consolidated Mines*[3]). For the appellants' contention to succeed, payment to the company must be treated as payment to the shareholders of the company, but a debt due to a company is not a debt due to all or any of its shareholders: *Salomon v Salomon & Co.* The company and the company alone is the creditor entitled to enforce payment of the debt and empowered to give to the debtor a good and valid discharge. Once this conclusion is reached it follows that payment to the plaintiff company is not payment to the alien enemy shareholders or for their benefit ...

It must, however, be clearly understood that any person who on behalf of the plaintiff company paid money to shareholders resident or carrying on business in Germany or to a company incorporated in Germany would be acting in defiance of the law, and none the less because payment is made in the name of the company. That would be a criminal offence and would be within the express prohibition of para 5, as defined by para 3. The plaintiff company has never claimed any such right and has explicitly disclaimed any such intention ...

BUCKLEY LJ delivered a dissenting judgment.

NOTE

The view of the majority of the Court of Appeal was rejected by the House of Lords, as we have seen (**19**).

The Trading with the Enemy Act 1939 adopts the view of the House of Lords in the *Daimler* case:

Trading with the Enemy Act 1939

2 *Definition of enemy*

(1) Subject to the provisions of this section, the expression 'enemy' for the purposes of this Act means—
(a) any state, or sovereign of a state, at war with His Majesty,
(b) any individual resident in enemy territory,
(c) any body of persons (whether corporate or unincorporate) carrying on business in any place, if and so long as the body is controlled by a person who, under this section, is an enemy, or
(d) any body of persons constituted or incorporated in, or under the laws of, a state at war with His Majesty;

3 [1902] AC 484 at 497, 501 and 505.

but does not include any person by reason only that he is an enemy subject.

QUESTION

Could a landlord be guilty of an offence under the Race Relations Act 1976 if he refused to lease premises to a company incorporated in England which was owned and controlled by three Russian businessmen?

An agency between a company and its shareholders or controllers may, exceptionally, be found to exist as a matter of fact.

21 Re FG (Films) Ltd [1953] 1 WLR 483, [1953] 1 All ER 615 (Chancery Division)

The applicant company sought to have the film 'Monsoon' registered as a British film under the Cinematograph Films Acts 1938–1948. The Board of Trade refused the application on the ground that the film had in reality been made by a large American company, Film Group Incorporated. By the terms of an agreement between the two companies, the American company had undertaken to provide finance and all the facilities required by the applicant to make the film. The applicant company sought a declaration that it was the 'maker' within the meaning of the Act.

VAISEY J: The applicants have a capital of £100, divided into 100 shares of £1 each, 90 of which are held by the American director and the remaining 10 by a British one. The third director has no shareholding. I now understand that they have no place of business apart from their registered office, and they did not employ any staff. It seems to me to be contrary, not only to all sense and reason, but to the proved and admitted facts of the case, to say or to believe that this insignificant company undertook in any real sense of that word the arrangements for the making of this film. I think that their participation in any such undertaking was so small as to be practically negligible, and that they acted, in so far as they acted at all in the matter, merely as the nominee of and agent for an American company called Film Group Incorporated, which seems (among other things) to have financed the making of the film to the extent of at least £80,000 under the auspices and direction of the said American director, who happened to be its president. The suggestion that this American company and that director were merely agents for the applicants is, to my mind, inconsistent with and contradicted by the evidence, and a mere travesty of the facts, as I understand and hold them to be.

The applicants' intervention in the matter was purely colourable. They were brought into existence for the sole purpose of being put forward as having undertaken the very elaborate arrangements necessary for the making of this film and of enabling it thereby to qualify as a British film. The attempt has failed, and the respondent's decision not to register 'Monsoon' as a British film was, in my judgment, plainly right.

In lieu of the declarations for which the applicants ask, I will declare that the applicants were not the makers of the film called 'Monsoon' and that that film is not a British film within the meaning of the Cinematograph Films Acts 1938 and 1948.

QUESTION

Can you identify any special feature of this case which might make it distinguishable from *Gramophone & Typewriter Co Ltd v Stanley* (**16**)?

NOTE

In this case a finding of agency allowed the court to 'lift the veil'. It is to be observed that a similar finding of agency by the trial judge in *Salomon*'s case (**12**) was rejected by the House of Lords. On this point, Kerr LJ in *J H Rayner* (*Mincing Lane*) *Ltd v Department of Trade and Industry* [1989] Ch 72 at 189 recently observed:

> The crucial point on which the House of Lords overruled the Court of Appeal in that landmark case was precisely the rejection of the doctrine that agency between a corporation and its members in relation to the corporation's contracts can be inferred from the control exercisable by the members over the corporation or from the fact that the sole objective of the corporation's contracts was to benefit the members. That rejection of the doctrine of agency to impugn the non-liability of the members for the acts of the corporation is the foundation of our modern company law.

We must therefore conclude that an agency must be shown on the evidence to exist and may not be inferred merely from control of a company or ownership of its shares. Of course, there is nothing in principle to prevent a company from being an agent of its controlling shareholders, just as it can be an agent of anyone else. Such an agency can be created by express agreement, as in fact happened in the well-known *Rylands v Fletcher* case or *Rainham Chemical Works Ltd v Belvedere Fish Guano Co Ltd* [1921] 2 AC 465, HL. There, the company whose factory blew up had agreed to occupy the land owned by its two shareholders as their agent. The existence of an agency does not violate the *Salomon* principle; on the contrary, it affirms that the company, being capable of acting as an agent, is a separate person. But if a judge were free to *infer* an agency from the mere fact of control, more or less at will, then the result would be that the veil could be lifted as often as he chose, and the law would be unpredictable.

One instance of this is, perhaps, *Smith, Stone and Knight Ltd v Birmingham Corpn* [1939] 4 All ER 116, where Atkinson J, on facts very similar to those of *DHN Food Distributors Ltd v Tower Hamlets London Borough Council* (**25**), allowed a holding company to claim compensation as if it were an owner-occupier, on the ground that its subsidiary (which occupied the land in question) was merely its agent for the purpose of carrying on its business. This decision of Atkinson J, which is in marked contrast to *Gramophone and Typewriter Co Ltd v Stanley* (**16**), has been the subject of some criticism, e g by Pickering, (1968) 31 MLR 481 at 494.

There was also a finding of agency in the tax case of *Firestone Tyre and Rubber Co Ltd v Lewellin* [1957] 1 All ER 561, [1957] 1 WLR 464, HL, where it was held that an English company which manufactured tyres in this country, and used them to fulfil orders for its American holding company, did so as the agent of the latter. But nothing in this decision was made to turn on the fact that the holding company had control of the English company.

The other argument which found support in the lower courts in *Salomon*'s case, based on a *trust* rather than an agency, will similarly fall to the ground unless a trust can be affirmatively proved. The evidence of such a trust in the case next cited was, to say the least, tenuous; but the court was plainly moved to find that it existed by the close analogy with an unincorporated members' club.

22 Trebanog Working Men's Club Ltd v MacDonald [1940] 1 KB 576, [1940] 1 All ER 454 (King's Bench Divisional Court)

The club was incorporated under the Industrial and Provident Societies Acts 1893–1913.[4] It bought liquor in its own name, paid for it by cheque drawn on its bank account, and served it to members in exchange for a money payment. The society was charged with selling liquor by retail without a licence, and was convicted. It appealed successfully to the Divisional Court.

LORD HEWART CJ read the judgment of the court (LORD HEWART CJ, HUMPHREYS and HILBERY JJ): The first general Act dealing with unlawful sales by retail of intoxicating liquor without a justices' licence was the Licensing Act 1872, which in s 3 created the offence now contained in s 65 of the Licensing (Consolidation) Act 1910 in almost identical terms. Ever since that date it has been a matter of general agreement that the transaction which takes place in a members' club, in which the property in the liquor is in all the members equally, when a member orders and pays for intoxicating liquor, is not a sale at all in the sense in which that word is used in s 3, but is rather to be deemed the transfer of a special property in the goods from all the other members of the club to the consumer in consideration of the price paid. The aspect of the matter is fully explained in the judgments of Field J and Huddleston B in *Graff v Evans*.[5] The club in that case was a bona fide members' club, but, by rule 7 of the club rules 'all property acquired by the club shall be vested in the trustees'—no doubt, as Field J observed in his judgment, for the purpose of enabling them to sue or take other legal proceedings with respect to injuries to the possession of the goods belonging to the club. Field J, in holding that no sale by retail of intoxicating liquor took place when a member ordered and paid for a drink, put the matter in this way: 'I think the true construction of the rules is that the members were the joint owners of the general property in all the goods of the club, and that the trustees were their agents with respect to the general property in the goods.' Huddleston B, in concurring, says: 'It seems to me clear that [the member] had a property or at least an interest in the goods which were transferred to him.' The correctness of that decision has never, so far as we are aware, been doubted ...

In our opinion, the decision in *Graff v Evans* applies to and governs the present case. Once it is conceded that a members' club does not necessarily require a licence to serve its members with intoxicating liquor, because the legal property in the liquor is not in the members themselves, it is difficult to draw any legal distinction between the various legal entities that may be entrusted with the duty of holding the property on behalf of the members, be it an individual, or a body of trustees, or a company formed for the purpose, so long as the real interest in the liquors remains, as in this case it clearly does, in the members of the club. There is no magic in this connection in the expressions 'trustee' or 'agent'. What is essential is that the holding of the property by the agent or trustee must be a holding for and on behalf of, and not a holding antagonistic to, the members of the club. We are dealing here with a quasi-criminal case, where the court seeks to deal with the substance of a transaction rather than the legal form in which it may be clothed ...

4 A second appeal concerned a charge based upon similar facts against the Monkwearmouth Conservative Club Ltd, which was incorporated under the Companies Acts. The cases were treated as indistinguishable and disposed of together.
5 (1882) 8 QBD 373.

NOTE

Three years earlier, Lord Hewart CJ had been one of the members of the Divisional Court which heard *Wurzel v Houghton Main Home Delivery Service Ltd* [1937] 1 KB 380, [1936] 3 All ER 311, DC. In this case, miners had formed two co-operative associations to run lorries for the delivery of coal to their homes, for which a payment based on mileage was made. The one association was unincorporated, and the court ruled that the lorry was being used by its co-owners, the members, to haul their own coal, and so there was no 'carriage of goods for hire or reward' in breach of the licensing laws. But the other association had been formed as a company, and it was convicted because it (as the owner of the lorry) was an entity separate from its members (who owned the coal). No argument based upon the existence of a trust was addressed to the court.

In *The Abbey, Malvern Wells Ltd v Ministry of Local Government and Planning* [1951] Ch 728, [1951] 2 All ER 154 Danckwerts J held that, where all the shares in a company were held on educational trusts, and the management of the company was in the hands of the trustees, the court could lift the veil of incorporation so as to impress the *company's* property with the terms of the trusts. This decision overlooks the possibility that the trustees might (quite properly) have decided to sell the shares, or some of them, and effectively have nullified the court's ruling.

QUESTION

If the Trebanog Working Men's Club Ltd owned a vehicle which it used to deliver supplies of liquor to its members' homes for consumption there, would it need (a) a retail liquor licence; (b) a licence to carry goods for hire or reward? Would it matter how payments for the supplies were reckoned?

The corporate veil may be disregarded if the company is used as a means to perpetrate a fraud.[6]

23 Re Darby, ex p Brougham [1911] 1 KB 95 (King's Bench Division)

Darby and Gyde (both undischarged bankrupts, with a number of convictions for fraud) registered in Guernsey a company called City of London Investment Corporation Ltd. It had only seven shareholders and had issued a mere £11 of its nominal capital of £100,000. Darby and Gyde were its only directors and entitled to all of its profits. The corporation so formed then purported to register and float in England a £30,000 company under the name of Welsh Slate Quarries Ltd, and to sell to it a quarrying licence and plant, bought for £3,500, at a price of £18,000. The prospectus inviting the public to take debentures in the Welsh company disclosed the role of the corporation as vendor and promoter, but did not mention the names of Darby and Gyde or the fact that it was they who were to receive the profit on the sale. The Welsh company failed and went into liquidation. The liquidator claimed in the bankruptcy of Darby for the secret profit which it was alleged that he, as a promoter, had made. It was objected on Darby's behalf that it was not he but the corporation who had been promoter; but this argument found no favour with the court.

6 This principle was applied to penetrate an elaborate network of some 80 interlocking trusts and companies in *Re a Company* [1985] BCLC 333, CA, strikingly illustrated by diagrams which are reproduced in the report of the case.

PHILLIMORE J: Now this case certainly does seem to me to be an advance upon the previous decisions. Darby and Gyde (who are two fraudulent persons, both of whom have been convicted of fraud in the present case, and of several previous crimes) registered in Guernsey a company called the City of London Investment Corporation, of which they were the proprietors. It was merely an alias for themselves just as much as if they had announced in the *Gazette* that they were in future going to call themselves 'Rothschild & Co'. It was merely a name under which they carried on business, and I am quite clear in my own mind that that was their object, and that, whenever they represented that some business was being done by or through the corporation and concealed the fact that it was being done by or through Darby and Gyde, they were by that mere fact probably perpetrating a fraud. I say this because their names and their persons were so well known generally that the chance of detection and the chances of repudiation were great in connection with any commercial transactions in which they engaged. The fraud here is that what they did through the corporation they did themselves and represented it to have been done by a corporation of some standing and position, or at any rate a corporation which was more than and different from themselves. Having registered that corporation, and being minded to perpetrate a very great fraud, they, as such corporation, agreed to buy a trivial interest in a Welsh slate quarry for a small sum in cash and a consideration in shares, and then as such corporation purported to sell this interest to the Welsh Slate Quarries Limited and thereby they made a very large profit. It is said that they concealed that profit and also that they concealed from the Welsh Slate Quarries Limited the fact that they were themselves the real vendors and promoters, and therefore it is contended that the liquidator is entitled to recover the profit from them ... Now they made that profit either directly or through the agency of the corporation, it does not matter which, and they may hold it if they disclosed it at the proper time ... [His Lordship then ruled that there had been no effective disclosure, and that Gyde and Darby were bound to account for the profit which the corporation had made.]

NOTE

See also *Aveling Barford Ltd v Perion Ltd* (**183**), where the veil of incorporation was disregarded in order to defeat the claims of an asset-stripper who had defrauded his company.

The veil of incorporation may also be lifted to prevent the deliberate evasion of a contractual obligation.

24 Gilford Motor Co v Horne [1933] Ch 935 (Court of Appeal)

The first defendant, E B Horne, had formerly been employed as managing director of the plaintiff company, and had covenanted in a written agreement not to solicit customers of the company after leaving its employment. When this employment was terminated, he began to set up his own business, undercutting the plaintiff's prices; but after taking legal advice, caused instead the formation of a company, J M Horne & Co Ltd (the second defendant) in which his wife and an employee were sole shareholders and directors. This company took over Horne's business and solicited the plaintiff's customers. Farwell J held that the covenant had been broken, but because in his view it was too wide and therefore against public policy, declined to enforce it against the defendants. The plaintiff appealed successfully against this latter ruling, and was granted an injunction against *both* defendants.

LORD HANWORTH MR: Farwell J heard the evidence about that company ... He says this:

> The defendant company is a company which, on the evidence before me, is obviously carried on wholly by the defendant Horne. Mrs Horne, one of the directors, is not, so far as any evidence I have had before me, taking any part in the business or the management of the business. The son, whose initials are 'JM', is engaged in a subordinate position in that company, and the other director, Howard, is an employee of the company. As one of the witnesses said in the witness-box, in all dealings which he had had with the defendant company the 'boss' or the 'guvnor', whichever term is the appropriate one, was the defendant Horne, and I have not any doubt on the evidence I have had before me that the defendant company was the channel through which the defendant Horne was carrying on his business. Of course, in law the defendant company is a separate entity from the defendant Horne, but I cannot help feeling quite convinced that at any rate one of the reasons for the creation of that company was the fear of Mr Horne that he might commit breaches of the covenant in carrying on the business, as for instance, in sending out circulars as he was doing, and that he might possibly avoid that liability if he did it through the defendant company. There is no doubt that the defendant company has sent out circulars to persons who were at the crucial time customers of the plaintiff company.

Now I have recalled that portion of the judgment of Farwell J, and I wish in clear terms to say that I agree with every word of it. I am quite satisfied that this company was formed as a device, a stratagem, in order to mask the effective carrying on of a business of Mr E B Horne. The purpose of it was to try to enable him, under what is a cloak or sham, to engage in business which, on consideration of the agreement which had been sent to him just about seven days before the company was incorporated, was a business in respect of which he had a fear that the plaintiffs might intervene and object.

Now that this action is brought by the plaintiffs, the Gilford Motor Company Ltd, to enforce the terms of clause 9 of the agreement of 30 May 1929, on the ground that the defendant Horne, and the company, as his agent and under his direction, have committed breaches of the covenant which I have read. [His Lordship held that the breaches were substantiated by the evidence, and rejected the defence that the covenant was too wide to be supportable in law. He accordingly granted an injunction, which he ruled should go against the company as well as Horne.]

LAWRENCE and ROMER LJJ delivered concurring judgments.

NOTE

This decision was followed in *Jones v Lipman* [1962] 1 All ER 442, [1962] 1 WLR 832, where the defendant, who had contracted to sell land to the plaintiff, later endeavoured to put the land beyond the reach of an order for specific performance by conveying it to a company which he had formed for this express purpose, and which he himself effectively owned and controlled. Ignoring the corporate veil, Russell J ordered specific performance against both the defendant and his company. It is common to refer to the company in cases such as this as a 'sham' or 'façade', set up (very often deliberately) to mask the underlying situation. In *Adams v Cape Industries plc* [1990] Ch 433 at 542, [1991] 1 All ER 929 at 1024, CA, the Court of Appeal expressed the view that 'where a façade is alleged, the motive of the perpetrator may be highly material'. For a further example, see *Re Bugle Press Ltd* (**260**).

The veil of incorporation may sometimes be lifted to allow a group of associated companies to be treated as one.

25 DHN Food Distributors Ltd v Tower Hamlets London Borough Council
[1976] 1 WLR 852, [1976] 3 All ER 462 (Court of Appeal)

DHN ran a wholesale cash-and-carry grocery business from premises owned by its wholly-owned subsidiary company ('Bronze'). Bronze had the same directors as DHN, but it carried on no business. Its only asset was the freehold properties which DHN occupied as its licensee. A second wholly-owned subsidiary owned vehicles used by DHN in its business, but it, too, carried on no operations of its own. The Council in 1970 compulsorily acquired the premises, and as a result DHN had to close down its business. Substantial compensation for disturbance (over and above the value of the land itself, which had already been paid to Bronze) could be claimed by DHN only if it had an interest in the land greater than that of a bare licensee. The Court of Appeal, reversing a ruling of the Lands Tribunal, held that the group of companies should be treated as a single economic entity, and that in consequence compensation for disturbance should be paid. In effect, DHN was treated as if it had owned the land itself.

SHAW LJ: [There] is the further argument[7] advanced on behalf of the claimants that there was so complete an identity of the different companies comprised in the so-called group that they ought to be regarded for this purpose as a single entity. The completeness of that identity manifested itself in various ways. The directors of DHN were the same as the directors of Bronze; the shareholders of Bronze were the same as in DHN, the parent company, and they had a common interest in maintaining on the property concerned the business of the group.

If each member of the group is regarded as a company in isolation, nobody at all could have claimed compensation in a case which plainly calls for it. Bronze would have had the land but no business to disturb; DHN would have had the business but no interest in the land.

In this utter identity and community of interest between DHN and Bronze there was no flaw at all. As Bronze did not trade and carried on no business, it had no actual or potential creditors other than its own parent, DHN. The directors of that company could at any time they chose have procured the transfer of the legal title from Bronze to itself. Mr Eyre again conceded that if they had gone through that formal operation the day before the notice to

7 [An alternative ground for the decision of the court was that DHN did have a sufficient interest in the land, on the basis of either an irrevocable licence or a resulting trust, to claim compensation for disturbance in its own right.]

treat was served on 12 October 1970, they would have had a secure claim for compensation for disturbance. Accordingly, they could in law have sought and obtained whatever advantages were derived up to that date from a separation of title and interest between the two companies and still quite legitimately have re-disposed matters right up till October 1970 so as to qualify for compensation. They could not have been criticised, still less prevented, if they had chosen to do so. Yet if the decision of the Lands Tribunal be right, it made all the difference that they had not. Thus no abuse is precluded by disregarding the bonds which bundled DHN and Bronze together in a close and, so far as Bronze was concerned, indissoluble relationship.

Why then should this relationship be ignored in a situation in which to do so does not prevent abuse but would on the contrary result in what appears to be a denial of justice? If the strict legal differentiation between the two entities of parent and subsidiary must, even on the special facts of this case, be observed, the common factors in their identities must at the lowest demonstrate that the occupation of DHN would and could never be determined without the consent of DHN itself. If it was a licence at will, it was at the will of the licensee, DHN, that the licence subsisted. Accordingly it could have gone on for an indeterminate time; that is to say, as long as the relationship of parent and subsidiary continued, which means for practical purposes for as long as DHN wished to remain in the property for the purposes of its business.

The President of the Lands Tribunal took a strict legalistic view of the respective positions of the companies concerned. It appears to me that it was too strict in its application to the facts of this case, which are, as I have said, of a very special character, for it ignored the realities of the respective roles which the companies filled. I would allow the appeal.

LORD DENNING MR and GOFF LJ delivered concurring judgments.

QUESTION

Can this decision be reconciled with the reasoning of Hughes J in *Hunt v T W Johnstone Co Ltd* (cited above, p 47)?

NOTE

Lord Denning began his judgment: 'This case might be called the "Three in one." Three companies in one. Alternatively, the "One in three." One group of three companies.' 'Group enterprise' is a common feature of modern commercial life, whether we think of domestic businesses within the United Kingdom or the great multinationals. We have already seen a number of examples in the cases: e g in *Gramophone and Typewriter Co Ltd v Stanley* (**16**), *Re F G (Films) Ltd* (**21**), *Lonrho Ltd v Shell Petroleum Co Ltd* (**17**), *Smith, Stone & Knight Ltd v Birmingham Corpn* (above, p 54), and *Firestone Tyre and Rubber Co Ltd v Lewellin* (above, p 54); and there will be many more in the pages to come.

A 'group' of companies may consist of a holding company and one or more subsidiaries and sub-subsidiaries, or of a number of companies which have substantially the same shareholders and directors; but it is obviously possible to have an infinite variety of other arrangements connecting either closely or loosely a number of companies which carry on associated businesses or different parts of the same business.

There are some statutory provisions governing groups: for instance, those requiring the publication of consolidated accounts (CA 1985, ss 227–230 and Sch 4A); and the tax laws have many rules dealing with such matters as the transfer of assets between member companies of a group (see, e g Income and Corporation Taxes Act 1988, ss 402 ff). Employment legislation, e g in regard to redundancy payments, sometimes treats as continuous employment a succession of jobs with a number of associated companies, and also the similar position where one employer company succeeds another following a takeover or reorganisation. In all these cases, the concepts of 'group' and 'associated company' will be formally defined for the purpose of the provision in question.

The case law gives a much more confused picture. The question whether the veil of incorporation should be lifted, so as to destroy the distinct identity of the separate companies within a group and treat the 'enterprise' as being in reality one concern, is one that has come before the courts on many occasions; but no clear principle emerges. The willingness of the Court of Appeal in the *DHN* case to treat all the companies as one contrasts sharply with its insistence on applying the *Salomon* principle in *Lonrho* (**17**). Indeed, in *Woolfson v Strathclyde Regional Council* 1978 SLT 159, 38 P & CR 521[8] the House of Lords upheld a decision of the Scottish courts delivered shortly after the *DHN* case in which the Scottish judges had pointedly declined to follow the English case, although the facts were quite similar.

In later parts of this book, we shall meet cases in which one company in a group has guaranteed the obligations of another (*Charterbridge Corpn Ltd v Lloyds Bank Ltd* (**69**); *Rolled Steel Products (Holdings) Ltd v British Steel Corpn* (**70**)), paid its debts (*Armour Hick Northern Ltd v Armour Trust Ltd* (below, p 363), or looked after the pay and pensions of its employees (*Re W & M Roith Ltd* (below, p 159); *Walker v Wimborne* (below, p 146)). The attitude of the courts has varied from an indulgent blurring of the differentiation between the member companies to a strict insistence that that differentiation be respected.

In Canada, industrial action has been held not to be 'secondary' picketing when directed by employees towards an associated company which belonged to the same group as their employer (*Canada Safeway Ltd v Local 373, Canadian Food and Allied Workers* (1974) 46 DLR (3d) 113), but the House of Lords showed no willingness to accede to a similar argument in *Dimbleby & Sons Ltd v National Union of Journalists* [1984] 1 All ER 751, [1984] 1 WLR 427, HL.[9]

In *Adams v Cape Industries plc* [1990] Ch 433, [1991] 1 All ER 929, CA, Cape, an English company, headed a group which included many wholly-owned subsidiaries. Some of these mined asbestos in South Africa, and others marketed the asbestos in various countries, including the US. Several hundred plaintiffs had been awarded damages by a Texas court for personal injuries suffered as a result of exposure to asbestos dust. The defendants included one of Cape's subsidiaries, NAAC. The Court of Appeal held that the judgment could not be enforced against the English parent, Cape, either on the basis of an argument that Cape had been 'present' in the US through its local subsidiaries (an argument which would have involved lifting the veil), or because it had carried on business in the US through the agency of NAAC. 'Our law', said Slade LJ, giving the judgment of the court (at 536, 544; 1019, 1026), 'for better or worse, recognises the creation of subsidiary companies, which though in one sense the creation of their parent companies, will nevertheless under the general law fall to be treated as separate legal entities with all the rights and liabilities which

---

8 This was not strictly a 'group enterprise' case. The occupier of the shop premises which were compulsorily acquired was a company of which W held 999 shares and his wife the remaining one. Part of the land was owned by W personally and the rest by a second company in which, again, W and his wife held all the shares. The judgments leave little doubt, however, that *DHN* would not have been followed even if the facts had been identical.

9 See also *The Maritime Trader* [1981] 2 Lloyd's Rep 153, [1981] Com LR 27, in which the court refused to order the arrest of a ship owned by the defendant company's subsidiary.

would normally attach to separate legal entities ... We do not accept as a matter of law that the court is entitled to lift the corporate veil as against a defendant company which is the member of a corporate group merely because the corporate structure has been used so as to ensure that the legal liability (if any) in respect of particular future activities of the group ... will fall on another member of the group rather than the defendant company. Whether or not this is desirable, the right to use a corporate structure in this manner is inherent in our law.'

There is much interest—though perhaps more in other parts of the world than there is in this country—in the question whether a holding company should be made liable for the debts of an insolvent subsidiary, or the 'enterprise' as a whole for the obligations of one of its members. The problem is well summarised in the following extract from the judgment of Templeman LJ in *Re Southard & Co Ltd* [1979] 3 All ER 556 at 565, [1979] 1 WLR 1198 at 1208, CA:

> English company law possesses some curious features, which may generate curious results. A parent company may spawn a number of subsidiary companies, all controlled directly or indirectly by the shareholders of the parent company. If one of the subsidiary companies, to change the metaphor, turns out to be the runt of the litter and declines into insolvency to the dismay of its creditors, the parent company and the other subsidiary companies may prosper to the joy of the shareholders without any liability for the debts of the insolvent subsidiary. It is not surprising that, when a subsidiary company collapses, the unsecured creditors wish the finances of the company and its relationship with other members of the group to be narrowly examined, to ensure that no assets of the subsidiary company have leaked away, that no liabilities of the subsidiary company ought to be laid at the door of other members of the group, and that no indemnity from or right of action against any other company, or against any individual, is by some mischance overlooked.
>
> The anxiety of the creditors will be increased where, as in the present case, all the assets of the subsidiary company are claimed by another member of the group in right of a debenture.

Generally speaking, English case-law has adhered to the *Salomon* principle in situations such as this and, as the *Multinational Gas* case (**143**) illustrates, has not developed principles[10] which would allow a court to lift the veil of incorporation. This contrasts with attitudes abroad, where factors such as 'domination' and 'under-capitalisation' (or 'thin incorporation') have been relied on to build up a body of rules under which other companies in a group have been held liable to back the obligations of the 'runt of the litter'. In New Zealand and Ireland, the Companies Acts have been amended so as to give the court a discretion to order that one company in a group should make a contribution to the assets of another which is in insolvent liquidation, or to order that the liquidations of two associated companies should proceed jointly, so that their assets and liabilities are pooled. The Cork Committee on Insolvency in its report (Cmnd 8558, 1982) did not suggest that this precedent should be followed in the United Kingdom, at least immediately, but did urge that the question be studied further.

The *DHN* case probably represents a high-water mark in the use of the technique of 'lifting the veil' on a discretionary basis in English law. It is unlikely to be followed. The courts have since had many opportunities to adopt a similar approach, but have consistently declined to do so; and on almost every occasion they have gone out of

---

10 Of course, in an appropriate case a parent may be held liable on the basis of a contractual promise or a representation that it would support its subsidiary (the well-known 'comfort letter'): a plea which failed in *Kleinwort Benson Ltd v Malaysia Mining Corpn Bhd* [1989] 1 All ER 785, [1989] 1 WLR 379, CA. If the subsidiary has gone into insolvent liquidation, the parent may be liable as a party to fraudulent trading under IA 1986, s 213, or (as a 'shadow director') liable for 'wrongful trading' under IA 1986, s 214. See below, p 578.

their way to stress the importance of the *Salomon* principle. The exceptions, they have said, must be confined to situations of fraud and cases where a company has been set up as a façade or sham, and they have seemed unwilling to make any finding of a 'façade' without evidence of some improper motive.

In the EEC, there are signs that the veil of incorporation may not be considered sacrosanct in a group situation. ICI was made to pay fines, even before the United Kingdom was a member of the Community, for the breach of the EEC competition laws by an overseas subsidiary.[11] And the Commission has in preparation a Draft Ninth Directive on the Conduct of Groups of Companies, which would in certain circumstances make a dominant company in a group liable for losses incurred by a dependent company.[12]

QUESTION

If FG (Films) Ltd (**21**) had incurred debts of £80,000 in making the film 'Monsoon' and had gone into liquidation leaving its creditors unpaid, should Film Group Inc have been made liable to the creditors?

C. Corporate acts and attributes: the company as a 'person'

It is a central feature of company law (and of the law of corporations generally), whether seen from a theoretical or a practical viewpoint, that incorporation creates a new and separate legal entity—a being capable of enjoying rights, exercising powers, and incurring duties and obligations. It is traditional to describe any subject of rights and duties as a legal 'person'. But it is one thing to attribute *legal* capacities to a company, and quite another to treat it as having *human* characteristics and qualities. It is unnecessary and, indeed, illogical to suppose that the latter step follows from the former; and yet—after a markedly hesitant beginning—the courts have now pursued the analogy with a physical person almost as far as it is possible to go, ascribing to a company human attributes such as a reputation or an intention to defraud which at an earlier stage were regarded as unthinkable. The extracts which follow show the progress of this development. The conclusions reached should not be regarded as either obvious or necessary; and at times it is instructive to ask whether as a matter of policy they are desirable.

QUESTION

A company is sometimes described as:
(a) a 'real person';
(b) an 'artificial person';
(c) a 'fictitious person'.
Consider the appropriateness of these expressions.

---

11 *ICI v EC Commission* (the *Dyestuffs* case) Cases 48, 49, 51–57/69: [1972] ECR 619.
12 For further reading on this topic, see T Hadden, *The Control of Corporate Groups* (London, 1983); D D Prentice, 'Groups of Companies: the English Experience', in K J Hopt (ed) *Groups of Companies in European Laws* (Berlin, 1982), p 99.

Blackstone, 'Commentaries on the Laws of England' (1768) Volume 1, p 476

'Of Corporations.'

[Footnotes in the original are omitted.]

There are also certain privileges and disabilities that attend an aggregate corporation, and are not applicable to such as are sole; the reason of them ceasing, and of course the law. It must always appear by attorney; for it cannot appear in person, being, as Sir Edward Coke says, invisible, and existing only in intendment and consideration of law. It can neither maintain, or be made defendant to, an action of battery or such like personal injuries; for a corporation can neither beat, nor be beaten, in it's body politic. A corporation cannot commit treason, or felony, or other crime, in it's corporate capacity: though it's members may, in their distinct individual capacities. Neither is it capable of suffering a traitor's or felon's punishment, for it is not liable to corporal penalties, nor to attainder, forfeiture, or corruption of blood. It cannot be executor or administrator, or perform any personal duties; for it cannot take an oath for the due execution of the office. It cannot be seised of lands to the use of another; for such kind of confidence is foreign to the end of it's institution. Neither can it be committed to prison;[13] for it's existence being ideal, no man can apprehend or arrest it. And therefore also it cannot be outlawed; for outlawry always supposes a precedent right of arresting, which has been defeated by the parties absconding, and that also a corporation cannot do: for which reasons the proceedings to compel a corporation to appear to any suit by attorney are always by distress on their lands and goods. Neither can a corporation be excommunicated; for it has no soul, as is gravely observed by Sir Edward Coke: and therefore also it is not liable to be summoned into the ecclesiastical courts upon any account; for those courts act only *pro salute animae,* and their sentences can only be enforced by spiritual censures: a consideration, which, carried to it's full extent, would alone demonstrate the impropriety of these courts interfering in any temporal rights whatsoever.

NOTE

Where corporate personality is ascribed to a *group* of persons, such as a limited liability company, a chartered body such as a university, or a municipality such as a city or borough, it is referred to as a 'corporation aggregate'. Where the law personifies an *office* occupied by a single person (e g the Crown, the Bishop of Ely), it is customarily called a 'corporation sole'.

Whether the word 'person' should be construed as including a corporate body depends on the context; there is a presumption that it does.

---

13 *Pace* Companies Act 1967, s 68(5) (now, alas, repealed): 'An insurance company which contravenes ... sub-s (1) or (2) above shall be guilty of an offence and liable on conviction on indictment to imprisonment for a term not exceeding two years ...'.

26 Pharmaceutical Society v London and Provincial Supply Association Ltd
(1880) 5 App Cas 857 (House of Lords)

The Pharmacy Act 1868 prohibited 'any person' from selling or keeping an open shop for retailing poisons unless such person was qualified and registered as a pharmaceutical chemist. The respondent company was prosecuted for an infringement of the Act. The sale of chemicals by the company was superintended by a registered chemist, who was a salaried employee and also a minority shareholder in the company. The House of Lords held that the company had not infringed the statute, provided that the individual seller was a qualified person within the Act.

LORD BLACKBURN: I own I have no great doubt myself ... that the word 'person' may very well include both a natural person, a human being, and an artificial person, a corporation. I think that in an Act of Parliament, unless there be something to the contrary, probably (but that I should not like to pledge myself to) it ought to be held to include both. I have equally no doubt that in common talk, the language of men not speaking technically, a 'person' does not include an artificial person, that is to say, a corporation. Nobody in common talk if he were asked, Who is the richest person in London, would answer, The London and North-Western Railway Co. The thing is absurd. It is plain that in common conversation and ordinary speech, 'a person' would mean a natural person: in technical language it may mean the artificial person: in which way it is used in any particular Act, must depend upon the context and the subject-matter. I do not think that the presumption that it does include an artificial person, a corporation, if that is the presumption, is at all a strong one. Circumstances, and indeed circumstances of a slight nature in the context, might shew in which way the word is to be construed in an Act of Parliament, whether it is to have the one meaning or the other. I am quite clear about this, that whenever you can see that the object of the Act requires that the word 'person' shall have the more extended or the less extended sense, then, whichever sense it requires, you should apply the word in that sense and construe the Act accordingly ...

But, my Lords, my conclusion, looking at this Act, is that it is clear to my mind that the word 'person' here is so used to show that it does not include a corporation, and that there is no object or intention of the statute which shows that it is requisite to extend the word to a sense which probably those who used it in legislation, were not thinking of at all. I do not think that the legislature was thinking of bodies corporate at all. Beginning with the preamble the Act says, 'Whereas it is expedient for the safety of the public that persons keeping open shop for the retailing, dispensing, or compounding of poisons, and persons known as chemists and druggists, should possess a competent practical knowledge of their business'. Stopping there it is quite plain that those who used that language were not thinking of corporations. A corporation may in one sense, for all substantial purposes of protecting the public, possess a competent knowledge of its business, if it employs competent directors, managers, and so forth. But it cannot possibly have a competent knowledge in itelf. The metaphysical entity, the legal 'person', the corporation, cannot possibly have a competent knowledge. Nor, I think, can a corporation be supposed to be a 'person known as a chemist and druggist' ... A body corporate may keep an open shop, and no mischief is done, if ... qualified persons perform or superintend the sale ...

NOTE

This case concerned the interpretation of a statute; but the views of Lord Blackburn have also served as a guide in the construction of other documents, e g in *Re Jeffcock's Trust* (1882) 51 LJ Ch 507, where a limited company was held to be a 'person' within the terms of a power to lease conferred by will. The courts have gone so far as to hold that a company is a 'person of full age' within the meaning of the Law of Property Act 1925 (*Re Earl of Carnarvon's Chesterfield Settled Estates* [1927] 1 Ch 138)[14] but have stopped short of holding that a company is capable of 'exercising itself in the duties of piety and true religion' (*Rolloswin Investments Ltd v Chromolit Portugal Cutelarias e Produtos Metalicos SARL* [1970] 2 All ER 673, [1970] 1 WLR 912), or of being deemed a rogue and a vagabond (*A-G v Walkergate Press Ltd* (1930) 142 LT 408: compare *R v Registrar of Companies, ex p More* (**2**)). In *Winkworth v Edward Baron Development Co Ltd* (below, p 255), Lord Templeman found no difficulty in ascribing to a limited company a 'conscience'. The Scottish courts have ruled that a company is incapable of shame, and so cannot be guilty of 'shameless conduct': *Dean v John Menzies (Holdings) Ltd* 1981 SLT 50 (below, p 78). But it has been held that a company has a reputation and so can sue in defamation: *D and L Caterers Ltd and Jackson v D'Ajou* [1945] KB 364, [1945] 1 All ER 563, CA (allegation that company had procured supplies on the black market).

The Interpretation Act 1978, s 5 and Sch 1, confirms the ruling in the *Pharmaceutical Society* case; and the statutory draftsmen nowadays regularly make a distinction between the term 'person' (which includes a corporate body) and 'individual' (which does not)—see, for example, Company Securities (Insider Dealing) Act 1985, s 1, and especially s 1(7).

(1) NATIONALITY, DOMICIL, ALIEN CHARACTER, RESIDENCE

A company's nationality is determined by the place of its registration, and it retains that nationality throughout its existence.

27 Kuenigl v Donnersmarck [1955] 1 QB 515, [1955] 1 All ER 46 (Queen's Bench Division)

[The facts are immaterial.]

MCNAIR J referred to *Daimler Co Ltd v Continental Tyre & Rubber Co Ltd* (**19**) and continued:

Neither of these passages in Lord Simon's or Lord Wright's speeches is dealing with the question which I have to deal with, namely, whether an English company found to have enemy character by reason of enemy control ceases to be in the eye of the English law an English company and subject to the prohibition which English law imposes on persons subject to that law. On this question there is, so far as I know, no direct authority, but such authority as there is in my judgment strongly suggests a negative answer. [His Lordship discussed the cases and continued:] Enemy character is not substituted for the original character, but is something added to it. An English company which has acquired enemy character continues to owe its very existence to English law (under which it was incorporated) and remains subject to all its obligations towards the Crown under the Companies Acts as an English company. It would, in my judgment, be absurd that the

---

14 See also *Re Lindsay Bowman Ltd* [1969] 3 All ER 601 at 604, [1969] 1 WLR 1443 at 1448, where Megarry J, referring to s 353(6) of the Act of 1948 [CA 1985, s 653], said: 'In obedience to Parliament, I must assume that the artificial and impersonal entity that we know as a limited company has been endowed with the capacity not merely of having feelings but also of feeling aggrieved even though it has ceased to exist.'

acquisition of enemy character should release it from the obligations attaching to an English company and enable it to do lawfully things which an English company not possessing enemy character was lawfully unable to do...

I think that it is ... clear that, in so far as nationality can by analogy be applied to a juristic person, its nationality is determined in an inalienable manner by the laws of the country from which it derives its personality ...

A company is capable of having a domicil. Its domicil is the place of its registration, and it retains that domicil throughout its existence.

28 Gasque v IRC [1940] 2 KB 80 (King's Bench Division)

A taxpayer cannot avoid income tax liability by transferring property so that income otherwise receivable by him becomes payable to a person 'resident or domiciled out of the United Kingdom': the income is deemed to remain that of the taxpayer (Finance Act 1936, s 18, now replaced by Income and Corporation Taxes Act 1988, s 739). Mrs Gasque had transferred property to MD Company Ltd, a company incorporated in Guernsey but doing some business in England. She claimed that it was domiciled in the United Kingdom, so that the statute did not apply, but the Commissioners of Inland Revenue ruled that it was domiciled in Guernsey, and assessed her to tax accordingly. The court upheld the view of the commissioners.

MACNAGHTEN J: The only question at issue on this appeal is whether the MD Company Ltd is a 'person resident or domiciled out of the United Kingdom' within the meaning of that section.

It was suggested by Mr Needham on behalf of the appellant that by the law of England a body corporate has no domicil. It is quite true that a body corporate cannot have a domicil in the same sense as an individual any more than it can have a residence in the same sense as an individual. But by analogy with a natural person the attributes of residence, domicil and nationality can be given, and are, I think, given by the law of England to a body corporate. It is not disputed that a company formed under the Companies Acts has British nationality, though, unlike a natural person, it cannot change its nationality. So, too, I think, such a company has a domicil—an English domicil if registered in England, and a Scottish domicil if registered in Scotland. The domicil of origin, or the domicil of birth, using with respect to a company a familiar metaphor, clings to it throughout its existence ...

In my opinion, the decision of the commissioners was right and ought to be affirmed.

A company may have an enemy or neutral character in time of war. This is determined not by any formal test but by reference to the character of the natural person or persons really in control.

Daimler Co Ltd v Continental Tyre and Rubber Co Ltd (19)

A company's 'residence' is where it 'really keeps house and does its real business'; its 'real business' is carried on where the central management and control actually abides.[15]

15 Other cases show that the 'central management and control' of a company may in fact be divided, so that its residence is in more than one country: see, e g *Union Corpn Ltd v IRC* [1952] 1 All ER 646, CA; (affd on other grounds [1953] AC 482, [1953] 1 All ER 729, HL).

29 De Beers Consolidated Mines Ltd v Howe [1906] AC 455 (House of Lords)

[The facts appear from the judgment.]

LORD LOREBURN LC: Now, it is easy to ascertain where an individual resides, but when the inquiry relates to a company, which in a natural sense does not reside anywhere, some artificial test must be applied.

Mr Cohen propounded a test which had the merits of simplicity and certitude. He maintained that a company resides where it is registered, and nowhere else. If that be so, the appellant company must succeed, for it is registered in South Africa.

I cannot adopt Mr Cohen's contention. In applying the conception of residence to a company, we ought, I think, to proceed as nearly as we can upon the analogy of an individual. A company cannot eat or sleep,[16] but it can keep house and do business. We ought, therefore, to see where it really keeps house and does business. An individual may be of foreign nationality, and yet reside in the United Kingdom. So may a company. Otherwise it might have its chief seat of management and its centre of trading in England under the protection of English law, and yet escape the appropriate taxation by the simple expedient of being registered abroad and distributing its dividends abroad. The decision of Kelly CB and Huddleston B in the *Calcutta Jute Mills v Nicholson*[17] and the *Cesena Sulphur Co v Nicholson*,[18] now thirty years ago, involved the principle that a company resides for purposes of income tax where its real business is carried on. Those decisions have been acted upon ever since. I regard that as the true rule, and the real business is carried on where the central management and control actually abides.

It remains to be considered whether the present case falls within that rule. This is a pure question of fact to be determined, not according to the construction of this or that regulation or by-law, but upon a scrutiny of the course of business and trading.

The case stated by the commissioners gives an elaborate explanation of the way in which this company carried on its business. The head office is formally at Kimberley, and the general meetings have always been held there. Also the profits have been made out of diamonds raised in South Africa and sold under annual contracts to a syndicate for delivery in South Africa upon terms of division of profits realised on resale between the company and the syndicate. And the annual contracts contain provisions for regulating the market in order to realise the best profits on resale. Further, some of the directors and life governors live in South Africa, and there are directors' meetings at Kimberley as well as in London. But it is clearly established that the majority of directors and life governors live in England, that the directors' meetings in London are the meetings where the real control is always exercised in practically all the important business of the company except the mining operations. London has always controlled the negotiation of the contracts with the diamond syndicates, has determined policy in the disposal of

---

16 ['Neither can it be a television entertainer or author'; per Viscount Dilhorne in *Newstead v Frost* [1980] 1 All ER 363 at 368, [1980] 1 WLR 135 at 139, HL. Nor a lorry driver: *Richmond upon Thames London Borough Council v Pinn & Wheeler Ltd* [1989] RTR 354.]
17 (1876) 1 Ex D 428.
18 Ibid.

diamonds and other assets, the working and development of mines, the application of profits, and the appointment of directors. London has also always controlled matters that require to be determined by the majority of all the directors, which include all questions of expenditure except wages, materials, and such-like at the mines, and a limited sum which may be spent by the directors at Kimberley.

The commissioners, after sifting the evidence, arrived at the two following conclusions, viz: (1) That the trade or business of the appellant company constituted one trade or business, and was carried on and exercised by the appellant company within the United Kingdom at their London office. (2) That the head and seat and directing power of the affairs of the appellant company were at the office in London, from whence the chief operations of the company, both in the United Kingdom and elsewhere, were in fact controlled, managed and directed.

These conclusions of fact cannot be impugned, and it follows that this company was resident within the United Kingdom for purposes of income tax, and must be assessed on that footing. I think, therefore, that this appeal fails . . .

LORD JAMES OF HEREFORD delivered a concurring opinion.

LORDS MACNAGHTEN, ROBERTSON and ATKINSON concurred.

QUESTIONS

(1) 'No taxation without representation.' If a company pays taxes and rates, should it not have a vote in parliamentary and local government elections?
(2) In many countries which have a written constitution, certain fundamental rights and freedoms are commonly guaranteed, such as freedom of speech, freedom to trade and do business, the privilege against self-incrimination, the right not to have property expropriated without compensation. Should companies enjoy any such constitutional guarantees? If so, which?[19]

(2) MENTAL STATE; MENS REA AND CRIMINAL LIABILITY

The mental state of a person who is 'the directing mind and will' of a corporation may be attributed to the corporation itself.

30 Lennard's Carrying Co Ltd v Asiatic Petrolem Co Ltd [1915] AC 705 (House of Lords)

The appellant company Lennard's Carrying Co Ltd owned a ship, the *Edward Dawson,* which (together with her cargo which belonged to the respondents) was destroyed at sea as a result of a fire caused by the defective condition of her boilers. The appellant company as owner would have been exonerated

---

19 In *R v Big M Drug Mart Ltd* (1985) 18 DLR (4th) 321, the Supreme Court of Canada held that the defendant company had standing to challenge a statute as unconstitutional, on the ground that it infringed the guarantee of freedom of religion and conscience in s 2(a) of the Canadian Charter of Rights and Freedoms, irrespective of any question whether a corporation can enjoy or exercise freedom of religion.

from liability by the terms of the Merchant Shipping Act 1894, s 502 (now repealed), if it could show that the loss happened without its 'actual fault or privity'. The House of Lords held that the concepts of fault and privity were capable in law of being attributed to a corporate body, but that on the facts the appellant had failed to show that it came within the exception.

VISCOUNT HALDANE LC: The appellants are a limited company and the ship was managed by another limited company, Messrs J M Lennard & Sons, and Mr J M Lennard, who seems to be the active director in J M Lennard & Sons, was also a director of the appellant company, Lennard's Carrying Company Limited. My Lords, in that state of things what is the question of law which arises? I think that it is impossible in the face of the findings of the learned judge, and of the evidence, to contend successfully that Mr J M Lennard has shown that he did not know or can excuse himself for not having known of the defects which manifested themselves in the condition of the ship, amounting to unseaworthiness. Mr Lennard is the person who is registered in the ship's register and is designated as the person to whom the management of the vessel was entrusted. He appears to have been the active spirit in the joint stock company which managed this ship for the appellants; and under the circumstances the question is whether the company can invoke the protection of s 502 of the Merchant Shipping Act to relieve it from the liability which the respondents seek to impose on it ...

Now, my Lords, did what happened take place without the actual fault or privity of the owners of the ship who were the appellants? My Lords, a corporation is an abstraction. It has no mind of its own any more than it has a body of its own; its active and directing will must consequently be sought in the person of somebody who for some purposes may be called an agent, but who is really the directing mind and will of the corporation, the very ego and centre of the personality of the corporation. That person may be under the direction of the shareholders in general meeting; that person may be the board of directors itself, or it may be, and in some companies it is so, that that person has an authority co-ordinate with the board of directors given to him under the articles of association, and is appointed by the general meeting of the company, and can only be removed by the general meeting of the company. My Lords, whatever is not known about Mr Lennard's position, this is known for certain, Mr Lennard took the active part in the management of this ship on behalf of the owners, and Mr Lennard, as I have said, was registered as the person designated for this purpose in the ship's register. Mr Lennard therefore was the natural person to come on behalf of the owners and give full evidence not only about the events of which I have spoken, and which related to the seaworthiness of the ship, but about his own position and as to whether or not he was the life and soul of the company. For if Mr Lennard was the directing mind of the company, then his action must, unless a corporation is not to be liable at all, have been an action which was the action of the company itself within the meaning of s 502. It has not been contended at the Bar, and it could not have been successfully contended, that s 502 is so worded as to exempt a corporation altogether which happens to be the owner of a ship, merely because it happens to be a corporation. It must be upon the true construction of that section in such a case as the present one that the fault or privity is the fault or privity of somebody who is not merely a servant or agent for whom the company is liable upon the footing respondeat superior, but somebody for whom the company is liable because his action is the very action of the company itself. It is not enough that the fault should be the fault of a servant in order to exonerate the owner, the fault must also be one which is not the fault of the owner, or a fault to which the owner is privy; and I take the view that when anybody sets up that section to excuse himself from the normal consequences of the maxim respondeat superior the burden lies upon him to do so.

Well, my Lords, in that state of the law it is obvious to me that Mr Lennard ought to have gone into the box and relieved the company of the presumption which arises against it that his action was the company's action. But Mr Lennard did not go into the box to rebut the presumption of liability and we have no satisfactory evidence as to what the constitution of the company was or as to what Mr Lennard's position was ... Under the circumstances I think that the company and Mr Lennard have not discharged the burden of proof which was upon them, and that it must be taken that the unseaworthiness, which I hold to have been established as existing at the commencement of the voyage from Novorossick, was an unseaworthiness which did not exist without the actual fault or privity of the owning company.

LORD DUNEDIN delivered a concurring opinion.

LORDS ATKINSON, PARKER OF WADDINGTON and PARMOOR concurred.

QUESTIONS

(1) Was Mr Lennard 'the directing mind and will' of J M Lennard & Sons, or of Lennard's Carrying Co Ltd, or of both? Was this question important?

(2) How far do you think that the decision in *Lennard's* case depended upon the fact that the onus of proof under the statute was on the appellants, who were required to prove a negative? If the onus had been on the respondents, who would have won the case?

31 H L Bolton (Engineering) Ltd v T J Graham & Sons Ltd [1957] 1 QB 159, [1956] 3 All ER 624 (Court of Appeal)

In this case a corporate landlord was held capable of 'intending' (through its managing directors) to occupy premises for its own use.

DENNING LJ: [The] question is whether the landlords have proved the necessary intention to occupy the holding for their own purpose. This point arises because the landlords are a limited company. Mr Albery says that there was no meeting of any board of directors to express the landlords' intention, and that therefore the landlords—the company—cannot say that it has the necessary intention.

[His Lordship stated the material facts on this part of the case and continued:]

Mr Albery says that there must at least be a board meeting. In view of the recent decision of this court in *Austin Reed Ltd v Royal Assurance Co Ltd*,[20] he has to concede that the decision of the board need not formally be recorded in a minute, but he says that, even though not formally recorded, there must be a board meeting by which there is a collective decision, and it is not

20 [1956] CA Transcript 217a.

sufficient that individual directors should individually be of one mind. The judge rejected that contention. He said: 'I am told its board only meets once a year and it seems to me that the mode of conducting its business is to leave nearly everything to its agents, and so far as its agents are concerned, I think there is no doubt about what they mean to do ...' Then he went on to say: 'So far as the agents of the company, the business managers, or the directors of the company who manage the business (to use a more accurate expression) [are concerned], they in their managerial capacity have certainly affirmed the intention to occupy the premises in question. An intention, of course, of a company as we all know cannot be formed in a company; a company is an abstract being, and the company itself must act by agents or it must act by its board of directors particularly in matters of importance. It is not necessary, so far as I understand it, that any resolution by the board should have been expressed by a minute, although it ought to be so. However, I do not want to be understood as finding, and I do not find, that the board of this company has ever met or passed any resolution that the company intends to occupy these premises for its own purpose. I do not propose to find that at any effective time the board of this company has passed a resolution of the intention to occupy these premises'—now these are the important words— 'but the business of the company has been so conducted and the position of the company is such that matters of this sort, which are business matters, are dealt with by the agents of the company, the people who manage the business. Their intention is quite clearly to occupy these premises as soon as they can ...'

So the judge has found that this company, through its managers, intend to occupy the premises for their own purposes. Mr Albery contests this finding, and he has referred us to cases decided in the last century; but I must say that the law on this matter and the approach to it have developed very considerably since then. A company may in many ways be likened to a human body. It has a brain and nerve centre which controls what it does. It also has hands which hold the tools and act in accordance with directions from the centre. Some of the people in the company are mere servants and agents who are nothing more than hands to do the work and cannot be said to represent the mind or will. Others are directors and managers who represent the directing mind and will of the company, and control what it does. The state of mind of these managers is the state of mind of the company and is treated by the law as such. So you will find that in cases where the law requires personal fault as a condition of liability in tort, the fault of the manager will be the personal fault of the company. [His Lordship referred to *Lennard's Carrying Co Ltd v Asiatic Petroleum Co Ltd* (**30**) and *R v ICR Haulage Ltd* (**33**) and continued:] So here, the intention of the company can be derived from the intention of its officers and agents. Whether their intention is the company's intention depends on the nature of the matter under consideration, the relative position of the officer or agent and the other relevant facts and circumstances of the case. Approaching the matter in that way, I think that although there was no board meeting, nevertheless, having regard to the standing of these directors in control of the business of the company, having regard to the other facts and circumstances which we know, whereby plans had been prepared and much work done, the judge was entitled to infer that the intention of the company was to occupy the holding for their own purposes. I am of opinion, therefore, that the judge's decision on this point was right ...

HODSON and MORRIS LJJ concurred.

A company is capable of having an intent to deceive.

32 DPP v Kent and Sussex Contractors Ltd [1944] KB 146, [1944] 1 All ER 119 (King's Bench Divisional Court)

The company was charged with offences under the petrol rationing regulations involving (a) making use of a false document with intent to deceive, and (b) making a statement which was known to be false in a material particular. The justices held that the company could not in law be guilty of these offences since there was implicit in them an act of will or state of mind which could not be imputed to a body corporate, and dismissed the informations. The prosecutor appealed by way of case stated to the Divisional Court, which ruled that a company was capable of committing the offences in question, it being sufficient that the particular officer responsible (in this case the transport manager) had the required intention or knowledge.

VISCOUNT CALDECOTE CJ: This special case raises the question whether a limited company, being a body corporate, can in law be guilty of the offences charged against the respondents, or whether a company is incapable of any act of will or state of mind such as that laid in the information. Mr Carey Evans submits that a company can only be held to be responsible in respect of the intention or knowledge of its agents, the officers of the company, to the same extent as a private individual is responsible for the acts of his agent, and, therefore, that the respondent company cannot be held to form the intention or to have the knowledge necessary to constitute the offences charged. He has not disputed the abstract proposition that a company can have knowledge and can form an intention to do an act. A company cannot be found guilty of certain criminal offences, such as treason or other offences for which it is provided that death or imprisonment is the only punishment, but there are a number of criminal offences of which a company can be convicted ...

In the present case the first charge against the company was of doing something with intent to deceive, and the second was that of making a statement which the company knew to be false in a material particular. Once the ingredients of the offences are stated in that way it is unnecessary, in my view, to inquire whether it is proved that the company's officers acted on its behalf. The officers are the company for this purpose. Mr Carey Evans stoutly maintained the position that a company cannot have a mens rea, and that a mens rea cannot be imputed to it even if and when its agents have been known to have one, but the question of mens rea seems to me to be quite irrelevant in the present case. The offences created by the regulation are those of doing something with intent to deceive or of making a statement known to be false in a material particular. There was ample evidence, on the facts as stated in the special case, that the company, by the only people who could act or speak or think for it had done both these things, and I can see nothing in any of the authorities to which we have been referred which requires us to say that a company is incapable of being found guilty of the offences with which the respondent company was charged. The case must go back to the justices with an intimation of our opinion to this effect, and for their determination on the facts.

HALLETT and MACNAGHTEN JJ delivered concurring judgments.

QUESTION

Was it true to say that 'the question of mens rea seems to be quite irrelevant in the present case'? If it had been thought relevant, would the decision have been the same?

A company can be indicted for a common law conspiracy to defraud.

33 R v ICR Haulage Ltd [1944] KB 551, [1944] 1 All ER 691 (Court of Criminal Appeal)

The company was convicted with others at Maidstone Assizes on an indictment charging a common law conspiracy to defraud. The conviction was upheld on appeal.

The judgment of the Court of Criminal Appeal (HUMPHREYS, CROOM-JOHNSON and STABLE JJ) was read by STABLE J: The question before us is whether a limited company can be indicted for a conspiracy to defraud ...

It was conceded by counsel for the company that a limited company can be indicted for some criminal offences, and it was conceded by counsel for the Crown that there were some criminal offences for which a limited company cannot be indicted. The controversy centred round the question where and on what principle the line must be drawn and on which side of the line an indictment such as the present one falls. Counsel for the company contended that the true principle was that an indictment against a limited company for any offence involving as an essential ingredient 'mens rea' in the restricted sense of a dishonest or criminal mind, must be bad for the reason that a company, not being a natural person, cannot have a mind honest or otherwise, and that, consequently, though in certain circumstances it is civilly liable for the fraud of its officers, agents or servants, it is immune from criminal process. Counsel for the Crown contended that a limited company, like any other entity recognised by the law, can as a general rule be indicted for its criminal acts which from the very necessity of the case must be performed by human agency and which in given circumstances become the acts of the company, and that for this purpose there was no distinction between an intention or other function of the mind and any other form of activity.

The offences for which a limited company cannot be indicted are, it was argued, exceptions to the general rule arising from the limitations which must inevitably attach to an artificial entity, such as a company. Included in these exceptions are the cases in which, from its very nature, the offence cannot be committed by a corporation, as, for example, perjury, an offence which cannot be vicariously committed, or bigamy, an offence which a limited company, not being a natural person, cannot commit vicariously or otherwise. A further exception, but for a different reason, comprises offences of which murder is an example, where the only punishment the court can impose is corporal, the basis on which this exception rests being that the court will not stultify itself by embarking on a trial in which, if a verdict of Guilty is returned, no effective order by way of sentence can be made. In our judgment these contentions of the Crown are substantially sound, and the existence of these exceptions, and it may be that there are others, is by no means inconsistent with the general rule ...

[His Lordship referred to the authorities, including *DPP v Kent and Sussex Contractors Ltd* (**32**) and *Pharmaceutical Society v London and Provincial Supply Association* (**26**), and continued:] In our judgment, both on principle and in accordance with the balance of authority, the present indictment was properly laid against the company, and the learned commissioner rightly refused to quash. We are not deciding that in every case where an agent of a limited company acting in its business commits a crime the company is automatically to be held criminally responsible. Our decision only goes to the invalidity of the indictment on the face of it, an objection which is taken before any evidence is led and irrespective of the facts of the particular case. [Whether] in any particular case there is evidence to go to a jury that the criminal act of an agent, including his state of mind, intention, knowledge or belief is the act of the company, and, in cases where the presiding judge so rules, whether the jury are satisfied that it has been proved, must depend on the nature of the charge, the relative position of the officer or agent, and the other relevant facts and circumstances of the case.[1] It was because we were satisfied on the hearing of this appeal that the facts proved were amply sufficient to justify a finding that the acts of the managing director were the acts of the company and the fraud of that person was the fraud of the company, that we upheld the conviction against the company, and, indeed, on the appeal to this court no argument was advanced that the facts proved would not warrant a conviction of the company assuming that the conviction of the managing director was upheld and that the indictment was good in law.

QUESTIONS

(1) Contrast the reasoning in these cases with the categorical statement of Blackstone (above, p 64): 'A corporation cannot commit treason, or felony, or other crime, in it's corporate capacity ...' Is it possible to account for the change? Why do you think that it was not until as late as 1944 that the breakthrough in making companies liable for crimes involving mens rea was made?

(2) What indications are there in the judgments that the decisions of the court in *Kent and Sussex Contractors* and *ICR Haulage* were based on *policy* considerations?

(3) If a company is capable of guilt, why not also shame? (See *Dean v John Menzies (Holdings) Ltd* (below, p 78).)

NOTE

The two cases last cited, and *Moore v I Bresler Ltd* [1944] 2 All ER 515, which was decided in the same year, established that a company may be guilty of a criminal offence, including an offence involving mens rea. (The doctrine of ultra vires might have been seen as an obstacle to imposing liability, but it does not seem to have been raised in any of the key cases—presumably because it had long been regarded as irrelevant to the corresponding question in tort: *Campbell v Paddington Corpn* (**36**).)

In later cases, there has been some uncertainty as to which officers, agents or servants of a company may be identified with the company itself for the purpose of

1 [This sentence was criticised as being too widely stated by Lord Reid in *Tesco Supermarkets Ltd v Nattrass* (**34**).]

ascribing to it a criminal intention. In *Moore v I Bresler Ltd* (above), the secretary of the company and a branch sales manager were so regarded; in *DPP v Kent and Sussex Contractors Ltd* (**32**) and in *The Lady Gwendolen* [1965] P 294, CA, the only officer concerned was the transport manager; and in *National Coal Board v Gamble* [1959] 1 QB 11, [1958] 3 All ER 203 it appears to have been assumed that a weighbridgeman's knowledge and intention were to be attributed to the Coal Board, although the contrary view was taken on the same point in *John Henshall (Quarries) Ltd v Harvey* [1965] 2 QB 233, [1965] 1 All ER 725. In the case next cited, the House of Lords had the opportunity to review the question. Their decision appears to assume the existence of a stratification of managerial functions which in the case of many companies may be far from obvious. It may well be begging the question to describe a transport manager as a 'superior officer' and the manager of a large retail shop as a 'subordinate'. In other contexts, the courts have not been so willing to see a significant difference between running a company's affairs and running part only of those affairs: see *Harold Holdsworth & Co (Wakefield) Ltd v Caddies* (**122**).

The mental state of one who occupies a subordinate position in the company will not be ascribed to the company itself.

34 Tesco Supermarkets Ltd v Nattrass [1972] AC 153, [1971] 2 All ER 127 (House of Lords)

Tesco, an incorporated company owning a chain of several hundred super-markets, was charged with an offence under the Trade Descriptions Act 1968, in selling a packet of washing powder for 3s 11d [19½p], when it had been advertised at 2s 11d (14½p). An assistant at the company's Northwich branch, Miss Rogers, had restocked the shelves with normally-priced packets after supplies of 'special offer' packets bearing a lower price had temporarily run out. She had not informed the branch manager, Mr Clements, of this, while he for his part had failed to detect the discrepancy between the 'special offer' posters and the price of the powder on the shelves. Mr Clements was in complete charge of this store and its 60 employees.

Under s 24 (1) of the Trade Descriptions Act, it is a defence for the accused to prove that the commission of the offence was due to the act or default of another person, and that the accused has taken all reasonable precautions and exercised all due diligence to avoid the commission of the offence. In quashing the conviction of Tesco, which had been upheld by the Divisional Court, the House of Lords ruled that for the purpose of the company's criminal liability, the branch manager did not represent its 'directing mind and will', but was merely a subordinate. It followed that the company could plead that the manager's acts were those of 'another person' within the terms of the statutory defence; and that it had discharged the burden of proving that it had taken all reasonable precautions and exercised all due diligence by showing that its managers had been issued with proper instructions.

LORD REID: Where a limited company is the employer difficult questions do arise in a wide variety of circumstances in deciding which of its officers or servants is to be identified with the company so that his guilt is the guilt of the company.

I must start by considering the nature of the personality which by a fiction the law attributes to a corporation. A living person has a mind which can have knowledge or intention or be negligent and he has hands to carry out his intentions. A corporation has none of these: it must act through living persons, though not always one or the same person. Then the person who acts is not speaking or acting for the company. He is acting as the company and his mind which directs his acts is the mind of the company. There is no question of the company being vicariously liable. He is not acting as a servant, representative, agent or delegate. He is an embodiment of the company or, one could say, he hears and speaks through the persona of the company, within his appropriate sphere, and his mind is the mind of the company. If it is a guilty mind then that guilt is the guilt of the company. It must be a question of law whether, once the facts have been ascertained, a person in doing particular things is to be regarded as the company or merely as the company's servant or agent. In that case any liability of the company can only be a statutory or vicarious liability.

In *Lennard's Carrying Co Ltd v Asiatic Petroleum Co Ltd* (**30**) the question was whether damage had occurred without the 'actual fault or privity' of the owner of a ship. The owners were a company. The fault was that of the registered managing owner who managed the ship on behalf of the owners and it was held that the company could not dissociate itself from him so as to say that there was no actual fault or privity on the part of the company ...

Reference is frequently made to the judgment of Denning LJ in *H L Bolton (Engineering) Co Ltd v T J Graham & Sons* (**31**). [His Lordship quoted part of the judgment, which is cited above, p 72, and continued:] In that case the directors of the company only met once a year: they left the management of the business to others, and it was the intention of those managers which was imputed to the company. I think that was right. There have been attempts to apply Lord Denning's words to all servants of a company whose work is brain work, or who exercise some managerial discretion under the direction of superior officers of the company. I do not think that Lord Denning intended to refer to them. He only referred to those who 'represent the directing mind and will of the company, and control what it does'.

I think that is right for this reason. Normally the board of directors, the managing director and perhaps other superior officers of a company carry out the functions of management and speak and act as the company. Their subordinates do not. They carry out orders from above and it can make no difference that they are given some measure of discretion. But the board of directors may delegate some part of their functions of management, giving to their delegate full discretion to act independently of instructions from them. I see no difficulty in holding that they have thereby put such a delegate in their place so that within the scope of the delegation he can act as the company. It may not always be easy to draw the line but there are cases in which the line must be drawn. *Lennard*'s case was one of them.

In some cases the phrase alter ego has been used. I think it is misleading. When dealing with a company the word alter is I think misleading. The person who speaks and acts as the company is not alter. He is identified with the company. And when dealing with an individual no other individual can be his alter ego. The other individual can be a servant, agent, delegate or representative but I know of neither principle nor authority which warrants the confusion (in the literal or original sense) of two separate individuals ...

In the next two cases a company was accused and it was held liable for the fault of a superior officer. In *DPP v Kent and Sussex Contractors Ltd* (**32**) he was the transport manager. In *R v ICR Haulage Ltd* (**33**) it was held that a company can be guilty of common law conspiracy. The act of the managing director was held to be the act of the company. I think that a passage in the judgment is too widely stated:

> [Whether] in any particular case there is evidence to go to a jury that the criminal act of an agent, including his state of mind, intention, knowledge or belief is the act of the company, and, in cases where the presiding judge so rules, whether the jury are satisfied that it has been proved, must depend on the nature of the charge, the relative position of the officer or agent, and the other relevant facts and circumstances of the case.

... I think that the true view is that the judge must direct the jury that if they find certain facts proved then as a matter of law they must find that the criminal act of the officer, servant or agent including his state of mind, intention, knowledge or belief is the act of the company. I have already dealt with the considerations to be applied in deciding when such a person can and when he cannot be identified with the company. I do not see how the nature of the charge can make any difference. If the guilty man was in law identifiable with the company then whether his offence was serious or venial his act was the act of the company but if he was not so identifiable then no act of his, serious or otherwise, was the act of the company itself ...

[His Lordship discussed a number of other cases and concluded:] The Divisional Court decided this case on a theory of delegation. In that they were following some earlier authorities. But they gave far too wide a meaning to delegation. I have said that a board of directors can delegate part of their functions of management so as to make their delegate an embodiment of the company within the sphere of the delegation. But here the board never delegated any part of their functions. They set up a chain of command through regional and district supervisors, but they remained in control. The shop managers had to obey their general directions and also take orders from their superiors. The acts or omissions of shop managers were not acts of the company itself.

In my judgment the appellants established the statutory defence. I would therefore allow this appeal.

LORD MORRIS OF BORTH-Y-GEST, VISCOUNT DILHORNE and LORDS PEARSON and DIPLOCK delivered concurring opinions.

NOTES

(1) In *R v HM Coroner for East Kent, ex p Spooner* (1987) 3 BCC 636, DC, the court expressed the view, without hearing full argument, that on appropriate facts a corporation could be found guilty of the crime of manslaughter. However, on the facts of that case (the sinking of the ferry *Herald of Free Enterprise*) it was not possible to establish the necessary mens rea against any person or persons who could be identified as 'the embodiment of the company itself'.

(2) The ratio decidendi of *Tesco Supermarkets Ltd v Nattrass* is not yet accepted as law in Scotland. The question was raised before the High Court of Justiciary in *Dean v John Menzies (Holdings) Ltd* 1981 SLT 50, where the defendant company was charged with the common law crime of 'shamelessly indecent conduct' by exposing copies of (inter alia) *Club International* and *Penthouse* for sale, which

were allegedly 'likely to deprave and corrupt the morals of the lieges and to create in their minds inordinate and lustful desires'. It was held (Lord Cameron dissenting) that the Sheriff had rightly dismissed the charge, but the majority of the court was divided as to whether this was because a sense of shame could not be imputed to a company or because the 'controlling mind fiction' of *Tesco* was not part of the law of Scotland.

QUESTIONS

(1) Lord Diplock in *Tesco Supermarkets Ltd v Nattrass* said ([1972] AC 153 at 199–200, [1971] 2 All ER 127 at 155):

> My Lords, a corporation incorporated under the Companies Act 1948 owes its corporate personality and its powers to its constitution, the memorandum and articles of association. The obvious and the only place to look to discover by what natural persons its powers are exercisable, is in its constitution. The articles of association, if they follow Table A, provide that the business of the company shall be managed by the directors and that they may 'exercise all such powers of the company' as are not required by the Act to be exercised in general meeting. Table A also vests in the directors the right to entrust and confer upon a managing director any of the powers of the company which are exercisable by them. So it may also be necessary to ascertain whether the directors have taken any action under this provision or any other similar provision providing for the coordinate exercise of the powers of the company by executive directors or by committees of directors and other persons, such as are frequently included in the articles of association of companies in which the regulations contained in Table A are modified or excluded in whole or in part.
>
> In my view, therefore, the question: what natural persons are to be treated in law as being the company for the purpose of acts done in the course of its business, including the taking of precautions and the exercise of due diligence to avoid the commission of a criminal offence, is to be found by identifying those natural persons who by the memorandum and articles of association or as a result of action taken by the directors, or by the company in general meeting pursuant to the articles, are entrusted with the exercise of the powers of the company.

Is this the same test as Lord Reid's? What do you consider that Lord Diplock meant by 'the powers of the company'? Who in the Tesco organisation was 'entrusted' with the exercise of the relevant power, and what was this power?

(2) Could the state of mind of the secretary of a company ever be attributed to the company? (See Table A, art 99, and the *Panorama* case (**148**).)
(3) Suppose that in another part of Northwich there was another supermarket with a staff of sixty run by John Smith Ltd, of which Mr John Smith was the principal shareholder and managing director, and that a similar error was made in pricing a packet of washing powder. Would John Smith Ltd be criminally liable?
(4) If a corporate body is to be convicted on the basis of a confession, whose confession is necessary?

A company cannot commit conspiracy with the one person who is solely responsible for its acts.

35 R v McDonnell [1966] 1 QB 233, [1966] 1 All ER 193 (Bristol Assizes)

The defendant was charged on an indictment containing, inter alia, two counts of conspiring with a company to defraud. Each of the companies was wholly under his direction and control. It was held that the charges could not be sustained.

NIELD J: [It] is essential to note that both counsel agree the facts necessary for the determination of these points, and in particular, without any doubt or equivocation, that the defendant was at all material times the sole person in either of the companies I have named responsible for any of the acts of the company and that no one else had any authority to act for the company or any responsibility for the acts of the company.

Four principal points arise. [Points 1–3 are omitted] ... The fourth, and the principal point in my opinion, is the submission that the conspiracy charges cannot stand since in the particular circumstances here the defendant and the company were, in effect, one and the same person with one and the same mind, and that a conspiracy in law requires the agreement of at least two persons and two minds ...

I am told that there is no English authority upon this particular point, and so one comes freshly to it, although assisted by some authority not directly in point and by persuasive authorities from overseas, to which I would attach great weight. It is important at the outset to emphasise two things. It is not a company which is here being proceeded against, it is an individual defendant; and further, this is a criminal trial and one of gravity so that problems of difficulty must at all times be resolved favourably to an accused person ...

I have ... considered all the cases which have been cited to me by counsel, and at the end one is presented with a new situation in that there is no English authority upon the point. I have reached the conclusion that ... these charges of conspiracy cannot be sustained, upon the footing that in the particular circumstances here, where the sole responsible person in the company is the defendant himself, it would not be right to say that there were two persons or two minds. If it were otherwise, I feel that it would offend against the basic concept of a conspiracy, namely, an agreement of two or more to do an unlawful act, and I think it would be artificial to take the view that the company, although it is clearly a separate legal entity, can be regarded here as a separate person or a separate mind, in view of the admitted fact that this defendant acts alone so far as these companies are concerned ...

QUESTIONS

(1) Half of the shares in Black & White Ltd are owned by Black and half by White, and they are its only directors. Can Black, White and the company be indicted for a conspiracy on the basis of acts of Black and White? Can Black and the company be indicted for a conspiracy on the basis of acts of Black at a time when White was away on holiday?

(2) It has been held that a person in total control of his one-man company is capable of stealing the property of the company (*Re A-G's Reference (No 2 of 1982)* [1984] QB 624, [1984] 2 All ER 216, CA): see below, p 84. Is this decision consistent with *R v McDonnell*?

NOTE

The *policy* of making corporate bodies liable to criminal prosecution in addition to or instead of those officers or agents who are personally at fault has been questioned by writers.[2] If both are proceeded against, and the officers are substantial shareholders, they are doubly punished; if the company only is prosecuted and the wrongdoers have no stake in it, the fine will, in effect, be levied wholly on innocent shareholders or customers, while if it is barely solvent, its creditors will suffer.

(3) Tort

A corporate body may be liable in tort.

36 Campbell v Paddington Corpn [1911] 1 KB 869 (King's Bench Divisional Court)

The plaintiff occupied premises in Edgware Road of which the balcony and front rooms could be let to persons wishing to view public processions. She had agreed to let a balcony to Mr Albert Ginger to watch the funeral procession of King Edward VII, but had to release him from the contract when the defendant corporation unlawfully erected a stand in the street outside, which blocked the view. In the county court, she was awarded £90 damages. The Corporation's appeal to the Divisional Court was dismissed.

AVORY J: Three objections are taken to this verdict. First, it is said that the defendants, the mayor, aldermen and councillors of the metropolitan borough of Paddington, being a corporation, are not liable because the borough council had no legal right to do what they did, and therefore the corporation cannot be sued. This stand was erected in pursuance of a formal resolution of the borough council. To say that, because the borough council has no legal right to erect it, therefore the corporation cannot be sued, is to say that no corporation can ever be sued for any tort or wrong. The only way in which this corporation can act is by its council, and the resolution of the council is the authentic act of the corporation. If the view of the defendants were correct no company could ever be sued if the directors of the company after resolution did an act which the company by its memorandum of association had no power to do. That would be absurd. The first objection therefore fails, and the defendants are liable to be sued ...
    [The second and third objections are not material.]

LUSH J delivered a concurring judgment, dismissing the appeal.[3]

A servant cannot have implied *authority to do an act which the company itself cannot lawfully do. The company is not liable in tort for such an act.*[4]

2 The arguments are well summarised in Glanville Williams, *Criminal Law,* 2nd ed (London, 1961), § 283. For further reading, see L H Leigh, *The Criminal Liability of Corporations in English Law* (London, 1969); C R N Winn, 'The Criminal Responsibility of Corporations' (1929) 3 CLJ 398; R S Welsh, 'The Criminal Liability of Corporations' (1946) 62 LQR 345; Sir R Burrows, 'The Responsibility of Corporations under Criminal Law' (1948) 1 Journal of Crim Sci 1; L H Leigh, 'The Criminal Liability of Corporations and other Groups' (1977) 9 Ottawa L Rev 247; L H Leigh, 'A Comparative View' (1982) 80 Mich L Rev 1508.
3 Part of the judgment of Lush J is cited below, p 82.
4 Distinguish the situation where the *act* is within the scope of the servant's authority but is performed in an unauthorised, or even a forbidden, *way: Limpus v London General Omnibus Co* (1862) 1 H & C 526 (omnibus driver racing en route contrary to instructions).

37 Poulton v London and South Western Rly Co (1867) LR 2 QB 534 (Court of Queen's Bench)

The railway company had statutory authority to *arrest a passenger* for non-payment of his fare, but only to *detain goods* for non-payment of freight. A station-master employed by the company arrested Poulton, mistakenly thinking that he had failed to pay for the carriage of his horse. The company was sued for damages for wrongful imprisonment and, when the jury returned a verdict for the plaintiff for £10, moved successfully for judgment non obstante verdicto on the ground that the station-master had acted without authority.

BLACKBURN J: In the present case an act was done by the station-master completely out of the scope of his authority, which there can be no possible ground for supposing the railway company authorised him to do, and a thing which could never be right on the part of the company to do. Having no power themselves, they cannot give the station-master any power to do the act. Therefore the wrongful imprisonment is an act for which the plaintiff, if he has a remedy at all, has it against the station-master personally, but not against the railway company.

MELLOR J: I am entirely of the same opinion. I think the distinction is clear; it limits the scope of authority, to be implied from the fact of being the station-master, to such acts as the company could do themselves, and I cannot think it ever can be implied that the company authorised the station-master to do that which they have no authority to do themselves.

SHEE J delivered a concurring judgment.

NOTE

In *Campbell v Paddington Corpn* (**36**), Lush J distinguished *Poulton*'s case in these words: '... In that case a station-master, being a servant of the defendants, without any authority from the defendants gave the plaintiff into custody for refusing to pay for the carriage of his horse. The question was whether the act of the station-master in giving the plaintiff into custody was within the scope of his employment. It was held that, as the defendants themselves could not lawfully have done the act, it could not be within the scope of their servant's employment to do it. That case was only an illustration of the principle that where the wrongful act is done without the express authority of the corporation, an authority from the corporation to do it cannot be implied if the act is outside the statutory powers of the corporation. That principle has no application to a case where the corporation has resolved to do and has, in the only way in which it can do any act, actually done the thing which is unlawful and which causes the damage complained of ... The resolution was the resolution of the corporation, and the act which caused the damage, no matter for whose benefit it was done, was the act of corporation and not of the individual councillors who resolved to do it.'

The principle established by *Campbell's* case extends to acts which are unlawful as well as to acts which prior to the coming into force of CA 1989 would have been beyond the company's capacity under the ultra vires doctrine (below, p 125). It therefore remains relevant despite the abolition of that doctrine. *Poulton's* case could still be authoritative in relation to an act of a servant which was outside the scope of his company's objects clause, since the scope of his employment would necessarily be restricted by any limitations in its memorandum. However, if the victim of the tort had been 'dealing with' the company (e g in a case of deceit or negligent misrepresentation), he could invoke CA 1985, s 35A.

(4) CONTRACTS AND THE EXECUTION OF DOCUMENTS

The general rule at common law was that a contract was not binding upon, or enforceable by, a corporation unless it was executed under the company's common seal. But this general rule was subject to exceptions, particularly in relation to routine contracts of relatively minor importance, and it was widely relaxed in favour of trading corporations. The position so far as concerns companies incorporated under the Companies Acts is now set out in CA 1985, ss 36–36B, 37–41. The use of a seal is now optional (s 36A(3)), and a company may make a contract with no more formality than is required in the case of an individual (s 36). Moreover, a 'purchaser' taking under a document in good faith and for valuable consideration is given very wide statutory protection by s 36A(6)—wide enough, it would appear, to include a document which is an outright forgery.

Companies Act 1985

36A *Execution of documents*

(2) A document is executed by a company by the affixing of its common seal.
(3) A company need not have a common seal, however, and the following subsections apply whether it does or not.
(4) A document signed by a director and the secretary of a company, or by two directors of a company, and expressed (in whatever form of words) to be executed by the company has the same effect as if executed under the common seal of the company.
(5) A document executed by a company which makes it clear on its face that it is intended by the person or persons making it to be a deed has effect, upon delivery, as a deed; and it shall be presumed, unless a contrary intention is proved, to be delivered upon its being executed.
(6) In favour of a purchaser a document shall be deemed to have been duly executed by a company if it purports to be signed by a director and the secretary of the company, or by two directors of the company, and, where it makes it clear on its face that it is intended by the person or persons making it to be a deed, to have been delivered upon its being executed.

A 'purchaser' means a purchaser in good faith for valuable consideration and includes a lessee, mortgagee or other person who for valuable consideration acquires an interest in property.

(5) SERVICE AND NOTICE

Companies Act 1985

725 *Service of documents*

(1) A document may be served on a company by leaving it at, or sending it by post to, the company's registered office.

38 J C Houghton & Co v Nothard, Lowe and Wills [1928] AC 1 (House of Lords)

[For the facts and another part of the decision, see below (**112**). These remarks of Viscount Sumner are of interest on the question of notice.]

VISCOUNT SUMNER: Has knowledge then been brought home to the respondent company . . .? In the case of a natural person, if information is intelligibly conveyed to and received by him, its source, whether a servant or a stranger, whether he is high or low, matters little, if at all. With an artificial incorporated person it must necessarily be otherwise, for an impersonal corporation cannot read or hear except by the eyes and ears of others. Who are to be the organs, by which it receives knowledge so as to affect its rights, may be specially determined by the articles of its constitution, but otherwise, in a matter where knowledge may lead to a modification of the company's rights according as it is or is not followed by action, the knowledge, which is relevant, is that of directors themselves, since it is their board that deals with the company's rights. The mind, so to speak, of a company is not reached or affected by information merely possessed by its clerks, nor is it deemed automatically to know everything that appears in its ledgers. What a director knows or ought in the course of his duty to know may be the knowledge of the company, for it may be deemed to have been duly used so as to lead to the action, which a fully informed corporation would proceed to take on the strength of it . . .

NOTES

(1) Two exceptions appear to have been recognised to the proposition in the last sentence quoted. One is when the knowledge of the director is acquired privately, in circumstances where he is under no duty to his company: see *Re David Payne & Co Ltd* [1904] 2 Ch 608, CA. The other is when the director is himself a wrongdoer, as was the position in *Houghton*'s case itself. Viscount Sumner observed later in his speech: 'It has long been recognised that it would be contrary to justice and common sense to treat the knowledge of such persons as that of their company, as if one were to assume that they would make a clean breast of their delinquency. Hence, for the purpose of estopping the company, some knowledge other than theirs has to be brought home to other directors, who can be presumed not to be concerned to suppress it . . .'

The reasoning in this case was applied in *Belmont Finance Corpn Ltd v Williams Furniture Ltd* (**176**) and in *Heron International Ltd v Grade* (**127**). It was also part of the basis of the decision in *Re A-G's Reference (No 2 of 1982)* [1984] QB 624, [1984] 2 All ER 216, CA.[5] The question there was whether a person in total control of a one-man company could in law steal its property. The court held that where the controller had acted dishonestly in relation to the company, his own knowledge was not to be attributed to the company, and it followed that a jury was not bound to conclude that the company must be taken to have consented to the controller's acts. The question of dishonesty was a separate issue, which should also be put to the jury—i e the question whether the defendant had established that he had an honest belief, based on the company's 'true' consent, that he was entitled to appropriate the company's funds.

(2) In regard to corporate agents generally (not necessarily directors) the position regarding knowledge and notice is summarised by Pearson J in *Regina Fur Ltd v Bossom* [1957] 2 Lloyd's Rep 466 at 484 as follows:

5 See G J Virgo, 'Stealing from the Small Family Business' [1991] CLJ 464.

The general effect of the authorities is, in my opinion, that in deciding whether in a particular case the knowledge of the agent is to be imputed to the company, or other principal, one should consider, mainly at any rate, (1) the position of the agent in relation to the principal and whether the agent had a wide or narrow sphere of operations, and (2) the position of the agent in relation to the relevant transaction and whether he represented the principal in respect of that transaction.

Plainly, this formulation gives the court considerable flexibility in any given case.

CHAPTER 3

The Company's Constitution and Powers

A. A company's constitutional documents

Prior to the Joint Stock Companies Act 1856, companies were formed on the basis of a *deed of settlement*—an elaborate form of partnership deed. The Act of 1844 provided for the registration of the deed of settlement and the grant of corporate status in return. The 1856 Act introduced a new constitutional framework based on two documents—the *memorandum of association* and the *articles of association*—and this pattern has continued under successive Companies Acts to the present day. The memorandum is the more fundamental document, as is reflected in decisions like *Guinness v Land Corpn of Ireland* (**40**) in which it was held that if there is any conflict between the terms of the memorandum and the articles, those of the memorandum are to prevail, and by statutory provisions such as CA 1985, s 125, which make it possible to 'entrench' rights by writing them into the memorandum with a prohibition or restriction on their alteration.

Originally, this question of alterability was perhaps the most important distinction between the two documents: apart from changing its name and increasing and reorganising its capital, a company could do nothing to alter any of the terms of the memorandum, while any of the articles could be changed simply by a special resolution of the members. Today, it is possible to alter virtually all the provisions of the memorandum by one procedure or another, and so this distinction is less important. Broadly speaking, however, we can say that by its memorandum a company proclaims to the world the *external* aspects of its constitution, such as its name, domicil, objects, status (as limited or unlimited, public or private, etc) and capital structure, while the articles are concerned with matters of *internal* organisation, which are primarily of interest to its own members and officers, e g the procedures for paying the subscription price for shares and for transferring shares, the convening and conduct of shareholders' and directors' meetings, the appointment, removal and remuneration of directors and the payment of dividends.

Sections 3 and 8 of the Act provide for regulations to be made by the Secretary of State prescribing model forms of memoranda and articles of association, and this has been done by the Companies (Tables A to F) Regulations 1985.

The memorandum of association

The forms of memorandum for (respectively) a private company limited by shares and a public company limited by shares are set out as Table B and Table F. But these very brief model forms bear only a superficial resemblance to those in customary use today: a century's experience of the ultra vires doctrine has led to a gross distortion of the objects clause, so that typically we find a memorandum looking like the specimen included in Appendix 1 (below, p 593). Every company must draw up its own memorandum and lodge it with the registrar in order to become incorporated.

The matters required by s 2 to be included in a company's memorandum are customarily set out, following Table B or Table F, in a number of clauses. These are:

(1) The *name clause*. The detailed rules about company names are contained in CA 1985, Part I, Ch II. These provisions leave it largely up to the incorporators of a proposed company to choose a name which complies with ss 25ff of the Act; and although the registrar does have a discretion to disallow a name on the ground that he considers it unlawful or offensive (s 26(1) (d), (e)), he does not undertake any positive vetting exercise—as he did prior to 1981— in an attempt to see that a new company's name is not too like that of an existing company. Instead, the latter is left to pursue its own remedy, if it chooses, e g by a passing-off action at common law. Students should treat older judicial decisions on the subject of company names with caution, for they may turn on the wording of legislation which has now been superseded.

(2) The *domicil clause*.[1] There is a threefold choice: a company may state that its registered office is to be (i) in England and Wales, (ii) in Wales or (iii) in Scotland. It is not possible for a company incorporated under CA 1985 to change its domicil by moving its registered office outside the jurisdiction of its incorporation—nor even, it appears, to move it from Wales to England once it has specified Wales in the domicil clause of its memorandum.

(3) The *objects clause*. This is discussed below, pp 125ff.

(4) The *liability clause*. This clause states simply whether the liability of the members is limited or unlimited.

(5) The *capital clause*.[2] A typical clause might read: 'The company's share capital is £50,000 divided into 50,000 shares of £1 each.' If the capital is divided into different classes, e g preference shares and ordinary shares, the rights attached to each class of shares may be set out in either the memorandum or the articles. It is possible to make these rights less easy to alter by setting them out in the memorandum, with an accompanying statement of the limitations on their alterability.[3]

(6) A *public company* must also state in its memorandum that it is to be a public company (s 1(3)(a)).

(7) The *association clause* or *subscription clause*. This states: 'We, the subscribers to this memorandum of association, wish to be formed into a company pursuant to this memorandum; and we agree to take the number of shares shown opposite our respective names.'

There follow the signatures of the subscribers, together with a statement of the number of shares that each agrees to take. This number may be, and commonly is, only one share, leaving any additional shares to be allotted at a later stage. The signatures are witnessed and the memorandum dated. It takes effect as a deed (s 14).

The articles of association

Table A contains a general-purpose set of articles of association. In contrast with the memorandum, a company need not have articles specially drafted

1 On a company's domicil, see further below, p 67.
2 The topic of capital is treated in more detail in chapter 7, below.
3 See below, p 423.

for it, although in practice most do. It may instead adopt, in whole or in part, the form of articles in Table A; and if in any respect it does not have articles dealing with its internal organisation, the appropriate parts of Table A are deemed to be its articles (s 8(2)). The relevant Table A for any particular company is that in force at the date of the company's registration. This means that even though Table A may be changed by amending legislation from time to time, the articles deemed to apply to a company will remain the same.

Table A may be taken as a reasonably typical set of articles of association. However, a private company will almost invariably contain some form of provision restricting the right of a member to transfer his shares, so that the essentially private nature of the association may be maintained. This used, prior to 1980, to be a statutory requirement for all private companies.

B. The memorandum and articles of association

(1) RELATIONSHIP BETWEEN THE MEMORANDUM AND ARTICLES

The articles of association cannot modify the memorandum. If there is any inconsistency, the terms of the memorandum prevail.

40 Guinness v Land Corpn of Ireland (1882) 22 Ch D 349 (Court of Appeal)

The memorandum stated that the objects of the company were the cultivation of lands in Ireland, and things incidental thereto, and that the capital of the company was £1,050,000 divided into 140,000 A shares of £5 each and 3,500 B shares of £100 each. The articles (by article 8) provided that the capital representing the B shares should be invested in a fund set up to guarantee the payment of a 5% preferential dividend to the holders of the A shares. One of the B shareholders brought these proceedings against the company to test whether it was competent for the company to apply its funds in the manner prescribed by article 8.

BOWEN LJ: Now it seems to me that ... only one interpretation can be put upon [CA 1985, s 2], namely, that in the case of a company which registers under that section the company is ipso facto precluded from devoting any of its capital to any other object than those stated in the memorandum of association. It seems to me that the collocation of the two things, the compulsory statement of the objects of the company in the first place, and the compulsory statement of the capital in the second place, produces at once the legal obligation that the company shall devote to those objects alone the capital which is subscribed, and I think that the other sections of the Act are based upon the assumption that this is so. [His Lordship said that the payment of dividends from the B capital was not an 'object' in this sense, and continued:]

We have then to consider the argument that the court may turn to the articles of association to see if they do not, so to say, supplement the memorandum, and for this particular purpose admit of being read with it. I shall only say a few words as to how far, in my opinion, the articles of association may be looked at and read together with the memorandum of association ... There is an essential difference between the memorandum and the articles. The memorandum contains the fundamental conditions upon which alone the company is allowed to be incorporated. They are conditions introduced for the benefit of the creditors, and the outside public, as well as of the shareholders. The articles of association are the internal regulations of the company. How can it be said that in all cases the fundamental conditions of the charter of incorporation, and the internal regulations of the company are to be construed together ... In any case it is, as it seems to me, certain that for anything which the Act of Parliament says shall be in the memorandum you must look to the memorandum alone. If the legislature has said that one instrument is to be dominant, you cannot turn to another instrument and read it in order to modify the provisions of the dominant instrument ...

COTTON LJ delivered a concurring judgment.

NOTE

The short answer which could be given in modern law to the company's contention is that a company has no power to pay dividends out of capital: see below, p 372. But at this date it was still an open question whether such a payment might not be made if the memorandum expressly authorised it. This accounts for the more elaborate reasoning of the judgment.

CA 1985, s 125(4)(a) provides a modest rider to the ruling in this case, in regard to the alteration of class rights (on this topic, see below, pp 423ff). A procedure contained in articles filed *contemporaneously* with the original memorandum may be relied on to alter class rights which might otherwise be regarded as 'entrenched' in the memorandum and so much more difficult to alter.

The superior status of the memorandum is confirmed, explicitly or by implication, at many places in the Act: see, e g CA 1985, ss 9, 17(2), 125.

(2) CONTRACTUAL EFFECT OF THE MEMORANDUM AND ARTICLES

Companies Act 1985

14 *Effect of memorandum and articles*

(1) Subject to the provisions of this Act, the memorandum and articles, when registered, bind the company and its members to the same extent as if they respectively had been signed and sealed by each member, and contained covenants on the part of each member to observe all the provisions of the memorandum and of the articles.

(2) Money payable by a member to the company under the memorandum or articles is a debt due from him to the company, and in England and Wales is of the nature of a specialty debt.

Any member has the right to enforce observance of the terms of the articles, by virtue of the contractual effect given to the articles by CA 1985, s 14.[4]

---

4 Section 14 refers to the memorandum as well as the articles, but in practice it is almost always in relation to the articles that questions under this section arise. For the sake of brevity, reference will be made only to the articles in the discussion which follows; but it should be borne in mind that the same considerations apply to the memorandum.

41 Wood v Odessa Waterworks Co (1889) 42 Ch D 636 (Chancery Division)

The articles empowered the directors with the sanction of a general meeting to declare a dividend 'to be paid' to the shareholders. The company passed an ordinary resolution proposing to pay no dividend but instead to give the shareholders debenture-bonds redeemable at par, by an annual drawing, extending over thirty years. Wood, a shareholder, sought an injunction to restrain the company from acting on the resolution. It was held that the proposal was inconsistent with the articles, and the injunction was accordingly granted.

STIRLING J: It was not disputed that profits available for the payment of a dividend by the company had been actually earned ... Neither was it disputed that the company had power to create a charge on the assets of the company, or to raise money by means of such charge, or to apply the money so raised in payment of a dividend. The question, simply, is whether it is within the power of a majority of the shareholders to insist against the will of a minority that the profits which have been actually earned shall be divided, not by the payment of cash, but by the issue of debenture-bonds of the company bearing interest at £5 per cent and repayable at par by an annual drawing extending over thirty years. It is to be inferred from the terms in which the bonds are offered for subscription that the company cannot issue them in the open market except at a discount of at least £10 per cent. Now the rights of the shareholders in respect of a division of the profits of the company are governed by the provisions in the articles of association. By s 16 of the Companies Act 1862 [CA 1985, s 14] the articles of association 'bind the company and the members thereof to the same extent as if each member had subscribed his name and affixed his seal thereto, and there were in such articles contained a covenant on the part of himself, his heirs, executors, and administrators, to conform to all the regulations contained in such articles, subject to the provisions of this Act'. Section 50 of the Act [CA 1985, s 9] provides the means for altering the regulations of the company contained in the articles of association by passing a special resolution, but no such resolution has in this case been passed or attempted to be passed; and the question is, whether this is a matter as to which the majority of the shareholders can bind those shareholders who dissent. The articles of association constitute a contract not merely between the shareholders and the company, but between each individual shareholder and every other; and the question which I have just stated must in my opinion be answered in the negative if there be in the articles a contract between the shareholders as to a division of profits, and the provisions of that contract have not been followed ... That then brings me to consider whether that which is proposed to be done in the present case is in accordance with the articles of association of the company. Those articles provide ... that the directors may, with the sanction of a general meeting, declare a dividend to be paid to the shareholders. Prima facie that means to be paid in cash. The debenture-bonds proposed to be issued are not payments in cash; they are merely agreements or promises to pay: and if the contention of the company prevails a shareholder will be compelled to accept in lieu of cash a debt of the company payable at some uncertain future period. In my opinion that contention ought not to prevail ...

The articles do not constitute a contract between the company and someone who is not a member.

42 Eley v Positive Government Security Life Assurance Co Ltd (1876) 1 Ex D 88 (Court of Appeal)

Article 118 of the company's articles provided: 'Mr William Eley, of No 27, New Broad Street, in the City of London, shall be the solicitor to the company, and shall transact all the legal business of the company, including parliamentary business, for the usual and accustomed fees and charges, and shall not be removed from his office except for misconduct.' Eley, the plaintiff, who had himself drafted the company's documents for registration, and who became a shareholder several months after its incorporation, sued the company for breach of contract in not employing him as its solicitor. In the Exchequer Division, it was held that the articles did not create any contract between Eley and the company. Eley appealed, but the Court of Appeal affirmed the decision.

LORD CAIRNS LC: This case was first rested on the 118th article. Articles of association, as is well known, follow the memorandum, which states the objects of the company, while the articles state the arrangement between the members. They are an agreement inter socios, and in that view, if the introductory words are applied to article 118, it becomes a covenant between the parties to it that they will employ the plaintiff. Now, so far as that is concerned, it is res inter alios acta, the plaintiff is no party to it. No doubt he thought that by inserting it he was making his employment safe as against the company; but his relying on that view of the law does not alter the legal effect of the articles. This article is either a stipulation which would bind the members, or else a mandate to the directors. In either case it is a matter between the directors and shareholders, and not between them and the plaintiff...

LORD COLERIDGE CJ and MELLISH LJ concurred.

NOTES

(1) The judgments do not deal with the question whether it was relevant that Eley did take shares in the company at a later stage and so became entitled to enforce whatever rights his membership conferred on him.
(2) This case is commonly cited as authority for the proposition that the articles could confer rights on Eley only qua member and not qua solicitor. But this reasoning forms no part of the ratio decidendi, and was first put forward in *Hickman's* case (**43**).

The effect of s 14 is to bind the company itself by the terms of the articles, as well as the members. But the contract which s 14 creates affects the members only in their capacity as members, *and not in any special or personal capacity (e g as director).*

43 Hickman v Kent or Romney Marsh Sheep-Breeders' Association [1915] 1
Ch 881 (Chancery Division)

The defendant association was incorporated as a non-profit-making
company. Article 49 of its articles of association provided that disputes
between the association and any of its members should be referred to arbitration. Hickman, a member, brought this action complaining of various
irregularities in the affairs of the association, including the refusal to register
his sheep in its published flock book, and a threat to expel him from membership. The association was granted a stay of proceedings on the ground
that the statutory provision corresponding to the present s 14 made article
49 an agreement to arbitrate, enforceable as between the association and a
member.

ASTBURY J:　This is a summons by the defendants to stay proceedings in the
action pursuant to s 4 of the Arbitration Act 1889 [now Arbitration Act 1950,
s 4]. The action is against the defendant association and their secretary
Chapman, and the plaintiff, who became a member in 1905, claims certain
injunctions and a declaration and other relief in respect of matters arising
out of and relating solely to the affairs of the association. In substance he
claims to enforce his rights under the association's articles ... [After stating
the objects of the association and reading article 49 as to arbitration, his
Lordship continued:] This is a common form of article in private companies,
and the objects of this association being what they are, it and its members
might be seriously prejudiced by a public trial of their disputes, and if this
summons fails, as the plaintiff contends that it should, these arbitration
clauses in articles are of very little, if any, value.

It is clear on the authorities that if there is a submission to arbitration
within the meaning of the Arbitration Act 1889, there is a prima facie duty
cast upon the court to act upon such an agreement ...

In the present case the defendants contend, first, that article 49, dealing as
it does with the members of the association, in their capacity of members
only, constitutes a submission within the meaning of the Arbitration Act,
or, secondly, that the contract contained in the plaintiff's application for
membership and the association's acceptance of it amounts to such a submission. The plaintiff contests both these propositions, and independently of
the particular dispute in this case, the arguments, especially upon the first of
these contentions, have raised questions of far-reaching importance.

I will first deal with the question as to the effect of article 49. [His Lordship
read s 14(1) of the 1908 Act (equivalent to the present s 14), and referred to
the long-standing dispute among leading textbook writers as to its precise
effect. He continued:]

The principal authorities in support of the view that the articles do not
constitute a contract between the company and its members are *Pritchard*'s
case,[5] *Melhado v Porto Alegre Rly Co*,[6] *Eley v Positive Life Assurance Co* (**42**)
and *Browne v La Trinidad*.[7]

In *Pritchard*'s case the articles of association of a mining company provided that the company should immediately after incorporation enter into
an agreement with De Thierry the vendor for the purchase of the mine for
£2,000 and 3,200 fully paid shares. The articles were signed by the vendor

5 (1873) 8 Ch App 956.
6 (1874) LR 9 CP 503.
7 (1887) 37 Ch D 1, CA.

and six other persons, and the directors allotted the 3,200 shares to the vendor or his nominees, but no further agreement was made with him. It was held, affirming the decision of Wickens V-C, that the articles of association did not constitute a contract in writing between the vendor and the company within s 25 of the Companies Act 1867, and that the shares could not therefore be considered as fully paid.[8] Mellish LJ in giving judgment said: 'I am of opinion that the articles of association cannot be considered as a contract in writing between De Thierry and the company for the sale of the mine to them. It may, no doubt, be the case, if no other contract was entered into, and if De Thierry signed these articles and they were acted upon, that a court of equity would hold that as between him and the company—from their acting upon it—there was a binding contract; but in themselves the articles of association are simply a contract as between the shareholders inter se in respect of their rights as shareholders. They are the deeds of partnership by which the shareholders agree inter se.'

[The discussion of *Melhado v Porto Alegre Rly Co* and *Eley v Positive Life Assurance Co* is omitted.]

In *Browne v La Trinidad* before the formation of the company an agreement was entered into between B and a person as trustee for the intended company, by which it was stipulated (inter alia) that B should be a director and should not be removable till after 1888. The sixth clause of the articles provided that the directors should adopt and carry into effect the agreement with or without modification, and that subject to such modification (if any) the provisions of the agreement should be construed as part of the articles. The agreement was acted upon, but no contract adopting it was entered into between the plaintiff and the company. It was held that treating the agreement as embodied in the articles, still there was no contract between B and the company that he should not be removed from being a director, the articles being only a contract between the members inter se, and not between the company and B ... Lindley LJ said: 'Having regard to the construction put upon [s 14] in the case of *Eley v Positive Life Assurance Co* and subsequent cases, it must be taken as settled that the contract upon which he relies is not a contract upon which he can maintain any action, either on the common law side or the equity side. There might have been some difficulty in arriving at that conclusion if it had not been for the authorities, because it happens that this gentleman has had shares allotted to him, and is therefore a member of the company. Having regard to the terms of s 16, there would be some force, or at all events some plausibility, in the argument that, being a member, the contract which is referred to in the articles has become binding between the company and him. Of course that argument is open to this difficulty that there could be no contract between him and the company until the shares were allotted to him, and it would be remarkable that, upon the shares being allotted to him, a contract between him and the company, as to a matter not connected with the holding of shares, should arise.'

Now in these four cases the article relied upon purported to give specific contractual rights to persons in some capacity other than that of shareholder, and in none of them were members seeking to enforce or protect rights given to them as members, in common with the other corporators. The actual decisions amount to this. An outsider to whom rights purport to be

---

8 [This section required the registration in advance of all contracts for the issue of shares for a consideration other than cash.]

given by the articles in his capacity as such outsider, whether he is or subsequently becomes a member, cannot sue on those articles treating them as contracts between himself and the company to enforce those rights. Those rights are not part of the general regulations of the company applicable alike to all shareholders and can only exist by virtue of some contract between such person and the company, and the subsequent allotment of shares to an outsider in whose favour such an article is inserted does not enable him to sue the company on such an article to enforce rights which are res inter alios acta and not part of the general rights of the corporators as such . . .

The wording of [s 14] is difficult to construe or understand. A company cannot in the ordinary course be bound otherwise than by statute or contract and it is in this section that its obligation must be found. As far as the members are concerned, the section does not say with whom they are to be deemed to have covenanted, but the section cannot mean that the company is not to be bound when it says it is to be bound, as if, etc, nor can the section mean that the members are to be under no obligation to the company under the articles in which their rights and duties as corporators are to be found. Much of the difficulty is removed if the company be regarded, as the framers of the section may very well have so regarded it, as being treated in law as a party to its own memorandum and articles.

It seems clear from other authorities that a company is entitled as against its members to enforce and restrain breaches of its regulations. See, for example, *MacDougall v Gardiner* (**235**), *Pender v Lushington* (**240**) and *Imperial Hydropathic Hotel Co, Blackpool v Hampson* (**84**). In the last case Bowen LJ said: 'The articles of association, by [s 14], are to bind all the company and all the shareholders as much as if they had all put their seals to them.'

It is also clear from many authorities that shareholders as against their company can enforce and restrain breaches of its regulations, and in many of these cases judicial expressions of opinion appear, which, in my judgment, it is impossible to disregard.

[His Lordship referred to a number of other cases, including *Wood v Odessa Waterworks Co* (**41**) and *Salmon v Quin & Axtens Ltd.*[9] He continued:]

In all these last mentioned cases the respective articles sought to be enforced related to the rights and obligations of the members generally as such and not to rights of the character dealt with in the four authorities first above referred to.

It is difficult to reconcile these two classes of decisions and the judicial opinions therein expressed, but I think this much is clear, first, that no article can constitute a contract between the company and a third person; secondly, that no right merely purporting to be given by an article to a person, whether a member or not, in a capacity other than that of a member, as, for instance, as solicitor, promoter, director, can be enforced against the company; and, thirdly, that articles regulating the rights and obligations of the members generally as such do create rights and obligations between them and the company respectively . . .

In the present case, the plaintiff's action is, in substance, to enforce his rights as a member under the articles against the association. Article 49 is a general article applying to all the members as such, and, apart from technicalities, it would seem reasonable that the plaintiff ought not to be allowed

9 [1909] 1 Ch 311, CA, affd (**95**).

in the absence of any evidence filed by him to proceed with an action to enforce his rights under the articles, seeing that the action is a breach of his obligation under article 49 to submit his disputes with the association to arbitration...

NOTE

It is apparent that for a considerable period before *Hickman*'s case there had been uncertainty about the scope and effect of the statutory provision which is now CA 1985, s 14. The controversy centred on three related questions:

(a) who were the parties to the 'statutory contract'—the members and the company, or just the members? (Note that the section does not say '... covenants on the part of each member *and the company*'.)
(b) were the members deemed to have covenanted with each other, or with the company, or both?
(c) could one member sue another directly on the contract, or could he enforce the statutory rights only through the company?

It is now settled that the company should be treated as a party to the contract contained in its own memorandum and articles: *Hickman*'s case (**43**); and that the contract contains rights which are directly enforceable by one member against another: *Rayfield v Hands* (**44**)—although on the latter point much may depend on what it is exactly that the right purports to confer.

But in his attempts to reconcile the decisions—or at the least the results reached—in the earlier cases, it has to be conceded that Astbury J paid little regard to the actual ratio decidendi of some of them, and added a gloss to the section which appears to contradict its express wording ('*all* the provisions of the memorandum and articles of association').[10] It is really quite remarkable that so shaky a first-instance decision has been tacitly accepted for the greater part of this century, and endorsed without any discussion by the Court of Appeal in *Beattie v E & F Beattie Ltd* [1938] Ch 708, [1938] 3 All ER 214. In the latter case the defendant, a director, also sought to invoke an arbitration clause contained in the articles, when he was sued by his company for the return of certain sums which it was alleged had been improperly paid to him. The court ruled that since he was being sued in his capacity of a *director* and not that of a *member*, he could not rely on the 'statutory contract'.

Hickman's case may have laid some earlier controversies to rest, but it has generated several new ones of its own.

First, there is an inherent conflict in the two propositions which may be deduced from the cases, viz (a) that any member has a right to have the provisions of the corporate constitution duly observed, and (b) that s 14 cannot be relied on to enforce the rights of a non-member, or the 'outsider-rights' of one who is a member (but also a director, solicitor, etc), which the articles purportedly confer.

Secondly, there are a number of cases which it is not easy to reconcile with the 'qua member' rule: e g *Pulbrook v Richmond Consolidated Mining Co* (**93**), *Imperial Hydropathic Hotel Co, Blackpool v Hampson* (**84**), *Quin & Axtens Ltd v Salmon* (**95**). In each of these rights more in the nature of management-rights than shareholder-rights were enforced.

10 R Gregory (1981) 44 MLR 526 argues that for these reasons the decision in *Hickman*'s case is insupportable, and that it should be reconsidered despite its long acceptance.

Some commentators (e g Lord Wedderburn, [1957] CLJ 194 at 212) seek to resolve the problem by saying that a member can sue under s 14 to enforce his right to have all the provisions of the corporate constitution observed, even where this would have the consequence of indirectly enforcing 'outsider-rights', so long as he *sues* in his capacity as a member. So, for instance, a disinterested member of the Positive Life company could have sued for an injunction to restrain the company from employing any solicitor other than the constitutionally-appointed Mr Eley, and by the same argument Mr Eley himself, suing qua member, could have obtained similar relief.

Others would argue that a solution to the conflict lies in a narrowing of proposition (a) above, and to say that it is not *every* provision of the memorandum and articles that can be enforced by a member, but only those which are of a 'constitutional' character. (This requires us to beg the question, e g by saying that the stipulation that Mr Eley should be solicitor was not part of the corporate constitution but peripheral to it.) More specifically, GD Goldberg, (1972) 35 MLR 362,[11] would confine the members' statutory contractual right to that of having the company's affairs conducted by the particular *organ* of the company which is specified as the appropriate body in the Act or in the memorandum or articles of association. GN Prentice, [1980] 1 Co Law 179, considers that it is necessary to go further, and ask whether the provision in question affects the power of the company to *function*: only then can a member sue to enforce a non-member right.

None of these arguments is really convincing, however far they may go towards reconciling the inconsistent decisions. Each of them involves writing even more by way of gloss into s 14 than Astbury J did, and reading more into some of the judgments than the judges themselves said. Section 14 was enacted to cover a gap which was thought to have been created when the memorandum and articles replaced the deed of settlement in 1856: neither it nor all the subsequent theorising has any relevance to the present-day world. Our legislators should go back to the drawing-board.

A similar gloss was put by the courts on CA 1948, s 210, the precursor of CA 1985, s 459 (see below, pp 495ff): a member bringing a complaint to the court under that section had to show that the conduct in question affected him qua member. Section 459 has been re-worded so as to meet many of the criticisms which were levelled at s 210, but no attempt was made to deal with this point. The judges have accordingly been obliged to construe the new section in the same way; but (at least in cases where the company is a 'quasi-partnership') some flexibility has been achieved by giving a fairly broad meaning to the concept of a 'membership' right. In *Ebrahimi v Westbourne Galleries Ltd* (**284**), the House of Lords did not feel constrained to put the same restriction on the statutory provision which allows a member to petition to have the company wound up.

Thirdly, it is not possible to say that every 'right' which the memorandum or articles purport to confer on a member is enforceable in an absolute sense.[12] This is because many constitutional irregularities are curable by a majority resolution of the shareholders, or even capable of being condoned by acquiescence or inertia. In *MacDougall v Gardiner* (**235**), for instance, a shareholder's undoubted right to call for a poll was denied him, for the court declined to come to his aid because the matter could be put right (if anyone

11 Mr Goldberg has reaffirmed his thesis in (1985) 48 MLR 158.
12 See R R Drury, 'The Relative Nature of the Shareholder's Right to Enforce the Company Contract' [1986] CLJ 219.

wanted to) by the company's own internal mechanisms. Even irregularities which the majority have no power to condone may be defeated by the procedural rule known as *Foss v Harbottle* (**232**), under which the shareholder may find that he has no access to the court unless he can carry the majority along with him (see below, p 491). Any claim that s 14 gives a member a 'right' to have the terms of the constitution observed is defective unless it acknowledges that the right is qualified in these senses.

One member may sue another on the contract created by the articles without joining the company as a party.

44 Rayfield v Hands [1960] Ch 1, [1958] 2 All ER 194 (Chancery Division)

Article 11 of the articles of association of Field-Davis Ltd provided: 'Every member who intends to transfer shares shall inform the directors who will take the said shares equally between them at a fair value...' Rayfield, a member, sought to compel the defendants, the three directors of the company, to purchase his shares in accordance with this provision. The court declared that they were bound to do so.

VAISEY J dealt first with a question of construction, and continued:
The next and most difficult point taken by the defendants, as to which it would appear that there is no very clear judicial authority, is that article 11, as part of the company's articles of association, does not do what it looks like doing, that is, to create a contractual relationship between the plaintiff as shareholder and vendor and the defendants as directors and purchasers. This depends on s 20(1) of the Companies Act 1948 [CA 1985, s 14]. [His Lordship read the section and passages from various textbooks. He continued:]
Now the question arises at the outset whether the terms of article 11 relate to the rights of members inter se (that being the expression found in so many of the cases), or whether the relationship is between a member as such and directors as such. I may dispose of this point very briefly by saying that, in my judgment, the relationship here is between the plaintiff as a member and the defendants not as directors but as members.
In *Re Leicester Club and County Racecourse Co*,[13] Pearson J, referring to the directors of a company, said that they 'continue members of the company, and I prefer to call them working members of the company', and on the same page he also said: 'directors cannot divest themselves of their character of members of the company. From first to last ... they are doing their work in the capacity of members, and working members of the company...' I am of opinion, therefore, that this is in words a contract or quasi-contract between members, and not between members and directors.
I have now to deal with the point for which there is considerable support in the cases, that the notional signing and sealing of the articles creates a contractual relation between the company on the one hand and the corporators (members) on the other, so that no relief can be obtained in the absence of company as a party to the suit. The defendants' case in so far as it is based on this point seems to be met by two recent decisions of the Court of Appeal.

13 (1885) 30 Ch D 629 at 633.

I refer first to *Smith and Snipes Hall Farm Ltd v River Douglas Catchment Board*,[14] and to the judgment of Denning LJ in that case, which was a case of a covenant made, not by or with but for the benefit of the plaintiffs, and thereby enabling them to sue without the intervention of the covenantee. Section 56 of the Law of Property Act 1925 was referred to in terms which it is not necessary for me to repeat here. This same principle is further exemplified by the case of *Drive Yourself Hire Co (London) Ltd v Strutt*,[15] see especially the judgment of Denning LJ as there reported.[16]

The case of the plaintiff may also be said to rest upon the well-known decision of *Carlill v Carbolic Smoke Ball Co*,[17] to which I need not refer except to say that it seems to me to be relevant here. To the like effect is *Clarke v Earl of Dunraven*,[18] upon which the plaintiff here also relied . . .

[His Lordship discussed a number of other cases, including *Hickman*'s case (**56**) and continued:]

The conclusion to which I have come may not be of so general an application as to extend to the articles of association of every company, for it is, I think, material to remember that this private company is one of that class of companies which bears a close analogy to a partnership; see the well-known passages in *Re Yenidje Tobacco Co* (**282**).

Nobody, I suppose, would doubt that a partnership deed might validly and properly provide for the acquisition of the share of one partner by another partner on terms identical with those of article 11 in the present case. I do not intend to decide more in the present case than is necessary to support my conclusion, though it may be that the principles upon which my conclusion is founded are of more general application than might be supposed from some of the authorities on the point.

I will make an appropriate declaration of the plaintiff's rights, or will order the defendants to give effect to them, and if necessary there must be an inquiry to ascertain the fair value of the shares . . .

NOTES

(1) The judge in this case circumvented the difficulty raised by *Hickman*'s case (**56**) and *Beattie v E & F Beattie Ltd* (above, p 95) by the blunt assertion that the article affected the directors 'not as directors but as members'. In the case before him, the directors did happen to be directors, and were, in fact, required by the company's articles to hold shares. But in many companies this is not so. The judgment as a whole rather too readily assumes that directors are bound to be members—something that was more likely to be true a century ago when the *Leicester Racecourse* case was decided than it is today.

(2) In *Newtherapeutics Ltd v Katz* [1991] Ch 226, [1990] 2 All ER 151, Knox J held that the appointment of a person to the office of director did not of itself establish a contractual relationship between him and the company. He might, and commonly would, also enter into a contract (e g of employment) with the company; but merely as officeholder such rights and duties as he had were not based on any contract, express or implied. Vaisey J's reference to *Carlill v Carbolic*

14 [1949] 2 KB 500, [1949] 2 All ER 179, CA.
15 [1954] 1 QB 250, [1953] 2 All ER 1475, CA.
16 [Lord Denning's dicta in these cases were disapproved in *Beswick v Beswick* [1968] AC 58, [1967] 2 All ER 1197, HL. But it is arguable that the decision in *Beswick*'s case as a whole gives strong support to the reasoning of Vaisey J here.]
17 [1893] 1 QB 256, CA.
18 [1897] AC 59, HL.

Smoke Ball Co and *Clarke v Earl of Dunraven* would not appear to be compatible with this ruling.

QUESTION

Given facts similar to *Rayfield v Hands*, except that Table A, article 77 applies, suppose that there are four directors: A, B and C, who hold shares, and D, who has none. Must each of the four directors buy a quarter of Rayfield's shares, or must A, B and C buy (i) a quarter each, (ii) a third each?

The court has no jurisdiction to rectify the memorandum or articles of association.

45 Scott v Frank F Scott (London) Ltd [1940] Ch 794 (Court of Appeal)

[The facts appear from the judgment.]

The judgment of the Court of Appeal (SCOTT, CLAUSON and LUXMOORE LJJ) was delivered by LUXMOORE LJ: The . . . question which falls to be considered is whether the defendants are entitled to have the articles of association rectified in the manner claimed by them. Bennett J [at first instance] said he was prepared to hold that the articles of association as registered were not in accordance with the intention of the three brothers who were the only signatories of the memorandum and articles of association, and down to the date of Frank Stanley Scott's death the only shareholders therein. Bennett J, however, held that the court has no jurisdiction to rectify articles of association of a company, although they do not accord with what is proved to have been the concurrent intention of all the signatories therein at the moment of signature. We are in complete agreement with this decision. It seems to us that there is no room in the case of a company incorporated under the appropriate statute or statutes for the application to either the memorandum or articles of association of the principles upon which a court of equity permits rectification of documents whether inter partes or not . . .

NOTE

If the understanding between the founders as to the basis on which a company is to be incorporated differs from the constitutional arrangements of the company when formed, this may be a reason for winding up the company on the 'just and equitable' ground (see below, pp 557ff). This was the case in *Re North End Motels (Huntly) Ltd* [1976] 1 NZLR 446, where a retired farmer subscribed for half the share capital of a company on the understanding that he would have an equal say in its management, but found that he was in a minority on the board of directors because his co-adventurer, a more experienced businessman, had secured a place for his own wife on the board.

(3) CONTRACTS BASED ON OR INCORPORATING THE ARTICLES[19]

19 The memorandum, although not specifically mentioned in the discussion, will ordinarily be governed by the same rules: see the note above, p 89.

A contract may be made between a company and a person (not necessarily a member) on the basis of the articles, so that the terms of the articles are incorporated expressly or impliedly into the contract. Such a contract may be inferred from the conduct of the parties.

46   Re New British Iron Co, ex p Beckwith [1898] 1 Ch 324 (Chancery Division)

The claimants had served the company as directors without any express agreement for remuneration, but article 62 of the company's articles of association provided that the remuneration of the board should be an annual sum of £1,000. They claimed arrears of directors' fees in the liquidation of the company, and succeeded on the ground that a contract incorporating the terms of article 62 was to be inferred.

WRIGHT J: Article 62 fixes the remuneration of the directors at the annual sum of £1,000. That article is not in itself a contract between the company and the directors; it is only part of the contract constituted by the articles of association between the members of the company inter se. But where on the footing of that article the directors are employed by the company and accept office the terms of article 62 are embodied in and form part of the contract between the company and the directors. Under the article as thus embodied the directors obtain a contractual right to an annual sum of £1,000 as remuneration ... The present case is ... not within s 38 of the Companies Act 1862 [IA 1986, s 74(2)(f)] because the remuneration is not due to the directors in their character as members. It is not due to them by their being members of the company, but under a distinct contract with the company.
  The claim must therefore be allowed.

A contract which incorporates by reference provisions of the company's articles must be taken to contemplate that the articles are alterable in the usual way. But an alteration of the articles cannot affect the contract retrospectively.

47   Swabey v Port Darwin Gold Mining Co (1889) 1 Meg 385 (Court of Appeal)

The articles provided that the directors were to be remunerated at the rate of £200 per annum. In July 1888 the company passed a special resolution altering the articles so that directors were thereafter to receive £5 per month. Swabey, a director, thereupon resigned office and claimed three months' accrued fees at the old rate. Stephen J rejected his claim, but he was successful in the Court of Appeal.

LORD HALSBURY LC: I am unable to agree with the conclusion at which Mr Justice Stephen has arrived. The argument which has been addressed to us proceeds upon the erroneous basis of treating the articles as a contract, and that as there is a power given by the Act to alter the articles, the contract they contained could be put an end to and varied by the altering resolution. The articles do not themselves constitute a contract, they are merely the regulations by which provision is made for the way the business of the company is to be carried on. A person who acts as director with those articles before him enters into a contract with the company to serve as a director, the remuneration to be at the rate contemplated by the articles. The person who does this has before him, as one of the stipulations of the contract, that it shall be possible for his employer to alter the terms upon which he is to serve, in which case he would have the option of continuing to serve, if he thought proper, at the reduced rate of remuneration. Those terms, however, could be altered only as to the future. In so far as the contract on those terms had already been carried into effect, it is incapable of alteration...

LORD ESHER MR: I am of the same opinion. The articles do not themselves form a contract, but from them you get the terms upon which the directors are serving. It would be absurd to hold that one of the parties to a contract could alter it as to service already performed under it. The company has power to alter the articles, but the directors would be entitled to their salary at the rate originally stated in the articles up to the time the articles were altered.

LINDLEY LJ concurred.

A company cannot, by altering its articles, justify a breach of contract.

48 Baily v British Equitable Assurance Co [1904] 1 Ch 374 (Court of Appeal)

The plaintiff, who was not a shareholder, had taken out a life policy with the company, whose by-laws (made under the authority of the original deed of settlement) provided that profits from such policies should be distributed to policyholders without deduction. In 1903 it was proposed to register the company under the Companies Act, with articles of association altering the by-laws so as to authorise the transfer of a percentage of such profits to a reserve fund. The plaintiff claimed a declaration that his policy was not affected by the altered articles. Kekewich J and the Court of Appeal granted the declaration.[20]

The judgment of the Court of Appeal (VAUGHAN WILLIAMS, STIRLING and COZENS-HARDY LJJ) was read by COZENS-HARDY LJ: It is ... contended that, as the company was registered under s 209 of the Companies Act 1862,[1] it thereby acquired power by special resolution to alter ... all or any of the by-laws, and that the plaintiff is seeking to restrain the company from altering by-law no 4 in exercise of this statutory power. And it is said that, apart from the statute, the deed of settlement itself contained a power to alter the by-law, of which power the plaintiff had notice. We cannot assent to this argument. As between the members of a company and the company, no doubt this proposition is to some extent true. The rights of a shareholder in respect of his shares, except so far as may be protected by the memorandum of association, are by statute made liable to be altered by special resolution: see *Allen v Gold Reefs of West Africa Ltd* (55).

But the case of a contract between an outsider and the company is entirely different, and even a shareholder must be regarded as an outsider in so far as he contracts with the company otherwise than in respect of his shares. It

---

20 This decision was reversed by the House of Lords (*British Equitable Assurance Co Ltd v Baily*, below) on the basis of a different construction of the policy. But the validity of the passage cited was not disputed by the House of Lords; and, indeed, Lord Macnaghten expressly approved it.

1 [This section directed the compulsory re-registration of certain companies under the 1862 Act.]

would be dangerous to hold that in a contract of loan or a contract of service or a contract of insurance validly entered into by a company there is any greater power of variation of the rights and liabilities of the parties than would exist if, instead of the company, the contracting party had been an individual. A company cannot, by altering its articles, justify a breach of contract...

In the present case there was a contract for value between the plaintiff and the company, relating to the future profits of a particular branch of the company's business, and the company ought not to be allowed, by special resolution or otherwise, to break that contract. The appeal must be dismissed.

NOTE

A contract may, of course, be construed as incorporating the terms of the articles whatever they may be, and however they may be varied from time to time. An alteration of the articles would then not be a breach of contract by the company at all (unless it were held to violate an implied term that the company would not alter its articles mala fide or unreasonably). *Baily*'s case went to the House of Lords, where the decision of the Court of Appeal was reversed on the basis of such a construction.[2]

49 British Equitable Assurance Co Ltd v Baily [1906] AC 35 (House of Lords)

LORD LINDLEY: My Lords, this appeal turns entirely on the contracts entered into between the insurance company and its participating policy-holders, represented by Mr Baily ... These contracts are to be found in the policies themselves. By each policy the company agree to pay the executors of the assured a fixed sum out of the funds of the company, 'and all such other sums, if any, as the said company by their directors may have ordered to be added to such amount by way of bonus or otherwise, according to their practice for the time being. Provided always, that this policy is made subject to the conditions and regulations hereon indorsed.' That is the contract between the parties; but the indorsed conditions and regulations are part of it, and the fifth is important. The company was formed as long ago as 1854, and the object of the fifth regulation is to limit the liability of the members of the company. But the regulation throws light on the position of the policy-holders and on what they can claim under their policies. The fifth indorsed condition or regulation in effect provides that the funds of the company, 'after satisfying prior claims and charges according to the provisions of the deed of settlement and by-laws of the company for the time being, shall alone be liable for the payment of the moneys payable under the policy...'[3]. The reference to the deed of settlement and by-laws for the time being is all-important; for the by-laws determine how the profits of the company are to be disposed of, and those by-laws are subject to alteration from time to time by an extraordinary meeting of the shareholders of the company... The policy-holders are not shareholders, and have no voice in making or altering by-laws; but the sum payable under any policy, in addition to the fixed sum mentioned in it, is made by the policy itself to depend upon what the directors may have ordered to be added to such sum, and that depends upon their

2 See also *Shuttleworth v Cox Bros & Co (Maidenhead) Ltd* (**58**).
3 [Note this early example of an attempt to limit the liability of members by contract before this was made possible by statute.]

practice for the time being. The practice of the directors in its turn depends on how the profits are to be ascertained and divided in accordance with the by-laws, which may be altered from time to time, as above pointed out.

My Lords, I am quite unable to adopt the view taken by the courts below as to the inability of the company to alter their by-laws as they have done, and, inter alia, to make a sinking fund without the consent of the policy-holders . . .

Of course, the powers of altering by-laws, like other powers, must be exercised bona fide, and having regard to the purposes for which they are created, and to the rights of persons affected by them. A by-law to the effect that no creditor or policy-holder should be paid what was due to him would, in my opinion, be clearly void as an illegal excess of power. But in this case it is conceded that the alteration contemplated, and sought to be restrained, is fair, honest and business-like, and will, in the opinion of the directors and shareholders of the company, be beneficial as well to the policy-holders as to the shareholders. The sole question is whether such an alteration infringes the rights of the policy-holders. In my opinion it clearly does not.

I am of opinion that the appeal should be allowed . . .

LORDS MACNAGHTEN and ROBERTSON delivered concurring opinions.

No term may be incorporated into a contract by implication from the articles of association so as to override an express term of the contract. For example, a contract appointing a person managing director for a prescribed term will prevail over a provision in the articles empowering the company to revoke such an appointment, and if such a person is removed from office before his term has expired, the company will be in breach of contract.

50 Nelson v James Nelson & Sons Ltd [1914] 2 KB 770 (Court of Appeal)

The plaintiff was by an agreement in writing appointed joint managing director of the company for 'so long as he shall remain a director of the company and retain his due qualification and shall efficiently perform the duties of the said office'. Article 85(B) of the company's articles provided that the board might from time to time appoint one or more managing directors for such period as they should deem fit, and might revoke such appointment. The board revoked Nelson's appointment and he sued for damages for wrongful dismissal. The Court of Appeal upheld the decision of Scrutton J awarding him £15,000 damages.

SWINFEN EADY LJ: The defendants by a resolution of their board on 10 September 1911 purported to revoke the appointment of the plaintiff as managing director of the company. There was no power of revocation contained in the agreement of 16 January 1908 under which the plaintiff was appointed. The plaintiff had entered into the agreement of 16 January 1908, which provided that he should hold the office so long as he remained a director of the company and retained his due qualification and efficiently performed the duties of his office. The defendants did not claim to terminate the appointment or to revoke it by virtue of any provision in the agreement, or by virtue of any contract whatever as between the plaintiff and the defendants. The contention is that, according to the true construction of the articles, the directors had only power to appoint the plaintiff to be a managing director subject to their right to revoke the appointment at any time; and that, if by entering into the agreement of 1908 they have purported to appoint the plaintiff without reserving to themselves the right to revoke the appointment at will, it is immaterial, because they had no power to do it. There is no question, they say, of the construction of the agreement, because it is conceded that according to the true construction of that agreement the appointment is not a revocable one. The point is that upon the true construction of the articles any appointment by the directors of a managing director may be revoked at any time...

Article 85(B) gives the board power to appoint one or more of their number to be managing director or managing directors 'for such period as they deem fit', and they 'may revoke such appointment'. That contemplates a definite period of appointment, and not an appointment at the will and pleasure of the board. 'Period' there means a definite period ... To my mind it is clear that these articles contemplate that the board may make an appointment of a managing director for a definite term. That is absolutely inconsistent with a power in the board to revoke the appointment at any time. If there were such a power its effect would be that the board would have no power to appoint for a term. If they had no power to appoint except upon the condition that the managing director should hold his office at the will and pleasure of the board—in other words, if they had power at any time to pass a resolution to determine the appointment—that would not be an appointment for a term. The term of the appointment in such a case would be purely nominal and fictitious if at any moment the board could say that, though the managing director was appointed for a term, he merely held office at their will and pleasure, and they thought it best in the interests of the company to determine the appointment...

For these reasons I am of opinion that the defendants have not the power which they claim to revoke the appointment during the currency of the term for which the appointment was made by merely passing the resolution.

LORD READING CJ and KENNEDY LJ delivered concurring judgments.

It may be a breach of contract for a company to alter its articles, or to act, personally or vicariously, upon a power created by altering its articles.

51 Southern Foundries (1926) Ltd v Shirlaw [1940] AC 701, [1940] 2 All ER 445 (House of Lords)

In 1933, the respondent was by a written agreement appointed managing director of the appellant company ('Southern') for ten years. In 1936, after Southern had been taken over by Federated Foundries Ltd ('Federated'), Southern altered its articles so as to include, inter alia, a new article 8 which empowered Federated by a written instrument to remove any director of Southern. In 1937 Federated exercised this power and removed the respondent from his directorship. He sued Southern for breach of contract and Federated for wrongly procuring the breach of contract. He was awarded £12,000 damages against both defendants, and the award was upheld by the Court of Appeal (Sir Wilfrid Greene MR dissenting) and by the House of Lords (Viscount Maugham and Lord Romer dissenting).

LORD ATKIN: My Lords, the question in this case is whether the appellant company have broken their contract with the respondent made in December 1933 that he should hold the office of managing director for ten years. The breach alleged is that under the articles adopted by the company, after the agreement, the respondent was removed from the position of director of the company by the Federated Foundries Ltd. There can be no doubt that the office of managing director could only be held by a director, and that upon the holder of the office of managing director ceasing for any cause to be a director the office would be ipso facto vacated. Under the articles in existence at the date of the agreement, by article 89 the office of a director could be vacated on the happening of six various events, bankruptcy, lunacy, etc, including the giving by the director of one month's notice to resign; while by article 105 the company by extraordinary resolution could remove him from his office. I feel no doubt that the true construction of the agreement is that the company agreed to employ the respondent and the respondent agreed to serve the company as managing director for the period of ten years. It was by the constitution of the company a condition of holding such office that the holder should continue to be a director: and such continuance depended upon the terms of the articles regulating the office of director. It was not disputed, and I take it to be clear law, that the company's articles so regulating the office of director could be altered from time to time: and therefore the continuance in office of the managing director under the agreement depended upon the provisions of the articles from time to time. Thus the contract of employment for the term of ten years was dependent upon the managing director continuing to be a director. This continuance of the directorship was a concurrent condition. The arrangement between the parties appears to me to be exactly described by the words of Cockburn CJ in *Stirling v Maitland*:[4] 'If a party enters into an arrangement which can only take effect by the continuance of an existing state of circumstances'; and in such a state of things the Lord Chief Justice said: 'I look on the law to be that ... there is an implied engagement on his part that he shall do nothing of his own motion to put an end to that state of circumstances under which alone the arrangement can be operative.' That proposition in my opinion is well-established law. Personally I should not so much base the law on an implied term, as on a positive rule of the law of contract that conduct of either promiser or promisee which can be said to amount to himself 'of his own motion' bringing about the impossibility of performance is in itself a breach. If A promises to marry B and before performance of that contract marries C, A is not sued for breach of an implied contract not to marry anyone else, but for breach of his contract to marry B. I think it follows that if either the company of its own motion removed the respondent from the office of director under article 105, or if the respondent caused his office of director to be vacated by giving one month's notice of resignation under article 89, either of them would have committed a breach of the agreement in question ...

The question that remains is whether if the removal by the company would have been a breach by the company, the removal under the altered articles by the Federated Foundries Ltd was a breach by the company. In this matter the Master of the Rolls agreed with the other members of the Court of Appeal; but all the members of this House are not agreed. My Lords, it is obvious that the question is not as simple as in the case just considered of

4 (1864) 5 B & S 840 at 852.

the removal being by the Southern Foundries Ltd; but I venture respectfully to think that the result must be the same. The office of director involves contractual arrangements between the director and the company. If the company removes the director it puts an end to the contract: and indeed the contract relations cannot be determined unless by events stipulated for in the contract, by operation of law, or by the will of the two parties. The altered article 8 which gives power to the Federated Foundries Ltd to remove from office any director of the company is, when analysed, a power to the Federated to terminate a contract between the Southern and its director. It is an act which binds the Southern as against its promisee; and if a wrong to the respondent if done by the Southern it surely must be a wrong to the respondent if done by the Federated who derive their power to do the act from the Southern only. If a landlord gives power to a tenant to discharge the landlord's servants, gardener or gamekeeper, it is the master, the landlord, who is bound by the consequences of that discharge whether rightful, or whether wrongful, and so involving the payment of damages ... The action of the Federated was, I think I may say avowedly, taken for the sole purpose of bringing the managing director's agreement to an end. I do not think that it could be said that the Southern committed any breach by adopting the new articles. But when the Federated acted upon the power conferred upon them in the new articles they bound the Southern if they acted in such a way that action by the Southern on the same articles would be a breach. It is not a question of agency but of acting under powers conferred by contract to interfere with a contract between the party granting the power and a third person ...

LORD PORTER: The general principle therefore may, I think, be thus stated. A company cannot be precluded from altering its articles thereby giving itself power to act upon the provisions of the altered articles—but so to act may nevertheless be a breach of the contract if it is contrary to a stipulation in a contract validly made before the alteration.

Nor can an injunction be granted to prevent the adoption of the new articles and in that sense they are binding on all and sundry, but for the company to act upon them will none the less render it liable in damages if such action is contrary to the previous engagements of the company. If, therefore, the altered articles had provided for the dismissal without notice of a managing director previously appointed, the dismissal would be intra vires the company but would nevertheless expose the company to an action for damages if the appointment had been for a term of (say) ten years and he were dismissed in less ...

LORD WRIGHT delivered a concurring opinion.

VISCOUNT MAUGHAM and LORD ROMER dissented.

NOTE

A *managing director* is an executive officer of a company with a seat on the board, who normally works full-time for the company at a salary. The position of a managing director is discussed in more detail below, pp 236ff. Under the articles of association of most companies, he will automatically lose his office if for any reason he ceases to be a director: see, e g Table A, article 84.

The *Shirlaw* case was followed by Diplock J in *Shindler v Northern Raincoat Co*

Ltd [1960] 2 All ER 239, [1960] 1 WLR 1038, where the managing director had a written service agreement appointing him for ten years. In contrast, in the case next cited, the appointment was an informal one, and the only source from which the terms of the contract could be determined was the articles themselves. There was therefore no breach of contract when the company exercised a power to remove him which was expressly contained in the articles.

52 Read v Astoria Garage (Streatham) Ltd [1952] Ch 637, [1952] 2 All ER 292 (Court of Appeal)

The defendant company's articles included article 68 of Table A of the 1929 Act, which provided that the directors might appoint a managing director for such term and at such remuneration as they might think fit; '... but his appointment shall be subject to determination ipso facto if he ceases from any cause to be a director, or if the Company in general meeting resolve that his tenure of the office of managing director ... be determined'. Read was appointed managing director at a salary of £7 per week by a resolution of the board. Seventeen years later the board, with the approval of the company in general meeting, gave him notice terminating his employment. It was held that he had no claim for wrongful dismissal.

JENKINS LJ: There is no record anywhere of any terms on which the plaintiff was appointed managing director beyond the minute of resolution no 4 which was passed at the first meeting of the directors by which the plaintiff was appointed managing director at a salary of £7 a week from 1 February 1932, and the articles of association of the company. The company's articles adopted Table A, with certain modifications. Amongst the articles of Table A adopted was article no 68. [His Lordship read the article.]

It is argued by Mr Harold Brown for the plaintiff that, notwithstanding the provisions of article 68, there was a contract between the plaintiff and the defendant company in the nature of a contract of general hiring—a plain contract of employment, one of the terms of which was that the plaintiff's employment should not be determined by the defendant company except by reasonable notice. The judge came to the conclusion that the terms of the plaintiff's appointment were not such as to entitle him to any notice in the event of the company choosing under article 68 to resolve in general meeting that his tenure of office as managing director be determined, and, in my judgment, the judge was clearly right ...

The directors purported by a resolution of the board to appoint him managing director. In my view, it is really clear beyond argument that the directors must be taken to have been making that appointment with reference to the provisions of article 68 of Table A—it was only under that article that they could make the appointment. Accordingly, in my view, the resolution, containing as it did no other special terms beyond the fixing of the remuneration of £7 a week, and containing nothing whatever amplifying, or inconsistent with, the provisions of article 68, must be taken to have been an appointment of the plaintiff as managing director on the terms of article 68, and accordingly it was an appointment upon terms, inter alia, that it should be subject to termination if the company in general meeting resolved that the plaintiff's tenure of the office of managing director be determined ...

We were referred to various authorities on this topic which, in one form or another, has been fairly often before the courts. The first was the well-known case of *Nelson v James Nelson & Sons Ltd* (**50**) ...

It is to be observed that this was a case in which there was an actual agreement with the plaintiff that he should be managing director for a period which was inconsistent with the unfettered exercise by the directors of their power under the articles to revoke the appointment of a managing director; and it seems to me that this is a vital distinction from the present case, in which there is no vestige of any contract beyond the minute of the resolution making the appointment and the article by reference to which, in my view, the appointment was made ...

In my view, on the facts of this case, the position was simply that the plaintiff was appointed to be managing director in accordance with article 68 of the 1929 Table A with such tenure of office as was provided for by that article, and had no special right to receive any particular notice of the termination of his employment in the event of the company deciding to determine it and doing so by a resolution in general meeting. Accordingly, in my view, the learned judge came to a right conclusion on the plaintiff's second claim; and in the result the appeal fails on both points, and should be dismissed.

MORRIS LJ concurred.

NOTE

For a further case on the dismissal of a managing director, see *Shuttleworth v Cox Bros & Co (Maidenhead) Ltd* (**58**).

(4) ALTERATION OF THE MEMORANDUM AND ARTICLES

When the memorandum of association was first introduced as the basic constitutional document of a company by the Joint Stock Companies Act 1856, none of its provisions could be altered apart from the company's name and the capital clause. It is now possible to alter any of the clauses of the memorandum, except that fixing the company's domicil, by the use of the appropriate procedure—which is invariably rather formal and elaborate. Thus, the name can be changed under CA 1985, s 28, the objects clause under s 4, the company's status as limited or unlimited, public or private and so on by the various procedures set out in Part II of the Act, and the capital provisions under ss 121, 125 and 135.

The alteration of a company's objects required confirmation by the court in all cases until 1948, when the present procedure (now CA 1985, s 4) was substituted.[5] This allows a company to alter its objects by special resolution, and the court becomes involved only if the holders of 15% or more of the issued share capital of any class make an objection by applying to the court within 21 days. The court then has an absolute discretion to confirm or disallow the alteration.

It is perhaps significant that the only reported cases on the exercise of the court's discretion, under both the present and the previous procedures, seem to have been concerned with non-commercial organisations. In *Re Cyclists' Touring Club* [1907] 1 Ch 269 an association formed to promote cycling was not allowed to expand its objects so as to let motorists become members,

5 The power to alter the objects clause was formerly restricted by reference to certain 'purposes' which were set out in s 4, but these restrictions were removed by CA 1989, s 110(2).

since the judge accepted evidence that the interests of cyclists and motorists were to some extent antithetical. In *Re Hampstead Garden Suburb Trust Ltd* [1962] Ch 806, [1962] 2 All ER 879 a change in the objects of a home-owners' community trust was disallowed on a rather technical construction of the statutory provisions, the unspoken reasons perhaps being that the alteration was part of a scheme to bring about a deal with property developers concerning those parts of the land yet to be built upon.

In contrast with this restrictive approach to changes in the memorandum, the legislation has always allowed the articles to be altered by special resolution, subject to no statutory constraints except for such protection as is given by s 125 in regard to changes affecting 'class rights'. (On this topic, see below, p 423.) The judges have therefore been left with the task of formulating general rules controlling the power of majority shareholders to alter articles; but unfortunately the principles which emerge are anything but clear. As a rule, the courts have been content to fall back on such broad general phrases as 'bona fide for the benefit of the company as a whole', apparently without appreciating that these expressions mask rather than explain the decisions which they are in fact making. The difficulty which is posed by the juxtaposition of the 'benefit of the company' test with the basic concept of the shareholder's vote as a property right is all too rarely faced in the judgments (with the notable exception of *Peter's American Delicacy Co Ltd v Heath* (**54, 59**)). If it had been, there can be little doubt that the cases which follow would have yielded more intelligible principles.

A contract by a company not to alter its articles will not be enforced by injunction.

53 Punt v Symons & Co Ltd [1903] 2 Ch 506 (Chancery Division)

By articles 95 and 97 of the defendant company's articles, GG Symons as governing director was given the power to appoint and remove directors, and after his death the same power was exercisable by his executors. The company had also agreed in a separate contract, relating to the purchase of Symons' business, that it would not alter these articles. After the death of Symons, friction arose between his executors and the directors, which led to a proposal from the directors to rescind the articles in question by special resolution. The executors moved for an injunction.[6]

BYRNE J: The first point taken is that passing the resolution would be a breach of the contract which was entered into with the testator; and that the plaintiffs as executors are entitled to enforce the terms of the agreement by restraining any alteration of the articles. I think the answer to this argument is—that the company cannot contract itself out of the right to alter its articles, though it cannot, by altering its articles, commit[7] a breach of contract. It is well established as between a company and a shareholder, the right not depending upon a special contract outside the articles, that this is the case. It has not been, so far as I know, the precise subject of reported decision as between a contractor and a company where the contract is independent of

6 They succeeded on another ground, viz that the directors had issued new shares to 'pack' the shareholders' meeting: see below (**139**).
7 [For 'commit', we should here read 'justify': see the note below, p 121.]

and outside the articles ... [His Lordship referred to *Allen v Gold Reefs of West Africa* (**55**); and to an unreported decision *Re Ladies' Dress Association Ltd*, in which a contract not to alter any article was not enforced. He continued:] That appears, so far as I can judge, to be a decision upon the point now before me. Whether that be so or not, I am prepared to hold that in the circumstances of the present case the contract could not operate to prevent the article being altered under the provisions of s 50 of the Companies Act 1862 [CA 1985, s 9], whatever the result of that alteration may be ... I consider that the principle of the decision in *Allen v Gold Reefs of West Africa* applies to a case between the company and an outside party on a separate contract, as well as to a case between a company and a shareholder on the contract contained in the articles, and that it applies in the present case...

[See also *Baily v British Equitable Assurance Co* (**48**) and *Southern Foundries (1926) Ltd v Shirlaw* (**51**).]

NOTES

The opinion expressed in this case is supported by the emphatic dictum of Lord Porter in *Southern Foundries (1926) Ltd v Shirlaw* (**51**), above. It is therefore to be preferred, it is submitted, to the contrary view of Sargant J in *British Murac Syndicate Ltd v Alperton Rubber Co Ltd* [1915] 2 Ch 186, which was based on the mistaken view that *Punt*'s case had been overruled by *Baily v British Equitable Assurance Co* (**48**).

However, it does not follow that a contractual undertaking by a company that its articles will not be altered might not be enforced in other ways. Lord Porter clearly thought that, if a company *acted upon* its altered articles in a way which was in breach of an existing contract, a remedy in damages would lie; and this must in principle be correct. And, in principle also, an injunction might in such circumstances be granted, in the discretion of the court, restraining the company from acting upon its altered articles.

In the *Cumbrian Newspapers* case (**216**), Scott J observed:

the right to alter articles by special resolution is not a right of the company; it is a right of the members. A contract made by the company cannot deprive the members of that right. It is of course, possible that a company might, nevertheless, contract that an article would not be altered.

These remarks are consistent with the view expressed above.

This and the other cases discussed in the present section were concerned with the question whether a promise by a *company* not to alter its own articles is enforceable. Whether a similar set of undertakings by all or some of a company's *shareholders* that they will not alter their company's articles is enforceable is quite a different question. On principle, there is no doubt that it should be: see the discussion of shareholder agreements (below, pp 180ff). It is even arguable, on the authority of *Snelling v John G Snelling Ltd* [1973] QB 87, [1972] 1 All ER 79, that the company itself could rely indirectly on such an agreement, even though not a party to it.

A stipulation in the articles that a particular provision is unalterable is ineffective.

54 Peter's American Delicacy Co Ltd v Heath (1939) 61 CLR 457 (High Court of Australia)

[For the facts and other parts of the decision, see below, (**59**).]

LATHAM CJ: The Companies Act 1936 (NSW), s 20 [CA 1985, s 9] provides: 'Subject to the provisions of this Act and to the conditions contained in its memorandum, a company may by special resolution alter or add to its articles.' A company cannot deprive itself of this statutory power either by agreement or by a provision contained in the articles (*Malleson v National Insurance and Guarantee Corpn* [1984] 1 Ch 200; *Allen v Gold Reefs of West Africa Ltd* (55)). It is not possible by articles of association, to make an unalterable article. If it is desired to place the rights of particular shareholders beyond the risk of being affected by an alteration of articles it is possible to include a provision in the memorandum of association which will have that effect. Section 20 empowers a company to alter its articles only subject to the conditions contained in the memorandum of association...

The power to alter a company's articles must be exercised 'bona fide for the benefit of the company as a whole'. An alteration so made is valid and binding on the members and may affect their existing rights as members. It may, however, amount to a breach of an independent contract.

55 Allen v Gold Reefs of West Africa Ltd [1900] 1 Ch 656 (Court of Appeal)

Article 29 of the company's articles of association gave it 'a first and paramount lien' for debts owing by a member to the company 'upon all shares (not being fully paid) held by such members'. The company altered this article by deleting the words 'not being fully paid'. Only one shareholder, Zuccani (who had died insolvent), was affected by this alteration: he had had fully paid shares allotted to him when the company was formed, and had later acquired other shares on which calls were overdue. His executors challenged the company's right to claim a lien on his fully paid shares pursuant to the altered article. Kekewich J held that the company could not enforce its lien. The Court of Appeal reversed this decision, and upheld the alteration.

LINDLEY MR: The articles of a company prescribe the regulations binding on its members: Companies Act 1862, s 14 [CA 1985, s 7]. They have the effect of a contract (see s 16 [CA 1985, s 14]); but the exact nature of this contract is even now very difficult to define. Be its nature what it may, the company is empowered by the statute to alter the regulations contained in its articles from time to time by special resolutions (ss 50 and 51 [CA 1985, ss 9, 378]); and any regulation or article purporting to deprive the company of this power is invalid on the ground that it is contrary to the statute: *Walker v London Tramways Co.*[8]
   The power thus conferred on companies to alter the regulations contained in their articles is limited only by the provisions contained in the statute and the conditions contained in the company's memorandum of association. Wide, however, as the language of s 50 is, the power conferred by it must, like all other powers, be exercised subject to those general principles of law and equity which are applicable to all powers conferred on majorities and enabling them to bind minorities. It must be exercised, not only in the manner required by law, but also bona fide for the benefit of the company as a whole, and it must not be exceeded. These conditions are always implied, and are

8 (1879) 12 Ch D 705. [See also *Punt v Symons & Co Ltd* (53).]

seldom, if ever, expressed. But if they are complied with I can discover no ground for judicially putting any other restrictions on the power conferred by the section than those contained in it. How shares shall be transferred, and whether the company shall have any lien on them, are clearly matters of regulation properly prescribed by a company's articles of association. This is shown by Table A in the Schedule to the Companies Act ... Speaking, therefore, generally, and without reference to any particular case, the section clearly authorises a limited company, formulated with articles which confer no lien on fully paid-up shares, and which allow them to be transferred without any fetter, to alter those articles by special resolution, and to impose a lien and restrictions on the registry of transfers of those shares by members indebted to the company.

But then comes the question whether this can be done so as to impose a lien or restriction in respect of a debt contracted before and existing at the time when the articles are altered. Again, speaking generally, I am of opinion that the articles can be so altered, and that, if they are altered bona fide for the benefit of the company, they will be valid and binding as altered on the existing holders of paid-up shares, whether such holders are indebted or not indebted to the company when the alteration is made. But, as will be seen presently, it does not by any means follow that the altered article may not be inapplicable to some particular fully paid-up shareholder. He may have special rights against the company, which do not invalidate the resolution to alter the articles, but which may exempt him from the operation of the articles as altered.

The conclusion thus arrived at is based on the language of s 50, which, as I have said already, the court, in my opinion, is not at liberty to restrict. This conclusion, moreover, is in conformity with such authorities as there are on the subject...

But, although the regulations contained in a company's articles of association are revocable by special resolution, a special contract may be made with the company in the terms of or embodying one or more of the articles, and the question will then arise whether an alteration of the articles so embodied is consistent or inconsistent with the real bargain between the parties. A company cannot break its contracts by altering its articles,[9] but, when dealing with contracts referring to revocable articles, and especially with contracts between a member of the company and the company respecting his shares, care must be taken not to assume that the contract involves as one of its terms an article which is not to be altered.

It is easy to imagine cases in which even a member of a company may acquire by contract or otherwise special rights against the company, which exclude him from the operation of a subsequently altered article. Such a case arose in *Swabey v Port Darwin Gold Mining Co* (**47**) where it was held that directors, who had earned fees payable under a company's articles, could not be deprived of them by a subsequent alteration of the articles, which reduced the fees payable to directors.

I take it to be clear that an appliation for an allotment of shares on the terms of the company's articles does not exclude the power to alter them nor the application of them, when altered, to the shares so applied for and allotted. To exclude that power or the application of an altered article to

9 [Later cases (e g (**48**), (**51**)) make it plain that this sentence should be understood to mean 'a company *cannot justify* a breach of contract by pleading the valid alteration of its articles', and not 'a company *cannot alter* its articles if to do so would break an existing contract'.]

particular shares, some clear and distinct agreement for that exclusion must be shown, or some circumstances must be proved conferring a legal or equitable right on the shareholders to be treated by the company differently from the other shareholders.

This brings me to the last question which has to be considered, namely, whether there is in this case any contract or other circumstance which excludes the application of the altered article to Zuccani's fully paid-up vendor's shares. [His Lordship ruled that there was no such special circumstance, and continued:]

The fact that Zuccani's executors were the only persons practically affected at the time by the alterations made in the articles excites suspicion as to the bona fides of the company. But, although the executors were the only persons who were actually affected at the time, that was because Zuccani was the only holder of paid-up shares who at the time was in arrear of calls. The altered articles applied to all holders of fully paid shares, and made no distinction between them. The directors cannot be charged with bad faith.

After carefully considering the whole case, and endeavouring in vain to discover grounds for holding that there was some special bargain differentiating Zuccani's shares from others, I have come to the conclusion that the appeal from the decision of the learned judge, so far as it relates to the lien created by the altered articles, must be allowed . . .

ROMER LJ delivered a concurring judgement.

VAUGHAN WILLIAMS LJ dissented.

56 Sidebottom v Kershaw, Leese & Co Ltd [1920] 1 Ch 154 (Court of Appeal)

The defendant company had altered its articles by introducing a provision which gave the directors power to buy out at a fair price the shareholding of any member who competed with the company's business. The plaintiffs, who were minority shareholders and who carried on a competing business, unsuccessfully challenged the validity of the alteration.

LORD STERNDALE MR: There are two objections to this alteration: one is a very broad one indeed. It is that whatever alterations a company may be empowered to make in its articles varying the terms upon which its members may hold their shares, it cannot alter its articles so as to provide a means of what was called 'expelling', as in this case, by buying out a particular member and making him cease to be a member. I cannot find that such an exception as that is anywhere stated in any of the authorities as existing . . . but there is no doubt—in fact I think it is established by *Phillips v Manufacturers' Securities Ltd*[10]—that a power such as this is a perfectly valid power in the case of original articles, and it seems to me that prima facie if it could be in the original articles, it could be introduced into the altered articles provided only it is done bona fide for the benefit of the company as a whole. Therefore, in my opinion, it comes back to the same thing. The introduction into an altered article of a power of buying a person out or expelling him can only be held invalid if the alteration is not made bona fide for the benefit of the company . . .

A second argument was addressed to us, which was this: I think Mr Jenkins

10 (1917) 116 LT 290, CA.

rather deprecated it being put in this form, but in my opinion this is what it came to: An alteration cannot be for the benefit of the company as a whole if in fact it is a detriment to one of the members of the company, because the company as a whole means the whole body of corporators and every individual corporator, and if one of them has detriment occasioned to him by the alteration, it cannot be for the benefit of the company as a whole. I must say that I find it very difficult to follow that argument, but it seems to me to be exactly met by *Allen v Gold Reefs of West Africa* (55), because undoubtedly the alteration that was made there was not for the benefit of the shareholder, of whom the plaintiff, Mr Allen, was the executor, because it made his fully paid-up shares subject to a lien to which they were not subject before, and thereby, as I have pointed out, made it possible to get rid of Mr Allen, or Mr Allen's testator, altogether by compulsorily buying up his shares if the debt were not satisfied.

In my opinion, the whole of this case comes down to rather a narrow question of fact, which is this: When the directors of this company introduced this alteration giving power to buy up the shares of members who were in competing businesses did they do it bona fide for the benefit of the company or not? It seems to me quite clear that it may be very much to the benefit of the company to get rid of members who are in competing businesses ... I think there can be no doubt that a member of a competing business or an owner of a competing business who is a member of the company has a much better chance of knowing what is going on in the business of the company, and of thereby helping his own competition with it, than if he were a non-member; and looking at it broadly, I cannot have any doubt that in a small private company like this the exclusion of members who are carrying on competing businesses may very well be of great benefit to the company. That seems to me to be precisely a point which ought to be decided by the voices of the business men who understand the business and understand the nature of competition, and whether such a position is or is not for the benefit of the company. I think, looking at the alteration broadly, that it is for the benefit of the company that they should not be obliged to have amongst them as members persons who are competing with them in business, and who may get knowledge from their membership which would enable them to compete better.

That brings me to the last point. It is said that that might be so were it not for the fact that the directors and the secretary have said, 'This is directed against Mr Bodden', and therefore it is not done bona fide for the benefit of the company, but it is done to get rid of Mr Bodden.[11] If it were directed against Mr Bodden for any malicious motive I should agree with that—the thing would cease to be bona fide at once; but these alterations are not as a rule made without some circumstances having arisen to bring the necessity of the alteration to the minds of the directors. I do not read this as meaning anything more than this: 'It was the position of Mr Bodden that made us appreciate the detriment that there might be to the company in having members competing with them in their business, and we passed this, and our intention was, if it became necessary, to use it in the case of Mr Bodden; that is what we had in our minds at the time; but we also had in our minds that Mr Bodden is not the only person who might compete, and therefore we passed this general article in order to enable us to apply it in any case where

11 [Bodden was not, in fact, a plaintiff.]

it was for the good of the company that it should be applied.' It is a question of fact. I come to the conclusion of fact to which I think the Vice-Chancellor came, that the directors were acting perfectly bona fide, that they were passing the resolution for the benefit of the company; but that no doubt the occasion of their passing it was because they realised in the person of Mr Bodden that it was a bad thing to have members who were competing with them...

For these reasons I think this is a valid article. I think the alteration was within the competence of the company, and therefore this appeal must be allowed with costs here and below.

WARRINGTON LJ and EVE J delivered concurring judgments.

NOTE

It is rather curious that in both this case and *Allen*'s case (above) there are references to the good faith of the *directors*, when it is plain from the rest of the judgments that it is the bona fides of the majority shareholders who pass the special resolution that is crucial. Of course, it would be easy to imagine a situation where the directors have an improper motive in introducing the proposal for change, and simply carry the opinion of the majority along with them. This may be what is being alluded to in the two cases. In fact, the directors in *Sidebottom*'s case held over half of the company's issued shares, and the majority in favour of the resolution was overwhelming.

In the case next cited, Peterson J favoured an objective test of what was 'for the benefit of the company'. This view was disapproved in *Shuttleworth v Cox Bros & Co Ltd* (**58**), but it has, in the view of some writers, been to some extent revived by the reformulated test suggested in *Greenhalgh v Arderne Cinemas Ltd* (**60**).

57 Dafen Tinplate Co Ltd v Llanelly Steel Co (1907) Ltd [1920] 2 Ch 124 (Chancery Division)

The defendant company altered its articles so as to introduce a power enabling the majority of the shareholders to require any member (with one named exception) to transfer his shares at a fair value to an approved transferee. The plaintiff company, which held shares in the defendant company, and had transferred its custom as a purchaser of steel from the defendants to a rival company, opposed the alteration. Peterson J upheld its objection, because *in his own view* the alteration was wider than necessary.

PETERSON J: In *Sidebottom*'s case (**56**) the Court of Appeal sanctioned an alteration of the articles of association which enabled the directors to require a shareholder who carried on a competing business, or was a director of a company carrying on a competing business, to transfer his shares, and it did so on the ground that the alteration was for the benefit of the company as a whole. It has been suggested that the only question in such a case as this is whether the shareholders bona fide or honestly believed that that alteration was for the benefit of the company. But this is not, in my view, the true meaning of the words of Lindley MR or of the judgment in *Sidebottom*'s case. The question is whether in fact the alteration is genuinely for the benefit of the company...

The question of fact then which I have to consider is whether the alteration of the articles which enables the majority of the shareholders to compel any shareholder to transfer his shares, can properly be said to be for the benefit of the company. It may be for the benefit of the majority of the shareholders to acquire the shares of the minority, but how can it be said to be for the benefit of the company that any shareholder, against whom no charge of acting to the detriment of the company can be urged, and who is in every respect a desirable member of the company, and for whose expropriation there is no reason except the will of the majority, should be forced to transfer his shares to the majority or to anyone else? Such a provision might in some circumstances be very prejudicial to the company's interest. For instance, on an issue of new capital, the knowledge that he might be expropriated as soon as his capital was on the point of producing profitable results might well exercise a deterrent influence on a man who was invited to take shares in the company ... In my view it cannot be said that a power on the part of the majority to expropriate any shareholder they may think proper at their will and pleasure is for the benefit of the company as a whole. To say that such an unrestricted and unlimited power of expropriation is for the benefit of the company appears to me to be confusing the interests of the majority with the benefit of the company as a whole. In my opinion the power which, in this case, has been conferred upon the majority of the shareholders by the alteration of the articles of association in this case is too wide and is not such a power as can be assumed by the majority. The power of compulsory acquisition by the majority of shares which the owner does not desire to sell is not lightly to be assumed whenever it pleases the majority to do so. The shareholder is entitled to say non haec in foedera veni; and while on the authorities as they stand at present it is possible to alter the articles in such a way as to confer this power, if it can be shown that the power is for the benefit of the company as a whole, I am of opinion that such a power cannot be supported if it is not established that the power is bona fide or genuinely for the company's benefit ...

58 Shuttleworth v Cox Bros & Co (Maidenhead) Ltd [1927] 2 KB 9 (Court of Appeal)

The plaintiff had been removed from the position of 'permanent' director, to which he had been appointed by the articles, in the circumstances described by Atkin LJ. This action followed the discovery of irregularities in the accounts between him and the company. He claimed that his dismissal was wrongful. The Court of Appeal, affirming Avory J, upheld the validity of the company's action.

ATKIN LJ: The plaintiff was a director of the defendant company from May 1921, when the company was incorporated, until 1926. Up to 1924 he was a director on the terms of article 18, which provided that he and others should be the first directors of the company, that they should be permanent directors, and that each of them should be entitled to hold office so long as he should live, unless he should become disqualified from any of the causes specified in article 22. At that time article 22 provided that the office of director should be vacated in any of the events specified in the six clauses of the article. In 1924 the company passed an altered article by a special resolution ... adding to the six clauses of article 22 a seventh clause: 'If he shall be requested in writing by all the other directors to resign his office.' Some ten or eleven months after article 22 was altered he was requested in writing to resign his office. He claims in this action that the clause added to the article is invalid, and that he still remains a director ...

[The] contract that they shall be permanent directors at a salary is contained in the articles only ... In these circumstances the proper inference appears to be that there was a contract that the plaintiff should be a permanent director, but a contract contained in articles which could be altered by a special resolution of the company in accordance with the provisions of the Companies Act; and inasmuch as the contract contemplated the permanent office being vacated in one of six contingencies, it is not inconsistent with the contract that the article should be altered so as to add a seventh contingency. In other words, it is a contract made upon the terms of an alterable article, and therefore neither of the contracting parties can complain if the article is altered. Consequently I cannot find that there has been any breach of contract in making the alteration.

The only other question is whether the article is upon general principles objectionable as being not honestly made within the powers of the company. Here the limits to the power of the company to alter its articles have to be considered. Certain limits there are, and they have been laid down in several cases, notably by Lindley MR in *Allen v Gold Reefs of West Africa Ltd* (55) ... There in a reasoned and lucid judgment the Master of the Rolls uses the phrase 'bona fide for the benefit of the company'. But neither this court nor any other court should consider itself fettered by the form of words, as if it were a phrase in an Act of Parliament which must be accepted and construed as it stands. We must study what its real meaning is by the light of the principles which were being laid down by the Master of the Rolls when he used the phrase ... The only question is whether or not the shareholders, in considering whether they shall alter articles, honestly intend to exercise their powers for the benefit of the company. If they do then, subject to one or two reservations which have been explained, the alteration must stand. It is not a matter of law for the court whether or not a particular alteration is for the benefit of the company; nor is it the business of a judge to review the decision of every company in the country on these questions. And even if the question were not for the shareholders themselves, but for some other body, it must be a question of fact. In this case there is a finding of fact by the jury that the alteration was for the benefit of the company; but I do not decide the case on that ground. In my view the question is solely for the shareholders acting in good faith. The circumstances may be such as to lead to one conclusion only, that the majority of the shareholders are acting so oppressively that they cannot be acting in good faith; or, to put it in another way, it may be that their decision must be one which could [not] be taken by persons acting in good faith with a view to the benefit of the company. But these are matters outside and apart from the question, Does this or that tribunal consider, in the light of events which have happened, that the alteration was or was not for the benefit of the company? With great respect to a very learned judge I cannot agree with the judgment of Peterson J to the contrary on this point.[12] In my view the passage which has been cited from the judgment of Lord Sterndale MR in *Sidebottom*'s case (56) makes it clear that in his view the ultimate decision is to be the decision of the majority of the shareholders ...

BANKES and SCRUTTON LJJ delivered concurring judgments.

12 In *Dafen Tinplate Co Ltd v Llanelly Steel Co (1907) Ltd* (57).

59 Peter's American Delicacy Co Ltd v Heath (1939) 61 CLR 457 (High Court of Australia)

As a result of an oversight by the draftsman, the company's articles of association contained inconsistent provisions governing the distribution of profits. Profits distributed as *dividends* were payable in proportion to the amounts paid up on shares, but distributions of *capitalised* profits ('bonus shares') were to be in proportion to the nominal value of shares held. The issued capital consisted of 511,000 fully paid and 169,000 partly paid shares. At a general meeting the articles were altered by special resolution so that the distribution of capitalised profits was to be made on the same basis as cash dividends, i e in proportion to the amounts paid up on shares. Some holders of partly paid shares objected, and their objection was upheld at first instance; but on appeal the High Court ruled that the alteration was valid.

[For another part of the decision, see (**54**).]

RICH J: Company law confers a power of alteration on a general meeting of shareholders requiring for any positive alteration a three-fourths majority. There is no other body to whom the question can be submitted. No rights given by articles of association can prevail against a three-fourths majority and it is well understood that all are subject to it. It is true that the power of alteration must be exercised bona fide with a view to the advancement of the company considered as a whole and not with a view to the advancement of the interests of a majority of voters or of a section of the company only ... But in deciding what is for the interest of the company and what is bona fide, the constitution of the company, the condition and effect of the various articles of association and the extent to which rights are conferred upon different classes of shareholders are relevant and important ... Where the very problem which arises contains as inherent in itself all the elements of a conflict of interests between classes of shareholders these authorities do not mean that the power of alteration is paralysed, they mean only that the purpose of bringing forward the resolution must not be simply the enrichment of the majority at the expense of the minority. The resolution in the present case was brought forward to solve a difficulty and make possible a capitalisation. It can hardly be supposed that the only solution of such a difficulty which can be lawfully adopted is that which gives the minority an advantage at the expense of the majority. In my opinion the case presents nothing but an ordinary example of an honest attempt on the part of the directors to clear up a difficulty by securing an alteration of the articles not unjust to any class of shareholders, but at the same time conserving the interests of the shareholders who form the great majority of the company ...

In my opinion the appeal should be allowed.

DIXON J: Primarily a share in a company is a piece of property conferring rights in relation to distributions of income and of capital. In many respects the proprietary rights are defined by the articles of association, and it is easy to see that a power of alteration might be used for the aggrandisement of a majority at the expense of a minority. For example, if there were no check upon the use of the power, it is conceivable that a three-fourths majority might adopt an article by which the shares which they alone held would participate, to the exclusion of other shares, in the surplus assets in winding up or even in distributions of profit by way of dividend. Again, authority might be obtained under an alteration so as to convert the assets or operations of a company into a source of profit not of the company but of persons forming part of or favoured by the majority. It has seemed incredible that alterations of such a nature could be made by the exercise of the power. But reliance upon the general doctrine that powers shall be exercised bona fide and for no bye or sinister purpose brings its own difficulties. The power of alteration is not fiduciary. The shareholders are not trustees for one another, and, unlike directors, they occupy no fiduciary position and are under no fiduciary duties. They vote in respect of their shares, which are property, and the right to vote is attached to the share itself as an incident of property to be enjoyed and exercised for the owner's personal advantage. No doubt the exercise of the right affects the interests of others too, and it may be that an analogy may be found in other powers which though given to protect the donee's own interests affect the property rights of others, as, for instance, does a mortgagee's power of sale. Some such analogy probably gave rise to the suggestion made in Buckley on *The Companies Acts* that the limitation on the power is that the alteration must not be such as to sacrifice the interests of the minority to those of a majority without any reasonable prospect of advantage to the company as a whole...

Apart altogether from altering articles of association, the voting strength of a majority of shareholders may be used in matters of management and administration to obtain for themselves advantages which otherwise would enure for the benefit of all the members of the company, and in some circumstances such an attempt on the part of the majority to secure advantages to the prejudice of the minority conflicts with ordinary notions of fair dealing and honesty. Often when this is done the thing attempted will be found by its nature to fall outside the power of the members in general meeting and even outside the corporate powers of the company. But this is not necessarily the case, and a thing not of its own nature ultra vires may be invalidated by the effect which it produces or is intended to produce in benefiting some shareholders at the expense of others or individuals at the expense of the company...

An example of a misuse of power on the part of shareholders constituting a majority in the administration of a company's affairs is the unjustifiable refusal to allow an action to be maintained in the name of the company to redress a wrong to it by one of themselves[13]...

In these formulations of general principle there is an assumption that vested in the company or in the minority of shareholders, as the case may be, is an independent title to property, to rights or to remedies, and the ground of the court's intervention is that by the course adopted by the majority, the company or the minority will be deprived of the enjoyment of that to which they are so entitled. The conduct of the majority is then given some dyslogistic description such as 'fraudulent', 'abuse of powers' or 'oppression'. A chief purpose of articles of association is to regulate the rights of shareholders inter se, and their relations to the profits and surplus assets of the company are governed by the provisions of the articles. A power to alter articles of association is necessarily a power to alter the rights of shareholders inter se, including their mutual rights in respect of profits and surplus assets. It is therefore evident that some difficulty must arise in applying to resolutions for the alteration of articles a statement of principle which assumes the independent existence of rights which should not be impaired or

13 [See below, pp 472 ff.]

destroyed. Prima facie rights altogether dependent upon articles of association are not enduring and indefeasible but are liable to modification or
destruction; that is, if and when it is resolved by a three-fourths majority that
the articles should be altered. To attempt to distinguish between alterations
which deserve the epithet fraudulent or oppressive or unjust and those
deserving no moral censure without explaining the considerations upon which
the distinction depends, is to leave the whole question to general notions of
fairness and propriety ... To base the application of these descriptions to a
particular resolution upon the fact that it involves a modification or defeasance of rights of a valuable or important nature, is in effect to go back to the
discarded distinction between articles affecting the constitution and those
affecting the administration of the company or to a distinction very like it.
To base the application of the epithets upon the circumstance that the
majority obtain a benefit by the change seems to involve some departure
from the principle that the vote attached to a share is an incident of property
which may be used as the shareholder's interests may dictate ...

The chief reason for denying an unlimited effect to widely expressed powers
such as that of altering a company's articles is the fear or knowledge that an
apparently regular exercise of the power may in truth be but a means of
securing some personal or particular gain, whether pecuniary or otherwise,
which does not fairly arise out of the subjects dealt with by the power and is
outside and even inconsistent with the contemplated objects of the power. It
is to exclude the purpose of securing such ulterior special and particular
advantages that Lord Lindley used the phrase 'bona fide for the benefit of
the company as a whole'. The reference to 'benefit as a whole' is but a very
general expression negativing purposes foreign to the company's operations,
affairs and organisations. But unfortunately, as appears from the foregoing
discussion, the use of the phrase has tended to cause misapprehension. If
the challenged alteration relates to an article which does or may affect an
individual, as, for instance, a director appointed for life or a shareholder
whom it is desired to expropriate, or to an article affecting the mutual rights
and liabilities inter se of shareholders or different classes or descriptions of
shareholders, the very subject-matter involves a conflict of interests and
advantages. To say that the shareholders forming the majority must consider
the advantage of the company as a whole in relation to such a question seems
inappropriate, if not meaningless, and at all events starts an impossible
inquiry. The 'company as a whole' is a corporate entity consisting of all the
shareholders. If the proposal put forward is for a revision of any of the
articles regulating the rights inter se of shareholders or classes of shareholders,
the primary question must be how conflicting interests are to be adjusted,
and the adjustment is left by law to the determination of those whose interests
conflict, subject, however, to the condition that the existing provision can be
altered only by a three-fourths majority. Whether the matter be voting rights,
the basis of distributing profits, the basis of dividing surplus assets on a
winding-up, preferential rights in relation to profits or to surplus assets, or
any other question affecting mutual interests, it is apparent that though the
subject-matter is among the most conspicuous of those governed by articles
and therefore of those to which the statutory power is directed, yet it involves
little if anything more than the redetermination of the rights and interests of
those to whom the power is committed. No one supposes that in voting
each shareholder is to assume an inhuman altruisim and consider only the
intangible notion of the benefit of the vague abstraction called by Lord

Robertson in *Baily*'s case **(48)** 'the company as an institution'. An investigation of the thoughts and motives of each shareholder voting with the majority would be an impossible proceeding . . . [When] the very question to be determined is a conflict of interests, unless the subject-matter is held outside the power, the purpose of the resolution, as distinguished from the motives of the individuals, often must be to resolve the conflict in favour of one and against the other interest.

In my opinion it was within the scope and purpose of the power of alteration for a three-fourths majority to decide the basis of distributing shares issued for the purpose of capitalising accumulated profits or profits arising from the sale of goodwill, and in voting for the resolution shareholders were not bound to disregard their own interests. I am far from saying that the resolution for the alteration of the articles would have been bad if the existing articles had been uniform and clear in requiring that, however the 'capitalisation' was effected, the basis of distribution should be the number of shares respectively subscribed for by members. But the facts of the case were that by one method, the older indirect method, a capitalisation might have been effected which would mean a distribution according to capital paid up. Doubts were felt about the propriety of adopting this course, and doubts were agitated as to the meaning of the article providing for the direct method. If there were no capitalisation, the accumulated profits would not be distributed in proportion with capital subscribed. In these circumstances the holders of partly paid shares had no 'right' to receive the profits in proportion with capital paid up. As the articles stood they were entitled only to receive shares in that proportion if and when issued by way of direct capitalisation. That event would never be likely to occur; for the holders of fully paid shares were perfectly entitled to prevent it and would no doubt do so. In these circumstances it appears to me that the resolution involved no oppression, no appropriation of an unjust or reprehensible nature and did not imply any purpose outside the scope of the power . . .

LATHAM CJ delivered a concurring judgment.

MCTIERNAN J concurred.

QUESTION

Is it consistent to say that the power to alter articles 'shall be exercised bona fide and for no bye or sinister purpose' and (in the next sentence) 'the power of alteration is not fiduciary'?

60 Greenhalgh v Arderne Cinemas Ltd[14] [1951] Ch 286, [1950] 2 All ER 1120 (Court of Appeal)

The articles of the defendant (a private company) provided that existing members should have pre-emptive rights if a member wished to sell his shares. Mallard, the managing director, had negotiated with an outsider, Sol Sheckman, for the sale to Sheckman of a controlling interest in the company

---

14 This was the last of many actions between the parties. The parties were involved in seven actions, five of which went to the Court of Appeal; Greenhalgh lost all but the first (Gower, *Modern Company Law* (4th edn, 1979), pp 624–6). See further below, **(219)**.

at 6*s* [30 p] per share, and to give effect to this agreement had procured the passing of a special resolution which in effect negatived the pre-emptive rights of the existing members. One of the latter, Greenhalgh, claimed a declaration that the resolutions were invalid as a fraud on the minority.[15] The Court of Appeal, affirming Roxburgh J, refused a declaration.

EVERSHED MR: The burden of that case is that the resolution was not passed bona fide and in the interests of the company as a whole, and there are, as Mr Jennings has urged, two distinct approaches.

The first line of attack is this, and it is one to which, he complains, Roxburgh J paid no regard: this is a special resolution, and, on authority, Mr Jennings says, the validity of a special resolution depends upon the fact that those who passed it did so in good faith and for the benefit of the company as a whole. The cases to which Mr Jennings referred are *Sidebottom v Kershaw, Leese & Co Ltd* (**56**), Peterson J's decision in *Dafen Tinplate Co Ltd v Llanelly Steel Co (1907) Ltd* (**57**) and, finally, *Shuttleworth v Cox Bros & Co (Maidenhead) Ltd* (**58**). Certain principles, I think, can be safely stated as emerging from those authorities. In the first place, I think it is now plain that 'bona fide for the benefit of the company as a whole' means not two things but one thing. It means that the shareholder must proceed upon what, in his honest opinion, is for the benefit of the company as a whole. The second thing is that the phrase 'the company as a whole' does not (at any rate in such a case as the present) mean the company as a commercial entity, distinct from the corporators: it means the corporators as a general body. That is to say, the case may be taken of an individual hypothetical member and it may be asked whether what is proposed is, in the honest opinion of those who voted in its favour, for that person's benefit.

I think that the matter can, in practice, be more accurately and precisely stated by looking at the converse and by saying that a special resolution of this kind would be liable to be impeached if the effect of it were to discriminate between the majority shareholders and the minority shareholders, so as to give to the former an advantage of which the latter were deprived. When the cases are examined in which the resolution has been successfully attacked, it is on that ground. It is therefore not necessary to require that persons voting for a special resolution should, so to speak, dissociate themselves altogether from their own prospects and consider whether [the proposal is] for the benefit of the company as a going concern. If, as commonly happens, an outside person makes an offer to buy all the shares, prima facie, if the corporators think it a fair offer and vote in favour of the resolution, it is no ground for impeaching the resolution that they are considering their own position as individuals.

Accepting that, as I think he did, Mr Jennings said, in effect, that there are still grounds for impeaching this resolution: first, because it goes further than was necessary to give effect to the particular sale of the shares; and, secondly, because it prejudiced the plaintiff and minority shareholders in that it deprived them of the right which, under the subsisting articles, they would have of buying the shares of the majority if the latter desired to dispose of them.

What Mr Jennings objects to in the resolution is that if a resolution is passed altering the articles merely for the purpose of giving effect to a particular transaction, then it is quite sufficient (and it is usually done) to

15 For the meaning of this phrase, see below, pp 476 ff.

limit it to that transaction. But this resolution provides that anybody who wants at any time to sell his shares can now go direct to an outsider, provided that there is an ordinary resolution of the company approving the proposed transferee. Accordingly, if it is one of the majority who is selling, he will get the necessary resolution. This change in the articles, so to speak, franks the shares for holders of majority interests but makes it more difficult for a minority shareholder, because the majority will probably look with disfavour upon his choice. But, after all, this is merely a relaxation of the very stringent restrictions on transfer in the existing article, and it is to be borne in mind that the directors, as the articles stood, could always refuse to register a transfer. A minority shareholder, therefore, who produced an outsider was always liable to be met by the directors (who presumably act according to the majority view) saying, 'We are sorry, but we will not have this man in.' ...

As to the second point, I felt at one time sympathy for the plaintiff's argument, because, after all, as the articles stood he could have said: 'Before you go selling to the purchaser you have to offer your shares to the existing shareholders, and that will enable me, if I feel so disposed, to buy, in effect, the whole of the shareholding of the Arderne company.' I think that the answer is that when a man comes into a company, he is not entitled to assume that the articles will always remain in a particular form; and that, so long as the proposed alteration does not unfairly discriminate in the way which I have indicated, it is not an objection, provided that the resolution is passed bona fide, that the right to tender for the majority holding of shares would be lost by the lifting of the restriction. I do not think that it can be said that that is such a discrimination as falls within the scope of the principle which I have stated ...

ASQUITH and JENKINS LJJ concurred.

NOTE

See also *Clemens v Clemens Bros Ltd* (**88**), where the issue before the court was similar, although no alteration of the articles was involved; the court, although purporting to apply the same principles, reached the opposite conclusion.

We should bear in mind that all[16] the events complained of in the sorry history of Mr Greenhalgh and his company took place before there was any statutory provision allowing the court to grant relief to a minority shareholder on the ground of 'oppression' (CA 1948, s 210) or 'unfairly prejudicial' conduct (CA 1985, s 459): see below, p 495. It is hard to believe that this jurisdiction would not be exercised in favour of such a shareholder today.

Greenhalgh v Arderne Cinemas Ltd is a very difficult judgment. We can put some of the problems which it raises in the form of questions, but it is not possible to give any confident answer to most of them.

QUESTIONS

(1) The first test posed by Lord Evershed seems to be a subjective one: the shareholders' bona fide opinion is determinative. In the next paragraph, with talk of

16 In the case of the last in the round of the many resolutions, just *one day* before CA 1948, s 210 came into force! Did the controllers of Arderne Cinemas Ltd have 'the foresight of a Hebrew prophet'?

discrimination, the test is apparently an objective one. Are the two passages consistent with each other, or is the court having the best of both worlds?

(2) Is it possible to reconcile 'the corporators as a general body' (distinct from 'the company as a commercial entity') and 'the company as a going concern'? What weight do you think should be given to the phrase 'at any rate in such a case as the present'? Are Lord Evershed's remarks intended to be confined to special resolutions, or to special resolutions altering articles, or to apply generally to all resolutions?

(3) A plaintiff does not go to court unless he has a grievance. Would it not be true to say that in all the *unsuccessful* cases in which an alteration has been challenged, as well as the successful ones, the minority were complaining of discrimination?

(4) Whom should the court identify as 'the individual hypothetical member' in a case such as *Clemens v Clemens Bros Ltd* (**88**), where the only two actual shareholders have fallen out?

61 Rights and Issues Investment Trust Ltd v Stylo Shoes Ltd [1965] Ch 250, [1964] 3 All ER 628 (Chancery Division)

The defendant company passed special resolutions increasing the issued share capital and (in order that the voting strength of the existing 'management shares' should be preserved notwithstanding the new issue) doubling the voting rights of the management shares. The resolutions were carried by a large majority at a meeting of the company and approved by a class meeting of the ordinary shareholders;[17] the holders of management shares did not vote on either occasion. The court ruled that the resolution altering the voting rights was valid.

PENNYCUICK J: I am not persuaded that there has been here any discrimination against or oppression of the holders of the ordinary shares. What has happened is that the members of this company, other than the holders of the management shares, have come to the conclusion that it is for the benefit of this company that the present basis of control through the management shares should continue to subsist notwithstanding that the management shares will henceforward represent a smaller proportion of the issued capital than heretofore. That, it seems to me, is a decision on a matter of business policy to which they could properly come and it does not seem to me a matter in which the court can interfere. So far as I am aware there is no principle under which the members of a company acting in accordance with the Companies Act and the constitution of the particular company and subject to any necessary consent on the part of a class affected, cannot, if they are so minded, alter the relative voting powers attached to various classes of shares. Of course, any resolution for the alteration of voting rights must be passed in good faith for the benefit of the company as a whole, but, where it is so, I know of no ground on which such an alteration would be objectionable and no authority has been cited to that effect. So here this alteration in voting powers has been resolved upon by a great majority of those members of the company who have themselves nothing to gain by it so far as their personal interest is concerned and who, so far as one knows, are actuated only by consideration of what is for the benefit of the company as a whole. I cannot see any ground on which that can be said to be oppressive . . .

17 On 'class meetings', see below, pp 423 ff.

NOTE

It is apparent from such cases as *North-West Transportation Co Ltd v Beatty* (**129**) and *Northern Counties Securities Ltd v Jackson & Steeple Ltd* (**87**) that the holders of the management shares were under no legal obligation to abstain from voting. Their self-denying act was, however, a very effective piece of window-dressing. In contrast with the rule which normally governs the acts of *directors*, there is no common law rule that a vote by an interested shareholder renders a decision invalid, or even raises a presumption of mala fides. The only situation in which it is clearly improper to exercise the voting rights attached to shares (fraud apart) is where the validity of the shares concerned is at stake, when to allow the vote would be to beg the very question in issue: see *Hogg v Cramphorn Ltd* (**140**) and *Bamford v Bamford* (**100**).

It has from time to time been suggested that it would be a desirable change in the law to allow some issues to be resolved by submitting them to the votes of 'independent' shareholders only. But this would be very difficult to enforce (consider, e g relatives, nominees, trustees and friends of 'interested' members), and it would deprive those with most at stake from a meaningful say in their company's affairs.

There are, however, one or two special situations where the holders of 'interested' shares are disfranchised: by statute (CA 1985, ss 164(5), 174(2)),[18] and by the rules of The Stock Exchange in regard to 'Class 4' transactions, i e dealings by a listed company in property or borrowings in which a director or substantial shareholder has an adverse interest: *Admission of Securities to Listing*, section 6, chapter 1, para 7.

In *Smith v Croft (No 2)* (**249**) Knox J held that it was proper for the court, in deciding whether to allow a minority shareholder's action to be brought as an exception to the Rule in *Foss v Harbottle* (below, pp 454ff), to have regard to the views of 'independent' shareholders, i e those who were not involved in the proposed litigation as defendants or as persons closely connected with them. The judgment (and that of the Court of Appeal in *Prudential Assurance Co Ltd v Newman Industries Ltd (No 2)* (**247**) on which it is based) comes very close to suggesting that this issue is to be resolved by summoning a meeting, perhaps under the direction of the court, at which the defendants and those in their camp should be disfranchised. This was something that the Court of Appeal said that it had no power to do in *Mason v Harris* (1879) 11 Ch D 97, but it appears to have become an accepted part of modern judicial thinking.

C. Objects and powers

(1) The Objects Clause and the Doctrine of Ultra Vires

Background—the ultra vires doctrine

The Companies Act 1985, s 2(1)(c), like every Companies Act since that of 1856, requires a company to include in its memorandum a statement of its objects. Table B, we must assume, shows us the sort of thing that the legislators had in mind:

> The company's objects are the carriage of passengers and goods in motor vehicles between such places as the company may from time to time determine and the

---

18 But note that these provisions (which deal with resolutions by a company to repurchase a member's shares), disfranchise only the *shares* that are affected and not the *holder*, who may vote with any other shares which stand in his name. In parts of insolvency law there are similar restrictions on the voting powers of *creditors* who are persons connected with the company: see the Insolvency Rules 1986, rr 1.19(4), 2.28(1A).

doing of all such other things as are incidental or conducive to the attainment of that object.

This would seem a reasonable enough requirement. Those who invest as shareholders in a company are plainly entitled to know what kind of enterprise it is that they are entrusting their money to—an investor in a gold-mining company, it has been said, would not wish to see his savings 'frittered away' in a fish and chip business; and similarly those who give credit to a company may reasonably expect some indication of the scope of the activities of the enterprise with which they are dealing. But the objects clause did not survive long merely as a statement for the information of investors and creditors. It soon became the basis for the development of the 'ultra vires' doctrine, which dominated the thinking in important areas of company law for over a century; and even though the reforms made by CA 1989 have deprived the doctrine of this central role, it has not disappeared altogether.[19]

The ultra vires doctrine was a rule concerned with the *capacity* of the company. It imposed artificial limitations on the acts and things which a company was regarded in law as capable of doing. Of course, as we saw in an earlier chapter, there are some acts which in the nature of things a company, or any other kind of corporation, simply cannot perform (e g marry or commit the crime of rape). But the ultra vires doctrine declared that, in addition to these natural limitations on a company's capacity, it was also to be regarded as incapable of doing anything which was not within the scope of its objects clause, or reasonably incidental thereto. The doctrine, in other words, restricted the powers of the company to matters covered by its stated objects, and any act which was outside those objects was not simply beyond the authority of the directors as a corporate organ, but beyond the capacity of the company itself—in the eyes of the law a nullity, having no effect whatever. It followed that not even the unanimous decision of the shareholders could authorise or ratify such an act, as the House of Lords established in the leading case of *Ashbury Rly Carriage & Iron Co Ltd v Riche* (**62**) in 1875.[20]

Although the doctrine was concerned to confine the activities of a company within its stated *objects*, it necessarily had the effect also of restricting the

19 The doctrine of ultra vires continues to apply to charitable companies (CA 1989, s 111) and to some other bodies such as building societies, and remnants of the doctrine survive in CA 1985, ss 35(3) and 322A: see the discussion below.

20 The doctrine had been applied rather earlier to 'statutory' companies incorporated by special Act of Parliament, where it had an important role to play, for these companies commonly had powers to acquire land compulsorily for the purposes of constructing the railways, canals, etc for which they were formed, and it was vital that the courts could keep the exercise of such powers under strict control. It did not apply to the 'deed of settlement' companies which were the forerunners of the modern company, since such companies, being in essence partnerships, were always free to change their constitution by agreement among the members. The *Ashbury Rly Carriage* case had the double effect of confirming that the doctrine applied to companies incorporated by registration under the Companies Acts, and also that the ultra vires act of a company could not be validated even by a unanimous ratification.

The doctrine of ultra vires has never been applied to companies incorporated by royal charter (except in regard to powers conferred upon them by statute: *Hazell v Hammersmith & Fulham LBC* [1991] 1 All ER 545, [1991] 2 WLR 372, HL). A chartered corporation which ventured into activities not authorised by its charter ran the (largely theoretical) risk that the charter might be forfeited on the initiative of the Crown, but the transactions which it entered into were not invalidated. However, it is possible that the judges, when laying down the ultra vires doctrine, did recall the scandals associated with the 'trafficking' in obsolete charters which went back to the days before the Bubble Act of 1720, and wanted to ensure that similar abuses did not arise with registered and statutory companies.

company's *powers*. The line between objects and powers is a difficult—perhaps an impossible—one to draw. The courts did make the concession that a company should be deemed to have implied powers to do anything reasonably incidental to its declared objects (*A–G v Great Eastern Rly Co* (**63**)) so that, for instance, a trading company could borrow money for the purposes of its trading business, but even then the position was not always clear. Could a company with surplus funds invest them in the shares of another company? Was this something which it had power to do, incidentally to its main business, or did it need to state in its memorandum that investing in shares was one of its objects? The draftsmen of company memoranda, confronted with such uncertainties, chose not to take any risks. They could put the matter beyond doubt by enlarging the objects clause and specifically including the making of investments as one of the objects of the company; and they did. Naturally, objects clauses became longer and longer. The judges saw it as their role to fight a rearguard action against these attempts to undermine the ultra vires doctrine. They protested frequently at the length and prolixity of the drafting—a futile gesture, and a rather unbecoming attitude for them to take, since most of them must, as counsel, have spent much professional time earlier on in their careers in drafting and settling the very terms which they now sought to condemn! But those concerned in the formation of companies have since early times consistently wanted to ensure that the capacity of their companies should be as nearly unfettered as possible. In addition to enumerating the objects at great length,[1] the draftsmen have had recourse to such devices as (i) specifying what are essentially powers as *objects* of the company (*Re Introductions Ltd* (**67**), the *Rolled Steel* case (**70**)), (ii) including clauses designed to ensure that none of the specified objects shall be construed restrictively, e g by being read as ancilliary to other objects (a 'main objects' clause: see *Cotman v Brougham* (**64**)), and (iii) authorising the company (or sometimes more specifically the directors) to determine the limits to which the company's objects may from time to time be extended (a 'subjective objects' clause: see *H A Stephenson & Son Ltd v Gillanders Arbuthnot & Co* (**65**), *Bell Houses Ltd v City Wall Properties Ltd* (**66**)). These drafting devices were received by the courts with unfavourable comment but, on the whole, grudging support, and went a considerable way to mitigate the harshness of the ultra vires rule by minimising the occasions when it could be invoked.

The judges for their part sought with equal persistence to cling to what was left of the doctrine, partly out of a perhaps misplaced sense of rectitude, but more justifiably because it was, after all, the strongest weapon they had to cope with cases of blatant corporate wrongdoing.

Reform of the law

The fact that the ultra vires doctrine came to strike so infrequently, and that when it did it did so with random effect, made it a hazard for the very people it was supposed to protect—the company's own shareholders (see *Bell Houses* (**66**), at first instance) and its unsuspecting creditors (such as those in *Re Jon Beauforte* (**71**))— who might naturally enough assume that a company with a well-drafted constitution would have the power to do anything at all. Accordingly, the case for abolishing it altogether has for decades been an unanswerable one.

1 See, for example, the extract on p 593 below.

The Cohen Committee (Cmd 6659 (1945), para 12) recommended that every company 'should, notwithstanding anything omitted from its memorandum of association, have as regards third parties the same powers as an individual. Existing provisions in memoranda as regards the powers of companies ... should operate solely as a contract between a company and its shareholders as to the powers exercisable by the directors.' This recommendation was not implemented because the government at the time recognised that to abrogate the ultra vires principle without at the same time modifying the rule that all persons dealing with a company were deemed to have constructive notice of its memorandum (below, p 200) would be pointless: the other party to a contract would still be deemed to know that the *directors* had no *authority* to contract with him in a matter not covered by the objects clause; and the constructive notice rule was thought too important to jettison without further consideration. So the 1948 Act left the ultra vires doctrine in place.

The Jenkins Committee (Cmnd 1749 (1962), para 42) recommended a different reform, which would have replaced the constructive notice doctrine with an elaborate set of statutory rules, but rather oddly did not urge the abolition of the ultra vires doctrine itself. Nothing came of this recommendation, either. Meantime, countries all around the Commonwealth were taking steps to discard both doctrines by one technique or another, such as enacting comprehensive lists of statutory objects applicable to all companies, declaring companies to have the full legal capacity of a natural person, allowing 'unlimited objects' clauses, making the objects clause optional, and even (in the case of the Isle of Man) banning the registration of objects clauses altogether.

When the United Kingdom acceded to the Treaty of Rome in 1972, it was necessary to make modifications to the doctrines of ultra vires and constructive notice in order to comply with article 9 of the First EEC Company Law Directive (below). Article 9 was concerned (inter alia) to ensure that a third party dealing with a company should not be disadvantaged by the possibility that the company was acting beyond its capacity. This was effected by s 9(1) of the European Communities Act 1972 (later consolidated as CA 1985, s 35). But the drafting of this provision was defective in a number of respects (for instance, in being expressed to apply only to a transaction 'decided on by the directors', and it operated only in favour of third parties acting in good faith: the company itself could not invoke the section for its own benefit). It was acknowledged that the object of the reform was 'to implement the requirements of the Directive, and no more';[2] and arguably the section did not achieve even that.[3] The result was most unsatisfactory: the harshest effects of the ultra vires doctrine were, no doubt, in part avoided, but the doctrine itself was allowed to survive.

It was not until 1989 that further reform came, following recommendations made by Professor Prentice in his Report, published in 1986. These recommendations also dealt with the doctrine of constructive notice (below, pp 200 ff) and the apparent authority of corporate representatives (below, pp 214 ff). Section 35 of CA 1985 was recast, so as to prevent the validity of any act done by a company from being called into question on the ground of lack of capacity (see below, p 151). But, once again, the ultra vires doctrine has not been abolished: it survives for some internal purposes (see s 35(2),

2 Letter from Sir Geoffrey Howe, then Solicitor-General, to the author dated 2 June 1972.
3 The EC Commission has so ruled: see G Morse (1978) 3 EL Rev 60. See also D Wyatt, 'The First Directive and Company Law' (1978) 94 LQR 182.

(3) (below), and compare s 322A(5)(d)), and it continues to apply to charitable companies (s 35(4)) and to bodies not governed by the Companies Acts, such as industrial and provident societies, building societies and friendly societies.

The abolition of the traditional connection between a company's objects clause and its capacity does not mean that those acting on behalf of the company will now have carte blanche to do what they like in the company's name. A member always had, in the past, a right to go to court to seek an injunction to prevent his company from entering into what would have been an ultra vires transaction, and this right is preserved by statute in the new s 35(2) (subject to a proviso for the benefit of third parties where the company is already committed by a legal obligation to perform the act in question). It is also declared by s 35(3) to be the duty of directors to observe any limitations on their powers flowing from the company's memorandum; and this is reinforced by a double-barrelled provision relating to ratification. First, the act itself is now made capable of ratification, in contrast with the common law rule of non-ratifiability, but a *special* resolution is required. Secondly, any resolution to relieve the directors or any other person from liability arising from a breach of this duty must also take the form of a special resolution, which must be separate from that effecting the ratification.

One further reform effected by CA 1989 was the enactment of a new provision, CA 1985, s 3A, designed to encourage companies having commercial objects to abandon the traditionally voluminous objects clause. This is discussed below, p 155.

The problem for the student of company law is to decide just how much of the massive body of case law which the doctrine generated in its heyday it remains important for him to know. It will, unhappily, still be necessary at times to construe a company's objects clause, particularly in the context of directors' duties, for there are now not only general rules defining such duties but also special rules where the breach of duty involves 'failing to observe any limitations on their powers flowing from the company's memorandum' (s 35(3)). So knowledge of some, at least, of the old cases will be required for this purpose. Of the cases which follow, *Ashbury Rly Carriage and Iron Co Ltd v Riche* (**62**) and *A-G v Great Eastern Rly Co* (**63**) are retained primarily for their historical interest, *Re Jon Beauforte (London) Ltd* (**71**) is cited as an example of the injustice which could be worked by the ultra vires rule, and the remainder because they illustrate the approach of the courts to the construction of objects clauses.

It is worth making two further points. First, although we may regard the ultra vires doctrine as being for most purposes 'yesterday's law', we cannot overlook its all-pervasive influence in the shaping of our company law and its philosophy. We have only to read the judgments in *Guinness v Land Corpn of Ireland Ltd* (**40**), for instance (articles to be construed as subordinate to memorandum), or *Trevor v Whitworth* (below, p 341) (maintenance of capital), to realise that the same reasoning which gave rise to the ultra vires doctrines underpins many other principles which continue to be of central importance to the subject; and no-one is likely to suggest that company law will discard these cognate doctrines simply because it has now outgrown the ultra vires rule. Secondly, even in the latterday period when ultra vires had lost most of its clout, it remained the most potent weapon in the armoury of the courts against the irresponsible dissipation of corporate assets: see, e g *International Sales and Agencies Ltd v Marcus* (**72**) and *Rolled Steel Products (Holdings) Ltd v British Steel Corpn* (**70**). The problem which these cases highlight will not go away with the disappearance of the ultra vires doctrine; and so judges will now have to have recourse to other, less well tried, rules and concepts, and perhaps invent some new ones, to cope with them. This issue is considered further below, pp 376 ff.

Cases illustrating the ultra virus doctrine

A company incorporated under the Companies Acts had power at common law to do only those things which were authorised by the memorandum of association. Anything not so authorised, expressly or implicitly, was ultra vires the company and could not be ratified or made effective even by the unanimous agreement of the members.

62 Ashbury Rly Carriage and Iron Co Ltd v Riche (1875) LR 7 HL 653 (House of Lords)

The company was incorporated under the Act of 1862. Clause 3 of the memorandum provided as follows: 'The objects for which the company is established are to make and sell, or lend on hire, railway-carriages and waggons, and all kinds of railway plant, fittings, machinery, and rolling-stock; to carry on the business of mechanical engineers and general contractors; to purchase and sell, as merchants, timber, coal, metals, or other materials; and to buy and sell any such materials on commission, or as agents.' Clause 4 of the articles was in these terms: 'An extension of the company's business beyond or for other than the objects or purposes expressed or implied in the memorandum of association shall take place only in pursuance of a special resolution.' The company agreed to provide Riche with finance for the construction of a railway in Belgium. It later repudiated the agreement and, when sued for damages, pleaded that it was ultra vires the company to enter into such a contract. In the lower courts the argument turned principally on the question whether the contract, though unauthorised, had been approved by the shareholders under article 4; but in the House of Lords it was ruled that the contract was void and that ratification, even if it had taken place, would have been wholly ineffective.

LORD CAIRNS LC: My Lords, I agree ... that a contract of this kind was not within the words of the memorandum of association. In point of fact it was not a contract in which, as the memorandum of association implies, the limited company were to be the employed, they were the employers. They purchased the concession of a railway—an object not at all within the memorandum of association; and having purchased that, they employed, or they contracted to pay, as persons employing, the plaintiffs in the present action, as the persons who were to construct it. That was reversing entirely the whole hypothesis of the memorandum of association, and was the making of a contract not included within, but foreign to, the words of the memorandum of association.

Those being the results of the documents to which I have referred, I will ask your Lordships now to consider the effect of the Act of Parliament—the Joint Stock Companies Act of 1862—on this state of things ... Your Lordships are well aware that this is the Act which put upon its present permanent footing the regulation of joint stock companies, and more especially of those joint stock companies which were to be authorised to trade with a limit to their liability.

The provisions under which that system of limiting liability was inaugurated, were provisions not merely, perhaps I might say not mainly, for the benefit of the shareholders for the time being in the company, but were enactments intended also to provide for the interests of two other very important bodies; in the first place, those who might become shareholders in succession to the persons who were shareholders for the time being; and secondly, the outside public, and more particularly those who might be creditors of companies of this kind. And I will ask your Lordships to observe, as I refer to some of the clauses, the marked and entire difference there is between the two documents which form the title deeds of companies of this description—I mean the memorandum of association on the one hand, and the articles of association on the other hand. With regard to the memorandum of association, your Lordships will find, as has often already been pointed out, although it appears somewhat to have been overlooked in the present case, that that is, as it were, the charter, and defines the limitation of the powers of a company to be established under the Act. With regard to the articles of association, those articles play a part subsidiary to the memorandum of association. They accept the memorandum of association as the charter of incorporation of the company, and so accepting it, the articles proceed to define the duties, the rights and the powers of the governing body as between themselves and the company at large, and the mode and form in which the business of the company is to be carried on, and the mode and form in which changes in the internal regulations of the company may from time to time be made. With regard, therefore, to the memorandum of association, if you find anything which goes beyond that memorandum, or is not warranted by it, the question will arise whether that which is so done is ultra vires, not only of the directors of the company, but of the company itself. With regard to the articles of association, if you find anything which, still keeping within the memorandum of association, is a violation of the articles of association, or in excess of them, the question will arise whether that is anything more than an act extra vires the directors, but intra vires the company.

The clauses of the statute to which it is necessary to refer are four: in the first place, the sixth clause [CA 1985, s 1(1)]. That provides that 'Any seven or more persons associated for any lawful purpose may, by subscribing their names to a memorandum of association, and otherwise complying with the requisitions of this Act in respect of registration, form an incorporated company, with or without limited liability.' My Lords, this is the first section which speaks of the incorporation of the company; but your Lordships will observe that it does not speak of that incorporation as the creation of a corporation with inherent common law rights, such rights as are by common law possessed by every corporation, and without any other limit than would by common law be assigned to them, but it speaks of the company being incorporated with reference to a memorandum of association; and you are referred thereby to the provisions which subsequently are to be found upon the subject of that memorandum of association.

The next clause which is material is the eighth [CA 1985, s 2(1)]: 'Where a company is formed on the principle of having the liability of its members limited to the amount unpaid on their shares, hereinafter referred to as a company limited by shares, the Memorandum of Association shall contain the following things' (I pass over the first and second, and I come to the third item which is to be specified): 'The objects for which the proposed company is to be established.' That is, therefore, the memorandum which the persons are to sign as a preliminary to the incorporation of the company. They are to state 'the objects for which the proposed company is to be established'; and the existence, the coming into existence, of the company is to be an existence and to be a coming into existence for those objects and for those objects alone.

Then, my Lords, the eleventh section [CA 1985, s 14(1)] provides: 'The memorandum of association ... shall, when registered, bind the company and the members thereof to the same extent as if each member had subscribed his name and affixed his seal thereto, and there were in the memorandum contained, on the part of himself, his heirs, executors, and administrators, a covenant to observe all the conditions of such memorandum, subject to the provisions of this Act.' Your Lordships will observe, therefore, that it is to be a covenant in which every member of the company is to covenant that he will observe the conditions of the memorandum, one of which is that the objects for which the company is established are the objects mentioned in the memorandum, and that he not only will observe that, but will observe it subject to the provisions of this Act. Well, but the very next provision of the Act contained in the twelfth section[4] is this: 'Any company limited by shares may so far modify the conditions contained in its memorandum of association, if authorised to do so by its regulations as originally framed, or as altered by special resolution in manner hereinafter mentioned, as to increase its capital by the issue of new shares of such amount as it thinks expedient, or to consolidate and divide its capital into shares of larger amount than its existing shares, or to convert its paid-up shares into stock, but, save as aforesaid, and save as is hereinafter provided in the case of a change of name, no alteration shall be made by any company in the conditions contained in its memorandum of association.' The covenant, therefore, is not merely that every member will observe the conditions upon which the company is established, but that no change shall be made in those conditions; and if there is a covenant that no change shall be made in the objects for which the company is established, I apprehend that that includes within it the engagement that no object shall be pursued by the company, or attempted to be attained by the company in practice, except an object which is mentioned in the memorandum of association.

Now, my Lords, if that is so—if that is the condition upon which the corporation is established—if that is the purpose for which the corporation is established—it is a mode of incorporation which contains in it both that which is affirmative and that which is negative. It states affirmatively the ambit and extent of vitality and power which by law are given to the corporation, and it states, if it is necessary so to state, negatively, that nothing shall be done beyond that ambit, and that no attempt shall be made to use the corporate life for any other purpose than that which is so specified.

Now, my Lords, with regard to the articles of association, observe how completely different the character of the legislation is. [His Lordship referred to provisions in the statute corresponding to CA 1985, s 9 and continued:] Of the internal regulations of the company the members of it are absolute

---

4 [Equivalent to CA 1985, ss 121 and 2(7); but the memorandum may now be altered in many other respects.]

masters, and, provided they pursue the course marked out in the Act, that is to say, holding a general meeting and obtaining the consent of the shareholders, they may alter those regulations from time to time; but all must be done in the way of alteration subject to the conditions contained in the memorandum of association. That is to override and overrule any provisions of the articles which may be at variance with it. The memorandum of association is, as it were, the area beyond which the action of the company cannot go; inside that area the shareholders may make such regulations for their own government as they think fit.

My Lords, that reference to the Act will enable me to dispose of a provision in the articles of association in the present case which was hardly dwelt upon in argument, but which I refer to in order that it may not be supposed to have been overlooked. It appears that there has come into the articles of association of this company one which is in these words: 'An extension of the company's business beyond or for other than the objects or purposes expressed or implied in the memorandum of association shall take place only in pursuance of a special resolution.' In point of fact, no resolution for the extension of the business of the company was in this case come to; but even if it had been come to, it would have been entirely inept and inefficacious. There was, in this fourth article, an attempt to do the very thing which, by the Act of Parliament, was prohibited to be done—to claim and arrogate to the company a power under the guise of internal regulation to go beyond the objects or purposes expressed or implied in the memorandum.

Now, my Lords, bearing in mind the difference which I have just taken the liberty of pointing out to your Lordships between the memorandum and the articles, we arrive at once at all which appears to me to be necessary for the purpose of deciding this case ... I assume the contract in itself to be perfectly legal, to have nothing in it obnoxious to the doctrine involved in the expressions which I have used. The question is not as to the legality of the contract; the question is as to the competency and power of the company to make the contract. Now, I am clearly of the opinion that this contract was entirely, as I have said, beyond the objects in the memorandum of association. If so, it was thereby placed beyond the powers of the company to make the contract. If so, my Lords, it is not a question whether the contract ever was ratified or was not ratified. If it was a contract void at its beginning, it was void because the company could not make the contract. If every shareholder of the company had been in the room, and every shareholder of the company had said, 'That is a contract which we desire to make, which we authorise the directors to make, to which we sanction the placing the seal of the company', the case would not have stood in any different position from that in which it stands now. The shareholders would thereby, by unanimous consent, have been attempting to do the very thing which, by the Act of Parliament, they were prohibited from doing ...

LORDS CHELMSFORD, HATHERLEY, O'HAGAN and SELBORNE delivered concurring opinions.

In addition to the powers specifically conferred by the memorandum, a company had power, even at common law, to do whatever could fairly be regarded as incidental to its express objects.

63 A-G v Great Eastern Rly Co (1880) 5 App Cas 473 (House of Lords)

The company was incorporated by statute to acquire the undertakings of two existing railway companies and to construct and run certain other railways. The question before the court was whether it was within its powers, as defined by the incorporating statute,[5] to hire out locomotives and rolling stock to another railway company operating in the same area.

LORD SELBORNE LC: I assume that your Lordships will not now recede from anything that was determined in the *Ashbury Rly Carriage and Iron Co v Riche* (**62**). It appears to me to be important that the doctrine of ultra vires, as it was explained in that case, should be maintained. But I agree with Lord Justice James that this doctrine ought to be reasonably, and not unreasonably, understood and applied, and that whatever may fairly be regarded as incidental to, or consequential upon, those things which the legislature has authorised, ought not (unless expressly prohibited) to be held, by judicial construction, to be ultra vires...

[His Lordship went on to hold that the activities in question were in any case within the company's *express* power.]

LORDS BLACKBURN and WATSON delivered concurring opinions.

A declaration in the memorandum of association that each part of the objects clause is to be construed as a substantive clause and not deemed auxiliary or subsidiary to the object primarily specified is effective to prevent a restrictive construction of the objects clause.[6]

64 Cotman v Brougham [1918] AC 514 (House of Lords)

[The facts appear from the opinion of Lord Finlay.]

LORD FINLAY LC: My Lords, the Essequibo Rubber and Tobacco Estates Limited is a company which was registered on 6 April 1910. The memorandum of association is one of a type which unfortunately has become common. The Companies (Consolidation) Act 1908 requires that the memorandum of association should set out, inter alia, 'the objects of the company' (s 3) [CA 1985, s 2(1)(c)]. The memorandum of this company in clause 3 set out a vast variety of objects, and wound up with the following extraordinary provision: 'The objects set forth in any sub-clause of this clause shall not, except when the context expressly so requires, be in any wise limited or restricted by reference to or inference from the terms of any other sub-clause, or by the name of the company. None of such sub-clauses or the objects therein specified or the powers thereby conferred shall be deemed subsidiary or auxiliary merely to the objects mentioned in the first sub-clause of this

---

 5 The statute may be taken as equivalent to a memorandum of association. The case was important in confirming that the strict doctrine as enunciated in *Ashbury Rly Carriage and Iron Co v Riche* applied to statutory companies.
 6 The ratio decidendi of this case is confined to the ultra vires rule. As appears from the speech of Lord Parker of Waddington, the court must also construe the objects clause of the memorandum when proceedings are brought to have the company wound up under IA 1986, s 122(1)(g) (the 'just and equitable' ground) (see below, p 557). The relevant question then is whether the 'main object' or 'substratum' of the company has failed. For this purpose a clause such as that considered in *Cotman v Brougham* is ineffective, and will not prevent the court from determining the 'main object' of the company as a matter of substance.

clause, but the company shall have full power to exercise all or any of the powers conferred by any part of this clause in any part of the world, and notwithstanding that the business, undertaking, property or acts proposed to be transacted, acquired, dealt with or performed do not fall within the objects of the first sub-clause of this clause.'

Warrington LJ expressed some doubt in his judgment in this case whether a memorandum setting out such a profusion of objects was a compliance with the Act, and it is possible that in some future case the question may arise on application for a mandamus if the registrar should refuse registration, taking the ground that the Act requires that the memorandum should be in such a form that the real objects of the company are made intelligible to the public.

In the present case no such question arises. The registrar accepted the memorandum of association and gave a certificate of incorporation, and that certificate is conclusive. The seventeenth section of the Act [CA 1985, s 13(7)] enacts that 'A certificate of incorporation given by the registrar in respect of any association shall be conclusive evidence that all the requirements of this Act in respect of registration and of matters precedent and incidental thereto have been complied with, and that the association is a company authorised to be registered and duly registered under this Act.' All that the courts can do is to construe the memorandum as it stands.

In the present case the question is whether it was intra vires of the Essequibo Rubber Company to [underwrite an issue of shares in] another company, the Anglo-Cuban Oil Bitumen and Asphalt Company Limited...

The question depends upon the interpretation to be put upon the third clause of the memorandum of association. This clause has thirty heads dealing with a multitude of objects and of powers. It is only necessary to refer to the eighth and twelfth heads of that clause, in addition to the general provision at the end of the clause which I have already quoted ... [His Lordship read sub-clauses (8) and (12), both of which specifically authorised dealings in shares, and continued:] I agree with both courts below in thinking that it is impossible to say that the acquisition of these powers was ultra vires of the Essequibo Company.

It is well worthy of consideration whether, if it should appear that the law as it stands is not sufficient to cope with such abuses as are exemplified in the memorandum now in consideration, the Companies Act should not be amended so as to bring the practice into conformity with what must have been the intention of the framers of the Act. But the only question before us now is the construction of the memorandum as it stands, and in my opinion this appeal must be dismissed with costs.

LORD PARKER OF WADDINGTON: My Lords, Mr Whinney in his able argument suggested that, in considering whether a particular transaction was or was not ultra vires a company, regard ought to be had to the question whether at the date of the transaction the company could have been wound up on the ground that its substratum had failed. Upon consideration I cannot accept this suggestion. The question whether or not a company can be wound up for failure of substratum is a question of equity between a company and its shareholders. The question whether or not a transaction is ultra vires is a question of law between the company and a third party. The truth is that the statement of a company's objects in its memorandum is intended to serve a double purpose. In the first place it gives protection to subscribers, who learn from it the purposes to which their money can be applied. In the second place it gives protection to persons who deal with the company, and who can infer from it the extent of the company's powers. The narrower the objects expressed in the memorandum the less is the subscribers' risk, but the wider such objects the greater is the security of those who transact business with the company. Moreover, experience soon showed that persons who transact business with companies do not like having to depend on inference when the validity of a proposed transaction is in question. Even a power to borrow money could not always be safely inferred, much less such a power as that of underwriting shares in another company. Thus arose the practice of specifying powers as objects, a practice rendered possible by the fact that there is no statutory limit on the number of objects which may be specified. But even thus, a person proposing to deal with a company could not be absolutely safe, for powers specified as objects might be read as ancillary to and exercisable only for the purpose of attaining what might be held to be the company's main or paramount object, and on this construction no one could be quite certain whether the court would not hold any proposed transaction to be ultra vires. At any rate, all the surrounding circumstances would require investigation. Fresh clauses were framed to meet this difficulty, and the result is the modern memorandum of association with its multifarious list of objects and powers specified as objects and its clauses designed to prevent any specified object being read as ancillary to some other object. For the purpose of determining whether a company's substratum be gone, it may be necessary to distinguish between power and object and to determine what is the main or paramount object of the company, but I do not think this is necessary where a transaction is impeached as ultra vires. A person who deals with a company is entitled to assume that a company can do everything which it is expressly authorised to do by its memorandum of association, and need not investigate the equities between the company and its shareholders.

The only other point which I need mention is the company's name. In construing a memorandum of association the name of the company, being part of the memorandum, can, of course, be considered. But where the operative part of the memorandum is clear and unambiguous, I do not think its obvious meaning ought to be cut down or enlarged by reference to the name of the company. It should be remembered that the name is susceptible of alteration, and it would be impossible to hold that such alteration could diminish or enlarge a company's powers. On the other hand, the name may be very material if it be necessary to consider what is the company's main or paramount object in order to see whether its substratum is gone.

I think the appeal should be dismissed with costs.

LORD WRENBURY delivered a concurring opinion.

LORD ATKINSON concurred.

QUESTION

Was it right for Lord Parker to say: 'The narrower the objects expressed in the memorandum the less is the subscribers' risk, but the wider such objects the greater is the security of those who transact business with the company'? (See, e g *Bell Houses Ltd v City Wall Properties Ltd* (**66**), as decided at first instance, and *Re Horsley & Weight Ltd* (**68**).) If the protection of these interests *was* the justification of the ultra vires rule, where did the doctrine go wrong?

The objects of the company may be formulated so as to leave to the company itself, or the directors, the power to define activities into which the company may extend[7] its business.

65 H A Stephenson & Son Ltd v Gillanders Arbuthnot & Co (1931) 45 CLR 476 (High Court of Australia)

The appellant company was established to carry on the trade of a produce merchant in Western Australia. It entered into speculative contracts with the respondents in Calcutta for the purchase of jute. The memorandum contained no express power to deal in jute, but clause (j) read: 'To carry on any other business whether manufacturing or otherwise as the company may deem expedient.' The question was whether the jute purchases were intra vires the company by virtue of this provision. The court held that they were.

DIXON J: When the company was formed it was provided with a memorandum of association consisting of a jumble of objects assembled from former precedents with a seeming disregard of symmetry, coherence and, at times, even orthography and correct transcription. With the purpose of carrying on the business of produce, grain and provision merchants in all branches, there is included the function of bacon-curing. Then follow clauses directed to authorise the company to become a flour-miller, a pastoralist, a farmer, a cattle-rearer, a dealer in live or dead stock, particularly in horses, cattle, sheep and pigs. It is then empowered to erect abattoirs, freezing-houses, warehouses and other buildings necessary or expedient for the purposes of the company, to acquire ships and carry on the business of shipowners and lightermen, and to conduct agencies in connection with the foregoing businesses. But none of these include speculation in jute. The final clause in the memorandum contains an ancillary power of a familiar type. Although it is very widely expressed, it yet remains ancillary in its character, and therefore cannot authorise distinct and independent activities. Standing tenth among the twenty-nine 'objects' which the memorandum ascribed to the company is this: 'To carry on any other business whether manufacturing or otherwise as the company may deem expedient.' It is upon this power or object that the validity of the respondent's contracts appears to depend . . .

As it can be affirmed that the company contracted with the respondent in the course of carrying on another business which the company deemed expedient, why should not the clause suffice to answer the contention of ultra vires? Two replies are given. First it is said that the clause cannot mean what its words, read apart from the rest of the memorandum, appear literally to say. Next it is said that if they do, then the clause is nugatory because it states no definite object but is equivalent to saying that the company may do all things so long as it does them for gain. This second contention is founded upon the view that when the Companies Act requires the memorandum to state the objects for which the proposed company is to be established, it refers to defined purposes capable of ascertainment. The dictum of North J

---

7 It is probable that, notwithstanding this decision and that next cited, the *initial* objects of the company must be specified and that a 'subjective' objects clause standing on its own would not be a 'statement' of the objects of the company as required by CA 1985, s 2(1)(c): see *Re Crown Bank* (cited by Dixon J in the present case). But after the issue of a certificate of incorporation the point of non-compliance with the Act would not be open to a party in ordinary litigation: see above, p 9.

in the *Crown Bank* case[8] was cited: 'I take that to mean this—that certain objects must be specified as those in which business is to be done. If the memorandum were to state, as the objects of the company, that it was to carry on any business whatever which the company might think would be profitable to the shareholders, in my opinion that would not be a statement of the objects of the company as required by the Act of Parliament.' . . .

[His Honour mentioned some of the accepted principles for the construction of documents and continued:] But when an attempt is made to apply such principles to the construction of the memorandum of H A Stephenson & Son Ltd, the difficulties are great in assigning a scope to the instrument or in discovering a fitness of matter or thing in the random collection of seemingly unrelated purposes which it contains. In face of clauses which specify flourmilling, farming, dealing in and making machinery, and shipowning, it seems impossible to regard the purpose of carrying on the business of a produce merchant as predominant. Doubtless it is the initial purpose, the immediate purpose which the promoters had in view, and the first purpose which the company proceeded to fulfil. But the other objects, although perhaps when written they were no more than expressions of distant hopes, cannot be treated as subservient. Secondary in point of time and illusory in point of fact they may be. In potency they rank as equal with and independent of the object with which the memorandum begins and of one another. Further they are directed to subjects which defy any construction *ejusdem generis*. Shipbuilding, farming and flour-milling are not pursuits which can be assigned to one genus. They are genera. Yet it is not for a court to resign as hopeless the task of rationalising the clauses of the memorandum, and to content itself with condemning them as grotesque and meaningless analects. It is not unreasonable to find in the instrument an intention so to constitute the company as to enable it, if it could, to go from its primary business onwards by an expansion of its undertaking in any direction where commercial enterprise might conceivably lead a produce merchant. Thus, the produce merchant may become a farmer, the grain merchant a miller, the farmer a dealer in live stock; the dealer in live stock may slaughter and freeze carcassses; grain merchant, miller and carcass butcher may need freight and charter ships. The scope of the memorandum is to give capacity to allow of an imaginary progress through a gamut of activities. In the case of specific powers the company might, of course, have proceeded per saltum or from one to another, or its undertaking might have expanded by the more usual process of gradual extension into trades or businesses with which its existing activites bring a connection, contact or association. If such is the rationale of the memorandum, the widely expressed general power to carry on any other business should be interpreted as an attempt to provide against the possibility of avenues for extension appearing which have not been foreseen and expressly authorised. It cannot be construed as merely ancillary: because another clause exists conferring all incidental powers and, although tautology and redundancy are to be expected in memoranda of association, two such clauses cannot be supposed. The true meaning of the object would appear to

8 (1890) 44 Ch D 634 at 645. [This case shows that as early as a century ago the long-winded objects clause was an established phenomenon. North J said (at 644–5): 'We have here the enumeration of things so large, that when I put it to [counsel] whether he could say that it would not extend to authorise the company to establish and work a line of balloons passing backwards and forwards between the earth and the moon, he admitted that he could not say it would not.']

be to authorise the company to carry on any business found to be connected or associated with any existing business of the company. When it speaks of such business as the company may deem expedient, it fails to supply in terms any criterion of expediency. The rest of the memorandum suggests that it does not simply mean such businesses as the company may choose to carry on, but such businesses as it may consider convenient to carry on because they are connected with or arise out of the course of business adopted by the company. Wide as such a definition is, it does not appear to be considered too indefinite to pass muster as a lawful object, and upon this memorandum no greater restriction of the general words is justified ...

Is not the speculative purchase of jute the kind of business which might reasonably be expected to arise out of its purchases for actual use or for supply to those who needed sacks? It is not an activity ancillary or conducive to that purpose; but is it not another step in the extension of an undertaking to which that purpose might be considered naturally to lead? On the whole I think this question should also be answered Yes. It follows that the respondent's contracts with the company were intra vires and their proof was properly admitted.

The appeal should be dismissed with costs.

STARKE and EVATT JJ delivered concurring judgments.

RICH and MCTIERNAN JJ dissented.

66 Bell Houses Ltd v City Wall Properties Ltd [1966] 2 QB 656, [1966] 2 All ER 674 (Court of Appeal)

Both companies carried on business as property developers. The plaintiff company had agreed to introduce the defendants to a financier who could provide a bridging loan amounting to £1m, in return for which the defendants promised to pay a fee of £20,000. When sued for the fee, the defendants pleaded that a mortgage-broking transaction such as this was ultra vires the plaintiff. It was not covered by the memorandum in express terms, but the company relied on subclause (c) of clause 3, which is quoted in the judgment below. Mocatta J upheld the plea of ultra vires and ruled in favour of the defendants—with the consequence that the company would have gone unrewarded for the services that it had provided. The plaintiff appealed, and the Court of Appeal, reversing Mocatta J, held that clause 3 (c) did give it the necessary power.[9]

SALMON LJ: Sub-clause (c) is of great importance and reads as follows: 'To carry on any other trade or business whatsoever which can, in the opinion of the board of directors, be advantageously carried on by the company in connection with or as ancillary to ... the general business of the company.'

As a matter of pure construction, the meaning of these words seems to me to be obvious. An object of the plaintiff company is to carry on any business which the directors genuinely believe can be carried on advantageously in connection with or as ancillary to the general business of the company. It may be that the directors take the wrong view and in fact the business in question cannot be carried on as the directors believe. But it matters not how mistaken the directors may be. Providing they form their view honestly, the

---

9 *H A Stephenson & Son Ltd v Gillanders Arbuthnot & Co* (**65**) does not appear to have been cited at any stage of this case.

business is within the plaintiff company's objects and powers. This is so plainly the natural and ordinary meaning of the language of sub-clause (c) that I would refuse to construe it differently unless compelled to do so by the clearest authority. And there is no such authority . . .

DANCKWERTS LJ delivered a concurring judgment.

SELLERS LJ concurred.

Some powers—such as the power to borrow—may be construed by the court as incidental powers, even though declared by the memorandum to be objects.

67 Re Introductions Ltd [1970] Ch 199, [1969] 1 All ER 887 (Court of Appeal)

[The facts appear from the judgment.]

HARMAN LJ: The company started its career in 1951 in connection with the Festival of Britain and facilities to be offered to visitors from abroad in connection with that event. It had an issued capital of £400. Subsequently for some years after 1953 it carried on a business connected with deck chairs at a seaside resort. From 1958 to 1960 it carried on no business, but in the latter year there was a transfer of shares and a new board was elected which decided to make use of the company for a venture connected with pigs. It has always been the ambition apparently of the commercial community to stretch the objects clause of a memorandum of association, thus obtaining the advantage of limited liability with as little fetter on the activities of the company as possible. But still you cannot have an object to do every mortal thing you want, because that is to have no object at all. There was one thing that the plaintiff company could not do and that was to breed pigs. The venture of pig breeding is the type of adventure which has always drawn money from the pockets of the British public, who apparently much prefer to regard themselves as owners of an apple or an apple tree or a pig rather than a mere share in a company. Anyhow, this venture, like other similar ventures, has been a disastrous failure, and the company was ordered to be wound up in 1965.

In 1960 the then new directors approached the defendant bank with a view to opening an account. This became in due course of time heavily overdrawn, and the bank, requiring security, was offered two debentures secured on the company's assets. It is common ground that before the security was given the bank was furnished with a copy of the memorandum and articles of association and also became aware, and expressly aware, that the company was carrying on as its sole business the business of pig breeding, which it has now acknowledged was ultra vires the company's powers in its memorandum. The bank has, however, relied on the fact that there is in the objects clause of the memorandum a sub-clause (N) empowering the company in general terms to borrow, in particular by the issue of debentures, and to secure the loan by charge. There is also in this memorandum a form of words which is common enough, and has been for many years; the words at the end of the objects clause are these: 'It is hereby expressly declared that each of the preceeding sub-clauses shall be construed independently of and shall be in no way limited by reference to any other sub-clause and that the objects set out in each sub-clause are independent objects of the company.' Of course, the original idea of that form of words was to avoid the old difficulty, which was that there was a main objects clause and all the others were ancillary to the main objects; and many questions of ultra vires arose out of that.

It was argued, therefore, that the only obligation of the bank was to satisfy itself that there was an express power to borrow money, and that this power was converted into an object by the concluding words of the objects clause which I have read. It was said that, if this was so, not only need the bank inquire no further but also that it was unaffected by the knowledge which it had that the activity on which the money was to be spent was one beyond the company's powers.

The judge rejected this view, and I agree with him. He based his judgment, I think, on the view that a power or an object conferred on a company to borrow cannot mean something in the air: borrowing is not an end in itself and must be for some purpose of the company; and since this borrowing was for an ultra vires purpose, that is an end of the matter.

Mr Walton, I think, agreed that if sub-clause (N) must in truth be construed as a power, such a power must be for a purpose within the company's memorandum. He says that it is 'elevated into an object' (to use his own phrase) by the concluding words of the objects clause in the memorandum, and this object, being an independent object of the company, will protect the lender and that that is its purpose. I answer that by saying that you cannot convert a power into an object merely by saying so. . . .

I agree with the judge that it is a necessarily implied addition to a power to borrow, whether express or implied, that you should add 'for the purposes of the company'. This borrowing was not for a legitimate purpose of the company: the bank knew it, and, therefore, cannot rely on its debentures. I would dismiss the appeal.

RUSSELL LJ ... If the borrowing sub-clause had expressly stated that it did not include borrowing for use in an undertaking ultra vires the company, it would have been plainly unarguable that the bank's security was valid, the bank being fully aware that the borrowing was only for use in the pig breeding business and being at least deemed to be aware that such business was wholly ultra vires the company. But in every borrowing sub-clause, that which I have stated as having been expressly stated is implicit, whether or not the objects clause contains the proviso that is contained here. Putting the matter round the other way, supposing the borrowing clause had purported expressly to include borrowing for use in a business ultra vires the company, no lender could conceivably rely upon such a provision, which would have to be ignored as mere nonsense.

KARMINSKI LJ concurred.

NOTES

(1) In *Rolled Steel Products (Holdings) Ltd v British Steel Corpn* (**70**) Vinelott J at first instance said ([1982] Ch 478 at 497, [1982] 3 All ER 1057 at 1075):

> The question whether a stated 'object' is truly an independent object or purpose is always a question of construction. Even borrowing and lending moneys are activities capable of being pursued as independent objects—for instance, in the case of a bank or finance company; but commonly, where a sub-clause of the memorandum of association of a company states that one of the objects of the

company is 'to lend or advance' or 'to borrow and raise' money it is artificial to construe the sub-clause as anything other than a power conferred for the furtherance of what are in truth its 'substantive objects' or purposes.

(2) The approach of *Re Introductions Ltd* to the construction of objects clauses, including the 'demotion' in appropriate cases of 'objects' to 'incidental powers', has been endorsed in later cases, including *Rolled Steel Products* (**70**). However, the judgments delivered in the Court of Appeal in that case make the distinction between objects and powers for most purposes unimportant, and declare that the decision itself in *Introductions* should be seen as having rested not on ultra vires grounds but on the basis that the directors had abused their powers or exceeded their authority. See the discussion below, pp 149–150, especially Note (4).

(3) One type of corporate 'object' which may call for particular attention in this connection is that of making gifts and paying pensions and gratuities, as the case next cited illustrates.

The making of gratuitous payments may be a substantive object of a company.

68 Re Horsley & Weight Ltd [1982] Ch 442, [1982] 3 All ER 1045 (Court of Appeal)

The company's memorandum included among its objects, by clause 3(o): 'to grant pensions to employees and ex-employees and directors and ex-directors . . .' and further provided (by what is referred to in the judgment as a 'separate objects clause') that all the objects should be read and construed as separate and distinct objects. The respondent Mr Stephen Horsley had served the company as a director and worked for it as an estimator for many years. The other directors were Mr Campbell-Dick and Mr Frank Horsley (who were the only two shareholders of the company at the material time) and their two wives. Just before the respondent was due to retire from active work at the age of 65, Mr Campbell-Dick and Mr Frank Horsley, purporting to act on behalf of the company, took out a retirement pension policy for his benefit at a cost of over £10,000. The company went into liquidation a year later and in these proceedings the liquidator attacked the validity of the pension payment. The Court of Appeal, affirming Oliver J, held that it had not been ultra vires the company to take out the pension.

[For another part of the decision, see below, (**98**)]

BUCKLEY LJ: . . . It has now long been a common practice to set out in memoranda of association a great number and variety of 'objects', so called, some of which (for example, to borrow money, to promote the company's interests by advertising its products or services, or to do acts or things conducive or incidental to the company's objects) are by their very nature incapable of standing as independent objects which can be pursued in isolation as the sole activity of the company. Such 'objects' must, by reason of their very nature, be interpreted merely as powers incidental to the true objects of the company and must be so treated notwithstanding the presence of a separate objects clause: *Introductions Ltd v National Provincial Bank Ltd* (**67**). Where there is no separate objects clause, some of the express 'objects' may upon construction fall to be treated as no more than powers which are ancillary to the dominant or main objects of the company: see, for example, *Re German Date Coffee Co* (**279**).

Ex hypothesi an implied power can only legitimately be used in a way which is ancillary or incidental to the pursuit of an authorised object of the company, for it is the practical need to imply the power in order to enable the company effectively to pursue its authorised objects which justifies the implication of the power. So an exercise of an implied power can only be intra vires the company if it is ancillary or incidental to the pursuit of an authorised object. So also, in the case of express 'objects' which upon construction of the memorandum or by their very nature, are ancillary to the dominant or main objects of the company, an exercise of any such powers can only be intra vires if it is in fact ancillary or incidental to the pursuit of some such dominant or main object.

On the other hand, the doing of an act which is expressed to be, and is capable of being, an independent object of the company cannot be ultra vires, for it is by definition something which the company is formed to do and so must be intra vires. I shall use the term 'substantive object' to describe such an object of a company.

The question, therefore, is whether para (o) of clause 3 of the company's memorandum of association in the present case contains a substantive object or merely an ancillary power. Having regard to the presence of the separate objects clause, the former of these alternatives must be the case unless the subject matter of para (o) is of its nature incapable of constituting a substantive object . . .

Mr Evans-Lombe [counsel for the liquidator] . . . submits that, properly construed, para (o) should be read as conferring merely an ancillary power . . . Mr Evans-Lombe . . . submits that the decision indicates that a capacity to grant pensions to employees or ex-employees, or to directors or ex-directors, is of its nature a power enabling the company to act as a good employer in the course of carrying on its business, and as such is an incidental power which must be treated as though it were expressly subject to a limitation that it can only be exercised in circumstances in which a grant of a pension will benefit the company's business. I do not feel able to accept that contention. Paragraph (o) must be read as a whole. It includes not only pensions and other disbursements which will benefit directors, employees and their dependants, but also making grants for charitable, benevolent or public purposes or objects. The objects of a company do not need to be commercial; they can be charitable or philanthropic; indeed, they can be whatever the original incorporators wish, provided that they are legal. Nor is there any reason why a company should not part with its funds gratuitously or for non-commercial reasons if to do so is within its declared objects.

Mr Evans-Lombe relies upon the finding of Oliver J that there is no evidence that the company did or could derive any benefit or that the question was considered by anyone connected with the transaction. He says that the provision of the pension must accordingly be accepted as having been purely gratuitous, that is to say, a gift which could and did confer no consequent benefit upon the company. Accepting this to have been the case, the transaction nonetheless falls, in my view, precisely within the scope of para (o) and, in my judgment, the purposes referred to in that paragraph are such as to be capable of subsisting as substantive objects of the company and, having regard to the separate objects clause, must be so construed. For these reasons the liquidator fails, in my view, on the ultra vires point . . .

CUMMING-BRUCE and TEMPLEMAN LJJ delivered concurring judgments.

NOTE

The transaction in *Re Horsley & Weight Ltd* might now be open to attack under IA 1986, s 238, as being 'at an undervalue'.

In the Court of Appeal in *Brady v Brady* (**174**), Nourse LJ expressed views which suggest that the ratio of *Re Horsley & Weight Ltd* may have a restricted application. He said:

> In its broadest terms the principle is that a company cannot give away its assets. So stated, it is subject to the qualification that in the realm of theory a memorandum of association may authorise a company to give away all its assets to whomsoever it pleases, including its shareholders. But in the real world of trading companies, charitable or political donations, pensions to widows of ex-employees and the like apart, it is obvious that such a power would never be taken. The principle is only a facet of the wider rule, the corollary of limited liability, that the integrity of a company's assets, except to the extent allowed by its constitution, must be preserved for the benefit of all those who are interested in them, most pertinently its creditors.

The House of Lords reversed the decision of the Court of Appeal in this case without commenting on these remarks.

QUESTION

'Borrowing is not an end in itself and must be for some purpose of the company.' Compare this statement from the judgment of Harman LJ (**67**) with that of Vinelott J in the *Rolled Steel* case (**70**): 'Even borrowing and lending moneys are activities capable of being pursued as independent objects, for instance, in the case of a bank.' Is the distinction a valid one? What does a bank borrow money *for*?

The state of mind of those acting on behalf of a company, e g its directors, is irrelevant to the question of capacity.

69 Charterbridge Corpn Ltd v Lloyds Bank Ltd [1970] Ch 62, [1969] 2 All ER 1185 (Chancery Division)

The plaintiff company asked the court to declare that a legal charge, given by a company referred to as 'Castleford' to the defendant bank as security for the due performance of its obligations under a guarantee, was void, being ultra vires Castleford. The guarantee was itself security for the indebtedness to the bank of another company ('Pomeroy') and other companies in the same group as Castleford, all of which were controlled and run by Mr Pomeroy. It was alleged that the guarantee and charge were ultra vires because at the time when they were given, Mr Pomeroy had not bona fide intended to further the interests of Castleford. The court held that this was irrelevant.

PENNYCUICK J: Mr Pomeroy, in causing Castleford to enter into the guarantee, and, later on, the legal charge, was looking to the interests of the group as a whole. He considered it in the interest of the group as a whole that Castleford should enter into these transactions and that the other companies in the group should enter into comparable transactions. He did not, at the time of the transaction, take into consideration the interest of Castleford separately from that of the group. Mr Watkins and Mr Barber[10] likewise looked to the group as a whole. They believed the transactions to be proper ones. They likewise did not at the time of the transactions take into consideration the interest of Castleford separately from that of the group.

To avoid any possible misunderstanding, these findings do not, of course, imply that either Mr Pomeroy or the bank officers believed that the transactions were prejudicial to Castleford. They simply did not give separate consideration to the interest of Castleford ...

It will be borne in mind that the present action is based exclusively upon the contention that it was ultra vires Castleford, i e outside its corporate powers, to give the guarantee and legal charge. On this footing the guarantee and legal charge were a nullity.

Apart from authority, I should feel little doubt that where a company is carrying out the purposes expressed in its memorandum, and does an act within the scope of a power expressed in its memorandum, that act is an act within the powers of the company. The memorandum of a company sets out its objects and proclaims them to persons dealing with the company and it would be contrary to the whole function of a memorandum that objects unequivocally set out in it should be subject to some implied limitation by reference to the state of mind of the parties concerned.

Where directors misapply the assets of their company, that may give rise to a claim based on breach of duty. Again, a claim may arise against the other party to the transaction, if he has notice that the transaction was effected in breach of duty. Further, in a proper case, the company concerned may be entitled to have the transaction set aside. But all that results from the ordinary law of agency and has not of itself anything to do with the corporate powers of the company.

[His Lordship discussed the earlier cases and continued:] I conclude upon this view of the authorities that they contain nothing which makes it necessary for me to accept the second head advanced by Mr Goulding. In my judgment, the state of mind of the directors of Castleford and of the bank's offficers is irrelevant upon this issue of ultra vires.

That is sufficient to dispose of the action; but in case I am wrong on my view of the law, I must proceed to express a conclusion upon the contention that in creating the guarantee and legal charge, the directors were not acting with a view to the benefit of Castleford. That is a question of fact, and the burden of proof lies on the plaintiff company. As I have already found, the directors of Castleford looked to the benefit of the group as a whole and did not give separate consideration to the benefit of Castleford. Mr Goulding contended that in the absence of separate consideration, they must, ipso facto, be treated as not having acted with a view to the benefit of Castleford. That is, I think, an unduly stringent test and would lead to really absurd results, i e unless the directors of a company addressed their minds specifically to the interest of the company in connection with each particular transaction, that transaction would be ultra vires and void, notwithstanding that the transaction might be beneficial to the company. Mr Bagnall for the bank contended that it is sufficient that the directors of Castleford looked to the benefit of the group as a whole. Equally I reject that contention. Each company in the group is a separate legal entity and the directors of a particular company are not entitled to sacrifice the interest of that company. This

10 [Officers of the defendant bank.]

becomes apparent when one considers the case where the particular company has separate creditors. The proper test, I think, in the absence of actual separate consideration, must be whether an intelligent and honest man in the position of a director of the company concerned, could, in the whole of the existing circumstances, have reasonably believed that the transactions were for the benefit of the company. If that is the proper test, I am satisfied that the answer here is in the affirmative...

NOTE

The *Charterbridge* case may be contrasted with the Australian High Court's decision in *Walker v Wimborne* (1976) 50 ALJR 446. In this case, directors were held liable on a misfeasance summons for moving funds between companies in the same group, and for using funds of some of the companies for the payment of wages and salaries of persons who were not bona fide employees of those companies, but worked elsewhere in the same group. (Exceptionally, it was held to be in order for one of the companies to pay a pension to a retiring director, although his services seem to have been rendered to the group as a whole.) In the course of his judgment, Mason J said:

> The word 'group' is generally applied to a number of companies which are associated by common or interlocking shareholdings, allied to unified control or capacity to control. In such a case the payment of money by company A to company B to enable company B to carry on its business may have derivative benefits for company A as a shareholder in company B if that company is enabled to trade profitably or realise its assets to advantage. Even so, the transaction is one which must be viewed from the standpoint of company A and judged according to the criterion of the interest of that company...
>
> [The] emphasis given by the primary judge to the circumstance that the group derived a benefit from the transaction tended to obscure the fundamental principles that each of the companies was a separate and independent legal entity, and that it was the duty of the directors of Asiatic to consult its interests and its interests alone in deciding whether payments should be made to other companies. In this respect it should be emphasised that the directors of a company in discharging their duty to the company must take account of the interest of its shareholders and its creditors. Any failure by the directors to take into account the interests of creditors will have adverse consequences for the company as well as for them. The creditor of a company, whether it be a member of a 'group' of companies in the accepted sense of that term or not, must look to that company for payment. His interests may be prejudiced by the movement of funds between companies in the event that the companies become insolvent.

However, it should be emphasised that *Walker v Wimborne* was not concerned with corporate capacity, but with directors' duties. In *Charterbridge* itself Pennycuick J made it clear that these were distinct issues, as the case next cited confirms.

An act which comes within the scope of a power conferred expressly or impliedly by the company's constitution is not beyond the company's capacity by reason of the fact that the directors entered into it for some improper purpose.

70 Rolled Steel Products (Holdings) Ltd v British Steel Corpn [1986] Ch 246, [1985] 3 All ER 52 (Court of Appeal)

Clause 3(κ) of the memorandum of RSP empowered it to give guarantees. It guaranteed the obligation to BSC of an associated company, SSS, and gave security over its property in transactions which were in no way for its own advantage but did benefit one of its own directors, Shenkman. All the shareholders of RSP were aware of the irregularity of these transactions, and so also was BSC. Vinelott J at first instance [1982] Ch 478, [1982] 3 All ER 1057 held that the knowledge of BSC that the transactions did not further the objects of RSP made them ultra vires and void, and incapable of validation by the shareholders' consent. The Court of Appeal, though ruling that the transactions were unenforceable on other grounds (**105**), held that they were not ultra vires, and declared that the line of cases on which the judge had relied (including *Re Introductions Ltd* (**67**)) should not be understood as establishing that an improper purpose could affect the question of a company's capacity.

BROWNE-WILKINSON LJ: . . . In my judgment, much of the confusion that has crept into the law flows from the use of the phrase 'ultra vires' in different senses in different contexts. The reconciliation of the authorities can only be achieved if one first defines the sense in which one is using the words 'ultra vires'. Because the literal translation of the words is 'beyond the powers', there are many cases in which the words have been applied to transactions which, although within the capacity of the company, are carried out otherwise than through the correct exercise of the powers of the company by its officers: indeed, that is the sense in which the judge seems to have used the words in this case. For reasons which will appear, in my judgment, the use of the phrase 'ultra vires' should be restricted to those cases where the transaction is beyond the capacity of the company and therefore wholly void.

A company, being an artificial person, has no capacity to do anything outside the objects specified in its memorandum of association. If the transaction is outside the objects, in law it is wholly void. But the objects of a company and the powers conferred on a company to carry out those objects are two different things: see *Cotman v Brougham* (**64**). If the concept that a company cannot do anything which is not authorised by law had been pursued with ruthless logic, the result might have been reached that a company could not (i e, had no capacity) to do anything otherwise than in *due* exercise of its powers. But such ruthless logic has not been pursued and it is clear that a transaction falling within the objects of the company is capable of conferring rights on third parties even though the transaction was an abuse of the powers of the company: see, for example, *Re David Payne & Co Ltd*.[11] It is therefore established that a company has capacity to carry out a transaction which falls within its objects even though carried out by the wrongful exercise of its powers.

In my judgment, for this purpose the position of a company is analogous to that of a human being who has fiduciary powers. If two trustees convey trust property in breach of trust, the conveyance is not void. As human beings they have the capacity to transfer the legal estate: their capacity to transfer flows from their status as human beings, not from the powers conferred on them as trustees. Even if their powers under the trust instrument did not authorise the conveyance, the legal estate will vest in the transferee. Beneficiaries under the trust would be entitled, if they learnt in time, to restrain the execution of such conveyance in excess of the powers of the trustees. If the beneficiaries only discovered the position after the conveyance, the transferee, if he took with notice, would be personally liable as a con-

11 [1904] 2 Ch 608, CA.

structive trustee and the property conveyed could be recovered: but the conveyance would not be a nullity. So in the case of a limited company, if a transaction falls within the objects of the company (and is therefore within its capacity) it is effective to vest rights in a third party even if the transaction was carried out in excess or abuse of the powers of the company. If the members of the company learn of what is proposed in time, they will be able to restrain such transaction: if they only discover the facts later, their remedy lies against those who have wrongly caused the company to act in excess or abuse of the company's powers. If a third party has received the company's property with notice of the excess or abuse of powers, such third party will be personally liable as a constructive trustee and the company will be able to recover the property: see *Belmont Finance Corpn Ltd v Williams Furniture Ltd (No 2)* (**145**).

However, the analogy between companies and trustees is not complete. As an artificial person, a company can only act by duly authorised agents. Apart from questions of ostensible authority, directors like any other agents can only bind the company by acts done in accordance with the formal requirements of their agency, e g, by resolution of the board at a properly constituted meeting. Acts done otherwise than in accordance with these formal requirements will not be the acts of the company. However, the principles of ostensible authority apply to the acts of directors acting as agents of the company and the rule in *Turquand's* case (**102**) establishes that a third party dealing in good faith with directors is entitled to assume that the internal steps requisite for the formal validity of the directors' acts have been duly carried through. If, however, the third party has actual or constructive notice that such steps had not been taken, he will not be able to rely on any ostensible authority of the directors and their acts, being in excess of their actual authority, will not be the acts of the company.

The critical distinction is, therefore, between acts done in excess of the capacity of the company on the one hand and acts done in excess or abuse of the powers of the company on the other. If the transaction is beyond the capacity of the company it is in any event a nullity and wholly void: whether or not the third party had notice of the invalidity, property transferred or money paid under such a transaction will be recoverable from the third party. If, on the other hand, the transaction (although in excess or abuse of powers) is within the capacity of the company, the position of the third party depends upon whether or not he had notice that the transaction was in excess or abuse of the powers of the company. As between the shareholders and the directors, for most purposes it makes no practical difference whether the transaction is beyond the capacity of the company or merely in excess or abuse of its power: in either event the shareholders will be able to restrain the carrying out of the transaction or hold liable those who have carried it out. Only if the question of ratification by all the shareholders arises will it be material to consider whether the transaction is beyond the capacity of the company since it is established that, although all the shareholders can ratify a transaction within the company's capacity, they cannot ratify a transaction falling outside its objects.

In this judgment I therefore use the words 'ultra vires' as covering only those transactions which the company has no capacity to carry out: i e, those things the company cannot do at all as opposed to those things it cannot do properly.

The two badges of a transaction which is ultra vires in that sense are (1) that the transaction is wholly void and (consequentially) (2) that it is irrelevant whether or not the third party had notice. It is therefore in this sense that the transactions in *Re David Payne & Co Ltd* and *Charterbridge Corpn Ltd v Lloyds Bank Ltd* (**69**) were held not to be ultra vires. The distinction between the capacity of the company and abuse of powers was also drawn by Oliver J in *Re Halt Garage* (*1964*) *Ltd* (**123**)...

For these reasons, in considering a claim based on ultra vires, the first step must be to determine what are the objects (as opposed to the powers) of a company. Not all activities mentioned in the objects clause are necessarily objects in the strict sense: some of them may only be capable of existing as, or on their true construction are, ancillary powers: *Cotman v Brougham* and *Re Introductions Ltd.* And this may be the position even if the memorandum of association contains the usual 'separate objects' clause: such a clause is not capable of elevating into an object of the company that which is in essence a power: see *Re Introductions Ltd.*

If, on construction of the objects clause, the transactions fall within the objects (as opposed to the powers), it will not be ultra vires since the company has the capacity to enter into the transaction. If the objects clause contains provisions (whether objects or powers) which show that a transaction of the kind in question is within the capacity of the company, that transaction will not be ultra vires....

The main difficulty in reconciling the authorities is *Re Introductions Ltd.* In my judgment, however, the decision in that case accords with the views I have expressed. The bank seeking to enforce the debenture had actual knowledge that the company was going to use the borrowed moneys for a purpose (pig breeding) which was wholly outside its main objects. The provision relating to borrowing in the memorandum of association was construed as being an ancillary power to borrow for the purposes of the company's business. Accordingly, the lender had actual notice of all the facts necessary to appreciate that the borrowing was in excess of the powers, ie, an abuse of powers. It is to be noted that in the Court of Appeal judgments the transaction is nowhere categorised as ultra vires and void. Indeed, ... the Court of Appeal held that the liability of the bank depended on the fact that it had notice. Buckley J at first instance described the borrowing as being ultra vires: but, in my judgment, this was merely an unguarded use of language since he also regarded the bank's knowledge of the facts as being a crucial element rendering the debenture unenforceable ... In my judgment, the *Introductions* case is not a decision relating to ultra vires in the strict sense: it is an example of a case in which a third party has entered into a transaction with a company with actual notice that the transaction was an abuse of power and accordingly could not enforce the transaction against the company...

Applying those principles to the present case, in my judgment, no question of ultra vires arises.

SLADE and LAWTON LJJ delivered concurring judgments.

NOTES

(1) Whether they acknowledged it or not, the members of the Court of Appeal in this case were making a break with the past and laying down a new rule. Their

reasoning is undoubtedly more logical, but their treatment of earlier, binding, Court of Appeal decisions such as *Re Introductions Ltd* (**67**) is questionable and, indeed, is impossible to reconcile with the ruling of the House of Lords in the well-known case of *Sinclair v Brougham* [1914] AC 398, HL.

(2) The events in *Rolled Steel Products* occurred before the European Communities Act 1972 came into force—i e before there was any provision in the law corresponding to CA 1985, ss 35–35A. But this would not have saved BSC, since the court held that it had not been 'acting in good faith'.

(3) The judgments in *Rolled Steel Products* refer throughout to ratification by the *unanimous* consent of all the shareholders. It is not clear whether the members of the court had in mind precedents such as *Multinational Gas* (**143**) and *Re Horsley & Weight Ltd* (**68**), where the consent had to be unanimous because it was given informally (below, p 166), or whether they were intending to lay down a new rule. On previous authority, a resolution validly passed by majority vote at a general meeting would be effective to ratify: see *North-West Transportation Co Ltd v Beatty* (**129**) and *Bamford v Bamford* (**100**). On this point, see further below, p 155.

(4) The distinction made in cases such as *Re Introductions Ltd* (**67**) between a substantive object and a 'mere' power loses a lot of point in the light of the decision in *Rolled Steel*, but it will remain of some relevance to the question whether the directors have exceeded or abused their corporate powers (see below, p 156). A ruling by the court that a particular act is within the objects of the company, rather than its powers (as in *Re Horsley & Weight Ltd* (**68**)) may strengthen the directors' case but will not, it is submitted, be conclusive of the issue.

(5) None of the judgments in the *Rolled Steel Products* case makes any mention of the decision of Roxburgh J in *Re Jon Beauforte (London) Ltd*, a case notorious for the way in which the 'constructive notice' doctrine (below, p 200) was applied to produce an inequitable result. Although the case is now no longer authoritative in view of CA 1985, s 35, it is worth citing as an example of the operation of the ultra vires rule at its worst.

71 Re Jon Beauforte (London) Ltd [1953] Ch 131, [1953] 1 All ER 634 (Chancery Division)

The company's memorandum authorised it to carry on the business of costumiers and gown-makers. It decided to undertake the business of veneered panel makers, which was admittedly [12] ultra vires, and for this purpose erected a factory at Bristol. The case concerned (inter alia) a proof of debt lodged in the liquidation of the company for the supply of coke to the factory. The coke had been ordered by the company on paper headed 'Veneered Panel Manufacturers'.

[Counsel for the suppliers of coke argued: These claimants were never aware of the purpose for which the coke would be used.

ROXBURGH J: They received letters from the company so headed as to make the purpose of the factory quite clear.

Counsel: There is nothing in the memorandum forbidding the company to buy coke; it might well be used for legitimate purposes. Under the Companies

---

12 The memorandum contained a 'subjective' objects clause in terms indistinguishable from that on which the plaintiff's successful argument was based in *Bell Houses Ltd v City Wall Properties Ltd* (**66**). It is ironical that *Jon Beauforte*, which has drawn nothing but unfavourable comment as an example of the working of the ultra vires doctrine, might have been decided the other way in the light of *Bell Houses*, and, indeed, could have been so decided at the time if the authority of *H A Stephenson & Son Ltd v Gillanders Arbuthnot & Co* (**65**) had been accepted.

Act 1948 a number of duties are imposed on a company which entail office work, so that an office must be maintained which requires heat. There is nothing to show that the coke was used for ultra vires purposes.]

It was held that the proof should be rejected.

ROXBURGH J: [The] argument is that the company needed fuel for its legitimate business, and that the fuel merchant cannot be prejudiced by its misapplication. I need not consider what the position might have been if the fuel merchant had not had clear notice that the business, which the company was carrying on and for which the fuel was required, was that of veneered panel manufacturers. The correspondence shows that they had notice of that, and as they had constructive notice of the contents of the memorandum of association, they had notice that the transaction was ultra vires the company...

Reform of the law: the First EEC Directive

First EEC Council Directive No 68/151/EEC

ARTICLE 9

1 Acts done by the organs of the company shall be binding upon it even if those acts are not within the objects of the company, unless such acts exceed the powers that the law confers or allows to be conferred on those organs.

However, Member States may provide that the company shall not be bound where such acts are outside the objects of the company, if it proves that the third party knew that the act was outside those objects or could not in view of the circumstances have been unaware of it; disclosure of the statutes[13] shall not of itself be sufficient proof thereof.

2 The limits on the powers of the organs of the company, arising under the statutes or from a decision of the competent organs, may never be relied on as against third parties, even if they have been disclosed.

3 If the national law provides that authority to represent a company may, in derogation from the legal rules governing the subject, be conferred by the statutes on a single person or on several persons acting jointly, that law may provide that such a provision in the statutes may be relied on as against third parties on condition that it relates to the general power of representation; the question whether such a provision in the statutes can be relied on as against third parties shall be governed by Article 3.[14]

European Communities Act 1972[15]

9 *Companies Act 1985*

(1) In favour of a person dealing with a company in good faith, any transaction decided on by the directors shall be deemed to be one which it is within

13 [I e, the memorandum and articles.]
14 [Article 3 refers to the registration of documents in a central register to be maintained by each member state, and the publication of particulars thereof in the national Gazette. This is provided for in the case of the United Kingdom by CA 1985, s 42 (below, p 232).]
15 [This subsection was later re-enacted as CA 1985, s 35—a provision now replaced by the new ss 35–35B.]

the capacity of the company to enter into, and the power of the directors to bind the company shall be deemed to be free of any limitation under the memorandum or articles of association; and a party to a transaction so decided on shall not be bound to enquire as to the capacity of the company to enter into it or as to any such limitation on the powers of the directors, and shall be presumed to have acted in good faith unless the contrary is proved.

Companies Act 1985 (as amended by CA 1989, s 108, following the Prentice Report)

35 *A company's capacity not limited by its memorandum*

(1) The validity of an act done by a company shall not be called into question on the ground of lack of capacity by reason of anything in the company's memorandum.

(2) A member of a company may bring proceedings to restrain the doing of an act which but for subsection (1) would be beyond the company's capacity; but no such proceedings shall lie in respect of an act to be done in fulfilment of a legal obligation arising from a previous act of the company.

(3) It remains the duty of the directors to observe any limitations on their powers flowing from the company's memorandum; and action by the directors which but for subsection (1) would be beyond the company's capacity may only be ratified by the company by special resolution.

A resolution ratifying such action shall not affect any liability incurred by the directors or any other person; relief from any such liability must be agreed to separately by special resolution.

Section 9(1) of the European Communities Act 1972 (and, by inference, CA 1985, s 35) does not protect a person who receives property belonging to a company in circumstances which make him accountable for it as a constructive trustee.

72 International Sales and Agencies Ltd v Marcus [1982] 3 All ER 551, [1982] 2 CMLR 46 (Queen's Bench Division)

The late Mr Aziz Fancy had in his lifetime borrowed £30,000 from the defendants, a moneylending company controlled by Marcus, and had died insolvent without repaying the money. Fancy had been the principal shareholder in the two plaintiff companies. His close friend, Munsey, was also a shareholder and a director, and after Fancy's death he ran the two businesses single-handed. Munsey drew cheques on the accounts of the two plaintiff companies to repay the £30,000 owed by Fancy. In proceedings brought by the plaintiffs to recover the payments, Lawson J held that they had been made ultra vires and in breach by Munsey of his fiduciary duties as a director; and that, since Marcus knew this, the defendants were liable as constructive trustees to account for the sums they had received.[16] Section 9(1) of the

---

16 The duties of directors are discussed below, pp 247ff, and the liability of third parties as constructive trustees at pp 304 ff.

European Community Act 1972 (CA 1985, s 35) did not protect the defendants because it had no application to liability under a constructive trust.

LAWSON J: The only conclusion it is possible to draw is that Mr Munsey for no consideration handed over the plaintiffs' moneys to the defendants without any obligation...

It is important to consider the consequences of these dealings because this has bearing on the other questions I have to consider. Remembering that at all material times from early November Mr Marcus, as I find, knew that Mr Fancy's estate was insolvent, the effect of the dealings under review was not only to deprive the plaintiff companies of their moneys and the use of their moneys, but the other consequences were to the extent that there was any value in the estate's shareholdings in the plaintiff companies (the shares were in fact charged to secured creditors) this would be diminished and to that extent the assets falling into the estate would be smaller in value. Secondly, the defendants would get priority over all the other creditors of the deceased's estate. Thirdly, the defendants would get their loan repaid in full whereas the other creditors of the estate would receive a dividend, if only a small one.

I am quite satisfied, and I hold, that the issue of the cheques by Mr Munsey with intent that they should be cashed by the defendants and taken in repayment of their loan to the deceased, Aziz Fancy, was a clear breach of Mr Munsey's duty to the plaintiffs as their director. It is, to my mind, unarguable that a director who gives away his company's money without the consent of the shareholders is not in breach of his fiduciary duty as constructive trustee of the money in the banking accounts of the companies over which he has control.

The nature of the dealings should also be approached from the aspect of the vires of the company which may be important. I earlier indicated the nature of each of the plaintiff companies' main businesses. Their respective memoranda of association, in addition to setting out their main objects, contained common-form exhaustive lists of ancillary objects, including, for example, lending money and giving credit, giving guarantees and indemnities, making, drawing and so forth negotiable instruments and doing all such things as may be deemed incidental or conducive to the attainment of the companies' objects. I find it impossible to form a view that the handouts, as I shall now call them, with which I am concerned, could conceivably fall under the umbrella of the objects clause of either of these plaintiffs.

[His Lordship then considered the authorities governing the position of the defendants as third parties, including *Selangor United Rubber Estates Ltd v Cradock (a bankrupt) (No 3)* (**144**) and *Belmont Finance Corpn Ltd v Williams Furniture Ltd (No 2)* (**145**) and continued:] I conclude then that the defendants became constructive trustees of the £30,000 which they received on the ground that they, through [Mr Marcus], had actual notice that this receipt was a consequence of Mr Munsey's breach of trust. In *principle* therefore the defendants are accountable to the plaintiffs for the £30,000 they received. I would add that at the very least Mr Marcus was turning a blind eye to the obvious, but I have been forced to a more unfavourable view, that is to say that he actually knew of Mr Munsey's breach of trust and duty.

I now turn to the question raised by the amended defence, which is whether the defendants' liability to the plaintiffs to account for the moneys they knowingly received in breach of trust is affected by the provisions of s 9(1) of the European Communities Act 1972 [CA 1985, s 35]. This Act was passed to give effect in England to EEC Council Directive 68/151 of 9 March 1968. [His Lordship read the section, and continued:]

It is to be observed that the section (indeed the Act in which it is set) does not in fact reproduce, first, the statement of purposes which precedes the text of the actual articles in the directive; second, the heading of Section II of the directive (this is the section of the directive which contains art 9, which is the ancestor of s 9(1) of the 1972 Act) is: 'Validity of obligations entered into by a company'; third, there is an important qualification in the first paragraph of art 9 of the directive (which broadly corresponds with s 9(1) of the 1972 Act) which appears in the second paragraph of art 9. The introductory words of Directive 68/151 make it clear that what the directive is concerned with is the obligations of companies. For example, one of the recitals provides:

> Whereas the co-ordination of national provisions concerning disclosure, the validity of obligations entered into by, and the nullity of, such companies is of special importance ... [and further on:] whereas the protection of third parties must be ensured by provisions which restrict to the greatest possible extent the grounds, on which obligations entered into in the name of the company are not valid ...

In my judgment, those passages and the heading of Section II of the directive are reflected effectively in the words: 'In favour of a person dealing with a company in good faith, any transaction decided on ...' This is directed at transactions with companies which obviously will result in the companies being under obligations which before the enactment of the 1972 Act they might have been able to avoid by the application of the old ultra vires doctrine. The other passage in the directive which is not reflected in s 9(1) relates to the state of mind of the person dealing with the company. The second paragraph of art 9(1) reads:

> However, Member States may provide that the company shall not be bound where such acts are outside the objects of the company, if it provides that the third party knew that the acts were outside those objects ... [and it goes on:] or could not in view of the circumstances have been unaware of it ...

Whilst art 9(1) reflects 'if it proves that the third party knew the act was outside those objects', it does not directly reflect or reflect in so many words, the alternative, 'or could not in view of the circumstances have been unaware of it'. Which seems to me very close to turning a blind eye. In my judgment I am entitled to look at the Council's directive as an aid to the interpretation of s 9(1) of the 1972 Act. I conclude, first, that s 9(1) relates only to legal obligations of the company under transactions with third parties, whether or not they be within or without its powers; second, that s 9(1) is designed to give relief to innocent third parties entering into transactions with companies against the operation in England of the old ultra vires doctrine; third, that the test of lack of good faith in somebody entering into obligations with a company will be found either in proof of his actual knowledge that the transaction was ultra vires the company or where it can be shown that such a person could not, in view of all the circumstances, have been unaware that he was party to a transaction ultra vires.

It seems to me, so far as the amended defence is concerned, I have to ask a number of questions. First, does s 9(1) of the 1972 Act at all affect the principles of constructive trust in relation to the recipients of companies' moneys knowingly paid in breach of trust, as happened, I find, in this case? ... In my judgment, the answer to this question is No. Constructive trust situations may or may not arise in an ultra vires context. The basic principles governing the two doctrines are, I find, quite different. I am satisfied that s 9(1) of the 1972 Act was designed to deal not with the operation of the doctrine of constructive trust, but only with the effect of the [doctrine] of ultra vires. In my judgment, in the light of the EEC Council's directive, this conclusion is a plain one.

[The remainder of the judgment, which dealt with aspects of s 9(1) that have since been repealed, is omitted.]

(2) OBJECTS: GENERAL COMMERCIAL COMPANIES

The Act of 1989 has added a new s 3A to CA 1985 which can be seen as a well-meaning attempt to encourage the draftsmen of company memoranda to abandon the traditional long-winded objects clause. It provides that where a company's memorandum states that the object of the company is to carry on business as a general commercial company, (a) the object of the company is to carry on any trade or business whatsoever, and (b) the company has power to do all such things as are incidental or conducive to the carrying on of any trade or business by it.

It appears, however, that the draftsmen have not taken the bait. Many have sought to have the best of both worlds, by continuing to use their old lengthy precedents and adding a further clause listing the carrying on of business as a general commercial company as an additional object!

QUESTIONS

(1) In what respects, if any, does s 3A make a change in the law?
(2) You are asked to advise the directors of a company whose memorandum contains the single object specified in s 3A whether they may (a) make a gift to charity, (b) guarantee the overdraft of another company, and (c) pay for an annuity to provide a pension for the retiring managing director. What advice would you give?

(3) CORPORATE POWERS

The decision of the House of Lords in *Ashbury Rly Carriage and Iron Co Ltd v Riche* (**62**) put paid to any suggestion that a company might have all the powers of a natural person, or even be presumed to have such powers except to the extent that they were taken away by the law or the company's memorandum. It is true that in *A–G v Great Eastern Rly Co* (**63**) it was very shortly afterwards conceded that a company should be regarded as having power to do anything reasonably incidental to the objects stated in the memorandum, but the confusion between objects and powers has persisted ever since, and has not been dispelled by the legislative amendments of 1989. The new s 35 only goes so far as to state that the *validity* of a corporate *act* shall not be called into question on the ground of lack of capacity; it does not say (as have many reforming statutes overseas), that a company shall be deemed by law to *have* the full capacity of a natural person. Section 35(3) speaks of limitations on the directors' powers 'flowing from the company's memorandum'; and since it would be wholly out of line with established practice to find any limitations on the directors' authority set out in the memorandum, as distinct from the articles, this phrase can only be taken as referring to limitations on the company's own powers which are set out in or derived from the objects clause itself—which, of course, must necessarily impose equivalent restrictions on the powers of the directors. This is linked in the same subsection with the further provision that any action which but for s 35(1) would be beyond the company's capacity may only be ratified by the company by *special* resolution.

Cases such as *Charterbridge Corpn Ltd v Lloyds Bank Ltd* (**69**), *Re Horsley & Weight Ltd* (**68**) and the *Rolled Steel* case (**70**), which discuss the question of corporate powers, will still therefore be relevant when there is a question whether an act of the directors which is in excess of their powers (i e authority) requires ratification by an ordinary or a special resolution.

However, if we read carefully the judgments in some cases, and particularly that of Browne-Wilkinson LJ in *Rolled Steel*, we find references to acts which are an *abuse* of the company's powers, and not just in excess of those powers. This may be a different concept; and it is certainly one which can be distinguished from acts which are an abuse of the *directors'* powers under the articles, in the sense that the directors are usurping some function which is constitutionally the responsibility of the shareholders (*Hogg v Cramphorn Ltd* (**140**)) The implications of this distinction, particularly in regard to the question of ratification, have not been fully explored. Where the directors abuse their own powers, as in *Hogg v Cramphorn Ltd*, it is well settled that the shareholders can ratify by ordinary resolution (*Bamford v Bamford* (**100**)). Where they *exceed* the company's powers (i e act beyond its capacity), their act was not capable of ratification at common law, but can now be ratified by special resolution (s 35(3)). But where they *abuse* its powers (of which a good example might be using its money to pay a shareholder's debt, as in *International Sales and Agencies Ltd v Marcus* (**72**)), it would surely be just as much an abuse for the shareholders to purport to ratify the act as for the directors to commit it in the first place. Browne-Wilkinson LJ in *Rolled Steel*, however, thought that such an act might be ratified by the *unanimous* vote of the shareholders. This suggestion (unless he was thinking of a unanimous *informal* resolution) would be a novelty having no counterpart elsewhere in company law and is, it is submitted, misplaced. Such unanimity might mean that the act could not be challenged in a derivative suit (below, p 463) because no shareholder would be able to come to the court 'with clean hands'; but it would surely not bind a liquidator (or possibly a new board, following a change of control). It would surely be better to say that the shareholders, even if they act unanimously, are no more competent to act in abuse of the company's powers than the directors. The ruling of the Australian court in *Kinsela v Russell Kinsela Pty Ltd* (below, p 254) could be cited in support of this view; but the reasoning in this and similar cases is coloured by the fact that the company was on the verge of insolvent liquidation at the material time. We will have to await further cases before we can say how far this notion of abuse of the company's powers is recognised as a separate concept in law and, if so, what the position is regarding ratification when the abuse is perpetrated by the directors.

(4) Gratuitous Payments and Analogous Transactions

Problems of some complexity may arise when a company makes a gift, such as a donation to a charity or a political party, or when it enters into a transaction which, although perhaps not strictly gratuitous, has an altruistic character—such as guaranteeing someone else's bank overdraft. Agreements to pay remuneration to a company's staff or officers may also be open to challenge (or, at least, arouse suspicion) on the ground that the sums may not have been genuinely earned; and, a fortiori, the payment of bonuses and pensions in recognition of past services may also be called into question as being unauthorised or unmerited.

The cases show that the courts have, over the years, viewed such payments with no great enthusiasm, and sometimes with outright hostility. The reasons for this are varied. Creditors, of course, stand to be prejudiced if corporate assets are given away, but they are given only limited protection by the rules of company law and virtually no direct access to the courts to have these rules enforced while the company is a going concern. Naturally enough, therefore, the courts will be astute to intervene indirectly on their behalf (e g in a suit brought by a liquidator) and to seek to upset such transactions, especially in cases where the company has become insolvent not long after the gifts were made.

Perhaps the strongest factor influencing the judges, more especially in the Victorian period, has been the difficulty of reconciling notions of altruism with the capitalist ethic. It seems to have been accepted practically without question until only a decade or two ago that the sole purpose of any company was to make the greatest possible profits for its shareholders. Even today this approach is by no means dead, and most people would assume that this was at least a company's predominant purpose. A corporate gift which diminishes profits violates this philosophy, unless it can be justified on the ground that it is likely to bring a greater benefit in the longer term. Nowadays, opinion has changed, and there is general support for the view that 'responsible' companies ought not to neglect 'wider' interests such as those of their employees, clients and customers, the community, the environment and so on; but even so the 'shareholders' money' attitude can still influence questions such as the propriety of corporate gifts to charity or donations to political parties: why, it is asked, should company directors, or even majority shareholders, decide where this benevolence is to be bestowed, when there are likely to be other shareholders who would choose to do something quite different with their share of the money if it were paid out to them?

Of course, the 'shareholders' money' approach rests on the basic assumption that companies *are* formed with the paramount aim of earning profits, and that the investors contribute their capital on that understanding. This may be apt in the vast majority of instances; but we should not forget that the Companies Acts do allow the corporate form to be used for all sorts of purposes, and there is nothing that says business and profits must come first. It is adopted by many purely charitable organisations, and could clearly be used also by an enterprise which allowed its investors a limited return, after which its excess profits were to go to philanthropy or to some other object. Many co-operatives are registered companies, established to run businesses that make *no* profit. And there is no reason why a 'one-man' company should not have as its objects *both* the carrying on of its founder's business *and* the support of his family—especially after his death—and any other objects of his benevolence.

The decision in *Re Horsley & Weight Ltd* (**68**) confirmed that, even at common law, the making of gratuitous payments can be construed as a corporate object if the company's memorandum is framed in sufficiently explicit terms. But prior to this decision, it was the ultra vires doctrine which was relied on by the judges to strike down many such transactions. Unhappily, in their zeal to keep corporate generosity within what they saw as proper bounds, they allowed a degree of confusion to creep into their reasoning, failing (for instance) to distinguish between corporate capacity and the directors' authority, in some cases, and between a company's express powers and its implied powers in others. It was not until the Court of Appeal re-stated the law in the *Rolled Steel* case (**70**) that some logic was restored to the subject; but the result of this was that the occasions on which ultra vires could be invoked to upset these gratuitous transactions were likely thereafter to be very few. With the abolition of the ultra vires rule, it cannot now be invoked at all. The courts will have to have recourse instead to the rules on directors' authority and abuse of their powers, to the 'maintenance of capital' rules (below, pp 341 ff), the statutory 'wrongful trading' provision, and perhaps to other, newer concepts, in order to counter the misapplication of corporate assets by transactions of this kind. We shall return to this topic in a later chapter.[17]

Meantime, a brief summary of some of the older cases may be worth noting, even if they are now mainly only of historical interest.

Hampson v Price's Patent Candle Co (1876) 45 LJ Ch 437. A trading company with no express power to pay gratuities was held to be acting within its implied powers in paying a bonus of one week's wages to its workmen.

Hutton v West Cork Rly Co (1883) 23 Ch D 654, CA.[18] A similar case, but this time it was held that such a power could not be implied after the company had ceased to be a going concern. Powers could be implied only as incidental to the company's business, and not when it had no business. Some passages from the celebrated judgment of Bowen LJ are still of interest. He said:

> The money which is going to be spent is not the money of the majority. That is clear. It is the money of the company, and the majority want to spend it. What would be the natural limit of their power to do so? They can only spend money which is not theirs but the company's, if they are spending it for the purposes which are reasonably incidental to the carrying on of the business of the company. That is the general doctrine. Bona fides cannot be the sole test, otherwise you might have a lunatic conducting the affairs of the company, and paying away its money with both hands in a manner perfectly bona fide yet perfectly irrational. The test must be what is reasonably incidental to, and within the reasonable scope of carrying on the business of the company...
>
> Most businesses require liberal dealings ... Take this sort of instance. A railway company, or the directors of the company, might send down all the porters at a railway station to have tea in the country at the

---

17 See below, p 376.
18 *Hutton*'s case is also a leading authority for the traditional rule that directors have no right to be paid for their services, unless payment is authorised by the company's articles. See further below, p 236.

expense of the company. Why should they not? It is for the directors to judge, provided it is a matter which is reasonably incidental to the carrying on of the business of the company; and a company which always treated its employees with Draconian severity, and never allowed them a single inch more than the strict letter of the bond, would soon find itself deserted—at all events, unless labour was very much more easy to obtain in the market than it often is. The law does not say that there are to be no cakes and ale, but there are to be no cakes and ale except such as are required for the benefit of the company.

Now that I think is the principle to be found in the case of *Hampson v Price's Patent Candle Co* [above]. The Master of the Rolls there held that the company might lawfully expend a week's wages as gratuities for their servants; because that sort of liberal dealing with servants eases the friction between masters and servants, and is, in the end, a benefit to the company. It is not charity sitting at the board of directors, because as it seems to me charity has no business to sit at boards of directors qua charity. There is, however, a kind charitable dealing which is for the interest of those who practise it, and to that extent and in that garb (I admit not a very philanthropic garb) charity may sit at the board, but for no other purpose . . .

Hutton's case was followed in the present century by Plowman J in *Parke v Daily News Ltd* [1962] Ch 927, [1962] 2 All ER 929, where the company was again moribund, and it was proposed to devote the whole of the purchase-moneys received from the sale of its newspaper businesses to the benefit of employees displaced by the transaction. (This was before the days of statutory redundancy payments.)

[Note: *Hutton*'s and *Parke*'s cases are no longer good law, because of the provisions of CA 1985, s 719, which specifically reverses them.]

Evans v Brunner, Mond & Co Ltd [1921] 1 Ch 359. Eve J held that it was reasonably incidental to the objects of a large chemical company to make substantial donations to universities and other institutions for general scientific research. The learned judge brushed aside arguments that it was the community at large, rather than the company or anyone connected with it, who would be benefited; that the company's trade rivals would derive an equal advantage from the expenditure; and that such indirect gain as the company might secure was out of all proportion to the cost.

Re Lee, Behrens & Co [1932] 2 Ch 46. The directors had voted an annuity to the widow of the company's former managing director. The company had express power to make such provision, but Eve J, in a judgment which was for many years thought to be a ruling on ultra vires, struck the payment down as being not 'reasonably incidental to the carrying on of the company's business' and not 'for the benefit of and to promote the prosperity of the company'. This reasoning, if it was intended to relate to the company's *capacity*, was plainly inappropriate where there was an express power, and it has been rejected in many modern cases. If the decision is defensible at all, it must be on the ground that the directors had acted in breach of duty: see the *Rolled Steel Products* case (**70**).

A similar criticism applies to *Re W & M Roith Ltd* [1967] 1 All ER 427, [1967] 1 WLR 432, where the company had altered its memorandum specifically in order to take power to pay a widow's pension, and had entered into a service agreement with her husband some two months before his death which included a provision for payment of the pension. He had in fact worked for the company and a sister-company for more than twenty years previously. Plowman J followed *Re Lee, Behrens & Co* uncritically. The case must now be regarded as of dubious authority.

Simmonds v Heffer [1983] BCLC 298. The League against Cruel Sports (a company limited by guarantee) was empowered to make donations to other bodies with similar objects. A contribution to the Labour Party's funds to advertise that party's commitment to animal welfare was held to be within the League's implied powers, but a second, unconditional donation to the Party was held ultra vires.

CHAPTER 4
Management

A. Introduction

In chapter 2 we saw how the law recognised that a company, as a 'person' in its own right, was capable of owning property, making contracts, committing wrongs and conducting litigation, and that mental states and many other human qualities could be ascribed to it. We now look at these matters from the practical angle, and at the way in which this artificial legal person functions: how its corporate will is manifested, its decisions taken and its acts performed. Plainly, a company cannot do anything at all except through those human beings who are its members and officers and, vicariously, through its agents and servants.

The articles of association of the company establish the institutional framework through which it is to function. If we take Table A as a typical set of articles, we can see that it contains details about meetings of members, about the appointment of directors and their duties and proceedings, about the executive officers and the secretary and the use of the corporate seal. Many of these provisions are modelled on those of the old deeds of settlement, and antedate the Companies Acts. We might have expected to find much of this detail spelt out in the legislation itself—as is the case in many other jurisdictions. But the approach in our Acts has been largely to assume that a company's constitution will follow the traditional lines, and to make very few rigid rules about these matters. The result is that the corporate draftsman enjoys a degree of flexibility which to outside commentators seems quite surprising. Not many legislators overseas would have allowed such disparate entities as the multinationals, the Trebanog Working Men's Club Ltd (**22**) and Lee's Air Farming Ltd (**14**) to flourish for long under the same statute without seeking to classify them into categories and to formulate different rules about the way in which each of them should be run. We can see indications of this penchant for regimentation in the first batch of EEC Directives which have already been implemented here.

In the nature of things, a company must have members, as the Act recognises (CA 1985, ss 22–24), and it is a legal requirement that it must have directors (s 282)—although they may be called something else, such as 'Governors' (s 741(1)) and a secretary (s 283).

The members (or shareholders) and the directors collectively are the two 'organs' of the company which share between them the most important corporate functions, and (except in the case of the wholly-owned subsidiary and the company with only one director) each normally acts by decisions (resolutions) taken at meetings. Very commonly, the organ constituted by the shareholders is termed 'the company in general meeting' and that of the directors 'the board of directors' or 'the board'. The *meeting* is thus seen as the focus of corporate decision-making. In earlier times, shareholders' meetings were often well attended, with vigorous debate and meaningful voting.

Nowadays, the 'meetings' of very small companies are perfunctory affairs, if held at all; while the attendance at the meetings of large companies is commonly unrepresentative and the 'business' a routine rubber-stamping of the directors' proposals. But the old concepts die hard: both the courts and the legislative reformers strive to preserve some vestiges of the democratic ideal in their attitude to corporate governance, even when it seems to be plain on all sides that the struggle is a hopeless one.

The general meeting and the board of directors are often referred to as 'organs' of the company, a term which signifies their constitutional authority to act *as* the company rather than merely to represent the company as its agent under an authority derived from some superior corporate source (the most that can be said of, for instance, a secretary: see Table A, article 99). The term 'organ' is also used, rather more loosely, in relation to those corporate officers whose mental state is attributed to the company for the purposes of criminal liability (see above, pp 73 ff); indeed, this topic is called by some writers 'the organic theory'.

B. The general meeting

At common law, a corporate body may act by a majority vote given at a meeting duly summoned.

78 A-G v Davy (1741) 2 Atk 212 (Lord Chancellor)

[The facts as given in the report were as follows:]

King Edward VI by charter incorporated twelve persons by name, to elect a chaplain for the church of Kirton, in Lincolnshire, and by another clause three of the twelve were to choose a chaplain to officiate in the church of Sandford, within the parish of Kirton, with the consent and approbation of the major part of the inhabitants of Sandford.

Upon a late vacancy, two of the three chose a chaplain, with the consent of the major part of the inhabitants of Sandford, the third dissented; and the question was, Whether this was a good choice.

LORD HARDWICKE LC: It cannot be disputed that wherever a certain number are incorporated, a major part of them may do any corporate act; so if all are summoned, and part appear, a major part of those that appear may do a corporate act, though nothing be mentioned in the charter of the major part.

This is the common construction of charters, and I am of opinion that the three are a corporation for the purpose they are appointed, and that the major part of them may do any corporate act; this was a corporate act, and the choice too was confirmed, and consequently not necessary that all the three should join; ... it is not necessary that every corporate act should be under the seal of the corporation, nor did this need the corporation seal.

To constitute a meeting, there must prima facie be more than one person present.

79 Sharp v Dawes (1876) 2 QBD 26 (Court of Appeal)

A meeting of a cost-book mining company governed by the Stannaries Acts[1] was summoned for the purpose, inter alia, of making a call. It was attended by only one member, Silversides, and the secretary (who was not a member); and the following proceedings took place, as recounted in a notice sent to all members:

> At a general meeting of the shareholders, held at 2, Gresham Buildings, Basinghall Street, London, EC, on Wednesday, the 30th day of December, 1874, pursuant to notice,
>
>   R H Silversides, Esq, in the chair,
> The notice convening the meeting having been read,
> The minutes of the last meeting were confirmed.
> The financial statement, ending the 28th of November, shewing a balance of £83 11s 5d against the shareholders, having been read, it was
> Resolved—'That the same be received and passed.'
> Captain William Taylor's report having been read, it was
> Resolved—'That the same be received and passed, and, together with the financial statement, be printed and circulated among the shareholders.'
> Resolved—'That a call of 4s 6d per share be now and is hereby made payable to the secretary, and that a discount of 5% be allowed if paid by the 20th of January, 1875.'
> Resolved—'In consequence of the death of Lieut-Col E T Nicolls, and until the appointment of a shareholder to act in his stead, that all cheques be signed by Mr R H Silversides and Mr Granville Sharp jointly.'
>   (Signed) R H Silversides, Chairman.
> Resolved—'That a vote of thanks be given to the chairman.'
>   (Signed) Granville Sharp, Secretary.

The call was in due course made on a shareholder, Dawes, who refused to pay it. It was held that the meeting was a nullity and that therefore the call was invalid.

LORD COLERIDGE CJ: This is an attempt to enforce against the defendant a call purporting to have been made under s 10 of the Stannaries Act 1869. Of course it cannot be enforced unless it was duly made within the Act. Now, the Act says that a call may be made at a meeting of a company with special notice, and we must ascertain what within the meaning of the Act is a meeting, and whether one person alone can constitute such a meeting. It is said that the requirements of the Act are satisfied by a single shareholder going to the place appointed and professing to pass resolutions. The sixth and seventh sections of the Act show conclusively that there must be more than one person present; and the word 'meeting' prima facie means a coming together of more than one person. It is, of course, possible to show that the word 'meeting' has a meaning different from the ordinary meaning, but there is nothing here to show this to be the case. It appears therefore to me that this call was not made at a meeting of the company within the meaning of the Act. The order of the court below must be reversed.

MELLISH LJ: In this case, no doubt, a meeting was duly summoned, but only

---

1 These tin-mining companies were unincorporated, and governed by special statutes.

one shareholder attended. It is clear that, according to the ordinary use of English language, a meeting could no more be constituted by one person than a meeting could have been constituted if no shareholder at all had attended. No business could be done at such a meeting, and the call is invalid.

BRETT and AMPHLETT JJA concurred.

NOTE

There is equally no 'meeting' when the one person present holds proxies from other members: *Re Sanitary Carbon Co* [1877] WN 223 (in this case, *all* the other shareholders); or where all but one of the shareholders have left the room where the meeting is being held: *Re London Flats Ltd* [1969] 2 All ER 744, [1969] 1 WLR 711. But, as Lord Coleridge CJ recognised, the word 'meeting' may in some contexts require to be construed differently. For instance in *East v Bennett Bros Ltd* [1911] 1 Ch 163, where the company's memorandum authorised changes in the capital structure with the sanction of an extraordinary resolution of the holders of the shares of any class affected, passed at a separate meeting of such holders, it was held sufficient that the single holder of all the preference shares should have formally given his assent. A similar approach is needed to resolve the problems of directors' meetings where the company has only one director, or only one who is competent to act.

The Twelfth EEC Company Law Directive on Single-Member Companies, when implemented, contemplates that the sole member may exercise the powers of the general meeting. Decisions so taken must be recorded in minutes or drawn up in writing.

Note also that in certain circumstances the Secretary of State under CA 1985, s 367, and the court under s 371, may direct a meeting to be held in a special manner, and in particular may direct that one person shall be deemed to constitute a meeting. For a recent example where the court made such an order, see *Re Sticky Fingers Restaurant Ltd* [1991] BCC 754.

In Canada, it has been held that two persons cannot hold a 'meeting' by telephone: *Re Associated Color Laboratories Ltd* (1970) 12 DLR (3d) 388. This decision surely misses the point, for the essence of a meeting is not physical presence, but the ability of all the members to participate simultaneously, and instantaneously, in the proceedings—a need which modern communications technology is well-fitted to meet, even where there are several participants.[2] It also fails to meet an obvious commercial need. It is therefore not surprising that the ruling has been reversed, as regards directors' meetings, by the Canada Business Corporations Act, s 109(9).

In *Byng v London Life Association Ltd* (**86**), more shareholders turned up to attend a meeting than could be accommodated in the cinema which had been notified as the venue. Overflow rooms with audio-visual links had been arranged, but these facilities did not work; and, in any case, some people could not get in and had to stay outside in the foyer. The Court of Appeal held, inter alia, that (i) the assembly in the cinema was a 'meeting' which was capable of being adjourned to another place, even though (since many members who wished to attend were excluded) it was not capable of proceeding to business; and (ii) that it was not essential to a meeting that all members should be present in one room or face to face, provided that proper audio-visual links were in place which would enable everyone present to see and hear what was going

---

2 More recently, in the Australian case *Magnacrete Ltd v Douglas-Hill* (1988) 15 ACLR 325 at 333, Perry J has said: 'The law has not yet advanced to the position whereby board meetings of directors may lawfully be held by separate phone calls to directors … It may be that a meeting of directors would be held on a conference telephone but that is not the position here.' In *Re Equiticorp International plc* [1989] 1 WLR 1010, [1989] BCLC 597, Millett J referred to directors being present at a meeting 'either in person or by telephone', but it appears that the meeting had been duly convened and was probably quorate without taking those 'present by telephone' into account.

on and participate in the proceedings. Browne-Wilkinson V-C said [1990] Ch 170 at 183, [1989] 1 All ER 560 at 565:

> The rationale behind the requirement for meeting in the Companies Act 1985 is that the members shall be able to attend in person so as to debate and vote on matters affecting the company. Until recently this could only be achieved by everyone being physically present in the same room face to face. Given modern technological advances, the same result can now be achieved without all the members coming face to face: without being physically in the same room they can be electronically in each other's presence so as to hear and be heard and to see and be seen. The fact that such a meeting could not have been foreseen at the time the first statutory requirements for meetings were laid down, does not require us to hold that such a meeting is not within the meaning of the word 'meeting' in the Act of 1985. ...
>
> I have no doubt therefore that, in cases where the original venue proves inadequate to accommodate all those wishing to attend, valid general meetings of a company can be properly held using overflow rooms provided, first, that all due steps are taken to direct to the overflow rooms those unable to get into the main meeting and, second, that there are adequate audio-visual links to enable those in all the rooms to see and hear what is going on in the other rooms. Were the law otherwise, with the present tendency towards companies with very large numbers of shareholders and corresponding uncertainty as to how many shareholders will attend meetings, the organisation of such meetings might prove to be impossible.

(1) FORMALITY

The notice convening a meeting must be sufficiently full and specific to enable the shareholder receiving it to decide whether or not he ought in his own interest to attend.

80 Tiessen v Henderson [1899] 1 Ch 861 (Chancery Division)

The Violet Consolidated Gold Mining Co Ltd was in difficulties, and meetings were summoned to put before the shareholders alternative schemes for reconstruction. The scheme which was approved was one in which certain of the directors had a strong financial interest, but this fact was not disclosed in the notice convening the meeting: the notice revealed that the 'guarantors' of the new scheme were to have a 'right of call' or share option on 50,000 of the new company's shares, but not that three of the directors were interested as such 'guarantors'. Kekewich J held the resolution invalid.

KEKEWICH J: The question is merely whether each shareholder as and when he received the notice of the meeting, in which I include the circular of the same date, had fair warning of what was to be submitted to the meeting. A shareholder may properly and prudently leave matters in which he takes no personal interest to the decision of the majority. But in that case he is content to be bound by the vote of the majority; because he knows the matters about which the majority are to vote at the meeting. If he does not know that, he has not a fair chance of determining in his own interest whether he ought to attend the meeting, make further inquiries, or leave others to determine the matter for him ...

The shareholder must be regarded as a man of ordinary prudence. Treating it as a commercial matter, he has invested his money in this company; the company is in difficulties, and reconstruction is necessary, and what he has to consider when the notice and circular come to him is whether, on the whole, this is the best thing that can be done. He is either to vote himself in person or by proxy, or he is to leave it to the majority to decide. It seems to me impossible to exclude from the matters which he ought, as a prudent man, to consider, the question whether some of his directors should be remunerated by means of this call on shares ... Why should any shareholder reading this circular think for a moment that two of his directors ... were to have a large proportion of the 50,000 shares on which there was to be a call in favour of the guarantors? He is told that the guarantors were the Henderson company. He is not told that the guarantors were to be some of his own directors, and that they were to derive a personal benefit. Of course I am told, and with perfect honesty no doubt, that these gentlemen only wished to do the best for the company, that they were largely interested in it, and they thought it the best thing to do. True; but they did so for a commission, or for remuneration; and they were not prepared to do the best they could without being paid for it ...; and those facts were not stated in the circular. If a meeting properly convened, and properly instructed as to the purpose for which it is convened, chooses to assent to this, there is no reason why it should not do so; but I think it ought to have this opportunity of considering the point. The man I am protecting is not the dissentient, but the absent shareholder—the man who is absent because, having received and with more or less care looked at this circular, he comes to the conclusion that on the whole he will not oppose the scheme, but leave it to the majority. I cannot tell whether he would have left it to the majority of the meeting to decide if he had known the real facts. He did not know the real facts; and, therefore, I think the resolution is not binding upon him ...

A company is bound in a matter intra vires by the unanimous but informal agreement of its members.

81 Re Express Engineering Works Ltd [1920] 1 Ch 466 (Court of Appeal)

Five persons, who were the only directors and shareholders of the company, resolved at a directors' meeting to purchase certain property from a syndicate in which they were themselves interested. The company's articles disqualified a director from voting as a director in relation to any contract in which he was interested. The liquidator sought to have the transaction set aside; but the court held that the unanimous, though informal, agreement of the five *as members* bound the company.

LORD STERNDALE MR: It was contended on the one hand that the issue of the debentures was invalid for this reason, that all the directors being interested parties were precluded by article 9 from voting, and that though the five persons acting together as corporators undoubtedly could make the contract they could only do so in a properly constituted general meeting. On the other hand it was argued that the contract could not be called invalid if every shareholder knew of and sanctioned it; and further, that whatever the draftsman of the minutes may have styled the meeting, it was in fact a meeting of all the corporators, and they were able, whatever they might call themselves, to waive technicalities and meet together and make any contract they chose. As authority for that the appellant relied upon what was said by Lindley LJ in delivering the judgment of the court in *Re George Newman & Co*:[3]

> It may be true, and probably is true, that a meeting, if held, would have done anything which Mr George Newman desired; but this is pure speculation, and the liquidator, as representing the company in its corporate capacity, is entitled to insist upon and to have the benefit of the fact that even if a general meeting could have sanctioned what was done, such sanction was never obtained. Individual assents given separately may preclude those who give them from complaining of what they have sanctioned; but for the purpose of binding a company in its corporate capacity individual assents given separately are not equivalent to the assent of a meeting.

There were, however, two differences between that case and the present one. First, the transaction there was ultra vires,[4] and, secondly, in that case there never was a meeting of the corporators. In the present case these five persons were all the corporators of the company and they did all meet, and did all agree that these debentures should be issued. Therefore it seems that the case came within the meaning of what was said by Lord Davey in *Salomon v Salomon & Co* (**12**). 'I think it an inevitable inference from the circumstances of the case that every member of the company assented to the purchase, and the company is bound in a matter intra vires by the unanimous agreement of its members.' It is true that a different question was there under discussion, but I am of opinion that this case falls within what Lord Davey said. It was said here that the meeting was a directors' meeting, but it might well be considered a general meeting of the company, for although it was referred to in minutes as a board meeting, yet if the five persons present had said, 'We will now constitute this a general meeting', it would have been within their powers to do so, and it appears to me that that was in fact what they did. The appeal must therefore be dismissed.

WARRINGTON and YOUNGER LJJ delivered concurring judgments.

A meeting is unnecessary if all the members in fact assent to the transaction.

82 Parker & Cooper Ltd v Reading [1926] Ch 975 (Chancery Division)

The company had issued a debenture to Reading as security for a loan; it was sealed and signed by two directors as prescribed by the articles but the seal had not been affixed in their presence as the articles required. It was also alleged that the two directors had not been validly appointed. The transaction had been discussed between all the four shareholders from time to time, and they had all individually assented, but no general meeting had been held. The liquidator disputed the validity of the debenture, but it was held to be enforceable.

ASTBURY J [after stating the facts and holding that everything had been done with the utmost bona fides and solely for the benefit of the company]:   For

---

3 [1895] 1 Ch 674 at 686.
4 [The company had made Newman, a director, a gift of £3,500 to spend on his house.]

the purposes of my judgment, I will assume that the defendants Reading and Botterill were not validly or formally appointed directors. But they believed that they were, and they continued during the remaining history of the company to act as such. I will assume again that the sealing of the debenture was quite irregular. The company had the benefit of the money. The debenture was issued with the assent of every shareholder, and the question is whether the plaintiffs, or rather the liquidator, ought to succeed in obtaining a declaration that the debenture and the resolution authorising it were inoperative and invalid, so that the creditors may get the advantage of the defendant Reading's £1,750 and deprive him of the security on which he made that advance.

Unless I am bound by authority to give this relief I certainly do not propose to do so.

It is, however, suggested that I am so bound, because the shareholders' assent to the irregular transactions was not given at any actual meeting. [His Lordship discussed *Re George Newman & Co* (referred to above, p 167) and *Re Express Engineering Works Ltd* (**81**) and continued:] All three judges [in *Re Express Engineering Works Ltd*] no doubt refer to the fact that there had been a meeting. But I cannot think that they came to their decision because the five shareholders happened to meet together in one room or one place, as distinct from agreeing to the transaction inter se in such manner as they thought fit ...

Now the view I take of both these decisions is that where the transaction is intra vires and honest, and especially if it is for the benefit of the company, it cannot be upset if the assent of all the corporators is given to it. I do not think it matters in the least whether that assent is given at different times or simultaneously ...

[See also *Re Halt Garage (1964) Ltd* (**123**); *Re Horsley & Weight Ltd* (**98**); *Rolled Steel Products (Holdings) Ltd v British Steel Corpn* (**105**); *Multinational Gas and Petrochemical Co v Multinational Gas and Petrochemical Services Ltd* (**143**).]

NOTES

Some glosses may be added to this line of cases.
(1) In *EBM Co Ltd v Dominion Bank* [1937] 3 All ER 555, it was emphasised that the informal consent of the members must be unanimous. In this case, the three principal shareholders held between them over $726,000 of issued capital, and were accustomed to running the company's affairs as if it were a three-man partnership. In fact, the wives of two of them held one share each. It was held fatal to the validity of a security given to the respondent bank that the consent of the three principal shareholders only had been given, notwithstanding that the holdings of the other two were altogether insignificant.
(2) In *Re Duomatic Ltd* [1969] 2 Ch 365, [1969] 1 All ER 161, it was held that a company would normally be bound by the informal agreement of all its *voting* members, but that even so, non-voting members were entitled to receive the disclosure stipulated for by CA 1985, s 312.
(3) The principle has been applied to special and extraordinary resolutions: see *Cane v Jones* (**83**).
(4) At least where the question is one of acquiescence in a corporate irregularity, it may not be necessary to show that a particular shareholder positively assented to the proposal, if he stood by, knowing that he had power to stop it, while the other

members gave it support. This appears from *Re Bailey, Hay & Co Ltd* [1971] 3 All ER 693, [1971] 1 WLR 1357.

(5) There is probably a similar rule about directors' resolutions (see below, p 185), but the question is not so clearly settled. For most companies, the question is resolved by an enabling article in the form of Table A, art 93.

(6) The common law rule is largely duplicated by Table A, art 53. But it is doubtful whether either the rule or such an article would allow an informal unanimous agreement to be treated as equivalent to a formal resolution where the Act appears to require a particular resolution to be passed *at a meeting*: see e g CA 1985, s 121(4), and a fortiori where the Act stipulates that a particular procedure shall be followed (e g a document produced at the meeting) before the resolution is passed: see e g s 319 (approval of director's service contract). In an attempt to overcome this problem, CA 1985, ss 381A–381C and Sch 15A now enable private companies to take decisions by unanimous written resolution for all purposes, except resolutions to remove a director or auditor. Unhappily, however, this legislative reform introduces the complication that notice of such a resolution must be given to the auditors (s 381B)—a requirement which may delay the procedure for as much as seven days. However, it is generally thought that the validity of resolutions passed in accordance with the common law rule or Table A, art 53 is preserved by s 381C(2).

(7) The Twelfth EEC Company Law Directive on Single-Member Companies, when implemented, will require decisions taken by the sole member, when exercising the powers of the general meeting, to be recorded in minutes or drawn up in writing.

QUESTION

If a meeting is held, a resolution can be carried by a majority, so long as a quorum is present. Why should it not be sufficient for (i) a number sufficient to make up a quorum, or (ii) a number representing a majority, to reach agreement informally?

An informal, unanimous shareholders' agreement may be effective as an extraordinary or special resolution.

83 Cane v Jones [1980] 1 WLR 1451, [1981] 1 All ER 533 (Chancery Division)

In 1946, two brothers, Percy and Harold Jones, formed a company to run the family business. Each was a director and the shareholding was divided equally between members of Percy's family and members of Harold's family. The articles gave the chairman a casting vote at both directors' and shareholders' meetings; but Harold's daughter Gillian (the plaintiff, Mrs Cane) claimed that an agreement had been made between all the shareholders in 1967 which provided (inter alia) that the chairman should cease to be entitled to use his casting vote, so that Percy (who was currently chairman) did not have a decisive vote in the company's affairs. The court held that this was so, and that the informal agreement had had the same effect as a special resolution altering the articles. It was immaterial that the statutory obligation to register such resolutions had not been complied with.

MICHAEL WHEELER QC (sitting as a deputy judge of the High Court): ... Now as to the arguments about the effect of the 1967 agreement. Mr Weaver contends that it operated as an alteration of the articles on what was conveniently called in argument 'the *Duomatic* principle' based on *Re Duomatic*

Ltd[5] and the principle is, I think, conveniently summarised in a short passage in the judgment in that case of Buckley J where he says, [1969] 2 Ch 365 at 373:

> ... I proceed upon the basis that where it can be shown that all share-holders who have a right to attend and vote at a general meeting of the company assent to some matter which a general meeting of the company could carry into effect, that assent is as binding as a resolution in general meeting would be.

Applying that principle to the present case, Mr Weaver says that the agreement of all the shareholders embodied in the 1967 agreement had the effect, so far as requisite, of overriding the articles. In other words, it operated to deprive the chairman for the time being of the right to use his casting vote ...

For the first and third defendant, Mr Potts ... answers ... that on its true interpretation in relation to a special or extraordinary resolution the *Duomatic* principle only applies if there has been (i) a resolution, and (ii) a meeting; and that here he says, with some truth, there was neither a resolution nor a meeting of the four shareholders ...

[His Lordship referred to CA 1948, ss 10 and 141 [CA 1985, ss 9 and 378], and to a number of decided cases, and continued:] The first of Mr Potts's two arguments—namely that there must be a 'resolution' and a 'meeting'—does not appear to have been raised in any of the ... reported cases which were concerned with special or extraordinary resolutions. But it is not an argument to which I would readily accede because in my judgment it would create a wholly artificial and unnecessary distinction between those powers which can, and those which cannot, be validly exercised by all the corporators acting together.

For my part I venture to differ from Mr Potts on the first limb of his argument, namely that articles can *only* be altered by special resolution. In my judgment, s 10 of the Act is merely laying down a procedure whereby *some only* of the shareholders can validly alter the articles: and if, as I believe to be the case, it is a basic principle of company law that all the corporators, acting together, can do anything which is intra vires the company, then I see nothing in s 10 to undermine this principle ...

Some light is also, I think, thrown on the problem by s 143(4) of the Act of 1948 [CA 1985, s 380(4)]. Section 143 deals with the forwarding to the Registrar of Companies of copies of every resolution or agreement to which the section applies: and sub-s (4) reads:

> This section shall apply to—(a) special resolutions; (b) extraordinary resolutions; (c) resolutions which have been agreed to by all the members of a company, but which, if not so agreed to, would not have been effective for their purpose unless, as the case may be, they had been passed as special resolutions or as extraordinary resolutions; ...

Paragraph (c) thus appears to recognise that you can have a resolution, at least, which has been agreed to by all the members and is as effective as a special or extraordinary resolution would have been ...

I should add in passing that a copy of the 1967 agreement was never, as far as I am aware, sent to the Registrar of Companies for registration. It may

5 [1969] 2 Ch 365, [1969] 1 All ER 161.

be that there is a gap in the registration requirements of s 143. But be that as it may, the fact that the 1967 agreement was drafted as an agreement and not as a resolution, and that the four signatories did not sign in each other's presence does not in my view prevent that agreement overriding pro tanto— and so far as necessary—the articles of the company; in my judgment Mr Potts's first argument fails and ... the chairman of the company has no casting vote at board or general meetings ...

QUESTIONS

(1) Did the judge rule that the agreement *was* a special resolution, or only that it was as good as one?
(2) Suppose that Thomas, a stranger, bought out all Percy's family's shares and was appointed chairman, without any knowledge of the events of 1967. Would he have a casting vote? Could he rely on CA 1985, s 14 to enforce the 'articles'?

(2) POWERS OF THE GENERAL MEETING

Where the articles limit the powers of the company in general meeting, they cannot be disregarded even by a majority sufficiently large to alter the articles. A formal alteration must be made and then acted upon.

84 Imperial Hydropathic Hotel Co, Blackpool v Hampson (1882) 23 Ch D 1 (Court of Appeal)

The articles provided that the directors were to hold office for a period of three years and to retire by rotation. At a general meeting specially summoned for this and other purposes, resolutions were carried for the removal of two directors (who were not due for retirement under the articles) and the election of others in their place. The company in this action claimed a declaration that the directors had been validly removed. It was held that the articles could not be disregarded in this way.[6]

COTTON LJ: There is nothing in the Act or in the articles which directly enables a general meeting to remove directors; but the way it is put is this— that there is power in these articles, as there is power in the Act, by a meeting duly called to pass a resolution altering the articles; and it is said that here there was a resolution which would have been effectual to alter the articles that these directors whom the articles did not authorise to be removed should be removed. Now in my opinion it is an entire fallacy to say that because there is power to alter the regulations, you can by a resolution which might alter the regulations, do that which is contrary to the regulations as they stand in a particular and individual case. It is in no way altering the regulations. The alteration of the regulations would be by introducing a provision, not that some particular director be discharged from being a director, but that directors be capable of being removed by the vote of a general meeting. It is a very different thing to pass a general rule applicable to every one who comes within it, and to pass a resolution against a particular individual, which would be a *privilegium* and not a law. Now here there was no attempt to pass any resolution at this meeting which would affect any director, except those

6 But see now CA 1985, s 303, which gives a special power to remove a director notwithstanding the terms of the articles.

who are aimed at by the resolution, no alteration of the regulations was to bind the company to those regulations as altered; and assuming, as I do for the present purpose, as the second meeting seems to have been regular according to the notice, that everything was regularly done, what was done cannot be treated in my opinion as an alteration first of the regulations, and then under that altered regulation as a removal of the directors ...

JESSEL MR and BOWEN LJ delivered concurring judgments.

[See also *Boschoek Pty Co Ltd v Fuke* (**99**)]

NOTE

The division of powers between the general meeting and the board of directors is discussed below, pp 186 ff.

(3) ROLE OF THE CHAIRMAN

It is the chairman's function to preserve order and to take care to see that proceedings are properly conducted and that the sense of the meeting is properly ascertained; but he has no power to take into his own hands decisions which the meeting itself is competent to make.

85 National Dwellings Society v Sykes [1894] 3 Ch 159 (Chancery Division)

[The facts appear from the judgment.]

CHITTY J: A question of some importance has been mooted in this case, with regard to the powers of the chairman over a meeting. Unquestionably it is the duty of the chairman, and his function, to preserve order, and to take care that the proceedings are conducted in a proper manner, and that the sense of the meeting is properly ascertained with regard to any question which is properly before the meeting. But, in my opinion, the power which has been contended for is not within the scope of the authority of the chairman—namely, to stop the meeting at his own will and pleasure. The meeting is called for the particular purposes of the company. According to the constitution of the company, a certain officer has to preside. He presides with reference to the business which is there to be transacted. In my opinion, he cannot say, after that business has been opened, 'I will have no more to do with it; I will not let this meeting proceed; I will stop it; I declare the meeting dissolved, and I leave the chair.' In my opinion, that is not within his power. The meeting by itself ... can resolve to go on with the business for which it has been convened, and appoint a chairman to conduct the business which the other chairman, forgetful of his duty or violating his duty, has tried to stop because the proceedings have taken a turn which he himself does not like ...

A chairman may adjourn a meeting on his own initiative where the meeting itself is unable to consider the question, but it is his duty when doing so to take care to ensure that the adjourned meeting will be properly representative of the membership.

86 Byng v London Life Association Ltd [1990] Ch 170, [1989] 1 All ER 560
(Court of Appeal)

An extraordinary general meeting of the company had been summoned
for 12 noon at Cinema 1, The Barbican Centre, London. Because of an
unexpectedly large turn-out of some 800 members, this venue was too small.
At 12.45 pm Dawson, the chairman, acting on his own initiative and without
following the procedure prescribed by article 18 of the company's articles,
announced that he was adjourning the meeting to 2.30 pm at the Café Royal,
about one mile away. Only 600 people could attend this adjourned meeting,
at which certain resolutions were passed. Byng and others sought declarations
that these resolutions were invalid. The Court of Appeal upheld their contentions, ruling that although the chairman had a common law power to
adjourn the meeting in circumstances such as these where the views of the
members could not be ascertained, and despite the fact that he had acted
throughout on advice and in good faith, he had failed in his duty to take into
account all relevant considerations, such as the fact that members who were
unable to attend the afternoon meeting could not arrange proxies in the time
available, with the consequence that the adjourned meeting would not be
representative.

BROWNE-WILKINSON VC: In my judgment, were it not for article 18, Mr
Dawson would at common law have had power to adjourn the meeting at
the cinema since the inadequacy of the space available rendered it impossible
for all those entitled to attend to take part in the debate and to vote. A
motion for adjournment could not be put to the meeting as many who would
be entitled to vote on the motion were excluded. Therefore, at common law
it would have been the chairman's duty to regulate the proceedings so as to
give all persons entitled a reasonable opportunity of debating and voting.
This would have required him either to abandon the meeting or to adjourn
it to a time and a place where the members could have a reasonable opportunity to debate or vote. I see no reason to hold that in all circumstances the
meeting must be abandoned: in my judgment the chairman can, in a suitable
case, merely adjourn such meeting.

What then is the effect of article 18 which expressly confers on the chairman
power to adjourn but only with the consent of a quorate meeting? Mr Potts
submits that the chairman's power to adjourn having been expressly laid
down and expressly circumscribed, there is no room for the chairman to have
any implied power at common law . . .

Like the judge, I reject this submission. In my judgment article 18 regulates
the chairman's powers of adjournment to the extent that its machinery is
effective to cover the contingencies which occur. Therefore if the circumstances are such that it is possible to discover whether or not the meeting
agrees to an adjournment, article 18 lays down a comprehensive code. But if
the circumstances are such that the wishes of the meeting cannot be validly
ascertained, why should article 18 be read as impairing the fundamental
common law duty of the chairman to regulate proceedings so as to enable
those entitled to be present and to vote to be heard and to vote? . . . Say that
there was a disturbance in a meeting which precluded the taking of any vote
on a motion to adjourn. Would this mean that the meeting had to be
abandoned even though a short adjournment would have enabled peace to
be restored and the meeting resumed? Again, say that in the present case the
adjoining Barbican theatre had been available . . . so that a short adjournment

to the theatre would have enabled an effective meeting of all members wishing to attend to be held that morning. Can it really be the law that because a valid resolution for such an adjourment could not be passed in the cinema (many members entitled to vote being excluded from the cinema) no such adjournment could take place?

I do not find that any principle of construction requires me to hold that an express provision regulating adjournment when the views of the meeting can be ascertained necessarily precludes the existence of implied powers when consent of the meeting cannot be obtained . . . Accordingly, I reach the conclusion that in any circumstances where there is a meeting at which the views of the majority cannot be validly ascertained, the chairman has a residual common law power to adjourn 'so as to give all persons entitled a reasonable opportunity of voting' and, I would add, speaking at the meeting . . .

Since such power is only exercisable for the purpose of giving the members a proper opportunity to debate and vote on the resolution, there must in my judgment be very special circumstances to justify a decision to adjourn the meeting to a time and place where, to the knowledge of the chairman, it could not be attended by a number of the members who had taken the trouble to attend the original meeting and could not even lodge a proxy vote. To overlook this factor is to leave out of account a matter of central importance. True it is that those who were available for the afternoon meeting would have been inconvenienced by an adjournment to another date or the convening of a wholly new meeting since they would either have to have attended at the fresh meeting or to have lodged proxies. But in my judgment this could not outweigh the central point that the form of the adjournment was such as undoubtedly to preclude certain members from taking any part in the meeting either by way of debate or by way of vote . . .

Accordingly, although Mr Dawson acted in complete good faith, his decision to adjourn to the Café Royal on the same date was not one which, in my judgment, he could reasonably have reached if he had properly apprehended the restricted nature and purpose of his powers. Therefore in my judgment his decision was invalid . . .

MUSTILL and WOOLF LJJ delivered concurring judgments.

(4) VOTING AND PROXIES

A shareholder's vote is a property right which, prima facie, may be exercised in his own interest and as he thinks fit. A shareholder voting as such is under no fiduciary duty to the company, and this is true also of a director when voting as a shareholder.

87 Northern Counties Securities Ltd v Jackson & Steeple Ltd [1974] 1 WLR 1133, [1974] 2 All ER 625 (Chancery Division)

The defendant company had given an undertaking to the court to use its best endeavours to obtain a stock exchange quotation for its shares, and to allot a certain number of these shares to the plaintiffs. It was necessary, under stock exchange rules, for the issue of the shares to be consented to by the defendant company in general meeting. After the company had for more than a year failed to take any steps to comply with its undertaking, the plaintiffs moved for orders against the company and its directors (a) that they should summon the required meeting; (b) that they should send a circular to members calculated to induce them to vote in favour of the resolution, and warning them that the defeat of the resolution would amount to a contempt of court; and (c) restraining the directors, as shareholders, from voting against the resolution. The court granted orders that the meeting be summoned and that a circular be sent inviting the members to support the resolution, but ruled that neither the members generally nor the directors voting as members would be in contempt of court if they opposed the resolution.

WALTON J: Mr Price [counsel for the plaintiffs] argued that, in effect, there are two separate sets of persons in whom authority to activate the company itself resides. Quoting the well known passages from Viscount Haldane LC in *Lennard's Carrying Co Ltd v Asiatic Petroleum Co Ltd* (**30**) he submitted that the company as such was only a juristic figment of the imagination, lacking both a body to be kicked and a soul to be damned. From this it followed that there must be some one or more human persons who did, as a matter of fact, act on behalf of the company, and whose acts therefore must, for all practical purposes, be the acts of the company itself. The first of such bodies was clearly the body of directors, to whom under most forms of articles—see art [70] of Table A, or article 86 of the defendant company's articles which is in similar form—the management of the business of the company is expressly delegated. Therefore, their acts are the defendant company's acts; and if they do not, in the present instance, cause the defendant company to comply with the undertakings given by it to the court, they are themselves liable for contempt of court. And this, he says, is well recognised: see RSC, Ord 45, r 5(1), whereunder disobedience by a corporation to an injunction may result directly in the issue of a writ of sequestration against any director thereof. It is of course clear that for this purpose there is no distinction between an undertaking and an injunction: see note 45/5/3 in *The Supreme Court Practice* (1973).

This is, indeed, all well established law, with which Mr Instone [counsel for the directors] did not quarrel, and which indeed his first proposition asserted. But, continues Mr Price, this is only half of the story. There are some matters in relation to which the directors are not competent to act on behalf of the company, the relevant authority being 'the company in general meeting', that is to say, a meeting of the members. Thus in respect of all matters within the competence—at any rate those within the exclusive competence—of a meeting of the members, the acts of the members are the acts of the company, in precisely the same way as the acts of the directors are the acts of the company. Ergo, for any shareholder to vote against a resolution to issue the shares here in question to the plaintiffs would be a contempt of court, as it would be a step taken by him knowingly which would prevent the defendant company from fulfilling its undertaking to the court. Mr Price admitted that he could find no authority which directly assisted his argument, but equally confidently asserted that there was no authority which precluded it.

Mr Instone indicted Mr Price's argument as being based upon 'a nominalistic fallacy'. His precise proposition was formulated as follows: 'Whilst directors have special responsibilities as executive agents of the defendant company to ensure that the company does not commit a contempt of court, a shareholder, when the position has been put before the shareholders generally, who chooses to vote against such approval will not himself be in contempt of court.' ...

In my judgment, these submissions of Mr Instone are correct. I think that, in a nutshell, the distinction is this: when a director votes as a director for or against any particular resolution in a directors' meeting, he is voting as a person under a fiduciary duty to the company for the proposition that the company should take a certain course of action. When a shareholder is voting for or against a particular resolution he is voting as a person owing no fiduciary duty to the company and who is exercising his own right of property, to vote as he thinks fit. The fact that the result of the voting at the meeting (or at a subsequent poll) will bind the company cannot affect the position that, in voting, he is voting simply in exercise of his own property rights.

Perhaps another (and simpler) way of putting the matter is that a director is an agent, who casts his vote to decide in what manner his principal shall act through the collective agency of the board of directors; a shareholder who casts his vote in general meeting is not casting it as an agent of the company in any shape or form. His act therefore, in voting as he pleases, cannot in any way be regarded as an act of the company ...

I now come to paragraph 4 of the notice of motion, which seeks an order restraining the individual respondents [ie the directors] and each of them from voting against the resolution. Mr Price says that, as the executive agents of the defendant company, they are bound to recommend to its shareholders that they vote in favour of the resolution to issue the shares, and hence, at the least, they cannot themselves vote against it, for they would thereby be assisting the defendant company to do that which it is their duty to secure does not happen. If, as executive officers of the defendant company, they are bound to procure a certain result if at all possible, how can they, as individuals, seek to frustrate that result?

I regret, however, that I am unable to accede to Mr Price's arguments in this respect ... I think that a director who has fulfilled his duty as a director of a company, by causing it to comply with an undertaking binding upon it is nevertheless free, as an individual shareholder, to enjoy the same unfettered and unrestricted right of voting at general meetings of the members of the company as he would have if he were not also a director ...

[See also *Pender v Lushington* (**240**), *North-West Transportation Co Ltd v Beatty* (**129**), *Burland v Earle* (**242**) and *Peter's American Delicacy Co Ltd v Heath* (**59**).]

NOTE

These cases appear to establish a general rule that a shareholder is free to use the votes attached to his shares as he thinks fit and that he may, if he wishes, use them to advance his own interests. This proposition is certainly true of most business and policy decisions, such as whether to make a purchase or whom to appoint a director, but there are a number of particular limitations on the shareholder's freedom to vote as he chooses, some of which are well recognised and others of more questionable standing. It is not easy to unite these exceptions by any common theme, although it is probably significant that they belong mostly in the area of intra-corporate disputes, where one group of shareholders is complaining that the others have used their more powerful voting strength to gain an unfair advantage.

Some of these special situations are:

(a) Majority shareholders may not use their votes to appropriate to themselves property which belongs to the company or to condone their own fraud (*Cook v Deeks* (**131**); *Menier v Hooper's Telegraph Works* (**243**)).

(b) Where there is a resolution on an issue which affects the rights of members inter se, such as an alteration of the articles or a variation of class rights, the majority must act 'bona fide in the interests of the company (or class) as a whole' (*Allen v Gold Reefs of West Africa Ltd* (**55**); *British America Nickel Corpn Ltd v O'Brien* (**217**)).

(c) Where it is sought to bring an action against persons who have allegedly committed wrongs against the company—or at least those wrongs coming within the elusive 'fraud on the minority' category—they may not use their votes to stop the action being brought (an exception to the rule in *Foss v Harbottle* (**232**): see below, pp 476 ff).

(d) There are certain *statutory* remedies which may be sought by a shareholder when he is disadvantaged as a result of some act of the majority even though is within their legal powers, e g winding up on the 'just and equitable' ground (*Ebrahimi v Westbourne Galleries Ltd* (**284**)) and relief against 'unfairly prejudicial' conduct (see, on an earlier but similar provision, *Scottish Co-op Wholesale Society Ltd v Meyer* (**250**) and, on the present section, below, pp 495 ff).

(e) *Clemens v Clemens Bros Ltd,* which is cited next, and *Re Halt Garage (1964) Ltd* (**123**) appear to impose vaguer limitations on the shareholders' voting powers: the first, that votes must not be used 'oppressively', and the second, that they must be used for 'genuine' purposes. Neither is a very weighty authority, and hardly strong enough to make any significant inroad into the line of cases which lay down the general rule.

It would be wrong to deduce from any of the exceptional situations listed above that a shareholder is ever under a *duty* to vote against his own interests, in the altruistic way disowned by Dixon J in the *Peter's American Delicacy* case (**59**)—although this is a trap which judges occasionally do fall into (**181**). The realistic choice which faces a controlling shareholder in this type of situation may well be between abandoning or modifying the proposal on the one hand and, on the other, taking a calculated risk and pressing ahead in the way he wants, in the knowledge that the burden of proof on any minority shareholder seeking to challenge a decision has traditionally been a difficult one to discharge. However, both the case next cited and the growing body of case-law under CA 1985, s 459 (the 'unfair prejudice' section: see below, pp 495 ff) suggest that the balance may be tipping towards the minority.

A decision carried by the votes of majority shareholders may be set aside if it is 'oppressive' of the minority.

88 Clemens v Clemens Bros Ltd [1976] 2 All ER 268 (Chancery Division)

The plaintiff held 45% and her aunt ('Miss Clemens') 55% of the shares in the defendant company. The company's articles gave existing members a pre-emptive right if another member wished to transfer his shares. The plaintiff therefore had an expectation of total control of the company after her aunt's death, and 'negative control' (i e the power to block a special resolution) in the aunt's lifetime. The aunt and four non-shareholders were the directors. The directors proposed that the company's capital should be increased by issuing 200 ordinary shares to each of these four directors, and 850 ordinary shares to an employees' trust; and resolutions to this effect were passed by the aunt's votes at a general meeting. Although it was claimed that the object of the resolutions was in the company's interests (namely, to give the directors and employees a stake in the company) the court took the view that the real object was to deprive the plaintiff of her degree of control, and the resolutions were set aside.

FOSTER J: For the plaintiff it was submitted that the proposed resolutions were oppressive, since they resulted in her losing her right to veto a special or extraordinary resolution and greatly watered down her existing right to purchase Miss Clemens's shares under article 6. For the defendants it was submitted that if two shareholders both honestly hold differing opinions, the view of the majority must prevail and that shareholders in general meeting are entitled to consider their own interests and vote in any way they honestly believe proper in the interests of the company.

There are many cases which have discussed a director's position. A director must not only act within his powers but must also exercise them bona fide in what he believes to be the interests of the company. The directors have a fiduciary duty, but is there any, or any similar, restraint on shareholders exercising their powers as members at general meetings? [His Lordship read extracts from the judgments in a number of cases, including *Greenhalgh v Arderne Cinemas* (**60**),[7] and continued:]

I think that one thing which emerges from the cases to which I have referred is that in such a case as the present Miss Clemens is not entitled to exercise her majority vote in whatever way she pleases. The difficulty is in finding a principle, and obviously expressions such as 'bona fide for the benefit of the company as a whole', 'fraud on a minority' and 'oppressive' do not assist in formulating a principle.

I have come to the conclusion that it would be unwise to try to produce a principle, since the circumstances of each case are infinitely varied. It would not, I think, assist to say more than that in my judgment Miss Clemens is not entitled as of right to exercise her votes as an ordinary shareholder in any way she pleases. To use the phrase of Lord Wilberforce,[8] that right is 'subject ... to equitable considerations ... which may make it unjust ... to exercise [it] in a particular way'. Are there then any such considerations in this case?

I do not doubt that Miss Clemens is in favour of the resolutions and knows and understands their purport and effect; nor do I doubt that she genuinely would like to see the other directors have shares in the company and to see a trust set up for long service employees. But I cannot escape the conclusion that the resolutions have been framed so as to put into the hands of Miss Clemens and her fellow directors complete control of the company and to deprive the plaintiff of her existing rights as a shareholder with more than 25% of the votes and greatly reduce her rights under article 6. They are specifically and carefully designed to ensure not only that the plaintiff can never get control of the company but to deprive her of what has been called her negative control. Whether I say that these proposals are oppressive to the plaintiff or that no one could honestly believe they are for her benefit matters not. A court of equity will in my judgment regard these considerations as sufficient to prevent the consequences arising from Miss Clemens using her legal right to vote in the way that she has and it would be right for a court of equity to prevent such consequences taking effect.

7 [See the note at the conclusion of this extract.]
8 *Ebrahimi v Westbourne Galleries Ltd* (**284**).

NOTE

This case may have reached a just result on the merits (although even that is doubtful, for there was a long history of non-cooperation by the niece), but it is very difficult to defend the judge's use of the authorities. The citation of *Greenhalgh* (**60**) draws on a line of decisions concerned with special resolutions for the alteration of articles, which had never before been applied to other types of resolution. Further, it is surely misunderstood, for having read the passage from *Greenhalgh's* case in which Evershed MR suggested the test of the 'individual hypothetical shareholder', Foster J commented: 'If that is right, the question in the instant case must be posed thus: did Miss Clemens, when voting for the resolutions, honestly believe that those resolutions, when passed, would be for the benefit of the plaintiff?' With respect, it must be observed that the plaintiff was no more a 'hypothetical' shareholder than Miss Clemens herself; and if the test had been understood in this sense in *Greenhalgh's* case itself, the decision must surely have gone in Greenhalgh's favour. These cases show how unhelpful the 'hypothetical shareholder' test is, especially in regard to small companies.

Again, in quoting Lord Wilberforce, the judge is borrowing from the winding up cases, contrary to the ruling in *Bentley-Stevens v Jones* (below, p 570). In this regard, the case is similar to *Pennell v Venida Investments Ltd* (below, p 287).

QUESTIONS

(1) Did Foster J consider that a shareholder in the position of Miss Clemens was under a duty to (i) the company, or (ii) her fellow-shareholder? What was the nature of this duty?

(2) Did the niece owe the company, or her fellow-shareholder, any corresponding duty?

(3) Can the *Clemens* and *Greenhalgh* (**60**) cases be reconciled?

A contract by a shareholder to vote in a particular way, or as directed by another person, is binding and may be enforced by a mandatory injunction.[9]

89 Puddephatt v Leith [1916] 1 Ch 200 (Chancery Division)

The plaintiff had mortgaged shares in the company to the defendant and transferred them into his name. By a contemporaneous letter, the defendant had undertaken to vote the shares as directed by the plaintiff. The court ordered him to comply with the undertaking.

SARGANT J, [after stating the facts and holding that the undertaking to vote in accordance with the plaintiff's wishes contained in the letter constituted a collateral agreement binding on the defendant, continued]: In my opinion, therefore, the right of the plaintiff is clear, and the only remaining question is whether she is entitled to a mandatory injunction to enforce her right. It is not disputed that she is entitled to a prohibitive injunction, and in my opinion she is also entitled to a mandatory injunction. Prima facie this court is bound ... to give effect to a clear right by way of a mandatory injunction. There are no doubt certain exceptions from this rule, as in the case of a

9 Contrast the position as regards *directors*; below, p 276.

contract of service, because in such cases it is impossible for the court to make its order effective, but ... in the present case, inasmuch as there is one definite thing to be done, about the mode of doing which there can be no possible doubt, I am of opinion that I ought to grant not only the prohibitive but also the mandatory injunction claimed by the plaintiff, and I make an order accordingly.

NOTES

(1) The specific undertaking given in this case displaced the normal rule that a mortgagee of shares may exercise the voting rights in respect of those shares free of any dictation from the mortgagor: *Siemens Bros & Co Ltd v Burns* [1918] 2 Ch 324, CA. Similarly, an *unpaid* vendor of shares who remains on the register retains the voting rights (*Musselwhite v CH Musselwhite & Son Ltd* [1962] Ch 964). But where the purchaser has paid the full price, the vendor holds the shares as a bare trustee (*Hawks v McArthur* (**228**)), and must vote the shares as directed by the purchaser (*Re Piccadilly Radio plc* [1989] BCLC 683).

(2) This case concerned a single shareholder. A contract between several shareholders, agreeing to co-ordinate their votes, or delegating to one the power to cast votes for all—commonly known as a 'voting trust'—is lawful. It is more widely used in the United States than in this country, and can be a powerful tool either to concentrate control behind the management, or to use as a countervailing force against it.

(3) It is also possible for the members of a company to enter into a 'shareholder agreement' or 'unanimous shareholder agreement',[10] by which they contract with each other that they will ensure that the company's affairs are run in a particular way: for instance, that each member of a three-man company will be entitled to a seat on the board for himself or his nominee (compare the arrangement in *Re A and BC Chewing Gum Ltd* (below, p 570)—surely a less clumsy approach than the English draftsman's solution to the same problem in *Bushell v Faith* (**120**)). The shareholder agreement is not a constitutional document (and so is not vulnerable to alteration by majority vote as the articles are), but it is enforceable as a contract—by injunction, where appropriate—and relevant to proceedings where a winding up order is sought on the 'just and equitable' ground (as in *Re A and BC Chewing Gum Ltd*). On the other hand, its terms cannot bind a third party without notice, such as a purchaser of shares. Judges do sometimes *imply* a shareholders' agreement and give effect to it (e g in *Pennell Securities Ltd v Venida Investments Ltd* (below, p 287).

The shareholder agreement is used, almost as a matter of routine, to supplement the constitutional documents in Canada and the US, and its importance is recognised by the legislation in those jurisdictions. We on this side of the Atlantic have been slower to recognise its potential as a drafting and planning aid, but its use is now standard for some purposes, e g joint ventures and management buy-outs.

QUESTION

Should the arrangement in *Cane v Jones* (**85**) have been seen as a shareholders' agreement in this sense? What would its effect then have been?

90 Re Dorman Long & Co Ltd [1934] Ch 635 (Chancery Division)

[These remarks were made in reference to a scheme of arrangement under

10 On this topic, see P D Finn, 'Shareholder Agreements' (1978) 6 ABL Rev 97.

CA 1985, ss 425–427, but they are applicable generally to meetings of large companies.]

MAUGHAM J: It may be observed that when the Joint Stock Companies Arrangement Act 1870 was passed, in the majority of cases all the persons concerned with an arrangement could go to the meeting, listen to what was said and vote for or against the arrangement according to the views which they were persuaded to take. In these days, in many of the cases that come before me, only a fraction of the persons who are concerned can get into the room where the meeting is proposed to be held, and in the great majority of cases, the proxies given to the directors before the meeting begins have in effect settled the question of the voting once for all. It is perhaps not unfair to say that in nearly every big case not more than 5% of the interests involved are present in person at the meeting. It is for that reason that the court takes the view that it is essential to see that the explanatory circulars sent out by the board of the company are perfectly fair and, as far as possible, give all the information reasonably necessary to enable the recipients to determine how to vote. I am assuming, of course, that following the usual procedure, explanatory circulars are sent out, because, I may observe, there is nothing in the Act to render them essential. In a sense, in all these cases, the dice are loaded in favour of the views of the directors: the notices and circulars are sent out at the cost of the company, the board have had plenty of time to prepare the circulars, all the facts of the case are known to them, proxy forms are made out in favour of certain named directors and, although it is true that the word 'for' or 'against' may be inserted in the modern proxy form, the recipients of the circulars very often are in doubt as to whether the persons named as proxies are bound to put in votes by proxy with which they are not in agreement. If we contrast with that position the position of a class of objectors, it is to be observed that a member of the class who receives a notice of the meeting and a circular from the directors is generally alone: he has no funds with which to fight the case and he has no information, except, sometimes, that information which has been contained in reports and balance sheets which have probably long ago been relegated to the waste paper basket. In any case, he has a minimum of information, his personal interest in the matter may be exceedingly small, probably he knows few persons in the same position as himself and, if he manages to get into touch with them, they together have to raise funds for the purposes of an opposition, which is often an expensive matter. They have then to get the names and addresses of the members of the class who are concerned, and to frame and send out a circular representing their views. Very often there is scarcely sufficient time for those purposes between the moment when the notice of the meeting reaches objectors by post and the date of the meeting. Proxies sent out by the directors can easily be lodged forty-eight hours before the meeting. It is quite plain that opponents may find it most difficult, after they have come together and have raised the necessary funds and have agreed on a circular and have sent out their notices, to lodge such proxies as they may have been able to obtain forty-eight hours before the meeting.

In my opinion the court ought to bear in mind these considerations when it has before it, as it often has, a case where the whole matter is really determined by the proxies that have been given before the meeting is held . . .

NOTE

In an attempt to redress the imbalance to which Maugham J refers, the Act now gives members holding together at least 5% of a company's shares (or a minimum of 100 members with an average stake of at least £100 paid up) the right to have a statement circulated to members: see CA 1985, s 376. But the requisitionists must be prepared to face the burden (which may be quite considerable) of paying the expenses incurred, unless the company resolves otherwise (s 376(1)). The cost of distributing one such circular to the shareholders of the Burmah Oil company in 1978 was put at £16,592— a figure which would have doubled, at least, at today's prices.[11]

Proxies

The articles of most companies allow a member to be represented at meetings and to vote through an agent called a *proxy,* and this right is recognised and confirmed by CA 1985, s 372. The word 'proxy' is also used to refer to the document signed by the shareholder to give the representative his authority to act. (For typical forms of proxy, see Table A, articles 60, 61.) Advocates of greater 'shareholder democracy' regard the proxy system as an important weapon in their cause, since it ensures that account is taken of the views of any members who are unable to attend a meeting personally. But even so, as Maugham J explained in the extract above, the directors still have the advantage in many respects.

A shareholder may ordinarily revoke a proxy by exercising his right to vote in person.

91 Cousins v International Brick Co Ltd [1931] 2 Ch 90 (Chancery Division and Court of Appeal)

Article 76 of the company's articles of association provided that a vote given in accordance with the terms of a proxy should be valid notwithstanding the previous revocation of the proxy, provided that no intimation in writing of the revocation should have been received at the company's office before the meeting.

At a meeting called for 20 October 1930 for the purpose (inter alia) of electing a director, the plaintiff held proxies representing 102,138 votes in favour of the election of one Carr. The meeting was adjourned until 3 November for a poll to be taken. Before the meeting was reconvened, shareholders whose votes amounted to 36,991 purported by written notice to the company to revoke the proxies which they had previously given to the plaintiff, and others with 11,396 votes not only revoked their proxies in a similar way but also attended the adjourned meeting and cast their votes personally against an amendment which proposed Carr's election. The chairman (a) rejected the plaintiff's proxies for the 36,991 votes; (b) rejected his proxies for the 11,396 votes; but (c) accepted the 11,396 votes cast personally by the shareholders; and he declared Carr not to have been elected. Luxmoore J (whose decision was upheld by the Court of Appeal) held that the chairman,

11 J M L Stone [1980] New LJ 152.

though wrong as regards (a), was right as regards (b) and (c), with the result that the amendment was still lost.

LUXMOORE J: I accept the argument on behalf of the plaintiff that the 36,991 votes he tendered on behalf of those persons who had given in proxies but who did not tender their votes in person at the adjourned meeting ought to have been received on the poll of the chairman, for the purported revocation of these proxies was not in accordance with the provisions of the article 76 ... [But] this is not decisive of the plaintiff's case, for if these votes are admitted, but the 11,396 are refused, the voting in favour of the amendment would be 89,072, while the voting against it remains unchanged at 96,604.

It is essential therefore to consider the position with regard to the 11,396 votes. It is clear on the authority of the case to which I have already referred that the purported notices of revocation in respect of those votes were ineffective by themselves to prevent the plaintiff Cousins from using the votes concerned on the poll, and therefore the only question is as to the effect of the tender of these votes in person by the shareholders who executed the proxies. Is there anything in the articles as between a shareholder and the company to preclude a shareholder who has given a proxy from attending a meeting or an adjourned meeting and voting in person, notwithstanding the fact that he has given a proxy? There is no authority touching the particular point, but on principle I do not think there is any ground in such a case for refusing the shareholder's vote and accepting that of the proxy. The proxy is merely the agent of the shareholder who appoints him. As between himself and the proxy he can determine the agency, and the agent is not entitled to vote if the agency is in fact determined. The shareholder, as between himself and the company, has the option of voting in person or by proxy. If he votes in person quite obviously he cannot also vote by proxy. As between himself and the company if he allows the proxy to vote, and the company accepts that vote, he cannot afterwards claim to vote personally. But this is not what happened in the present case. The shareholders in question and their proxies tendered votes in respect of the same shares, and it was not until the votes came to be considered that the company had to determine which of the votes had to be accepted. A company finding votes cast in respect of the same shares is bound to consider which votes are to be accepted, and where the votes of a shareholder are cast by that shareholder himself in a manner justified by the articles, I think the company is, in the absence of any particular circumstances, bound to accept those votes, notwithstanding that a person who has been validly appointed as proxy in respect of the same shares has also purported to vote. The right of the shareholder to vote in person must, in my judgment, and in the absence of any special contract between himself and the company expressly precluding the right to vote in person where a proxy has been validly given, be paramount to the right of the proxy to vote in respect of the shares in question ...

It follows from what I have said, that in my judgment the 11,396 votes which were cast by shareholders who had given the plaintiff Cousins proxies in respect of those shares were properly accepted by the company, and that the votes tendered by the plaintiff Cousins in respect of the same shares under those proxies were validly rejected.

In the result, the amendment for the appointment of the plaintiff H G T Carr as a director was in fact defeated on the poll ...

C. The board of directors

A board meeting may be held informally, but cannot be constituted on a casual encounter between the directors if one of them objects.

92 Barron v Potter [1914] 1 Ch 895 (Chancery Division)

The articles of the British Seagumite Co Ltd provided that the quorum at directors' meetings should be two, and also conferred upon the board the power to appoint additional directors. In 1914 the only two directors were Potter, who was chairman, and Canon Barron, who lived in the country and refused to attend board meetings with Potter. On 23 February, Barron came to London to attend a shareholders' meeting, fixed for the following day, which he had himself convened. On his arrival at Paddington station he was met on the platform by Potter, who said, walking by his side along the platform: 'I want to see you, please.' Barron replied, 'I have nothing to say to you.' Potter then said, 'I formally propose that we add the Reverend Charles Herbert, Mr William George Walter Barnard and Mr John Tolehurst Musgrave as additional directors to the board of the British Seagumite Company Limited. Do you agree or object?' Barron replied, 'I object and I object to say anything to you at all.' Potter then said, 'In my capacity as chairman, I give my casting vote in their favour and declare them duly elected.' He continued to walk with Barron a few steps and then said, 'That is all I want to say; thank you. Good day.'

A second 'meeting', at which a substantially similar exchange of remarks took place, was 'held' when Potter buttonholed Barron just before the shareholders' meeting on the following day. It was held that neither of these informal encounters between the directors could be treated as a valid board meeting, and that the 'appointments' were accordingly nullities.

WARRINGTON J: Mr Potter originally insisted that what took place on the platform of Paddington station was a directors' meeting at which a sufficient proposal was made for the appointment of the three persons named as additional directors, and that if Canon Barron did not vote it was competent for Mr Potter to vote and carry the resolution, or if Canon Barron did vote, then it was competent for Mr Potter to carry it by his own casting vote. It is not, however, now contended that what took place on that occasion was a valid appointment of the additional directors, but it is contended that what took place the next day immediately before the general meeting did amount to a valid appointment ... [His Lordship then referred to what took place between Canon Barron and Mr Potter immediately before the general meeting on 24 February and continued:] What then took place is said to have been a directors' meeting at which a valid appointment was made of the three additional directors proposed by Mr Potter. The answer, in my opinion, is that there was no directors' meeting at all for the reason that Canon Barron to the knowledge of Mr Potter insisted all along that he would not attend any directors' meeting with Mr Potter or discuss the affairs of the company with him, and it is not enough that one of two directors should say 'This is a directors' meeting' while the other says it is not. Of course if directors are willing to hold a meeting they may do so under any circumstances, but one of them cannot be made to attend the board or to convert a casual meeting into a board meeting, and in the present case I do not see how the meeting in question can be treated as a board meeting. In my opinion therefore the true conclusion is that there was no board meeting, but that Canon Barron came with the deliberate intention of not attending a board meeting. If he had received the notice sent to him by Mr Potter summoning him to a board meeting different considerations might have arisen, but he had not received it and came with the fixed intention of not attending any such meeting. There was therefore no board meeting at which Canon Barron was present. Mr Potter was alone present, so that there was no quorum, and I must hold that the three additional directors named by him were not validly appointed ...

[The remainder of the decision is cited below, (**101**).]

NOTE

There is no English case which establishes categorically that the informal and unanimous consent of the directors is for all purposes equivalent to a resolution passed at a meeting duly convened and held, although the remarks of Lord Denning in *H L Bolton (Engineering) Co Ltd v T J Graham & Sons Ltd* (**31**) and the unreported case which he there cites come very close to saying so, as do some remarks of Browne-Wilkinson V-C in *TCB Ltd v Gray* (**117**).[12] These statements are, it is submitted, to be preferred to those in some older cases which suggest that the directors cannot act without meeting. In practice, most companies have an article like Table A, article 93, which allows the directors to record their consent to a decision in writing.

However, in *Guinness plc v Saunders* (**124**),[13] the Court of Appeal declined to accept that a statutory requirement of disclosure to 'a meeting of directors' (CA 1985, s 317(1)) could be deemed to have been complied with simply because every individual member of the board knew of the matter. Fox LJ said ([1988] 2 All ER 940 at 944, [1988] 1 WLR 863 at 868) that disclosure to 'a meeting of the directors of the company' is 'a wholly different thing from knowledge by individuals and involves the opportunity for positive consideration of the matter by the board as a body'.

A director may bring a personal action against his fellow directors to restrain them from wrongfully excluding him from board meetings.

93 Pulbrook v Richmond Consolidated Mining Co (1878) 9 Ch D 610 (Chancery Division)

The company's articles fixed as the qualification of a director the holding 'as registered member in his own right' shares to the nominal amount of £500. Pulbrook had mortgaged his qualification shares, and delivered to the mortgagee an unregistered transfer. The directors, on learning of this, refused to allow him to sit on the board. Jessel MR held (1) that he still held the shares 'in his own right', and (2) that he had suffered an individual wrong for redress of which he could sue in his own name.[14]

JESSEL MR: This is a motion which raises some points of great importance. The first question is, whether a director who is improperly and without cause

12 See also *Re Bonelli's Telegraph Co, Collie's Claim* (1871) LR 12 Eq 246 at 258. In *Re Tivoli Freeholds Ltd* [1972] VR 445 at 459–460 Menhennit J held that such a resolution was valid and binding.
13 The House of Lords affirmed the decision of the Court of Appeal on grounds which did not raise this question.
14 On this point, see below, pp 470 ff.

excluded by his brother directors from the board from which they claim the right to exclude him, is entitled to an order restraining his brother directors from so excluding him.

In this case a man is necessarily a shareholder in order to be a director, and as a director he is entitled to fees and remuneration for his services, and it might be a question whether he would be entitled to the fees if he did not attend meetings of the board. He has been excluded. Now, it appears to me that this is an individual wrong, or a wrong that has been done to an individual. It is a deprivation of his legal rights for which the directors are personally and individually liable. He has a right by the constitution of the company to take a part in its management, to be present, and to vote at the meetings of the board of directors. He has a perfect right to know what is going on at these meetings. It may affect his individual interest as a share-holder as well as his liability as a director, because it has been sometimes held that even a director who does not attend board meetings is bound to know what is done in his absence.

Besides that, he is in the position of a shareholder, or a managing partner in the affairs of the company, and he has a right to remain managing partner, and to receive remuneration for his services. It appears to me that for the injury or wrong done to him by preventing him from attending board meetings by force, he has a right to sue. He has what is commonly called a right of action, and those decisions which say that, where a wrong is done to the company by the exclusion of a director from board meetings, the company may sue and must sue for that wrong, do not apply to the case of wrong done simply to an individual. There may be cases where, by preventing a director from exercising his functions in addition to its being a wrong done to the individual, a wrong is also done to the company, and there the company have a right to complain. But in a case of an individual wrong, another shareholder cannot on behalf of himself and others, not being the individuals to whom the wrong is done, maintain an action for that wrong. That being so, in my opinion, the plaintiff in this case has a right of action.

[His Lordship then ruled that he still held the qualification shares 'in his own right', and so had been properly elected a director. He accordingly granted an injunction.]

NOTE

It is probably impossible to square all the remarks in this judgment either with the ratio decidendi of *Hickman*'s case (**43**) or with the view (commonly associated with Lord Wedderburn: see his article in [1957] CLJ 194, 212) that every member of a company has a right to have the provisions of the corporate constitution observed. (On these questions see further above, pp 95 ff and below, pp 471 ff.) The difficulties can be highlighted by supposing that in the case above the company's articles did not require a director to hold shares, and that the excluded director held none.

D. Division of powers between the general meeting and the board

Companies (Tables A to F) Regulations 1985

Table A

70 Subject to the provisions of the Act, the memorandum and the articles and to any directions given by special resolution, the business of the company shall be managed by the directors who may exercise all the powers of the company. No alteration of the memorandum or articles and no such direction shall invalidate any prior act of the directors which would have been valid if that alteration had not been made or that direction had not been given. The powers given by this regulation shall not be limited by any special power given to the directors by the articles and a meeting of directors at which a quorum is present may exercise all powers exercisable by the directors.

Where (as in Table A, article 70) the general management of the company is vested in the directors, the shareholders have no power by ordinary resolution to give directions to the board or to overrule its business decisions.

94 Automatic Self-Cleansing Filter Syndicate Co Ltd v Cuninghame [1906] 2 Ch 34 (Court of Appeal)

Article 96 of the company's articles of association vested in the directors 'the management of the business and the control of the company' in terms similar to the present Table A, article 70; and article 97(1) specifically empowered them to sell any property of the company on such terms and conditions as they might think fit. At a general meeting of the company a resolution was passed directing the board to sell the company's undertaking to a new company formed for the purpose, but the directors disapproved of the proposed terms and declined to carry out the sale. It was held that the shareholders had no say in the matter, which was for the board alone to decide.

COLLINS MR: This is an appeal from a decision of Warrington J, who has been asked by the plaintiffs, Mr McDiarmid and the company, for a declaration that the defendants, as directors of the company, are bound to carry into effect a resolution passed at a meeting of the shareholders in the company on 16 January . . .

The point arises in this way. At a meeting of the company a resolution was passed by a majority—I was going to say a bare majority, but it was a majority—in favour of a sale to a purchaser, and the directors, honestly believing, as Warrington J thought, that it was most undesirable in the interests of the company that that agreement should be carried into effect, refused to affix the seal of the company to it, or to assist in carrying out a resolution which they disapproved of; and the question is whether under the memorandum and articles of association here the directors are bound to accept, in substitution of their own view, the views contained in the resolution of the company. Warrington J held that the majority could not impose that obligation upon the directors, and that on the true construction of the articles the directors were the persons authorised by the articles to effect this sale, and that unless the other powers given by the memorandum were invoked by a special resolution, it was impossible for a mere majority at a meeting to override the views of the directors. That depends, as Warrington J put it, upon the construction of the articles. [His Lordship read the relevant articles and continued:] Therefore in the matters referred to in article 97(1) the view of the directors as to the fitness of the matter is made the standard; and furthermore, by article 96 they are given in express terms the full powers which the company has, except so far as they 'are not hereby or by statute expressly directed or required to be exercised or done by the company', so that the directors have absolute power to do all things other than those that are expressly required to be done by the company; and then comes the limitation on their general authority—'subject to such regulations as may from time to time be made by extraordinary resolution'. Therefore, if it is desired to alter the powers of the directors, that must be done not by a resolution carried by a majority at an ordinary meeting of the company, but by an extraordinary resolution. In these circumstances it seems to me that it is not competent for the majority of the shareholders at an ordinary meeting to affect or alter the mandate originally given to the directors, by the articles of association. It has been suggested that this is a mere question of principal and agent, and that it would be an absurd thing if a principal in appointing an agent should in effect appoint a dictator who is to manage him instead of his managing the agent. I think that that analogy does not strictly apply to this case. No doubt for some purposes directors are agents. For whom are they agents? You have, no doubt, in theory and law one entity, the company, which might be a principal, but you have to go behind that when you look to the particular position of directors. It is by the consensus of all the individuals in the company that these directors become agents and hold their rights as agents. It is not fair to say that a majority at a meeting is for the purposes of this case the principal so as to alter the mandate of the agent. The minority also must be taken into account. There are provisions by which the minority may be overborne, but that can only be done by special machinery in the shape of special resolutions. Short of that the mandate which must be obeyed is not that of the majority—it is that of the whole entity made up of all the shareholders. If the mandate of the directors is to be altered, it can only be under the machinery of the memorandum and articles themselves. I do not think I need say more.

One argument used by Warrington J strongly supports that view. He says in effect: 'There is to be found in these articles a provision that a director can only be removed by special resolution. What is the use of that provision if the views of the directors can be overridden by a mere majority at an ordinary meeting? Practically you do not want any special powers to remove directors if you can do without them and differ from their opinion and compel something other than their view to be carried into effect.' That argument appears to me to confirm the view taken by the learned judge . . .

COZENS-HARDY LJ delivered a concurring judgment.

NOTE

The argument of Warrington J referred to in the last paragraph cited above is no longer applicable in view of CA 1985, s 303, which authorises the removal of a director by ordinary resolution, whatever the articles may provide. While the authority of the decision itself in *Cuninghame*'s case is no doubt unimpaired, a majority of the shareholders may nowadays ensure that their views prevail by removing the board, or threatening to use their power to do so.

The decision in *Cuninghame*'s case marked the beginning of a departure from the traditional nineteenth-century view which regarded the shareholders in general meeting as constituting 'the company' and the directors as their delegates or agents.

The older view is well illustrated by the wording of s 90 of the Companies Clauses Consolidation Act 1845, which reads as follows:

90 *Powers of the company to be exercised by the directors*

The directors shall have the management and superintendence of the affairs of the company, and they may lawfully exercise all the powers of the company, except as to such matters as are directed by this or the special Act to be transacted by a general meeting of the company; but all the powers so to be exercised shall be exercised in accordance with and subject to the provisions of this and the special Act; and the exercise of all such powers shall be subject also to the control and regulation of any general meeting specially convened for the purpose, but not so as to render invalid any act done by the directors prior to any resolution passed by such general meeting.

Consistent with this older view are the remarks of Cotton LJ in *Isle of Wight Rly Co v Tahourdin* (1883) 25 Ch D 320, CA, a case on s 90 of the Act of 1845 (above). The directors had succeeded at first instance in securing an injunction to restrain the holding of a meeting which had been requisitioned by a number of shareholders. He said (at 329):

We are of opinion that this injunction ought not to have been granted. It is a very strong thing indeed to prevent shareholders from holding a meeting of the company, when such a meeting is the only way in which they can interfere, if the majority of them think that the course taken by the directors, in a matter which is intra vires of the directors, is not for the benefit of the company ...

Directors have great powers, and the court refuses to interfere with their management of the company's affairs if they keep within their powers, and if a shareholder complains of the conduct of the directors while they keep within their powers, the court says to him, 'If you want to alter the management of the affairs of the company go to a general meeting, and if they agree with you they will pass a resolution obliging the directors to alter their course of proceeding' ...

Three further points may be made about *Cuninghame*'s case:

(a) It is not the *law* which has changed between 1883 (the date of *Tahourdin*'s case) and today, so much as commercial practice. All that the courts have done is to recognise that practice. There is nothing in the law which would prevent a company from having a provision in its articles which gave supervisory powers in the widest terms to its shareholders, or allowed them to override the directors' decisions—indeed, article 70 itself has such a provision (but a special resolution is needed).

(b) Article 70 uses the words 'the business of the company shall be managed by the directors ...'. The ruling in *Cuninghame*'s case does not apply to decisions outside the company's business and its management. In *Re Emmadart Ltd* [1979] Ch 540, [1979] 1 All ER 599, it was held that directors had no power under such an article to resolve to put their company into liquidation.

(c) Until the revision of Table A in 1985, the wording of the article corresponding to the present article 70 was ambiguous: there was a power reserved to the company in general meeting to prescribe 'regulations' binding on the directors (see, e g CA 1948, Table A, article 80). But what was meant by 'regulations' in this context was never settled; and some commentators (e g Goldberg, (1970) 33 MLR 177, Sullivan, (1977) 93 LQR 569) argued that if due weight were given to this provision, article 80 ought to be construed as giving the shareholders power to override the autonomy apparently conferred on the directors by *Cuninghame*'s case. Their view was supported by the first-instance decision of Neville J in *Marshall's Valve Gear Co Ltd v Manning, Wardle & Co Ltd* [1909] 1 Ch 267. The problem is still very much a live one, for there are probably upwards of half a million companies extant which have articles in this old form. But all the indications are that a modern court would not go out of its way to restore the nineteenth-century position in the face of the shift in business practice over the last hundred years; and in the recent case of *Breckland Group Holdings Ltd v London & Suffolk Properties Ltd* [1989] BCLC 100, Harman J held that *Marshall*'s case could not stand against the overwhelming weight of authority to the contrary.

Following *Cuninghame*'s case, the Court of Appeal in *Gramophone and Typewriter Co Ltd v Stanley* (16) declined to 'lift the veil' so as to identify a subsidiary with its holding company, partly on the ground that the control of the affairs of the subsidiary was confided to its *directors*. The same approach was adopted in the cases which follow.

95 Quin & Axtens Ltd v Salmon [1909] AC 442 (House of Lords)

The company's two managing directors, Salmon and Axtens, held between them the bulk of the company's ordinary shares. Article 75 of the articles provided that the business of the company should be managed by the directors, who might exercise all the powers of the company 'subject to such regulations (being not inconsistent with the provisions of the articles) as may be prescribed by the company in general meeting'. Article 80 stated that no resolution of a meeting of the directors having for its object (inter alia) the acquisition or letting of certain premises should be valid if either Salmon or Axtens dissented. The directors resolved to acquire and to let various properties, but Salmon dissented. An extraordinary general meeting was then held at which the shareholders by a majority passed similar resolutions. The House of Lords, upholding the decision of the Court of Appeal, held that the shareholders' resolutions were inconsistent with the articles and granted an injunction restraining the company from acting on them.

LORD LOREBURN LC: My Lords, I do not see any solid ground for complaint against the judgment of the Court of Appeal.

The bargain made between the shareholders is contained in articles 75 and 80 of the articles of association, and it amounts for the purpose in hand to this, that the directors should manage the business; and the company, therefore, are not to manage the business unless there is provision to that effect. Further the directors cannot manage it in a particular way—that is to say, they cannot do certain things if Mr Salmon or Mr Axtens objects. Now I cannot agree with Mr Upjohn in his contention that the failure of the directors upon the objection of Mr Salmon to grant these leases of itself remitted the matter to the discretion of the company in general meeting. They could still manage the business, but not altogether in the way they desired. . .

LORDS MACNAGHTEN, JAMES OF HEREFORD and SHAW OF DUNFERMLINE concurred.

96 John Shaw & Sons (Salford) Ltd v Shaw [1935] 2 KB 113 (Court of Appeal)

As part of the settlement of a dispute concerning sums owing to the plaintiff company by Peter, John and Percy Shaw (three brothers who were shareholders in and directors of the plaintiff company), the articles were altered so as to hand over all control of the financial affairs of the company and the management of its business to three independent persons known as 'permanent directors'. Two of the brothers, however, later failed to accept certain other provisions of the settlement, and as a result it was resolved at a meeting of the permanent directors that the present action should be instituted against them. But before the hearing of the suit the shareholders held an extraordinary meeting, at which a resolution was passed directing the board to discontinue the action forthwith. Du Parcq J disregarded the shareholders' resolution and gave judgment for the plaintiff company. The defendants appealed.

GREER LJ: [This] cause of action, whether likely to succeed or not, was one in respect of which the permanent directors were, in my opinion, empowered to commence and carry on.

I am therefore of opinion that the learned judge was right in refusing to dismiss the action on the plea that it was commenced without the authority of the plaintiff company. I think the judge was also right in refusing to give effect to the resolution of the meeting of the shareholders requiring the chairman to instruct the company's solicitors not to proceed further with the action. A company is an entity distinct alike from its shareholders and its directors. Some of its powers may, according to its articles, be exercised by directors, certain other powers may be reserved for the shareholders in general meeting. If powers of management are vested in the directors, they and they alone can exercise these powers. The only way in which the general body of the shareholders can control the exercise of the powers vested by the articles in the directors is by altering their articles, or, if opportunity arises under the articles, by refusing to re-elect the directors of whose actions they disapprove. They cannot themselves usurp the powers which by the articles are vested in the directors any more than the directors can usurp the powers vested by the articles in the general body of shareholders . . .

[Roche LJ agreed, for other reasons, that the action had been competently brought, while Slesser LJ, again for other reasons, thought that it had not. But he agreed, or 'inclined to the view', that the shareholders could not interfere with a power conferred by the articles on the permanent directors, except by altering the articles. The court unanimously held, however, that the defendants were entitled to succeed on the substantive issue of the case, and allowed the appeal.]

NOTE

The above cases may be taken to have established that, where the directors in pursuance of a power conferred upon them have instituted litigation in the company's name, the shareholders in general meeting may not interfere and direct that the proceedings be discontinued. But in the converse case, where the majority of the shareholders have instituted or consented to the institution of proceedings in the company's name, and the *directors* object to their being continued, the law is less clear. Certainly if the directors are themselves defendants or if the allegation is that they are party to a wrong against the company, the rule in *Foss v Harbottle* (**232**) appears to allow the majority shareholders the ultimate say and even, where the directors are themselves majority shareholders, to permit a minority shareholder to bring a derivative action. This view receives indirect support from the case next cited, but the decision in fact turned mainly on the special terms of the article in *Cuninghame*'s case.

QUESTION

Consider Table A, articles 70 and 84. If a company appoints a managing director under these provisions, will it (on the reasoning of Greer LJ) have two, or three, 'organs' with independent functions and powers?

The company in general meeting may by ordinary resolution ratify an act of the directors which is within the powers of the company but beyond the authority or competence of the directors.

97 Grant v United Kingdom Switchback Railways Co (1888) 40 Ch D 135 (Court of Appeal)

Article 100 of the articles of association of Thompson's Patent Gravity Switchback Railways Co (the second defendant) disqualified any director from voting at a board meeting in relation to any contract in which he was interested. The directors of this company agreed to sell the company's undertaking to the United Kingdom Co (the first defendant) despite the fact that they were the promoters of the purchasing company. [The remaining facts appear from the judgment.]

COTTON LJ: This is an appeal from a decision of Mr Justice Chitty refusing an injunction to restrain Thompson's Company and the United Kingdom Company from carrying into effect a contract for the sale of part of the undertaking of the former company to the latter. The ground of the application was that the directors of Thompson's Company had no authority to enter into the contract, as the articles prohibited a director from voting upon a contract in which he was interested, and here all the directors but one were interested. An application for an injunction was made in the Long Vacation, and ordered to stand over till the Michaelmas Sittings, the companies undertaking not to act upon the agreement in the meantime, but being left at liberty to call meetings of their shareholders with reference to the agreement. A general meeting of the shareholders of Thompson's Company was accordingly held, and passed a resolution approving and adopting the agreement, and authorising the directors to carry it into effect. Mr Justice Chitty under these circumstances refused an injunction, and the plaintiff has appealed.

It was urged for the appellant that the directors could not, being interested, make a contract which would bind their company, and that a general meeting could not, by a mere ordinary resolution, affirm that contract, for this would be an alteration of the articles, which could only be effected by a special resolution. This is a mistake. The ratifying of a particular contract which had been entered into by the directors without authority, and so making it an act of the company, is quite a different thing from altering the articles. To give the directors power to do things in future which the articles did not authorise them to do would be an alteration of the articles, but it is no alteration of the articles to ratify a contract which has been made without authority.

It was urged that the contract was a nullity, and could not be ratified. That is not the case. There was a contract entered into on behalf of the company, though it was one which could not be enforced against the company. Article 100 prevented the directors from binding the company by the contract, but there was nothing in it to prevent the company from entering into such a contract. Two passages in *Irvine v Union Bank of Australia*[15] were referred to. Being in the same judgment, they must be taken together, and they appear to me to express what I have said—that power to do future acts cannot be given to directors without altering the articles, but that a ratification of an unauthorised act of the directors only requires the sanction of an ordinary resolution of a general meeting, if the act is within the powers of the company.

LINDLEY and BOWEN LJJ delivered concurring judgments.

98 Re Horsley & Weight Ltd [1982] Ch 442, [1982] 3 All ER 1045 (Court of Appeal)

[For the facts and another part of the decision, see (**68**).]

BUCKLEY LJ: I now turn to the second head of Mr Evans-Lombe's argument, viz that the purchase of the pension was effected by Mr Campbell-Dick and Mr Frank Horsley without the authority of the board of directors or of the company in general meeting, and was an act of misfeasance which was not validated as against the company's creditors by virtue of the fact that Mr Campbell-Dick and Mr Frank Horsley were the only shareholders. Ignoring for the moment that Mr Campbell-Dick and Mr Frank Horsley were the only shareholders, the transaction in question was indeed carried out by them without the sanction of any board resolution, whether antecedent, contemporary or by way of subsequent ratification. It was an unauthorised act which they were, as two only of the company's five directors, incompetent to carry out on the company's behalf. It therefore cannot stand unless it has in some way been ratified. The question is whether the fact that Mr Campbell-Dick and Mr Frank Horsley were the only shareholders of the company has the effect of validating the transaction.

Mr Evans-Lombe has submitted that there is a general duty incumbent on directors of a company, whether properly described as owed to creditors or not, to preserve the company's capital fund (which he identifies as those assets which are not distributable by way of dividend) and not to dispose of it otherwise than for the benefit or intended benefit of the company. He submits that creditors dealing with the company are entitled to assume that directors will observe that duty; and that creditors, although they are not entitled to interfere in the day to day management of a company which is not in liquidation, are entitled through a liquidator to seek redress in respect of a breach of the duty. Consequently, Mr Evans-Lombe submits, the members of the company cannot, even unanimously, deprive the creditors of any remedy so available to them.

On this part of the case Mr Evans-Lombe mainly relies upon *Re Exchange Banking Co, Flitcroft's Case* (**182**) . . . The facts of that case were very different from those of the present case and the principles applicable were, in my opinion, also different. A company cannot legally repay contributed capital to the contributors otherwise than by way of an authorised reduction of capital. Nothing of that kind occurred in the present case. There is nothing in the statute or in the general law which prevents a company or its directors expending contributed capital in doing anything which is an authorised object of the company. In the present case the cost of effecting the pension policy

15 (1877) 2 App Cas 366, PC.

was, in my view, incurred in the course of carrying out an express object of the company.

It is a misapprehension to suppose that the directors of a company owe a duty to the company's creditors to keep the contributed capital of the company intact. The company's creditors are entitled to assume that the company will not in any way repay any paid-up share capital to the shareholders except by means of a duly authorised reduction of capital. They are entitled to assume that the company's directors will conduct its affairs in such a manner that no such unauthorised repayment will take place. It may be somewhat loosely said that the directors owe an indirect duty to the creditors not to permit any unlawful reduction of capital to occur, but I would regard it as more accurate to say that the directors owe a duty to the company in this respect and that, if the company is put into liquidation when paid-up capital has been improperly repaid, the liquidator owes a duty to the creditors to enforce any right to repayment which is available to the company. On the other hand, a company and its directors acting on its behalf, can quite properly expend contributed capital for any purpose which is intra vires the company. As I have already indicated, the purchase of the pension policy was, in my view, intra vires the company. It was not, however, within the powers of Mr Campbell-Dick and Mr Frank Horsley acting not as members of the board of directors but as individual directors. Unless the act was effectually ratified it cannot bind the company. They were, however, the only two shareholders. A company is bound in a matter which is intra vires the company by the unanimous agreement of its members (per Lord Davey in *Salomon v Salomon & Co Ltd* (**12**); and see *Re Express Engineering Works Ltd* (**81**)) even where that agreement is given informally: *Parker & Cooper Ltd v Reading* (**82**). That both Mr Campbell-Dick and Mr Frank Horsley assented to the transaction in question in the present case is beyond dispute. They both initialled the proposal form and they both signed the cheques for the premiums. Their good faith has not been impugned, nor, in my view, does the evidence support any suggestion that in effecting the policy they did not honestly apply their minds to the question whether it was a fair and proper thing for the company to do in the light of the company's financial state as known to them at the time. In my judgment, their assent made the transaction binding on the company and unassailable by the liquidator ...

CUMMING-BRUCE and TEMPLEMAN LJJ delivered concurring judgments, in the course of which they made the following comments:

CUMMING-BRUCE LJ:　On these facts it is unnecessary to decide whether, had misfeasance by the directors been proved, it was open to them in their capacity as shareholders to ratify their own negligence and so to prejudice the claims of creditors. It would surprise me to find that the law is to be so understood.

TEMPLEMAN LJ:　If, however, there had been evidence and a finding of misfeasance and it appeared that the payment of £10,000 in the event reduced the fund available for creditors by that sum, or by a substantial proportion of that sum, I am not satisfied that the directors convicted of such misfeasance, albeit with no fraudulent intent or action, could excuse themselves because two of them held all the issued shares in the company and as shareholders ratified their own gross negligence as directors which inflicted loss on creditors. I should be sorry to find the scope of s 333 [1A 1986, s 212] so restricted and need not do so on this occasion.

An ordinary resolution which purports to ratify an irregular act of the directors is ineffective if it itself contravenes the articles.

99 Boschoek Pty Co Ltd v Fuke [1906] 1 Ch 148 (Chancery Division)

The directors had purported to appoint Fuke managing director at a remuneration of £700 per annum, although he did not hold 'in his own right' the number of qualification shares prescribed by the articles, and also despite the fact that the maximum remuneration of the whole board was fixed by the articles at £500. The company later confirmed the appointment by resolutions passed unanimously at a general meeting; but the court ruled that the resolutions were invalid.

SWINFEN EADY J: The ... ground on which the plaintiff company has objected to the validity of the ... resolutions passed at this meeting is that they could only have been properly passed after the articles had been altered by special resolution. The company in general meeting could not appoint, and could not ratify, as from December 1901, the appointment of Fuke as managing director at £700 per annum as he had not the necessary qualification, and the maximum remuneration of the whole board was fixed by the articles at £500. The articles, until altered, bound the shareholders in general meeting as much as the board. The present case is unlike that of *Irvine v Union Bank of Australia*[16], to which reference was made, as in that case the limitation of the power of borrowing and mortgaging was merely a limitation of the authority of the directors, and not a limitation of the general powers of the company. It was argued that the acts of the directors in excess of their authority might be ratified by the company and rendered binding, and that contention succeeded. Articles must first be altered by special resolution before the altered articles can be acted upon: *Imperial Hydropathic Hotel Co, Blackpool v Hampson* (**84**).

The general meeting may also ratify an act of the directors which is voidable as an irregular exercise of their powers.[17]

100 Bamford v Bamford [1970] Ch 212, [1969] 1 All ER 969 (Court of Appeal)

The directors of Bamfords Ltd (referred to in the judgment as 'the company') issued 500,000 shares at par to F H Burgess Ltd, one of the principal distributors of the company's products. They did so in exercise of a power vested in them by the articles, but (so the plaintiffs alleged) improperly, being primarily for the purpose of forestalling a take-over bid by J C Bamford (Excavators) Ltd. When the validity of the allotment was challenged by the issue of a writ, the directors convened a shareholders' meeting at which the allotment was ratified and approved. (The newly issued shares were not

16 (1877) 2 App Cas 366, PC.
17 For a comparative study, see H Mason, 'Ratification of Directors' Acts' (1978) 41 MLR 61.

voted.[18]) The Court of Appeal held as a preliminary point of law, on the assumption that the facts alleged were true, that such a ratification would be effective.

HARMAN LJ: ... [This] is a tolerably plain case. It is trite law, I had thought, that if directors do acts, as they do every day, especially in private companies, which, perhaps because there is no quorum, or because their appointment was defective, or because sometimes there are no directors properly appointed at all, or because they are actuated by improper motives, they go on doing for years, carrying on the business of the company in the way in which, if properly constituted, they should carry it on, and then they find that everything has been so to speak wrongly done because it was not done by a proper board, such directors can, by making a full and frank disclosure and calling together the general body of the shareholders, obtain absolution and forgiveness of their sins; and provided the acts are not ultra vires the company as a whole everything will go on as if it had been done all right from the beginning. I cannot believe that that is not a commonplace of company law. It is done every day. Of course, if the majority of the general meeting will not forgive and approve, the directors must pay for it.

[His Lordship referred to *Regal (Hastings) Ltd v Gulliver* (132) and continued:] So it seems to me here that these directors, on the assumptions which we have to make, made this allotment in breach of their duty—mala fide, as it is said. They made it with an eye primarily on the exigencies of the takeover war and not with a single eye to the benefit of the company, and, therefore, it is a bad allotment. But it *is* an allotment. There is no doubt that the directors had power to allot these shares. There is no doubt that they did allot them. There is no doubt that the allottees are on the register and are for all purposes members of the company. The only question is whether the allotment, having been made, as one must assume, in bad faith, is voidable and can be avoided at the instance of the company—at their instance only and of no one else, because the wrong, if wrong it be, is a wrong done to the company. If that be right, the company, which had the right to recall the allotment, has also the right to approve of it and forgive it; and I see no difficulty at all in supposing that the ratification by the decision of December 15 in the general meeting of the company was a perfectly good 'whitewash' of that which up to that time was a voidable transaction. And that is the end of the matter ...

RUSSELL LJ delivered a concurring judgment.

KARMINSKI LJ concurred.

[For another part of the decision, see (236).]
[See also *North-West Transportation Co Ltd v Beatty* (129), *Burland v Earle* (242) and the *Multinational Gas* case (143).]

NOTES

(1) The principle established by these cases is subject to the limitations recognised in such cases as *Cook v Deeks* (131) and *Menier v Hooper's Telegraph Works* (243): the power to ratify cannot validate acts of fraud or expropriation.
(2) CA 1985, s 35(3) establishes a special rule where the directors' act would have

---

18 Compare *Hogg v Cramphorn Ltd* (140), and see the note above, p 125.

been beyond the company's capacity under the (now repealed) doctrine of ultra vires: such action may only be ratified by the company by *special* resolution. It is further provided that a *separate* special resolution is necessary to absolve the directors from any liabilty for breach of duty.

QUESTION

Suppose that the purchase of the pension in *Re Horsley & Weight Ltd* (**98**) had not been authorised by the company's memorandum. Would the informal assent of the two shareholders have been effective to satisfy the transaction under s 35(3)? Would it also have relieved them from liability for breach of duty?

The company in general meeting may act if there is no board competent or able (e g because of deadlock) to exercise the powers conferred upon it.

101 Barron v Potter [1914] 1 Ch 895 (Chancery Division)

The two directors of the company were not on speaking terms, so that effective board meetings could not be held. [This aspect of the case is dealt with above, (**92**).] The plaintiff, Canon Barron, had requisitioned a shareholders' meeting at which additional directors had purportedly been appointed, but the defendant objected that the power to make such appointments was vested by the company's articles in the directors. It was held that, in view of the deadlock, the power in question reverted to the general meeting, and so the appointments were valid.

WARRINGTON J [having held that no proper board meeting had been held: see above, (**92**)]: The question then arises, Was the resolution passed at the general meeting of the company a valid appointment? The argument against the validity of the appointment is that the articles of association of the company gave to the board of directors the power of appointing additional directors, that the company has accordingly surrendered the power, and that the directors alone can exercise it. It is true that the general point was so decided by Eve J in *Blair Open Hearth Furnace Co v Reigart*,[19] and I am not concerned to say that in ordinary cases where there is a board ready and willing to act it would be competent for the company to override the power conferred on the directors by the articles except by way of special resolution for the purpose of altering the articles. But the case which I have to deal with is a different one. For practical purposes there is no board of directors at all. The only directors are two persons, one of whom refuses to act with the other, and the question is, What is to be done under these circumstances? On this point I think that I can usefully refer to the judgment of the Court of Appeal in *Isle of Wight Rly Co v Tahourdin* [above, p 189], not for the sake of the decision, which depended on the fact that it was a case under the Companies Clauses Consolidation Act 1845, but for the sake of the observations of Cotton and Fry LJJ upon the effect of a deadlock such as arose in the present case. Cotton LJ says: 'Then it is said that there is no power in the meeting of shareholders to elect new directors, for that under the 89th

19 (1913) 108 LT 665.

section[20] the power would be in the remaining directors. The remaining directors would no doubt have that power if there was a quorum left. But suppose the meeting were to remove so many directors that a quorum was not left, what then follows? It has been argued that in that case, there being no board which could act, there would be no power of filling up the board so as to enable it to work. In my opinion that is utterly wrong. A power is given by the 89th section to the remaining directors "if they think proper so to do" to elect persons to fill up the vacancies. I do not see how it is possible for a non-existent body to think proper to fill up vacancies. In such a case a general meeting duly summoned for the purpose must have power to elect a new board so as not to let the business of the company be at a deadlock ...'. Those observations express a principle which seems to me to be as applicable to the case of a limited company incorporated under the Companies (Consolidation) Act 1908 as to a case falling under the Companies Clauses Consolidation Act 1845, and moreover to be a principle founded on plain common sense. If directors having certain powers are unable or unwilling to exercise them—are in fact a non-existent body for the purpose—there must be some power in the company to do itself that which under other circumstances would be otherwise done. The directors in the present case being unwilling to appoint additional directors under the power conferred on them by the articles, in my opinion, the company in general meeting has power to make the appointment ...

NOTE

A similar decision was reached in *Foster v Foster* [1916] 1 Ch 532, where there was a dispute over which of two directors should be appointed managing director, there being three directors in all. Although the power to appoint was conferred by the company's articles upon the directors, another article forbade a director from voting in respect of any contract in which he was interested. It was therefore not possible to carry any motion, in view of the disqualification of one director and the opposition of another. Peterson J held that in these circumstances competence to deal with the matter reverted from the board to the general meeting.

QUESTIONS

(1) Warrington J's reasoning is based largely on the decision in *Tahourdin*'s case which, as he points out, depended on the Companies Clauses Consolidation Act 1845 (above, p 189). Was he right to treat the case of a company registered under the Companies Acts as indistinguishable?
(2) Suppose a situation the reverse of that in *Barron v Potter* (**101**), where the shareholders cannot act but there is a board of directors capable of functioning. Could the directors exercise powers reserved by the articles to the general meeting? If not, what could be done to resolve matters?

Reform of the law

In this section we have seen how the constitutional provisions of modern companies, with the backing of the law, put all the say in the running of the company's business into the hands of the directors, and leave the shareholders a very minor part, typically

---

20 [Section 89 of the Act of 1845, which empowers the remaining directors to fill up interim vacancies on the board: compare Table A, article 79.]

the declaration of a dividend, the election or re-election of directors and the appointment of auditors—although even in these matters there may be little for them to do except rubber-stamp the recommendations of the directors. In other words, the role of the shareholder has become more and more that of a passive investor (no doubt partly from choice, but also from apathy and a sense of impotence) while power has progressively come to be concentrated in the directors, and especially the executive directors. The larger and more widely-dispersed the shareholding of the company, the more marked this difference between 'ownership' and 'control' usually is. (In the post-war period, the trend has in part been reversed by the growth of the institutional shareholders such as the pension funds, unit trusts and insurance companies.[1])

Reformers, motivated both by idealistic notions of 'shareholder democracy' as an end in itself, and also by a sense that directors do have too much power over 'other people's money', which is at times abused ('the unacceptable face of capitalism') have urged for new legislation that consciously seeks to put a larger share of real control into the hands of the shareholders. Thus, by the 1948 Act, shareholder approval was required for some kinds of 'golden handshake' (CA 1985, ss 312 ff), and the members were empowered to remove any director by ordinary resolution (CA 1985, s 303). The 1980 and 1981 Acts, implementing in part the second and fourth EEC Directives and in part some home-grown reforms, brought in many more provisions of this kind, e g CA 1985, s 80 (issue of additional capital), s 319 (directors' long-term service contracts), s 320 (directors' substantial property transactions) s 142 (serious losses of capital) and ss 164–166 (repurchase of shares): these are all matters in which companies legislation now insists that shareholders have a say. The procedures for these shareholder-authorisations are sometimes quite rigidly prescribed, and the consequences of failing to observe the formalities very severe. The costs of compliance, both in cash and in time, may prove to be a heavy price to pay for the gain in theoretical terms: certainly it is true to say that in many North American jurisdictions reformers have pressed for a reduction in shareholder-consents in the interests of business efficiency.

In some European companies codes, and most notably that of West Germany, the problems associated with the concentration of power in the hands of the board of directors have been tackled in another way. In these systems, there is provision for a 'two-tier' management structure, consisting of a managerial (or executive) board and a supervisory board, the former having charge of matters of day-to-day management and the latter being responsible for the control of the executive board and, in particular, having the power of appointment and removal of its personnel. The Draft Fifth EEC Directive on Company Law, in its original form (9 October 1972), contained proposals for the adoption of this model for public companies by all the member states of the European Economic Community. Such a change, if implemented in the United Kingdom, would have introduced a further 'organ' into our hierarchy of corporate management, and would have called for a basic reconsideration of the principles laid down by the cases cited above.

The whole question of the revision of board structure is now inseparably linked with the issue of employee participation in management, or 'industrial democracy'. In the United Kingdom, this question was referred by the Government to a committee ('the Bullock Committee'), which reported in 1977 (*Report of the Committee of Inquiry into Industrial Democracy* (Cmnd 6706), 1977). The members of this committee were unable to reach unanimity. The majority recommended that companies with a workforce of more than two thousand should be required by statute to have a single board of directors, to which shareholders and trade unions should appoint an equal number of representatives, supplemented by a third co-opted group (the so-called '2X+Y' formula). One member of the committee also favoured a unitary board, but thought that employee representation should be on a minority rather than a parity basis. Three members representing employer-interests recommended that there should

---

1 On this subject, see J H Farrar and M Russell, 'The Impact of Institutional Investment on Company Law' (1984) 5 Co Law 107.

be no mandatory change in company law, but that a legislative framework for a two-tier board should be introduced which might be adopted by companies on a voluntary basis. The recommendations of the majority did not meet with general support, and the Labour government to which the Bullock Committee reported published instead proposals which might have led to reforms involving the introduction of a two-tier board.[2] Subsequent Conservative administrations, however, have made it clear in their own consultative documents that they are opposed to the introduction of any compulsory legislation in this area, and that they believe that employee participation is best promoted voluntarily.

However, the matter is still being pressed within the EEC, in connection with both the Fifth Directive and another draft directive known as the 'Vredeling' Directive, and also with the proposed 'European Company Statute'. In more recent drafts, the original Fifth Directive requirement of mandatory representation of employees on a supervisory board has been modified: there are now alternatives proposed of (i) employee representation on a one-tier board, (ii) where there is a two-tier board, employee representation on the supervisory board, (iii) works councils and (iv) collective agreements giving analogous rights to employee representatives. The most recent draft also includes provisions governing the powers and duties of the various corporate organs and their members, and the rights of minorities, some of which would require extensive alterations of English company law. The Vredeling Directive (which applies to all the larger employers and not only to companies) is concerned with the question of informing and consulting employees on all decisions likely to have serious repercussions on the workforce.

In the meantime, the concern for employees' interests has been shown only by some very modest provisions in the Companies Acts, such as CA 1985, s 309 (directors to have regard to interests of employees) and CA 1985, s 719, IA 1986, s 187 (companies to have power to make over assets to employees on a cessation of business or in a liquidation). The directors' annual report must give certain information about its employment policies and employee involvement (CA 1985, Sch 7, Pts III–V). And there are inducements in the tax legislation to establish employee share-ownership schemes.

For further reading, see the *Biedenkopf Report on Co-determination in Germany* (1970, translated into English 1977); the EEC *Draft Fifth Directive on Company Law* (1989); EEC Commission Green Paper, *Employee Participation and Company Structure* (1975); S Simitis, 'Workers' Participation in the Enterprise—Transcending Company Law?' (1975) 38 MLR 1; P L Davies, 'Employee Representation on Company Boards and Participation in Corporate Planning' (1975) 38 MLR 254; E Batstone and P L Davies, *Industrial Democracy: the European Experience* (1976); R Lewis and J Clark, 'The Bullock Report' (1977) 40 MLR 323; T Hadden, *Company Law and Capitalism* (2nd edn, 1977), chapter 13; A J Boyle, 'The Draft Fifth Directive' (1992) 13 Co Law 6.

E. The doctrine of constructive notice and its abolition

In *Ernest v Nicholls* (1857) 6 HL Cas 401 the House of Lords ruled that a person dealing with a company should be deemed to have notice of that company's registered constitutional documents. The case itself concerned a deed of settlement company incorporated by registration under the Act of 1844, but the 'doctrine of constructive notice' which it established was naturally applied to companies formed with a memorandum and articles of association under the later Companies Acts: anyone dealing with a company was deemed to have notice of the contents of its memorandum and articles.

2 White Paper, *Industrial Democracy,* 1978.

It was not at all a necessary step to reason that, because the law gave everyone the *opportunity* to find out about a company's registered documents, there was a corresponding *duty* to do so; and perhaps only an English chancery judge, to whom the notion of constructive notice would have been so very familiar, would so readily have run the two ideas together, and disregarded the obvious non sequitur. Commercial law generally regards the concept of constructive notice with disfavour; and there is much to be said for the view that, since company transactions (especially as regards outsiders) are mostly of a commercial nature, a rule which deemed the world at large to have constructive notice of the registered documents should not have been allowed to gain a footing, still less to have become a cornerstone of the law. However, we must remember that, at the time when the doctrine was established, most companies (including the one concerned in *Ernest v Nicholls*) did not have limited liability, and so there was some reason in having a rule of law which called for those dealing with a company to make an effort to see that whoever purported to represent a company did indeed have the competence and authority to act for it. But once limited liability became the norm, and especially after it became the usual practice for shares to be paid up in full, the real trading risk shifted from the shareholders to the creditors, and the constructive notice doctrine ceased to have any proper justification. Businessmen need to make decisions promptly and for them the documents held by the registrar are accessible only at too great a cost in time and trouble. But for so long as the doctrine remained in place, there was a risk that it could be invoked against them, sometimes with patently unjust results: see e g *Re Jon Beauforte Ltd* **(71)**

The presumption of notice applied in the first place to the company's memorandum and articles, and to at least some special resolutions (*Irvine v Union Bank of Australia* (1877) 2 App Cas 366, PC). It was later extended to apply to the particulars of registered charges (see below, p 411). But it was never certain what other material held by the registrar came within the rule, or whether it extended to information which was available for inspection at the company's own registered office. These questions are now academic, in view of the changes effected by CA 1989.

Most jurisdictions have abolished the constructive notice rule altogether. In England, the argument for reform was first raised by the Jenkins Committee in 1962 as a necessary corollary to that committee's proposal for the reform of the ultra vires doctrine. But, as we have seen (above, p 128), no step was taken by the legislature until our entry to the EEC required certain modifications to be made to our domestic company law in order to comply with the First Directive. Accordingly, s 9(1) of the European Communities Act 1972 (above, p 151) not only gave protection to 'a person dealing with a company in good faith', where the *capacity* of the company was in issue, but also declared that in favour of such a person 'the power of the directors to bind the company shall be deemed to be free of any limitation under the memorandum or articles of association', at least as regards a transaction 'decided on by the directors'. But this first attempt at reform was flawed because phrases such as the last quoted raised doubts as to its scope, despite manful endeavours by the courts[3] to give effect to the spirit of the directive. So it was no surprise that when Professor Prentice's report on the reform of

3 See, e g *TCB Ltd v Gray* **(109)**.

the law of ultra vires was published (above, p 128), he recommended that the doctrine of constructive notice should be totally abolished.[4]

The reforms introduced by CA 1989 were no doubt intended to give effect to the Prentice recommendations and abolish the doctrine once and for all; but unhappily they have given rise to a great deal of uncertainty. Instead of a single provision consigning the rule to oblivion categorically and without qualification, we find that the draftsman has had two (or, if we count s 416, three) separate bites at the cherry—ss 35B and 711A.

Companies Act 1985

35B *No duty to enquire as to capacity of company or authority of directors*

A party to a transaction with a company is not bound to enquire as to whether it is permitted by the company's memorandum or as to any limitation on the powers of the board of directors to bind the company or authorise others to do so.

711A *Exclusion of deemed notice*

(1) A person shall not be taken to have notice of any matter merely because of its being disclosed in any document kept by the registrar of companies (and thus available for inspection) or made available by the company for inspection.
(2) This does not affect the question whether a person is affected by notice of any matter by reason of a failure to make such inquiries as ought reasonably to be made.

It will be seen that whereas s 35B is not expressly made subject to any qualification, the question-begging language of s 711A(2) is capable of being construed in such a way as largely to take away whatever benefit is conferred by s 711A(1). Subsection (2) may have been intended only to deal with the case where a person turns a 'Nelsonian' blind eye, or to preserve the former law where someone has been 'put on inquiry', but the vague wording gives no real clue as to what is intended. In consequence, there has been much uncertainty as to the scope of the reforms which CA 1989 has actually brought about. It would seem reasonable to say that s 35B should be treated as self-standing and that its clear words ought not to be read down by introducing into that section the qualification imposed by s 711A(2): in other words, that so long as the point at issue involves only *restrictions imposed by the company's memorandum* or *limitations on the powers of the board* to bind the company or authorise others to do so, no 'further inquiries' need be made. But it appears that those who in the past have been in the habit of making thorough searches and inquiries before concluding transactions with companies—notably solicitors and banks—are not yet persuaded that the new law has made it safe for them to discontinue this practice.

4 This recommendation did not extend to the register of charges, which was outside Professor Prentice's remit, and which has since been the subject of a separate reform in the new CA 1985, s 416: see below, p 411.

F. The 'indoor management' rule

The doctrine of constructive notice might have been challenged much earlier in its history but for the fact that its harshest effects were mitigated by the development, almost contemporaneously with the doctrine itself, of the 'indoor management' or 'internal management' rule, sometimes known as the rule in *Royal British Bank v Turquand* (**102**). This rule allows a person dealing with a company to assume, in the absence of circumstances putting him on inquiry, that all matters of internal management and procedure have been duly complied with (*Omnia praesumuntur rite et solemniter esse acta*). So, although under the doctrine of constructive notice such a person was taken to be aware of the provisions of the company's memorandum and articles, and thus of any restrictions contained in those documents, he was not bound to inquire further. He could take it for granted that its officers had been duly appointed, that meetings had been properly summoned and conducted and that resolutions had been passed by requisite majorities.

The development of the rule, and of various limitations on its application, can be seen in the cases (**102**) to (**108**) which follow.

The question must be asked: what is the standing of the rule, and the scope for its application, if we accept that the doctrine of constructive notice has been abolished? If the rule was itself only a qualification to the doctrine, will it not have been swept away also? For various reasons, it is probably wrong to take this view.

In the first place, although it is true that the rule did operate to mitigate the effects of the doctrine of constructive notice, this was never its only function. It is a rule of wider scope. A person dealing with a company is, and always has been, subject to uncertainty as to whether its officers have been properly appointed, its resolutions duly passed, etc, whether or not the question arises in connection with a provision in the company's memorandum or articles; but he has to take it for granted that the internal affairs *have* been regularly conducted (and, for that matter, must accept that the company's internal affairs are none of his business). The issues which arose in *Mahony v East Holyford Mining Co* (**103**), for instance, did not depend upon the bank having had knowledge or notice of any particular provision in the company's constitutional documents, and the same issues could still arise today after the doctrine of constructive notice has been abolished.

Secondly, although the indoor management rule is commonly regarded as operating only in favour of a person dealing with a company in good faith (see, e g, *Rolled Steel Products (Holdings) Ltd v British Steel Corpn* (**105**)), the presumption of regularity in fact applies in a much wider range of situations. It may be necessary to fall back on the common law rule for the protection of someone who is not 'dealing with' a company (s 35A) or a 'party to a transaction' with it (s 35B), as in the Australian case *Australian Capital Television Pty Ltd v Minister of Transport and Communications* (1989) 7 ACLC 525, where the *Turquand* rule was applied in favour of a third party.

However, it is plain that the occasions on which the indoor management rule will be pleaded are likely to be rare in the future, for a number of reasons.
(1) There will no longer be any need to raise it, as so often in the past, by way of rejoinder to a contention that the person was affected by the constructive notice doctrine.
(2) In any case, since the important decision in *Freeman & Lockyer v*

Buckhurst Park Properties (Mangal) Ltd (**115**) it has become very common to use arguments based on the law of agency rather than the internal management rule to resolve questions in this area.

(3) Furthermore, there are now a considerable number of statutory provisions designed to protect third parties against possible internal irregularities in a company's decision-making. See, e g, CA 1985, ss 35A(3), 322A(8) (limitations on directors' powers deriving from the memorandum and articles of association, shareholders' resolutions, class resolutions, and shareholder agreements), s 36A(6) (documents purporting to be signed by two officers binding in favour of 'purchaser'), s 184(3)(b) (certification of an instrument of transfer of shares) and s 285 (directors or managers defectively appointed). The more such specific provisions there are, and the more widely they are drafted, the less will be the need to fall back on the common law.

Along with the *Turquand* rule itself, the present scope of the 'exceptions' to the rule must similarly be clarified. It is plain from the *Rolled Steel* case (**105**) that a person who knows or has notice of the irregularity in question or has been put on inquiry (*B Liggett (Liverpool) Ltd v Barclays Bank Ltd* (**104**)) will continue to be barred from relying on the rule. But the former 'exception' which denied protection to a person who could have discovered the irregularity by inspecting the company's registered documents (*Irvine v Union Bank of Australia* (1877) 2 App Cas 366, PC) has plainly been abolished along with the constructive notice rule.

A person dealing with a company is entitled to assume, in the absence of facts putting him on inquiry, that there has been due compliance with all matters of internal management and procedure required by the articles.

102 Royal British Bank v Turquand (1856) 6 E & B 327 (Exchequer Chamber)

Turquand was sued, as the official manager of a coal mining and railway company incorporated under the Act of 1844, on a bond for £2,000 which had been given by the company to the plaintiff bank to secure its drawings on current account. The bond was given under the seal of the company and signed by two directors and the secretary, but the company alleged that under the terms of its registered deed of settlement the directors had power to borrow only such sums as had been authorised by a general resolution of the company, and in this case no sufficiently specific resolution had been passed. The Court of Exchequer Chamber, affirming the judgment of the Court of Queen's Bench, held that even so the company was bound by the bond.

JERVIS CJ: I am of opinion that the judgment of the Court of Queen's Bench ought to be affirmed. I incline to think that the question which has been principally argued both here and in that court does not necessarily arise, and need not be determined. My impression is (though I will not state it as a fixed opinion) that the resolution set forth in the replication goes far enough to satisfy the requisites of the deed of settlement. The deed allows the directors to borrow on bond such sum or sums of money as shall from time to time, by a resolution passed at a general meeting of the company, be authorised to be borrowed: and the replication shows a resolution, passed at a general meeting, authorising the directors to borrow on bond such sums for such periods and at such rates of interest as they might deem expedient, in accordance with the deed of settlement and the Act of Parliament; but the resolution does not otherwise define the amount to be borrowed. That seems to me enough. If that be so, the other question does not arise. But whether it be so or not we need not decide; for it seems to us that the plea, whether we consider it as a confession and avoidance or a special non est factum, does not raise any objection to this advance as against the company. We may now take for granted that the dealings with these companies are not like dealings with other partnerships, and that the parties dealing with them are bound to read the statute and the deed of settlement. But they are not bound to do more. And the party here, on reading the deed of settlement, would find, not a prohibition from borrowing, but a permission to do so on certain conditions. Finding that the authority might be made complete by a resolution, he would have a right to infer the fact of a resolution authorising that which on the face of the document appeared to be legitimately done.

POLLOCK CB, ALDERSON and BRAMWELL BB, and CRESSWELL and CROWDER JJ concurred.

103 Mahony v East Holyford Mining Co (1875) LR 7 HL 869 (House of Lords)

The liquidator of the respondent company sued Mahony as public officer of the National Bank, Dublin, alleging that the bank had paid moneys from the company's account without due authorisation. The bank had acted upon a letter signed by one Wall as secretary of the company, enclosing a copy of a 'resolution' of the board of directors. This 'resolution' named three directors, and instructed the bank to pay cheques signed by any two of them and countersigned by the secretary. Specimen signatures were attached. The instruction was entirely in accordance with the company's memorandum and articles, and would have been in order, except that there had never been any proper appointment of directors or a secretary by the company, the roles having been simply assumed by those who had formed the company. The House of Lords held that the company was bound by cheques which the bank had honoured in accordance with the instructions contained in the letter.

LORD HATHERLEY: My Lords, it appears to me ... that the judgment in this case should be entered for the defendant.

It is a point of very great importance that those who are concerned in joint stock companies and those who deal with them should be aware of what is essential to the due performance of their duties, both as customers or dealers with the company, and as persons forming the company, and dealing with the outside world respectively. On the one hand, it is settled by a series of decisions, of which *Ernest v Nicholls*[5] is one and *Royal British Bank v Turquand* (102) a later one, that those who deal with joint stock companies are bound to take notice of that which I may call the external position of the company. Every joint stock company has its memorandum and articles of association; every joint stock company, or nearly every one, I imagine (unless it adopts the form provided by the statute, and that comes to the same thing) has its

5 (1857) 6 HL Cas 401, HL.

partnership deed under which it acts.[6] Those articles of association and that partnership deed are open to all who are minded to have any dealings whatsoever with the company, and those who so deal with them must be affected with notice of all that is contained in those two documents.

After that, the company entering upon its business and dealing with persons external to it, is supposed on its part to have all those powers and authorities which, by its articles of association and by its deed, it appears to possess; and all that the directors do with reference to what I may call the indoor management of their own concern, is a thing known to them and known to them only; subject to this observation, that no person dealing with them has a right to suppose that anything has been or can be done that is not permitted by the articles of association or by the deed . . .

This being the case, a banker dealing with a company must be taken to be acquainted with the manner in which, under the articles of association, the moneys of the company may be drawn out of his bank for the purposes of the company. My noble and learned friend on the woolsack has read those articles by which, in this case, the bankers were informed that cheques might be drawn upon the bank by three directors of the company. And the bankers must also be taken to have had knowledge, from the articles, of the duties of the directors, and the mode in which the directors were to be appointed. But, after that, when there are persons conducting the affairs of the company in a manner which appears to be perfectly consonant with the articles of association, then those so dealing with them, externally, are not to be affected by any irregularities which may take place in the internal management of the company. They are entitled to presume that that of which only they can have knowledge, namely, the external acts, are rightly done, when those external acts purport to be performed in the mode in which they ought to be performed. For instance, when a cheque is signed by three directors, they are entitled to assume that those directors are persons properly appointed for the purpose of performing that function, and have properly performed the function for which they have been appointed . . .

But what do the bankers find in the case now before us? They find on the face of the deed how the directors are to be appointed; they find that the first directors are to be appointed by the majority of the first seven persons (that is to say, by four of them) who signed the articles of association; they find, both by the articles of association and by the second prospectus which was issued . . . that the place of business was fixed at 12, Grafton Street. That was an external fact with which they might well acquaint themselves. They might well have been justified in entertaining doubts as to whether they should transact business with the company if they had found it carrying on business in any other place, supposing they had not been made acquainted with any change of abode. But they go to No 12, Grafton Street, and they find there an office, and they find there a person acting as secretary, who is the same person as the person described as the secretary in the second prospectus, issued after the company was formed. They find there certain persons in constant attendance, namely, six out of the seven persons who signed the

6 [Lord Hatherley's reference to the company's 'partnership deed' is obscure. Companies incorporated before the Act of 1856 registered a deed of settlement instead of a memorandum and articles of association, and this could properly be referred to as a 'partnership deed'; but the allusion to a 'form provided by the statute' can only be to what is now Table A. It seems best to assume that by 'articles' his Lordship means 'memorandum' and by 'deed of partnership', 'articles'.]

articles of association. I believe all the seven were at one time or another in attendance, but six were there constantly. And one of the witnesses says (I need not turn to his evidence for this purpose), that Mr Hoare and another person, as to whom they were informed that they were the directors, were there acting as directors. Finding then a certain number of persons acting as directors, who had been represented to them to be directors, and finding four other persons who might well have elected them to be directors (having the authority and the power to do so), on the spot daily, sitting by and seeing them performing those directorial functions, what conclusion could they come to but that those directors had been duly appointed? ...

Then the bankers get a notice from a person who calls himself the secretary, and who says he gives them a resolution under the authority of which, and according to the form there stated, the cheques are to be drawn. I pass by altogether, as really immaterial in the inquiry, the circumstance that a fraud may have been intended on the part of the company in the way in which the letter was expressed. That could have no effect upon the bankers; the jury found by the verdict that the bankers acted entirely in good faith upon the representations contained in that letter. It has been noticed that that letter does not mention, in words, that the resolution was passed by a vote of the board of directors. But the subject-matter of it was the drawing of cheques; the mode of providing for the drawing of cheques is treated of in the articles, and it is there laid down that that duty is to be performed by the directors. The bankers were furnished with the names of three so-called 'directors', who sent their signatures in order that the bankers might have an opportunity of verifying the signatures upon any cheques that might be drawn. If the bankers went there and found the secretary sitting there, as the evidence tells us he did all day long from ten till six, and performing the duties of a secretary, and if they found some of these other gentlemen sitting there appearing to be performing the duties of directors, and if they saw those four other gentlemen who might have appointed them as directors sitting there also, witnessing them performing the duties of directors, I must ask what more could be required on the part of those who were dealing with the company, and who had obtained all the external information they could upon the subject. If we are not now to hold that the bankers are to be protected in honouring the drafts of these three persons, who, they were informed, were authorised to draw cheques, I do not know how any person, dealing with a company, can be safe against being bound to inquire into all the minute transactions which may have taken place indoors ...

LORD CAIRNS LC and LORDS CHELMSFORD and PENZANCE delivered concurring opinions.

The presumption of regularity cannot be relied on by a person who has notice of the irregularity or has been put on inquiry.

104 B Liggett (Liverpool) Ltd v Barclays Bank Ltd [1928] 1 KB 48 (King's Bench Division)

The original directors of the plaintiff company were Liggett and Melia, and the articles empowered the directors at any time to appoint an additional director. The bank was instructed to honour cheques signed by the two directors, but Liggett was in the habit of issuing cheques signed only by himself which Melia would subsequently countersign at the bank, sometimes after they had been paid. In July 1925 Melia instructed the bank that cheques were not to be paid without his signature, but the former practice was at times still followed. In September 1925 Liggett as chairman of the board wrote informing the bank that his wife had been appointed an additional director. Melia was unaware of this letter and of the alleged 'appointment' of Mrs Liggett. The bank thereafter honoured cheques signed by Mr and Mrs Liggett. The bank was sued by the company for paying these cheques without authority; and it was held liable, on the ground that it had been put on inquiry.

WRIGHT J: The primary defence set up by the defendant bank is one based upon an application of the well-known rule which is often referred to as the rule in the *Royal British Bank v Turquand* (**102**), a rule which has been applied in a great many cases to which I have been referred ... The rule as relied on by the defendant bank is that the defendant bank having had the articles of association were entitled to assume that the notice of 1 September 1925 sent to them by the chairman was a valid and proper notice, because according to the articles of association it was possible if the proper steps in the matter of internal management had been taken by the directors of the company that Mrs Liggett should have been duly appointed an additional director, as the notice stated. I am relieved from any examination of the exact definition of this very respectable but perhaps somewhat ambiguous rule of law, because the plaintiff company in answer to that contention have alleged that the defendant bank in any case is not entitled to the benefit of that rule by reason of the fact that the defendant bank were put on inquiry by the circumstances of the case and were negligent in not investigating the position before they accepted and acted upon the notice of the appointment of a new director. On that issue I put two questions to the jury, and the questions were these: 'Was the bank put on inquiry, whether the appointment of Mrs Liggett was in order?' The jury answered: 'Yes.' 'Secondly, whether the bank was guilty of negligence in paying the bills and cheques complained of?' and again the jury answered 'Yes.' Whatever may be the exact scope of the rule in *Turquand*'s case I think it is quite clear on principle and on the authorities I have already referred to that it can never be relied upon by a person who is put on inquiry. The rule proceeds on a presumption that certain acts have been regularly done, and if the circumstances are such that the person claiming the benefit of the rule is really put on inquiry, if there are circumstances which debar that person from relying on the prima facie presumption, then it is clear, I think, that he cannot claim the benefit of the rule; and if, therefore, the answers of the jury to the questions which I put to them stand, it is clear, I think, that this defence will not avail the defendants here ...

105 Rolled Steel Products (Holdings) Ltd v British Steel Corpn [1986] Ch 246, [1985] 3 All ER 52 (Court of Appeal)

[For the facts and another part of the decision, see above, (**70**).]

SLADE LJ: Mr Shenkman unquestionably had a personal interest in the proposed guarantee and debenture which fell for consideration at the board meeting of the plaintiff on 22 January 1969. Under article 17 of the plaintiff's articles of association he was entitled to vote as a director in regard to these transactions and to be counted in the quorum of two directors required by article 18(a), notwithstanding his personal interest, if, but only if he declared his interest 'in manner provided by s 199 of the Companies Act 1948' [CA 1985, s 317]. The manner provided by that section is this. Under s 199(1) the director has to declare 'the nature of his interest at a meeting of the directors of the company'. Section 199(2), so far as material, provides:

> In the case of a proposed contract the declaration required by this section to be made by a director shall be made at the meeting of the directors at which the question of entering into the contract is first taken into consideration ...

The judge, as I have said, accepted the evidence of Mr Shenkman that there had been no meeting of the board of the plaintiff before 22 January 1969 at which the desirability of the plaintiff giving a guarantee had been considered; and that he had made no declaration of his personal interest at the board meeting of 22 January 1969. I can see no grounds for challenging either of these findings of fact. Mr Shenkman and Mr Ilya Shenkman were the only two directors present and voting at the last-mentioned board meeting ...

In these circumstances, on the facts as found by the judge, it is, in my opinion, clear that the no due authorisation point as pleaded in the statement of claim is well-founded in law, and the only averment pleaded in the unamended defence in answer to that point, namely that 'the guarantee and the debenture were duly executed by the plaintiff', is *not* well founded in law.

The only remaining questions in this context are whether the judge was right by his judgment to give leave to amend the defence so as to plead that Colvilles was entitled to rely on the resolution as a resolution passed at a properly constituted board of directors at which, Mr Shenkman and Mr Ilya Shenkman having been the only directors present, a proper disclosure of Mr Shenkman's interest had been made; and, if so, to decide that this amendment provided a complete answer in law to the claim against the defendants, in so far as that claim was founded on the no due authorisation point.

The possible relevance of the rule in *Royal British Bank v Turquand* (**103**) in the present context is obvious. The following statement of the rule taken from *Halsbury's Laws of England,* 2nd ed, vol V (1932), p 423, was approved by the House of Lords in *Morris v Kanssen*[7] per Lord Simonds:

> ... persons contracting with a company and dealing in good faith may assume that acts within its constitution and powers have been properly and duly performed and are not bound to inquire whether acts of internal management have been regular.

Lord Simonds later pointed out the rationale of the rule: 'The wheels of business will not go smoothly round unless it may be assumed that that is in order which appears to be in order.'

However, s 9(1) of the European Communities Act 1972 [CA 1985, s 35] apart, persons dealing with a company registered under the Companies Acts must be taken not only to have read both the memorandum and articles of a company, but to have understood them according to their proper meaning: see *Palmer's Company Law,* 23rd ed (1982), vol 1, para 28–02 and the cases there cited.

Colvilles[8] and BSC, therefore, must be taken to have known that, under

---

7 [1946] AC 459 at 474, [1946] 1 All ER 586 at 592 (below, p 211).
8 [Colvilles was a steel company which was later taken over by BSC.]

the articles of the plaintiff, a quorum of two was required for the transaction of the business of its directors, and of the provisions of those articles relating to the declaration of a personal interest. They were well aware of the personal interest of Mr Shenkman in the transactions proposed on 22 January 1969.

The signed minutes of the board meeting of that day, a copy of which was subsequently supplied to Colvilles' solicitors (and indeed had been drafted by them) made no mention whatever of any declaration of a personal interest by Mr Shenkman. Since Colvilles and its legal advisers must be taken to have had knowledge of the relevant provisions of the plaintiff's articles, they must also be taken to have known that the resolution could not have been validly passed *unless Mr Shenkman had duly declared his personal interest at that board meeting or a previous board meeting.*

If, therefore, the defendants are to be allowed both to take and succeed on the *Turquand*'s case point, this must mean that, in the circumstances subsisting in late January 1969, they were *as a matter of law* entitled to assume (contrary to the fact and without further inquiry) that Mr Shenkman had duly declared his personal interest either at the board meeting of 22 January 1969 or at some previous board meeting of the plaintiff.

This contention might well have been unanswerable if the rule in *Turquand*'s case were an absolute and unqualified rule of law, applicable in all circumstances. But, as the statement of the rule quoted above indicates, it is not. It is a rule which only applies in favour of persons dealing with the company in good faith.[9] If such persons have notice of the relevant irregularity, they cannot rely on the rule ...

[His Lordship held that, in any event, the judge had been wrong to allow the amendment to the pleadings.]

LAWTON and BROWNE-WILKINSON LJJ delivered concurring judgments.

The presumption of regularity cannot be relied on by 'insiders', i e persons who by virtue of their position in the company are in a position to know whether or not the internal regulations have been observed.

106 Howard v Patent Ivory Manufacturing Co (1888) 38 Ch D 156 (Chancery Division)

[The facts appear from the judgment.]

KAY J: But then a very much more serious question has been raised, and that is this. These debentures were issued by the directors, and it is said that the power of the directors to issue debentures is limited, and the limit is very plain when you look at article 95, which is as follows. The directors are empowered 'to borrow from time to time on behalf of the company such sums of money, not exceeding in the whole at any one time £1,000, as the directors think necessary or advisable, also to raise such further moneys as may be authorised from time to time by resolution of any general meeting of shareholders summoned for the purpose'. So that when the directors have borrowed up to £1,000, and there are existing loans unpaid to that amount, the borrowing power of the directors is exhausted, and no more can be borrowed without the authority of a general meeting of shareholders. Then

9 [See the comment above, p 203.]

the next clause is, 'To secure repayment of any moneys so borrowed, together with the interest, by debentures'. Therefore the directors could only issue valid debentures for moneys borrowed by themselves, without the assent of a general meeting, to the extent of the borrowing power. Beyond that, in order to authorise themselves to borrow and to issue debentures, there must be the assent of the general meeting.

Now in this case, unfortunately for the holders of these debentures, they are all directors, and therefore the well-known authorities which make it unnecessary to see whether the internal regulations of a company have been observed or not do not apply; because, of course, the directors must be taken to know that the internal requirements of the company had not been observed in the case of these debentures. Accordingly, I am very sorry to say that I cannot treat the debentures as valid to the extent of more than £1,000. How that sum is to be allotted between the different parties I do not know. I have heard nothing on that point. I must treat the issue of the debentures as being invalid within the knowledge of the directors beyond the amount of £1,000. There must be a declaration that the first ten only of the thirty-five debentures, taking them according to their numbers, are valid.

NOTE

In *Morris v Kanssen* [1946] AC 459, [1946] 1 All ER 586, C and S, who were purporting to act as the company's directors although they had not been properly appointed, resolved to co-opt M as a third director; and C, S and M then allotted shares to M. The House of Lords ruled that the fact that M himself had acted as a director in this transaction precluded him from relying on the rule in *Turquand*'s case, even though in the circumstances he had plainly had no time to make any inquiry into the company's affairs, and certainly not enough to have enabled him to discover the irregularities in the standing of C and S as directors. It was also pointed out that if the items on the directors' agenda had been taken in a different order, with the allotment preceding the appointment of M to the board, he would have been protected as an 'outsider'. In comparison with this decision, the following case seems to have been remarkably indulgent to the plaintiff.

A person who, though a director of a company, is not acting as such may be treated as an 'outsider' for the purpose of the rule.

107 Hely-Hutchinson v Brayhead Ltd [1968] 1 QB 549, [1967] 3 All ER 98 (Chancery Division and Court of Appeal)

[For other parts of the decision, see **(116)** and **(130)**.]

The plaintiff (referred to in the judgment as Lord Suirdale) was suing to enforce two letters of indemnity which had been negotiated and signed on behalf of the defendant company by its chairman, Richards. Roskill J in this part of his judgment rejected an argument that the plaintiff, merely because he happened to be a director of the defendant company, should be presumed to know that Richards had not been authorised[10] to act in the matter.

ROSKILL J referred to passages in the judgments in *Morris v Kanssen* (above)

10 The Court of Appeal held that Richards *had* authority (see below, **(116)**), and so found it unnecessary to consider this question.

and *Howard v Patent Ivory Co* (**106**), and continued: The present defendants rely upon this statement of the law as showing that a director dealing with a company of which he is a director must be taken for all purposes to have knowledge of the powers and obligations of and limitations on those powers under the articles. As I read Lord Simonds' speech in *Morris v Kanssen,* his Lordship was expressly dealing with a case where the director, Morris, had been acting on behalf of the company in relation to the matter there in question, namely, the purported allotment of shares to himself. Similarly in *Howard*'s case the directors, including Jordan, were acting as directors on behalf of the company in connection with the issue and allotment of the debentures to Jordan and others. But do those cases go so far as to compel a court to say that where a director of a company not acting as such but in his personal and individual capacity makes a contract with that company which in relation to that contract acts not by that director but by another director who is in fact the chairman and chief executive of that company, the individual director is to be treated as possessed of constructive knowledge (for Lord Suirdale had no actual knowledge) of any defect in the authority of that other director, so as to exclude the operation of the rule in *Turquand*'s case (**103**), notwithstanding that other director's representations as to his authority? It is quite plain that Lord Simonds was not dealing with such a case, because he said: 'Your Lordships have not in this case to consider what the result might be if such a director had not himself purported to act on behalf of the company in the unauthorised transaction.' Nor do I think that Kay J [in *Howard*'s case] had such a case in mind.

Lord Suirdale did not act on behalf of Brayhead in relation to the allegedly unauthorised transaction. But both Mr Finer and, in his admirable argument following his leader, Mr Instone said it was enough to exclude the operation of the rule in *Turquand*'s case that Lord Suirdale was a party to the transaction and was a director of Brayhead, even though he did not act for Brayhead. With the utmost respect to that argument and the skill with which it was advanced both by Mr Finer and Mr Instone, I find nothing in these cases which compels me to go so far as they have invited me to go. In some cases—and of course *Morris*'s case is one and *Howard*'s case is another—a director is quite plainly anything but a 'stranger', or an 'outsider', or a 'third party', but I do not think the mere fact that a man who is a director of a company makes a contract with that company in a capacity other than that of a director automatically affects him, in the capacity in which he is contracting, with constructive knowledge of such disabilities and limitations as he might be deemed to know were he also acting for the company in the transaction in question. As Mr MacCrindle said in the course of his reply, to extend this doctrine in the way suggested would have very far-reaching ramifications on ordinary day-to-day business transactions and would or might involve very often considerable inquiry before a contract could be signed as to what the respective position and authority was of a particular individual by whom it was proposed that a contract should be signed. I regard the decisions in *Morris v Kanssen* and in *Howard*'s case as decisions where, on the facts of those particular cases, the rights sought to be enforced by the plaintiffs concerned arose from acts done by them as directors which were so closely interwoven with their duties and acts as directors as to make it impossible for the directors involved to say that they were not for all purposes to be treated as possessed of knowledge of the limitations upon their powers as directors. In the present case Brayhead's agreement with

Lord Suirdale had nothing to do with his duties and obligations as a director of Brayhead. What he was doing was to agree to advance money to an associated company of Brayhead of which he was chairman and managing director against a guarantee and indemnity from Brayhead, who were expected to become the parent company of that associated company. He was acting, as I think, otherwise than in his capacity as a director of Brayhead in making that agreement. He was acting as an individual, for it was he who was going to advance the money in consideration of the agreement into which Mr Richards was purporting to enter on behalf of Brayhead. He was going to be the other contracting party. I think, therefore, that this argument fails . . .

The presumption of regularity does not apply in the case of forgery.

108 Ruben v Great Fingall Consolidated [1906] AC 439 (House of Lords)

The question was whether the company was estopped by a share certificate to which the company's seal had been affixed without authority and the forged signatures of two directors added.

[For a more detailed account of this case, see (**224**).]

LORD LOREBURN LC: I cannot see upon what principle your Lordships can hold that the defendants are liable in this action. The forged certificate is a pure nullity. It is quite true that persons dealing with limited liability companies are not bound to inquire into their indoor management, and will not be affected by irregularities of which they had no notice. But this doctrine, which is well established, applies only to irregularities that otherwise might affect a genuine transaction. It cannot apply to a forgery . . .

[See also *Kreditbank Cassel v Schenkers* (**113**) and *South London Greyhound Racecourses Ltd v Wake* (below, p 440).]

NOTE

The dictum of Lord Loreburn is probably too wide, for the company may (it is submitted) be estopped from relying on the fact of forgery if the forged document has been represented as genuine by an officer or agent of the company having actual or ostensible authority to do so. The *British Thomson-Houston* case (**114**) shows that an officer with no apparent authority to act on behalf of the company may yet have actual authority to represent that his own act is authorised. The *Kreditbank* and *South London Greyhound Racecourses* cases are even less defensible, for the 'forgeries' in those cases consisted of documents to which genuine signatures had been written without authority. The High Court of Australia, in *Northside Developments Pty Ltd v Registrar-General* (1990) 64 ALJR 427 has held that the 'forgery' exception to the *Turquand* rule is not applicable in such a case, and that it should be governed by the normal rules of agency. It is in any event difficult to reconcile these cases with the general rules governing vicarious liability for an agent's fraud, as laid down in, e g *Lloyd v Grace Smith & Co* [1912] AC 716, HL. (See the discussion below, p 440.)

G. Application of agency principles to companies

The 'indoor management' rule, or rule in *Royal British Bank v Turquand*, appears in its simplest form in relation to such questions as the due execution of documents, the passing of authorising resolutions and the regularity of elections and appointments. In all these cases, if nothing has occurred which is evidently contrary to the provisions of the registered documents, the outsider may assume the regularity of all matters internal to the company and its organisation. Where, however, the issue is whether a single person has, or is deemed to have, authority to represent the company as its representative or agent, these questions of indoor management may become confused with other questions arising from the ordinary laws of agency. The position may be illustrated by various examples. If a person has been appointed to the office of secretary or managing director and acts as such, but there was some technical defect in the procedure by which he was appointed, the indoor management rule will apply so as to protect an outsider dealing with him. On the other hand, when a person has been appointed as the company's agent either specially, to act in a particular transaction, or generally, e g to manage a branch office, the questions whether he has exceeded the authority conferred upon him and, if so, whether the company as principal is nevertheless bound vis-à-vis a third party, are matters which ought to be determined by the ordinary rules of agency. A more complex problem arises when a person holding *some* office in the company (commonly a director) purports to act on behalf of the company in a matter which is not within the scope of such an officer's usual activities, but *would* be within the normal functions of another office to which he might have been appointed—e g a managing director. Such a person may, depending on the evidence, be regarded as either (1) a managing director defectively appointed, (2) a person held out by the company[11] as a managing director although never appointed as such, or (3) an officer of limited powers who has without authority simply exceeded those powers. On the first view, the matter is one governed by the indoor management rule;[12] on the second, by the rules of agency;[13] and in either case the third party with whom he deals will be protected. On the third view, the company will not be bound whichever set of rules is applied. It is perhaps not surprising that the cases sometimes fail to keep the *Turquand* and the agency principles distinct.

The four cases which follow seem to have been argued and decided primarily on the basis of the indoor management rule, but they should all now be reconsidered in the light of the judgments in *Freeman & Lockyer v Buckhurst Park Properties (Mangal) Ltd* (**115**), where the problems raised in cases of this nature were reformulated as issues of agency.

---

11 He may be 'held out' by the company's documents; by the board or other duly constituted authority; he may in rare cases (see (**114**)) lawfully have authority to hold *himself* out; or there may be circumstances which estop the board or other organ of the company from denying that he is a managing director.

12 It has been held that, in order to succeed under this head, the third party must have actual knowledge of the article conferring the power to delegate: see (**112**).

13 In this case, knowledge of the existence of a power to delegate is unnecessary.

111 Biggerstaff v Rowatt's Wharf Ltd [1896] 2 Ch 93 (Court of Appeal)

In consideration of cash advances made to the defendant company, Davy (the defendant's managing director) signed letters hypothecating various debts to Harvey, Brand & Co. By the articles the directors (who had power to hypothecate debts) were authorised to appoint a managing director and to delegate to him such of their powers as they thought fit. There was no minute showing what powers had been delegated to Davy and none of his appointment as managing director, but he had acted as such. The Court of Appeal (reversing North J) held that the hypothecations were valid.

[Another part of the decision is cited below, (**194**).]

LOPES LJ: The question as to the hypothecation of debts is quite distinct. It is said that the managing director had no power to hypothecate them. There is no doubt that Mr Davy was the managing director and acted as such, and according to the articles the directors could have given him the power which he purported to exercise. There is an absence of evidence that they had done so; but is that enough to make his acts void? In *Lindley on Companies,* 5th ed, p 159, the law is thus laid down: 'Upon principle, therefore, where persons are in fact employed by directors to transact business for a company the authority of those persons to bind a company within the scope of their employment cannot be denied by the company, unless—(1) their employment was altogether beyond the powers of the directors; or unless, (2) the persons employed have been appointed irregularly, and those who dealt with them had notice of the irregularity. Where the power to appoint an agent for a given purpose exists, irregularity in its exercise is immaterial to a person dealing with the agent bona fide and without notice of the irregularity in his appointment' . . .

Every word of that applies here. It cannot be said but that Mr Davy was acting within the limits of his apparent authority, or that Harvey, Brand & Co were not acting bona fide, or that they had not a right to assume that Mr Davy was duly appointed.

LINDLEY and KAY LJJ delivered concurring judgments.

112 Houghton & Co v Nothard Lowe & Wills Ltd [1927] 1 KB 246 (Court of Appeal)

[Affirmed on other grounds by the House of Lords, [1928] AC 1.]

Mr Maurice Lowe was a director of the defendant company and also of another company referred to in the judgments as 'the preserving company'. As security for an advance made by the plaintiffs to the preserving company, Lowe purported to assign to the plaintiffs the right to receive and dispose of all the fruit shipments consigned to either of the companies; but he had no actual authority to commit the defendant company to such a contract. The secretary of the defendant company later wrote a letter to the plaintiffs purporting to confirm the agreement, but he too had no actual authority to do so.[14] The plaintiffs claimed the right to enforce the contract against the

14 More recently, the company secretary has been recognised as filling a more important role than was so in an earlier period: see below, (**148**). An outsider might well be entitled to rely on such a letter today, as being within the secretary's usual authority; but at present the courts have only conceded the secretary's wider authority in administrative matters, while leaving the question of 'commercial' communications open.

defendant company. Wright J held that it was bound by the act of Lowe who, though only an ordinary director and not a managing director, was 'the representative and plenipotentiary' of the defendant company; the board was empowered by the articles to delegate its functions to a single director, and it was immaterial that the plaintiffs had no knowledge of the articles. The Court of Appeal reversed his decision.

[Part of the judgment of the House of Lords is cited above, (**38**).]

SARGANT LJ: Turning now to a more minute examination of the judgment of Wright J, the steps by which he arrives at the conclusion that the defendant company were bound as towards the plaintiffs are as follows. [His Lordship mentioned a preliminary point, which he later held not to be supported by the evidence, and continued:] In the next place he relies on the fact that under the articles of association of the defendant company (both as incorporating Table A and under a special article number 28) their board of directors might have delegated their power to enter into such a contract to any person, including a single director or their secretary. And, thirdly, he draws the conclusion that, although this power to delegate was unknown to Mr Dart or to anyone else acting for the plaintiffs, yet Mr Dart and the plaintiffs were entitled to treat this as a matter of internal management only and to assume that Mr Maurice Lowe and the secretary in fact possessed the power to bind the defendant company ...

Next as to the power to delegate which is contained in the articles of association. In a case like this where that power of delegation had not been exercised, and where admittedly Mr Dart and the plaintiff firm had no knowledge of the existence of that power and did not rely on it, I cannot for myself see how they can subsequently make use of this unknown power so as to validate the transaction. They could rely on the fact of delegation, had it been a fact, whether known to them or not. They might rely on their knowledge of the power of delegation, had they known of it, as part of the circumstances entitling them to infer that there had been a delegation and to act on that inference, though it were in fact a mistaken one. But it is quite another thing to say that the plaintiffs are entitled now to rely on the supposed exercise of a power which was never in fact exercised and of the existence of which they were in ignorance at the date when they contracted. No case was cited to us in which a binding obligation has been constructed out of so curious a combination; and I cannot see any principle on which an obligation could be so constructed ...

Cases where the question has been as to the exact formalities observed when the seal of a company has been affixed, such as *Royal British Bank v Turquand* (**102**) ..., are quite distinguishable from the present case ... Perhaps the nearest approach to the present case is to be found in *Biggerstaff v Rowatt's Wharf Ltd* (**111**). But there the agent whose authority was relied on had been acting to the knowledge of the company as a managing director, and the act done was one within the ordinary ambit of the powers of a managing director in the transaction of the company's affairs. It is I think clear that the transaction there would not have been supported had it not been in this ordinary course, or had the agent been acting merely as one of the ordinary directors of the company. I know of no case in which an ordinary director, acting without authority in fact, has been held capable of binding a company by a contract with a third party, merely on the ground that that third party assumed that the director had been given authority by the board to make the contract ...

The result is that the decision of the learned judge must be reversed, with costs here and below.

BANKES LJ delivered a concurring judgment.

ATKIN LJ concurred.

NOTE

It was also stressed, particularly by Bankes LJ, that both the unusual nature of the transaction (involving the application of the property of one company towards payment of the debt of another) and the circumstances in which it was negotiated were such as to put the plaintiff on inquiry. The House of Lords [1928] AC 1 (Lord Shaw of Dunfermline dissenting) upheld the decision of the Court of Appeal but on other grounds: that the contract did not on its face purport to name the defendant company as a party, and further that the defendant company was not estopped from denying that it was a party, since the only person who had notice of the transaction sufficient to raise an estoppel was Lowe himself, and in the circumstances his knowledge was not attributable to the company: see (**38**).

QUESTIONS

(1) The directors' power to delegate functions to a single director and their power to appoint a managing director are both matters dependent on the terms of the company's articles (see Table A, articles 72, 84). Is it consistent for the courts to hold that it should be necessary for a third party to have actual knowledge of an article empowering delegation, but not necessary (see (**115**)) to have actual knowledge of an article authorising the appointment of a managing director?

(2) To what extent do you think that each of these cases was decided on (i) indoor management, (ii) agency, principles?

(3) Many companies list the names of their directors on their stationery. Is this of any legal consequence?

113 Kreditbank Cassel GmbH v Schenkers Ltd [1926] 2 KB 450 (King's Bench Division) and [1927] 1 KB 826 (Court of Appeal)

The plaintiffs, a German bank, sued the defendant company as drawers and indorsers of seven bills of exchange, each purportedly signed on behalf of the defendant by Clarke, the manager of its Manchester branch office. Clarke had in fact no authority to sign bills on the company's behalf. Wright J held that his signature bound the company; but the Court of Appeal reversed his decision.

WRIGHT J:[15] The rule in *Turquand*'s case is of peculiar importance in the case of negotiable instruments. A limited company is not competent to draw, accept or indorse bills of exchange unless by the memorandum it is given special power to do so. If it is so given it must depend on the articles who may sign such instruments on behalf of the company. The memorandum and articles are public documents, and every one dealing in such matters with a

---

15 Wright J delivered this judgment before the Court of Appeal had reversed his earlier decision in *Houghton*'s case (above).

limited company is taken in law to be acquainted with their terms. But once it appears that the company has the necessary power, and that the person purporting to bind the company by his signature to the negotiable instrument on the company's behalf falls within the category of persons who under the articles might be properly so empowered if the appropriate steps by way of internal management have been taken, the company will be bound. On any other basis the position of persons dealing with the negotiable paper of a limited company would be very difficult and business could not go on. The rule is subject to the obvious limitation that the person so dealing must have no actual or constructive notice that the professing agent of the company has not authority in fact: *A L Underwood Ltd v Bank of Liverpool and Martins*[16] ...

Mr Pritt contended that in the present case the view just expressed would carry with it the consequence that the bills of exchange in question might have been signed as on behalf of the company by the messenger or office boy. If that were the true effect of article 18, no doubt that result would follow. But I do not think it is the true effect. The mere description of messenger or office boy would take the case out of the category of persons who would ordinarily be entrusted with the power under the article, and would further carry with it notice of irregularity according to business usage. It is enough here to say, for the reasons I have given, that the Manchester manager is a person who falls within a fair construction of article 18[17] ...

[This decision was reversed by the Court of Appeal:]

ATKIN LJ: The bills themselves, it is plain to my mind, were forgeries; they were false and fraudulent documents; they were concocted by Clarke for the purpose of defrauding the defendants, who had nothing to do with the bills or the consideration for them. There was no reason therefore why the defendants should pay them. But it is said that they are nevertheless liable. One reason for seeking to impose liability upon them is this; it is said: 'You, the defendants, are a limited company, and as such you are in a much more awkward position than if you were a firm, because you have an article in your articles of association empowering the directors to determine who may sign bills of exchange on behalf of the company, and, therefore, anyone who purports to sign a bill of exchange in the name of the company is deemed to have authority to do so.' Carried to its logical conclusion, that would be a most alarming doctrine for companies, for anyone who has the pen of a ready writer need only sit down and write a bill of exchange in the name of a company having an article in this form, and the company would, presumably, be bound when the bill got into the hands of a holder for value without notice, even although the bill was an absolute forgery. The article cannot have that extended bearing, and if some limitation were not placed upon it, not merely the office boy but anyone might purport to sign on behalf of the company. Such a view is not correct. Wright J limited the application of the doctrine to such a person as falls within the category of those who under the article might properly be empowered if the appropriate steps were

16 [1924] 1 KB 775.
17 [Which reads: 'The directors shall have power to determine who shall be entitled to sign ... on the company's behalf bills, notes, ... acceptances, indorsements (etc).']

taken. I agree that that view is probably right. But who is the person who might properly be authorised? We are thrown back on the persons who ordinarily, apart from the articles, in view of their position in the company, would be acting within the scope of their apparent authority in signing a bill. That question must be determined apart from the actual terms of the article, which merely empowers the directors to pick out a person to whom authority may be given to sign bills. Accepting the proposition I have mentioned Wright J was in my view wrong, in the absence of evidence, in assuming that the manager of a branch business is a person who has ostensible authority to sign bills on behalf of his company. Much depends, of course, upon the evidence as to the nature of the business and the actual position occupied by the particular person. But in the absence of evidence I am not prepared to hold that the manager of a provincial branch, even if he is in such an important position as manager of the Manchester branch of a forwarding agency, has authority to draw bills to bind his company. The actual evidence in this case was that the company never signed bills at all, and in the absence of evidence that the person has ostensible authority to draw bills I should think that he plainly has not authority to do so. Therefore, we have the ordinary case of a person having purported to exercise an authority to bind the company in fraud of the company outside the scope of his ordinary ostensible authority ...

The true limits of the doctrine as to the effect of an article which empowers the company or its directors to nominate a person to have authority to do a particular act on behalf of the company are, I think, made quite plain in the judgments in *Houghton & Co v Nothard, Lowe & Wills* (**112**). It is therefore unnecessary to consider further the doctrine as to the knowledge of the articles of association of a company ... But we have the authority of the House of Lords in *Ruben*'s case (**108**) for saying that the doctrine that you need not investigate whether or not the conditions regulating the internal management of the company have been strictly carried out in accordance with the articles has no application in the case of a document which is an obvious forgery. In this case the defendants are entitled to say: 'These are not our bills and we are not precluded from denying the authority of the person who purported to sign them on our behalf.'

For these reasons I think that the appeal should be allowed and judgment entered for the defendants.

BANKES and SCRUTTON LJJ delivered concurring judgments.

NOTE

It appears to be fairly plain that, despite the references to the internal management rule, the question which both Wright J and the Court of Appeal really asked was: what acts are within the 'usual' authority of a branch manager such as Clarke? They differed only in the answers which they gave to this question. Atkin LJ's description of the document as a 'forgery' is far from helpful: it may be thought to beg the very question before the court; it again focuses attention on the indoor management rule when the issue is otherwise treated as one of agency; and, as has been observed (above, p 213) it is out of step with developments in other branches of the law of vicarious liability to make an exception of forgery cases.

114 British Thomson-Houston Co Ltd v Federated European Bank Ltd [1932] 2 KB 176 (Court of Appeal)

The defendant company had guaranteed the debt of another company in a letter to the plaintiffs signed by N Pal, the chairman of the defendant's board of directors. The defendant's articles empowered the board to delegate to a single director. When sued on the guarantee, the defendant pleaded that Pal had no authority to execute guarantees on behalf of the company. The Court of Appeal, affirming Macnaghten J, held the defendant bound.

GREER LJ: If it were necessary for the decision of this case to apply the first ruling, as stated in the headnote to *Houghton & Co v Nothard, Lowe & Wills Ltd* (**112**), I should find myself in some difficulty. One of the propositions of law there stated is: 'Although a person who contracts with an individual director or servant of a company, knowing that the board of directors has power to delegate its authority to such an individual, may under certain circumstances assume that that power of delegation has been exercised and that he may safely deal with the individual in question as representing the company, he cannot rely on the supposed exercise of such power if he did not know of the existence of the power at the time that he made the contract.' If I rightly understand the decision in that case, it proceeds upon that proposition as good law. But it is not necessary for me to inquire whether it was an essential element in the ratio decidendi, because there are in this case adequate grounds upon which we can rest a decision apart from *Houghton's* case. In the case before us the guarantee was signed by a person who was the chairman of the board of directors. Someone must represent the company for the purpose of conducting correspondence, it may be a secretary, or the managing director, or some other officer; and he must have authority to bind the company by letters written on its behalf. The person chosen by the defendants for this purpose was the chairman of the board, and the defendants have represented by their chairman that the plaintiffs could rely on the guarantee of the defendants as the act of the defendants and are responsible for those acts which they have held him out as having authority to perform. That is enough to decide this case.

SCRUTTON and SLESSER LJJ delivered concurring judgments.

NOTE

It appears that the one signature of the chairman was held to constitute both the execution of the guarantee and the representation of the company that Pal had authority to act on the company's behalf.

115 Freeman & Lockyer v Buckhurst Park Properties (Mangal) Ltd [1964] 2 QB 480, [1964] 1 All ER 630 (Court of Appeal)

The defendant company had been formed to buy and resell a large estate by two men: Kapoor, a property developer, and Hoon, who had contributed half of the capital but played no active part in the company's business. Kapoor, Hoon and a nominee of each were appointed the four directors of the company, and under the articles all four were needed to constitute a quorum. Hoon spent much time abroad, leaving all the day-to-day management of the company's affairs to be conducted by Kapoor. After an initial plan for the immediate resale of the land had fallen through, Kapoor decided to develop the estate and engaged the plaintiffs, a firm of architects and surveyors, to apply for planning permission. The company later refused to pay the plaintiffs' fees on the ground that Kapoor had had no authority to engage them. The county court judge held that the company was bound. The Court of Appeal affirmed his decision.

DIPLOCK LJ: The county court judge made the following findings of fact: (1) that the plaintiffs intended to contract with Kapoor as agent for the company, and not on his own account; (2) that the board of the company intended that Kapoor should do what he could to obtain the best possible price for the estate; (3) that Kapoor, although never appointed as managing director, had throughout been acting as such in employing agents and taking other steps to find a purchaser; (4) that Kapoor was so acting was well known to the board ...

The county court judge did not hold (although he might have done) that actual authority had been conferred upon Kapoor by the board to employ agents. He proceeded on the basis of apparent authority, that is, that the defendant company had so acted as to be estopped from denying Kapoor's authority. This rendered it unnecessary for the judge to inquire whether actual authority to employ agents had been conferred upon Kapoor by the board to whom the management of the company's business was confided by the articles of association.

I accept that such actual authority could have been conferred by the board without a formal resolution recorded in the minutes, although this would have rendered them liable to a default fine under s 145(4) of the Companies Act 1948 [CA 1985, s 317(7)]. But to confer actual authority would have required not merely the silent acquiescence of the individual members of the board, but the communication by words or conduct of their respective consents to one another and to Kapoor. [His Lordship discussed the evidence and continued:] I myself do not feel that there is adequate material to justify the court in reaching the conclusion of fact (which the county court judge refrained from making) that actual authority to employ agents had been conferred by the board on Kapoor.

This makes it necessary to inquire into the state of the law as to the ostensible authority of officers and servants to enter into contracts on behalf of corporations. It is a topic on which there are confusing and, it may be, conflicting judgments of the Court of Appeal ... We are concerned in the present case with the authority of an agent to create contractual rights and liabilities between his principal and a third party whom I will call 'the contractor'. This branch of the law has developed pragmatically rather than logically owing to the early history of the action of assumpsit and the consequent absence of a general jus quaesitum tertii [sic] in English law. But it is possible (and for the determination of this appeal I think it is desirable) to restate it upon a rational basis.

It is necessary at the outset to distinguish between an 'actual' authority of an agent on the one hand, and an 'apparent' or 'ostensible' authority on the other. Actual authority and apparent authority are quite independent of one another. Generally they co-exist and coincide, but either may exist without the other and their respective scopes may be different. As I shall endeavour to show, it is upon the apparent authority of the agent that the contractor normally relies in the ordinary course of business when entering into contracts.

An 'actual' authority is a legal relationship between principal and agent created by a consensual agreement to which they alone are parties. Its scope is to be ascertained by applying ordinary principles of construction of contracts, including any proper implications from the express words used, the usages of the trade, or the course of business between the parties. To this agreement the contractor is a stranger; he may be totally ignorant of the existence of any authority on the part of the agent. Nevertheless, if the agent does enter into a contract pursuant to the 'actual' authority, it does create contractual rights and liabilities between the principal and the contractor ...

An 'apparent' or 'ostensible' authority, on the other hand, is a legal relationship between the principal and the contractor created by a representation, made by the principal to the contractor, intended to be and in fact acted upon by the contractor, that the agent has authority to enter on behalf of the principal into a contract of a kind within the scope of the 'apparent' authority, so as to render the principal liable to perform any obligations imposed upon him by such contract. To the relationship so created the agent is a stranger. He need not be (although he generally is) aware of the existence of the representation but he must not purport to make the agreement as principal himself. The representation, when acted upon by the contractor by entering into a contract with the agent, operates as an estoppel, preventing the principal from asserting that he is not bound by the contract. It is irrelevant whether the agent had actual authority to enter into the contract.

In ordinary business dealings the contractor at the time of entering into the contract can in the nature of things hardly ever rely on the 'actual' authority of the agent. His information as to the authority must be derived either from the principal or from the agent or from both, for they alone know what the agent's actual authority is. All that the contractor can know is what they tell him, which may or may not be true. In the ultimate analysis he relies either upon the representation of the principal, that is, apparent authority, or upon the representation of the agent, that is, warranty of authority.

The representation which creates 'apparent' authority may take a variety of forms of which the commonest is representation by conduct, that is, by permitting the agent to act in some way in the conduct of the principal's business with other persons. By so doing the principal represents to anyone who becomes aware that the agent is so acting that the agent has authority to enter on behalf of the principal into contracts with other persons of the kind which an agent so acting in the conduct of his principal's business has usually 'actual' authority to enter into.

In applying the law as I have endeavoured to summarise it to the case where the principal is not a natural person, but a fictitious person, namely, a corporation, two further factors arising from the legal characteristics of a corporation have to be borne in mind. The first is that the capacity of a corporation is limited by its constitution, that is, in the case of a company incorporated under the Companies Act, by its memorandum and articles of association; the second is that a corporation cannot do any act, and that includes making a representation, except through its agent. [Lord Diplock discussed aspects of the ultra vires and constructive notice doctrines (now, of course, repealed), and continued:]

The second characteristic of a corporation, namely, that unlike a natural person it can only make a representation through an agent, has the consequence that in order to create an estoppel between the corporation and the contractor, the representation as to the authority of the agent which creates his 'apparent' authority must be made by some person or persons who have 'actual' authority from the corporation to make the representation. Such 'actual' authority may be conferred by the constitution of the corporation itself, as, for example, in the case of a company, upon the board of directors, or it may be conferred by those who under its constitution have the powers of management upon some other person to whom the constitution permits them to delegate authority to make representations of this kind. It follows that where the agent upon whose 'apparent' authority the contractor relies has no 'actual' authority from the corporation to enter into a particular kind of contract with the contractor on behalf of the corporation, the contractor cannot rely upon the agent's own representation as to his actual authority. He can rely only upon a representation by a person or persons who have actual authority to manage or conduct that part of the business of the corporation to which the contract relates.

The commonest form of representation by a principal creating an 'apparent' authority of an agent is by conduct, namely, by permitting the agent to act in the management or conduct of the principal's business. Thus, if in the case of a company the board of directors who have 'actual' authority under the memorandum and articles of association to manage the company's business permit the agent to act in the management or conduct of the company's business, they thereby represent to all persons dealing with such agent that he has authority to enter on behalf of the corporation into contracts of a kind which an agent authorised to do acts of the kind which he is in fact permitted to do usually enters into in the ordinary course of such business. The making of such a representation is itself an act of management of the company's business. Prima facie it falls within the 'actual' authority of the board of directors, and unless the memorandum or articles of the company either make such a contract ultra vires the company or prohibit the delegation of such authority to the agent,[18] the company is estopped from denying to anyone who has entered into a contract with the agent in reliance upon such 'apparent' authority that the agent had authority to contract on behalf of the company.

If the foregoing analysis of the relevant law is correct, it can be summarised by stating four conditions which must be fulfilled to entitle a contractor to enforce against a company a contract entered into on behalf of the company by an agent who had no actual authority to do so. It must be shown:

(1) that a representation that the agent had authority to enter on behalf of the company into a contract of the kind sought to be enforced was made to the contractor;

(2) that such representation was made by a person or persons who had 'actual' authority to manage the business of the company either generally or in respect of those matters to which the contract relates;

(3) that he (the contractor) was induced by such representation to enter into the contract, that is, that he in fact relied upon it; and

(4) that under its memorandum or articles of association the company was not deprived of the capacity either to enter into a contract of the kind

18 [These remarks must now be read in the light of the new ss 35–35B, CA 1985.]

sought to be enforced or to delegate authority to enter into a contract of that kind to the agent.[19]

The confusion which, I venture to think, has sometimes crept into the cases is in my view due to a failure to distinguish between these four separate conditions, and in particular to keep steadfastly in mind (a) that the only 'actual' authority which is relevant is that of the persons making the representation relied upon, and (b) that the memorandum and articles of association of the company are always relevant (whether they are in fact known to the contractor or not) to the questions (i) whether condition (2) is fulfilled, and (ii) whether condition (4) is fulfilled, and (but only if they are in fact known to the contractor) may be relevant (iii) as part of the representation on which the contractor relied.

In each of the relevant cases the representation relied upon as creating the 'apparent' authority of the agent was by conduct in permitting the agent to act in the management and conduct of part of the business of the company. Except in *Mahony v East Holyford Mining Co Ltd* (**103**), it was the conduct of the board of directors in so permitting the agent to act that was relied upon. As they had, in each case, by the articles of association of the company full 'actual' authority to manage its business, they had 'actual' authority to make representations in connection with the management of its business, including representations as to who were agents authorised to enter into contracts on the company's behalf. The agent himself had no 'actual' authority to enter into the contract because the formalities prescribed by the articles for conferring it upon him had not been complied with. In *British Thomson-Houston Co v Federated European Bank Ltd* (**114**), where a guarantee was executed by a single director, it was contended that a provision in the articles, requiring a guarantee to be executed by two directors, deprived the company of capacity to delegate to a single director authority to execute a guarantee on behalf of the company, that is, that condition (4) above was not fulfilled; but it was held that other provisions in the articles empowered the board to delegate the power of executing guarantees to one of their number, and this defence accordingly failed. In *Mahony*'s case no board of directors or secretary had in fact been appointed, and it was the conduct of those who, under the constitution of the company, were entitled to appoint them which was relied upon as a representation that certain persons were directors and secretary. Since they had 'actual' authority to appoint these officers, they had 'actual' authority to make representations as to who the officers were. In both these cases the constitution of the company, whether it had been seen by the contractor or not, was relevant in order to determine whether the persons whose representations by conduct were relied upon as creating the 'apparent' authority of the agent had 'actual' authority to make the representations on behalf of the company. In *Mahony*'s case, if the persons in question were not persons who would normally be supposed to have such authority by someone who did not in fact know the constitution of the company, it may well be that the contractor would not succeed in proving condition (3), namely, that he relied upon the representations made by those persons, unless he proved that he did in fact know the constitution of the company ...

19 [This fourth requirement will not now be relevant, in the light of the reforms mentioned in the preceding footnote, except in the case where the 'contractor' cannot bring himself within CA 1985, s 35A (e g because he was not dealing in good faith).]

The cases where the contractor's claim failed, namely *Houghton & Co v Nothard, Lowe & Wills Ltd* (**112**), *Kreditbank Cassel GmbH v Schenkers Ltd* (**113**) and the *Rama Corpn* case,[20] were all cases where the contract sought to be enforced was not one which a person occupying the position in relation to the company's business which the contractor knew that the agent occupied, would normally be authorised to enter into on behalf of the company. The conduct of the board of directors in permitting the agent to occupy that position, upon which the contractor relied, thus did not of itself amount to a representation that the agent had authority to enter into the contract sought to be enforced, that is, condition (1) was not fulfilled. The contractor, however, in each of these three cases sought to rely upon a provision of the articles giving to the board power to delegate wide authority to the agent as entitling him to treat the conduct of the board as a representation that the agent had had delegated to him wider powers than those usually exercised by persons occupying the position in relation to the company's business which the agent was in fact permitted by the board to occupy. Since this would involve proving that the representation on which he in fact relied as inducing him to enter into the contract comprised the articles of association of the company as well as the conduct of the board, it would be necessary for him to establish first that he knew the contents of the articles (that is, that condition (3) was fulfilled in respect of any representation contained in the articles) and secondly that the conduct of the board in the light of that knowledge would be understood by a reasonable man as a representation that the agent had authority to enter into the contract sought to be enforced, that is that condition (1) was fulfilled. The need to establish both these things was pointed out by Sargant LJ in *Houghton*'s case in a judgment which was concurred in by Atkin LJ; but his observations, as I read them, are directed only to a case where the contract sought to be enforced is not a contract of a kind which a person occupying the position which the agent was permitted by the board to occupy would normally be authorised to enter into on behalf of the company ...

In the present case the findings of fact by the county court judge are sufficient to satisfy the four conditions, and thus to establish that Kapoor had 'apparent' authority to enter into contracts on behalf of the company for their services in connection with the sale of the company's property, including the obtaining of development permission with respect to its use. The judge found that the board knew that Kapoor had throughout been acting as managing director in employing agents and taking other steps to find a purchaser. They permitted him to do so, and by such conduct represented that he had authority to enter into contracts of a kind which a managing director or an executive director responsible for finding a purchaser would in the normal course be authorised to enter into on behalf of the company. Condition (1) was thus fulfilled. The articles of association conferred full powers of management on the board. Condition (2) was thus fulfilled. The plaintiffs, finding Kapoor acting in relation to the company's property as he was authorised by the board to act, were induced to believe that he was authorised by the company to enter into contracts on behalf of the company for their services in connection with the sale of the company's property, including the obtaining of development permission with respect to

20 *Rama Corpn Ltd v Proved Tin and General Investments Ltd* [1952] 2 QB 147, [1952] 1 All ER 554 (a case similar to *Houghton*'s case (**112**) concerning a contract negotiated by a single non-executive director).

its use. Condition (3) was thus fulfilled. The articles of association, which contained powers for the board to delegate any of the functions of management to a managing director or to a single director, did not deprive the company of capacity to delegate authority to Kapoor, a director, to enter into contracts of that kind on behalf of the company. Condition (4) was thus fulfilled.

I think the judgment was right, and would dismiss the appeal.

WILLMER and PEARSON LJJ delivered concurring judgments.

116 Hely-Hutchinson v Brayhead Ltd [1968] 1 QB 549, [1967] 3 All ER 98 (Chancery Division and Court of Appeal)

Richards was chairman of directors of the defendant company and its chief executive or 'de facto managing director', who often committed the company to contracts on his own initiative and only disclosed the matter to the board subsequently. The board acquiesced in this practice. The plaintiff (referred to in the judgment as Lord Suirdale) was chairman and managing director of another company, 'Perdio', which it was planned should eventually be merged with the defendant. As part of an agreement to put more money into Perdio, the plaintiff (who had been made a director of the defendant company) was given certain letters (referred to as C 23 and C 26) signed by Richards, by which the defendant agreed to guarantee the repayment of money owed to the plaintiff and to indemnify him against certain losses. When sued on these undertakings, the defendant alleged that Richards had had no authority to make the contract in question. Roskill J held that Richards had *apparent* authority to bind his company; the Court of Appeal affirmed his decision, but on the ground that he had *actual* authority.

[For other parts of the decision in this case, see above, (**107**), and below, (**130**).]

ROSKILL J: The set-up in Brayhead is easy to envisage. It was an industrial holding company with a large number of subsidiaries. Its directors were in the main working directors, each in charge of a section of the holding company's subsidiaries. One would look after electronics, another engineering, and so on. They would all come back to Mr Richards for advice and—which is more important— decisions from time to time on matters concerning their own particular group. The final decision—and the final decision most especially on any matter concerning finance—was Mr Richards' and nobody else's. Sometimes, I dare say, the directors persuaded him to take or to refrain from taking a particular step; no doubt, like any wise chief executive, he sought and obtained advice before he made up his mind; but in all these cases the final decision, I am quite satisfied, rested with him and with nobody else.

If one goes through the minutes and documents which have been put before me, one can see repeated examples of Mr Richards acting in this way. Sometimes, of course, the matter would come back to the board for formal ratification after he had committed Brayhead perhaps technically without express authority. On other occasions, of which there are a number of examples in the minutes, he plainly committed Brayhead and then, as it were, reported the matter afterwards ... I have no doubt that the board knew that he was doing this sort of thing all the time, and that whenever he thought it was necessary he assumed, or purported to assume, authority to bind Brayhead, and that the board allowed him to do it and acquiesced in his doing it. That is not to say, to use Mr Finer's phrase yesterday, that all the directors were 'Yes men'; I am sure they were nothing of the kind. Mr Richards was a forceful personality; he knew his own mind. I think he quite clearly was allowed by Brayhead to hold himself out as having ostensible or apparent authority to enter into commitments of the kind which he entered into or purported to enter into, when he signed C 23 and C 26 ...

[The Court of Appeal affirmed the decision of Roskill J, but on the grounds that Richards had *actual* authority.]

LORD DENNING MR: I need not consider at length the law on the authority of an agent, actual, apparent or ostensible. That has been done in the judgments of this court in *Freeman & Lockyer v Buckhurst Park Properties (Mangal) Ltd* (**115**). It is there shown that actual authority may be expressed or implied. It is *express* when it is given by express words, such as when a board of directors pass a resolution which authorises two of their number to sign cheques. It is *implied* when it is inferred from the conduct of the parties and the circumstances of the case, such as when the board of directors appoint one of their number to be managing director. They thereby impliedly authorise him to do all such things as fall within the usual scope of that office. Actual authority, express or implied, is binding as between the company and the agent, and also as between the company and others, whether they are within the company or outside it.

Ostensible or apparent authority is the authority of an agent as it *appears* to others. It often coincides with actual authority. Thus, when the board appoint one of their number to be managing director, they invest him not only with implied authority, but also with ostensible authority to do all such things as fall within the usual scope of that office. Other people who see him acting as managing director are entitled to assume that he has the usual authority of a managing director. But sometimes ostensible authority exceeds actual authority. For instance, when the board appoint the managing director, they may expressly limit his authority by saying he is not to order goods worth more than £500 without the sanction of the board. In that case his *actual* authority is subject to the £500 limitation, but his *ostensible* authority includes all the usual authority of a managing director. The company is bound by his ostensible authority in his dealings with those who do not know of the limitation ...

Apply these principles here. It is plain that Mr Richards had no express authority to enter into these two contracts on behalf of the company: nor had he any such authority implied from the nature of his office. He had been duly appointed chairman of the company but that office in itself did not carry with it authority to enter into these contracts without the sanction of the board ... The judge held that Mr Richards had ostensible or apparent authority to make the contract, but I think his findings carry with it the necessary inference that he had also actual authority, such authority being implied from the circumstance that the board by their conduct over many months had acquiesced in his acting as their chief executive and committing Brayhead Ltd to contracts without the necessity of sanction from the board.

LORDS WILBERFORCE and PEARSON delivered concurring judgments.

NOTES

(1) In *British Bank of the Middle East v Sun Life Assurance Co of Canada (UK) Ltd* [1983] BCLC 78, HL, it was held that a branch manager of a multinational insurance company had no 'usual' authority to represent to a bank that a subordinate employee had actual authority to execute undertakings to pay moneys to the bank. The evidence was that all such undertakings were in practice executed by insurance companies at their head office.

(2) We should remember that acts of the directors or other agents of a company which are beyond their actual authority can be ratified: see above, pp 192 ff.

(3) The Prentice Report (above, p 128), in addition to recommending the abolition of the doctrine of constructive notice, suggested that the law should be changed so that a company should be bound by the acts of an individual director. However, the amendments made by CA 1989 did not incorporate any provision along these lines.

QUESTIONS

(1) Is it right to think in terms of the 'usual' authority of a managing director? Is it not likely that the terms of appointment of managing directors will vary from case to case? (see article 72 of Table A, and *Harold Holdsworth & Co (Wakefield) Ltd v Caddies* (**122**)).

(2) Was Lord Diplock right to say (above, p 224) that in *Mahony*'s case (**103**), the *directors* held the agent out as having apparent authority? What was the nature or source of the directors' own authority to do so?

(3) If Richards had implied actual authority to make the contract in *Hely-Hutchison v Brayhead Ltd*, should not the trial judge in *Freeman & Lockyer* (**115**) have made a similar finding about Kapoor?

(4) In *British Thomson-Houston* (**114**), did the chairman have *actual* authority to sign the letter?

H. Statutory reform

Article 9 of the First EEC Company Law Directive (cited above, p 151), as well as dealing with 'acts not within the objects of the company', provided that 'the limits on the powers of the organs of the company ... may never be relied on as against third parties, even if they have been disclosed'. This provision was first enacted as part of UK domestic legislation by s 9(1) of the European Communities Act 1972 (also cited on p 151), and later consolidated as the former CA 1985, s 35. Each of these sections ran together into a single sentence provisions relating to the capacity of the company and the authority of the directors and was marred, as we have seen, by the inclusion of phrases such as 'decided on by the directors' which had no counterpart in the directive itself.

The Companies Act 1989, following the recommendations of the Prentice report, introduced amendments which separate the two issues: the new s 35 (above, p 152) deals with acts which are not within a company's capacity, while s 35A focuses on the question of authority—not only the authority of the directors themselves, but also that of others acting under powers delegated by the board. It reads as follows:

35A *Power of directors to bind the company*

(1) In favour of a person dealing with a company in good faith, the power of the board of directors to bind the company, or authorise others to do so, shall be deemed to be free of any limitation under the company's constitution.
(2) For this purpose—
  (a) a person 'deals with' a company if he is a party to any transaction or other act to which the company is a party;
  (b) a person shall not be regarded as acting in bad faith by reason only of his knowing that an act is beyond the powers of the directors under the company's constitution; and
  (c) a person shall be presumed to have acted in good faith unless the contrary is proved.
(3) The references above to limitations on the directors' powers under the company's constitution include limitations deriving—
  (a) from a resolution of the company in general meeting or a meeting of any class of shareholders, or
  (b) from any agreement between the members of the company or of any class of shareholders.
(4) Subsection (1) does not affect any right of a member of the company to bring proceedings to restrain the doing of an act which is beyond the powers of the directors; but no such proceedings shall lie in respect of an act to be done in fulfilment of a legal obligation arising from a previous act of the company.
(5) Nor does that subsection affect any liability incurred by the directors, or any other person, by reason of the directors' exceeding their powers.

It will be seen that, unlike the new s 35, s 35A brings forward from the former section the stipulation that it operates only 'in favour of a person dealing in good faith'. But it is wider in scope than its predecessor, and its meaning is made much clearer, by reason of the detailed provisions of subsections (2) and (3).

The extracts from the judgments in *TCB Ltd v Gray* (**117**) and *Barclays Bank Ltd v TOSG Trust Fund Ltd* (below, p 231) which follow were decided under the section in its unamended form, but they are relevant as showing readiness on the part of the judges to interpret the new law generously.

Section 35A is to be construed broadly so as to obviate the commercial inconvenience caused by the old rule of constructive notice.

117 TCB Ltd v Gray [1986] Ch 621, [1986] 1 All ER 587 (Chancery Division; affd on other grounds [1987] Ch 458n, [1988] 1 All ER 108, CA)

Gray was sued on a guarantee which he had given to the plaintiff TCB to secure the indebtedness of a company called Link, of which Gray was a director. The debenture evidencing Link's debt had been signed by one Rowan purporting to act as Gray's attorney, but Link's articles required a director to sign personally. The court ruled that TCB, which had acted on the debenture in good faith, was protected by s 9(1) of the European Communities Act 1972 [CA 1985, s 35A].

BROWNE-WILKINSON V-C: The debenture was not signed by any director of Link, but by an attorney for a director. There is no power in the articles of

Link for a director to act by an attorney. Therefore, says Mr Brodie, on the principle delegatus non potest delegare the seal was not affixed in accordance with the requirements of the articles; accordingly the debenture is not the act of Link.

Apart from s 9(1) of the European Communities Act 1972, there would be much force in these submissions. But in my judgment that section provides a complete answer. Under the old law, a person dealing with a corporation was required to look at the company's memorandum and articles to satisfy himself that the transaction was within the corporate capacity of the company and was to be carried through in accordance with the requirements of its articles. The rigour of those requirements was only tempered to the extent that the rule in *Royal British Bank v Turquand* (**102**) allowed third parties to assume that acts of internal management had been properly carried out. It has been generally assumed that the old law has to a large extent been swept away by s 9(1) of the Act of 1972 ... Section 9(1) was passed to bring the law of England into line with article 9 of Council Directive 68/151/EEC. In approaching the construction of the section, it is in my judgment relevant to note that the manifest purpose of both the directive and the section is to enable people to deal with a company in good faith without being adversely affected by any limits on the company's capacity or its rules for internal management. Given good faith, a third party is able to deal with a company through its 'organs' (as the directive describes them) or directors. Section 9(1) achieves this in two ways: first it 'deems' all transactions to be authorised; second, it deems that the directors can bind the company without limitations. The second part of the subsection reinforces this by expressly abolishing the old doctrine of constructive notice of the contents of a company's memorandum and articles. It being the obvious purpose of the subsection to obviate the commercial inconvenience and frequent injustice caused by the old law, I approach the construction of the subsection with a great reluctance to construe it in such a way as to reintroduce, through the back door, any requirement that a third party acting in good faith must still investigate the regulating documents of a company.

Mr Brodie, whilst accepting that TCB had no actual or imputed knowledge of any irregularity in the execution of the debenture, at first submitted that TCB did not act 'in good faith' within the meaning of the section since TCB was put on inquiry by the unusual manner in which the debenture had been executed. He said that TCB should have looked at the articles and would then have discovered the irregularity. Accordingly, he submitted, they were not acting 'in good faith'. On further consideration Mr Brodie abandoned this argument, to my mind rightly. The last words of the second part of s 9(1) expressly provide that good faith is to be presumed: the second part further provides that the person dealing with the company is *not* bound to inquire as to limitations on the powers of directors. In my judgment, it is impossible to establish lack of 'good faith' within the meaning of the subsection solely by alleging that inquiries ought to have been made which the second part of the subsection says need not be made.

Mr Brodie's next submission was that, in order for s 9(1) to apply at all, the first requirement is that there must be a transaction by the company. Since Link never sealed the debenture in the only way authorised by the articles, there was here no transaction by Link at all; the debenture was not the act of Link. If this argument is right, it drives a coach and horses through the section. In every dealing with the company the third party would have to look at its articles to ensure that the company was binding itself in an authorised manner. In my judgment the section does not have that effect. The section is dealing with purported actions by a company which, having regard to its internal documents, may be a nullity, e g acts outside its corporate capacity. In such a case under the old law the purported act of the company would not be the act of the company at all. Yet the first part of s 9(1) deems it so to be. Similarly a document under seal by the company executed otherwise than in accordance with its articles was not, under the old law, the act of the company: but s 9(1) deems it so to be since the powers of the directors are deemed to be free from limitations, i e as to the manner of affixing the company's seal. In my judgment, s 9(1) of the Act applies to transactions which a company purports to enter into and deems them to be validly entered into ...

Accordingly the necessary basis for s 9(1) of the Act of 1972 to apply, as between Link and TCB, exists. It follows that the debenture was valid, and Mr Gray's second line of defence also fails.

NOTE

In *Barclays Bank Ltd v TOSG Trust Fund Ltd* [1984] BCLC 1 at 17, Nourse J made the following observations on the meaning of the phrase 'in good faith':

[Counsel for the defendants] said that even if the assignment agreement was ultra vires the trust fund nevertheless, in favour of the agency, it is deemed, by virtue of s 9(1) of the European Communities Act 1972 to have been intra vires, on the ground that at all material times the agency acted in 'good faith', that is to say that it genuinely and honestly believed that it was within the trust fund's corporate powers to enter into the assignment agreement. Counsel for the plaintiffs, on the other hand, says that before s 9(1) can apply the agency must have acted not only genuinely and honestly, but in circumstances where it neither knew nor ought to have known of the lack of vires. That means, he says, that the agency must have acted not only genuinely and honestly, but reasonably as well ...

Section 9(1) was enacted in pursuance of Art 9(1) of the European Economic Community's First Council Directive on Companies 68/151. There was some discussion as to whether I should rely on the Directive in order to construe s 9(1) of the 1972 Act. But I think it was ultimately agreed on all sides that, as in the case of an Act of Parliament which is passed to give effect to an international convention or the like, I should only do so if the language of the Act is either ambiguous or doubtful in some other respect; cf *The Banco*.[1] In my judgment the expression 'in good faith' is one whose meaning is well established and understood in our law. It does not admit of any ambiguity or doubt. I do not therefore need to rely on the Directive in the present case. I would add that, having read both the French original and the English translation, I am not at all sure that it would have taken me any further ...

My view of that question is this. In the case of a transaction decided on by the directors s 9(1) has abolished the rule that a person who deals with a company is automatically affected with constructive notice of its objects clause. But, by retaining the requirement of good faith, it nevertheless ensures that a defence based on absence of notice shall not be available to someone who has not acted genuinely and honestly in his dealings with the company. Notice and good faith, although two separate beings, are often inseparable. There is a most valuable account of their liaison in the speech of Lord Wilberforce in the recent case of

1 [1971] P 137, [1971] 1 All ER 524, CA.

Midland Bank Trust Co Ltd v Green.[2] What it comes to is that a person who deals with a company in circumstances where he ought anyway to know that the company has no power to enter into the transaction will not necessarily act in good faith. Sometimes, perhaps often, he will not. And a fortiori where he actually knows. Next, a person who acts in good faith will sometimes, perhaps often, act in a manner which can also be described as being reasonable. But I emphatically refute the suggestion, if such it is, that reasonableness is a necessary ingredient of good faith. That would require the introduction of an objective standard into a subjective concept and it would be contrary to everything which the law has always understood of that concept. In my judgment a person acts in good faith if he acts genuinely and honestly in the circumstances of the case. Beyond that it is neither possible nor desirable to attempt an examination of the circumstances in which s 9(1) may or may not apply.

[The decision of Nourse J was reversed on another point: [1984] 1 All ER 628, CA; affd [1984] AC 626, [1984] 1 All ER 1060, HL; but no comment was made about this passage in any of the judgments on appeal.]

I. Official notification

The European Communities Act 1972, having in s 9(1) taken much of the sting out of the doctrine of constructive notice of registered company documents, went on in s 9(3)–(4) (now CA 1985, s 42) to introduce an additional disclosure regime, that of 'official notification', which states that a company may not rely on certain constitutional changes, and other events, unless they have been properly notified to the registrar and published by him in the *Gazette*. It would have been a natural enough step, given the precedent of *Ernest v Nicholls*, for an English court to infer that a company *could* rely on the events against a third party once they had been properly notified, so that the constructive notice rule had been revived, at least in relation to the events listed in the new provision. The Court of Appeal, however, in *Official Custodian for Charities v Parway Estates Ltd* (**118**), has held that s 42 is negative in its application, operating against a company but not in its favour, and that the official notification of events in the *Gazette* does not constitute notice of their happening to all the world.

Official notification in the Gazette *under CA 1985, s 42, does not constitute notice of the events in question to all the world. The only effect of the section is to prevent a company from relying on the event if it has not been gazetted.*

118 Official Custodian for Charities v Parway Estates Ltd [1985] Ch 151, [1984] 3 All ER 679 (Court of Appeal)

The question was whether the plaintiffs, as landlords of a large property in Shepherd's Bush, had waived their right to forfeit a lease in the event of the liquidation of the defendant company, their tenant. An order for the compulsory liquidation of the company had been made on 26 February 1979 and official notification of this event was gazetted on 8 March. The appointment of a liquidator was gazetted the following August. But the landlords were unaware of these matters and went on accepting rent until

2 [1981] AC 513 at 528, 529, HL.

mid-1981. It was held that the landlords should not be deemed to have notice of the events gazetted and so they had not waived their right to forfeit.

DILLON LJ: It is common ground that ... receipt by the plaintiffs of rent after the defendant had gone into liquidation cannot have operated as a waiver of the right to forfeit the lease if at the time that the rent was received the plaintiffs had had no notice that the defendant had gone into liquidation.

It is also common ground that before s 9 of the European Communities Act 1972 [CA 1985, s 42] came into force, the registration in the Companies Registry and subsequent promulgation in the London Gazette of the fact that a company was in liquidation or of the appointment of a liquidator did not operate as notice to all the world, and more particularly did not operate as notice to the company's landlord, that the company was in liquidation. This was decided in *Ewart v Fryer*.[3] The effect of s 9 of the 1972 Act is therefore crucial to the argument.

Section 9 was enacted in anticipation of the entry of this country into the European Economic Community, in order to comply with [EEC Council Directive 68/151] which was adopted on 9 March 1968. Section 9 deals with a number of different aspects of company law covered by the Directive. The provisions directly relevant to the present case are those of sub-ss (3) and (4) but subs (1) [CA 1985, s 35] is also of importance ...

Mr Nugee QC [Counsel for the tenant] submits that on the true construction of s 9 official notification of an event is to be treated as giving notice of that event to all the world. In this submission he has the support of *Palmer's Company Law,* 23rd ed (1982), vol 1, who say on pp 184, 185–186:

> The European Communities Act 1972, s 9 introduced a new notion into company law, viz that of official notification. The provisions dealing with that subject are contained in sub-s (3) ... and (4) of s 9. The object of this measure is to give persons in the United Kingdom and the other member states of the EEC official intimation that an important change in the constitution of the company has occurred ...
>
> Only when the official notification has become fully effective, can the company absolutely rely on any of the events listed in s 9(4) ... and is a third party treated as having constructive notice of the event in question. Before the official notification becomes fully effective, the company can rely on any of those events only if certain conditions are satisfied. Official notification becomes fully effective after the expiration of a period of grace which is 15 days ...

It is to be noted that the statement in *Palmer*:

> The object of this measure is to give persons in the United Kingdom and the other member states of the EEC official notification that an important change in the constitution of the company has occurred,

does not wholly accord with the wording of the Directive. A version of the Directive in the English language and apparently taken from the Official Journal of the European Communities has been put before us. In this the provisions which have led to s 9(3) and (4) appear in a section headed 'Disclosure', and the relevant recital states:

3 [1901] 1 Ch 499, CA; affd sub nom *Fryer v Ewart* [1902] AC 187, HL.

Whereas the basic documents of the company should be disclosed in order that third parties may be able to ascertain their contents and other information concerning the company, especially particulars of the persons who are authorised to bind the company.

Even without reference to the Directive, I have no doubt, on the wording of s 9, that that section was primarily intended for the protection of persons dealing with a company rather than for the protection of the company. This is apparent not least from the opening words of s 9(1) 'in favour of a person dealing with a company in good faith' and from the opening words of s 9(4) 'A company shall not be entitled to rely against other persons on the happening of any of the following events . . .'.

The question then is whether, even so, it is implicit in s 9(4), or necessary in order to give effect to s 9(4), that, after an official notification of an event has become fully effective, all persons must be treated as having constructive notice of that event. Three matters can be urged in support of the argument, viz: (i) if an event has not been officially notified a company can still rely on it as against a person who has actual knowledge of it, and so official notification is in a sense treated as the counterpart of actual knowledge, in enabling the company to rely on the event; (ii) during the period of grace before the official notification has become fully effective, the person concerned can prevent the company relying on the event by showing that he was unavoidably prevented from knowing of the event, absence of knowledge of the event being treated in the period of grace as countervailing the official notification; and (iii) it is difficult to think of circumstances in which a company will wish to rely as against a third party on the happening of the event of its own liquidation and in which the real issue will not be the third party's knowledge of that event rather than the happening of the event itself.

This question whether official notification of a relevant event constitutes notice of that event to all the world, is an important question. If indeed the notification does constitute notice to all, the very many landlords who are not in the habit of studying the London Gazette regularly or effecting regular searches of the files of their company tenants in the Companies Registry will be at risk of inadvertently waiving the forfeiture of leases by accepting rent after the company tenant has gone into liquidation.

The deputy judge, after considering the wording of s 9(4) and the views expressed in *Palmer's Company Law* . . ., concluded that sub-s (4) did not impute knowledge to anyone and did not impute notice to anyone. It was essentially negative in its impact. It provided that a company cannot rely upon a relevant event if it is not in the Gazette but it did not make the positive counter proposition that a company can rely upon that event—it can rely on everyone having notice of that event—merely because it is in the Gazette. I agree with the deputy judge's analysis of the subsection and with his conclusion.

I would add two further comments. In the first place, I do not think that the link, such as it is, in s 9(4), between official notification of a relevant event, and actual knowledge of the event if it has not been officially notified, requires that official notification should be treated as importing notice of the event to everyone. The object of the legislation is that persons dealing with a company should be officially given an opportunity of finding out important information concerning the company but there is no sense in hampering the company vis-à-vis those who have actual knowledge of the relevant event.

Hence the qualification of the restriction imposed by the subsection on the company. It is not necessary to treat official notification as the equivalent of actual knowledge in all circumstances.

In the second place, among the events, other than liquidation and the appointment of a liquidator, listed in s 9(4) as events on which a company cannot rely in the absence of official notification are the making of any alteration in the memorandum of association of the company, including, of course, its objects clause, and the making of any change among the company's directors. But it is plain to my mind from s 9(1) that a person dealing in good faith with a company is not to be treated as having constructive notice (as under the previous ultra vires doctrine of English law) of the terms of the company's objects clause, whether in its original form or as from time to time altered, and is not to be treated as having constructive notice of the composition from time to time of the board of directors of the company. The tenor of the section is thus against imputing constructive notice of relevant events to persons dealing with a company, while ensuring that they have an opportunity to find out information about those events.

I thus agree with the deputy judge that the tenant's defence of waiver fails . . .

KERR and STEPHENSON LJJ concurred.

QUESTION

What is the effect of s 42 on a resolution such as that held to have been passed in *Cane v Jones* (**83**)?

CHAPTER 5

Directors and Other Officers

A. Directors: appointment, tenure and remuneration

Apart from providing that a public company must have at least two directors, and a private company at least one (s 282), and stipulating that vacancies on the board of a public company shall not normally be filled by a simple resolution appointing a number of candidates en bloc (s 292), the Companies Act has little to say about the appointment of directors; and so the matter is left to the articles of the particular company. The appointment of *managing* directors is usually a question for the board (Table A, articles 72 and 84); but of course the appointee must be a director, appointed by the customary constitutional process, to be eligible; and if he ceases to be a director he will automatically lose office as a managing director as well (see above, pp 106ff).

The most important statutory provision regarding the *removal* of directors is s 303. A director has ordinarily no claim to any kind of tenure, unless he has a service contract (see above, pp 103ff). Even then, he cannot specifically enforce his right to remain in office, but has merely a claim for damages for breach.[1] It is obvious that a director could be made virtually irremovable if he had a service contract that ran for a very long period, for the company could get rid of him only by paying a prohibitive sum as compensation. A board of directors acting in collusion could see to it that every member of the board was protected in this way. To avert this risk, the legislation provides that no service contact may be made to run for more than five years without the prior authorisation of a members' resolution (s 319); and to keep the shareholders informed, s 318 directs that service contracts should be kept continually available for them to inspect.

The law maintains a presumption (the legacy of a more leisured era) that directors are expected to work for nothing (see *Hutton v West Cork Rly Co*, above, p 158). This is ordinarily displaced by a provision in the articles (e g Table A, article 82) which authorises the company in general meeting to determine the rate of payment. More important will be the question of the remuneration of the managing and other executive directors. This, in a typical company's articles, is left to the *directors* to determine: see, e g Table A, article 84, and cf *Guinness plc v Saunders* (**124**). Note also the requirement in Sch 6, Part I of disclosure in the company's accounts of the remuneration paid to directors; and s 311, which prohibits the payment of directors' remuneration free of tax.

A director may be protected from being removed from office by attaching special voting rights to his shares. Such a provision is valid despite s 303.

1 The removal of a director from a salaried office may also, in a small company, justify the making of a winding-up order on the 'just and equitable' ground: see below, pp 557 ff, and sometimes also amount to 'unfairly prejudicial' conduct within CA 1985, s 459 (below, pp 495 ff).

120 Bushell v Faith [1970] AC 1099, [1970] 1 All ER 53 (House of Lords)

Bush Court (Southgate) Ltd had a capital of £300 in £1 shares, held as to 100 each by Faith and his sisters, Mrs Bushell and Dr Bayne. Article 9 of the articles of association provided: 'In the event of a resolution being proposed at any general meeting of the company for the removal from office of any director, any shares held by that director shall on a poll in respect of such resolution carry the right to three votes per share ...' Faith was thus able to record 300 votes and outvote his sisters, who recorded 200 votes between them, by demanding a poll on a motion to remove him from office. Ungoed-Thomas J held that article 9 was invalid because it infringed s 303; but his decision was reversed on appeal. The House of Lords (Lord Morris of Borth-y-Gest dissenting) upheld the effectiveness of the article.

LORD DONOVAN: My Lords, the issue here is the true construction of s 184 of the Companies Act 1948 [CA 1985, s 303] and I approach it with no conception of what the legislature wanted to achieve by the section other than such as can reasonably be deduced from its language.

Clearly it was intended to alter the method by which a director of a company could be removed while still in office. It enacts that this can be done by the company by ordinary resolution. Furthermore, it may be achieved notwithstanding anything in the company's articles, or in any agreement between the company and the director.

Accordingly any case (and one knows there were many) where the articles prescribed that a director should be removable during his period of office only by a special resolution or an extraordinary resolution, each of which necessitated inter alia a three to one majority of those present and voting at the meeting, is overriden by s 184. A simple majority of the votes will now suffice; an ordinary resolution being, in my opinion, a resolution capable of being carried by such a majority. Similarly any agreement, whether evidenced by the articles or otherwise, that a director shall be a director for life or for some fixed period is now also overreached.

The field over which s 184 operates is thus extensive for it includes, admittedly, all companies with a quotation on the Stock Exchange.

It is now contended, however, that it does something more; namely, that it provides in effect that when the ordinary resolution proposing the removal of the director is put to the meeting each shareholder present shall have one vote per share and no more: and that any provision in the articles providing that any shareholder shall, in relation to *this* resolution, have 'weighted' votes attached to his shares, is also nullified by s 184. A provision for such 'weighting' of votes which applies generally, that is, as part of the normal pattern of voting, is accepted by the appellant as unobjectionable: but an article such as the one here under consideration which is special to a resolution seeking the removal of a director falls foul of s 184 and is over-ridden by it.

Why should this be? The section does not say so, as it easily could. And those who drafted it and enacted it certainly would have included among their numbers many who were familiar with the phenomenon of articles of association carrying 'weighted votes'. It must therefore have been plain at the outset that unless special provision were made, the mere direction that an ordinary resolution would do in order to remove a director would leave the section at risk of being made inoperative in the way that has been done here. Yet no such provision was made, and in this Parliament followed its practice of leaving to companies and their shareholders liberty to allocate voting rights as they pleased . . .

LORDS REID and UPJOHN delivered concurring opinions.

LORD GUEST concurred.

LORD MORRIS OF BORTH-Y-GEST (dissenting): Some shares may . . . carry a greater voting power than others. On a resolution to remove a director shares will therefore carry the voting power that they possess. But this does not, in my view, warrant a device such as article 9 introduces. Its unconcealed effect is to make a director irremovable. If the question is posed whether the shares of the respondent possess any added voting weight the answer must be that they possess none whatsoever beyond, if valid, an ad hoc weight for the special purpose of circumventing s 184. If article 9 were writ large it would set out that a director is not to be removed against his will and that in order to achieve this and to thwart the express provision of s 184 the voting power of any director threatened with removal is to be deemed to be greater than it actually is. The learned judge thought that to sanction this would be to make a mockery of the law. I think so also.

If the appointment of a person as managing director is void because made without proper authority, he may be entitled to remuneration on a quantum meruit basis for work actually done.

121 Craven-Ellis v Canons Ltd [1936] 2 KB 403, [1936] 2 All ER 1066 (Court of Appeal)

[The facts appear from the judgment.]

GREER LJ: The signatories to the memorandum and articles, being entitled to elect the first directors, nominated Mr Phillip du Cros, the plaintiff, and Mr A W Wheeler as the first directors on 15 August 1928, and on 23 August the directors co-opted Sir Arthur de Cros as a director. Under the articles these directors could act without qualification for two months, but after that time they became incapable of acting as directors as none of them had acquired the necessary qualification. The only issued shares of the company were in the two signatories to the memorandum, but there is little room for doubt that these gentlemen were nominees of the du Cros'. Be this as it may it is clear that on the expiration of the two months, the directors having no qualification ceased to be directors, and were unable to bind the company except as de facto directors by agreements with outsiders or with shareholders . . . On 14 April 1931 an agreement was executed under the seal of the company, purporting to be between the company and the plaintiff, stating the terms on which he was to act by resolution of the unqualified directors. The plaintiff in this action sought to recover from the defendant company the remuneration set out in the agreement, and as an alternative, sought to recover for his services on a quantum meruit. Until the company purported to put an end to his engagement he continued to perform all the services mentioned in the agreement.

The company, having had the full benefit of these services, decline to pay either under the agreement or on the basis of a quantum meruit. Their defence to the action is a purely technical defence, and if it succeeds the Messrs du Cros as the principal shareholders in the company, and the company, would be in the position of having received and accepted valuable services and refusing, for purely technical reasons, to pay for them.

As regards the services rendered between 31 December 1930 and 14 April 1931, there is, in my judgment, no defence to the claim. These services were rendered by the plaintiff not as managing director or as a director, but as an estate agent, and there was no contract in existence which could present any obstacle to a claim based on a quantum meruit for services rendered and accepted.

As regards the plaintiff's services after the date of the contract, I think the plaintiff is also entitled to succeed. The contract, having been made by directors who had no authority to make it with one of themselves who had notice of their want of authority, was not binding on either party. It was, in fact, a nullity, and presents no obstacle to the implied promise to pay on a quantum meruit basis which arises from the performance of the services and the implied acceptance of the same by the company.

It was contended by Mr Croom-Johnson on behalf of the respondents that, inasmuch as the services relied on were purported to be done by the plaintiff under what he and the directors thought was a binding contract, there could be no legal obligation on the defendants on a quantum meruit claim. The only one of the numerous authorities cited by Mr Croom-Johnson that appears to support his contention is the judgment of a Divisional Court in *Re Allison, Johnson & Foster Ltd, ex p Birkenshaw.*[2] The court consisted of Lord Alverstone, Wills and Kennedy JJ, and the judgment was delivered by Kennedy J. In giving judgment that learned judge, expressing not merely his own opinion, but that of the other two judges, said: 'There can be no implied contract for payment arising out of acceptance of the work done where the work was done upon an express request which turns out to be no request at all, but which down to the time when the whole of the work had been done was supposed by both parties to be valid and operative.' This passage appears to involve the proposition that in all cases where parties suppose there is an agreement in existence and one of them has performed services, or delivered goods in pursuance of the supposititious agreement there cannot be any inference of any promise by the person accepting the services or the goods to pay on the basis of a quantum meruit. This would certainly be strictly logical if the inference of a promise to pay on a quantum meruit basis were an inference of fact based on the acceptance of the services or of the goods delivered under what was supposed to be an existing contract; but in my judgment the inference is not one of fact, but is an inference which a rule of law imposes on the parties where work has been done or goods have been delivered under what purports to be a binding contract, but is not so in fact ...

I accordingly think that the defendants must pay on the basis of a quantum meruit not only for the services rendered after 31 December 1930, and before the date of the invalid agreement, but also for the services after that date. I think the appeal should be allowed, and judgment given for such a sum as

---

2 [1904] 2 KB 327.

shall be found to be due on the basis of a quantum meruit in respect of all services rendered by the plaintiff to the company until he was dismissed ...

GREENE LJ delivered a concurring judgment.

TALBOT J concurred.

QUESTION

The judgment rests in part upon the assumption that 'the company' accepted the plaintiff's services. Which organ or agent of the company could in the circumstances be deemed to have done so? (There were some outside shareholders.)

NOTE

The plaintiff as an 'insider' was deemed to have constructive notice both of the supposed directors' want of competence, and of his own ineligibility for appointment because he was not a director. In the light of *Hely-Hutchinson v Brayhead Ltd* (**107**) he might not now be considered an 'insider'.

In *Re Richmond Gate Property Co Ltd* [1964] 3 All ER 936, [1965] 1 WLR 335, Plowman J held that a managing director was not entitled to remuneration on a quantum meruit basis, because the articles of the company provided that a managing director was to receive 'such remuneration ... as the directors may determine', and the company had gone into liquidation without any consideration of the matter by the directors. The existence of an express arrangement about remuneration, the judge held, ruled out any possibility of an alternative claim based on a quantum meruit. The case depends in part on a misunderstanding of *Craven Ellis v Canons Ltd* (**121**) and is, it is submitted, open to criticism on other grounds also, so that its authority is questionable.

The functions of a managing director are not fixed by law, but depend on the particular terms of his appointment.

122 Harold Holdsworth & Co (Wakefield) Ltd v Caddies [1955] 1 WLR 352, [1955] 1 All ER 725 (House of Lords)

[The facts appear from the opinion of Earl Jowitt.]

EARL JOWITT: My Lords, the appellants are a limited company carrying on business as worsted yarn spinners at Balne Mills, Wakefield, Yorkshire. In 1947 the appellant company had purchased from the respondent the entire share capital of a company known as the British Textile Manufacturing Co Ltd, whom I refer to as the Textile Company. The business of the Textile Company, which was carried on at Irvine, Ayrshire, was the manufacture of knitted articles of wool clothing. The appellant company thus became, and remained at all material times, the beneficial owners of all the shares in the Textile Company. They were also beneficial owners of all the shares in two other limited companies ...

By an agreement between the appellant company and the respondent dated April 1, 1949, which was to operate as from October 1, 1948, the respondent was appointed managing director of the appellant company ... Clause 1 of that agreement was in the following terms:

> [The respondent] shall be and he is hereby appointed a managing director of the [appellant] company and as such managing director he shall

perform the duties and exercise the powers in relation to the business of the company and the businesses (howsoever carried on) of its existing subsidiary companies at the date hereof which may from time to time be assigned to or vested in him by the board of directors of the company.

Other clauses in that agreement provided that the respondent was to hold the said office for five years; that he was to devote his whole time and attention to his duties under the agreement and in all respects to conform to, and comply with, the directions and regulations of the board; and that he was to receive a salary of £2,500 per annum together with a commission on profits ... Differences of opinion arose between the respondent and his fellow directors of the appellant company, and culminated in the passing of a resolution by the appellant company's board in the following terms:

Management at Balne Mills: The board decided that the managing director confine his attentions to British Textile Manufacturing Co Ltd only. Permanent arrangements for management at Balne Mills will be made later. Meanwhile the board requested Mr RP Pitcher to assume responsibility for local supervision. The managing director wished it recorded that as a director he did not agree with the decision.

The respondent regarded this resolution as a repudiation of the agreement and, by letter of 19 June 1950, intimated to the appellant company that, as they had so repudiated the agreement, he regarded himself as no longer bound to give, and intimated that he would not give, his services to the appellant company.

My Lords ... I am clearly of the opinion that the resolution did not constitute any breach of the agreement. I think that, on the true construction of cl 1 of the agreement of 1949, the respondent was to perform such duties and exercise such powers in relation to the business of the appellant company, and to perform such duties and exercise such powers in relation to the business of the Textile Company and the other subsidiaries, as might from time to time be vested in him by the appellant company's board. In directing the respondent on 10 May 1950, to confine his attention to the Textile Company, the board of the appellant company were, in my opinion, merely exercising the right given to them by the agreement.

The Lord President (Lord Cooper) took a different view, because he considered that the appointing of managing director was

a well recognised title in company administration, carrying responsibilities of a familiar nature and involving sundry obligations and liabilities under the Companies Act. The [respondent] was not appointed to perform such duties, if any, as the board might assign to him.

The Lord President, having formed this view, no doubt considered that the resolution which called on the respondent to devote his whole time to the affairs of the Textile Company prevented him from carrying out those responsiblities, obligations and liablities which, on this view, he had the right to perform for the appellant company, by virtue of his office as their managing director. My Lords, with the greatest respect for the Lord President, I do not think that the respondent, by the mere fact that he was appointed managing director of the appellant company, had any responsibilities, obligations or liabilities which would prevent the appellant company ordering him to devote his full time to a subsidiary, and I am of the opinion that the appellant company had, by cl 1 of the agreement, expressly preserved their right to call on the respondent to devote his time to the affairs of the Textile Company if they judged this course desirable.

Being of the opinion that there was no relevant breach of contract averred, I think the action should have been dismissed without proof, and, accordingly, I would allow the appeal.

VISCOUNT KILMUIR LC and LORDS MORTON OF HENRYTON and REID delivered concurring opinions.

LORD KEITH OF AVONHOLM dissented.

QUESTION

Are the decisions in *Biggerstaff v Rowatt's Wharf Ltd* (**111**), *Freeman & Lockyer v Buckhurst Park Properties* (*Mangal*) *Ltd* (**115**) and *Hely-Hutchinson v Brayhead Ltd* (**116**) consistent with the ruling in this case?

It is permissible to pay directors remuneration when the company has made no profits, and even when the company is not solvent. The amount of remuneration is for the shareholders to fix, and need not be determined by the market value of those services. But an award of remuneration must be 'genuine' and not a 'disguised gift' or an unlawful return of capital to a shareholder.

123 Re Halt Garage (1964) Ltd [1982] 3 All ER 1016 (Chancery Division)

Mr and Mrs Charlesworth were the only directors and shareholders of the company, and initially they had both worked in the business, drawing sums as directors' remuneration under express powers in the memorandum and articles. In 1967 Mrs Charlesworth became ill and ceased to take an active part in the business, but she remained a director and continued to draw remuneration at a reduced rate. From 1968 onwards, the company became unprofitable, and in 1971 it went into insolvent liquidation. The liquidator claimed that Mrs Charlesworth had no right to be paid after she had given up work, and also that Mr Charlesworth had been paid more than the market value of his services, and sought restitution of the sums allegedly overpaid. The payments to Mr Charlesworth were upheld, even those made after the company had ceased to be profitable. But Mrs Charlesworth was obliged to refund that part of the money paid to her which the judge held was not a 'genuine award of remuneration' but a 'disguised gift out of capital'.

OLIVER J: Now there is no presumption that directors' remuneration is payable only out of divisible profits ...

Counsel for the liquidator does not go to the extent, in fact, of suggesting that when a company has fallen on bad times the directors must either close the business down immediately or go on trying to pull it round for nothing ... What I think counsel's submission comes to is this, that while the company has divisible profits remuneration may be paid on any scale which the shareholders are prepared to sanction within the limits of available profits, but that, as soon as there cease to be divisible profits, it can only lawfully be paid on a scale which the court, applying some objective standard of benefit to the company, considers to be reasonable. But assuming that the sum is bona fide voted to be paid as remuneration, it seems to me that the amount, whether it be mean or generous, must be a matter of management for the company to determine in accordance with its constitution which expressly authorises payment for directors' services. Shareholders are required to be honest but, as counsel for the respondents suggests, there is no requirement that they must be wise and it is not for the court to manage the company.

Counsel for the liquidator submits, however, that if this is right it leads to the bizarre result that a meeting of stupid or deranged but perfectly honest shareholders can, like Bowen LJ's lunatic director,[3] vote to themselves, qua directors, some perfectly outlandish sum by way of remuneration and that in a subsequent winding up the liquidator can do nothing to recover it. It seems to me that the answer to this lies in the objective test which the court necessarily applies. It assumes human beings to be rational and to apply ordinary standards. In the postulated circumstances of a wholly unreasonable payment, that might, no doubt, be prima facie evidence of fraud, but it might also be evidence that what purported to be remuneration was not remuneration at all but a dressed-up gift to a shareholder out of capital ...

This, as it seems to me, is the real question in a case such as the present. The real test must, I think, be whether the transaction in question was a genuine exercise of the power. The motive is more important than the label. Those who deal with a limited company do so on the basis that its affairs will be conducted in accordance with its constitution, one of the express incidents of which is that the directors may be paid remuneration. Subject to that, they are entitled to have the capital kept intact. They have to accept the shareholders' assessment of the scale of the remuneration, but they are entitled to assume that, whether liberal or illiberal, what is paid is genuinely remuneration and that the power is not used as a cloak for making payments out of capital to the shareholders as such ...

[His Lordship referred to Mrs Charlesworth's illness, and continued:] The fact is that, however valuable and exacting may have been the services which Mrs Charlesworth had rendered in the past, her continued directorship contributed nothing to the company's future, beyond the fact that she was and remained responsible as a director and was able to make up the necessary quorum for directors' meetings (of which remarkably few took place if the minutes are any accurate guide).

On the other hand, it is said that the Companies Act 1948 imposes on every company incorporated under its provisions an obligation to have a director and it contemplates that those who assume the responsibilities of office, whether they carry them out well or ill, may be paid for that service in such way and in such measure as the company's regulations prescribe or permit. Here the company's constitution conferred on it in express terms a power to award to a director a reward or remuneration for the bare fact of holding office, and that power the company purported to exercise. If it be legitimate for the company to award some remuneration, however nominal, to Mrs Charlesworth for acting as a director and taking on herself, for good or ill, the responsibilities which that office entails, at what point, counsel for the respondents asks, does it become beyond the company's power to do that which its constitution permits it to do and how can the court take on itself the discretion as to quantum which is vested in the shareholders, there being,

3 [In *Hutton v West Cork Rly Co* (see above, p 158).

ex concessis, no mala fides? I have not found the point an easy one, but on the view that I take of the law the argument of counsel for the respondents is very difficult to meet *if* the payments made really were within the express power conferred by the company's constitution.

But of course what the company's articles authorise is the fixing of 'remuneration', which I take to mean a reward for services rendered or to be rendered; and, whatever the terms of the resolutions passed and however described in the accounts or the company's books, the real question seems to me to be whether the payments really were 'directors' remuneration' or whether they were gratuitous distributions to a shareholder out of capital dressed up as remuneration.

I do not think that it can be said that a director of a company cannot be rewarded as such merely because he is not active in the company's business. The mere holding of office involves responsibility even in the absence of any substantial activity, and it is indeed in part to the mere holding of office that Mrs Charlesworth owes her position as a respondent in these proceedings. I can see nothing as a matter of construction of the article to disentitle the company, if the shareholders so resolve, from paying a reward attributable to the mere holding of the office of director, for being, as it were, a name on the notepaper and attending such meetings or signing such documents as are from time to time required. The director assumes the responsibility on the footing that he will receive whatever recompense the company in general meeting may think appropriate. In this case, however, counsel for the liquidator is entitled to submit that the sums paid to Mrs Charlesworth were so out of proportion to any possible value attributable to her holding of office that the court is entitled to treat them as not being genuine payments of remuneration at all but as dressed-up dividends out of capital . . .

[His Lordship considered the evidence, and ruled that only £10 out of the £30 per week which had been paid to Mrs Charlesworth while she was ill was genuinely 'remuneration'. He ordered her to repay the balance.]

QUESTIONS

(1) Mrs Charlesworth was a shareholder. Could Oliver J have reached the same conclusion if she had not held any shares?
(2) Earlier in his judgment, Oliver J said:

> It is a commonplace in private family companies, where there are substantial profits available for distribution by way of dividend, for the shareholder directors to distribute those profits by way of directors' remuneration rather than by way of dividend, because the latter course has certain fiscal disadvantages. But such a distribution may, and frequently does, bear very little relation to the true market value of the services rendered by the directors . . . Yet it is very difficult to see why the payment of directors' remuneration, on whatever scale the company in general meeting chooses, out of funds which could perfectly well be distributed by way of dividend, should be open to attack merely because the shareholders, in their own interests, choose to attach to it the label of directors' remuneration . . .

> Does this mean that different rules apply if a company has undistributed profits?
(3) Could Mrs Charlesworth have kept the payments if:
   (a) the company had been solvent at the time they were made;
   (b) the shareholders had believed that the company was solvent, when in fact it was not?

NOTES

(1) The payments to Mrs Charlesworth would now be caught (as a 'transaction at an undervalue') by IA 1986, s 238, subject to the time limits fixed by that section. In an appropriate case s 423 of that Act might also be applicable: this section has no time limits but requires proof of an intention to put assets beyond the reach of the company's creditors.
(2) The reasoning of Oliver J was followed by Hoffmann J in *Aveling Barford Ltd v Perion Ltd* (**183**) to strike down as not 'genuine' and as an unauthorised return of capital a sale of land made at an undervalue by a company to another company controlled by its principal shareholder. It is possible that we may see emerging here a new doctrine which may be invoked where corporate assets are wrongfully depleted for the benefit of insiders.

Where the power to pay directors' remuneration is conferred by the articles of association upon the directors themselves, the terms of the articles must be strictly observed.

124 Guinness plc v Saunders [1990] 2 AC 663, [1990] 1 All ER 652 (House of Lords)

In January 1986, the board of Guinness appointed a committee of three directors, Saunders, Roux and Ward, to handle the day-to-day decisions in connection with a take-over bid which Guinness had made for another company, Distillers. The bid was ultimately successful. Ward had been paid a fee of £5.2m for his part in the bid, which he said had been agreed by the committee. The company's articles empowered the board of Guinness to fix the remuneration of individual directors and contained several provisions allowing it to delegate various of its functions. The House of Lords declined to construe the articles in a way that invested the committee with power to pay remuneration to one of its own members, and ordered Ward to repay the £5.2m.

LORD TEMPLEMAN: ... Mr Ward admits receipt of £5.2m from Guinness and pleads an agreement by Guinness that he should be paid this sum for his advice and services in connection with the bid. Mr Ward admits that payment was not authorised by the board of directors of Guinness.

The articles of association of Guinness provide:

Remuneration of directors. 90. The board shall fix the annual remuneration of the directors provided that without the consent of the company in general meeting such remuneration (excluding any special remuneration payable under article 91 and article 92) shall not exceed the sum of £100,000 per annum. ...
91. The board may, in addition to the remuneration authorised in article 90, grant special remuneration to any director who serves on any committee or who devotes special attention to the business of the company or who otherwise performs services which in the opinion of the board are outside the scope of the ordinary duties of a director. Such special remuneration may be made payable to such director in addition to or in substitution for his ordinary remuneration as a director, and may be made payable by a lump sum or by way of salary, or commission or participation in profits, or by any or all of those modes or otherwise as the board may determine.

Articles 90 and 91 of the articles of association of Guinness depart from the Table A articles recommended by statute, which reserve to a company in general meeting the right to determine the remuneration of the directors of the company. But by article 90 the annual remuneration which the directors may award themselves is limited and by article 91 special remuneration for an individual director can only be authorised by the board. A committee, which may consist of only two or, as in the present case, three members, however honest and conscientious, cannot assess impartially the value of its work or the value of the contribution of its individual members. A director may, as a condition of accepting appointment to a committee, or after he has accepted appointment, seek the agreement of the board to authorise payment for special work envisaged or carried out. The shareholders of Guinness run the risk that the board may be too generous to an individual director at the expense of the shareholders but the shareholders have, by article 91, chosen to run this risk and can protect themselves by the number, quality and impartiality of the members of the board who will consider whether an individual director deserves special reward. Under article 91 the shareholders of Guinness do not run the risk that a committee may value its own work and the contribution of its own members. Article 91 authorises the board, and only the board, to grant special remuneration to a director who serves on a committee.

It was submitted that article 2 alters the plain meaning of article 91. In article 2 there are a number of definitions each of which is expressed to apply 'if not inconsistent with the subject or context'. The expression 'the board' is defined as 'The directors of the company for the time being (or a quorum of such directors assembled at a meeting of directors duly convened) or any committee authorised by the board to act on its behalf.'

The result of applying the article 2 definition to article 91, it is said, is that a committee may grant special remuneration to any director who serves on a committee or devotes special attention to the business of the company or who otherwise performs services which in the opinion of the committee are outside the scope of the ordinary duties of a director. In my opinion the subject and context of article 91 are inconsistent with the expression 'the board' in article 91 meaning anything except the board. Article 91 draws a contrast between the board and a committee of the board. The board is expressly authorised to grant special remuneration to *any* director who serves on *any* committee. It cannot have been intended that any committee should be able to grant special remuneration to any director, whether a member of the committee or not. The board must compare the work of an individual director with the ordinary duties of a director. The board must decide whether special remuneration shall be paid in addition to or in substitution for the annual remuneration determined by the board under article 90. These decisions could only be made by the board surveying the work and remuneration of each and every director. Article 91 also provides for the board to decide whether special remuneration should take the form of participation in profits; the article could not intend that a committee should be able to determine whether profits should accrue to the shareholders' fund or be paid out to an individual director. The remuneration of directors concerns all the members of the board and all the shareholders of Guinness. Article 2 does not operate to produce a result which is inconsistent with the language, the subject and the context of article 91. Only the board possessed power to award £5.2m to Mr Ward. . . .

[Lord Templeman ruled further that (i) none of Guinness's other articles conferred a power on the committee to pay Ward remuneration; (ii) Ward was not entitled to sue Guinness for professional services rendered as a solicitor; (iii) Saunders, as chairman, had no actual or ostensible authority to agree that Ward should be paid the sum; and (iv) that since the articles made express provision for the way in which directors should be remunerated, Ward had no claim by way of quantum meruit.]

LORD GOFF OF CHIEVELEY delivered a concurring opinion.

LORDS KEITH OF KINKEL, BRANDON OF OAKBROOK and GRIFFITHS concurred.

NOTE

Many companies, and especially public companies, have a 'remuneration committee' to which they entrust the delicate task of fixing the directors' remuneration. It is normally composed mainly, if not exclusively, of non-executive directors. The powers of such a committee will depend upon the company's articles and its terms of reference in the particular case; but most commonly it will only make recommendations to either the board or the general meeting. The committee in the *Guinness* case, of course, was charged with quite a different function.

B. Directors: obligations and duties

The directors *as a body* are under an equitable duty to act bona fide in the interests of the company (see below, p 284). This phrase is reminiscent of the obligation imposed upon the majority voters at a shareholders' or class meeting (see above, p 111); but there is at least one vital difference between the two situations.[4] Whereas there is no rule that a shareholder who has a personal interest in a matter is precluded from voting, or even a presumption that a vote given in such a case is biased or affected by mala fides, there is an irrebuttable presumption of irregularity in the case of a director, which forbids any inquiry whatever into his good faith, even where the disinterested directors constitute a quorum without him. The articles may, however, modify this equitable rule (as in practice is invariably done: see Table A, articles 85, 94) by empowering the company to act through a quorum of directors, and even by expressly permitting an interested director to take part. Even so, the basic duty to act bona fide in the company's interests continues to apply. It is also established that directors must exercise their powers 'for proper purposes', an obligation which is viewed sometimes as a variant of the duty to act bona fide and at other times as something distinct from it.

A director *as an individual* is in a fiduciary position in relation to his company. This has various consequences in equity. First, any contract in which he has an interest adverse to that of the company is voidable in the absence of disclosure, or of authorisation in the company's articles. (The equitable rule is supplemented by a statutory duty of disclosure and abstention with criminal sanctions for breach: see s 317 of the Act.) Secondly, it follows from the director's fiduciary position that he may not make a secret

---

4 The concept of 'the company' (or 'the company as a whole') may vary also in the different uses of the phrases.

profit, or divert an opportunity or advantage from the company to himself. There is, however, no equitable obligation imposed upon a director to *avoid* putting himself into a position where he may be faced with potentially conflicting loyalties. Directors' fiduciary duties are owed, under the traditional rules, to their *company* and not to the shareholders, either individually or collectively. But in some respects this view may be too narrow, and in certain circumstances a duty owed directly to shareholders may arise on the facts of a particular case.

A number of specific obligations are imposed upon directors, and sometimes other officers, by statute–e g in regard to insider trading (below, p 539). The sanctions for breaches of such duties may be civil, or criminal, or both; and these statutory obligations do not displace the common law and equitable rules which have developed through the courts but have been superimposed on them without any thought having been given to the relationship between the two. This makes life very difficult for the practitioner, who may have to work through more than one checklist in order to see that he has covered all aspects of the law, and burdensome for the student, who has several sets of rules to learn when in any rational system one would be enough.

In endeavouring to fix directors with duties of care, skill and diligence, the courts concerned, being courts of Chancery, naturally turned to the analogy of trustees, but the parallel has not proved to be very appropriate. A trustee must be honest, and adhere strictly to the terms of his trust: the corresponding rules in company law are that a director must be honest, and act lawfully and within the terms of his own authority and the constitution of the company. To this limited extent, the rules of equity have served some purpose. But whereas a trustee is properly held only to the layman's standard of honesty, a director (at least in the case of a public company) ought nowadays to be fixed with the professional man's standards of skill and care.[5] This, however, requires a common law approach, and the development of the concept of the 'reasonable' business man whose behaviour is to be the yardstick. The cases have so far gone only a limited way towards establishing this new approach.

These common law duties of care and skill have now been supplemented by recent statutory innovations.The insolvency legislation of 1985–86 in certain circumstances empowers the court to review, with hindsight, the conduct of directors in the period leading up to a situation of corporate 'insolvency' and to penalise a director who has failed to come up to standards of proper behaviour. First, if a company is wound up insolvent, an order imposing personal liability on a director may be made if it is found that there has been 'wrongful trading' under IA 1986, s 214 (below, p 578). Secondly, if a company goes into insolvent liquidation or if an administration order is made against it or an administrative receiver is appointed, a director whose conduct in relation to that and perhaps other companies makes him 'unfit to be concerned in the management of a company' may have a disqualification order made against him (below, p 310). For the purpose of applying these

---

5 In other respects, the trustees' code is too severe. Trustees must conserve property, while directors must take business risks. Trustees must act unanimously, or seek the court's guidance; but directors may act by a quorum, and must accept the principle of majority rule. See further LS Sealy, 'The Director as Trustee' [1967] CLJ 83.

sanctions, the conduct of a director may be assessed by objective as well as subjective standards.

The directors of a company are not normally in a fiduciary position towards the shareholders individually.

125 Percival v Wright [1902] 2 Ch 421 (Chancery Division)

The plaintiffs offered to sell their shares, and the defendants, who were the chairman of the board and two other directors, agreed to buy them at £12.50 per share. After completion of the transfers, the plaintiffs discovered that at the time the board had been negotiating with an outsider for the sale to him of the company's whole undertaking at a price which represented well over £12.50 per share, but this information had not been disclosed to the plaintiffs. In fact, the takeover negotiations ultimately proved abortive. The plaintiffs claimed that the directors stood in a fiduciary relationship towards them as shareholders, and sought to avoid the transfers on the ground of non-disclosure; but the court held that there was no fiduciary relationship between directors and the shareholders individually.

SWINFEN EADY J: The position of the directors of a company has often been considered and explained by many eminent equity judges. [His Lordship discussed a number of cases dealing with directors' duties to their company, and continued:]

The plaintiffs' contention in the present case goes far beyond this. It is urged that the directors hold a fiduciary position as trustees for the individual shareholders, and that, where negotiations for sale of the undertaking are on foot, they are in the position of trustees for sale. The plaintiffs admitted that this fiduciary position did not stand in the way of any dealing between a director and a shareholder before the question of sale of the undertaking had arisen, but contended that as soon as that question arose the position was altered. No authority was cited for that proposition, and I am unable to adopt the view that any line should be drawn at that point. It is contended that a shareholder knows that the directors are managing the business of the company in the ordinary course of management, and impliedly releases them from any obligation to disclose any information so acquired. That is to say, a director purchasing shares need not disclose a large casual profit, the discovery of a new vein, or the prospect of a good dividend in the immediate future, and similarly a director selling shares need not disclose losses, these being merely incidents in the ordinary course of management. But it is urged that, as soon as negotiations for the sale of the undertaking are on foot, the position is altered. Why? The true rule is that a shareholder is fixed with knowledge of all the directors' powers, and has no more reason to assume that they are not negotiating a sale of the undertaking than to assume that they are not exercising any other power. It was strenuously urged that, though incorporation affected the relations of the shareholders to the external world, the company thereby becoming a distinct entity, the position of the share-holders inter se was not affected, and was the same as that of partners or shareholders in an unincorporated company. I am unable to adopt that view. I am therefore of opinion that the purchasing directors were under no obligation to disclose to their vendor shareholders the negotiations which ultimately proved abortive. The contrary view would place directors in a most invidious position, as they could not buy or sell shares without disclosing negotiations, a premature disclosure of which might well be against the best interests of the company. I am of opinion that directors are not in that position.

There is no question of unfair dealing in this case. The directors did not approach the shareholders with the view of obtaining their shares. The shareholders approached the directors, and named the price at which they were desirous of selling. The plaintiffs' case wholly fails, and must be dismissed with costs.

Directors may, however, in particular circumstances owe fiduciary duties to the shareholders individually, as, e g when they undertake to act as the shareholders' agents.

126 Allen v Hyatt (1914) 30 TLR 444 (Privy Council)

The appellants, directors of Lakeside Canning Co Ltd, who were negotiating an amalgamation with another company, induced the respondents, who were shareholders in the company, to give them options to buy their shares at par by representing that this would assist their negotiations. When the final terms were agreed upon with the other company, the directors exercised their options and made a handsome profit.The Judicial Committee affirmed the view of the three courts below in Ontario that the appellants must account for the profit to the respondents.

The opinion of the board was delivered by VISCOUNT HALDANE LC: The action was brought by the respondents for a declaration that the appellants were trustees for the shareholders of the Lakeside Canning Company of the profits derived from the Dominion Company, and for an account and consequential relief.

Mr Justice Sutherland tried the case and, after hearing evidence, found the facts substantially as follows: That general and similar representations were made by the appellants to each of the respondents, to the effect that the former as directors wanted the options from the shareholders in order to deal on behalf of all the shareholders with the representatives of the Dominion Company; that the appellants expected to realise the par value of the shares and the 7% interest, and that all the shareholders, including themselves, were to share pro rata in the amount they realised; that the appellants did not inform the other shareholders that they were buying their shares on their own account, and that they had entered into a secret arrangement by which they kept concealed from the other shareholders the information which it was their duty, as directors, to disclose, and that the appellants were thereby guilty of fraud ...

The Court of Appeal took the same view and held that although in other circumstances it might be that the fiduciary duty of the directors was a duty to the company and not to individual shareholders, yet in circumstances such as those of the case before them the directors became the agents in the transaction of the shareholders, when they took the options from them ...

[Their] Lordships did not think it necessary to say more, so far as the questions of fact were concerned, than that, having heard the arguments and considered the evidence, they saw no ground for not accepting the concurrent findings of the three courts which had already decided that issue. They agreed with the Court of Appeal in thinking that the respondents were entitled to treat the appellants as trustees for them, and, subject to the question of procedure, to ask for the relief they obtained.

The appellants appeared to have been under the impression that the directors of a company were entitled in all circumstances to act as though they owed no duty to individual shareholders. No doubt the duty of the directors was primarily one to the company itself. It might be that in circumstances such as those of *Percival v Wright* (**125**) they could deal at arm's length with a shareholder. But the facts in the present case were widely different from those in *Percival v Wright*, and their Lordships thought that the directors must here be taken to have held themselves out to the individual shareholders as acting for them on the same footing as they were acting for the company itself, that was, as agents ...

NOTE

In *Coleman v Myers* [1977] 2 NZLR 225, the defendants were directors of a family company. The first defendant make a take-over offer to all the other shareholders and ultimately succeeded in acquiring total control of the company. The plaintiffs were minority shareholders who had reluctantly agreed to sell when the first defendant invoked statutory powers of compulsory purchase under a section equivalent to CA 1985, s 429. They then brought an action against the defendants alleging, inter alia, breaches of fiduciary duty owed by the defendants as directors to themselves as shareholders. Mahon J at first instance considered that *Percival v Wright* (**125**) had been wrongly decided, although he found in favour of the defendants on other grounds. On appeal, the New Zealand Court of Appeal did not regard *Percival v Wright* as having been wrong on its own particular facts, but did hold that a fiduciary relationship had existed between the directors and the shareholders in the special circumstances of *Coleman*'s case: the company was a private company with shares held largely by members of the one family, the other members of the family had habitually looked to the defendants for business advice, and information affecting the true value of the shares had been withheld from the shareholders by the defendants. The defendants were accordingly held liable to compensate the plaintiffs. In the course of his judgment, WOODHOUSE J, referring to *Percival v Wright*, said:

'In my opinion it is not the law that anybody holding the office of director of a limited liability company is for that reason alone to be released from what otherwise would be regarded as a fiduciary responsibility owed to those in the position of shareholders of the same company. Certainly their status as directors did not protect the defendants in a Canadian case which finally made its way to the Privy Council: see *Allen v Hyatt* (**126**). The decision in that case turned upon the point that the directors of the company had put themselves in a fiduciary relationship with some of their shareholders because they had undertaken to sell shares of the shareholders in an agency capacity. But there is nothing in the decision to suggest that in the case of a director the fiduciary relationship can arise only in an agency situation. On the other hand, the mere status of company director should not produce that sort of responsiblity to a shareholder and in my opinion it does not do so. The existence of such a relationship must depend, in my opinion, upon all the facts of the particular case.

'When dealing with this part of the present case, Mahon J himself came to the conclusion that *Percival v Wright* had been wrongly decided. Then he expressed his opinion generally upon the point in the following way:

The essential basis of breach of fiduciary duty is the improper advantage taken by the defendant of a confidence reposed in him either by, or for the benefit of, the plaintiff. When one considers the legal relationship between the shareholder in a limited liability company and the directors entrusted with the management of that company, it appears to me that in any transaction involving sale of shares between director and shareholder, the director is the repository of confidence and trust necessarily vested in him by the shareholder, or by his legal status, in relation to the existence of information affecting the true value of those shares.

He then qualified that conclusion by restricting it to those holding office as directors in private companies. It may be that he intended some qualification beyond that but if he did not then, with respect, I think myself the conclusion is too broadly stated.

'As I have indicated it is my opinion that the standard of conduct required from a director in relation to dealings with a shareholder will differ depending upon all the surrounding circumstances and the nature of the responsibility which in a real and practical sense the director has assumed towards the shareholders. In the one case there may be a need to provide an explicit warning and a great deal of information concerning the proposed transaction. In another there may be no need to speak at all. There will be intermediate situations. It is, however, an area of the law where the courts can and should find some practical means of giving effect to sensible and fair principles of commercial morality in the cases that come before them; and while it may not be possible to lay down any general test as to when the fiduciary duty will arise for a company director or to prescribe the exact conduct which will always discharge it when it does, there are nevertheless some factors that will usually have an influence upon a decision one way or the other. They include, I think, dependence upon information and advice, the existence of a relationship of confidence, the significance of some particular transaction for the parties and, of course, the extent of any positive action taken by or on behalf of the director or directors to promote it. In the present case each one of those matters had more than ordinary significance and when they are taken together they leave me in no doubt that each of the two directors did owe a fiduciary duty to the individual shareholders.'

Directors whose company is the 'target' in a take-over bid may owe duties to their company's shareholders.

127 Heron International Ltd v Lord Grade [1983] BCLC 244 (Court of Appeal)

Associated Communications Corpn plc (ACC) was the subject of rival take-over bids from companies referred to in the judgment as 'Bell' and 'Heron'. The capital of ACC consisted of 150,000 voting shares and over 54 million non-voting shares. Article 29 (A) of the company's articles provided that the transfer of any voting share could only be made to a person nominated by the directors and with the approval of the Independent Broadcasting Authority (IBA).

The judgment of the court (LAWTON, TEMPLEMAN and BRIGHTMAN LJJ) was read by LAWTON LJ, and in the course of it he said: Under article 29 (A) if a shareholder desires to sell his shares, it is for the directors and not the IBA to decide who shall be the purchaser and transferee . . . Thus, [if] the directors are purporting to operate under article 29 (A) . . ., they must consider whether a transfer should be allowed to take place to an intended transferee. In the present case, for example, the directors as a whole were under a duty to decide whether to sanction a sale by any director of voting shares to Bell. This duty to determine which person shall acquire and be registered as the holder of voting shares in ACC is a fiduciary power which the directors must exercise in the interests of the company and in the interests of the shareholders of the company. The fact that the directors as individuals held between them a majority of the voting shares did not authorise them to reflect their individual inclinations. The directors as directors had a duty to consider whether, in exercise of the fiduciary power vested in them by article 29, they should agree to voting shares being transferred to Bell. In the declaration which the directors signed on 11 February 1982 they appear to be unaware of the fiduciary duties imposed upon them by article 29 because they assert that they will accept the Bell offer irrespective of what advice they may be obliged to give other shareholders. They could not advise shareholders to refuse Bell's offer and, at the same time, as directors allow their own voting shares to be transferred to Bell. Either it is in the interests of ACC and of all their shareholders, voting and non-voting, that Bell should take over ACC or it is in the interests of them all that Heron should take over ACC; and it is in the interests of all shareholders that they should not be deprived of an opportunity to sell their shares to the highest bidder . . .

Where directors have decided that it is in the interests of the company that the company should be taken over, and where there are two or more bidders, the only duty of the directors, who have powers such as those contained in article 29, is to obtain the best price. The directors should not commit themselves to transfer their own voting shares to a bidder unless they are satisfied that he is offering the best price reasonably obtainable. Where the directors must only decide between rival bidders, the interests of the company must be the interests of the current shareholders. The future of the company will lie with the successful bidder. The directors owe no duty to the successful bidder or to the company after it has passed under the control of the successful bidder. The successful bidder can look after himself, and the shareholders who reject the bid and remain as shareholders do so with their eyes open, having rejected that price which the directors consider to be the best price reasonably obtainable. Thus, as a result of article 29, the directors owed a duty to the general body of shareholders who were shareholders on 13 January 1982 to obtain for the shareholders the opportunity to accept or reject the best bid reasonably obtainable.

The directors of ACC could not consistently with their duty decide to sell and transfer their individual voting shares to Bell at 66p and, at the same time, advise other shareholders to reject the Bell bid on the grounds that the price was lower than the price obtainable from Heron.

This does not mean that the directors were bound to refuse to commit themselves or to commit the company to Bell on 13 January 1982. What it does mean is that, when the directors considered the ultimatum presented by Mr Holmes à Court [a director of Bell] on 13 January 1982, they should have asked themselves whether there was a reasonable possibility of obtaining a higher bid either from Heron or a third party or from Bell, or whether it was vitally necessary, in the interests of the company and of the existing shareholders, that the Bell offer should be immediately embraced.

[His Lordship examined the evidence, and concluded that the directors had not acted unreasonably or in breach of duty in deciding that the bid from Bell should be accepted.]

NOTES

For further cases dealing with the duties of directors in a take-over, see *Re a Company* (**262**) and *Dawson International plc v Coats Patons plc* (**263**). These cases show that the directors' duty to the shareholders in *Heron International Ltd v Lord Grade* depended upon the special power contained in the company's article 29 (A).

Reference should also be made to *Mills v Mills* (**138**), in which it was recognised that in matters affecting the relative rights of different categories of members, where no considerations of the paramount interests of the company as a corporate body arise, the directors owe a duty to act fairly as between the different classes of shareholders.

Directors' 'duties' to creditors

There are dicta in a number of cases to the effect that directors are under a duty to have regard to the interests of *creditors* of their company. Sometimes this is put more loosely as a duty *owed to* the creditors. But in many other cases the suggestion that directors owe a duty to creditors is emphatically rejected: see, e g *Charterbridge Corpn Ltd v Lloyds Bank Ltd* (**69**), *Re Halt Garage (1964) Ltd* (**123**), *Re Horsley & Weight Ltd* (**98**), the *Multinational Gas* case (**143**) and *Kuwait Asia Bank EC v National Mutual Life Nominees Ltd* (**136**). Each of these statements must be taken in its context. It would be contrary to all reason to burden directors with any duty towards creditors when their company is solvent: their function is to make judgments about business risks, and to take those risks. Those who give credit to limited liability companies are plainly aware of this. The dicta in the five cases cited above confirm this. Moreover, the law gives no standing to the creditors, individually or collectively, to sue to redress a breach of any such supposed duty.

The picture is different when a company is insolvent, or nearly so. It is in keeping with recent trends in the law of insolvency (e g in relation to 'wrongful trading': see below, p 578) for a judge to say that the directors of an ailing company must have regard to the interests of the company's creditors—not because any duty directly owed to the creditors has come into being,[6] but because ('lifting the veil' and looking at the situation broadly) it is the creditors' position in the company's liquidation which will be affected by the directors' acts. Even so, the only duty of the directors that the law is able to recognise continues to be that owed to the company, and it is only indirectly, through a liquidator acting on behalf of the company (or, perhaps, an administrator or a receiver) that the creditors' interests are represented.

Judicial statements that directors are obliged to have regard to the interests of their company's creditors will be found invariably to have been made in the context just described. One example appears in the extract from *Walker v Wimborne* cited above, p 146. Among others we may note the following:[7]

Kinsela v Russell Kinsela Pty Ltd (1986) 10 ACLR 395 at 401, 404 (NSW CA), per Street CJ:

> The learned judge at first instance held, as I have noted, that he was bound by authority to hold that the approval by all the shareholders validated an action which would otherwise be beyond the powers of the directors provided that there had been a full and frank disclosure to the shareholders of all the circumstances relevant to the proposed transaction ...

---

6 Dicta to this effect in *Nicholson v Permakraft (NZ) Ltd* [1985] 1 NZLR 242 at 249, per Cooke J are, it is submitted, too wide.

7 See also *Brady v Brady* (**174**); *West Mercia Safetywear Ltd v Dodd* [1988] 4 BCC 30 at 33, CA, per Dillon LJ.

The authorities to which his Honour submitted, notwithstanding the generality of their enunciations of principle, were not intended to, and do not, apply in a situation in which the interests of the company as a whole involve the rights of creditors as distinct from the rights of shareholders. In a solvent company the proprietary interests of the shareholders entitle them as a general body to be regarded as the company when questions of the duty of directors arise. If, as a general body, they authorise or ratify a particular action of the directors, there can be no challenge to the validity of what the directors have done. But where a company is insolvent the interests of the creditors intrude. They become prospectively entitled, through the mechanism of liquidation, to displace the power of the shareholders and directors to deal with the company's assets. It is in a practical sense their assets and not the shareholders' assets that, through the medium of the company, are under the management of the directors pending either liquidation, return to solvency, or the imposition of some alternative administration ...

It is, to my mind, legally and logically acceptable to recognise that, where directors are involved in a breach of their duty to the company affecting the interests of shareholders, then shareholders can either authorise that breach in prospect or ratify it in retrospect. Where, however, the interests at risk are those of creditors I see no reason in law or in logic to recognise that the shareholders can authorise the breach. Once it is accepted, as in my view it must be, that the directors' duty to a company as a whole extends in an insolvency context to not prejudicing the interests of creditors ... the shareholders do not have the power or authority to absolve the directors from that breach.

Winkworth v Edward Baron Development Co Ltd [1987] 1 All ER 114 at 118 (HL), [1986] 1 WLR 1512 at 1516, per Lord Templeman:

[A] company owes a duty to its creditors, present and future. The company is not bound to pay off every debt as soon as it is incurred, and the company is not obliged to avoid all ventures which involve an element of risk, but the company owes a duty to its creditors to keep its property inviolate and available for the repayment of its debts. The conscience of the company, as well as its management, is confided to its directors. A duty is owed by the directors to the company and to the creditors of the company to ensure that the affairs of the company are properly administered and that its property is not dissipated or exploited for the benefit of the directors themselves to the prejudice of the creditors.

Directors' duties towards employees

Section 309(1) of CA 1985 provides that 'the matters to which the directors of a company are to have regard in the performance of their functions include the interests of the company's employees in general, as well as the interests of its members'.

Much of the interest in this provision, which was introduced by the Act of 1980, centres on the question of enforcement (below, p 472). It seems plain from its wording that the directors are not merely *permitted* to consider the employees' interest but *bound* to do so; but the borderline between 'may' and 'must' in this context is probably meaningless, for there is no requirement that the interests of the employees should be *preferred* to those of the members, and there will be many cases in which a decision adverse to the employees will be justifiable by reference to the benefits of long term profitability and thus the interests of the members.

QUESTIONS

(1) What difference has the enactment of s 309(1) made in theory or in practice to company law?
(2) Insofar as directors may be said to be under a duty to have regard to the interests of creditors, do not shareholders have a similar duty? (See *Re Halt Garage (1964) Ltd* (**123**), and contrast the *Kuwait Asia Bank* case (**136**).)

(1) CONTRACTS INVOLVING DIRECTORS

We consider first the position at common law. There is a degree of overlap between the principles established by the cases and the rules laid down by statute (mostly implementing the second EEC directive), which are noted at pp 261, 309, below.

A contract made by a company with one of its directors or with a company or firm in which he is interested is voidable at the instance of the company.

128 Aberdeen Rly Co v Blaikie Bros (1854) 1 Macq 461 (House of Lords)

The respondents, Blaikie Bros, had agreed to manufacture iron chairs for the railway company at £8.50 per ton, and sued to enforce the contract. The railway company pleaded that it was not bound by the contract because, at the time when it was made, the chairman of its board of directors was managing partner of the respondents. This plea was upheld by the House of Lords.

LORD CRANWORTH LC: This, therefore, brings us to the general question, whether a director of a railway company is or is not precluded from dealing on behalf of the company with himself, or with a firm in which he is a partner.

The directors are a body to whom is delegated the duty of managing the general affairs of the company.

A corporate body can only act by agents, and it is of course the duty of those agents so to act as best to promote the interests of the corporation whose affairs they are conducting. Such agents have duties to discharge of a fiduciary nature towards their principal.[8] And it is a rule of universal application that no one, having such duties to discharge, shall be allowed to enter into engagements in which he has, or can have, a personal interest conflicting, or which possibly may conflict, with the interests of those whom he is bound to protect.

So strictly is this principle adhered to that no question is allowed to be raised as to the fairness or unfairness of a contract so entered into.

It obviously is, or may be, impossible to demonstrate how far in any

8 *York and North Midland Rly Co v Hudson* (1853) 16 Beav 485.

particular case the terms of such a contract have been the best for the interest of the cestui que trust, which it was possible to obtain.

It may sometimes happen that the terms on which a trustee has dealt or attempted to deal with the estate or interests of those for whom he is a trustee, have been as good as could have been obtained from any other person—they may even at the time have been better.

But still so inflexible is the rule that no inquiry on that subject is permitted. The English authorities on this head are numerous and uniform.

The principle was acted on by Lord King in *Keech v Sandford*,[9] and by Lord Hardwicke in *Whelpdale v Cookson*,[10] and the whole subject was considered by Lord Eldon on a great variety of occasions ...

It is true that the questions have generally arisen on agreements for purchases or leases of land, and not, as here, on a contract of a mercantile character. But this can make no difference in principle. The inability to contract depends not on the subject-matter of the agreement, but on the fiduciary character of the contracting party, and I cannot entertain a doubt of its being applicable to the case of a party who is acting as manager of a mercantile or trading business for the benefit of others, no less than to that of an agent or trustee employed in selling or letting land.

Was then Mr Blaikie so acting in the case now before us?—if he was, did he while so acting contract on behalf of those for whom he was acting with himself?

Both these questions must obviously be answered in the affirmative. Mr Blaikie was not only a director, but (if that was necessary) the chairman of the directors. In that character it was his bounden duty to make the best bargains he could for the benefit of the company.

While he filled that character, namely, on 6 February 1846, he entered into a contract on behalf of the company with his own firm, for the purchase of a large quantity of iron chairs at a certain stipulated price. His duty to the company imposed on him the obligation of obtaining these chairs at the lowest possible price.

His personal interest would lead him to an entirely opposite direction, would induce him to fix the price as high as possible. This is the very evil against which the rule in question is directed, and here I see nothing whatever to prevent its application.

I observe that Lord Fullerton seemed to doubt whether the rule would apply where the party whose act or contract is called in question is only one of a body of directors, not a sole trustee or manager.

But, with all deference, this appears to me to make no difference. It was Mr Blaikie's duty to give to his co-directors, and through them to the company, the full benefit of all the knowledge and skill which he could bring to bear on the subject. He was bound to assist them in getting the articles contracted for at the cheapest possible rate. As far as related to the advice he should give them, he put his interest in conflict with his duty, and whether he was the sole director or only one of many, can make no difference in principle.

The same observation applies to the fact that he was not the sole person contracting with the company; he was one of the firm of Blaikie Brothers, with whom the contract was made, and so interested in driving as hard a bargain with the company as he could induce them to make ...

9 (1726) Sel Cas Ch 61.
10 (1747) 1 Ves Sen 9.

LORD BROUGHAM delivered a concurring opinion.

NOTE

It has been held that a contract is also voidable where a director has a conflicting *duty* (e g to another company, or to the beneficiaries of a trust of which he is trustee): *Transvaal Land Co v New Belgium (Transvaal) Land and Development Co* [1914] 2 Ch 488, CA.

Although the principle formulated by Lord Cranworth is expressed in unqualified terms, it is recognised both as a general rule of equity, and more particularly as regards company law, that *disclosure* of his interest by the fiduciary party may validate the contract. In relation to a director, the traditional rule is that disclosure to a disinterested quorum of directors is insufficient (see the cases cited below). This interpretation may perhaps be open to reconsideration in the light of *Shaw & Sons (Salford) Ltd v Shaw* (**96**) and similar decisions: but in practice the question is unlikely to arise since most modern articles (e g Table A, article 85) authorise disclosure to the rest of the board and expressly or by implication declare contracts made in compliance with this procedure to be valid.

A contract which is voidable because of a director's interest may be ratified by the company in general meeting. The director is not debarred from voting as a shareholder at such a meeting.

129 North-West Transportation Co Ltd v Beatty (1887) 12 App Cas 589 (Privy Council)

[The facts appear from the judgment.]

The opinion of their Lordships was delivered by SIR RICHARD BAGGALLAY: The plaintiff, Henry Beatty, is a shareholder in the North-West Transportation Company Limited, and he sues on behalf of himself and all other shareholders in the company, except those who are defendants. The defendants are the company and five shareholders, who, at the commencement of the action, were the directors of the company. The claim in the action is to set aside a sale made to the company by James Hughes Beatty, one of the directors, of a steamer called the *United Empire*, of which, previously to such sale, he was sole owner.

The general principles applicable to cases of this kind are well established. Unless some provision to the contrary is to be found in the charter or other instrument by which the company is incorporated, the resolution of a majority of the shareholders, duly convened, upon any question with which the company is legally competent to deal, is binding upon the minority, and consequently upon the company, and every shareholder has a perfect right to vote upon any such question, although he may have a personal interest in the subject-matter opposed to, or different from, the general or particular interests of the company.

On the other hand, a director of a company is precluded from dealing, on behalf of the company, with himself, and from entering into engagements in which he has a personal interest conflicting, or which possibly may conflict, with the interests of those whom he is bound by fiduciary duty to protect; and this rule is as applicable to the case of one of several directors as to a managing or sole director. Any such dealing or engagement may, however, be affirmed or adopted by the company, provided such affirmance or adoption is not brought about by unfair or improper means, and is not illegal or fraudulent or oppressive towards those shareholders who oppose it.

The material facts of the case are not now in dispute ...

It is proved by uncontradicted evidence, and is indeed now substantially admitted, that at the date of the purchase the acquisition of another steamer to supply the place of the *Asia* was essential to the efficient conduct of the company's business; that the *United Empire* was well adapted for that purpose; that it was not within the power of the company to acquire any other steamer equally well adapted for its business; and that the price agreed to be paid for the steamer was not excessive or unreasonable ...

It is clear upon the authorities that the contract entered into by the directors on 10 February could not have been enforced against the company at the instance of the defendant JH Beatty, but it is equally clear that it was within the competency of the shareholders at the meeting of the 16th to adopt or reject it. In form and in terms they adopted it by a majority of votes, and the vote of the majority must prevail, unless the adoption was brought about by unfair or improper means.

The only unfairness or impropriety which, consistently with the admitted and established facts, could be suggested, arises out of the fact that the defendant JH Beatty possessed a voting power as a shareholder which enabled him, and those who thought with him, to adopt the bye-law,[11] and thereby either to ratify and adopt a voidable contract, into which he, as a director, and his co-directors had entered, or to make a similar contract, which latter seems to have been what was intended to be done by the resolution passed on 7 February.

It may be quite right that, in such a case, the opposing minority should be able, in a suit like this, to challenge the transaction, and to show that it is an improper one, and to be freed from the objection that a suit with such an object can only be maintained by the company itself.

But the constitution of the company enabled the defendant JH Beatty to acquire this voting power; there was no limit upon the number of shares which a shareholder might hold, and for every share so held he was entitled to a vote; the charter itself recognised the defendant as a holder of 200 shares, one-third of the aggregate number; he had a perfect right to acquire further shares, and to exercise his voting power in such a manner as to secure the election of directors whose views upon policy agreed with his own, and to support those views at any shareholders' meeting; the acquisition of the *United Empire* was a pure question of policy, as to which it might be expected that there would be differences of opinion, and upon which the voice of the majority ought to prevail; to reject the votes of the defendant upon the question of the adoption of the bye-law would be to give effect to the views of the minority, and to disregard those of the majority.

[See also *Burland v Earle* (**242**).]

---

11 [This was a company incorporated by letters patent. The 'bye-law' was a decision reached provisionally by the directors which had to be confirmed by the shareholders in general meeting.]

QUESTIONS

(1) In *Aberdeen Rly Co v Blaikie Bros* (**128**), Lord Cranworth said: 'So strictly is this principle adhered to that no question is allowed to be raised as to the fairness or unfairness of a contract so entered into.' Is it consistent with that view that the question of fairness should have been discussed in this case?

(2) In what circumstances might the exercise by Beatty of his voting power have been 'oppressive'? (Consider *Clemens v Clemens Bros Ltd* (**88**), *Cook v Deeks* (**131**), *Daniels v Daniels* (**246**).)

(3) How do you think that a judge is to decide whether the case before him involves 'a pure question of policy' or does not? (Compare *Cook v Deeks* (**131**).)

Non-compliance by a director with the statutory obligation to disclose his interest in a contract under CA 1985, s 317 does not render the contract void; but it remains voidable under the principles of equity.

130 Hely-Hutchinson v Brayhead Ltd [1968] 1 QB 549, [1967] 3 All ER 98 (Court of Appeal)

[For the facts and other parts of the decision, see (**107**) and (**116**).]

LORD DENNING MR: Accepting that Mr Richards had actual authority to make these contracts, there still remains the second point: Lord Suirdale was a director of Brayhead. He had an interest in these contracts and did not disclose it. He failed to comply with s 199 of the Companies Act 1948 [CA 1985, s 317] and with article 99 of the articles of association. He did not disclose the nature of his interest to any board meeting as he should have done. His failure is a criminal offence. It renders him liable to a fine not exceeding £100. But how does it affect the contract? . . .

It seems to me that when a director fails to disclose his interest, the effect is the same as non-disclosure in contracts uberrimae fidei, or non-disclosure by a promoter who sells to the company property in which he is interested: see *Re Cape Breton Co*;[12] *Burland v Earle* (**242**). Non-disclosure does not render the contract void or a nullity. It renders the contract voidable at the instance of the company and makes the director accountable for any secret profit which he has made.

At first sight article 99 does present difficulties. It says that: 'A director may contract with and be interested in any contract or proposed contract with the company either as vendor, purchaser or otherwise, and shall not be liable to account for any profit made by him by reason of any such contract or proposed contract, provided that the nature of the interest of the director in such contract or proposed contract be declared at a meeting of the directors as required by and subject to the provisions of s 199 of the Act.'

On the wording it might be suggested that there is no contract unless the director discloses his interest. In other words, that disclosure is a condition precedent to the formation of a contract. But I do not think that is correct. All that article 99 does is to validate every contract when the director makes proper disclosure. If he discloses his interest, the contract is not voidable,

12 (1885) 29 Ch D 795 (above, p 28).

nor is he accountable for profits. But if he does not disclose his interest, the effect of the non-disclosure is as before: the contract is voidable and he is accountable for secret profits.

In this case, therefore, the effect of the non-disclosure by Lord Suirdale was not to make the contract void or unenforceable. It only made the contract voidable. Once that is held, everyone agrees that it is far too late to avoid it. It is impossible to put the parties back in the same position or anything like it. The contracts are, therefore, valid and, I would add, enforceable. So Lord Suirdale can sue upon them.

LORDS WILBERFORCE and PEARSON delivered concurring judgments.

[See also *Rolled Steel Products (Holdings) Ltd v British Steel Corpn* (**70**).]

NOTES

(1) The decision in *Hely-Hutchinson v Brayhead Ltd* on this point was approved by the House of Lords in *Guinness plc v Saunders* (**124**). Ward, a former director of Guinness, claimed to be entitled to retain a sum of £5.2m which, he alleged, had been paid to him as a fee under a consultancy contract made betwen him and the company. The Court of Appeal, affirming Browne-Wilkinson V-C, had held that Ward's failure to disclose the contract to a meeting of Guinness's board of directors (as was required both by CA 1985, s 317 and by the company's articles) was fatal to his claim. But in the House of Lords Lord Goff pointed out that the effect of the failure by Ward to disclose his interest would have been to render the contract voidable and not void, with the consequence that the £5.2m could not be claimed back unless Guinness was willing and able to make restitutio in integrum. (However, Guinness did succeed on other grounds (see **124**), viz that there had never been proper authorisation to pay the money to Ward.)

(2) Attention must be drawn to the statutory provision in CA 1985, s 320, which was introduced by CA 1980 to implement a requirement of the Second EEC Directive. Where a director (or a person 'connected with' a director) enters into a 'substantial' property transaction (defined in s 320(2)) with his company, he is required (in addition to his obligations under s 317 and to whatever the articles may stipulate) to obtain shareholder approval beforehand (s 320) or ratification 'within a reasonable period' afterwards. Failing this, the Act provides both that the transaction shall be voidable and that he (together with the other directors) shall be liable to account to the company for any gain that he has made or to indemnify it against any loss that it has suffered (s 322(1)–(3)). There is a very crude overlap between this position and the common-law principles illustrated by the cases cited in this chapter, but it is not difficult to find detailed points of difference by studying the text of the Act.

(3) A further statutory provision dealing with contracts involving a director (or a person 'connected with' a director) and his company is CA 1985, s 322A, introduced by CA 1989. Where a company enters into a transaction which includes such a person as one of its parties, and the board of directors, in connection with the transaction, exceed any limitation on their powers under the company's constitution, the transaction is voidable at the instance of the company and the person in question, together with any director of the company who authorised the transaction, may incur personal liability to the company.

QUESTIONS

(1) What would be the effect of lapse of time on a contract affected by s 320?
(2) How far, if at all, can the obligations of s 320 be modified by provisions in the articles?
(3) The decisions in *Re Cape Breton Co* (1885) 29 Ch D 795 and *Ladywell Mining Co v Brookes* (1887) 35 Ch D 400 (above, p 28) are authorities on directors' contracts as well as those involving promoters. If a director's contract is 'substantial', does s 322(3) nullify the effect of these cases?
(4) If the facts of *Guinness plc v Saunders* were to recur, would s 322A be applicable?
(5) If a board of directors exceeds its powers, is not the resulting transaction *void* under the ordinary rules of agency? (Cf the *Rolled Steel* case (**70**).) What, if anything, is achieved by declaring (as s 322A does) that it is voidable?

(2) SECRET PROFITS

A director, being in a fiduciary position, is accountable to the company for any secret profit which he has made by reason of that position. Where directors acquire for themselves property or rights which they are regarded as holding in equity on behalf of their company, they cannot by using their votes as shareholders cause the company to waive its rights.

131 Cook v Deeks [1916] 1 AC 554 (Privy Council)

The defendants, three of the four directors of the Toronto Construction Company, who were named Deeks, Deeks and Hinds, resolved to break their business relations with the fourth director, the plaintiff Cook. The company had built up considerable goodwill with the Canadian Pacific Railway Company as a result of the satisfactory performance of a series of construction contracts, each of which had been negotiated with the railway company's representative by one of the defendants. The last of these contracts, the Shore Line contract, was negotiated in the same way, but when the arrangements were completed, the defendants took it in their own names and not that of the company. Cook claimed that the company was entitled to the benefit of the contract, and that a shareholders' resolution (which the defendants had carried by their own votes) purporting to confirm that the company claimed no interest in the contract was ineffective. The Privy Council upheld both contentions, reversing the decisions of the courts in Ontario in favour of the defendants.

The opinion of their Lordships was delivered by LORD BUCKMASTER, who stated the facts, and continued: Two questions of law arise out of this long history of fact. The first is whether, apart altogether from the subsequent resolutions, the company would have been at liberty to claim from the three defendants the benefit of the contract which they had obtained from the Canadian Pacific Railway Company; and the second, which only arises if the first be answered in the affirmative, whether in such event the majority of the shareholders of the company constituted by the three defendants could ratify and approve of what was done and thereby release all claim against the directors.

It is the latter question to which the Appellate Division of the Supreme

Court of Ontario have given most consideration, but the former needs to be carefully examined in order to ascertain the circumstances upon which the latter question depends.

It cannot be properly answered by considering the abstract relationship of directors and companies; the real matter for determination is what, in the special circumstances of this case, was the relationship that existed between Messrs Deeks and Hinds and the company that they controlled. Now it appears plain that the entire management of the company, so far as obtaining and executing contracts in the east was concerned, was in their hands, and indeed, it was in part this fact which was one of the causes of their disagreement with the plaintiff. The way they used this position is perfectly plain. They accelerated the work on the expiring contract of the company in order to stand well with the Canadian Pacific Railway when the next contract should be offered, and although Mr McLean was told that the acceleration was to enable the company to get the new contract, yet they never allowed the company to have any chances whatever of acquiring the benefit, and avoided letting their co-director have any knowledge of the matter. Their Lordships think that the statement of the trial judge upon this point is well founded when he said that 'it is hard to resist the inference that Mr Hinds was careful to avoid anything which would waken Mr Cook from his fancied security', and again, that 'the sole and only object on the part of the defendants was to get rid of a business associate whom they deemed, and I think rightly deemed, unsatisfactory from a business standpoint'. In other words, they intentionally concealed all circumstances relating to their negotiations until a point had been reached when the whole arrangement had been concluded in their own favour and there was no longer any real chance that there could be any interference with their plans. This means that while entrusted with the conduct of the affairs of the company they deliberately designed to exclude, and used their influence and position to exclude, the company whose interest it was their first duty to protect ...

It is quite right to point out the importance of avoiding the establishment of rules as to directors' duties which would impose upon them burdens so heavy and responsibilities so great that men of good position would hesitate to accept the office. But, on the other hand, men who assume the complete control of a company's business must remember that they are not at liberty to sacrifice the interests which they are bound to protect, and, while ostensibly acting for the company, divert in their own favour business which should properly belong to the company they represent.

Their Lordships think that, in the circumstances, the defendants TR Hinds and GS and GM Deeks were guilty of a distinct breach of duty in the course they took to secure the contract, and that they cannot retain the benefit of such contract for themselves, but must be regarded as holding it on behalf of the company.

There remains the more difficult consideration of whether this position can be made regular by resolutions of the company controlled by the votes of these three defendants. The Supreme Court have given this matter the most careful consideration, but their Lordships are unable to agree with the conclusion which they reached.

In their Lordships' opinion the Supreme Court has insufficiently recognised the distinction between two classes of case and has applied the principles applicable to the case of a director selling to his company property which was in equity as well as at law his own, and which he could dispose of as he thought fit, to the case of the director dealing with property which, though his own at law, in equity belonged to his company. The cases of *North-West Transportation Co v Beatty* (**129**) and *Burland v Earle* (**242**) both belonged to the former class. In each, directors had sold to the company property in which the company had no interest at law or in equity. If the company claimed any interest by reason of the transaction, it could only be by affirming the sale, in which case such sale, though initially voidable, would be validated by subsequent ratification. If the company refused to affirm the sale the transaction would be set aside and the parties restored to their former position, the directors getting the property and the company receiving back the purchase price. There would be no middle course. The company could not insist on retaining the property while paying less than the price agreed. This would be for the court to make a new contract between the parties.[13] It would be quite another thing if the director had originally acquired the property which he sold to his company under circumstances which made it in equity the property of the company. The distinction to which their Lordships have drawn attention is expressly recognised by Lord Davey in *Burland v Earle* and is the foundation of the judgment in *North-West Transportation Co v Beatty*, and is clearly explained in the case of *Jacobus Marler Estates v Marler*[14] ...

If, as their Lordships find on the facts, the contract in question was entered into under such circumstances that the directors could not retain the benefit of it for themselves, then it belonged in equity to the company and ought to have been dealt with as an asset of the company. Even supposing it be not ultra vires of a company to make a present to its directors, it appears quite certain that directors holding a majority of votes would not be permitted to make a present to themselves. This would be to allow a majority to oppress the minority. To such circumstances the cases of *North-West Transportation Co v Beatty* and *Burland v Earle* have no application. In the same way, if directors have acquired for themselves property or rights which they must be regarded as holding on behalf of the company, a resolution that the rights of the company should be disregarded in the matter would amount to forfeiting the interest and property of the minority of shareholders in favour of the majority, and that by the votes of those who are interested in securing the property for themselves. Such use of voting power has never been sanctioned by the court, and, indeed, was expressly disapproved in the case of *Menier v Hooper's Telegraph Works* (**243**).

If their Lordships took the view that, in the circumstances of this case, the directors had exercised a discretion or decided on a matter of policy (the view which appears to have been entertained by the Supreme Court) different results would ensue, but this is not a conclusion which their Lordships are able to accept. It follows that the defendants must account to the Toronto Company for the profits which they have made out of the transaction ...

QUESTIONS

(1) Would the position have been any different if the defendants had told Cook beforehand of their plans? Or if the matter had been put to a shareholders' meeting

13 [Cf the discussion above, p 28.]
14 (1913) 85 LJPC 167n.

in advance, and the defendants had used their majority votes to carry a resolution giving them a 'clearance' to proceed independently of the company?

(2) Can you suggest circumstances in which the directors might be said to have 'exercised a discretion or decided on a matter of policy', with the result that the defendants could have had the benefit of the Shore Line contract for themselves?

132 **Regal (Hastings) Ltd v Gulliver** [1942] 1 All ER 378, [1967] 2 AC 134n (House of Lords)

The appellant company ('Regal') owned a cinema in Hastings, and the directors decided to acquire two others in the same area and sell all three to an outsider as a going concern. For this purpose, they formed a subsidiary company, Hastings Amalgamated Cinemas Ltd ('Amalgamated') to lease the other two cinemas; but the landlord insisted on either a personal guarantee of the rent from the directors, or the paid-up capital of Amalgamated being £5,000. Regal was unable to pay for more than 2,000 £1 shares in Amalgamated from its own resources, and so the directors, not wishing to give the requested guarantees, agreed to take up the other 3,000 shares between themselves. In the event, four directors took 500 shares each personally, the chairman Gulliver found outside subscribers for 500, and the remaining 500 were offered by the board to Garton, the company's solicitor. Some three weeks later, the proposal for a sale of the actual cinemas was abandoned, and was replaced by an agreement to sell to the purchasers all the shares in the two companies. As a result, the directors and others who had subscribed for the 3,000 shares in Amalgamated made a profit of £2 16s 1d [£2.80] per share. Regal, now under the control of the purchasers, then issued a writ claiming reimbursement of this profit from the four directors, Gulliver and Garton. The action was based alternatively in negligence, misfeasance, and money had and received. Before the House of Lords, only the last of these claims was argued, and the four directors (but not Gulliver or Garton) were held severally liable to account.

LORD RUSSELL OF KILLOWEN: The case has, I think, been complicated and obscured by the presentation of it before the trial judge. If a case of wilful misconduct or fraud on the part of the respondents had been made out, liability to make good to Regal any damage which it had thereby suffered could, no doubt, have been established; and efforts were apparently made at the trial, by cross-examination and otherwise, to found such a case. It is, however, due to the respondents to make it clear at the outset that this attempt failed. The case was not so presented to us here. We have to consider the question of the respondents' liability on the footing that, in taking up these shares in Amalgamated, they acted with bona fides, intending to act in the interest of Regal.

Nevertheless, they may be liable to account for the profits which they have made, if, while standing in a fiduciary relationship to Regal, they have by reason and in course of that fiduciary relationship made a profit. This aspect of the case was undoubtedly raised before the trial judge, but, in so far as he deals with it in his judgment, he deals with it on a wrong basis. Having stated at the outset quite truly that what he calls 'this stroke of fortune' only came the way of the respondents because they were the directors and solicitors of the Regal, he continues thus: 'But in order to succeed the plaintiff company must show that the defendants both ought to have caused and could have caused the plaintiff company to subscribe for these shares, and that the neglect to do so caused a loss to the plaintiff company. Short of this, if the plaintiffs can establish that, though no loss was made by the company, yet a profit was corruptly made by the directors and the solicitor, then the company can claim to have that profit handed over to the company, framing the action in such a case for money had and received by the defendants for the plaintiffs' use.' Other passages in his judgment indicate that, in addition to this 'corrupt' action by the directors, or, perhaps, alternatively, the plaintiffs in order to succeed must prove that the defendants acted mala fide, and not bona fide in the interests of the company, or that there was a plot or arrangement between them to divert from the company to themselves a valuable investment. However relevant such considerations may be in regard to a claim for damages resulting from misconduct, they are irrelevant to a claim against a person occupying a fiduciary relationship towards the plaintiff for an account of the profits made by that person by reason and in course of that relationship.

In the Court of Appeal, upon this claim to profits, the view was taken that in order to succeed the plaintiff had to establish that there was a duty on the Regal directors to obtain the shares for Regal. Two extracts from the judgment of Lord Greene MR shows this. After mentioning the claim for damages, he says: 'The case is put on an alternative ground. It is said that, in the circumstances of the case, the directors must be taken to have been acting in the matter of their office when they took those shares; and that accordingly they are accountable for the profits which they have made ... There is one matter which is common to both these claims which, unless it is established, appears to me to be fatal. It must be shown that in the circumstances of the case it was the duty of the directors to obtain these shares for their company.' Later in his judgment he uses this language: 'But it is said that the profit realised by the directors on the sale of the shares must be accounted for by them. That proposition involves that on 2 October, when it was decided to acquire these shares, and at the moment when they were acquired by the directors, the directors were taking to themselves something which properly belonged to the company.' Other portions of the judgment appear to indicate that upon this claim to profits, it is a good defence to show bona fides or absence of fraud on the part of the directors in the action which they took or that their action was beneficial to the company, and the judgment ends thus: 'That being so, the only way in which these directors could secure that benefit for their company was by putting up the money themselves. Once that decision is held to be a bona fide one, and fraud drops out of the case, it seems to me there is only one conclusion, namely, that the appeal must be dismissed with costs.'

My Lords, with all respect I think there is a misapprehension here. The rule of equity which insists on those, who by use of a fiduciary position make a profit, being liable to account for that profit, in no way depends on fraud, or absence of bona fides; or upon such questions or considerations as whether the profit would or should otherwise have gone to the plaintiff, or whether the profiteer was under a duty to obtain the source of the profit for the plaintiff, or whether he took a risk or acted as he did for the benefit of the plaintiff, or whether the plaintiff has in fact been damaged or benefited by his action. The liability arises from the mere fact of a profit having, in the stated circumstances, been made. The profiteer, however honest and well-intentioned, cannot escape the risk of being called upon to account.

The leading case of *Keech v Sandford*[15] is an illustration of the strictness of this rule of equity in this regard, and of how far the rule is independent of these outside considerations. A lease of the profits of a market had been devised to a trustee for the benefit of an infant. A renewal on behalf of the infant was refused. It was absolutely unobtainable. The trustee, finding that it was impossible to get a renewal for the benefit of the infant, took a lease for his own benefit. Though his duty to obtain it for the infant was incapable of performance, nevertheless he was ordered to assign the lease to the infant, upon the bare ground that, if a trustee on the refusal to renew might have a lease for himself, few renewals would be made for the benefit of cestuis que trust. Lord King LC said, at p 62: 'This may seem hard, that the trustee is the only person of all mankind who might not have the lease: but it is very proper that the rule should be strictly pursued, and not in the least relaxed ...' One other case in equity may be referred to in this connection, viz *Ex p James*,[16] decided by Lord Eldon LC. This was a case of a purchase of a bankrupt's estate by the solicitor to the commission, and Lord Eldon LC refers to the doctrine thus, at p 345: 'This doctrine as to purchases by trustees, assignees, and persons having a confidential character, stands much more upon general principles than upon the circumstances of any individual case. It rests upon this: that the purchase is not permitted in any case however honest the circumstances; the general interests of justice requiring it to be destroyed in every instance; as no court is equal to the examination and ascertainment of the truth in much the greater number of cases.'

Let me now consider whether the essential matters, which the plaintiff must prove, have been established in the present case. As to the profit being in fact made there can be no doubt. The shares were acquired at par and were sold three weeks later at a profit of £2 16*s* 1*d* per share. Did such of the first five respondents as acquired these very profitable shares acquire them by reason and in course of their office of directors of Regal? In my opinion, when the facts are examined and appreciated, the answer can only be that they did ...

It now remains to consider whether in acting as directors of Regal they stood in a fiduciary relationship to that company. Directors of a limited company are the creatures of statute and occupy a position peculiar to themselves. In some respects they resemble trustees, in others they do not. In some respects they resemble agents, in others they do not. In some respects they resemble managing partners, in others they do not. [His Lordship considered a number of the authorities and continued:]

In the result, I am of opinion that the directors standing in a fiduciary relationship to Regal in regard to the exercise of their powers as directors, and having obtained these shares by reason and only by reason of the fact that they were directors of Regal and in the course of the execution of that office, are accountable for the profits which they have made out of them. The equitable rule laid down in *Keech v Sandford* and *Ex p James* and similar authorities applies to them in full force. It was contended that these cases were distinguishable by reason of the fact that it was impossible for Regal to get the shares owing to lack of funds, and that the directors in taking the shares were really acting as members of the public. I cannot accept this argument. It was impossible for the cestui que trust in *Keech v Sandford* to

15 (1726) Sel Cas Ch 61.
16 (1803) 8 Ves 337.

obtain the lease, nevertheless the trustee was accountable. The suggestion that the directors were applying simply as members of the public is a travesty of the facts. They could, had they wished, have protected themselves by a resolution (either antecedent or subsequent) of the Regal shareholders in general meeting. In default of such approval, the liability to account must remain. The result is that, in my opinion, each of the respondents Bobby, Griffiths, Bassett and Bentley is liable to account for the profit which he made on the sale of his 500 shares in Amalgamated.

The case of the respondent Gulliver, however, requires some further consideration, for he has raised a separate and distinct answer to the claim. He says: 'I never promised to subscribe for shares in Amalgamated. I never did so subscribe. I only promised to find others who would be willing to subscribe. I only found others who did subscribe. The shares were theirs. They were never mine. They received the profit. I received none of it.' If these are the true facts, his answer seems complete. The evidence in my opinion establishes his contention ... As regards Gulliver, this appeal should, in my opinion be dismissed ...

There remains to consider the case of Garton. He stands on a different footing from the other respondents in that he was not a director of Regal. He was Regal's legal adviser; but, in my opinion, he has a short but effective answer to the plaintiffs' claim. He was requested by the Regal directors to apply for 500 shares. They arranged that they themselves should each be responsible for £500 of the Amalgamated capital, and they appealed, by their chairman, to Garton to subscribe the balance of £500 which was required to make up the £3,000. In law his action, which has resulted in a profit, was taken at the request of Regal, and I know of no principle or authority which would justify a decision that a solicitor must account for profit resulting from a transaction which he has entered into on his own behalf, not merely with the consent, but at the request of his client.

My Lords, in my opinion the right way in which to deal with this appeal is (i) to dismiss the appeal as against the respondents Gulliver and Garton with costs, (ii) to allow it with costs as against the other four respondents, and (iii) to enter judgment as against each of these four respondents for a sum of £1,402 1s 8d with interest at 4% ...

LORD PORTER: My Lords, I am conscious of certain possibilities which are involved in the conclusion which all your Lordships have reached. The action is brought by the Regal company. Technically, of course, the fact that an unlooked for advantage may be gained by the shareholders of that company is immaterial to the question at issue. The company and its shareholders are separate entities. One cannot help remembering, however, that in fact the shares have been purchased by a financial group who were willing to acquire those of the Regal and the Amalgamated at a certain price. As a result of your Lordships' decision that group will, I think, receive in one hand part of the sum which has been paid by the other. For the shares in Amalgamated they paid £3 16s 1d per share, yet part of that sum may be returned to the group, though not necessarily to the individual shareholders, by reason of the enhancement in value of the shares in Regal—an enhancement brought about as a result of the receipt by the company of the profit made by some of its former directors on the sale of Amalgamated shares. This, it seems, may be an unexpected windfall, but whether it be so or not, the principle that a person occupying a fiduciary relationship shall not make a profit by reason thereof is of such vital importance that the possible consequence in the present case is in fact as it is in law an immaterial consideration.

VISCOUNT SANKEY and LORDS MACMILLAN and WRIGHT delivered concurring opinions.

NOTE

In an editorial note to the All ER report of this case, it is stated: 'As their Lordships point out, no question as to the right to retain this profit could have arisen if the respondents had taken the precaution of obtaining the approval of the appellant company in general meeting, and this would have been a mere matter of form, since they doubtless controlled the voting.' In contrast, in *Prudential Assurance Co Ltd v Newman Industries (No 2)* (**247**) Vinelott J at first instance said [1980] 2 All ER 841 at 862: 'I can see nothing in the report which indicates that the defendant directors controlled the voting and, as I understand this passage in the speech of Lord Russell of Killowen, he contemplated that the defendant directors might have protected themselves by a resolution in general meeting precisely because they had not control of the majority of the votes.' What the true factual situation was may never be known; and (perhaps more relevantly) what Lord Russell *thought* the facts were we shall quite certainly never know.

Although there is superficially a close resemblance between this case and *Cook v Deeks* (**131**), it is most difficult to attempt to reconcile them on points of detail, and especially to deal satisfactorily with this question of ratification. The nature of the claim brought in *Regal* may be of relevance: we should note that the defendants were held *severally* liable in *money had and received* proceedings, i e accountable in each case as *debtor* for what he had received. On this basis, the observation that the transaction could have been authorised or ratified by the company in general meeting is consistent with some earlier authorities, such as *Lister & Co v Stubbs* (1890) 45 Ch D 1. Had the claim in negligence succeeded, *all five* of the directors would have been *jointly and severally* liable for the loss suffered by the company, but the company, might, it seems, still have ratified (see the *Multinational Gas* case (**143**); but *Daniels v Daniels* (**246**) may suggest the contrary); while had the court been prepared to hold, analogously with *Cook v Deeks*, that the business opportunity which the defendants exploited 'belonged' in equity to the company, all *six* defendants could have been held jointly and severally liable as constructive trustees for the value of the 'property' improperly paid away, and the shareholders could not have ratified. But the distinction between the two cases is perhaps impossible to pin down: the task is not made easier by the absence of any reference to *Cook v Deeks*, or to the constructive trust remedy, in the judgments. It is plain that Lord Russell of Killowen would have taken a different view of the matter had he thought that the profit had been 'corruptly' made, or that there had been a 'plot or arrangement to divert from the company to themselves a valuable investment' (above, p 266); but even on this view he was contemplating a remedy by way of 'damages for misconduct', which is not what was awarded in *Cook v Deeks*. To say that in *Cook v Deeks* the directors were under a 'duty' to give their company the benefit of the opportunity, but that there was no corresponding duty in *Regal*, is not merely to beg the question, but also to ignore the result reached in the latter case: there was plainly a 'duty' in both cases, albeit perhaps different 'duties' with different sanctions. It seems also to beg the question to say that the opportunity in *Cook v Deeks* 'belonged in equity' to the company: this too readily assumes that our jurisprudence has accepted the concept of an 'opportunity' as property; and it also does not explain why the opportunity in *Regal* was not so regarded. Unless, therefore, it is thought that the finding of bona fides was crucial, it is difficult to say why the impropriety in *Regal* was assumed to be capable of ratification (whether or not by the directors' own votes as shareholders), while that in *Cook v Deeks* was held not to be.

Regal was followed and applied in *Canadian Aero Service Ltd v O'Malley* and in *Industrial Development Consultants Ltd v Cooley*, both mentioned below; but in each of these cases the issue was more straightforward because the officers in question had an express mandate from the board to negotiate for the acquisition of the particular contract on behalf of their company, rather than a self-assumed undertaking; and there was also no question of ratification.

In *Canadian Aero Service Ltd v O'Malley* (1973) 40 DLR (3d) 371, the president and the executive vice-president of the plaintiff company ('Canaero') had been engaged on behalf of Canaero in negotiating for a large aerial surveying and mapping contract with the government of Guyana, to be financed by the external aid programme of the Canadian government. Instead of securing the contract for Canaero, they resigned their managerial posts and formed their own company ('Terra'), to which they successfully diverted the contract. The Supreme Court of Canada held that their fiduciary duty had survived their resignation and that that duty was enforceable against Terra as well as the individual defendants. The remedy took the form of an award of damages for breach of duty, rather than an account of profits. Key factors in this case were (1) that what the defendants had diverted for their own benefit was a 'maturing business opportunity' which their company was actively pursuing; (2) that they were participants in the negotiations on behalf of the company; (3) that their resignation had been 'prompted or influenced' by a wish to acquire the opportunity for themselves; and (4) that it was their position with the company rather than a 'fresh initiative' which led them to the opportunity which they later acquired.

These elements were all present in *Industrial Development Consultants Ltd v Cooley* [1972] 2 All ER 162, [1972] 1 WLR 443 where Cooley, an architect, was managing director of the plaintiff company, which was in business as building and development consultants. As the company's representative, he took part in negotiations with officers of the Eastern Gas Board, endeavouring to secure for the company contracts to build four large depots; but these negotiations were unsuccessful because the Board would not engage a firm of consultants (as distinct from a private architect). Shortly afterwards, the work was offered to Cooley in his private capacity. Cooley obtained a release from his employment (by falsely representing that he was in ill health), and was later given the contract by the Gas Board. Roskill J held that he was accountable to the company for the whole of his benefits under the contract or, alternatively, liable in damages for breach of his service contract. The amount awardable under the second head would, however, have been relatively small – it was put by the judge at 'a 10% chance'—because the likelihood that the company might itself have secured the contract was so remote.

In contrast with *Canaero* and *Cooley*, the director in *Island Export Finance Ltd v Umunna* [1986] BCLC 460 was allowed to keep the profit which he had derived from contracts that he had obtained for himself after he had resigned as the managing director of his company, IEF. Although these contracts (to supply postal boxes to the Cameroons postal authorities) were of the same kind, and made with the same party, as an earlier contract which he had secured for the IEF while working as its managing director, Hutchinson J accepted evidence that IEF was not actively seeking further orders either when Umunna resigned or when he later obtained the contracts and that the resignation was for unrelated reasons. He had also not made improper use of any confidential information.

More recently, in *Balston Ltd v Headline Filters Ltd* [1990] FSR 385 Head, an employee and director of Balston who had worked for it for 17 years, gave notice terminating his employment and resigned his directorship. He had already agreed to lease premises where he intended to set up his own business, but he said in evidence that he had not then decided what that business was to be. Shortly afterwards one of Balston's customers telephoned Head after being notified by Balston that it would continue to supply him with a particular kind of filter tubes for only a limited further period. As a result of this call, Head commenced business making the filter tubes and supplied them to the customer. Falconer J held that it was not a breach of fiduciary duty for a director to form an intention to set up business in competition with his company after his directorship had ceased, and that there was no maturing business opportunity which Head had improperly diverted to himself.

Of the cases which follow, *New Zealand Netherlands Society 'Oranje' Inc v Kuys* shows that a director may secure a release or immunity from potential accountability by proper negotiation with a competent organ of the company, while *Peso*'s case deals with the difficult question whether an opportunity, once declined by the company, may then be taken up by one of the directors on his own account, without any such negotiation.

QUESTIONS

(1) Would it have mattered whether the directors of *Regal* had voted as shareholders on a resolution to ratify their acts?
(2) On what legal basis might *damages* be awarded against the defendants in cases like *Regal, Canaero* and *Cooley*?
(3) If the original proposal to sell the cinemas, rather than the shares, had gone through, would the four directors have been under any liability and, if so, for what?
(4) Of the four 'key factors' identified in *Canaero* (above), which were missing in *Island Exports Finance Ltd v Umunna* and in *Balston Ltd v Headline Filters Ltd* (above)?
(5) Jane is a director of three investment companies. She is approached in confidence by two young scientists whose company needs a major injection of finance to develop a newly discovered drug. After investigating the project, she forms the view that it is likely to be a highly profitable venture for one of the three companies. What advice should Jane be given?

A company may, by agreement, release a director or other officer from a fiduciary duty which he would otherwise owe.

133 New Zealand Netherlands Society 'Oranje' Inc v Kuys [1973] 1 WLR 1126, [1973] 2 All ER 1222 (Privy Council)

Kuys had been the secretary of a Dutch residents' society ('the Auckland Society') and the editor of its newsletter ('the Holland Bulletin') from 1963 until 1966. In December 1966, the Bulletin ceased publication because of financial difficulties. On 5 January 1967, it was decided to form a new society (the appellant), of which Kuys was to be the secretary and one of the committee members. It was also agreed (as the trial judge found) that a newspaper should be produced, to be called the 'Windmill Post', that the paper should be Kuys' property, and that for the first six months the society should support the paper by taking 2000 copies for its members. In June 1967, Kuys left the appellant society, which then decided to publish a rival newspaper under the same name. Kuys was granted an injunction restraining the society from this action, it being held that, notwithstanding his possible fiduciary position vis-à-vis the society, he had effectively been given a dispensation from any duty in regard to the newspaper venture by the terms of the agreement. He was not, therefore, under any obligation to hold the newspaper or its title, the 'Windmill Post', on trust for the society.

The opinion of their Lordships was delivered by LORD WILBERFORCE: The appellant ... pleaded ... that Kuys, by virtue of his position as secretary and member of committee of the society, was in a fiduciary position. He had acquired the ownership of the newspaper while he held this position and by virtue of it. Admittedly it would be possible for the society to release him from accountability and to allow him to keep the ownership for himself: but this could only be done by an arrangement freely arrived at after full disclosure of all relevant matters. There had not, it was said, been that full disclosure ...

Their Lordships are in agreement with these contentions in so far as they stress the necessity to give consideration to the nature of the relationship between Kuys and the society and to the question whether that relationship imposed upon him, in relation to the particular transaction under investigation, duties of a fiduciary character. The obligation not to profit from a position of trust, or, as it is sometimes relevant to put it, not to allow a conflict to arise between duty and interest, is one of strictness. The strength, and indeed the severity, of the rule has recently been emphasised by the House of Lords: *Boardman v Phipps*.[17] It retains its vigour in all jurisdictions where the principles of equity are applied. Naturally it has different applications in different contexts.

The present case is concerned with an officer of an incorporated, non-profitmaking society. Kuys was not paid for his services but he was a trusted employee; and he was ready to agree that he had duties of trust and confidence placed in him. On the other hand the scope of his responsibility and the dividing line between that and his own personal interests were loosely defined. It appears from the evidence that he was able to run a small insurance business of his own: also it appears that he was permitted a personal interest in the group travel service which he managed for the society. A person in his position may be in a fiduciary position quoad a part of his activities and not quoad other parts: each transaction, or group of transactions, must be looked at ...

It is, then, necessary to consider the relationship of Kuys and the society in regard to the publication of a newspaper. In their Lordships' opinion, there was at least the potentiality of a fiduciary relationship. The Auckland Society had for several years published the newsheet called the Holland Bulletin—this was at the centre of its activity. Kuys was for some time the editor of the Bulletin and there is no doubt that he was so in his capacity as secretary. It was contemplated that in one form or another the new society, which became the appellant society, should be associated with a newspaper: its stated objects included taking over the publication of the Holland Bulletin. It was obvious and essential that any newspaper would largely depend for its viability upon subscriptions by the society's members and that they would subscribe partly at least because it contained the society's news.

Another source of finance would be advertising, and there was evidence that the main likely clients, the airlines, were interested in supporting the society. Thus, in these circumstances, if Kuys had proceeded to launch a newspaper, without any special arrangement, there would be at the least a case for saying that to claim or retain the benefit of it for himself would be a breach of fiduciary duty.

17 [1967] 2 AC 46, [1966] 3 All ER 721; see the note below, p 275.

On the other hand, what has already been said as to Kuys' position and responsibilities left open the way for a special arrangement, and, equally, such an arrangement was, on the judge's findings, made. It was straightforward and, in the circumstances, reasonable. The Bulletin could not be carried on: to produce a newspaper obviously involved the risk of loss. The contract limited the society's commitment to the purchase of 2,000 copies at 1s [5p] each for six months. Kuys was to secure what advertising and other income he could to cover all outgoings and his own remuneration. He was not to come down upon the society for any losses. As one witness said, he was not to cry on its shoulder. The newspaper was to be his for ill and for good.

There was much discussion at the trial as to what was to happen at the end of the period of six months. But the judge's finding (supported by the evidence) was that the reconsideration then to be given to the situation was limited to the amount, if any, of the society's support. That the ownership of the newspaper should revert to the society was certainly not agreed, and if it was not agreed, either, in terms, that the ownership should remain with Kuys, no other conclusion was possible from the terms which were agreed. There was therefore, in their Lordships' opinion, established a set of facts which would fully displace any potential fiduciary obligation on Kuys to hold the newspaper in trust for the society ...

NOTE

In *Queensland Mines Ltd v Hudson* (1978) 18 ALR 1, 52 ALJR 399, PC, the plaintiff company was set up as a joint venture by A Ltd, a company controlled by Hudson, and F Ltd, a company controlled by Korman. Hudson, as managing director of Queensland Mines, was involved in negotiations with the Tasmanian government for licences to mine iron ore. Just before the licences were issued, Korman and his company F Ltd ran into financial difficulties and Korman told Hudson that he had not the financial resources to proceed with the venture. Hudson took the licences in his own name. He later resigned as managing director of Queensland Mines and formed his own new company, which at considerable risk and expense exploited the licences and earned profits. The Privy Council held (i) that the opportunity to make the profits had come to Hudson through his position as managing director of Queensland Mines, but (ii) that since the board of that company had known of Hudson's interest at all times (and had resolved a year after the issue of the licences that Queensland Mines 'should not pursue the matter [i e the licences] any further'), Hudson was not accountable for his profit.

QUESTIONS

(1) Was Kuys, in the view of Lord Wilberforce:
    (a) not in a fiduciary position at all?
    (b) in a fiduciary position because he was a committee member?
    (c) in a fiduciary position as a secretary or as a 'trusted employee', or as both?
(2) Which organ of the society released (i) Kuys, (ii) Hudson, from his actual or potential fiduciary obligations? Was it competent in law to do so?
(3) Would the knowledge of the board of Queensland Mines of Hudson's interest, without the resolution, have been sufficient to allow Hudson to keep his profit?

A director is free to make an investment on his own account after his company has considered the same proposition and bona fide decided against it.

134 Peso Silver Mines Ltd v Cropper (1966) 58 DLR (2d) 1 (Supreme Court of Canada)

The board of directors of the appellant company Peso was approached by an outsider named Dickson, who wished to sell to it 126 prospecting claims near to the company's own mining territories. The proposal was rejected by the company after bona fide consideration by the board. Later, a syndicate (which included Cropper, the respondent) was formed by Dr Aho, the company's geologist, to purchase Dickson's claims; and a company called Cross Bow Mines Ltd was incorporated by the syndicate for the purpose. Cropper was a director of Peso and had taken part in the earlier decision of its board. Control of Peso later passed to a company referred to as 'Charter', who caused this action to be brought, claiming that Cropper was accountable to the company for the Cross Bow shares which he had thus obtained. The Supreme Court of Canada decided that he held them on his own behalf and was not bound to account.[18]

The judgment of the court (CARTWRIGHT, MARTLAND, JUDSON, RITCHIE and HALL JJ) was delivered by CARTWRIGHT J: On the facts of the case at bar I find it impossible to say that the respondent obtained the interests he holds in Cross Bow and Mayo by reason of the fact that he was a director of the appellant and in the course of the execution of that office.

When Dickson, at Dr Aho's suggestion, offered his claims to the appellant it was the duty of the respondent as director to take part in the decision of the board as to whether that offer should be accepted or rejected. At that point he stood in a fiduciary relationship to the appellant. There are affirmative findings of fact that he and his co-directors acted in good faith, solely in the interests of the appellant and with sound business reasons in rejecting the offer. There is no suggestion in the evidence that the offer to the appellant was accompanied by any confidential information unavailable to any prospective purchaser or that the respondent as director had access to any such information by reason of his office. When, later, Dr Aho approached the appellant it was not in his capacity as a director of the appellant, but as an individual member of the public whom Dr Aho was seeking to interest as a co-adventurer.

The judgments in the *Regal* case **(132)** in the Court of Appeal are not reported but counsel were good enough to furnish us with copies. In the course of his reasons Lord Greene MR said: 'To say that the company was entitled to claim the benefit of those shares would involve this proposition: Where a board of directors considers an investment which is offered to the company and bona fide comes to the conclusion that it is not an investment which their company ought to make, any director, after that resolution is come to and bona fide come to, who chooses to put up the money for that investment himself must be treated as having done it on behalf of the company, so that the company can claim any profit that results to him from it. That is a proposition for which no particle of authority was cited; and

---

18 See S Beck, 'The Saga of *Peso Silver Mines*: Corporate Opportunity Reconsidered' (1971) 49 Can B Rev 80; and, by the same author, 'The Quickening of the Fiduciary Obligation' (1975) 53 Can B Rev 771.

goes, as it seems to me, far beyond anything that has ever been suggested as to the duty of directors, agents, or persons in a position of that kind.'

In the House of Lords, Lord Russell of Killowen concluded his reasons with the following paragraph: 'One final observation I desire to make. In his judgment Lord Greene MR stated that a decision adverse to the directors in the present case involved the proposition that, if directors bona fide decide not to invest their company's funds in some proposed investment, a director who thereafter embarks his own money therein is accountable for any profits which he may derive therefrom. As to this, I can only say that to my mind the facts of this hypothetical case bear but little resemblance to the story with which we have had to deal.'

I agree with Bull JA[19] when after quoting the two above passages he says: 'As Greene MR was found to be in error in his decision, I would think that the above comment by Lord Russell on the hypothetical case would be superfluous unless it was intended to be a reservation that he had no quarrel with the proposition enunciated by the Master of the Rolls, but only that the facts of the case before him did not fall within it.'

As Bull JA goes on to point out, the same view appears to have been entertained by Lord Denning MR in *Phipps v Boardman*.[20]

If the members of the House of Lords in *Regal* had been of the view that in the hypothetical case stated by Lord Greene the director would have been liable to account to the company, the elaborate examination of the facts contained in the speech of Lord Russell of Killowen would have been unnecessary.

The facts of the case at bar appear to me in all material respects identical with those in the hypothetical case stated by Lord Greene and I share the view which he expressed that in such circumstances the director is under no liability. I agree with the conclusion of the learned trial judge and of the majority in the Court of Appeal that the action fails ...

NOTE

Boardman v Phipps [1967] 2 AC 46, [1966] 3 All ER 721, referred to above, was not a company law case but it is of interest as an application of the principle of *Regal (Hastings) Ltd v Gulliver* (132). B, a solicitor, and P, acting together as agents for the trustees of an estate, attended the annual general meeting of a company in which the estate had a minority holding of shares. Later, they obtained information about share prices from the company. They formed the opinion that the company could be made more profitable and, acting honestly and without concealment (but not having first obtained the 'informed consent' of all the trustees), used their own money to bid for and eventually to acquire a controlling interest in it. Ultimately, they succeeded in making considerable profits for both themselves and the estate from capital distributions on their respective holdings of shares. By a majority of three to two, the House of Lords held that they must account to the trust for the profit which they had made from their own investment: the profit had been made by reason of their fiduciary position as agents and by reason of the opportunity and the knowledge which had come to them while acting in that capacity.

---

19 [Bull JA was one of the majority judges in the court below (British Columbia Court of Appeal (1965) 56 DLR 2d 117).]
20 [1965] Ch 992; affd by the House of Lords [1967] 2 AC 46: see the note below.

QUESTION

Can the decision in the *Peso Silver Mines* case be reconciled with *Boardman v Phipps* (above), *Aberdeen Rly Co v Blaikie Bros* (**128**) and the passage from *Keech v Sandford* quoted in *Regal (Hastings) Ltd v Gulliver* (**132**), above, p 267?

(3) Conflicting Loyalties

A director may not fetter his discretion by a contract with an outsider.

135 Kregor v Hollins (1913) 109 LT 225 (King's Bench Division and Court of Appeal)

Hollins had invested £5,000 in a company, and he agreed to pay Kregor £200 to act as a director of the company on his nomination. Kregor sued to recover this remuneration and succeeded, the jury finding that the agreement did not contemplate that he should put Hollins' interests above those of the company.

AVORY J, addressing the jury, said:

If he was to look after the interests of the defendant in the sense that he was to prefer them to the interests of the whole body of shareholders—that is to say, if they came into conflict that he was to promote the defendant's interests rather than the interests of the whole body of shareholders which were in conflict—then in my opinion it was an unlawful agreement.

The Court of Appeal (HAMILTON LJ and BRAY J, VAUGHAN WILLIAMS LJ dissenting) held that the bargain was in any event not corrupt in that the company had assented to and approved it; the majority did not refer to these remarks of Avory J, but they were approved by Vaughan Williams LJ.

NOTE

A similar decision is the Irish case of *Clark v Workman* [1920] 1 IR 107, in which it was held improper for directors to give an 'undertaking' to a third party that they would see that his interests would be 'looked after'.

In *Horn v Henry Faulder & Co Ltd* (1908) 99 LT 524 the company appointed Horn manager of its confectionery department under a 14 year contract, with full power to conduct the business 'without in any way being interfered with' by the directors. When he claimed that he had been wrongfully 'interfered with' in breach of this contract, Neville J held that it was unenforceable.

See also *Scottish Co-operative Wholesale Society Ltd v Meyer* (**250**), in which the special position of a 'nominee director'[1] is discussed. That case confirms the view that a nominated director must not put his principal's interests above those of the company (or, to be more accurate, that members of the company may be able to invoke s 459 if this happens).

But in Australia and New Zealand there are cases which suggest that this may be too narrow a view. The whole object of having a director appointed to represent a special interest may have been the furtherance of some ulterior corporate good, and in such circumstances it may be justifiable to put that interest first. Thus in *Levin v*

1　On nominee directors, see E Boros, 'The Duties of Nominee and Multiple Directors' (1989) 10 Co Law 211, (1990) 11 Co Law 6, and P Crutchfield, 'Nominee Directors: the Law and Commercial Reality' (1991) 12 Co Law 136.

Clark [1962] NSWR 686, directors nominated to the board to represent the interests of a secured creditor were held not to be in breach of any fiduciary duties to the company when they acted to enforce the security: the company, by accepting the credit on the terms in question, had waived its right to have the unqualified loyalty of those directors.

Again, in *Berlei Hestia (NZ) Ltd v Fernyhough* [1980] 2 NZLR 150 at 165–166, Mahon J (without deciding the point) adverted to the possiblity that the normal fiduciary duties might be modified where a company had been set up as a joint venture between two or more participants on the understanding that each of them would be separately represented on its board by nominee directors. He said:

> Notwithstanding that the Australian directors are the nominees of the Australian company, they nevertheless have responsibilities to the whole body of share-holders. That principle seems to be settled in England by *Scottish Co-operative Wholesale Society Ltd v Meyer* (**250**) and by *Boulting v Association of Cine-matograph, Television and Allied Technicians*.[2] But despite the width of that proposition, there have been attempts to bring this theoretical doctrine of undiv-ided responsibility into harmony with commercial reality, upon the basis that when articles are agreed upon whereby a specified shareholder or group of shareholders is empowered to nominate its own directors, then there may be grounds for saying that in addition to the responsibility which such directors have to all shareholders as represented by the corporate entity, they may have a special responsibility towards those who nominated them. Such a view proceeds on the basis that the articles were so constructed with the intent and belief that the institution of such a special responsibility towards one class of shareholders was conducive to the interests of the company as a whole. For an illustration of this line of thinking I refer to the dicta of Jacobs J in *Levin v Clark* [above] and in *Re Broadcasting Station 2GB Pty Ltd.*[3] In the present case this business undertaking, stripped of its corporate shell, is a trading partnership between two organisations operating in different countries. They agreed, when the company was incorporated, that each partner nominate three directors, and they impliedly agreed, as the articles show, that one class of directors was at liberty to bring the board's functions to a stand-still when a disagreement arose, and that dis-agreement would almost certainly have its origin in a dispute between the two sets of shareholders. These consequences were all well known to the corporators when the articles were drawn. As a matter of legal theory, as opposed to judicial precedent, it seems not unreasonable for all the corporators to be able to agree upon an adjusted form of fiduciary liability, limited to circumstances where the rights of third parties vis-à-vis the company will not be prejudiced. The stage has already been reached, according to some commentators, where nominee directors will be absolved from suggested breach of duty to the company merely because they act in furtherance of the interest of their appointors, provided that their conduct accords with a bona fide belief that the interests of the corporate entity are likewise being advanced. Cf Finn, *Fiduciary Obligations* (1977) para 114 ...

The case law on this particular topic is as yet indecisive ...

The New Zealand Law Commission, in recommending changes in company law, has proposed that a nominee director should be free to disclose confidential information to his nominating shareholder where that relationship has been disclosed in a register of directors' interests, and that in such circumstances the nominating shareholder should come under the same obligations as if he were a director as regards the abuse of confidential information, insider dealing, and certain other specified duties.

---

2 [1963] 2 QB 606, [1963] 1 All ER 716, CA.
3 [1964–5] NSWR 1648.

QUESTIONS

(1) If a company's constitution provides for the election of employee representatives to the board, is there a case for adopting the reasoning in *Levin v Clark*?

(2) Directors sometimes confer upon a 'management company' all their powers of management, pursuant to a 'management agreement'. (For an example, see *Lee Panavision Ltd v Lee Lighting Ltd* (below, p 295).) Does such an arrangement infringe the principle of *Kregor v Hollins*?

A substantial shareholder in a company who appoints a nominee director to its board owes no duty to anybody for the way in which the nominee performs his duties as a director. It makes no difference that the director is an employee of the shareholder who nominates him.

136 Kuwait Asia Bank EC v National Mutual Life Nominees Ltd [1991] 1 AC 187, [1990] 3 All ER 404 (Privy Council)

The Kuwait Asia bank owned 40% of the shares in AICS, a New Zealand company which had taken money on deposit from the public. The plaintiff company, NMLN, had acted as trustee for the depositors pursuant to requirements of the New Zealand securities legislation. House and August, employees of the bank, were appointed by the bank to be two of the five directors of AICS; the remaining three were nominees of another large shareholder, Kumutoto. When AICS went into liquidation, NMLN settled claims brought by the depositors for breach of its duties as their trustee, and in these proceedings NMLN sought contribution from, inter alios (i) House and August and (ii) the bank, contending that it (NMLN) had relied on certificates of AICS's financial position which were inaccurate and for which the directors bore collective responsibility. The Judicial Committee held that while a prima facie case existed against House and August, no claim lay against the bank. The bank was not vicariously liable for any breach of duty which might be proved against the two directors whom it had nominated, and this was so even though they were also its employees; and it did not qua shareholder owe duties to anybody.

The opinion of the Judicial Committee was delivered by LORD LOWRY: ... Their Lordships now proceed to consider the causes of action pleaded by the plaintiff against the bank. Two general principles may first be stated. (1) A director does not by reason only of his position as director owe any duty to creditors or to trustees for creditors of the company. (2) A shareholder does not by reason only of his position as shareholder owe any duty to anybody . . . .

But although directors are not liable *as such* to creditors of the company, a director may by agreement or representation assume a special duty to a creditor of the company. A director may accept or assume a duty of care in supplying information to a creditor analogous to the duty described by the House of Lords in *Hedley Byrne & Co Ltd v Heller & Partners Ltd*.[4] In that case, but for an express disclaimer of liability, a bank which supplied a reference of creditworthiness in respect of a customer of the bank would have

4 [1964] AC 465, [1963] 2 All ER 575, HL.

been under an implied duty of care towards the person who sought and relied upon the reference.

In the present case, a duty of care owed by House and August to the trustees can only be sought in the trust deed entered into between AICS and the plaintiff. The statement of claim contains the following allegations:

> 10. Pursuant to the provisions of clause 3.5.1 of the trust deed, AICS was required to furnish [the plaintiff] with monthly reports certified as true and correct by two of its directors in relation to the matters set out in the said clause 3.5.1 ('the monthly certificates').

The statement of claim annexes particulars of the names of the directors of AICS who signed monthly certificates. House and August did not sign any of the monthly certificates. ...

The plaintiff intends at the trial to show that House and August must have known or ought to have known that the quarterly certificates were furnished on behalf of all the directors of AICS including House and August, and that in those circumstances House and August assumed and accepted a special duty owed to the plaintiff and the depositors to take reasonable care to see that the statements in the quarterly certificates were accurate. The plaintiff also proposes to show that House and August did not exercise reasonable care, the quarterly certificates were not accurate and the plaintiff relied upon the quarterly certificates and therefore did not take timely action under the trust deed to protect the interest of the depositors and is entitled to a contribution from House and August to meet the liability incurred and settled by the plaintiff for the sum of $6.75m.

Of course, the plaintiff may fail to show either the existence or the breach of the duty alleged to have been accepted by House and August. It may be that House and August relied, and were entitled to rely, upon information received from their co-directors or from Deloittes [AICS's auditors]. House and August might be able to show that the plaintiff received sufficient information and that the loss to the depositors could have been averted or reduced if the plaintiff had properly evaluated the information and facts supplied to them. There are other allegations against House and August in the statement of claim, and there may be other defences open to House and August. There is no doubt that the plaintiff, by its statement of claim, has established an arguable case against House and August arising out of the fact that the quarterly certificates were furnished on behalf of all the directors of AICS.

As against the bank, the statement of claim pleaded that the bank was liable to contribute to the loss suffered by the plaintiff in settling the claims of the depositors against the plaintiff for all or any of the following reasons: (1) House and August were appointed to the board of directors of AICS by the bank, were employed by the bank and carried out their duties as directors in the course of their employment by the bank. (2) House and August were, as directors of AICS, the agents of the bank which was the principal. (3) As a substantial shareholder ... the bank owed a duty of care to the plaintiff and to the depositors

> to ensure that the business of AICS was not conducted negligently or recklessly or in such a manner as to materially disadvantage the interests of those unsecured depositors.

(4) House and August were persons occupying a position of directors of AICS who were accustomed to act in accordance with the bank's directions,

and therefore the bank was a director of AICS within the meaning of section 2 of the Companies Act 1955.[5]

As to (1) the power of appointing a director of a company may be exercised by a shareholder or a person who is not a shareholder by virtue of the articles of association of the company, or by virtue of the control of the majority of the voting shares of the company, or by virtue of the agreement or acquiescence of other shareholders. In the present case, the bank and Kumutoto, who together controlled AICS, decided that the bank should nominate two directors. In the absence of fraud or bad faith (which are not alleged here), a shareholder or other person who controls the appointment of a director owes no duty to creditors of the company to take reasonable care to see that directors so appointed discharge their duties as directors with due diligence and competence. One shareholder may lock away his paid up shares and go to sleep. Another shareholder may take an active interest in the company, insist on detailed information and deluge the directors with advice. The active shareholder is no more liable than the sleeping shareholder. In *Salomon v Salomon & Co Ltd* (12), Lord Watson said:

> Any person who holds a preponderating share in the stock of a limited company has necessarily the intention of taking the lion's share of its profits without any risk beyond loss of the money which he has paid for, or is liable to pay upon his shares ...

In *Rainham Chemical Works Ltd v Belvedere Fish Guano Co Ltd*,[6] where it was argued that shareholders were liable for a tort committed by a company, Lord Buckmaster said:

> It not infrequently happens in the course of legal proceedings that parties who find they have a limited company as debtor with all its paid up capital issued in the form of fully-paid shares and no free capital for working suggest that the company is nothing but an alter ego for the people by whose hand it has been incorporated, and by whose action it is controlled. But in truth the Companies Acts expressly contemplate that people may substitute the limited liability of a company for the unlimited liability of the individual, with the object that by this means enterprise and adventure may be encouraged.

The liability of a shareholder would be unlimited if he were accountable to a creditor for the exercise of his power to appoint a director and for the conduct of the director so appointed. It is in the interests of a shareholder to see that directors are wise and that the actions of the company are not foolish; but this concern of the shareholder stems from self-interest, and not from duty. The House of Lords, in the recent case of *JH Rayner (Mincing Lane) Ltd v Department of Trade and Industry*[7] (the *International Tin Council* case), reiterated that a corporation is a legal person, that no one can sue on a contract save the parties to the contract, and that therefore the members of a corporation are not liable as members for the debts of the corporation. It does not make any difference if the directors appointed by a shareholder are employed by the shareholder and are allowed to carry out their duties as

---

5 [Section 2 of CA 1955 (NZ) includes within the definition of 'director' a person who in the UK would be termed a 'shadow director': see CA 1985, s 741(2).]

6 [1921] 2 AC 465 at 475, HL.

7 [1990] 2 AC 418, [1989] 3 All ER 523, HL.

directors while in the shareholder's employment. House and August owed three separate duties. They owed in the first place to AICS the duty to perform their duties as directors without gross negligence; the liability of a director to his company is set forth in the judgment of Romer J in *Re City Equitable Fire Insurance Co Ltd* (**142**). They owed a duty to the plaintiff to use reasonable care to see that the certificates complied with the requirements of the trust deed. Finally, they owed a duty to their employer, the bank, to exercise reasonable diligence and skill in the performance of their duties as directors of AICS.

If House and August did not exercise reasonable care to see that the quarterly certificates were accurate, they committed a breach of the duty they owed to the plaintiff and may have committed a breach of the duty they owed to AICS and a breach of the duty they owed to the bank to exercise reasonable diligence and skill. But these duties were separate and distinct and different in scope and nature. The bank was not responsible for a breach of the duties owed by House and August to AICS or to the plaintiff any more than AICS or the plaintiff were responsible for a breach of duty by House and August. If House and August committed a breach of the duty which was imposed on them and the other directors of AICS and was owed to the plaintiff under and by virtue of the trust deed they did so as individuals and as directors of AICS and not as employees of the bank; House and August were not parties to the trust deed, nor was the bank. House and August were allowed by the bank to perform their duties to AICS in the bank's time and at the bank's expense. It was in the interests of the bank that House and August should discharge with diligence and skill the duties which they owed to AICS, but these facts do not render the bank liable for breach by House and August of the duty imposed on them by the trust deed. In the performance of their duties as directors and in the performance of their duties imposed by the trust deed, House and August were bound to ignore the interests and wishes of their employer, the bank. They could not plead any instruction from the bank as an excuse for breach of their duties to AICS and the plaintiff. Of course, if the bank exploited its position as employers of House and August to obtain an improper advantage for the bank or to cause harm to the plaintiff then the bank would be liable for its own misconduct. But there is no suggestion that the bank behaved with impropriety ...

(2) Then it is said that House and August were the agents of the bank. But, as directors of AICS, they were the agents of AICS and not of the bank. As directors of AICS, House and August were agents of AICS for the purposes of the trust deed and, by the express terms of the trust deed, responsibility for the accuracy of the quarterly certificates was assumed by the directors of AICS. House and August accepted responsibility for the quarterly certificates as directors of AICS and not as agents or employees of the bank.

(3) Next it was said that the bank owed a personal duty of care to the plaintiff. For the protection of the depositors the plaintiff stipulated for and obtained by the trust deed a duty of care in the preparation of the quarterly certificates by the directors of AICS. The plaintiff may or may not have known that two of the directors of AICS were employed by the bank and that the bank would allow those two directors to carry out their duties as directors while in the employment of the bank. Any of these circumstances, even if known, could change at any time. The plaintiff may or may not have

known that the bank was beneficially interested in 40 per cent of the shares of AICS. That circumstance also could change at any time. The plaintiff did not rely on any of these circumstances. ... An employer who is also a shareholder who nominates a director owes no duty to the company unless the employer interferes with the affairs of the company. A duty does not arise because the employee may be dismissed from his employment by the employer or from his directorship by the shareholder or because the employer does not provide sufficient time or facilities to enable the director to carry out his duties. It will be in the interests of the employer to see that the director discharges his duty to the company but this again stems from self-interest and not from duty on the part of the employer.

[His Lordship ruled, finally, that the bank was not in the position of a 'shadow director'. The proceedings against the bank were accordingly struck out as disclosing no valid cause of action.]

A director is not under an obligation to refrain from competing with his company or from becoming a director of a rival company.

137 Bell v Lever Bros Ltd [1932] AC 161 (House of Lords)

The principal questions in issue in this well-known case are not important for present purposes; but Lord Blanesburgh made the following observations relating to the position of the appellants as directors of the respondent company's subsidiary, 'Niger'. He pointed out that, apart from the specific provisions of their contract of employment, they were under no legal or equitable obligation to refrain from dealing in the same commodities as their company.

LORD BLANESBURGH: The point here to be noted is that these transactions involved no contract or engagement in which, either for profit or loss, Niger was at all concerned. The contracts were all contracts by which the appellants alone were bound for their own benefit or burden to some outside party exclusive of Niger altogether. And this distinction is vital: because the liability of a director in respect of profits made by him from a contract in which his company also is concerned is one thing: his liability, if any there be, in respect of his profits from a contract in which the company has no interest at all is quite another. In the first case, unless by the company's regulations the director is permitted, subject to or without conditions, to retain his profit, he must account for it to the company. In the second case, the company has no concern in his profit and cannot make him accountable for it unless it appears—this is the essential qualification—that in earning that profit he has made use either of the property of the company or of some confidential information which has come to him as a director of the company.

   Now, unfortunately, the learned judge here, so far as his observations had precision, directed the jury as if the offending transactions were in the first class, and not, as was the fact, in the second ... The relevant duties of a director were laid down by him in terms of the following quotation which he read to the jury. Their duties were: 'So to act as to promote the best interests of the company. No one having such duties to perform can be allowed to enter into engagements in which he has or can have a personal interest which conflicts or may possibly conflict with the interests of those whom he is bound to protect. No question is liable on such occasion to be raised to the fairness or unfairness of the dealing. It may be possible to demonstrate how far the interest of the company is affected. No inquiry on that subject is permitted.'

Now, the learned judge did not give the source of his quotation, and I have not succeeded in tracing it. But both from its wording, and also from its close similarity to Lord Cranworth's locus classicus on the subject printed in the headnote to *Aberdeen Rly Co v Blaikie Bros* (**128**), I can have little doubt that, like Lord Cranworth's statement, the quotation is concerned with a company's contracts in which, on the other side of the table, a director is interested, and with reference to which the company's regulations are silent. The quotation is not addressed to a director's own contracts with outsiders in which the company has no financial interest at all ...

And this brings me to the position of a director in relation to contracts of the second class, with which we are here alone concerned. The principle will be found in the case usually cited in relation to it, although reported only in the Weekly Notes, of *London and Mashonaland Exploration Co v New Mashonaland Exploration Co*,[8] where it was held that, it not appearing from the regulations of the company that a director's services must be rendered to that company and to no other company, he was at liberty to become a director even of a rival company, and it not being established that he was making to the second company any disclosure of information obtained confidentially by him as a director of the first company he could not at the instance of that company be restrained in his rival directorate. What he could do for a rival company, he could, of course, do for himself. And in the present case that principle is not affected by the agreements of each appellant with Levers to devote all his time during business hours to the Niger service. There is no corresponding provision in the regulations of Niger, and it was not because the offending instructions were instructed during the day and not in the evening that they are impugned. It was not suggested that the appellants were in any way precluded by virtue of their engagement from at any time entering into private speculations of their own in outside things as, e g stocks and shares. Indeed any such suggestion was expressly disclaimed by the respondents ... Accordingly I reach the conclusion that, so far, the appellants in relation to the offending transactions were under no liability whatever to Niger ...

NOTE

In view of the decision in *Hivac Ltd v Park Royal Scientific Instruments Ltd* [1946] Ch 169, [1946] 2 All ER 350, CA, which held—admittedly in the context of a highly competitive area of commerce—that *employees* may be restrained from working for a business competing with that of their employer, doubts have been expressed whether the views of Lord Blanesburgh should continue to represent the law: see, e g *Abbey Glen Property Corpn v Stumborg* [1976] 2 WWR 1 at 47 per McDonald J.

8 [1891] WN 165.

(4) THE DUTY TO ACT BONA FIDE

It is well-established law that directors, acting as a board, must exercise their powers 'bona fide in what they consider is in the interests of the company' and 'not for any collateral purpose'. Such propositions appear in many leading cases, such as *Re Smith & Fawcett Ltd* (**220**), as well as in those cited in this section. It is, however, an oversimplification to put the issue in these terms, as the following comments show:

(1) The phrase 'bona fide in the interests of the company' is also used as a yardstick by which the propriety of decisions of the members in general meeting is judged; yet the expression has a different meaning in the two contexts: for whereas the self-interest of a shareholder may be consistent with bona fides, the opposite rule is strictly applied against a director: see above, p 247.

(2) 'The interests of the company' may not have the same meaning in all cases. It may refer to the interest of the corporate body as a separate entity (**69**) or to those of the shareholders collectively (**59**), and in some cases the interests of the company as such may not be directly involved at all—e g in regard to the allocation of a surplus between different classes of shareholders. Here, as *Mills v Mills* (**138**) shows, a criterion of fairness must be substituted for 'the interests of the company'.

(3) The application of a test based on 'the interests of the company' unnaturally assumes that directors' decisions are motivated by a single factor. The possibility that they may act from a combination of motives, or that the individual directors who support a resolution may be influenced by different considerations, is overlooked. In the case of mixed motives, therefore, the court's inquiry must go deeper, and endeavour to identify a dominant motive: this, in cases with similar facts, may lead to seemingly inconsistent results.

(4) The reference to a 'collateral purpose' is ambiguous: it may be seen merely as the counterpart in negative terms of the 'bona fide' test, or as a separate test involving considerations of law. This issue is discussed further below, at p 290.

Directors must exercise their powers bona fide in what they consider is in the interests of the company, and not for any collateral purpose.

[See *Re Smith & Fawcett Ltd* (**220**), and compare also the three cases next cited.]

Where mixed motives are involved, regard should be had to the directors' main purpose. As between different categories of shareholders, the directors' duty is to act fairly.

138 Mills v Mills (1938) 60 CLR 150 (High Court of Australia)

The plaintiff, Ainslie Mills, and his uncle, Neilson Mills (the defendant) were two of the directors and the largest shareholders of a family company. Neilson Mills (who was managing director) held mostly ordinary shares, and Ainslie Mills mostly preference shares. A resolution was passed by a majority of the directors, including Neilson Mills, by which accumulated profits (which would have gone to the ordinary shareholders had the same sums been paid as dividends) were capitalised and distributed to the ordinary shareholders in the form of fully paid bonus shares. This resolution, whilst not affecting the position as regards dividends, greatly strengthened the voting power of the ordinary shareholders (and in particular of Neilson Mills), and it also diminished the rights of the preference shareholders to share in assets in a winding up. Lowe J found that the majority directors had acted honestly in what they believed to be the best interests of the company, and he held that the fact that Neilson Mills stood to gain from their decision did not invalidate it. This view was upheld by the High Court.

LATHAM CJ: The learned judge asked the question whether the resolution was passed in the interests of the company. He expanded this question by asking: 'Was it passed in the honest exercise of the directors' discretion, to distribute reserves which were no longer needed, or was it passed with the sole view of creating voting power which would inure for the benefit of Neilson Mills and those supporting him?' I think that the form of this question is not entirely appropriate. In fact, reserves were not distributed in consequence of the resolution. All that was done by the resolution was to distribute new shares to the ordinary shareholders in proportion to their existing shares. The assets in the reserve fund were retained in the business. Further, the alternatives which this question submits for consideration are not completely exhaustive. A resolution may have been passed honestly in the exercise of the directors' discretion but also with the view of creating voting power to which it was thought that ordinary shareholders, in view of the relative extent of their interests in the assets of the company, were fairly entitled. Again, even though the view of the directors in passing the resolution was not *solely* that of creating voting power which could be used by them as desired, yet, if the substantial object of the directors was to bring about this result, the resolution might be held to be invalid ...

It is urged that the rule laid down by the cases is that directors must act always and solely in the interests of the company and never in their own interest ...

It must, however, be recognised that as a general rule, though not invariably ... directors have an interest as shareholders in the company of which they are directors. Most sets of articles of association actually require the directors to have such an interest, and it is generally desired by shareholders that directors should have a substantial interest in the company so that their interests may be identified with those of the shareholders of the company. Ordinarily, therefore, in promoting the interests of the company, a director will also promote his own interests. I do not read the general phrases which are to be found in the authorities with reference to the obligations of directors to act solely in the interests of the company as meaning that they are prohibited from acting in any matter where their own interests are affected by what they do in their capacity as directors. Very many actions of directors who are shareholders, perhaps all of them, have a direct or indirect relation to their own interests. It would be ignoring realities and creating impossibilities in the administration of companies to require that directors should not advert to or consider in any way the effect of a particular decision upon their own interests as shareholders. A rule which laid down such a principle would paralyse the management of companies in many directions. Accordingly, the judicial observations which suggest that directors should consider only the interests of the company and never their own interests should not be pressed to a limit which would create a quite impossible position.

Directors are required to act not only in matters which affect the relations of the company to persons who are not members of the company but also in relation to matters which affect the rights of shareholders inter se. Where there are preference and ordinary shares a particular decision may be of such a character that it must necessarily affect adversely the interests of one class of shareholders and benefit the interests of another class. In such a case it is difficult to apply the test of acting in the interests of the company. The question which arises is sometimes not a question of the interests of the company at all, but a question of what is fair as between different classes of shareholders. Where such a case arises some other test than that of 'the interests of the company' must be applied, and the test must be applied with knowledge of the fact already mentioned that the law permits directors, and by virtue of provisions in articles of association often requires them, to hold shares, ordinary or preference, as the case may be. A director who holds one or both classes of such shares is not, in my opinion, required by the law to live in an unreal region of detached altruism and to act in a vague mood of ideal abstraction from obvious facts which must be presented to the mind of any honest and intelligent man when he exercises his powers as a director. It would be setting up an impossible standard to hold that, if an action of a director were affected in any degree by the fact that he was a preference or ordinary shareholder, his action was invalid and should be set aside ... The question is: What was 'the moving cause' of the action of the directors? (See per Lord Shaw in *Hindle v John Cotton Ltd*)[9]. If this principle is applied to the findings of the learned judge, his decision upon this aspect of the case is seen to be right ...

DIXON J: When the law makes the object, view or purpose of a man, or of a body of men, the test of the validity of their acts, it necessarily opens up the possibility of an almost infinite analysis of the fears and desires, proximate and remote, which, in truth, form the compound motives usually animating human conduct. But logically possible as such an analysis may seem, it would be impracticable to adopt it as a means of determining the validity of the resolutions arrived at by a body of directors, resolutions which otherwise are ostensibly within their powers. The application of the general equitable principle to the acts of directors managing the affairs of a company cannot be as nice as it is in the case of a trustee exercising a special power of appointment. It must, as it seems to me, take the substantial object, the accomplishment of which formed the real ground of the board's action. If this is within the scope of the power, then the power has been validly exercised. But if, except for some ulterior and illegitimate object, the power would not have been exercised, that which has been attempted as an ostensible exercise of the power will be void,[10] notwithstanding that the directors may incidentally bring about a result which is within the purpose of the power and which they consider desirable ...

RICH and STARKE JJ delivered concurring judgments.

EVATT J concurred.

9 1919 56 SLR 625.
10 [More accurately, 'voidable': see *Bamford v Bamford* (**100**).]

NOTE

In the unreported case *Pennell Securities Ltd v Venida Investments Ltd* (25 July 1974, noted by Burridge (1981) 44 MLR 40), the directors proposed to convene an extraordinary general meeting to pass resolutions increasing the company's capital by creating new shares which would be offered to existing members (as a 'rights issue') on a nine-for-one basis. The directors knew that the plaintiffs (who had a 49% shareholding) would probably not be able to find the money to take up their proportion of the new shares: if they could not, their minority holding would be cut to under 10%. The company itself, of course, stood to benefit from the majority's massive cash injection, and there would be considerable tax savings for the group of companies controlled by the majority if the scheme were allowed to go ahead. But Templeman J granted the plaintiffs injunctions to prevent the directors from proceeding with the resolutions. He held that the directors' dominant object was to benefit their own group of companies, and he took the view also that the proposal would violate an agreement made tacitly between the members of the company on its formation that the plaintiffs' minority stake should remain at 49% unless they agreed otherwise.[11]

Directors may exercise their powers only for a proper purpose.

139 Punt v Symons & Co Ltd [1903] 2 Ch 506 (Chancery Division)

[For the facts and another part of the decision, see (**53**). In order to secure the passing of a special resolution, the directors had issued new shares to five additional members. This was held to be an abuse of their powers.]

BYRNE J: I now come to the last and most important point. It is argued on the evidence that but for the issue by the directors of the shares under their powers as directors, and, therefore, in their fiduciary character under the general power to issue shares, it would have been impossible to pass the resolution proposed; and that the shares were not issued bona fide, but with the sole object and intention of creating voting power to carry out the proposed alteration in the articles. On the evidence I am quite clear that these shares were not issued bona fide for the general advantage of the company, but that they were issued with the immediate object of controlling the holders of the greater number of shares in the company, and of obtaining the necessary statutory majority for passing a special resolution while, at the same time, not conferring upon the minority the power to demand a poll. I need not go through the affidavits. I am quite satisfied that the meaning, object and intention of the issue of these shares was to enable the shareholders holding the smaller amount of shares to control the holders of a very considerable majority. A power of the kind exercised by the directors in this case, is one which must be exercised for the benefit of the company: primarily it is given them for the purpose of enabling them to raise capital when required for the purposes of the company. There may be occasions when the directors may fairly and properly issue shares in the case of a company constituted like the present for other reasons. For instance, it would not be at all an unreasonable thing to create a sufficient number of shareholders to enable statutory powers to be exercised; but when I find a limited issue of shares to persons who are obviously meant and intended to secure the

11 On this latter point, see above, p 180.

necessary statutory majority in a particular interest, I do not think that is a fair and bona fide exercise of the power . . .

If I find as I do that shares have been issued under the general and fiduciary power of the directors for the express purpose of acquiring an unfair majority for the purpose of altering the rights of parties under the articles, I think I ought to interfere. I propose to grant an injunction . . .

NOTE

Punt v Symons & Co Ltd was followed in *Piercy v Mills & Co Ltd* [1920] 1 Ch 77, where it was again held improper for directors to use their power to issue shares in order to rob the existing majority shareholders of their voting control.

140 Hogg v Cramphorn Ltd [1967] Ch 254, [1966] 3 All ER 420 (Chancery Division)

The directors of the defendant company, acting in good faith, had issued shares with special voting rights to the trustees of a scheme set up for the benefit of the company's employees, in an attempt (which proved successful) to forestall a take-over bid by one Baxter. This was held to be an improper use of the directors' power to issue shares, but to be capable of ratification by the shareholders in general meeting.

BUCKLEY J: I am satisfied that Mr Baxter's offer, when it became known to the company's staff, had an unsettling effect upon them. I am also satisfied that the directors and the trustees of the trust deed genuinely considered that to give the staff through the trustees a sizeable, though indirect, voice in the affairs of the company would benefit both the staff and the company. I am sure that Colonel Cramphorn and also probably his fellow directors firmly believed that to keep the management of the company's affairs in the hands of the existing board would be more advantageous to the shareholders, the company's staff and its customers than if it were committed to a board selected by Mr Baxter. The steps which the board took were intended not only to ensure that if Mr Baxter succeeded in obtaining a shareholding which, as matters stood, would have been a controlling shareholding, he should not secure control of the company, but also, and perhaps primarily, to discourage Mr Baxter from proceeding with his bid at all . . .

Accepting as I do that the board acted in good faith and that they believed that the establishment of a trust would benefit the company, and that avoidance of the acquisition of control by Mr Baxter would also benefit the company, I must still remember that an essential element of the scheme, and indeed its primary purpose, was to ensure control of the company by the directors and those whom they could confidently regard as their supporters. Was such a manipulation of the voting position a legitimate act on the part of the directors?

[His Lordship referred to *Punt v Symons & Co Ltd* (**139**) and *Piercy v Mills & Co Ltd* (above), and continued:] Unless a majority in a company is acting oppressively towards the minority, this court should not and will not itself interfere with the exercise by the majority of its constitutional rights or embark upon an inquiry into the respective merits of the views held or policies favoured by the majority and the minority. Nor will this court permit directors to exercise powers, which have been delegated to them by the company in circumstances which put the directors in a fiduciary position when exercising those powers, in such a way as to interfere with the exercise by the majority of its constitutional rights; and in a case of this kind also, in my judgment, the court should not investigate the rival merits of the views or policies of the parties ... It is not, in my judgment, open to the directors in such a case to say, 'We genuinely believe that what we seek to prevent the majority from doing will harm the company and therefore our act in arming ourselves or our party with sufficient shares to outvote the majority is a conscientious exercise of our powers under the articles, which should not be interfered with.'

Such a belief, even if well founded, would be irrelevant. A majority of shareholders in general meeting is entitled to pursue what course it chooses within the company's powers, however wrong-headed it may appear to others, providing the majority do not unfairly oppress other members of the company. These considerations lead me to the conclusion that the issue of the 5,707 shares, with the special voting rights which the directors purported to attach to them, could not be justified by the view that the directors genuinely believed that it would benefit the company if they could command a majority of the votes in general meetings ... The power to issue shares was a fiduciary power and if, as I think, it was exercised for an improper motive, the issue of these shares is liable to be set aside.

Mr Goulding, however, contends that the present case is distinguishable from those I have cited in an important respect. In both *Punt v Symons & Co Ltd* and *Piercy v S Mills & Co Ltd* the majority and the minority were already arrayed for battle on a specific issue when the latter attempted to create reinforcements by issuing additional shares. If the question whether that issue should be allowed to stand had been referred to a general meeting at which the newly issued shares were excluded from voting, the resulting answer would in each case have been a negative one. Such a meeting would have served no useful purpose. In the present case, on the other hand, no battle had been joined when the 5,707 shares were issued; the directors were merely fearful that Mr Baxter would acquire control and that in any ensuing battle they would find themselves outnumbered. In the event, as I said, Mr Baxter's offer lapsed. One cannot say what the result would have been if the directors had sought the approval of a general meeting before making the issue, and it is very possible that if the issue of the shares were now submitted to the company for approval it would be approved.

Mr Instone says, no doubt rightly, that the company in general meeting could not by ordinary resolution control the directors in the exercise of the powers under article 10. He goes on to say, with less justification, that what they could not ordain a majority could not ratify. There is, however, a great difference between controlling the directors' exercise of a power vested in them and approving a proposed exercise by the directors of such a power, especially where the proposed exercise of the power is of a kind which might be assailed if it had not the manifest approval of the majority. Had the majority of the company in general meeting approved the issue of the 5,707 shares before it was made, even with the proposed special voting rights attached (assuming that such rights could have been so attached conformably with the articles), I do not think that any member could have complained of the issue being made; for in these circumstances, the criticism that the directors were by the issue of the shares attempting to deprive the majority of their constitutional rights would have ceased to have any force. It follows that a majority in a general meeting of the company at which no votes were cast in respect of the 5,707 shares could ratify the issue of those shares. Before setting the allotment and issue of the 5,707 shares aside, therefore, I propose to allow the company an opportunity to decide in general meeting whether it approves or disapproves of the issue of these shares to the trustees. Mr Goulding will undertake on behalf of the trustees not to vote at such a meeting in respect of the 5,707 shares . . .

[The action of the directors was ratified by the shareholders at the subsequent meeting. Compare *Bamford v Bamford* (**100**).]

NOTE

These cases reveal an element of ambiguity in the term 'improper purpose' (or 'collateral purpose'). It may be seen as meaning an improper motive; and in some of the cases cited the expressions 'improper motive' and 'improper purpose' are used interchangeably. For example, the directors' motive may be to confer a benefit on themselves, or an outsider, or a certain faction of shareholders, or even to injure a particular party or interest (such as a take-over bidder), without any benefit to the company. In this type of situation, the expression 'improper purpose' is simply a restatement in negative terms of the 'bona fide' test.

A new approach has, however, been introduced as a result of the cases beginning with *Hogg v Cramphorn Ltd* (above),[12] in which good faith on the part of the directors was expressly found, or conceded, but their 'purpose' was nevertheless declared 'improper' and their decision struck down. Commentators have sought, in the light of the finding of good faith, to give another meaning to the term 'proper purpose', based on the notion that it is possible to define in the abstract, independently of any question of motive, the ends which a particular power may legitimately be used to attain. Thus, it has been suggested (although more recent decisions do not entirely support this view) that the power to create and issue new shares is conferred upon directors in order that they can raise money when the company needs it, and that to use this power for any other purpose may be 'improper'. The propriety of a particular purpose, in this sense, is a matter of construction of the articles and as such, a question of law.

In later cases, courts in Australia and Canada have upheld the validity of a decision by directors to use their powers in a way which brought about the defeat of a threatened takeover. In *Harlowe's Nominees Pty Ltd v Woodside (Lakes Entrance) Oil Co* (1968) 42 ALJR 123, the High Court of Australia rejected the view that any gloss should be put on the 'bona fide' test which would have the effect, as a matter of law, of 'laying down narrow lines within which the concept of a company's interests must necessarily fall'. And in *Teck Corpn Ltd v Millar* (1972) 33 DLR (3d) 288, Berger J rejected the approach of *Hogg v Cramphorn Ltd*, preferring the view that directors can be said to have abused their powers only where their purpose was not to serve the interest of their company; but he went on to hold that even on a contrary view of the law, the directors' purpose had on the facts been proper.

In the case next cited, the Privy Council had an opportunity to review the whole question. It will be seen that the result is to endorse the view that the 'proper' purposes

12 Note also the opinion given by the Board of Trade's inspector in his report on the *Savoy Hotel* affair (HMSO, 1954), where the directors had endeavoured by the device of a sale and lease-back to fetter the future use of the company's hotel property, in the bona fide belief that the alternative use planned by an intending take-over bidder would not be in the company's interest. This was thought an improper 'purpose' for the exercise by the directors of their power to dispose of corporate assets.

for which a power is conferred are to be determined as a matter of construction, whilst at the same time disowning its most extreme applications. This may allow the cases to be reconciled with each other—at least in the results achieved, if not in their reasoning—and with *Re Smith & Fawcett Ltd* (**220**).

It is submitted that these take-over cases miss the real issue by focusing on the scope of the power exercised by the directors on the particular occasion. It would surely have been more satisfactory to build on the basis of such cases as *John Shaw & Sons (Salford) Ltd v Shaw* (**96**), where the separate roles of the different constitutional organs are recognised, and to say that the question: Which shareholders should have control? is, at least prima facie,[13] no more the business of the directors in constitutional terms than management is the concern of the shareholders. The sanction of a shareholders' vote would then be required in all such cases, not under the guise of ratifying an ill-purposed act of the directors,[14] but because the decision involves a matter which was not within the directors' sphere of action. This point was recognised, but was not made the ratio decidendi, in the speech of Lord Wilberforce which follows. It is in keeping with this view that CA 1985 now stipulates (s 80) that in most cases the directors must obtain the authorisation of the company in general meeting before they allot equity shares or other equity-related securities.

141 Howard Smith Ltd v Ampol Petroleum Ltd [1974] AC 821, [1974] 1 All ER 1126 (Privy Council)

Rival take-over offers for all the issued shares in RW Miller (Holdings) Ltd had been made by Howard Smith Ltd and Ampol Ltd. Since Ampol, with an associated company ('Bulkships') already owned 55% of Millers' shares, there was no prospect that Howard Smith's offer would succeed; but a majority of Millers' directors favoured this offer, both because its terms were more generous and because of fears as to the future of Millers if it were to pass into Ampol's control. Millers' directors resolved to issue some $10m worth of new shares to Howard Smith: this served the dual purposes of providing Millers with much-needed capital to finance the completion of two tankers, and of converting the Ampol-Bulkships holding into a minority one, so that the Howard Smith offer was likely to succeed. In these proceedings, Ampol challenged the validity of the share issue. At first instance, Street J found that, while Millers' directors were not motivated from any consideration of self-interest or desire to retain control, their primary purpose was not to satisfy Millers' admitted need for capital but to destroy the majority holding of Ampol and Bulkships. He rejected as 'unreal and unconvincing' the directors' own statements to the contrary in the witness-box, and set aside the allotment. The Privy Council upheld his decision.

The opinion of their Lordships was delivered by LORD WILBERFORCE: The directors, in deciding to issue shares, forming part of Millers' unissued capital, to Howard Smith, acted under clause 8 of the company's articles of

13 The articles could, of course, provide otherwise—e g in relation to the approval of share transfers in a private company (and see also *Heron International Ltd v Lord Grade* (**127**)). But then, matters of management may similarly be reversed by the articles to the members.
14 There does not seem yet to have been any attempt in this country to introduce a parallel concept of 'proper purpose', as a test separate from that of bona fides, into shareholders' decisions. (There is an instance in Canada, in the questionable case *Western Mines Ltd v Shield Development Co Ltd* [1976] 2 WWR 300. In *Winthrop Investments Ltd v Winns Ltd* [1975] 2 NSWLR 666 at 701–703 (NSW CA), Mahoney JA accepted that the court does have power to intervene in such a case. Finn, *Fiduciary Obligations* (1977), 73 contends that shareholders' decisions should be subject to a similar test to those of the directors.)

association. This provides, subject to certain qualifications which have not been invoked, that the shares shall be under the control of the directors, who may allot or otherwise dispose of the same to such persons on such terms and conditions and either at a premium or otherwise and at such time as the directors may think fit. Thus, and this is not disputed, the issue was clearly intra vires the directors. But, intra vires though the issue may have been, the directors' power under this article is a fiduciary power: and it remains the case that an exercise of such a power, though formally valid, may be attacked on the ground that it was not exercised for the purpose for which it was granted. It is at this point that the contentions of the parties diverge. The extreme argument on one side is that, for validity, what is required is bona fide exercise of the power in the interests of the company; that once it is found that the directors were not motivated by self-interest—i e by a desire to retain their control of the company or their positions on the board—the matter is concluded in their favour and that the court will not inquire into the validity of their reasons for making the issue. All decided cases, it was submitted, where an exercise of such a power as this has been found invalid, are cases where directors are found to have acted through self-interest of this kind.

On the other side, the main argument is that the purpose for which the power is conferred is to enable capital to be raised for the company, and that once it is found that the issue was not made for that purpose, invalidity follows.

It is fair to say that under the pressure of argument intermediate positions were taken by both sides, but in the main the arguments followed the polarisation which has been stated.

In their Lordships' opinion neither of the extreme positions can be maintained. It can be accepted, as one would only expect, that the majority of cases in which issues of shares are challenged in the courts are cases in which the vitiating element is the self-interest of the directors, or at least the purpose of the directors to preserve their own control of the management . . .

Further it is correct to say that where the self-interest of the directors is involved, they will not be permitted to assert that their action was bona fide thought to be, or was, in the interest of the company; pleas to this effect have invariably been rejected . . .

But it does not follow from this, as the appellants assert, that the absence of any element of self-interest is enough to make an issue valid. Self-interest is only one, though no doubt the commonest, instance of improper motive: and, before one can say that a fiduciary power has been exercised for the purpose for which it was conferred, a wider investigation may have to be made . . .   On the other hand, taking the respondents' contention, it is, in their Lordships' opinion, too narrow an approach to say that the only valid purpose for which shares may be issued is to raise capital for the company. The discretion is not in terms limited in this way: the law should not impose such a limitation on directors' powers. To define in advance exact limits beyond which directors must not pass is, in their Lordships' view, impossible. This clearly cannot be done by enumeration, since the variety of situations facing directors of different types of company in different situations cannot be anticipated. No more, in their Lordships' view, can this be done by the use of a phrase—such as 'bona fide in the interest of the company as a whole', or 'for some corporate purpose'. Such phrases, if they do anything more than restate the general principle applicable to fiduciary powers, at best serve, negatively, to exclude from the area of validity cases where the directors are acting sectionally, or partially: i e improperly favouring one section of the shareholders against another ...

In their Lordships' opinion it is necessary to start with a consideration of the power whose exercise is in question, in this case a power to issue shares. Having ascertained, on a fair view, the nature of this power, and having defined as can best be done in the light of modern conditions the, or some, limits within which it may be exercised, it is then necessary for the court, if a particular exercise of it is challenged, to examine the substantial purpose for which it was exercised, and to reach a conclusion whether that purpose was proper or not. In doing so it will necessarily give credit to the bona fide opinion of the directors, if such is found to exist, and will respect their judgment as to matters of management; having done this, the ultimate conclusion has to be as to the side of a fairly broad line on which the case falls.

The main stream of authority, in their Lordships' opinion, supports this approach. In *Punt v Symons & Co Ltd* (**139**) Byrne J expressly accepts that there may be reasons other than to raise capital for which shares may be issued. In the High Court case of *Harlowe's Nominees Pty Ltd v Woodside (Lakes Entrance) Oil Co NL*,[15] an issue of shares was made to a large oil company in order, as was found, to secure the financial stability of the company. This was upheld as being within the power although it had the effect of defeating the attempt of the plaintiff to secure control by buying up the company's shares ...

Their Lordships were referred to the recent judgment of Berger J in the Supreme Court of British Columbia, in *Teck Corpn Ltd v Millar*.[16] This was concerned with the affairs of Afton Mines Ltd in which Teck Corporation Ltd, a resource conglomerate, had acquired a majority shareholding. Teck was indicating an intention to replace the board of directors of Afton with its own nominees with a view to causing Afton to enter into an agreement (called an 'ultimate deal') with itself for the exploitation by Teck of valuable mineral rights owned by Afton. Before this could be done, and in order to prevent it, the directors of Afton concluded an exploitation agreement with another company 'Canex'. One of its provisions, as is apparently common in this type of agreement in Canada, provided for the issue to Canex of a large number of shares in Afton, thus displacing Teck's majority. Berger J found: 'their [sc the directors'] purpose was to obtain the best agreement they could while ... still in control. Their purpose was in that sense to defeat Teck. But, not to defeat Teck's attempt to obtain control, rather it was to foreclose Teck's opportunity of obtaining for itself the ultimate deal. That was ... no improper purpose.' His decision upholding the agreement with Canex on this basis appears to be in line with the English and Australian authorities to which reference has been made ...

By contrast to the cases of *Harlowe* and *Teck*, the present case, on the evidence, does not, on the findings of the trial judge, involve any considerations of management, within the proper sphere of the directors. The purpose found by the judge is simply and solely to dilute the majority voting power held by Ampol and Bulkships so as to enable a then minority of

15 Above, p 290.
16 Above, p 290.

shareholders to sell their shares more advantageously. So far as authority goes, an issue of shares purely for the purpose of creating voting power has repeatedly been condemned ... And, though the reported decisions, naturally enough, are expressed in terms of their own facts, there are clear considerations of principle which support the trend they establish. The constitution of a limited company normally provides for directors, with powers of management, and shareholders, with defined voting powers having power to appoint the directors, and to take, in general meeting, by majority vote, decisions on matters not reserved for management. Just as it is established that directors, within their management powers, may take decisions against the wishes of the majority of shareholders, and indeed that the majority of shareholders cannot control them in the exercise of these powers while they remain in office (*Automatic Self-Cleansing Filter Syndicate Co Ltd v Cunninghame* (**94**)), so it must be unconstitutional for directors to use their fiduciary powers over the shares in the company purely for the purpose of destroying an existing majority, or creating a new majority which did not previously exist. To do so is to interfere with that element of the company's constitution which is separate from and set against their powers. If there is added, moreover, to this immediate purpose, an ulterior purpose to enable an offer for shares to proceed which the existing majority was in a position to block, the departure from the legitimate use of the fiduciary power becomes not less, but all the greater ... Directors are of course entitled to offer advice, and bound to supply information, relevant to the making of such a decision, but to use their fiduciary power solely for the purpose of shifting the power to decide to whom and at what price shares are to be sold cannot be related to any purpose for which the power over the share capital was conferred upon them. That this is the position in law was in effect recognised by the majority directors themselves when they attempted to justify the issue as made primarily in order to obtain much needed capital for the company. And once this primary purpose was rejected, as it was by Street J, there is nothing legitimate left as a basis for their action, except honest behaviour. That is not, itself, enough.

Their Lordships therefore agree entirely with the conclusion of Street J that the power to issue and allot shares was improperly exercised by the issue of shares to Howard Smith ...

NOTES

(1) In *Gaiman v National Association for Mental Health* [1971] Ch 317, [1970] 2 All ER 362 the council of management of the association, a company limited by guarantee, had used a power of expulsion contained in the articles to expel certain members who were Scientologists. Megarry J upheld the council's action, saying:

> Mr Pain relied heavily on *Hogg v Cramphorn Ltd* (**140**). In that case, an issue of shares with special voting rights which would alter the balance of power was set aside on the ground that it was an exercise of a fiduciary power with an improper motive, and, being so, it was immaterial that the directors believed in good faith that the issue was in the interests of the company. Without attacking the honour of the members of the council, Mr Pain contended that they had acted with improper motives; and he said that if the power exercised was a fiduciary power, it mattered not whether the object of the improper exercise of the power was to provide reinforcements for those exercising it or to decimate the opposition.

This contention ignores, as it seems to me, an essential distinction in the powers. In a passage in *Punt v Symons & Co Ltd* (**139**), cited by Buckley J in *Hogg v Cramphorn Ltd*, Byrne J pointed out that the directors' power to issue shares was primarily given to them for the purpose of enabling them to raise capital when required for the purposes of the company. The issue of shares with the object not of raising capital needed by the company, or any other proper purpose, but of affecting the balance of voting power, is thus an exercise of powers made with a purpose that is ulterior, and not a purpose for which the power was intended. In such a case, no genuine belief in the propriety of the act done can cure the defect. In the present case, the power is a direct power to deprive a member of his membership: it is not a power to reduce capital (if that could be good) which is being employed with the ulterior purpose of depriving a member of his membership.

The question, then, is whether that power of deprivation of membership has been exercised by the council in good faith for the purpose for which it was conferred.

(2) Where the directors are motivated by more than one purpose, the decision in *Howard Smith* indicates that regard is to be had to their *primary* purpose in deciding whether the court will intervene. However, in the recent case of *Whitehouse v Carlton Hotel Pty Ltd* (1987) 11 ACLR 715, the High Court of Australia appeared to favour a narrower interpretation. The majority (Mason, Deane and Dawson JJ) in a joint judgment said (at 721):

> In this court, the preponderant view has tended to be that the allotment will be invalidated only if the impermissible purpose or a combination of impermissible purposes can be seen to have been dominant—'the substantial object' (per Williams ACJ, Fullagar and Kitto JJ, *Ngurli Ltd v McCann*[17] quoting Dixon J in *Mills v Mills* (**138**) and see *Harlowe's Nominees*);[18] 'the moving cause' (per Latham CJ, *Mills v Mills*). The cases in which that view has been indicated have not, however, required a determination of the question whether the impermissible purpose must be *the* substantial object or moving cause or whether it may suffice to invalidate the allotment that it be one of a number of such objects or causes. As a matter of logic and principle, the preferable view would seem to be that, regardless of whether the impermissible purpose was the dominant one or but one of a number of significantly contributing causes, the allotment will be invalidated if the impermissible purpose was causative in the sense that, but for its presence, 'the power would not have been exercised' per Dixon J, *Mills v Mills*.

(3) *Howard Smith* was followed by the Court of Appeal in *Lee Panavision Ltd v Lee Lighting Ltd* [1991] BCC 620, where a company's directors proposed to renew a management agreement (which would commit the management of the company to outside control for an extended period) at a time when the directors knew that the shareholders were intending very shortly to remove them, and appoint a new board. 'The function of the directors', said Dillon LJ (at p 635), 'is to manage, but the appointment of the directors who are to do the managing is constitutionally a function of the shareholders in general meeting. Therefore it must have been unconstitutional for the directors, knowing ... that the shareholders were proposing as soon as they could to exercise their constitutional right to appoint new directors, to take all managerial powers away from any new directors who might be appointed by committing Lighting [the company] to the second management agreement.'

---

17 (1953) 90 CLR 425 at 445.
18 Above, p 290.

QUESTIONS

(1) Does it follow from the judgment of Megarry J in *Gaiman*'s case that the range of purposes which it is 'proper' for the directors to pursue can be enlarged by the draftsman of the articles?

(2) Was the judge in *Re Halt Garage* (*1964*) *Ltd* (**123**) applying a 'proper purposes' test when he examined the 'genuineness' of the payment of the directors' remuneration? If so, why did he not think that a similar payment made out of undistributed profits was wrong? If not, was he applying merely a 'bona fides' test?

(3) When, if ever, might it be proper for directors to use their powers to ensure that they retained control? Could it ever be their *duty* to do so?

(4) In the Australian case *FAI Insurances Ltd v Urquhart* (1987) 11 ACLR 25 (NSW CA) there was a contested election for four vacancies on the board. The remaining directors who were continuing in office supported the re-election of the retiring directors, and were opposed to the rival candidates nominated by a minority shareholder, whose policies they thought would be harmful to the company. The minority shareholder challenged the right of the continuing directors to spend the company's money on publicity, circulated to all the shareholders, taking sides in the campaign, and on soliciting votes by telephone. What would your view have been?

(5) The Director as Trustee of the Company's Property; Duties of Care, Skill and Diligence

[See also *Re Exchange Banking Co, Flitcroft's Case* (**182**).]

142 Re City Equitable Fire Insurance Co Ltd [1925] Ch 407 (Chancery Division)

The company had lost £1,200,000, owing partly to the failure of certain investments but mainly to the frauds of the chairman of directors, Bevan, 'a daring and unprincipled scoundrel'. In this action the liquidator sought to make the other directors liable for the losses on the ground of negligence.[19] The action failed because of a provision in the articles which exempted the directors from liability apart from losses caused by 'their own wilful neglect or default';[20] but the decision of Romer J is important as a summary of the common-law duties of directors in relation to care and skill.

ROMER J: It has sometimes been said that directors are trustees. If this means no more than that directors in the performance of their duties stand in a fiduciary relationship to the company, the statement is true enough. But if the statement is meant to be an indication by way of analogy of what those duties are, it appears to me to be wholly misleading. I can see but little resemblance between the duties of a director and the duties of a trustee of a will or of a marriage settlement. It is indeed impossible to describe the duty of directors in general terms, whether by way of analogy or otherwise. The position of a director of a company carrying on a small retail business is very different from that of a director of a railway company. The duties of a bank director may differ widely from those of an insurance director, and the duties of a director of one insurance company may differ from those of a director

19 The action also sought to make the auditors liable, and on these issues went to the Court of Appeal; but the auditors too were held, having acted honestly, to be exonerated by the special provision in the company's articles.

20 Such articles are now invalidated by statute: see CA 1985, s 310.

of another. In one company, for instance, matters may normally be attended to by the manager or other members of the staff that in another company are attended to by the directors themselves. The larger the business carried on by the company the more numerous, and the more important, the matters that must of necessity be left to the managers, the accountants and the rest of the staff. The manner in which the work of the company is to be distributed between the board of directors and the staff is in truth a business matter to be decided on business lines ...

In order, therefore, to ascertain the duties that a person appointed to the board of an established company undertakes to perform, it is necessary to consider not only the nature of the company's business, but also the manner in which the work of the company is in fact distributed between the directors and the other officials of the company, provided always that this distribution is a reasonable one in the circumstances, and is not inconsistent with any express provisions of the articles of association. In discharging the duties of his position thus ascertained a director must, of course, act honestly; but he must also exercise some degree of both skill and diligence. To the question of what is the particular degree of skill and diligence required of him, the authorities do not, I think, give any very clear answer. It has been laid down that so long as a director acts honestly he cannot be made responsible in damages unless guilty of gross or culpable negligence in a business sense. But as pointed out by Neville J in *Re Brazilian Rubber Plantations and Estates Ltd*,[1] one cannot say whether a man has been guilty of negligence, gross or otherwise, unless one can determine what is the extent of the duty which he is alleged to have neglected. For myself, I confess to feeling some difficulty in understanding the difference between negligence and gross negligence, except in so far as the expressions are used for the purpose of drawing a distinction between the duty that is owed in one case and the duty that is owed in another ... If, therefore, a director is only liable for gross or culpable negligence, this means that he does not owe a duty to his company, to take all possible care. It is some degree of care less than that. The care that he is bound to take has been described by Neville J in the case referred to above as 'reasonable care' to be measured by the care an ordinary man might be expected to take in the circumstances on his own behalf ...

There are, in addition, one or two other general propositions that seem to be warranted by the reported cases: (1) A director need not exhibit in the performance of his duties a greater degree of skill than may reasonably be expected from a person of his knowledge and experience. A director of a life insurance company, for instance, does not guarantee that he has the skill of an actuary or of a physician. In the words of Lindley MR: 'If directors act within their powers, if they act with such care as is reasonably to be expected from them, having regard to their knowledge and experience, and if they act honestly for the benefit of the company they represent, they discharge both their equitable as well as their legal duty to the company': see *Lagunas Nitrate Co v Lagunas Syndicate*.[2] It is perhaps only another way of stating the same proposition to say that directors are not liable for mere errors of judgment. (2) A director is not bound to give continuous attention to the affairs of his company. His duties are of an intermittent nature to be performed at periodical board meetings, and at meetings of any committee of the board upon

1 [1911] 1 Ch 425.
2 [1899] 2 Ch 392 at 435, CA.

which he happens to be placed. He is not, however, bound to attend all such meetings, though he ought to attend whenever, in the circumstances, he is reasonably able to do so. (3) In respect of all duties that, having regard to the exigencies of business, and the articles of association, may properly be left to some other official, a director is, in the absence of grounds for suspicion, justified in trusting that official to perform such duties honestly. In the judgment of the Court of Appeal in *Re National Bank of Wales Ltd*,[3] the following passage occurs in relation to a director who had been deceived by the manager, and managing director, as to matters within their own particular sphere of activity: 'Was it his duty to test the accuracy or completeness of what he was told by the general manager, and the managing director? This is a question on which opinions may differ, but we are not prepared to say that he failed in his legal duty. Business cannot be carried on upon principles of distrust. Men in responsible positions must be trusted by those above them, as well as those below them, until there is reason to distrust them. We agree that care and prudence do not involve distrust; but for a director acting honestly himself to be held legally liable for negligence, in trusting the officers under him not to conceal from him what they ought to report to him, appears to us to be laying too heavy a burden on honest businessmen.' ...

These are the general principles that I shall endeavour to apply in considering the question whether the directors of this company have been guilty of negligence ...

[His Lordship then considered a number of specific allegations and made various observations about points of detail. These must, of course, be understood to be applicable primarily to the facts before him, and to companies the size and nature of the City Equitable Co; but they are of value if only as illustrations of the extent of a director's duty in a typical case. Some of these observations follow.]

... [A] director who signs a cheque that appears to be drawn for a legitimate purpose is not responsible for seeing that the money is in fact required for that purpose or that it is subsequently applied for that purpose, assuming, of course, that the cheque comes before him for signature in the regular way having regard to the usual practice of the company. If this were not so, the business of a large company could not be carried on. In the case of an insurance company, for instance, the cheques to be signed at the board meeting would often include cheques in payment of insurance claims. If a claim appears to have been examined into and passed by the manager or other proper official for the purpose, a director who signs the necessary cheque in payment of the claim (the cheque being brought before him in the customary way) cannot be expected to investigate the whole matter over again, for the purpose of satisfying himself that the claim is well founded. A director must of necessity trust to the officials of the company to perform properly and honestly the duties allocated to those officials ...

It is the duty of each director to see that the company's moneys are from time to time in a proper state of investment, except in so far as the company's articles of association may justify him in delegating that duty to others. So far as the respondent directors, other than Mr Haig Thomas and Mr Grenside, are concerned, they were justified in delegating this general duty to the

3 [1899] 2 Ch 629 at 673.

finance committee, and thought that they had done so. The position of Mr Thomas and Mr Grenside was, however, very different. They knew that neither the board nor the finance committee were attending to the temporary investments and were content to leave the duty of doing so to Mr Bevan and Mr Mansell. In this they were wrong. Thinking, as they did, that the duty had not been delegated to the finance committee, they should have regarded it as being still reposed in the board as a whole. That Bevan and Mansell were persons enjoying the highest reputation is beside the mark. If the shareholders had desired to leave hundreds of thousands of pounds of the company's money under the sole control of Bevan, they would have done so. But the shareholders had preferred to have associated with Bevan a board of six or seven other directors, and it was not for these other directors to leave Bevan to discharge one of the most important of the duties that had been entrusted by the shareholders to the board as a whole, however reasonable and however safe it might have seemed to the directors to do so. Still less would it be permissible to leave the control of the company's temporary investments to the general manager. It is not any part of the functions of a manager of an insurance company to decide upon the method of investment of the company's cash resources. His advice and assistance will no doubt be sought. But the responsibility for the ultimate decision as to investment must rest with the directors or, when the articles permit, with a committee of the directors, and none the less that the investment is only a temporary one. In my judgment, Mr Haig Thomas and Mr Grenside were guilty of a breach of their duty in failing to control and safeguard the moneys of the company that were not in a state of permanent investment.

The Official Receiver ... seeks to charge the respondent directors ... upon the ground that it was a breach of their duty to allow securities of the company to be retained by their brokers. Had any one of the respondent directors been aware of the fact that securities were left in the hands of Ellis & Co for safe custody he would have been guilty of breach of duty if he had not insisted on the practice being summarily stopped. But in fact they were all ignorant that this was being done. The Official Receiver contends, however, that this ignorance does not protect them, as they ought to have initiated some system of safeguarding the company's securities under which it would have been impossible for Ellis & Co to obtain possession of them. This object could, no doubt, have been attained if the directors had taken the securities to the bank in person or had personally supervised the locking up of the securities in a safe, retaining sole control of the key. But it is not the duty of a director of such a company as the City Equitable to see in person to the safe custody of securities. That is one of the matters which the directors must almost of necessity leave to some official who is at the office daily, such as the manager, accountant or secretary. When an investment is made through the brokers, it would be quite impracticable for the directors to receive actual delivery of the securities. So too when investments are sold, delay and great inconvenience would result if the delivery of the securities to the brokers had to await a meeting of the board or of a committee of directors. The respondent directors would therefore be justified in trusting to Mr Mansell, their general manager, or Mr Lock, their accountant, to perform the duty of putting into safe custody the securities of the company. And this is what in fact the respondent directors appear to have done ...

NOTES

(1) In *Dorchester Finance Co Ltd v Stebbing* (1977), reported [1989] BCLC 498, a moneylending company had three directors, Stebbing, Parsons and Hamilton. Stebbing worked full time for the company; the other two paid very little attention to it and visited its premises only rarely. They signed cheque forms in blank at Stebbing's request, with which he made loans that were illegal and accordingly irrecoverable. No board meetings were held. All three directors were held liable to make good the company's losses. Foster J laid some stress on the fact that the two non-executive directors were experienced in accountancy; but it appears that this was not crucial to his decision. He said:

> For a chartered accountant and an experienced accountant to put forward the proposition that a non-executive director has no duties to perform I find quite alarming. It would be an argument which, if put forward by a director with no accountancy experience, would involve total disregard of many sections of the Companies Act 1948 . . . The signing of blank cheques by Hamilton and Parsons was in my judgment negligent, as it allowed Stebbing to do as he pleased. Apart from that, they not only failed to exhibit the necessary skill and care in the performance of their duties as directors, but also failed to perform any duty at all as directors of Dorchester. In the Companies Act 1948 the duties of a director whether executive or not are the same.

(2) In *Norman v Theodore Goddard (a firm)* [1991] BCLC 1028 Hoffmann J said that he was 'willing to assume' that the test of a director's duty of care, in considering what he ought reasonably to have known or inferred, empowered the court to take into account the knowledge, skill and experience which he actually had, in addition to that which a person carrying out his functions should be expected to have—a submission based on IA 1986, s 214(4), the 'wrongful trading' provision which applies in insolvency (below, p 578). If accepted, this test would introduce a partly objective element into the standard of care.

(3) Section 13 of the Supply of Goods and Services Act 1982 provides that, in a contract for the supply of a service where the supplier is acting in the course of a business, there is an implied term that the supplier will carry out the service with reasonable care and skill. But under regulations made by the Secretary of State (SI 1982/1771) this section is declared not to apply to 'the services rendered to a company by a director in his capacity as such'.

Although these provisions rather oddly assume that a director supplies a service to his company 'in the course of a business', and that he does so pursuant to a contract (contrast *Newtherapeutics Ltd v Katz,* above, p 98), we have here an endorsement by the legislature of the common law view that a director does not undertake to bring any particular skill to his office, coupled with a perhaps surprising denial of any obligation to exercise reasonable care. However, the words 'in his capacity as such' leave room for the implication of such terms in the contract of service of a director who is also an employee.

Acts of the directors made with the approval of the shareholders cannot be impugned on the grounds of negligence, for shareholders owe no duty of care to their company.

143 Multinational Gas and Petrochemical Co Ltd v Multinational Gas and Petrochemical Services Ltd [1983] Ch 258, [1983] 2 All ER 563 (Court of Appeal)

Three international oil companies established a joint venture to deal in liquified gas. They set up the plaintiff company to carry on the business, and the defendant company 'Services' to manage it and to provide advisory services. The three oil companies were the sole shareholders in both companies and appointed their directors. The plaintiff company went into liquidation owing approximately £114 m, and its liquidator sued its directors and also the defendant company, alleging that they had all been negligent. The Court of Appeal held that the action was not founded on any tort committed within the jurisdiction and so refused leave to serve the proceedings on those defendants who were abroad. But Lawton and Dillon LJJ also accepted an argument that there could be no complaint about commercial decisions, alleged to be negligent, which had been made by the directors with the approval of the three oil companies as shareholders.

LAWTON LJ: The submission in relation to the defendants was as follows. No allegation had been made that the plaintiff's directors had acted ultra vires or in bad faith. What was alleged was that when making the decisions which were alleged to have caused the plaintiff loss and giving instructions to Services to put them into effect they acted in accordance with the directions and behest of the three oil companies. These oil companies were the only shareholders. All the acts complained of became the plaintiff's acts. The plaintiff, although it had a separate existence from its oil company shareholders, existed for the benefit of those shareholders, who, provided they acted intra vires and in good faith, could manage the plaintiff's affairs as they wished. If they wanted to take business risks through the plaintiff which no prudent businessman would take they could lawfully do so. Just as an individual can act like a fool provided he keeps within the law so could the plaintiff, but in its case it was for the shareholders to decide whether the plaintiff should act foolishly. As shareholders they owed no duty to those with whom the plaintiff did business. It was for such persons to assess the hazards of doing business with them. It follows, so it was submitted, that the plaintiff, as a matter of law, cannot now complain about what they did at their shareholders' behest.

This submission was based on ... a long line of cases starting with *Salomon v A Salomon & Co Ltd* (**12**) and ending with the decision of this court in *Re Horsley & Weight Ltd* (**68**). In my judgment these cases establish the following relevant principles of law. First, that the plaintiff was at law a different legal person from the subscribing oil company shareholders and was not their agent (see *Salomon v A Salomon & Co Ltd*). Second that the oil companies as shareholders were not liable to anyone except to the extent and the manner provided by the Companies Act 1948 (see *Salomon v A Salomon & Co Ltd*). Third, that when the oil companies acting together required the plaintiff's directors to make decisions or approve what had already been done, what they did or approved became the plaintiff's acts and were binding on it (see by way of examples *A-G for Canada v Standard Trust Co of New York*,[4] *Re Express Engineering Works Ltd* (**81**) and *Re Horsley & Weight Ltd*). When approving whatever their nominee directors had done, the oil companies were not, as the plaintiff submitted, relinquishing any causes of action which the plaintiff may have had against its directors. When the oil companies, as shareholders, approved what the plaintiff's directors had done there was no cause of action because at that time there was no damage. What the oil

4 [1911] AC 498.

companies were doing was adopting the directors' acts and as shareholders, in agreement with each other, making those acts the plaintiff's acts.

It follows, so it seems to me, that the plaintiff cannot now complain about what in law were its own acts. Further, I can see no grounds for adjudging that the oil companies as shareholders were under any duty of care to the plaintiff. In coming to this conclusion I have kept in mind the doubts expressed by Cumming-Bruce and Templeman LJJ in *Re Horsley & Weight Ltd.* Their comments were obiter. Both my brethren were thinking of 'misfeasance' which probably does not cover 'an ordinary claim for damages simply': see *Re B Johnson & Co (Builders) Ltd.*[5] Having regard to the long line of authorities to which I have referred and the examples I have mentioned I do not share their doubts ...

DILLON LJ: It is not alleged that the joint venturers or the directors of the plaintiff acted fraudulently or in bad faith in any way or were guilty of fraudulent trading. What is alleged is that they all acted negligently in that they made five speculative decisions in relation to the six ships, when they knew or ought to have known that they did not have sufficient information to make sensible business decisions. The decisions which they took in good faith went, it is said, outside the range of reasonable commercial judgment.

The heart of the matter is therefore that certain commercial decisions which were not ultra vires the plaintiff were made honestly, not merely by the directors but by all the shareholders of the plaintiff at a time when the plaintiff was solvent. I do not see how there can be any complaint of that.

An individual trader who is solvent is free to make stupid, but honest, commercial decisions in the conduct of his own business. He owes no duty of care to future creditors. The same applies to a partnership of individuals.

A company, as it seems to me, likewise owes no duty of care to future creditors. The directors indeed stand in a fiduciary relationship to the company, as they are appointed to manage the affairs of the company and they owe fiduciary duties to the company though not to creditors, present or future,[6] or to individual shareholders. The duties owed by a director include a duty of care, as was recognised by Romer J in *Re City Equitable Fire Insurance Co Ltd* (**142**), though as he pointed out the nature and extent of the duty may depend on the nature of the business of the company and on the particular knowledge and experience of the individual director.

The shareholders, however, owe no such duty to the company. Indeed, so long as the company is solvent the shareholders are in substance the company ...

[Counsel for the plaintiff] has put before us some very interesting submissions on what the shareholders ought to have in mind if they seek to release a director from liability to the company for breach of duty, and the release is not to be ultra vires the company, and as to the extent of knowledge of the facts which the shareholders must have before they can validly release a director from such liability, i e they must know that there is said to have been something wrong with what the director did. It seems to me, however, that in the present case we never get to that point. The case set up is that all the shareholders, the joint venturers, made the impugned decisions at the outset ...

5 [1955] Ch 634 at 648, [1955] All ER 775 at 781.
6 [In *West Mercia Safetywear Ltd v Dodd* (1988) 4 BCC 30 Dillon LJ has since qualified these remarks by saying that they apply only to a company which is solvent at the relevant time.]

The well-known passage in the speech of Lord Davey in *Salomon v A Salomon & Co Ltd* that the company is bound in a matter intra vires by the unanimous agreement of its members is, in my judgment, apt to cover the present case whether or not Lord Davey had circumstances such as the present case in mind.

If the company is bound by what was done when it was a going concern, then the liquidator is in no better position. He cannot sue the members because they owed no duty to the company as a separate entity and he cannot sue the directors because the decisions which he seeks to impugn were made by, and with the full assent of, the members.

MAY LJ (dissenting): It is well established by such authorities as *Salomon v A Salomon & Co Ltd* and the many authorities to like effect to which we were referred that a company is bound, in a matter which is intra vires and not fraudulent, by the unanimous agreement of its members or by an ordinary resolution of a majority of its members. However, I do not think that this line of authority establishes anything more than that a company is bound by the legal results of a transaction so entered into: that is to say, for instance, by the terms of contract which is so approved; or that neither it nor for that matter its liquidator can challenge the legal consequences, such as a transfer of title, of a transaction to which its members have agreed to the extent that I have mentioned.

This, however, is very different from saying that where all the acts of the directors of a company, for instance, Services, have been carried out by them as nominees for, at the behest and with the knowledge of all the members of the company, namely the joint venturers, then forever the company as a separate legal entity is precluded from complaining of the quality of those acts in the absence of fraud or unless they were ultra vires. If we assume for the purposes of this argument that the directors of the plaintiff did commit breaches of the duty of care that they owed that company, as a result of which it suffered damage, then I agree with the submission made by counsel for the plaintiff that the company thereby acquired a cause of action against those directors in negligence. The fact that all the members of the company knew of the acts constituting such breaches, and indeed knew that those acts were in breach of that duty, does not of itself in my opinion prevent them from constituting the tort of negligence against the company or by itself release the directors from liability for it. Of course, in the circumstances of the present case, whilst the joint venturers retained effective control of the company they would be extremely unlikely to complain of the negligence of their nominees. But such restraint on their part could not and did not in my opinion amount to any release by the company of the cause of action which ex hypothesi had become vested in it against its directors. *Salomon*'s case and the subsequent authorities make it clear that a limited company is a person separate and distinct from its members, even though a majority of the latter have the power to control its activities so long as it is not put into liquidation and whilst they remain members and a majority. Once, however, the joint venturers ceased to be able to call the tune, either because the company went into liquidation or indeed, though it is not this case, because others took over their interests as members of the company, then I can see no legal reason why the liquidator or the company itself could not sue in respect of the cause of action still vested in it. I agree with counsel's submission that that cause of action was an asset of the company which could not be gratuitously released ...

NOTE

All three members of the Court of Appeal in this case referred to the doubts expressed obiter by Templeman and Cumming-Bruce LJJ in *Re Horsley & Weight Ltd* (**98**) whether directors holding a majority of shares were competent to ratify their own negligence. But their discussion of the dicta is inconclusive. May LJ appears to have shared the doubts, but Lawton and Dillon LJJ to have considered that they applied, if at all, only to 'misfeasance'—i e something more than mere negligence. This could perhaps be either (i) 'reckless' conduct coming somewhere near to fraud or (ii) negligent acts which benefit the directors themselves (*Daniels v Daniels* (**246**)).

QUESTIONS

(1) If the alleged acts of negligence were committed by the directors with the prior authorisation of the shareholders, do you consider the reasoning of Lawton LJ or that of May LJ more appropriate?
(2) If the alleged acts of negligence were committed by the directors on their own initiative and later approved by the shareholders, do you consider the reasoning of Lawton LJ or that of May LJ more appropriate?
(3) Were the directors in this case in breach of their duty not to fetter their discretion (above, p 276)?

The misapplication of corporate property by directors renders them liable to account to the company in equity on the same basis as governs a misapplication of trust funds by trustees.

A director acting in a transaction as the 'puppet' of a stranger is fixed with the stranger's knowledge that the transaction is improper.

A third party receiving or handling corporate property with knowledge that it is being applied for an improper purpose is liable to the company as a constructive trustee.

144 Selangor United Rubber Estates Ltd v Cradock (No 3) [1968] 1 WLR 1555, [1968] 2 All ER 1073 (Chancery Division)

Cradock bid for and obtained a controlling interest in the shareholding of Selangor, the plaintiff company, which he paid for improperly by the use of the company's own funds in the following way: his nominees, Barlow-Lawson and Jacob, were appointed to the Selangor board; at Cradock's direction, they advanced £232,500 of Selangor's money to a company called Woodstock; Woodstock lent the same sum to Cradock; and £195,000 of that sum was then paid to the former shareholders in Selangor, as the purchase price of their shares, through the medium of Contanglo, a banking firm specialising in take-overs. Soon afterwards, Selangor was compulsorily wound up and Cradock left England. The Board of Trade brought these proceedings in the company's name to recover the sum improperly paid away, against (a) Barlow-Lawson and Jacob, as directors, (b) Cradock (against whom judgment was given by default) and (c) Woodstock, Cantanglo and the District Bank (which had handled and met all the cheques by which the payments were made) as constructive trustees. The directors were held liable for the misapplication, being fixed by the court with knowledge of Cradock's improper purpose. The other defendants, though 'outsiders', were held liable as constructive trustees for having 'assisted with knowledge in a dishonest and fraudulent design' on the part of the directors and Cradock. [On this last point, the reasoning of Ungoed-Thomas J has since been disapproved: see the note below.]

UNGOED-THOMAS J: The first question of law that arises is how far directors are trustees of their companies' funds? It is clear and not disputed that they owe a fiduciary duty to the company to apply its assets only for the purposes of the company and are therefore liable for breach of that duty. But the question how far they are trustees bears upon the question how other defendants can be made liable as constructive trustees as claimed ...

Directors are clearly not trustees identically with trustees of a will or marriage settlement. In particular, so far as at present relevant, they have business to conduct and business functions to perform in a business manner, which are not normally at any rate associated with trustees of a will or marriage settlement. All their duties, powers and functions qua directors are fiduciary for and on behalf of the company. So property in their hands or under their control is theirs for the company, i e for the company's purposes in accordance with their duties, powers and functions. However much the company's purposes and the directors' duties, powers and functions may differ from the purposes of a strict settlement and the duties, powers and functions of its trustees, the directors and such trustees have this indisputably in common—that the property in their hands or under their control must be applied for the specified purposes of the company or the settlement; and to apply it otherwise is to misapply it in breach of the obligations to apply it for those purposes for the company or the settlement beneficiaries. So, even though the scope and operation of such obligation differs in the case of directors and strict settlement trustees, the nature of the obligation with regard to property in their hands or under their control is identical, namely, to apply it to specified purposes for others beneficially. This is to hold it on trust for the company or the settlement beneficiaries as the case may be. That is what holding it on trust means. That is why a misapplication of it is equally in each case a breach of trust ...

[Secondly], how far, as put in argument, the director who acts, without exercising any discretion, at the direction of a stranger to the company is, in respect of his liability for funds under his control (for which he is, as I have concluded, a trustee) to have ascribed to him the purpose of that stranger, or, as I prefer to put it and which comes to much the same thing in our case and is sufficient for present purposes, how far is he bound by the stranger's knowledge of the nature of the transaction?

In *Gray v Lewis* Mellish LJ said:[7] 'If a person allows himself to be the mere nominee of, and acts for another person, he must be bound by the notice which that other person for whom he acts has of the nature of the transaction.' And that was said with reference to a fraudulent and illegal transaction. The nominees in that case were not directors but purchasers of shares ...

7 (1873) 8 Ch App 1035 at 1056.

In my view a director acting in a transaction on the direction of a stranger is fixed with that stranger's knowledge of the nature of that transaction ...

[Thirdly] I come ... to the question how far a stranger to the trust can become liable as constructive trustee in respect of a breach of the trust.

It is essential at the outset to distinguish two very different kinds of so-called constructive trustees: (1) Those who, though not appointed trustees, take upon themselves to act as such and to possess and administer trust property for the beneficiaries, such as trustees de son tort. Distinguishing features for present purposes are (a) they do not claim to act in their own right but for the beneficiaries, and (b) their assumption to act is not of itself a ground of liability (save in the sense of course of liability to account and for any failure in the duty so assumed), and so their status as trustees precedes the occurrence which may be the subject of a claim against them. (2) Those whom a court of equity will treat as trustees by reason of their action, of which complaint is made. Distinguishing features are (a) that such trustees claim to act in their own right and not for beneficiaries, and (b) no trusteeship arises before, but only by reason of, the action complained of ...

Barnes v Addy[8] contains a formulation of the second category of constructive trusteeship, upon which the plaintiff relies. In that case Barnes was husband of the life tenant of the trust, was appointed sole trustee by Addy, the sole surviving trustee, and subsequently he misappropriated the trust fund. The question before the Court of Appeal was whether the solicitors engaged in respect of the appointment were liable to make good the amount misappropriated. Lord Selborne LC referred to both categories of constructive trustees. He said: 'That responsibility'—that is the responsibility of express trustees—'may no doubt be extended in equity to others who are not properly trustees, if they are found either making themselves trustees de son tort, or actually participating in any fraudulent conduct of the trustee to the injury of the cestui que trust. But, on the other hand, strangers are not to be made constructive trustees merely because they act as agents of trustees in transactions within their legal powers, transactions, perhaps of which a court of equity may disapprove, unless those agents receive and become chargeable with some part of the trust property, or unless they assist with knowledge in a dishonest and fraudulent design on the part of the trustees' ...

[His Lordship ruled that Woodstock, Contanglo and the District Bank were liable as constructive trustees on the ground that each of them had 'assisted with knowledge' in Cradock's 'dishonest and fraudulent design'—a part of his judgment that has since been criticised (see below). He observed, in regard to the defendant directors:] It seems to me ... that both Barlow-Lawson and Jacob were nominated as directors of the plaintiff to do exactly as they were told by Cradock, and that is in fact what they did. They exercised no discretion or volition of their own and they behaved in utter disregard of their duties as directors to the general body of stockholders or creditors or anyone but Cradock. They put themselves in his hands, not as their agent or adviser, but as their controller. They were puppets which had no movement apart from the strings and those strings manipulated by Cradock. They were voices without any mind but that of Cradock; and with that mind they are fixed in accordance with the view which I have already expressed on the law. They doubtless hoped for the best but risked the worst; and that worst has befallen them.

8　(1874) 9 Ch App 244.

NOTE

It will be observed that in the passage quoted by Ungoed-Thomas J from *Barnes v Addy,* two possible grounds for making a stranger liable as constructive trustee are identified, namely: (i) where he 'receives and becomes chargeable with some part of the trust property' (commonly called 'knowing receipt'); and (ii) where he 'assists with knowledge in a dishonest and fraudulent design on the part of the trustees' ('knowing assistance'). The *Belmont Finance (No 2)* decision (**145**) draws attention to the distinction between these two possible heads of liability. There have since been a number of decisions, mostly at first instance, concerned with the liability of a stranger as constructive trustee in similar circumstances, and a confused picture has emerged. Controversy has centred around the question whether different standards of notice or knowledge are to be applied in the two cases. In *Baden Delvaux & Lecuit v Société Général pour Favoriser le Développement du Commerce et de l'Industrie en France SA* [1983] BCLC 325 at 407, Peter Gibson J identified five different kinds of mental state which may be relevant in this context, as follows:

> (i) actual knowledge; (ii) wilfully shutting one's eyes to the obvious; (iii) wilfully and recklessly failing to make such inquiries as an honest and reasonable man would make; (iv) knowledge of circumstances which would indicate the facts to an honest and reasonable man; (v) knowledge of circumstances which would have put an honest and reasonable man on inquiry.

It is now generally accepted that in a case of knowing *assistance,* the defendant will not be liable unless his knowledge falls within categories (i), (ii) or (iii)—in other words, there must have been a degree of intentional wrongdoing on his part. In regard to knowing *receipt* however, the position is still unresolved. It is accepted that under this head, the breach of trust or fiduciary duty itself need not be fraudulent, but in respect of the type of knowledge required, opinions vary between those who consider that some want of probity on the part of the defendant is an essential element (thus confining the case to categories (i)–(iii)—*Baden Delvaux, Re Montagu's Settlement Trusts* [1987] Ch 264, and others who would allow (iv) and possibly also (v) to qualify as well (*Westpac Banking Corpn v Savin* [1985] 2 NZLR 41 (NZ CA), and cf *Belmont Finance (No 2)*, below)). For the latest, but surely not the last, discussion of the authorities see *Cowan de Groot Properties Ltd v Eagle Trust plc* [1991] BCLC 1045, where Knox J found it unnecessary to resolve the issue.

In the *Selangor* case Ungoed-Thomas J held the District Bank liable on the basis of 'knowing assistance' when at best it was only affected by *notice* of the irregularity of the transaction—that is, knowledge of type (iv) or (v); and his reasoning has since been disapproved by the Court of Appeal in *Lipkin Gorman v Karpnale Ltd* [1989] 1 WLR 1340 at 1355.[9] However, the bank could well have been held liable on the ground of 'knowing receipt', if knowledge of either type (iv) or (v) is all that is required under this head.[10]

145 Belmont Finance Corpn Ltd v Williams Furniture Ltd (No 2) [1980] 1 All ER 393 (Court of Appeal)

A company referred to as 'City' owned all the shares in Belmont. The directors of Belmont and others agreed to a complex transaction under which, inter alia, a property was sold to Belmont for £500,000 and all the shares in Belmont were sold by City to the vendors of that property for £489,000. The transaction was illegal for breach of the statutory provision which is now CA 1985, s 151 (below, p 353). The Court of Appeal, in other proceedings,

---

9 The appeal to the House of Lords in this case ([1991] 3 WLR 10) involved different parties and was concerned with a different point.
10 See C Harpum, 'The Stranger as Constructive Trustee' (1986) 102 LQR 114, 267.

held some of the defendants liable in conspiracy (below, **(176)**). The extract which follows deals with an alternative claim under which City was held not to be liable as a constructive trustee for Belmont in respect of the £500,000 which Belmont's directors had wrongly paid away, but liable on this basis for the £489,000 which it had itself received with knowledge of the circumstances. Dishonesty had not been established against City, but that was relevant only to the former type of constructive trust claim.

BUCKLEY LJ: I now come to the constructive trust point. If a stranger to a trust (a) receives and becomes chargeable with some part of the trust fund or (b) assists the trustees of a trust with knowledge of the facts in a dishonest design on the part of the trustees to misapply some part of a trust fund, he is liable as a constructive trustee (*Barnes v Addy*[11] per Lord Selborne LC).

A limited company is of course not a trustee of its own funds: it is their beneficial owner; but in consequence of the fiduciary character of their duties the directors of a limited company are treated as if they were trustees of those funds of the company which are in their hands or under their control, and if they misapply them they commit a breach of trust (*Re Lands Allotment Co*,[12] per Lindley and Kay LJJ). So, if the directors of a company in breach of their fiduciary duties misapply the funds of their company so that they come into the hands of some stranger to the trust who receives them with knowledge (actual or constructive[13]) of the breach, he cannot conscientiously retain those funds against the company unless he has some better equity. He becomes a constructive trustee for the company of the misapplied funds ...

In the present case, the payment of the £500,000 by Belmont ... being an unlawful contravention of s 54 (CA 1985, s 151), was a misapplication of Belmont's money and was in breach of the duties of the directors of Belmont. £489,000 of the £500,000 so misapplied found their way into the hands of City with City's knowledge of the whole circumstances of the transaction. It must follow, in my opinion, that City is accountable to Belmont as a constructive trustee of the £489,000 under the first of Lord Selborne LC's two heads.

There remains the question whether City is chargeable as a constructive trustee under Lord Selborne LC's second head on the ground that Belmont's directors were guilty of dishonesty ... and that City with knowledge of the facts assisted them in that dishonest design. As I understand Lord Selborne LC's second head, a stranger to a trust notwithstanding that he may not have received any of the trust fund which has been applied will be treated as accountable as a constructive trustee if he has knowingly participated in a dishonest design on the part of the trustees to misapply the fund; he must himself have been in some way a party to the dishonesty of the trustees. It follows from what I have already held that the directors of Belmont were guilty of misfeasance but not that they acted dishonestly. [His Lordship accordingly ruled that they were not liable on this ground.]

GOFF and WALLER LJJ delivered concurring judgments.

---

11 (1874) 9 Ch App 244.
12 [1894] 1 Ch 616.
13 [See the note to the *Selangor* case **(144)**, above.]

NOTE

The *Belmont Finance* ruling was followed also in *International Sales and Agencies Ltd v Marcus* (**72**) and formed an alternative ground of liability in *Rolled Steel Products (Holdings) Ltd v British Steel Corpn* (**70**), (**105**).

Statutory provisions affecting directors

CA 1985 contains many provisions regulating the activities of directors and imposing duties upon them. Some are sanctioned by criminal penalties only, while others may affect the validity of transactions or give rise to civil liability to pay damages or make restitution. These provisions have been allowed to accumulate and proliferate without adequate regard to their impact on each other or on the existing law as found in the cases. The result is that the full legal position in any situation can be assessed only by checking both the statutory rules and the common law. Even so, a fully comprehensive list of all the statutory provisions would be hard to draw up. The following are among the most important:

(a) CA 1985, ss 312–316 requires disclosure by directors and shareholder approval if payments are made to directors for loss of office in connection with a transfer of the company's undertaking, or on a take-over.

(b) Directors must disclose to the board their interests in contracts that the company is making or proposes to make: CA 1985, s 317.[14]

(c) Shareholder approval is required for directors' contracts of employment of more than five years' duration: CA 1985, s 319.

(d) Shareholder approval is required for 'substantial property transactions' involving directors: CA 1985, ss 320–322.

(e) A director is forbidden to deal in options on the shares of his company or of other companies in the same group: CA 1985, s 323.

(f) Loans by a company to its directors are in general forbidden: CA 1985, ss 330 ff (see below).

(g) Directors may be criminally liable for 'insider dealing': Company Securities (Insider Dealing) Act 1985 (see below, p 539).

(h) Directors may be liable to make good losses of capital, e g through issuing shares without complying with the statutory rules about payment (CA 1985, ss 99 ff) or for making an improper repurchase of shares out of capital (IA 1986, s 76(2)(b)).

There are, in addition, extensive disclosure obligations regarding directors' activities: see, e g CA 1985, ss 318 (service contracts), 324 (shareholdings) and Sch 6 (emoluments, pensions, loans).

Mention should also be made of the statutory creatures 'shadow directors' and 'connected persons'. A number of the provisions of CA 1985 which forbid or restrict certain acts on the part of directors are made to apply also to persons who fall into one or other of these categories.

A 'shadow director' is defined (s 741(2)), as 'a person in accordance with whose directions or instructions the directors of a company are accustomed to act'. Section 741(2), however, excludes a professional person on whose

---

14 Note also CA 1985, s 322A, which imposes special sanctions when, in contracting with a director or a person 'connected with' a director, the board of directors exceed their constitutional powers (above, p 261).

advice the directors act. The object of this provision is plainly to prevent the people who really exercise control from sheltering behind a puppet board.

A person is 'connected with' a director for the purposes, at least, of Part X of the Act and much of the insolvency legislation, in the circumstances laid down by s 346. These include the director's spouse, his children under 18, other companies with which the director is 'associated' (i e in which he has, with his 'connected persons', at least a 20% stake), any trustee of a family trust, and a partner.

It is important to bear in mind the possibility that statutory rules may affect these other people as well as the directors when one is using the legislation. The statutory provisions do not, however, affect matters at common law (but then the common law has some healthy rules of its own to cope with problems of this sort: see, e g *Gilford Motor Co Ltd v Horne* (**24**) and *Selangor United Rubber Estates Ltd v Cradock* (**144**)).

Loans to directors

Loans by a company to its directors and guarantees of a director's indebtedness are, in general, prohibited by statute (CA 1985, ss 330 ff). The ban extends to a number of analogous transactions and to 'shadow directors'. The rules for public companies (including private companies which form part of a public company group) are more extensive than those for private companies, covering also what the Act calls 'quasi-loans' and 'credit transactions' and dealings with 'connected persons' (defined in s 346). 'Indirect arrangements', which broadly have the same effect as those expressly prohibited by the Act, are also banned—e g a 'back to back' loan under which X agrees to make a loan to a director of Y Ltd in return for some benefit conferred by Y Ltd on X. There are exceptions for certain smaller transactions, such as loans for the purchase of season tickets, and more generous rules for moneylending companies. This regime, dating from the 1980 Act, is considerably more strict than that which obtained under the Act of 1948, and the old loopholes like loans 'to enable a director properly to perform his duties' have gone. There are also very elaborate disclosure rules which require such loans as are still permitted to be shown in the accounts of all companies.

It is sufficient for the purposes of most examination syllabuses for the student to know that this statutory minefield exists. Later, when he has graduated, he may choose to join the flourishing avoidance industry!

Disqualification of directors[15]

The courts have wide powers to order that directors of companies which have gone into insolvent liquidation and persons who have committed serious or persistent breaches of company law shall be banned from being a director of a company or being concerned (directly or indirectly) in its management. The legislation on disqualification orders is now consolidated in the Company Directors Disqualification Act 1986. Under this Act, the court may make an order against a person who has (i) been convicted of an indictable offence in connection with the formation or management of a company (s 2); (ii) been persistently in breach of his obligations under the Companies Acts, e g to file returns (ss 3, 5); (iii) been guilty of fraud or fraudulent trading revealed in a

---

15 See J Dine, 'The Disqualification of Company Directors' (1988) 9 Co Law 213; 'Disqualification of Directors' (1991) 12 Co Law 6.

winding up (s 4); (iv) been a director of a company which has 'become insolvent' and is found 'unfit' to be concerned in the management of a company (s 6); (v) similarly been found 'unfit' after a statutory investigation into the affairs of a company (s 8); (vi) been guilty of fraudulent or wrongful trading as defined in IA 1986, ss 213–214 (s 10). A disqualification order may ban the person from being a director or being concerned in the management of a company for up to 15 years in the more serious cases, such as fraudulent trading, and up to 5 years in others, such as persistent failure to file returns with the registrar.

Of these provisions, ss 6 and 8 are of particular interest because of the new concept of 'unfitness', which is elaborated in Schedule 1 to the Act. The relevant statutory rules amplify the directors' traditional common-law duties of care and skill (at least for the purpose of imposing the salutary sanction of disqualification, if not the common law's own remedies). A number of cases under the new legislation have been reported, including *Re Sevenoaks Stationers (Retail) Ltd* (**146**), in which the Court of Appeal laid down some guidelines for the exercise of this jurisdiction.

The Department of Trade and Industry Insolvency Service has a special unit charged with the task of enforcing this branch of the law. Whenever a company goes into receivership, administration or insolvent liquidation, a report on the conduct of every director has to be made to the Department by the insolvency practitioner concerned. Disqualification orders are currently being made at the rate of about 300 per annum.

The Registrar maintains a register of the names of all persons against whom disqualification orders are made (Company Directors Disqualification Act 1986, s 18).

146 Re Sevenoaks Stationers (Retail) Ltd [1991] Ch 164, [1991] 3 All ER 578 (Court of Appeal)

Cruddas, a chartered accountant, was a director of five companies which had become insolvent with a total net deficiency of £600,000. The defaults proved against him in respect of one or more of the companies included: failing to keep proper accounting records, failing to ensure that annual returns were filed and that annual accounts were prepared and audited, causing the companies to incur debts when he ought to have known that they were in severe financial difficulties, causing them to trade while insolvent, and failing to pay Crown debts in respect of PAYE and NIC contribution and VAT. The Court of Appeal upheld the judge's finding that he was 'unfit to be concerned in the management of a company' (Company Directors Disqualification Act 1986, s 6). A disqualification order for five years was imposed.

DILLON LJ: ... [This] appeal has an importance beyond its own facts, since it is the first appeal against a disqualification order which has come to this court. ...

I would for my part endorse the division of the potential 15 year disqualification period into three brackets, which was put forward by Mr Keenan for the official receiver to Harman J in the present case and has been put forward by Mr Charles for the official receiver in other cases, viz: (i) the top bracket of disqualification for periods over 10 years should be reserved for particularly serious cases. These may include cases where a director who has already had one period of disqualification imposed on him falls to be disqualified yet again. (ii) The minimum bracket of two to five years' disqualification should be applied where, though disqualification is mandatory, the case is, relatively, not very serious. (iii) The middle bracket of disqualification for from six to 10 years should apply for serious cases which do not merit the top bracket.

I will come back to the appropriate bracket and period of disqualification when I have considered the facts and other issues.

[His Lordship discussed the facts, and continued:]

It is beyond dispute that the purpose of s 6 is to protect the public, and in particular potential creditors of companies, from losing money through companies becoming insolvent when the directors of those companies are people unfit to be concerned in the management of a company. The test laid down in s 6—apart from the requirement that the person concerned is or has been a director of a company which has become insolvent—is whether the person's conduct as a director of the company or companies in question 'makes him unfit to be concerned in the management of a company.' These are ordinary words of the English language and they should be simple to apply in most cases. It is important to hold to those words in each case.

The judges of the Chancery Division have, understandably, attempted in certain cases to give guidance as to what does or does not make a person unfit to be concerned in the management of a company. Thus in *Re Lo-Line Electric Motors Ltd,*[16] Sir Nicolas Browne-Wilkinson V-C said:

> Ordinary commercial misjudgment is in itself not sufficient to justify disqualification. In the normal case, the conduct complained of must display a lack of commercial probity, although I have no doubt in an extreme case of gross negligence or total incompetence disqualification could be appropriate.

Then he said that the director in question

> has been shown to have behaved in a commercially culpable manner in trading through limited companies when he knew them to be insolvent and in using the unpaid Crown debts to finance such trading.

Such statements may be helpful in identifying particular circumstances in which a person would clearly be unfit. . . .

This is not a case in which it was alleged that Mr Cruddas had, in the colloquial phrase, 'ripped off' the public and pocketed the proceeds. On the contrary, and as the judge found, he had lost a lot of his own money . . . There was evidence that Mr Cruddas had remortgaged his home to raise money to pay creditors of the companies, and he claimed to have lost from £200,000 to £250,000 of his own money.

I turn next to the question of Crown debts. As to this the judge said:[17]

> In the circumstances I am faced with admitted deficiencies of a most serious character, including in particular Crown debts in total of an order of £120,000 which were left outstanding . . . It is, in my judgment, a badge of commercial immorality to cause moneys which have been taken under force of law from third parties (PAYE deductions, after all, are taken under compulsion of law from wages which are owed to

16 [1988] Ch 477 at 486, [1988] 2 All ER 692 at 696.
17 [1990] BCLC 668 at 671.

employees; VAT is taken under compulsion of law from members of the public who purchase goods as an addition to the price of the goods) to be not paid over to the Crown.

There have been differing views expressed by Chancery judges about the significance of Crown debts on a disqualification application and the phrase has tended to become something of a ritual incantation. In some earlier cases, Harman J regarded such Crown debts as 'quasi-trust moneys'. That view has not however been followed by other judges, and the official receiver does not seek to resurrect it. A different view was expressed by Hoffmann J in *Re Dawson Print Group Ltd,*[18] where he said, in a passage with which I entirely agree:

> but the fact is that, no doubt for good reasons, the Exchequer and the Commissioners of Customs and Excise have chosen to appoint traders to be tax collectors on their behalf with the attendant risk. That risk is, to some extent, compensated by the preference which they have on insolvency. There is, as yet, no obligation on traders to keep such moneys in a separate account, as there might be if they were really trust moneys. They are simply a debt owed by the company to the revenue or the Commissioners of Customs and Excise. I cannot accept that failure to pay these debts is regarded in the commercial world generally as such a breach of commercial morality that it requires in itself a conclusion that the directors concerned are unfit to be involved in the management of the company.

The official receiver cannot, in my judgment, automatically treat non-payment of any Crown debt as evidence of unfitness of the directors. It is necessary to look more closely in each case to see what the significance, if any, of the non-payment of the Crown debt is.

Mr Cruddas made a deliberate decision to pay only those creditors who pressed for payment. The obvious result was that the ... companies traded, when in fact insolvent and known to be in difficulties, at the expense of those creditors who, like the Crown, happened not to be pressing for payment. Such conduct on the part of a director can well, in my judgment, be relied on as a ground for saying that he is unfit to be concerned in the management of a company. But what is relevant in the Crown's position is not that the debt was a debt which arose from a compulsory deduction from employees' wages or a compulsory payment of VAT, but that the Crown was not pressing for payment, and the director was taking unfair advantage of that forbearance on the part of the Crown, and, instead of providing adequate working capital, was trading at the Crown's expense while the companies were in jeopardy. It would be equally unfair to trade in that way and in such circumstances at the expense of creditors other than the Crown. ...

[His Lordship reviewed the various defaults which had been established against the respondent, and fixed a disqualification period of five years. BUTLER-SLOSS and STAUGHTON LJJ concurred.]

18 [1987] BCLC 601.

Relief from liability

The court has a discretion to grant relief to directors and other officers from liability for breach of duty, similar to that which exists in relation to trustees, if they have 'acted honestly and reasonably and ought fairly to be excused': CA 1985, s 727. Relief from liability was sought, but refused, in a number of well-known cases, e g *Selangor United Rubber Estates Ltd v Cradock (No 3)* **(144)**, *Dorchester Finance Co Ltd v Stebbing* (above, p 300) and *Guinness plc v Saunders* **(124)**. In *Re Produce Marketing Consortium Ltd* [1989] 3 All ER 1, [1989] 1 WLR 745, Knox J ruled that, as a matter of principle, relief under s 727 could not be granted in favour of a director who was held liable to pay compensation for wrongful trading under IA 1986, s 214.

Contracting out of liability

A provision contained in a company's articles or in any contract with the company or otherwise exempting a director or any other officer of the company, or an auditor, from liability for breach of duty, etc is void: CA 1985, s 310. The widely-phrased language of this section has been much criticised: for instance, until the point was clarified in 1989 by the enactment of what is now s 310(3)(a), it appeared to make unlawful a director's insurance policy taken out against his possible liability for negligence. There is the further difficulty that the legislature in successive Companies Acts (and more recently in subordinate legislation) has included in Table A provisions which appear, at least on a prima facie reading, to be the very type of article which is outlawed by s 310. This is a conundrum which has generated a good deal of academic controversy. In *Movitex Ltd v Bulfield* **(147)** Vinelott J had the first opportunity to express a judicial view on the question. He resolved it by holding that the rule against self-dealing by a trustee or a director is properly seen as a *disability* or restriction on the conduct of a fiduciary and not a *duty*: articles which exclude or modify the application of this rule do not, therefore, infringe s 310.

147 Movitex Ltd v Bulfield [1988] BCLC 104

[The facts are immaterial. The company's articles included provisions (arts 98–100) which were very similar to arts 78 and 84 of the 1948 Table A (broadly equivalent in scope to art 85 of the 1985 Table A).]

VINELOTT J read CA 1948, s 205 [CA 1985, s 310] and continued: The argument advanced on behalf of Movitex can be shortly summarised as follows. The self-dealing rule is founded on and exemplifies the wider principle that 'no one who has a duty to perform shall place himself in a situation to have his interests conflicting with that duty' (see *Broughton v Broughton*).[19] To that should be added for completeness 'nor to have his duty to one conflicting with his duty to another' (see *Re Haslam & Hier-Evans*).[20] So, it is said, the fiduciary owes a duty to the person whose interest he is bound to protect not to place himself in a position in which duty and interest or duty and duty are in conflict. If he does place himself in such a position in relation to a particular transaction, the beneficiary may have the transaction set aside or compel the fiduciary to account for any profit he has made or, if no profit

19 (1855) 5 De GM & G 160 at 164, per Lord Cranworth.
20 [1902] 1 Ch 765.

has been realised but if restitution of the property is none the less impractical or inequitable, to make compensation. So, it is said, to the extent that a provision in the articles of a company permits a director to enter into a transaction in which one of their number has an interest or owes a duty to another the provision is one 'for exempting' the director from a liability which under the general law would otherwise attach to him in respect of a breach of his duty not to place himself in a position of conflict.

This argument, if sound, would have very startling consequences, for it would give rise to inconsistency between s 205 on the one hand and arts 78 and 84 of Table A, which correspond in their general purport though not in detail with arts 98 to 100 of Movitex's articles, on the other hand. Whether s 205 would then override or be overriden by arts 78 and 84 of Table A read in conjunction with s 8(2) of the 1985 Act, is a question which does not directly arise. The articles of Movitex exclude the regulations in Table A and arts 98 to 100 of Movitex's articles, though similar in their general purport to arts 78 and 84, cannot be said to be a mere repetition of them. But it would be at the lowest very paradoxical to find that s 205 conflicts with arts 78 and 84. The legislature in enacting the 1948 Act must have contemplated that the modifications of the self-dealing rule in arts 78 and 84 do not infringe s 205. Accordingly, if s 205 is fairly capable of a construction which avoids that conflict, that construction must clearly be preferred to one which does not.

This problem has attracted the attention of the authors and editors of some of the leading textbooks. The solution advanced by the editors of *Gore-Browne on Companies* (43rd edn) is that a provision may, without infringing s 205, reduce or abrogate a duty owed by a director, provided it does not exempt the director from liability for breach of it. That solution fails, I think, to give effect to the words, 'for exempting', and leads to the absurd result that an article could, without infringing s 205, modify a director's duty to use reasonable skill and care in the conduct of the company's affairs and so avoid a liability for damages for breach of duty which would otherwise arise, a conclusion which seems to me manifestly in conflict with the purpose of the section.

Counsel for the defendants took me through a number of early cases in which the scope and effect of an article modifying a director's duty to a company and exempting him from breach of that duty has been considered by the courts and in particular the decision of Romer J and of the Court of Appeal in *Re City Equitable Fire Insurance Co Ltd* (**142**) and to the report of the Greene Committee which led to the inclusion in the Companies Act 1929 of s 152, the legislative predecessor of s 205. If I may say so without disrespect to counsel's very thorough argument, it does not follow that because the purpose of s 152 was to nullify articles similar to the article on which the directors successfully relied in the *City Equitable Fire Insurance* case that that section and s 205 should be construed as invalidating only an article in those or similar terms. A patch may be intentionally wider than the visible hole to which it is applied.

I was at first inclined to find the solution to this conundrum in the principle ... that there is no breach of the self-dealing rule if a trustee enters into a transaction in which he has a personal interest with the consent of his beneficiary (if of full age and capacity and so capable of giving consent or with the authority of the court given on behalf of any who are not so capable).

The trustee, of course, must be able to show that he has made full disclosure and took no advantage of his position or of any information gained from it. The consent must be an informed consent freely given. If that condition is satisfied, the conflict between duty and interest is dissolved. The trustee is relieved from his duty to deal with the trust property for the benefit of the beneficiary to the extent that the beneficiary chooses freely and with full knowledge of the circumstances to concur in the transaction.

As I understand it, this is the ground which underlies the well-settled principle that a transaction entered into by a director on behalf of a company in which he has a personal interest is not liable to be avoided if the company was authorised by the company in general meeting to enter into it. The company in general meeting is for this purpose the beneficiary. The resolution in general meeting protects the director not because it operates to release him or absolve him from the consequences of a breach of the self-dealing rule but because, to the extent that the company in general meeting gives its informed consent to the transaction, there is no breach, the conflict of duty and interest is avoided.

It is at first sight tempting to construe arts 78 and 84 and arts 98 to 100 as substituting the board, at least to the extent that there is a quorum of independent directors, for the purpose of giving the concurrence of the company. But this is not a satisfactory solution. There are two reasons. First the rule is that the company is entitled to the unbiased judgment of every one of its directors. If it is the duty of a director not to place himself in a position of conflict, the duty is just as much breached by an article which permits a director to do so, if he does not vote or is not counted in the quorum, as it is by an article which permits him to vote and be counted in the quorum. Secondly even on that construction arts 78 and 84 and arts 98 to 100 would be invalid to the extent to which a director is in the cases specified entitled to vote and to be counted in the quorum on the resolution to enter into a transaction in which he has a personal interest. Indeed, one commentator has suggested that arts 78 and 84 are valid, save in this one respect.

The true solution is, I think, to be found in a passage in the judgment of Megarry V-C in *Tito v Waddell (No 2)*.[1]

[His Lordship quoted from the judgment (which included the following passage):]

> In my judgment, what equity does is to subject trustees to particular disabilities in cases falling within the self-dealing and fair-dealing rules ... Another aspect of the matter, producing the same result, is that the fair-dealing rule is essentially a rule of equity that certain persons (including trustees) are subject to certain consequences if they carry through certain transactions without, where appropriate, complying with certain requirements. The rule seems to me to be a general rule of equity and not a specific part of the law of trusts which lays down the duties of a trustee. Trusteeship is merely one of the categories of relationship which brings a person within the rule. There are many things that a trustee may do or omit to do which will have consequences for him as a trustee without the act or omission amounting to a breach of trust. I do not think that it could be said that a trustee is under a duty as trustee not to become bankrupt, so that his bankruptcy will constitute

1 [1977] Ch 106, [1977] 3 All ER 129.

a breach of trust; yet his bankruptcy may be a ground for removing him from his trusteeship.

[He continued:] Looked at in the light of this analysis of the self-dealing rule, the explanation of the apparent conflict between s 205 and arts 78 and 84 becomes clear. The true principle is that if a director places himself in a position in which his duty to the company conflicts with his personal interest or his duty to another, the court will intervene to set aside the transaction without inquiring whether there was any breach of the director's duty to the company. That is an overriding principle of equity. The shareholders of the company, in formulating the articles, can exclude or modify the application of this principle. In doing so they do not exempt the director from or from the consequences of a breach of a duty owed to the company ...

C. Other officers

Whether or not a particular person should be regarded as an 'officer' of a company depends on the context. CA 1985, s 744 tells us that for the purpose of the Act the term 'includes' a director, manager or secretary, but then unhelpfully does not go on to define 'manager'. In this section, we examine the role and functions of the secretary and the auditor.[2]

The *Panorama* case (below, (**148**)) has belatedly recognised the important position held in a modern company by the secretary, and in consequence the validity of a number of older cases must surely now be questioned: see, e g *Ruben v Great Fingall Consolidated* (**224**).

By statute, every company (unless it is 'dormant': CA 1985, s 250) is required to appoint an auditor (s 384), who must be professionally qualified under the provisions of CA 1989, Pt II (implementing the Eighth EEC Company Law Directive). The duties of auditors are set out in statutory form in CA 1985, s 237. The standard of care to be exercised by auditors is illustrated by the cases beginning with *Re London and General Bank (No 2)* (**149**), which are cited below. The more difficult question is to whom is the auditor's duty of care owed, for the purposes of civil liability—has been largely resolved by the decision of the House of Lords in *Caparo Industries plc v Dickman* (**152**), although some aspects of it may still require clarification.

The secretary of a company has usual authority to bind the company in matters concerned with administration.

148 Panorama Developments (Guildford) Ltd v Fidelis Furnishing Fabrics Ltd
[1971] 2 QB 711, [1971] 3 All ER 16 (Court of Appeal)

The secretary of the defendant company, Bayne, hired cars from the plaintiff, ostensibly for the company's business; but in fact he fraudulently used them

2 An auditor has been held to be an 'officer' of a company, for the purpose of particular statutory provisions, in a number of cases, e g *Re Thomas Gerrard & Son Ltd* (**151**). But the question whether he is for all purposes an officer is not free from doubt: see the wording of CA 1985, s 727. On auditors' liability, see further R Baxt, 'The Modern Company Auditor: A Nineteenth-Century Watchdog?' (1970) 33 MLR 413; N Savage, 'Auditors: a Critical Review of their Role' (1983) 4 Co Law 187; A Arora, 'The Regulation of the Company Auditor under the Companies Act 1989' [1991] JBL 272.

for his own purposes. The company was held bound by the contracts to pay the hire charges.

LORD DENNING MR: [Counsel] says that the company is not bound by the letters which were signed by Mr Bayne as 'Company Secretary'. He says that, on the authorities, a company secretary fulfils a very humble role: and that he has no authority to make any contracts or representations on behalf of the company. He refers to *Barnett v South London Tramways Co*[3] where Lord Esher MR said: 'A secretary is a mere servant; his position is that he is to do what he is told, and no person can assume that he has any authority to represent anything at all ...' Those words were approved by Lord Macnaghten in *George Whitechurch Ltd v Cavanagh*.[4] They are supported by the decision in *Ruben v Great Fingall Consolidated* (**224**). They are referred to in some of the textbooks as authoritative.

But times have changed. A company secretary is a much more important person nowadays than he was in 1887. He is an officer of the company with extensive duties and responsibilities. This appears not only in the modern Companies Act, but also by the role which he plays in the day-to-day business of companies. He is no longer a mere clerk. He regularly makes representations on behalf of the company and enters into contracts on its behalf which come within the day-to-day running of the company's business. So much so that he may be regarded as held out as having the authority to do such things on behalf of the company. He is certainly entitled to sign contracts connected with the administrative side of a company's affairs, such as employing staff, and ordering cars, and so forth. All such matters now come within the ostensible authority of a company's secretary.

Accordingly I agree with the judge that Mr RL Bayne, as company secretary, had ostensible authority to enter into contracts for the hire of these cars, and therefore, the company must pay for them. Mr Bayne was a fraud. But it was the company which put him in the position in which he, as company secretary, was able to commit the frauds. So the defendants are liable. I would dismiss the appeal, accordingly.

SALMON LJ: I think there can be no doubt that the secretary is the chief administrative officer of the company. As regards matters concerned with administration, in my judgment, the secretary has ostensible authority to sign contracts on behalf of the company. If a company is ordering cars so that its servants may go and meet foreign customers at airports, nothing, to my mind, is more natural than that the company should hire those cars through its secretary. The hiring is part of his administrative functions. Whether the secretary would have any authority to sign a contract relating to the commercial management of the company, for example, a contract for the sale or purchase of goods in which the company deals, does not arise for decision in the present case and I do not propose to express any concluded opinion upon the point; but contracts such as the present fall within the ambit of administration and I entertain no doubt that the secretary has ostensible power to sign on behalf of the company ...

MEGAW LJ concurred.

3 (1887) 18 QBD 815, CA.
4 Below, p 440.

*An auditor must use reasonable care and skill, and must certify to the share-
holders only what he believes to be true.*

149 Re London and General Bank (No 2) [1895] 2 Ch 673 (Court of Appeal)

This was an appeal by Theobald, one of the bank's auditors, from a judgment
in which Vaughan Williams J had held him liable to reimburse the company,
now in liquidation, for the amount of certain dividends which had been paid
out of capital after the shareholders had been presented with a balance-sheet
which Theobald had certified as correct. The appeal failed, except for a
variation in the sum for which he was held liable. The main respect in which
the accounts were defective was the entry of certain loans at their face value
when it was known that most of the amounts were not realisable. It was held
that none of the following matters absolved Theobald from liability: (1) that
he had included in his report the words 'The value of the assets as shown on
the balance-sheet is dependent upon realisation'; (2) that he had submitted
a full report to the *directors* in which the gravity of the company's position
was shown in detail; and (3) that the report (to the *directors*) had initially
expressed the view that no dividend should be paid, but the chairman later
persuaded the auditors to delete the sentence; and (4) that the chairman had
undertaken to explain the true position verbally to the shareholders in general
meeting. (In fact, he had done so only in ambiguous terms.)

LINDLEY LJ: It is no part of an auditor's duty to give advice, either to
directors or shareholders, as to what they ought to do. An auditor has
nothing to do with the prudence or imprudence of making loans with or
without security. It is nothing to him whether the business of a company is
being conducted prudently or imprudently, profitably or unprofitably. It is
nothing to him whether dividends are properly or improperly declared,
provided he discharges his own duty to the shareholders. His business is to
ascertain and state the true financial position of the company at the time of
the audit, and his duty is confined to that. But then comes the question, How
is he to ascertain that position? The answer is, By examining the books of
the company. But he does not discharge his duty by doing this without
inquiry and without taking any trouble to see that the books themselves show
the company's true position. He must take reasonable care to ascertain that
they do so. Unless he does this his audit would be worse than an idle farce.
Assuming the books to be so kept as to show the true position of a company,
the auditor has to frame[5] a balance-sheet showing that position according to
the books and to certify that the balance-sheet presented is correct in that
sense. But his first duty is to examine the books, not merely for the purpose
of ascertaining what they do show, but also for the purpose of satisfying
himself that they show the true financial position of the company ... An
auditor, however, is not bound to do more than exercise reasonable care and
skill in making inquiries and investigations. He is not an insurer; he does not
guarantee that the books do correctly show the true position of the company's
affairs; he does not even guarantee that his balance-sheet is accurate according
to the books of the company. If he did, he would be responsible for error on
his part, even if he were himself deceived without any want of reasonable

5 [It is not nowadays the auditor's role to draw up the balance-sheet: CA 1985, s 226 (1) places
  the responsibility for its preparation upon the directors, although as a practical matter this
  task will normally be entrusted to the company's accountants.]

care on his part, say, by the fraudulent concealment of a book from him. His obligation is not so onerous as this. Such I take to be the duty of the auditor: he must be honest—i e must not certify what he does not believe to be true, and he must take reasonable care and skill before he believes that what he certifies is true. What is reasonable care in any particular case must depend upon the circumstances of that case. Where there is nothing to excite suspicion very little inquiry will be reasonably sufficient, and in practice I believe businessmen select a few cases at haphazard, see that they are right, and assume that others like them are correct also. Where suspicion is aroused more care is obviously necessary; but, still, an auditor is not bound to exercise more than reasonable care and skill, even in a case of suspicion, and he is perfectly justified in acting on the opinion of an expert where special knowledge is required. Mr Theobald's evidence satisifies me that he took the same view as myself of his duty in investigating the company's books and preparing his balance-sheet. He did not content himself with making his balance-sheet from the books without troubling himself about the truth of what they showed. He checked the cash, examined vouchers for payments, saw that the bills and securities entered in the books were held by the bank, took reasonable care to ascertain their value, and in one case obtained a solicitor's opinion on the validity of an equitable charge. I see no trace whatever of any failure by him in the performance of this part of his duty: It is satisfactory to find that the legal standard of duty is not too high for business purposes, and is recognised as correct by businessmen. The balance-sheet and certificate of February 1892 (i e for the year 1891) was accompanied by a report to the directors of the bank. Taking the balance-sheet, the certificate and report together, Mr Theobald stated to the directors the true financial position of the bank, and if this report had been laid before the shareholders Mr Theobald would have completely discharged his duty to them. Unfortunately, however, this report was not laid before the shareholders ...

In this case I have no hesitation in saying that Mr Theobald did fail to discharge his duty to the shareholders in certifying and laying before them the balance-sheet of February 1892 without any reference to the report which he laid before the directors and with no other warning than is conveyed by the words 'The value of the assets as shown on the balance-sheet is dependent upon realisation'. [His Lordship referred to the details of the balance-sheet, and to the report made to the directors, including the warning that no dividend should be paid, and continued:] A dividend of 7% was, nevertheless, recommended by the directors, and was resolved upon by the shareholders at a meeting furnished with the balance-sheet and profit and loss account certified by the auditors, and at which meeting the auditors were present, but silent. Not a word was said to inform the shareholders of the true state of affairs. It is idle to say that these accounts are so remotely connected with the payment of the dividend as to render the auditors legally irresponsible for such payment. The balance-sheet and account certified by the auditors, and showing a profit available for dividend, were, in my judgment, not the remote but the real operating cause of the resolution for the payment of the dividend which the directors improperly recommended. The auditors' account and certificate gave weight to this recommendation, and rendered it acceptable to the meeting ...

RIGBY LJ delivered a concurring judgment.

LOPES LJ concurred.

It is not part of the duty of an auditor to take stock: in the absence of suspicion, he may rely on the certificate of a manager or other apparently responsible employee.

150 Re Kingston Cotton Mill Co (No 2) [1896] 2 Ch 279 (Court of Appeal)

[The facts appear from the judgment.]

LOPES LJ: [In] determining whether any misfeasance or breach of duty has been committed, it is essential to consider what the duties of an auditor are. They are very fully described in *Re London and General Bank* (**149**), to which judgment I was a party. Shortly they may be stated thus: It is the duty of an auditor to bring to bear on the work he has to perform that skill, care and caution which a reasonably competent, careful and cautious auditor would use. What is reasonable skill, care and caution must depend on the particular circumstances of each case. An auditor is not bound to be a detective, or, as was said, to approach his work with suspicion or with a foregone conclusion that there is something wrong. He is a watch-dog, but not a bloodhound. He is justified in believing tried servants of the company in whom confidence is placed by the company. He is entitled to assume that they are honest, and to rely upon their representations, provided he takes reasonable care. If there is anything calculated to excite suspicion he should probe it to the bottom; but in the absence of anything of that kind he is only bound to be reasonably cautious and careful.

In the present case the accounts of the company had been for years falsified by the managing director, Jackson, who subsequently confessed the frauds he had committed. It is only, however, just to him to say that they were not committed with a view to putting money in his own pocket, but for the purpose of making things appear better than they really were and in the hope of the company ultimately recovering itself. Jackson deliberately overstated the quantities and values of the cotton and yarn in the company's mills. He did this for many years. It was proved that there is a great wastage in converting yarn into cotton, and the fluctuations of the market in the prices of cotton and yarn are exceptionally great. Jackson had been so successful in falsifying the accounts that what he had done was never detected or even suspected by the directors. The auditors adopted the entries of Jackson and inserted them in the balance-sheet as 'per manager's certificate'. It is not suggested but that the auditors acted honestly and honestly believed in the accuracy and reliability of Jackson. But it is said that they ought not to have trusted the figures of Jackson, but should have further investigated the matter. Jackson was a trusted officer of the company in whom the directors had every confidence; there was nothing on the face of the accounts to excite suspicion, and I cannot see how in the circumstances of the case it can be successfully contended that the auditors are wanting in skill, care or caution in not testing Jackson's figures.

It is not the duty of an auditor to take stock; he is not a stock expert; there are many matters in respect of which he must rely on the honesty and accuracy of others. He does not guarantee the discovery of all fraud. I think the auditors were justified in this case in relying on the honesty and accuracy of Jackson, and were not called upon to make further investigation . . .

LINDLEY and KAY LJJ delivered concurring judgments.

An auditor who has been, or ought to have been, put on inquiry is under a duty to make an exhaustive investigation.

151 Re Thomas Gerrard & Son Ltd [1968] Ch 455, [1967] 2 All ER 525 (Chancery Division)

The company's managing director, Croston, had caused the company's books to be falsified in three ways: (1) by altering the half-yearly stock-taking figures so as to include non-existent stock; (2) by altering invoices relating to purchases of stock so that the amounts payable were made to appear just *after*, instead of just *before*, the half-yearly 'cut off' date; and (3) (the converse of (2)) by advancing *into* the half-yearly period sums due in respect of goods sold which were in fact invoiced *after* the 'cut off' date. The auditors ('Kevans') had accepted the explanations given by Croston and his brother-in-law Heyes (now deceased) regarding the altered invoices. The court held that Kevans had been negligent in relation to (2) and (without any finding in relation to (1) and (3)) held them liable to the company's liquidator in respect of dividends which the company had wrongly paid on the strength of the false accounts.

PENNYCUICK J referred to *Re Kingston Cotton Mill Co* (*No 2*) (**150**) and continued: This case appears, at any rate at first sight, to be conclusive in favour of Kevans as regards the falsification of the stock taken in isolation. Mr Walton, for the liquidator, pointed out that before 1900 there was no statutory provision corresponding to section 162 of the Companies Act 1948 [CA 1985, s 236]. That is so, but I am not clear that the quality of the auditor's duty has changed in any relevant respect since 1896. Basically that duty has always been to audit the company's accounts with reasonable care and skill. The real ground on which *Re Kingston Cotton Mill Co* (*No 2*) is, I think, capable of being distinguished is that the standards of reasonable care and skill are, upon the expert evidence, more exacting today than those which prevailed in 1896. I see considerable force in this contention. It must, I think, be open, even in this court, to make a finding that in all the particular circumstances the auditors have been in breach of their duty in relation to stock. On the other hand, if this breach of duty stood alone and the facts were more or less the same as those in *Re Kingston Cotton Mill Co* (*No 2*), this court would, I think, be very chary indeed of reaching a conclusion different from that reached by the Court of Appeal in *Re Kingston Cotton Mill Co* (*No 2*) . . .

I find it impossible to acquit Kevans of negligence as regards purchases of stock before the end of each current period of account and the attribution of the price to the succeeding period of account. I will assume in their favour that Mr Nightingale[6] was entitled to rely on the assurances of Mr Heyes and Mr Croston until he first came upon the altered invoices, but once these were discovered he was clearly put upon inquiry and I do not think he was then entitled to rest content with the assurances of Mr Croston and Mr Heyes, however implicitly he may have trusted Mr Croston. I find the conclusion inescapably alike on the expert evidence and as a matter of business common sense that at this stage he ought to have taken steps on the lines indicated by Mr Macnamara [an expert witness], that is to say, he should have examined the suppliers' statements and where necessary have communicated with the

6 [A partner in Kevans.]

suppliers. Having ascertained the precise facts so far as it was possible for him to do so, he should then have informed the board. It may be that the board would then have taken some action. But whatever the board did he should in each subsequent audit have made such checks and inquiries as would have ensured that any misattribution in the cut-off procedure was detected. He did not take any of these steps. I am bound to conclude that he failed in his duty. It is important in this connection to remember that this is not a case of some isolated failure in detection. The fraud was repeated half-yearly on a large scale for many years. The words which I have quoted from the judgment of Lindley LJ in *Re Kingston Cotton Mill Co (No 2)* are, I think, precisely in point. 'What in any particular case is a reasonable amount of care and skill depends on the circumstances of the case; that if there is nothing which ought to excite suspicion, less care may properly be considered reasonable than can be so considered if suspicion was or ought to have been aroused.' Here suspicion ought emphatically to have been aroused and the auditors ought to have taken the steps which I have indicated ...

[His Lordship accordingly held the auditors liable for the amount of the dividends wrongly paid.]

The auditors of a company owe no duty of care either to members of the public who rely on the accounts in deciding whether to invest in the company's shares, or to existing members of the company who may also rely on the accounts for the purpose of decisions in relation to present or future investment in the company.

152 Caparo Industries plc v Dickman [1990] 2 AC 605, [1990] 1 All ER 568 (House of Lords)

Touche Ross & Co had audited the 1983–84 accounts of Fidelity plc, a listed company, which showed a pre-tax profit of £1.3m. Both before and after the publication of these accounts, Caparo bought Fidelity shares in the market and subsequently made a take-over bid, as a result of which it acquired all the shares. In these proceedings Caparo alleged that it had paid too much for the shares because the trading figures should have shown a loss of £0.4m instead of a profit, and claimed damages from the auditors on the ground that they had been negligent in certifying that the accounts showed a true and fair view of Fidelity's financial position. The House of Lords, reversing in part the judgment of the Court of Appeal, held that the auditors owed Caparo no duty of care.

LORD BRIDGE OF HARWICH referred to a number of well-known cases, including *Hedley Byrne & Co Ltd v Heller & Partners* [1964] AC 465, [1963] 2 All ER 575, HL, and continued:

The salient feature of all these cases is that the defendant giving advice or information was fully aware of the nature of the transaction which the plaintiff had in contemplation, knew that the advice or information would be communicated to him directly or indirectly and knew that it was very likely that the plaintiff would rely on that advice or information in deciding whether or not to engage in the transaction in contemplation. In these circumstances the defendant could clearly be expected, subject always to the effect of any disclaimer of responsibility, specifically to anticipate that the plaintiff would rely on the advice or information given by the defendant for the very purpose for which he did in the event rely on it. So also the plaintiff, subject again to the effect of any disclaimer, would in that situation reasonably suppose that he was entitled to rely on the advice or information communicated to him for the very purpose for which he required it. The situation is entirely different where a statement is put into more or less general circulation and may foreseeably be relied on by strangers to the maker of the statement for any one of a variety of different purposes which the maker of the statement has no specific reason to anticipate. To hold the maker of the statement to be under a duty of care in respect of the accuracy of the statement to all and sundry for any purpose for which they may choose to rely on it is not only to subject him, in the classic words of Cardozo CJ to 'liability in an indeterminate amount for an indeterminate time to an indeterminate class': see *Ultramares Corpn v Touche*[7]; it is also to confer on the world at large a quite unwarranted entitlement to appropriate for their own purposes the benefit of the expert knowledge or professional expertise attributed to the maker of the statement. Hence, looking only at the circumstances of these decided cases where a duty of care in respect of negligent statements had been held to exist, I should expect to find that the 'limit or control mechanism ... imposed upon the liability of a wrongdoer towards those who have suffered economic damage in consequence of his negligence'[8] rested in the necessity to prove, in this category of the tort of negligence, as an essential ingredient of the 'proximity' between the plaintiff and the defendant, that the defendant knew that his statement would be communicated to the plaintiff, either as an individual or as a member of an identifiable class, specifically in connection with a particular transaction or transactions of a particular kind (e g in a prospectus inviting investment) and that the plaintiff would be very likely to rely on it for the purpose of deciding whether or not to enter upon that transaction or upon a transaction of that kind. ...

These considerations amply justify the conclusion that auditors of a public company's accounts owe no duty of care to members of the public at large who rely upon the accounts in deciding to buy shares in the company. If a duty of care were owed so widely, it is difficult to see any reason why it should not equally extend to all who rely on the accounts in relation to other dealings with a company as lenders or merchants extending credit to the company. A claim that such a duty was owed by auditors to a bank lending to a company was emphatically and convincingly rejected by Millett J in *Al Saudi Banque v Clarke Pixley* ...[9]

The main submissions for Caparo are that the necessary nexus of proximity between it and the appellants giving rise to a duty of care stems (1) from the pleaded circumstances indicating the vulnerability of Fidelity to a take-over bid and from the consequent probability that another company, such as Caparo, would rely on the audited accounts in deciding to launch a take-over bid, or (2) from the circumstance that Caparo was already a shareholder in Fidelity when it decided to launch its take-over bid in reliance on the accounts. ...

I should ... be extremely reluctant to hold that the question whether or not an auditor owes a duty of care to an investor buying shares in a public

7 (1931) 174 NE 441 at 444.
8 *Candlewood Navigation Corpn Ltd v Mitsui OSK Lines Ltd* [1986] AC 1 at 25, [1985] 2 All ER 935 at 945, PC.
9 [1990] Ch 313, [1989] 3 All ER 361.

company depends on the degree of probability that the shares will prove attractive either en bloc to a take-over bidder or piecemeal to individual investors. It would be equally wrong, in my opinion, to hold an auditor under a duty of care to anyone who might lend money to a company by reason only that it was foreseeable as highly probable that the company would borrow money at some time in the year following publication of its audited accounts and that lenders might rely on those accounts in deciding to lend. I am content to assume the high probability of a take-over bid in reliance on the accounts which the proposed amendment of the statement of claim would assert but I do not think it assists Caparo's case. . . .

[Lord Bridge referred to the statutory provisions dealing with the auditor's report (CA 1985, ss 235ff), and continued:] No doubt these provisions establish a relationship between the auditors and the shareholders of a company on which the shareholder is entitled to rely for the protection of his interest. But the crucial question concerns the extent of the shareholder's interest which the auditor has a duty to protect. The shareholders of a company have a collective interest in the company's proper management and in so far as a negligent failure of the auditor to report accurately on the state of the company's finances deprives the shareholders of the opportunity to exercise their powers in general meeting to call the directors to book and to ensure that errors in management are corrected, the shareholders ought to be entitled to a remedy. But in practice no problem arises in this regard since the interest of the shareholders in the proper management of the company's affairs is indistinguishable from the interest of the company itself and any loss suffered by the shareholders, e g by the negligent failure of the auditor to discover and expose a misappropriation of funds by a director of the company, will be recouped by a claim against the auditors in the name of the company, not by individual shareholders.

I find it difficult to visualise a situation arising in the real world in which the individual shareholder could claim to have sustained a loss in respect of his existing shareholding referable to the negligence of the auditor which could not be recouped by the company. But on this part of the case your Lordships were much impressed with the argument that such a loss might occur by a negligent undervaluation of the company's assets in the auditor's report relied on by the individual shareholder in deciding to sell his shares at an undervalue. The argument then runs thus. The shareholder, qua shareholder, is entitled to rely on the auditor's report as the basis of his investment decision to sell his existing shareholding. If he sells at an undervalue he is entitled to recover the loss from the auditor. There can be no distinction in law between the shareholder's investment decision to sell the shares he has or to buy additional shares. It follows, therefore, that the scope of the duty of care owed to him by the auditor extends to cover any loss sustained consequent on the purchase of additional shares in reliance on the auditor's negligent report.

I believe this argument to be fallacious. Assuming without deciding that a claim by a shareholder to recover a loss suffered by selling his shares at an undervalue attributable to an undervaluation of the company's assets in the auditor's report could be sustained at all, it would not be by reason of any reliance by the shareholder on the auditor's report in deciding to sell; the loss would be referable to the depreciatory effect of the report on the market value of the shares before ever the decision of the shareholder to sell was taken. A claim to recoup a loss alleged to flow from the purchase of over-valued shares, on the other hand, can only be sustained on the basis of the purchaser's reliance on the report. The specious equation of 'investment decisions' to sell or to buy as giving rise to parallel claims thus appears to me to be untenable. ....

LORDS ROSKILL, OLIVER OF AYLMERTON and JAUNCEY OF TULLICHETTLE delivered concurring opinions.

LORD ACKNER concurred.

NOTES

(1) In *Al Saudi Banque v Clark Pixley* [1990] Ch 313, [1989] 3 All ER 361, it was held that a company's auditors owed no duty of care to existing or future creditors who might foreseeably lend money to the company or continue its credit on the faith of its audited accounts.

(2) *Caparo Industries plc v Dickman* may be contrasted with *Morgan Crucible Co plc v Hill Samuel & Co Ltd* [1991] 1 All ER 148, [1991] 2 WLR 655, CA, where the court declined to rule, as a preliminary point of law, that the directors and financial advisers, including the auditors, of the target company in a contested take-over bid owed no duty of care towards the bidder (whose identity was publicly known) in making representations as to the target's position, as a result of which the bidder had allegedly been induced to offer more for the shares than they were worth.

CHAPTER 6

The Raising of Capital

We are here concerned mainly with public companies. A private company can raise funds only by private negotiation, since it is by law forbidden to advertise its securities (FSA 1986, s 170). If a public company wishes to raise money by the issue of shares or debentures, it may make: (a) a direct offer to the public, usually called an 'offer for subscription' or 'offer by prospectus'; (b) an 'offer for sale', where an issuing house subscribes for the whole of the new issue and then itself invites the public to buy from it, either at a fixed price or by tender (for an example, see below, pp 596 ff); (c) a 'placing' of the securities by an issuing house or broker without public advertisement. In addition, an established company may direct its appeal to its own members or debenture holders by (d) a 'rights issue', where the new securities are offered on a pro rata basis in relation to the offerees' existing holdings (see below, p 616) or (e) an 'open offer', which invites each shareholder to apply for any number of the new securities.[1]

It does not follow from the fact that a public company has raised capital by an issue of securities or from the fact that it has published a prospectus that there will be a market in those securities in which they can be traded after their issue. For this, it is normally necessary for application to be made to The Stock Exchange, either for a 'full' official listing or for admission to the Unlisted Securities Market,[2] depending on the size and status of the company and the proportion of its securities that are to be made available to the public. Exceptionally, a dealer may 'make a market' in a particular security without a listing; but for the holders this is very much a second-best arrangement.

The Financial Services Act 1986 makes a distinction between invitations addressed to the public to take securities issued by listed companies (i e those with a full official listing), on the one hand and other companies (including those quoted on the USM), on the other. The former (known as 'listing particulars') must comply with FSA 1986, Pt IV and with the listing requirements of The Stock Exchange (which embody, inter alia, the provisions of the three EEC Directives on the subject), while the latter (which are to continue to be known by the traditional label of 'prospectus'), are subject to separate statutory rules contained in FSA 1986, Pt V.[3]

An offer of securities to the public may sometimes be made, not by the company to raise further capital, but by the existing holders of those securities

---

1 A company allotting new equity shares must in principle offer them pro rata to its existing equity shareholders (CA 1985, ss 89 ff); but there are a number of exceptions to this statutory 'pre-emption rights' rule, and it may be waived by special resolution. See below, p 338.
2 The 'Third Market,' which formerly catered for the smallest category of listed companies, was phased out and ceased to exist early in 1991.
3 FSA 1986, Pt V is not yet in force, but will be presumed to be for the purposes of the present chapter. Until Pt V becomes operative, the relevant statutory provisions are CA 1985, Pt III and Sch 3.

in order to realise the some or all of the value of their investment. For example, the present shareholders may wish to retire from the business, or need funds to pay inheritance tax, etc and be unable to sell their shares privately. In these circumstances an offer for sale may be made independently of the company; but more often it will be combined with a flotation of the securities by the company itself and an application for admission to the appropriate market.

A. The issue of shares

A company is not bound to issue its shares at a premium even though a price above par could be obtained. The benefit conferred on the allottee of such shares is not obtained at the expense of the company's capital, even indirectly, and so is not a prohibited payment within the terms of CA 1985, s 98.

155 Hilder v Dexter [1902] AC 474 (House of Lords)

The company immediately after its incorporation issued one-sixth of its shares to selected private persons in order to obtain working capital. These shares were issued at par on the terms that the allottees should later have the option to take up further shares at par on a one for one basis. Hilder exercised his option at a time when the shares were worth £2 17s 6d [£2.87] per £1 share. Dexter, another shareholder, sought and obtained an injunction restraining Hilder and the company from carrying out the agreement on the ground that such an arrangement was forbidden by s 8(2) of the Act of 1900 [CA 1985, s 98]. The House of Lords reversed this decision and discharged the injunction.

LORD DAVEY: The advantage which the appellant will derive from the exercise of his option is certainly not a 'discount or allowance', because he will have to pay 20s [100p] in the pound for every share. Nor is it, in my opinion, a commission paid by the company, for the company will not part with any portion of its capital which is received by it intact, or indeed with any moneys belonging to it. But the words relied on are, 'either directly or indirectly', and the argument seems to be that the company, by engaging to allot shares at par to the shareholder at a future date, is applying or using its shares in such a manner as to give him a possible benefit at the expense of the company in this sense, that it foregoes the chance of issuing them at a premium. With regard to the latter point, it may or may not be at the expense of the company. I am not aware of any law which obliges a company to issue its shares above par because they are saleable at a premium in the market. It depends on the circumstances of each case whether it will be prudent or even possible to do so, and it is a question for the directors to decide. But the point which, in my opinion, is alone material for the present purpose is that the benefit to the shareholder from being able to sell his shares at a premium is not obtained by him at the expense of the company's capital. The prohibited application of the shares may be direct by allotting them as fully or partly paid up to the person underwriting the shares, or by allotting them in some other way with the intention that they shall ultimately find their way to such person or be applied in payment of his commission.

My Lords, it may be that in some particular case a contract such as that which your Lordships have before you would be open to impeachment as improvident, or an abuse, or in excess of the powers of management committed to the directors. In this case the question is as to the powers of the company itself, and not as to the due exercise of the directors' powers. I have come to the conclusion from a consideration of the language of s 8(2), that the prohibition therein contained extends only to the application, direct or indirect, of the company's capital in payment of a commission by the company, and the transaction impeached in this case is not within it . . .

The EARL OF HALSBURY LC and LORD BRAMPTON delivered concurring opinions.

LORD ROBERTSON concurred.

B. Commissions and discounts; underwriting

A company is, in general, forbidden to issue shares[4] at a discount; see CA 1985, s 98 and the cases cited below, pp 344 ff. But the professional people and institutions who handle new issues must, of course, be remunerated for their services or, where they take the risk of an issue not being fully subscribed for by the public (i e 'underwrite' the issue), be compensated for the risk which they take. Accordingly, s 97 authorises the payment of commissions and discounts up to a statutory limit (currently 10%), subject to certain safeguards.

C. Listing particulars and the prospectus

If a company seeks to raise capital by a direct offer of securities to the public, the document or advertisement which sets out the terms of the offer and makes the invitation to subscribe is traditionally called a *prospectus*. Until 1984,[5] a single set of statutory provisions governed all invitations to the public to subscribe for securities in a company, or to acquire them from the issuing house which was selling them under an offer for sale. The law required a prospectus to be issued, accompanying every form of application for shares or debentures, and very explicit and detailed information had to be given in the prospectus about the company and the securities in question. Both criminal and civil sanctions could be invoked if the prospectus requirements were not complied with, and if the information given in the prospectus was inaccurate or misleading there were common-law remedies available as well to any investor who had relied on it.

Much of this old law survives the recent statutory changes, but in order to put the subject into perspective it is now necessary to make a distinction between three different types of situation.

(1) Where the securities are to be admitted to official listing by The Stock Exchange, Pt IV of FSA 1986 applies, and both the company and the securities must conform to the rules laid down in The Stock Exchange's

---

4 But not debentures: see below, p 347.
5 The date when the three EEC 'listing Directives' were implemented in the UK. This was initially done by regulations (Stock Exchange (Listing) Regulations 1984, SI 1984/716), but these regulations have now been incorporated into The Stock Exchange's listing rules and given statutory backing by FSA 1986, Pt IV.

Admission of Securities to Listing (usually referred to as 'the Yellow Book'). These rules have statutory backing (FSA 1986, s 142(1)). A condition of listing is that the company must publish 'listing particulars' which give all the information that was formerly required by the 'prospectus' provisions of the Companies Act, and also satisfy the more stringent conditions of The Stock Exchange's own rules (which incorporate the three EEC 'listing Directives'). In addition to this legal safeguard, an investor in listed securities has further protection because (i) listing particulars are vetted before publication by The Stock Exchange itself, and (ii) a company can only be admitted to listing if it is sponsored by a member of the Exchange, whose own professional standing is thus put at risk.

Over and above the obligation to comply in detail with the listing particulars requirements, FSA 1986, s 146 imposes a general duty to ensure that listing particulars contain all the information that investors and their professional advisers would reasonably require in order to make an informed assessment of the securities and their value.

(2) Unlisted securities which are to be quoted on an 'approved exchange' (which will mean, in practice, the securities of USM companies) may not be advertised for subscription or sale unless a prospectus has been submitted to and approved by the exchange and also registered with the Registrar of Companies (FSA 1986, s 159). The detailed contents of the prospectus are to be laid down by regulations made by the Secretary of State (s 162), but he is empowered instead to authorise the issue of a prospectus which conforms to the exchange's own rules (s 162(3)).

(3) All other securities may not be offered for subscription or sale unless a prospectus has been registered which complies with rules laid down by the Secretary of State. This applies to both 'primary offers' (made by the company itself) and 'secondary offers' (made in various defined circumstances by an existing shareholder, including an issuing house which is acting as intermediary in an offer for sale). There is no provision for the vetting of this class of prospectus by The Stock Exchange or any similar body, but an advertisement relating to the securities concerned must either be issued by a person who is authorised under the Act or approved by such a person (FSA 1986, s 57).

D. Remedies and liabilities

A failure to comply with the statutory requirements relating to the registration and approval of listing particulars or prospectuses may lead, in the case of listed securities and those quoted on the USM, to a suspension of the listing or quotation. Disciplinary action may also be taken against the member of the exchange or other 'authorised person' who may have been concerned in the issue—and this could apply to an authorised person involved in an issue of unquoted securities.

There are criminal sanctions where there has been a failure to comply with these statutory provisions by an unauthorised person.

Where there have been inaccurate or misleading statements made in listing particulars or a prospectus, or omissions from the information which must by statute be disclosed, the Act provides civil remedies against the persons responsible—a term which includes the issuing company and, at least prima facie, all of its directors: FSA 1986, ss 150–152, 166–168. These sections run together what were formerly separate provisions dealing with misstatements and omissions, and are more comprehensive than the old law in other ways, e g in giving civil remedies against the company for the omission of statutory information.

In earlier periods, when the stock exchanges did not exercise effective control over the new issues market and it was not customary to utilise the services of professional issuing houses, investors who felt deceived or wronged had recourse to the civil courts, seeking common-law and equitable remedies such as rescission of their shareholding contracts or damages. An enormous volume of precedent was thus built up, including such celebrated cases as *Derry v Peek* (1889) 14 App Cas 337, HL and *Edgington v Fitzmaurice* (1885) 29 Ch D 459, CA, which students will already have met in their tort and contract courses, but which have now been rendered all but obsolete so far as company law is concerned. Even in the general law of misrepresentation, much of this learning has now been made redundant by the twin developments represented by *Hedley Byrne & Co Ltd v Heller & Partners Ltd* [1964] AC 465, [1963] 2 All ER 575, HL and the Misrepresentation Act 1967, not to mention earlier partial reforms which go back as far as the Directors' Liability Act 1890 (now incorporated into FSA 1986, ss 150–151, 166–167). Whilst therefore there is a very substantial body of law, civil and criminal, statutory, equitable and common law, ready to be called in aid by any shareholder who is wrongfully misled into making an unfortunate investment, the professionalisation of the investment industry in the present century has made recourse to it unnecessary. The only law which has been invoked at all commonly in recent times are the criminal provisions, such as those governing market manipulation and the making of reckless forecasts, which are appropriate to deal with such offenders as have managed to escape the preventive nets of the City institutions.

The cases which follow should not be thought representative of the great mainstream of misrepresentation decisions based on the prospectus scandals of the later nineteenth century. Rather, they highlight special rulings, some of them anomalous and possibly open to review, on questions peculiar to company law. Otherwise, the general principles of the law of misrepresentation may be assumed to apply.

The different proceedings available may be summarised as follows:

(a) *Remedies against the company or seller of the securities*[6]

 (i) Rescission of the contract and consequent rectification of the share register (for material misrepresentation of *any* kind).
 (ii) Damages for deceit (for *fraudulent* misrepresentation).
 (iii) Damages under the Misrepresentation Act 1967, s 2(2) (in lieu of rescission) and also possibly under s 2(1) of this Act (so-called 'negligent' misrepresentation).
 (iv) (Possibly) a claim in damages for breach of contract, on the basis that the statements in the prospectus have been incorporated as terms of the contract.
 (v) A fraudulent misrepresentation may be pleaded as a defence (e g to an action for calls).

6 See S Griffin, 'Damages for Misstatements in Company Prospectuses' (1991) 12 Co Law 209.

(Note that no civil remedy lies against the *company* for the omission of information required to be included in the listing particulars or prospectus: *Re South of England Natural Gas and Petroleum Co Ltd* [1911] 1 Ch 573.)

(b) Civil remedies against persons responsible for the listing particulars or prospectus

 (i) Damages for deceit.
 (ii) Damages for negligent misstatement (at common law).
(iii) Compensation under FSA 1986, ss 150, 166 for untrue statements in, or material omissions from, the listing particulars or prospectus.[7]

(c) Criminal liability of persons responsible[8]

 (i) Liability under FSA 1986, s 47 (1) for knowingly or recklessly making a statement, promise or forecast which is misleading, false or deceptive, or dishonestly concealing material facts, to induce a person to make an investment agreement.[9]
 (ii) Liability under Theft Act 1968, s 19, for written statements *known* to be false.
(iii) Liability under the Banking Act 1987, s 35 (originally the Protection of Depositors Act 1963, ss 1, 2), for fraudulent statements inducing investment on *deposit.*

A contract to take shares which has been induced by a material mis-representation[10] may be rescinded by the shareholder. But the contract is voidable and not void; and it is too late to exercise the right to rescind after the company has gone into liquidation.

156 Oakes v Turquand and Harding; Peek v The Same (1867) LR 2 HL 325 (House of Lords)

Overend, Gurney & Co Ltd was incorporated in July 1865 to take over the long-established banking business of Overend, Gurney & Co. The prospectus issued to the public concealed the fact that the business was insolvent and had been carried on at a loss for some years. Within a year after the incorporation of the company it stopped payment and went into liquidation. In order to meet the claims of its creditors, large calls were made on the

---

7 The appropriate measure of damages in the tort measure (ie the same as in an action of deceit): *McConnel v Wright* [1903] 1 Ch 546, CA (a case decided under the Directors' Liability Act 1890).
8 This list is not confined in its application to prospectuses, but applies to statements inducing investments of every kind.
9 S 47(1) replaces and extends the Prevention of Fraud (Investments) Act 1958, s 13, and also supersedes CA 1985, s 70.
10 In this case, fraud was proved. But in *Redgrave v Hurd* (1881) 20 Ch D 1, CA it was established that where only rescission is sought it is not necessary to show fraud as in an action of deceit. Until the enactment of the Misrepresentation Act 1967, it was necessary to make a distinction even in rescission cases between fraudulent and innocent mis-representation, for the right to rescind was more easily lost in the latter case; but all the most important points of difference have now been removed by that Act. The right to rescind for misrepresentation may now be lost as a result of (1) affirmation after the truth is discovered, (2) the supervening of third party rights, (3) restoration of the status quo becoming impossible. This case illustrates both (2) and (3).

numerous members of the public who had become shareholders. Many of them combined to form a defence association, which appointed Oakes (an original allottee of shares) and Peek (who had bought shares in the market) as representatives to conduct test cases on behalf of all the shareholders. In this case they claimed that their names should be taken off the list of contributories on the ground that their contracts to take and to purchase shares, respectively, had been induced by fraud, but it was held that they had lost the right to rescind.

(In later proceedings (*Peek v Gurney* (1873) LR 6 HL 377) Peek was again unsuccessful, this time in a claim against the directors. Among the score or so of other reported cases arising out of the same liquidation, the best-known is *Overend, Gurney & Co v Gibb and Gibb* (1872) LR 5 HL 480, in which the liquidators failed in a claim against the directors, alleging that they had been negligent in allowing the company to purchase the business.)

LORD CHELMSFORD LC: It is said that everything which is stated in the prospectus is literally true, and so it is. But the objection to it is, not that it does not state the truth as far as it goes, but that it conceals most material facts with which the public ought to have been made acquainted, the very concealment of which gives to the truth which is told the character of falsehood. If the real circumstances of the firm of Overend, Gurney & Co had been disclosed it is not very probable that any company founded upon it would have been formed. Indeed, it was admitted in the course of the argument that if the true position of the affairs of Overend, Gurney & Co had been published it would have entailed the ruin of the old firm, and would have been utterly prohibitory of the formation of the new. To which the only answer which fairly suggests itself is, 'Then no company ought ever to have been attempted, because it was only possible to entice persons to become shareholders by improper concealment of facts' ...

If this had been a case between Oakes and the company, in which he sought to be relieved from his contract, as in *Central Rly Co of Venezuela v Kisch*,[11] or the company had been suing him for calls, as in *Bwlch-y-Plwm Lead Mining Co v Baynes*,[12] he would have succeeded in the one case, and the company would have failed in the other, on the ground—which, I venture to think, was correctly laid down in the recent case of *Western Bank of Scotland v Addie*[13] in this House—that 'where a person has been drawn into a contract to purchase shares belonging to a company by fraudulent misrepresentations' (and I would here add, 'by fraudulent concealment') 'of the directors, and the directors seek to enforce that contract, or the person who has been deceived institutes a suit against the company to rescind the contract on the ground of fraud, the purchaser cannot be held to his contract, because a company cannot retain any benefit which they have obtained through the fraud of their agent'.

It is quite clear, therefore, that Oakes might originally have disaffirmed that contract, and divested himself of his shares, and that he never did any act to affirm it, nor was aware of the true state of the firm of Overend, Gurney & Co at the time of the formation of the new company, nor until after the failure ...

11 (1867) LR 2 HL 99.
12 (1867) LR 2 Exch 324.
13 (1862) LR 1 Sc & Div 145.

Such was the position of Oakes when the order for winding up the company was made on 22 June 1866. His name being upon the register of shareholders, was placed (as a matter of course) by the liquidators upon the list of contributories. A motion was made before Vice-Chancellor Malins to remove his name from the list, when his Honour refused to make any order, and from that refusal the present appeal is brought ...

On the part of the creditors, it is said that every person whose name is found upon the register at the time when the order for winding up is made is a shareholder, and liable to contribute towards the payment of the debts of the company to the extent of the sums due upon his shares, unless he can prove that his name was put upon the register without his consent.

On the part of the shareholders it is contended that a person who has been induced by fraud to enter into a contract to take shares, and whose name is afterwards placed upon the register, never becomes a shareholder, because his agreement, being obtained by fraud, is of no validity. In support of this proposition, the words of my noble and learned friend (Lord Cranworth) in *The Venezuela Rly Co v Kisch* were cited, where he said 'The case of the respondent is, that he never was a member, for that he was induced to take shares by fraudulent representations, which entitle him to repudiate and treat as null all which he was induced to do.' My noble and learned friend never meant to deny the distinction between void and voidable contracts, or to say that an agreement obtained by fraud is in no case any agreement at all. His language must be understood in its application to the case before him, in which the respondent seeking relief from the contract into which he had been drawn by fraud, was entitled, if he chose to repudiate it, to treat it as null and void ab initio, and therefore to say that he never was a member.

The distinction between void and voidable contracts is one which will be found very necessary to be borne in mind when we come to consider the words of the Companies Act 1862, upon which the question of Oakes' liability will ultimately turn. It is a settled rule of law, as Mr Justice Crompton said in *Clarke v Dickson*:[14] 'that a contract induced by fraud is not void, but voidable only at the option of the party defrauded'. If it were otherwise, if a contract induced by fraud were void, there would be an end of the question in this case, because a contract void in itself can have no valid beginning, and Oakes never would have become a shareholder of the company ...

Did the appellant then agree to become a member? His counsel answer this question in the negative; because they say that a person who is induced by fraud to enter into an agreement cannot be said to have agreed; the word 'agreed' meaning having entered into a binding agreement. But this is a fallacy. The consent which binds the will and constitutes the agreement is totally different from the motive and inducement which led to the consent. An agreement induced by fraud is certainly, in one sense, not a binding agreement, as it is entirely at the option of the person defrauded whether he will be found by it or not. In the present case, if the company formed on the basis of the partnership of Overend, Gurney & Co had realised the expectations held out by the prospectus, the appellant would probably have retained his shares, as he would have had an undoubted right to do. But when the order for winding up came, and found him with the shares in his possession, and his name upon the register, the agreement was a subsisting one. How could it then be said that he was not a person who had agreed to

14 (1858) EB & E 148.

become a member? To hold otherwise would be to disregard the long and well-established distinction between void and voidable contracts . . .

[His Lordship then held that the supervening rights of the creditors in a winding up barred the right of a member to avoid the contract on the ground of fraud. He concluded:] It only remains to observe that all that has been said with respect to Oakes applies with greater force to Peek, even if his situation as a purchaser of shares in the market did not preclude him from most of the objections which have been raised in Oakes' case.

LORD CRANWORTH and LORD COLONSAY delivered concurring opinions.

NOTES

(1) For over 100 years, the rule laid down in *Houldsworth v City of Glasgow Bank* (1880) 5 App Cas 317, HL, prevented a person who had been induced by fraud to take shares in a company from claiming damages against the company while he remained a member. The same principle was applied where damages for breach of contract were sought, based on the contract of shareholding: *Re Addlestone Linoleum Co* (1887) 37 Ch D 191, CA. The juridical basis of this rule was never satisfactorily explained. But it has now been reversed by CA 1985, s 111A.[15] There is one statutory exception: s 178 expressly excludes the possibility of a claim in damages when a company has broken an obligation to redeem or repurchase shares (but without prejudice to his other remedies, which may include an action for specific performance or an application for relief under s 459 (unfairly prejudicial conduct) or for winding up on the 'just and equitable' ground (below, p 557)).

(2) In *Peek v Gurney* (1873) LR 6 HL 377, the House of Lords held that a prospectus should be regarded as addressed only to those who might become allottees of shares directly from the company, and that it could not be relied on by someone who had bought shares from another source. But in *Andrews v Mockford* [1896] 1 QB 372, CA a different interpretation was put on the prospectus in question: it was held to have been addressed by the company and its promoters to those who might afterwards buy on the market as well as to prospective allottees. However, *Andrews v Mockford* was a case of fraudulent misrepresentation. In *Al-Nakib Investments (Jersey) Ltd v Longcroft* [1991] BCLC 7, Mervyn Davies J held that, in the light of *Caparo Industries plc v Dickman* (152), it was not open to a plaintiff who had bought shares in the market to rely on the prospectus in a negligence action: the duty of care owed by those responsible for the issue of the prospectus was owed only to those who used the prospectus for the purpose of subscribing for shares.

E. Allotment

Section 80 of CA 1985 stipulates that the authority of the company in general meeting, or of a provision in the articles, is necessary before directors may allot most categories of shares. The authority must be exercised within five years of the authorisation (or, where this is contained in the articles on the

---

15 Earlier inroads into the rule in *Houldsworth's* case were made by CA 1985, s 92 (failure by company to accord pre-emption rights to a member) and FSA 1986, ss 152, 168 (liability in respect of untrue or misleading statements in listing particulars or prospectus).

incorporation of the company, within five years from the date of incorporation).

The cases cited here deal with the contractual aspects of allotment. On the question of the consideration payable for the allotment of shares, see below, pp 344 ff.

The allotment of shares to an applicant is an acceptance by the company of his offer to take shares; it completes a binding and enforceable contract between them, but he does not become a member of the company until his name is entered on the share register.

157 Nicol's Case (1885) 29 Ch D 421 (Court of Appeal)

Wilkinson had applied for 100 £20 shares in the Florence Land & Public Works Co Ltd and had been sent a letter of allotment which called on him to pay the sum of £8 per share which was due on allotment. He was never put on the share register and the allotment money was never paid. The allotment was purportedly cancelled three years later by the directors, after which shares representing all the nominal capital were issued to others. In the liquidation of the company Wilkinson was held not to be liable as a contributory.

BOWEN LJ: It seems to me, in the first place ... that Mr Wilkinson never acquired the status of a member of the company. I think that he remained with contractual obligations to the company, which the company had for a time a right to enforce against him. But, secondly, I think that if he did acquire the status of a member, that status has been destroyed under the circumstances that have happened, and the appeal must, in any view of the case, fail. It is said that he became a member by signing the list of subscribers, and by the act of the directors in sending him a letter of allotment ... Taking the letter of allotment in the present case, I am by no means satisfied that it appropriated any shares to any subscriber of the subscription contract till something else had been done by him. But even assuming that it did, and that we have here a complete contract to take shares, followed by an appropriation of shares to him, still there was no entry on the register. Was the relation between the subscriber and the company still contractual? Was it still in fieri? or had he become a member of the corporation? According to the 23rd section of the Companies Act[16] I think he had not become a corporate member. If so, the only remaining question is whether that which passed afterwards is not evidence that the contract was put an end to by rescission ... I entertain the view that the contract was still in fieri, and I think the lapse of time and the conduct of the company in cancelling and re-allotting the shares, and the conduct of both classes of allottees, lead only to one conclusion, namely, that all parties had agreed that the contract should be put an end to, and therefore we get to a rescission of the contract ...

BAGALLAY and FRY LJJ delivered concurring judgments.

In the case of a 'rights' issue, the letter of rights addressed to a holder of existing

16 [Section 23 of the Act of 1862 was equivalent to s 22 of the Act of 1985. Note: the 'subscription contract' referred to was not the company's memorandum, but a separate document.]

securities is an offer by the company, capable of acceptance by the shareholder. But in an 'open offer',[17] the letter contains merely an invitation to treat, and the member's reply is, legally speaking, the offer.

158 Jackson v Turquand (1869) LR 4 HL 305 (House of Lords)

The Leeds Banking Co distributed to its shareholders a circular giving them an option to take up additional shares on a one for five basis, and further invited them to say 'whether, in the event of any shares remaining, you wish to have any more allotted you'. The appellants, who already held 145 shares, applied for twenty-nine shares pursuant to the option and a further six if available from the surplus. The company allotted both the twenty-nine and the six shares but in respect of the latter attached a condition as to forfeiture which had not been previously mentioned. The appellants never answered the company's letter notifying them of the allotment. In the subsequent liquidation of the company, they sought to evade liability for calls by pleading (inter alia) that there had been no concluded contract to take the shares in question. The House of Lords held that there was a binding contract in respect of the twenty-nine but not in respect of the six.

LORD HATHERLEY LC: Then the next question we have to consider is, whether or not a contract was entered into for the purchase of the shares in question. It was found that the directors had power to distribute a number of shares which had either never been issued or were forfeited, and were capable of being re-issued. On making a calculation of the number of those shares they ascertained to their own satisfaction that they could fairly offer to every proprietor a certain number of shares, first, upon his taking an aliquot part of the whole number at their disposal, in proportion to the number of shares that he already held. Then they found, or thought they might find, that after making such an appropriation, there would be the possibility of a surplus of shares, either arising from there being some odd number, or from the possibility—not at all an improbable one—of some of the shares being rejected, which might leave a residuum or surplus, which might again have to be allotted out. The course they took, therefore, was to write a letter which I can characterise in a few words . . . as amounting to nothing more than this: it plainly appears to me to be very distinctly expressed that they had at their disposal a certain number of shares which they could at once offer; those shares were to be at once offered—namely, the shares which were to be offered in proportion to the number of those already held by the shareholders—they could be offered to each individual shareholder, and he could be asked, 'Aye or no, will you accept them?' As to that, it was simply that they made the offer, and if it was accepted the bargain was concluded. There was another portion of shares which they could not offer, because they did not know themselves the amount that might be available. Therefore they made this proposition to the shareholders. As regards certain other shares, if there should be any surplus, tell us how many you propose to take; in other words, inviting the shareholders to make an offer for the shares not binding themselves. As to those shares, we should expect to find a shareholder would state what his offer was. As regards, therefore, the first class of shares, if the offer was accepted simpliciter, that would have constituted a contract in respect of those shares. And with respect to the other class of shares as to

17 For the meaning of these terms, see above, p 327.

which an offer emanating from the proprietor was to be returned in answer to the letter of the secretary of the company, that would have to be considered farther by the directors, and then it would be for them to say, 'Aye or no,' whether they would form a contract by issuing those reserved shares ...

[His Lordship then ruled that there was no completed contract in respect of the six shares, because the new term as to forfeiture had not been assented to.]

LORD WESTBURY delivered a concurring opinion.

LORDS CHELMSFORD, COLONSAY and CAIRNS concurred.

An application to take shares lapses if no allotment is made within a reasonable time.

159 Ramsgate Victoria Hotel Co Ltd v Montefiore (1866) LR 1 Exch 109 (Court of Exchequer)

The defendants, Montefiore and another, on 8 June applied for 50 £20 shares in the plaintiff company, but no allotment was made until 23 November. They refused to accept the shares or pay any calls.

The court (POLLOCK CB, MARTIN, CHANNELL and PIGOTT BB) held that an allotment must be made within a reasonable time, and that the interval from June to November was not reasonable, and therefore gave judgment for both the defendants.

F. Pre-emption rights

A pre-emption right is a right given to the shareholders of a company to subscribe for any new shares that the company issues in proportion to their existing shareholdings. It is most often found in relation to equity shares and normally applies only to new issues of shares of the same class. In this way, the balance of control between the respective shareholders can be kept constant. A pre-emption right may also prevent the 'watering' or dilution in value of existing shares, which will happen if the new shares are issued at a price which is below their true value.

Prior to 1980, shareholders were legally entitled to pre-emption rights only if this was expressly provided for in the company's articles; but it was also a requirement under The Stock Exchange's listing rules that equity shares of listed companies should be offered in the first instance on a pro rata basis to existing equity shareholders. The Act of 1980, implementing the Second EEC Directive (but extending its provisions to private as well as public companies), introduced a statutory pre-emption right to this country. The relevant provisions are now to be found in CA 1985, ss 89–96. The statutory right applies only to 'equity securities', ie equity shares and rights convertible into equity shares (s 94(2)). Equity shares held under an employees' share scheme are entitled to the benefit of pre-emption rights where there is a new issue, but the pre-emption rights rule does not apply to an allotment of equity shares made pursuant to such a scheme (s 89(5)).

Exceptions to the statutory obligation are as follows:

(a) shares allotted for a non-cash consideration (s 89(4));
(b) shares allotted for the purposes of an employees' share scheme (s 89(5));
(c) private companies may exclude the statutory right by a provision in the memorandum or articles (s 91);
(d) the shareholders may waive the requirement by special resolution, either generally or in relation to specified shares (s 95);
(e) the articles may empower the company, in giving the directors an authorisation to allot shares pursuant to s 80, to do so without applying the pre-emption procedure (s 95(1)).

CHAPTER 7

Capital and Dividends

A. Capital

The meanings of 'capital'

All companies having shares are incorporated with a 'nominal' or 'authorised' capital, which must be stated in the memorandum. This figure has little practical significance. It merely fixes a ceiling upon the amount of capital the company may raise by the issue of shares without further formalities.

The real money—or money's worth—which goes to provide the company with assets and working capital is that which is received as consideration for the issue of shares in the company. The 'issued capital' (or, in the case of the first shareholders, the 'subscribed capital') is the sum equivalent to the nominal value of all the shares that have been issued, and the 'paid-up capital' is so much of the issued capital as is represented by money which the shareholders have in fact paid: there may be an unpaid balance on each share which is not due for payment until a 'call' is made. Any premium (i e sum above the nominal value per share) is not part of the company's 'capital' in any of the above senses, but under CA 1985 it must be treated in the same way as 'capital' for many purposes (s 130). Further sums may be raised by borrowing. If the borrowing is of medium or long-term duration, it is customary to describe the sums raised as 'loan capital'.

So, in *Salomon*'s case (**12**), the authorised or nominal capital was £40,000 in 40,000 shares of £1 each; the subscribed capital was £7, the total issued capital was £20,007, which was fully paid up, and the loan capital (secured by the debenture) was a further £10,000.

It was very common practice in the early days for companies to issue shares on terms that only a small part of the capital—perhaps only 5% or 10% of the nominal value—was to be paid up, and so a very large sum of uncalled capital was left in reserve as a kind of 'guarantee fund' for creditors. This could have horrendous consequences for investors in the event of a liquidation (or, worst still, a spate of liquidations, as might occur in a slump). It also coloured much of the thinking in company law matters generally. Nowadays, the whole of the issue price of shares is normally payable on or soon after allotment, and so partly-paid shares are not at all common. In some jurisdictions, they have been banned altogether, primarily for the sake of simplifying the law, but perhaps also out of a desire that investors should not be over-committed with potential liabilities.

A *public company* must have a nominal capital which is not less than the statutory 'authorised minimum' amount fixed by CA 1985, ss 117–118. At present, the prescribed authorised minimum is £50,000. At least a quarter of this must be paid up (s 101). There is no minimum capital requirement for private companies.

It is not necessary that the capital of a company be designated in sterling, or in a single currency. A public company, however, must have at least £50,000 of its capital expressed in sterling to satisfy the requirements of ss 117–118. In *Re Scandinavian Bank Group plc* [1988] Ch 87, [1987] 2 All ER 70, Harman J ruled that it was in order for a public company to have a nominal capital denominated in a 'mixed basket' of currencies: £30m in shares of 10p, $US 30m in shares of 10 cents, Sw fr 30m in shares of 10 centimes, and Dm 30m in shares of 10 pfennigs each respectively.

Maintenance of capital

Most of the material in this chapter illustrates the concern of the law to see that those who take shares in a company do, in fact, contribute the subscription or issue price of their shares in money or money's worth, and that this sum or its equivalent is as far as possible maintained in the company's hands (consistently with all the risks associated with any business venture), and in particular that it is not returned to the members themselves directly or indirectly except through some statutory procedure, such as a reduction of capital (CA 1985, ss 135 ff) or a redemption or a repurchase of shares (ss 159 ff), which provides proper safeguards for creditors and others who might be prejudiced by the diminution of the company's assets. In this way, the law does its best for the corporate creditor, who is denied any direct recourse against the members by the principle of limited liability. There is, of course, only so much protection that the law can give. In addition to the normal business risks mentioned above, the historic figure representing the issued capital may be eroded in real terms by the effects of inflation. But these are risks which creditors necessarily accept; and our company law does provide for them a further measure of protection through the publicity given to company accounts and through the insolvency legislation.

The rules providing for 'maintenance of capital' referred to in the previous paragraph were formulated in the first place by the courts in the latter part of last century. But the second EEC Directive (No 77/9/EEC), which was adopted by the Council of Ministers on 13 December 1976, required the UK to make legislative provision, in quite explicit terms, about many matters relating to capital and the payment of dividends, by new rules which to some extent overlapped with the existing judge-made law and in other respects went much further. The Directive was implemented by the Companies Act 1980, which is now re-enacted in Pt V of the consolidating Act of 1985. English law is in fact more extensive than the Directive required, in that some of the new provisions were made to apply not just to public companies (as the Directive stipulated) but to private companies as well.

The printer's ink on the Companies Act 1980 was hardly dry when the Act of 1981, introduced by the same government, made further radical changes in the capital rules of company law. For the first time, English law allowed the repurchase by a company of its own shares.[1] This had been declared unlawful in *Trevor v Whitworth* (1887) 12 App Cas 409, and the common law ban had, indeed, been confirmed in statutory form by s 35 of the Act of 1980 (now CA 1985, s 143). These amending rules have been consolidated as CA 1985, ss 159 ff. And by the same Act of 1981 new (and far more detailed) provisions were enacted governing the issue of shares at a premium and the

---

1 A limited statutory exception, under which a company might issue redeemable preference shares, had existed since 1929. CA 1985, ss 159 ff now allows the issue of redeemable shares of any class.

giving by a company of financial assistance towards the purchase of its shares. Much of the earlier case-law was superseded as a result. It need hardly be said that, for the English student of company law, the greatest caution is needed when referring to decisions of the courts prior to 1980. It is not possible in this book to find space to reproduce all the new statutory rules—still less to try to explain their byzantine obfuscations; all that can be attempted here is to summarise them, and to cite some of the older judicial pronouncements which appear to have survived the new legislation.

It is illegal for a company to acquire its own shares, except as provided in the Companies Act.

See CA 1985, s 143, confirming the rule established at common law by *Trevor v Whitworth* (1887) 12 App Cas 409. This case settled a controversy which had existed, at least potentially, ever since the passing of the 1856 Act. It was only slowly recognised that the issue was not a domestic matter concerned with compliance with the articles, or even a question of vires dependent upon the powers set out in the memorandum, but a matter of legality under the Companies Act itself. The reasoning of the House of Lords in *Trevor v Whitworth* appears from the following passage in the speech of Lord Watson:[2]

> One of the main objects contemplated by the legislature, in restricting the power of limited companies to reduce the amount of their capital as set forth in the memorandum, is to protect the interests of the outside public who may become their creditors. In my opinion the effect of these statutory restrictions is to prohibit every transaction between a company and a shareholder, by means of which the money already paid to the company in respect of his shares is returned to him, unless the court has sanctioned the transaction. Paid-up capital may be diminished or lost in the course of the company's trading; that is a result which no legislation can prevent; but persons who deal with, and give credit to a limited company, naturally rely upon the fact that the company is trading with a certain amount of capital already paid, as well as upon the responsibility of its members for the capital remaining at call; and they are entitled to assume that no part of the capital which has been paid into the coffers of the company has been subsequently paid out, except in the legitimate course of its business.
>
> When a share is forfeited or surrendered, the amount which has been paid upon it remains with the company, the shareholder being relieved of liability for future calls, whilst the share itself reverts to the company, bears no dividend, and may be re-issued. When shares are purchased at par, and transferred to the company, the result is very different. The amount paid up on the shares is returned to the shareholder; and in the event of the company continuing to hold the shares (as in the present case) is permanently withdrawn from its trading capital. It appears to me that, as the late Master of the Rolls pointed out in *Re Dronfield Silkstone Coal Co,*[3] it is inconsistent with the essential nature of a company that it should become a member of itself. It cannot be registered as a shareholder to the effect of becoming debtor to itself for calls, or of being placed on the list of contributories in its own liquidation ...

2 (1887) 12 App Cas 409 at 423–442.
3 (1880) 17 Ch D 76 at 83.

When the return of capital is permitted

The Companies Act permits the return of capital by a company to its members by two procedures—one old and one fairly new. Each method calls for elaborate formality (and involves considerable expense) in the interests of safeguarding the rights of creditors and minority shareholders. These are:

(1) A 'reduction of capital', sanctioned in every case by an order of the court.[4] The relevant provisions of the Act, which are more or less self-explanatory, are ss 135 ff. Examples of the exercise of the court's discretionary powers under these provisions are **(178)**, **(179)**, **(180)**.
(2) A 'redemption'[5] or 'repurchase' of shares, made in accordance with ss 159 ff. Again, students are referred to the wording of the Act itself, although with the warning that these sections are long-winded and not easy to follow. Different rules apply to:
   (i) a purchase by a *public* company of its own shares *on the market*: an ordinary resolution is required (s 166);
   (ii) a purchase by a *public* company of its own shares *off the market*: a special resolution is necessary (s 164); and
   (iii) a purchase by a *private* company of its own shares: this is necessarily an off-market purchase and so a special resolution will also be required in this case. But whereas a public company must pay for the shares out of funds which might otherwise be distributed as dividends,[6] a private company is given the additional concession that it may repurchase out of capital: see ss 171 ff.

Note especially:

(a) The provision in s 170, which makes mandatory the establishment of a 'capital redemption reserve', in (i) and (ii) and, insofar as the repurchase is made out of distributable funds, also in (iii). In effect, this means that the company must have available a surplus equivalent to *double* the funds needed to effect the repurchase, and one half has to be set aside and treated as capital thereafter.
(b) The rule prohibiting the selling shareholder from voting the shares in question (ss 164(5), 165(2), 167(2), 174(2)).
(c) The requirement of auditors' and directors' certificates in (iii).
(d) The extensive disclosure and sanctioning provisions.

QUESTION

In *Re Halt Garage* (*1964*) *Ltd* **(123)**, the issued capital of the company was two £1 shares, of which Mrs Charlesworth held one. Was the judge right to describe the overpayment of £20 per week as a 'disguised return of capital' to her?

---

4 The procedure for a reduction of capital may also be used in other circumstances, e g to write off capital which has been lost or is no longer represented by available assets.
5 An expression used when the shares are *issued* on terms that they are, or are liable, to be bought back. Prior to 1980, only preference shares could be issued as redeemable.
6 Or out of the proceeds of a new issue of shares expressly made for the purpose, in which case the total capital issued will remain the same.

NOTE

In addition to the reduction of capital procedure and the provisions regarding repurchase of shares, the Act allows a company to accept a legacy or a gift of its own *fully-paid*[7] shares. There is not any real infringement of the principle of maintenance of capital in such a case, since the previous shareholder will have paid up the full nominal value of the shares, and nothing is paid back to him or paid out to anyone else. The statutory provision (s 143(3)) confirms the decision at common law in *Re Castiglione's Will Trusts* [1958] Ch 549, [1958] 1 All ER 480, in which a legacy of shares to be held by a nominee on behalf of the company itself was held not to violate the rule in *Trevor v Whitworth* (above).

Shares acquired by a *public* company or by a nominee on its behalf must normally be cancelled; but where a public company lawfully holds its own shares (eg in the circumstances described in the preceding paragraph), it must cancel or dispose of them within a maximum period of one year (three years in the case of shares which have been forfeited or surrendered in lieu of forfeiture), and pending cancellation or disposal no voting rights may be exercised in respect of those shares. If this were permitted, the directors of the company would have a voting power disproportionate to their personal stake as shareholders. (We may quite reasonably ask why the prohibition on voting is restricted to public companies.)

A statutory rule which has some links with this principle is that contained in CA 1985, s 23. This states that a body corporate cannot be a member of a company which is its holding company, either directly or through a nominee. The weakness of this provision, however, is that it is confined in its operation to 'holding companies' and their subsidiaries as these terms are defined by ss 736 ff of the Act. There is nothing in these definitions or in s 23 which stops company A from owning 40% of the shares in company B, which itself has 40% of the shares in company A. If a majority of the board of each of the two companies consists of the same persons, they can usually in practice wield unrestricted control of both companies, regardless of the size of their own individual shareholdings.

Analogous to the acquisition of its own shares by a company is the taking of security over them. This, too is forbidden by the Act in the case of public companies: see s 150; but there are exceptions when (a) the charge is to secure calls on partly-paid shares or (b) it is an ordinary business dealing by a moneylending company.

Shares may be *forfeited* for non-payment of calls (s 143(3)(d)). But there is no return of capital to the member in such a case: the company keeps whatever payments have already been made on the shares, and under the terms of the company's articles the forfeited shares may normally be re-issued to another holder.

QUESTIONS

(1) In the example given above, in which A Ltd and B Ltd have cross-shareholdings of 40% in each other, why is it that the board will usually have de facto control?
(2) Is there any infringement of the principle of maintenance of capital in such a case?

Payment for shares

A company may not issue shares at a discount.[8]

---

7 For the position where the shares are partly paid, see s 144: the nominee incurs personal liability.
8 See also CA 1985, ss 97–98, and note the exceptions there mentioned.

171 Ooregum Gold Mining Co of India Ltd v Roper [1892] AC 125 (House of Lords)

This action was brought by a holder of ordinary shares to test the validity of an issue of preference shares which had been made by the directors, in accordance with resolutions duly passed by the members, on the basis that each new share of £1 nominal value should be credited with 75p paid, leaving a liability of only 25p per share. The transaction was bona fide thought to be the best way of raising further funds for the company, especially since the ordinary shares stood at a great discount. The House of Lords held, however, that it was beyond the power of the company to issue the shares at a discount, and that in consequence the holders were liable for the full nominal amount of the shares.

LORD HALSBURY LC: My Lords, the question in this case has been more or less in debate since 1883, when Chitty J decided that a company limited by shares was not prohibited by law from issuing its shares at a discount. That decision was overruled, though in a different case, by the Court of Appeal in 1888, and it has now come to your Lordships for final determination.

My Lords, the whole structure of a limited company owes its existence to the Act of Parliament, and it is to the Act of Parliament one must refer to see what are its powers, and within what limits it is free to act. Now, confining myself for the moment to the Act of 1862, it makes one of the conditions of the limitation of liability that the memorandum of association shall contain the amount of capital with which the company proposes to be registered, divided into shares of a *certain fixed amount.* It seems to me that the system thus created by which the shareholder's liability is to be limited by the amount unpaid upon his shares, renders it impossible for the company to depart from that requirement, and by any expedient to arrange with their shareholders that they shall not be liable for the amount unpaid on the shares, although the amount of those shares has been, in accordance with the Act of Parliament, fixed at a certain sum of money. It is manifest that if the company could do so the provision in question would operate nothing.

I observe in the argument it has been sought to draw a distinction between the nominal capital and the capital which is assumed to be the real capital. I can find no authority for such a distinction. The capital is fixed and certain, and every creditor of the company is entitled to look to that capital as his security.

It may be that such limitations on the power of a company to manage its own affairs may occasionally be inconvenient, and prevent its obtaining money for the purposes of its trading on terms so favourable as it could do if it were more free to act. But, speaking for myself, I recognise the wisdom of enforcing on a company the disclosure of what its real capital is, and not permitting a statement of its affairs to be such as may mislead and deceive those who are either about to become its shareholders or about to give it credit.

I think ... that the question which your Lordships have to solve is one which may be answered by reference to an inquiry: What is the nature of an agreement to take a share in a limited company? and that that question may be answered by saying, that it is an agreement to become liable to pay to the company the amount for which the share has been created. That agreement is one which the company itself has no authority to alter or qualify, and I am therefore of opinion that, treating the question as unaffected by the Act of 1867, the company were prohibited by law, upon the principle laid down in *Ashbury Co v Riche* (**62**), from doing that which is compendiously described as issuing shares at a discount.

LORDS WATSON, HERSCHELL, MACNAGHTEN and MORRIS delivered concurring opinions.

NOTE

The position in which this company found itself is not at all an uncommon one: unprofitable trading has led to a depressed market price for the shares, and the company is seeking an injection of new funds to 'keep head above water' while the directors endeavour to surmount the immediate financial difficulties and find a way back to profitability.[9] The classical solution of an earlier generation was to issue preference shares, so that those who provided the new capital ranked ahead of the existing shareholders as regards both income and capital rights (below, pp 414 ff). Another possible solution—to issue new shares ranking pari passu with the existing shares but at a discounted price—is, on the authority of the above case, unlawful in England.

One way of making such a course of action possible would be for the law to authorise companies to create and issue *no par value* shares—something which is permitted in many jurisdictions and, indeed, compulsory in some. There is, after all, something unreal and simplistic about the concept of a par or nominal value. If the share in question was originally issued at a premium, or in exchange for a non-cash consideration, it may *never* have been worth its face value; and certainly after the date of its issue its market value will never again bear any relation to the historic figure which was once ascribed to it. If it were lawful for companies to issue shares of no par value, many of the misunderstandings associated with the concept of a nominal value would disappear, and in addition it would be possible for a company to issue shares, ranking pari passu, at a price of £1 in January, £1.05 in February and £0.90 in March (depending on what the market would stand), without any implication that there was a par value which was being enhanced by a premium or reduced by a discount.

Recommendations have been made at different times for such an innovation to be made here—e g by the Gedge Committee (1954, Cmd 9112), the Jenkins Committee (1962, Cmnd 1749, paras 32–34), and the Wilson Committee (1980, Cmnd 7937, para 735), as well as by professional bodies, but the response from successive governments has been nil.

Where shares of no par value are permitted, the 'maintenance of capital' rules still apply; but a concept of 'stated capital'—in effect, the issue price of the shares—is commonly entered in the accounts in place of 'issued capital', 'share premium account' and so on.

QUESTIONS

(1) When shares in British Telecom plc were sold to the public in 1984, the company was permitted to issue a simplified prospectus, for the benefit of the 'wider' public. This prospectus omitted to state that the nominal value of the shares was 25p. Why might it have been thought appropriate to withhold this information?

(2) The issue price of a 25p British Telecom share was £1.30. Were the shares expensive at that price?

9 As, in fact, happened in the *Ooregum* case: the company soon afterwards struck gold, and its ordinary shares rose in value from 12½p to £2.

(3) If a dividend of 10p is paid on a share of nominal value 25p, does this mean that the investor has done well?

There is ordinarily no prohibition on the issue of *debentures* at a discount, because the 'maintenance of capital' principle does not apply to loan capital. A company may find it attractive to create debentures on terms which give the holders the option at some later date of converting the debentures into shares at a predetermined rate of exchange. Such convertible debentures may not be issued, at a discount, on terms that they may be *immediately* exchanged for shares of an equivalent nominal value, for this would be only an indirect way of achieving an issue of shares at a discount (*Mosely v Koffyfontein Mines Ltd* [1904] 2 Ch 108). The rate at which the exchange of securities is to take place must, to be above challenge, represent a realistic assessment of future trends in the value of money and the market prices in securities.

QUESTIONS

(1) What might be the attractions of an issue of convertible debentures, rather than a straightforward issue of shares, for (a) the company, (b) the investor?
(2) The basis of conversion set out in the terms of issue of convertible debentures commonly prescribes a declining tariff, e g 75 shares for every £100 of debentures converted after three years, 70 shares per £100 converted after four years, 65 shares per £100 after five years. Why?

Issue of shares at a premium

The rule that shares may not be issued at a discount means that a company which allots a share of nominal value £1 must get £1 and nothing less for it; but there is no corresponding rule which says that the company must get £1 and nothing *more* for it. If investors can be found who are willing to pay the company £1.20 or £2 or £5 for a share of nominal value £1, the company is free to charge that sum. (Indeed, it may give the company's existing shareholders cause for complaint if a new issue of shares *is* made at par, for that would reduce (or 'water') the value of their shareholdings.[10])

The excess received by the company over the nominal value of the shares is called a *premium*, and there are provisions of the Act designed to ensure that such sums are treated for almost all purposes as capital in the company's hands and not in any sense as income or profit: see ss 130 ff. They must be shown in the company's accounts under a separate head as the 'share premium account' and (with the few exceptions stated in s 130(2) and subject to the relief allowed by ss 131–134) can be returned to members only by a formal reduction of capital.

Shareholders who have paid a premium for their shares have no right to the return of their premium in a winding up: at least in the absence of specific provision in the terms of issue, any surplus remaining after the return of the nominal amount of the shares is distributable on a rateable basis: *Re Driffield Gas Light Co* [1898] 1 Ch 451.

Shares may be issued 'at a premium' within the meaning of s 130, even though not issued for cash.

10 The directors would not breach any legal duty to the *company*: see *Hilder v Dexter* (**155**). The existing shareholders, however, might complain of 'unfairly prejudicial' treatment under s 459. The statutory 'pre-emption rights' provisions (ss 89 ff) are designed to ensure fairness in this and similar situations, but they will not always apply: see ss 89(4), (5), 91, 95, and the discussion above, p 338.

172 Henry Head & Co Ltd v Ropner Holdings Ltd [1952] Ch 124, [1951] 2
All ER 994 (Chancery Division)

The defendant company was formed to acquire by way of amalgamation the
shares of two shipping companies, and did so by exchanging the shares in
these companies for shares in itself of equivalent nominal value. In this way
it acquired assets worth some £7m in exchange for shares of a nominal value
of £1,750,000. The court held that the difference of just over £5m had rightly
been shown in the company's balance-sheet as carried to a share premium
account.

HARMAN J: The directors have been advised that they are bound to show
their accounts in that way, and not only they but the plaintiffs, who are large
shareholders, regard that as a very undesirable thing, because it fixes an
unfortunate kind of rigidity on the structure of the company, having regard
to the fact that an account kept under that name, namely, the Share Premium
Account, can only have anything paid out of it by means of a transaction
analogous to a reduction of capital. It is, in effect, as if the company had
originally been capitalised at approximately £7,000,000 instead of £1,750,000.

The question which I have to determine is whether the defendants were
obliged to keep their accounts in that way. That depends purely on s 56 of
the Companies Act 1948 [CA 1985, s 130], which is a new departure in
legislation and was, it is said, intended to make compulsory that which had
long seemed to be desirable, namely, the practice of putting aside as a reserve
and treating in the ordinary way as capital cash premiums received on the
issue of shares at a premium ...

Counsel for the plaintiff company asks who would suppose that a common
type of transaction of the sort now under consideration was the issue of
shares at a premium and says that nobody in the city or in the commercial
world would dream of so describing it. It is with a sense of shock at first
that one hears that this transaction was the issue of shares at a premium.
Everybody, I suppose, who hears those words thinks of a company which,
being in a strong trading position, wants further capital and puts forward its
shares for the subscription of the public at such a price as the market in those
shares justifies, whatever it may be [£1.50] a £1 share, £5 a £1 share, or any
price obtainable; and the [50p] or £4 above the nominal value of a share
which it acquires as a result of that transaction is no doubt a premium. That
is what is ordinarily meant by the issue of shares at a premium. The first
words of sub-s (1) are: 'Where a company issues shares at a premium'. If the
words had stopped there, one might have said that the subsection merely
refers to cash transactions of that sort, but it goes on to say 'whether for
cash or otherwise'.

What 'otherwise' can there be? It must be a consideration other than cash,
namely, goods or assets of some physical sort. Continuing, the sub-section
contains the words 'a sum equal to the aggregate amount or value of the
premiums on those shares shall be transferred to an account, to be called
"the share premium account"'. Apparently, if the shares are issued for a
consideration other than cash and the value of the assets acquired is more
than the nominal value of the shares issued, you have issued shares at a
premium; and I think that counsel for the plaintiff company was constrained
to admit that, in the ordinary case, that was so. This sub-section at least has
that much result; but he says that the line must be drawn somewhere. It

cannot apply, he says, where the issuing company has no assets at all other than the assets which it will acquire as the price of the issue of shares. 'Premium' (he argues) means something resulting from the excess value of its already existing assets over the nominal value of its shares. I am much attracted by that. I have every desire to reduce the effect of this section to what I cannot help thinking would be more reasonable limits, but I do not see my way to limiting it in that way. It is not stated to be a section which only applies after the company has been in existence a year, or after the company has acquired assets, or when the company is a going concern, or which does not apply on the occasion of a holding company buying shares on an amalgamation. Whether that is an oversight on the part of the legislature, or whether it was intended to produce the effect it seems to have produced, it is not for me to speculate. All I can say is that this transaction seems to me to come within the words of the section, and I do not see my way to holding as a matter of construction that it is outside it ...

NOTE

This case was followed in *Shearer* (*Inspector of Taxes*) *v Bercain Ltd* [1980] 3 All ER 295, a decision concerned with 'merger accounting'. B Ltd, which was incorporated as an investment holding company, acquired the entire share capital of L Ltd and A Ltd, worth all in all £96,000, in exchange for an issue of its own shares of nominal value £4,100. The difference of £92,000 was carried to a share premium account in the books of B Ltd. The bulk of the value of the acquired shares represented undistributed profits which those companies had earned before they were taken over. The Crown contended that B Ltd could, if it wished, have treated the £92,000 as distributable profits in its own hands and that therefore a 'shortfall assessment'[11] of tax could be made against B Ltd. Walton J rejected this argument and held that the *Henry Head* decision had the effect of compelling an acquiring company such as B Ltd to capitalise the pre-merger profits of the acquired companies by setting up a share premium account (as B Ltd had done).

This ruling, although in law unexceptionable in view of the earlier authority, caused some dismay in accounting circles because an 'exposure draft on merger acquisitions' issued some years before by the accountancy profession[12] had given its blessing to a practice of treating such profits as distributable by an acquiring company, at least where 90% or more of the equity shares had been taken over in the merger. As a result of representations by industry and the professions the law was amended in 1981, so as to allow some relief from the strict application of the share premium account rules in the special cases of mergers and of reconstructions within corporate groups. These new provisions are now contained in CA 1985, ss 131–134.

Shares issued in exchange for property

It is not necessary that shares should be allotted for cash. It is very common instead for the issue price to be satisfied by the transfer to the company of property, such as a business, previously owned by the allottee: this is what Mr Salomon (12) did. Or the new shares may be exchanged for shares in another company—see, for example, *Shearer v Bercain Ltd* (above).

---

11 A procedure (now not generally operative) by which the income of a closely-controlled company which had not been distributed to members could be assessed for tax as if it had been distributed.
12 ED 3, January 1971.

Two problems may arise here. If the property taken by the company as consideration is worth *more than* the nominal value of the new shares, then the shares will have been issued at a premium, and this will bring into play the burdensome and restrictive accounting provisions of ss 130 ff discussed above. If, on the other hand, the property is worth *less than* the nominal value of the shares (as may well have been true in Mr Salomon's case), then in practical terms the shares will have been issued at a discount, contrary to law. Creditors who assume that the shares have been paid for in full may then suffer loss, or at least be exposed to risk, and existing shareholders also may be prejudiced through the 'watering' of their own investment.

The common law leaves this problem to be determined by the business judgment and integrity of the directors (*Re Wragg,* (**173**)). This means that the rule against issuing shares at a discount can be fairly easily circumvented, for challenges to the board's decision are rarely mounted, and those that are face the formidable procedural obstacles of *Foss v Harbottle* (**232**): compare the analogous cases of *Pavlides v Jensen* (**245**) (sale of assets at alleged undervalue) and *Prudential Assurance Co Ltd v Newman Industries Ltd* (*No 2*) (**247**) (purchase of assets at alleged overvalue). The case for some form of statutory control has always seemed a strong one.

Such a step has now been taken in this country, in regard to *public* companies, as a result of the second EEC Directive (which was implemented in 1980). The relevant provisions are now ss 99–116 of the CA 1985. Some forms of consideration for the allotment of shares are banned altogether, e g an undertaking to do work for the company in the future (s 99(2)) and an undertaking of a long-term nature (other than a promise to pay cash) which may take five years or more to perform (s 102(1)). Other forms of 'non-cash' consideration have to be valued by an expert (ss 103, 104), and sometimes a second expert has to certify that the first one is competent (s 108(2))! Rules of even greater severity are laid down for subscribers to the memorandum (ss 104, 106). In all, it is a very elaborate (and costly) procedure that the Act spells out, in the most finicky detail: a pretty large sledgehammer to crack a fairly small nut.

It is not so important for the student to know all the finer points of the statutory procedure. But we cannot overlook the code of sanctions for a failure to comply—even with these finer points; and these are formidable. The allottee is obliged to pay to the company the nominal value of the shares and any premium, with interest, regardless of any benefit that the company may already have had (so that he may in effect have to pay for his shares twice over); and, in addition, a subsequent holder of the shares is jointly and severally liable with the allottee to pay the same amounts, unless he is (or has derived his title through) a bona fide purchaser for value without (actual) notice: see s 112. The only relief that those who are caught by these provisions have against what may be potentially a double liability to pay for their shares is that they have a right to make application to the court and ask for exemption from some or all of the statutory liability (s 113). In addition to these civil consequences, criminal penalties are imposed upon the company and its officers; and the transactions which infringe the statutory rules, though enforceable by the company against the allottee, are (by implication, and in the case of a contract with a subscriber to the memorandum, expressly) unenforceable or 'void' as against the company.

There is an exception from the valuation requirement in the case of a take-over in which all or part of the consideration for the shares allotted is the exchange of shares in the offeree company (s 103(3)); and it does not apply also in a merger.

It should be remembered that the rules stated above govern public companies only; private companies continue to be subject to the common law, as declared in the case next cited.

QUESTIONS

(1) Fred comes to an arrangement with the directors of XYZ plc that he will subscribe for 20,000 £1 ordinary shares in the company at their par value. He also agrees to sell to XYZ plc a leasehold shop property for a price of £20,000. On 1 April the shares are allotted to him in exchange for his cheque, payable to the company, for £20,000, and on the same day, the leasehold interest in the shop is transferred to the company in return for the company's cheque, payable to Fred, for £20,000. What legal issues arise?

(2) What do you consider is the policy reasoning behind CA 1985, s 104? Suppose that X and Y are the promoters of a public company and intend within a few days of its incorporation to transfer a business to it: is there any need to pay regard to s 104 if they take the precaution of ensuring that the memorandum is subscribed only by two clerks in their solicitor's office?

(3) Given the length and detail of most modern companies' objects clauses, when would it not be 'part of the company's ordinary business' to acquire assets such as those described in questions 1 and 2? (See s 104(6)(a).)

(4) Why do you think that the legislation requires a copy of the valuation to be sent to the proposed allottee (s 103(1)(c))? If the valuer's report advises the company that the transferor's property would be a snip at twice the price, can he withdraw from the transaction and negotiate for more? If the valuer negligently overvalues the property, could the allottee sue him in tort?

(5) Where there has been an infringement of s 103, could the company and the allottee effectively agree that the latter should be released from his liability under s 103(6) without going to court under s 113?

A company may buy property at any price it thinks fit, and pay for it in fully paid shares. Unless the transaction itself is impeached (e g on the ground of fraud), the actual value of the consideration received by the company for its shares cannot be inquired into. (This common law rule now governs private companies only.)

173 Re Wragg Ltd [1897] 1 Ch 796 (Court of Appeal)

Wragg and Martin had sold to the company on its incorporation their omnibus and livery-stable business for £46,300, which was paid partly in cash and debentures and partly by the allotment to them of the whole of the company's original capital of £20,000 in fully paid shares. The liquidator of the company later sought to show that the value of the business had been overstated by some £18,000; and he claimed either to be entitled to treat shares representing this amount as unpaid, or alternatively to charge Martin and Wragg as directors with misfeasance in connection with the purchase. Both claims failed.

LINDLEY LJ: I understand the law to be as follows. The liability of a shareholder to pay the company the amount of his shares is a statutory liability, and is declared to be a specialty debt (Companies Act 1862, s 16), and a short form of action is given for its recovery (s 70).[13] But specialty debts, like other debts, can be discharged in more ways than one—e g by payment, set-off, accord and satisfaction, and release—and, subject to the qualifications introduced by the doctrine of ultra vires, or, in other words, the limited capacity of statutory corporations, any mode of discharging a specialty debt is as available to a shareholder as to any other specialty debtor. It is, however, obviously beyond the power of a limited company to release a shareholder from his obligation without payment in money or money's worth. It cannot give fully paid-up shares for nothing and preclude itself from requiring payment of them in money or money's worth: *Re Eddystone Marine Insurance Co*,[14] nor can a company deprive itself of its right to future payment in cash by agreeing to accept future payments in some other way ...

From this it follows that shares in limited companies cannot be issued at a discount. By our law the payment by a debtor to his creditor of a lesser sum than is due does not discharge the debt; and this technical doctrine has also been invoked in aid of the law which prevents the shares of a limited company from being issued at a discount. But this technical doctrine, though often sufficient to decide a particular case, will not suffice as a basis for the wider rule or principle that a company cannot effectually release a shareholder from his statutory obligation to pay in money or money's worth the amount of his shares. That shares cannot be issued at a discount was finally settled in the case of the *Ooregum Gold Mining Co of India v Roper* (**171**), the judgments in which are strongly relied upon by the appellant in this case. It has, however, never yet been decided that a limited company cannot buy property or pay for services at any price it thinks proper, and pay for them in fully paid-up shares. Provided a limited company does so honestly and not colourably, and provided that it has not been so imposed upon as to be entitled to be relieved from its bargain, it appears to be settled by *Pell*'s case[15] and the others to which I have referred, of which *Anderson*'s case[16] is the most striking, that agreements by limited companies to pay for property or services in paid-up shares are valid and binding on the companies and their creditors ...

[If] a company owes a person £100, the company cannot by paying him £200 in shares of that nominal amount discharge him ... from his obligation as a shareholder to pay up the other £100 in respect of those shares. That would be issuing shares at a discount. The difference between such a transaction and paying for property or services in shares at a price put upon them by a vendor and agreed to by the company may not always be very apparent in practice. But the two transactions are essentially different, and whilst the one is ultra vires the other is intra vires. It is not law that persons cannot sell property to a limited company for fully paid-up shares and make a profit by the transaction. We must not allow ourselves to be misled by talking of value. The value paid to the company is measured by the price at which the company agrees to buy what it thinks it worth its while to acquire. Whilst the transaction is unimpeached, this is the only value to be considered ...

AL SMITH and RIGBY LJJ delivered concurring judgments.

13 [Section 16 corresponds to the present s 14; there is no equivalent of s 70 in the Act of 1985.]
14 [1893] 3 Ch 9.
15 (1869) 5 Ch App 11.
16 (1877) 7 Ch D 75.

Financial assistance by a company for the acquisition of its own shares

A statutory rule that has links with the maintenance of capital principle is that contained in s 151, which imposes a general prohibition against a company or any of its subsidiaries from giving financial assistance to a person directly or indirectly for the purpose of an acquisition of the company's own shares. Examples of the kind of transaction in question are:

(i) the company lends money to A to put A in funds so that he can buy shares from an existing member;
(ii) it guarantees B's bank overdraft, and on the security of this the bank advances money to B so that he can buy shares in the company;
(iii) it lends money to C so that C can repay a loan provided earlier by C's bank which C has already used to buy shares in the company;
(iv) it buys a piece of land from D, knowing that D will use the purchase money he receives to pay for shares in the company that he has agreed to buy.

The same kind of thing can occur in a take-over: the person who seeks to buy all the shares, or a controlling block of shares, in a company may wish to use some of the company's own funds or assets to pay for the shares or provide security for their price.

If, in examples (i) to (iii) above, the purchaser of the shares repays the money he has borrowed, then no harm may be done; but the risk is that the loan may never be repaid or that the bank may enforce the guarantee against the company after the customer himself has defaulted, and so the company will have lost money which was part of its capital, and the 'maintenance of capital' rule will be infringed. Similar consequences will follow in (iv) if the land is not worth what the company has paid D for it. So it is not surprising that a statutory prohibition similar to s 151 has been in the Companies Acts since 1929.

Earlier versions of this provision, however, up to and including s 54 of the Act of 1948, were notorious for the uncertainty of their language, which was wide enough to catch many quite innocent transactions. Responsible lending institutions and professional advisers were unwilling to be associated with schemes which might offend against the vague wording of the statute ('financial assistance for the purpose of *or in connection with* a purchase ...'), and so companies were often prevented from taking a course of action which made good business sense and was not morally objectionable. At the same time, the penalty of a £100 fine[17] was no real deterrent to the unscrupulous. The new statutory rules are intended to formulate more precisely the definition of the conduct which it is intended to prohibit: the words 'in connection with' have been deleted, and the emphasis is now on the purpose, or predominant purpose, for which the assistance is given, and the good faith of those concerned is relevant (s 153(1), (2)). In addition, later parts of s 151 spell out a number of types of financial assistance (e g the payment of lawful dividends) which are specifically allowed.

A further exception to the prohibition in s 151 is confined to solvent private companies: see ss 155 ff. Subject to some very tight safeguards, private companies may now make financial arrangements, such as loans, for the very purpose of assisting persons to buy their shares, if the company has net assets

---

17 The penalty has now been increased to a fine of unlimited amount plus, in the case of an individual offender, up to two years' imprisonment: see CA 1985, Sch 24.

that are not reduced as a result or, to the extent that they are reduced, if the assistance is provided out of distributable profits. This innovation reflects the desire of the Conservative government of the early 1980s to encourage 'management buyouts' and other 'hiving-down' arrangements, under which a business or part of it is sold off to the existing managers or to similar entrepreneurial figures who wish to become owner-executives of the business but cannot finance the purchase except through the direct or indirect use of the company's own assets as security.

All these statutory changes were introduced in 1981, and so far the new provisions have been discussed in only one case of significance, *Brady v Brady* (**174**). The student must therefore rely mainly on the wording of the Act itself for guidance—subject to the inevitable warning that he should not allow himself to be dismayed by the length and detail of the drafting. The other cases which follow all arose under the old law. To the extent that they deal with the civil consequences of an infringement of the statute, they may be regarded as still authoritative; but of course they should not be considered as illustrating the scope of the prohibition laid down in the present Act. They do also show the confusion on issues of policy which can be generated when the draftsman thoughtlessly makes liable under his criminal provision the very company whose protection it is his concern to promote!

The case of *Charterhouse Investment Trust Ltd v Tempest Diesels Ltd* [1986] BCLC 1 (in fact decided under the repealed CA 1948, s 54) throws some light on the meaning of 'financial assistance'. This case concerned a 'management buy-out' transaction under which Charterhouse hived off a subsidiary company, Tempest, by selling its entire shareholding to one of its managers, Allam. Hoffmann J was asked to decide whether a surrender of tax losses by Tempest to Charterhouse, as part of the transaction, constituted financial assistance. In ruling that it did not, he said:

> There is no definition of giving financial assistance in the section, although some examples are given. The words have no technical meaning and their frame of reference is in my judgment the language of ordinary commerce. One must examine the commercial realities of the transaction and decide whether it can properly be described as the giving of financial assistance by the company, bearing in mind that the section is a penal one and should not be strained to cover transactions which are not fairly within it.
>
> The *Belmont* case (**145**) shows that the sale of an asset by the company at a fair value can properly be described as giving financial assistance if the effect is to provide the purchaser of its shares with the cash needed to pay for them. It does not matter that the company's balance sheet is undisturbed in the sense that the cash paid out is replaced by an asset of equivalent value. In the case of a loan by a company to a creditworthy purchaser of its shares, the balance sheet is equally undisturbed but the loan plainly constitutes giving financial assistance. It follows that if the only or main purpose of such a transaction is to enable the purchaser to buy the shares, the section is contravened. But the *Belmont* case is of limited assistance in deciding whether or not an altogether different transaction amounts to giving financial assistance.
>
> The need to look at the commercial realities means that one cannot consider the surrender letter [relating to the tax losses] in isolation. Although it constituted a collateral contract, it was in truth part of a

composite transaction under which Tempest both received benefits and assumed burdens. It is necessary to look at this transaction as a whole and decide whether it constituted the giving of financial assistance by Tempest. This must involve a determination of where the net balance of financial advantage lay. I see no contradiction between this view and anything which was said in the *Belmont* case. In *Belmont* the company made cash available to the purchaser. This amounted to giving financial assistance and no less so because it was done without any net transfer of value by the company. On the facts of this case there is no question of cash being provided and the only way in which it can even plausibly be suggested that Tempest gave financial assistance is if it made a net transfer of value which reduced the price Mr Allam would have had to pay for the shares if the transaction as a whole had not taken place.

To bring a transaction involving financial assistance within the exception created by CA 1985, s 153(1)(a), (2)(a), a company's 'principal purpose' or 'larger purpose' must be something more than the reason why the transaction was entered into.

174 Brady v Brady [1989] AC 755, [1988] 2 All ER 617 (House of Lords)

A group of companies run by the Brady brothers, Bob and Jack, had a haulage and drinks business in Barrow-in-Furness. Following differences between the two brothers, it was agreed that they should divide the business in two, Jack taking the haulage side and Bob the drinks side. A complex scheme of reconstruction was drawn up under which assets were transferred from the principal company ('Brady') to a new company controlled by Bob. This transfer, it was conceded, involved the giving of financial assistance by Brady towards discharging the liability of its holding company ('Motoreal') for the price of shares which Motoreal had purchased in Brady, and so there was a prima facie infringement of CA 1985, s 151. Accordingly, when Jack brought proceedings for specific performance of the agreement, Bob argued that the transaction was illegal.[18] However, Jack contended that the financial assistance was an incidental part of a larger purpose of the company, namely the resolution of the conflict and deadlock between the brothers which was paralysing its business and threatening to lead to its liquidation, so that the exception set out in s 153(2)(a) applied. The House of Lords rejected this argument: the alleged 'larger purpose' was nothing more than the *reason why* the transaction was entered into. However, it ruled that an order for specific performance should be made because Brady was a solvent private company and could lawfully give financial assistance by following the procedure pre-scribed by ss 155–158.

LORD OLIVER OF AYLMERTON: Where I part company both from the trial judge and from the Court of Appeal is on the question of whether para (a) [of CA 1985, s 153(2)] can, on any reasonable construction of the subsection, be said to have been satisfied. As O'Connor LJ observed, the section is not altogether easy to construe. It first appeared as part of s 42 of the Companies

18 It was also claimed that the transfer by Brady of its assets was ultra vires. In the Court of Appeal, Nourse LJ had accepted this contention (see above, p 144); but the House of Lords held that the transfer was within the company's objects.

Act 1981 and it seems likely that it was introduced for the purpose of dispelling any doubts resulting from the query raised in *Belmont Finance Corpn Ltd v Williams Furniture Ltd (No 2)* **(145)** whether a transaction entered into partly with a genuine view to the commercial interests of the company and partly with a view to putting a purchaser of shares in the company in funds to complete his purchase was in breach of s 54 of the Companies Act 1948. The ambit of the operation of the section is, however, far from easy to discern, for the word 'purpose' is capable of several different shades of meaning. This much is clear, that para (a) is contemplating two alternative situations. The first envisages a principal and, by implication, a subsidiary purpose. The inquiry here is whether the assistance given was principally in order to relieve the purchaser of shares in the company of his indebtedness resulting from the acquisition or whether it was principally for some other purpose—for instance, the acquisition from the purchaser of some asset which the company requires for its business. That is the situation envisaged by Buckley LJ in the course of his judgment in the *Belmont Finance* case as giving rise to doubts. That is not this case, for the purpose of the assistance here was simply and solely to reduce the indebtedness incurred by Motoreal on issuing the loan stock. The alternative situation is where it is not suggested that the financial assistance was intended to achieve any other object than the reduction or discharge of the indebtedness but where that result (i e the reduction or discharge) is merely incidental to some larger purpose of the company. Those last three words are important. What has to be sought is some larger overall corporate purpose in which the resultant reduction or discharge is merely incidental. The trial judge found Brady's larger purpose to be that of freeing itself from the deadlock and enabling it to function independently and this was echoed in the judgment of O'Connor LJ where he observed that the answer 'embraces avoiding liquidation, preserving its goodwill and the advantages of an established business'. Croom-Johnson LJ found the larger purpose in the reorganisation of the whole group. My Lords, I confess that I have not found the concept of a 'larger purpose' easy to grasp, but if the paragraph is to be given any meaning that does not in effect provide a blank cheque for avoiding the effective application of s 151 in every case, the concept must be narrower than that for which the appellants contend.

The matter can, perhaps, most easily be tested by reference to s 153(1)(a) where the same formula is used. Here the words are 'or the giving of the assistance for that purpose' (i e the acquisition of shares) 'is but an incidental part of some larger purpose of the company'. The words 'larger purpose' must here have the same meaning as the same words in sub-s (2)(a). In applying sub-s (1)(a) one has, therefore, to look for some larger purpose in the giving of financial assistance than the mere purpose of the acquisition of the shares and to ask whether the giving of assistance is a mere incident of that purpose. My Lords, 'purpose' is, in some contexts, a word of wide content but in construing it in the context of the fasciculus of sections regulating the provision of finance by a company in connection with the purchase of its own shares there has always to be borne in mind the mischief against which s 151 is aimed. In particular, if the section is not, effectively, to be deprived of any useful application, it is important to distinguish between a purpose and the reason why a purpose is formed. The ultimate reason for forming the purpose of financing an acquisition may, and in most cases probably will, be more important to those making the decision than the immediate transaction itself. But 'larger' is not the same thing as 'more important' nor is 'reason' the same as 'purpose'. If one postulates the case of a bidder for control of a public company financing his bid from the company's own funds—the obvious mischief at which the section is aimed—the immediate purpose which it is sought to achieve is that of completing the purchase and vesting control of the company in the bidder. The reasons why that course is considered desirable may be many and varied. The company may have fallen on hard times so that a change of management is considered necessary to avert disaster. It may merely be thought, and no doubt would be thought by the purchaser and the directors whom he nominates once he has control, that the business of the company will be more profitable under his management than it was heretofore. These may be excellent reasons but they cannot, in my judgment, constitute a 'larger purpose' of which the provision of assistance is merely an incident. The purpose and the only purpose of the financial assistance is and remains that of enabling the shares to be acquired and the financial or commercial advantages flowing from the acquisition, whilst they may form the reason for forming the purpose of providing assistance, are a by-product of it rather than an independent purpose of which the assistance can properly be considered to be an incident.

Now of course in the instant case the reason why the reorganisation was conceived in the first place was the damage being occasioned to the company and its shareholders by reason of the management deadlock, and the deadlock was the reason for the decision that the business should be split in two, so that the two branches could be conducted independently. What prompted the particular method adopted for carrying out the split was the commercial desirability of keeping Brady in being as a corporate entity. That involved, in effect, Jack buying out Bob's interest in Brady and it was, presumably, the fact that he did not have free funds to do this from his own resources that dictated that Brady's own assets should be used for the purpose. No doubt the acquisition of control by Jack was considered, at any rate by Jack and Robert [Jack's nephew], who were and are Brady's directors, to be beneficial to Brady. Indeed your Lordships have been told that the business has thriven under independent management. But this is merely the result, and no doubt the intended result, of Jack's assumption of control and however one analyses the transaction the only purpose that can be discerned in the redemption of loan stock is the payment in tangible form of the price payable to enable the Brady shares to be acquired and ultimately vested in Jack or a company controlled by him. The scheme of reorganisation was framed and designed to give Jack and Robert control of Brady for the best of reasons, but to say that the 'larger purpose' of Brady's financial assistance is to be found in the scheme of reorganisation itself is to say only that the larger purpose was the acquisition of the Brady shares on their behalf. For my part, I do not think that a larger purpose can be found in the benefits considered to be likely to flow or the disadvantages considered to be likely to be avoided by the acquisition which it was the purpose of the assistance to facilitate. The acquisition was not a mere incident of the scheme devised to break the deadlock. It was the essence of the scheme itself and the object which the scheme set out to achieve. In my judgment therefore, sub-s (2)(a) of s 153 is not satisfied and if the matter rested there the appeal ought to fail on that ground.

[His Lordship went on to hold that an order for specific performance could, however, be made by following the procedure in CA 1985, ss 155–158.]

LORDS KEITH OF KINKEL, HAVERS, TEMPLEMAN and GRIFFITHS concurred.

A transaction which infringes s 151 is illegal and unenforceable.

175 Heald v O'Connor [1971] 1 WLR 497, [1971] 2 All ER 1105 (Queen's Bench Division)

The plaintiffs agreed to sell to the defendant all the shares in a company for £35,000; and simultaneously they agreed to make a secured loan, guaranteed by the defendant, of £25,000 to the company. When the company afterwards defaulted in paying instalments due in repayment of the loan, the plaintiffs sued to enforce the defendant's guarantee, and claimed to be entitled to enter summary judgment against him. The defendant, however, alleged that the loan had been made not to the company but to him personally so that he could pay for the shares, and he contended that the giving of security by the company in the circumstances was in breach of CA 1948, s 54 (CA 1985, s 151). Fisher J ruled that if the defendant's allegations were true the security would be illegal and void, and therefore granted leave to defend.

FISHER J: I proceed to consider the question of law on the assumption that the debenture was given to secure the repayment of the sum of £25,000 lent by the plaintiffs to the defendant in order to enable him to pay for the shares and that without such security the plaintiffs would not have been willing to make the loan. On this assumption I am satisfied that the company did give financial assistance within the words of s 54. Some meaning has to be given to the words in the section 'give financial assistance by means of the provision of security' and the meaning must be such as to cover some matter not already covered by the other words, 'loan' and 'guarantee'. It seems to me that a usual way, and maybe the only way, in which a company could give financial assistance by means of the provision of a security in circumstances which would not amount to the giving of financial assistance by means of a loan or guarantee would be by entering into a debenture such as the one in the present case.
    Is the debenture for this reason illegal and void? In *Victor Battery Co Ltd v Curry's Ltd*,[19] Roxburgh J held that a debenture given by a company as security for moneys lent to enable a person to purchase shares in the company was not illegal and void. He was impressed by the apparent injustice if the debenture were held to be illegal: the company which had contravened the section would benefit and the lender would suffer a loss which might greatly exceed the maximum penalty of £100. He held that the word 'security' in s 54 must mean a 'valid security' and he said: 'The section provides, not that it shall not be lawful for a company to provide a security in order to give financial assistance, but that it shall not be lawful for a company by means of the provision of security to give any financial assistance. In my judgment, "security" prima facie means "valid security", although I do not say that it must mean that. Moreover, the words of the section are not "purport to give financial assistance" but "give financial assistance" and I cannot see how an

19 [1946] Ch 242, [1946] 1 All ER 519.

invalid debenture could give any financial assistance. If, then, the section is, as I hold it is, referring to the provision of valid security and is treating the security as valid at the moment of the commission of the offence by the borrower, what is there to invalidate it subsequently? The section punishes the borrowing company on the footing that the security provided was and remains valid. Therefore, those principles of law to which Mr Slade, on behalf of the plaintiff company, referred me, cannot be imported, and I cannot believe that the legislature intended them to be imported, as they appear to lead to the extravagant consequences which I have indicated.'

The reasoning and conclusion of Roxburgh J in that case have been questioned in *Palmer's Company Law,*[20] and in three Commonwealth decisions, *Dressy Frocks Pty Ltd v Bock;*[1] *Shearer Transport Co Pty Ltd v McGrath*[2] and *E H Dey Pty Ltd v Dey,*[3] and more recently by Ungoed-Thomas J in *Selangor United Rubber Estates Ltd v Cradock (No 3)* (**177**). I am impressed by these criticisms and I propose to adopt them and to find in the contrary sense to Roxburgh J . . .

In summary, my reasoning is as follows: by the provision of a security in the circumstances in *Victor Battery Co Ltd v Curry's Ltd* and of this case the company undoubtedly gives financial assistance to the purchaser of the shares whether the security is valid or not. All that is necessary to make the financial assistance effective is that the lender should believe the security to be valid and on the strength of it make the loan. The apparent injustice which is the common result of the statutory prohibition of these particular kinds of transaction is not sufficient warranty for declining to apply the well-settled principle of law. The application of this principle in such circumstances as the present is likely to deter potential lenders from lending money on security which might be held to contravene the statute and is likely to be more efficacious in achieving the policy of the sections than the very small maximum penalty on the company . . .

Although a company which is a party to a transaction which infringes s 151 cannot enforce the illegal contract, it is not prevented by law from suing others who have participated in the wrongdoing, e g in an action for damages for conspiracy.

176 Belmont Finance Corpn Ltd v Williams Furniture Ltd [1979] Ch 250, [1979] 1 All ER 118 (Court of Appeal)

It was alleged that four of the defendants, with the connivance of two of the three directors of the plaintiff company, had sold its property worth £60,000 for a price of £500,000 and that the four had then used the money to purchase all the issued shares in the plaintiff. The company claimed damages for conspiracy against the defendants. It was held that the company could sue, despite the fact that it had been itself a party to the transaction which infringed the statute.

BUCKLEY LJ: In the course of the argument in this court counsel for the first

20 21st ed, (1968), 447.
1 (1951) 51 SRNSW 390.
2 [1956] VLR 316.
3 [1966] VR 464.

and second defendants conceded that the plaintiff company is entitled in this appeal to succeed on the conspiracy point, unless it is debarred from doing so on the ground that it was a party to the conspiracy, which was the ground that was relied upon by the judge.

The plaintiff company points out that the agreement was resolved on by a board of which the seventh and eighth defendants constituted the majority, and that they were the two directors who countersigned the plaintiff company's seal on the agreement, and that they are sued as two of the conspirators. It is conceded by Mr Miller for the plaintiff company that a company may be held to be a participant in a criminal conspiracy, and that the illegality attending a conspiracy cannot relieve the company on the ground that such an agreement may be ultra vires; but he says that to establish a conspiracy to which the company was a party, having as its object the doing of an illegal act, it must be shown that the company must be treated as knowing all the facts relevant to the illegality; he relies on *R v Churchill*[4] ... But I feel impelled to ask: can the plaintiff company sensibly be regarded as a party to the conspiracy, and in law ought it to be regarded as a party to the conspiracy?

Section 54 of CA 1948 [CA 1985, s 151] is designed for the protection of the relevant company whose shares are dealt with in breach of the section; that was so held in *Wallersteiner v Moir*.[5]

In the present case the object of the alleged conspiracy was to deprive the plaintiff company of over £400,000-worth of its assets, assuming always, of course, that it succeeds in establishing that allegation. The plaintiff company was the party at which the conspiracy was aimed. It seems to me that it would be very strange that it should also be one of the conspirators. The majority of the board which committed the company to carry out the project consisted of two of the alleged conspirators.

The judge said that the plaintiff company was a vital party to the agreement, and it could not be said that the other parties were conspirators but not the plaintiff company. With deference to the judge, who I think probably had very much less reference to authority in the course of the argument before him than we have had in this court, that view seems to me to be too simplistic a view, and not to probe far enough into the true circumstances of the case.

On the footing that the directors of the plaintiff company who were present at the board meeting on 11 October 1963 knew that the sale was at an inflated value, and that such value was inflated for the purpose of enabling the third, fourth, fifth and sixth defendants to buy the share capital of the plaintiff company, those directors must be taken to have known that the transaction was illegal under s 54.

It may emerge at a trial that the facts are not as alleged in the statement of claim, but if the allegations in the statement of claim are made good, the directors of the plaintiff company must then have known that the transaction was an illegal transaction.

But in my view such knowledge should not be imputed to the company, for the essence of the arrangement was to deprive the company improperly of a larger part of its assets. As I have said, the company was a victim of the conspiracy. I think it would be irrational to treat the directors, who were allegedly parties to the conspiracy, notionally as having transmitted this

---

4 [1967] 2 AC 224, [1967] 1 All ER 497 (sub nom *Churchill v Walton*).
5 [1974] 1 WLR 991. (For other proceedings between these parties, see below, p 494.)

knowledge to the company; and indeed it is a well-recognised exception from the general rule that a principal is affected by notice received by his agent that, if the agent is acting in fraud of his principal and the matter of which he has notice is relevant to the fraud, that knowledge is not to be imputed to the principal.

So in my opinion the plaintiff company should not be regarded as a party to the conspiracy, on the ground of lack of the necessary guilty knowledge.

GOFF LJ: [In] support of what Buckley LJ has said, I would wish to cite two short passages from *Wallersteiner v Moir*; the first passage is in the judgment of Lord Denning MR where he said:

> In *Essex Aero Ltd v Cross*,[6] Harman LJ said: 'the section was not enacted for the company's protection, but for that of its creditors; . . . the company . . . cannot enforce it.' I do not agree. I think the section was passed so as to protect the company from having its assets misused. If it is broken, there is a civil remedy by way of an action for damages.

Scarman LJ spoke to the same effect and said:

> There was, on these facts, a breach of duty by Dr Wallersteiner as a director. The companies were, also, in breach of the section. But the maxim 'potior est conditio defendentis' is of no avail to Dr Wallersteiner, for the section must have been enacted to protect company funds and the interests of shareholders as well as creditors. I do not agree with the dictum of Harman LJ in *Essex Aero Ltd v Cross* . . . to the effect that the section was enacted not for the company's protection but for that of its creditors.

ORR LJ delivered a concurring opinion.

A company which has been a party to a transaction which infringes s 151 may bring an action against its directors and other persons implicated for recovery of its property misapplied, on the grounds of breach of trust or constructive trust.

177 Selangor United Rubber Estates Ltd v Cradock (No 3) [1968] 1 WLR 1555, [1968] 2 All ER 1073 (Chancery Division)

[For the facts and another part of the judgment, see (**144**).]

UNGOED-THOMAS J: Does [this] principle, however, prevent an action succeeding for breach of trust in doing what is illegal?

In *Steen v Law*[7] directors of a company, incorporated in New South Wales, lent the company's funds which the directors had to give financial assistance to purchase the company's shares. The liquidator of the company claimed that there had thus been a breach of a New South Wales section, which, so far as material, was in the terms of s 54 [CA 1985, s 151]; and that the directors had thereby committed a breach of their fiduciary duty to the company and should reimburse the company the sums so illegally applied. It was not

6 [1961] CA Transcript 388.
7 [1964] AC 287, [1963] 3 All ER 770.

contended that the directors were absolved from accounting by reason of the illegality of the loan by the company. Such illegality was clearly before the Privy Council and, if available against such a claim, provided a complete answer to it. Yet the point was neither taken by the defendants nor by the Privy Council; and it seems to me for the very good reason that the company was not relying for its claim on the unlawful loan and the relationship of creditor and debtor thereby created, but upon the misapplication by the directors of the company's moneys by way of the unlawful loan. That is the position with regard to the plaintiff company's claim in our case. It was founding its claim, as in our case, not on a wrong done by it as a party to the unlawful loan, but as a wrong done to it by parties owing a fiduciary duty to it. The courts were being invited, as in our case, not to aid illegality but to condemn it. If this were not so, the courts would give redress to companies against directors for misapplication and breach of fiduciary duty which did not involve the company in illegality, but no redress if they were so serious as to involve the company in illegality.

I appreciate that, in the ordinary case of a claim by a beneficiary against a trustee for an illegal breach of trust, the beneficiary is not a party to the illegality; but that, when directors act for a company in an illegal transaction with a stranger, the company is itself a party to that transaction and therefore to the illegality. The company, therefore, could not rely on that transaction as 'the source of civil rights' and, therefore, for example, it could not successfully sue the stranger with regard to rights which it was claimed that the transaction conferred ... [But in] a claim based on an illegal breach of trust the claimant does not rely on a right conferred or created by that breach. On the contrary, he relies on a right breached by the breach, as the very words 'breach of trust' indicate. It is only on the footing that there is a breach of trust that the defence of illegality becomes relevant. So it is assumed, for present purposes, that there is a breach of trust against the plaintiff company by those who are directors and by those who are claimed to be constructive trustees. The constructive trustees are, it is true, parties with the plaintiff company itself to the transaction which is illegal. The plaintiff company's claim, however, for breach of trust is not made by it as a party to that transaction, or in reliance on any right which that transaction is alleged to confer, but against the directors and constructive trustees for perpetrating that transaction and making the plaintiff company party to it in breach of trust owing to the plaintiff company. The breach of trust includes the making of the plaintiff a party to the illegal transaction. So it seems to me clear on analysis that the plaintiff company is not precluded from relying on breach of trust by a party to an illegal transaction, to which the plaintiff itself is a party, when the breach includes the making of the plaintiff a party to that very transaction. Those who proved to be constructive trustees, sharing the responsibility with the directors for the breach of trust, share the liability too.

The result is that the plaintiff company in this case would not, by reason of illegality, be prevented from being reimbursed money paid by it unlawfully under a transaction to which it is a party. But this does not mean that this would nullify the ordinary operation of illegality with regard to companies and parties outside the company, and not being or treated as being a trustee to it. But it would prevent such operation shielding those whose position or conduct makes them responsible as owing a fiduciary duty or as constructive trustee ...

QUESTIONS

(1) In the light of the reasoning in *Belmont* (**176**), will a company ever have the mens rea necessary for it to be convicted under s 151?

(2) Tortuous plc lends £5,000 to Smith for the purpose of a purchase by Smith of Tortuous shares. Can it recover £5,000 or any sum from Smith (i) as repayment of the loan when due; (ii) as damages on the basis of *Belmont*; (iii) on the ground that Smith is liable to it as a constructive trustee, following *Selangor*?

(3) In *Armour Hick Northern Ltd v Armour Trust Ltd* [1980] 3 All ER 833, [1980] 1 WLR 1520, A Ltd was a subsidiary of B Ltd. B owed £93,000 to X, the owner of 7,000 shares in B. Y and Z wished to buy these shares, but X was unwilling to sell them unless the debt was first repaid. A accordingly paid off the debt out of its own funds. Y and Z then used their own money to buy the shares. Would there in your opinion be an infringement of CA 1985, s 151 on these facts?

Increase and reduction of capital

A company may *increase* the amount of its authorised capital with little formality: s 121 of the Act requires only an ordinary resolution. (In most cases the directors will, in addition, need authorisation from the shareholders to make the ensuing allotments: see s 80 and above, p 291.)

More formality is called for in the case of a *reduction* of capital—a step which a company may choose to take if it has sold off assets and wishes to return the proceeds to its members rather than reinvest the money in a new venture; or if it has suffered losses and wishes to write off the capital representing the lost assets. The Act in ss 135 ff lays down a strict procedure,[8] including an application to the court for approval, which is intended to safeguard the interests of creditors and minority shareholders. Where the rights of a *class* of shareholders are affected by a reduction, it may be necessary to have regard also to the provisions of s 125, but the approach of the courts to this topic (**180**) gives less scope to that section than its draftsman probably appreciated: see below, pp 423 ff:

The new statutory power to repurchase shares (above, p 343) offers an alternative method for returning money to shareholders: it may not be significantly less bothersome or costly, but for small companies there may be some tax advantages.

The cases which follow illustrate the approach of the courts in determining whether a resolution for the reduction of capital should be confirmed.

178 Scottish Insurance Corpn Ltd v Wilsons & Clyde Coal Co Ltd 1948 SC 360 (Court of Session), [1949] AC 462, [1949] 1 All ER 1068 (House of Lords)

The company's business had been nationalised, so that it could no longer earn profits. Its proposal to pay off the preference capital in anticipation of liquidation was opposed, partly because it was believed that this would rob the preference shareholders of a right to participate in 'surplus assets' in a liquidation. Endorsing this view, Lord President Cooper (dissenting) protested in this passage against the established judicial policy of non-intervention in reductions of capital. The House of Lords rejected this construction of the preference shareholders' rights (**215**) and held that the reduction was in any case fair.

---

8 *Unissued* share capital may be cancelled simply by an ordinary resolution: s 121.

LORD PRESIDENT (COOPER):   Every major Companies Act, beginning with the Act of 1867, has required that reduction of share capital (except by certain methods which are not in point) should be confirmed by the court. In the early days the courts took this jurisdiction very seriously and refused to confirm many reductions of capital, often on the dubious ground that they were ultra vires. This tendency was corrected in *British and American Trustee Corpn*;[9] *Balmenach-Glenlivet Distillery*;[10] *Poole v National Bank of China*;[11] and *Caldwell & Co*,[12] which progressively narrowed the scope of the court's powers, and inaugurated in company practice what might be called an era of self-determination and laissez-faire. Nevertheless, emphasis was again and again laid by the House of Lords upon the proposition that the courts had a 'discretion' to confirm or not to confirm, which it was their duty to apply in 'every proper case', and that this discretion fell to be exercised by reference to the test of whether the scheme would be 'fair and equitable', 'just and equitable', 'fair and reasonable' or 'not unjust or inequitable', expressions sometimes qualified and explained by the addition of the words 'in the ordinary sense of the term' or 'as a matter of business'. This was the safeguard on which Lord Herschell relied as a complete answer to the argument that the interests of a minority might be sacrificed to those of a majority (*British and American Trustee Corpn*). It is significant that the authority selected by Parliament to confirm reductions of capital is not the Registrar of Joint Stock Companies or any other administrative official, but the court; and it is abundantly plain from these decisions that the court's jurisdiction is a discretionary one, not confined to verifying the technical correctness of the formal procedure, nor even to determining according to strict law the precise rights of the contending parties, but involving the application of broad standards of fairness, reasonableness and equity, and the avoidance of what Lord Dunedin once described as 'a desolating logic' (*Balmenach-Glenlivet Distillery*).

Nothing could be clearer and more reassuring than these formulations of the duties of the court. Nothing could be more disappointing than the reported instances of their subsequent exercise. Examples abound of the refusal of the courts to entertain the plea that a scheme was not fair or equitable, but it is very hard to find in recent times any clear and instructive instance of the acceptance of such an objection. The explanations may be that the modern company meeting never deviates by a hair's breadth from fairness and equity, and that the 'proper case' for the exercise of the court's discretionary control never nowadays occurs; but I find it difficult to regard this explanation as convincing. It is important to observe that nearly all the cases in which the court has refused to listen to the complaint of a minority have been marked by one or both of two significant features: (a) that the dissentient minority was very small and usually merely obstructive, and (b) that the company was a going concern, recasting its capital structure in the general interests of the company as a trading entity, or staving off the threat of ruin in the interests of all concerned. When such features are present it is easy to understand the hint dropped by Eve J (*Thomas de la Rue & Co*)[13] that in ninety-nine cases out of a hundred the court should not interfere, and to

9 [1894] AC 399.
10 (1906) 8 F 1135.
11 [1907] AC 229.
12 1916 SC (HL) 120.
13 [1911] 2 Ch 361 at 366.

appreciate the importance rightly attached by Stirling LJ (*Welsbach Incandescent Gas Light Co*)[14] to the bona fide judgment of businessmen on a matter of business in which they themselves are largely interested.

I have stressed all this at the outset for two reasons: (1) Until I am instructed to the contrary I must continue to treat the discretionary jurisdiction of the court as not a paper safeguard but a living reality, and to apply it in every 'proper case'; and, by 'proper case', I understand a case in which the reduction is in a business sense unfair or inequitable to some of the affected interests. (2) The circumstances of the present case impress me as so exceptional that, if the power to refuse confirmation is not to be exercised here, I have difficulty in figuring circumstances in which it will ever be worth invoking it again ...

[This was a dissenting opinion. The House of Lords followed the majority members of the Court of Session (LORDS RUSSELL and KEITH) in holding that the proposed reduction was not unfair:]

LORD SIMONDS: The Companies Act 1929, no more than its predecessors, prescribes what is to guide the court in the exercise of its discretionary jurisdiction to confirm or to refuse to confirm a reduction in capital. But I agree with the learned Lord President that, important though its task is to see that the procedure, by which a reduction is carried through, is formally correct and that creditors are not prejudiced, it has the further duty of satisfying itself that the scheme is fair and equitable between the different classes of shareholders: see e g *British and American Trustee and Finance Corpn Ltd v Couper*.[15] But what is fair and equitable must depend upon the circumstances of each case and I propose, ignoring for the moment the particular factor introduced by the Coal Act, to consider the elements on which the appellants rely for saying that this reduction is not fair to them.

In the formal case which they have presented to the House the element of unfairness on which the appellants insist is that the reduction deprives them of their right to participate in the surplus assets of the company on liquidation and leaves the ordinary stockholders in sole possession of those assets. But in their argument both in the Court of Session and before your Lordships they have further relied on the fact that they have been deprived of a favourable 7% investment which they cannot hope to replace and might have expected to continue to enjoy. They further contend that the deprivation of these rights, which would in any case have been unmerited hardship, is rendered more unfair because it is likely to be followed at an early date by liquidation of the company or, as it is less accurately expressed, because it is itself only a step in the liquidation of the company.

The first plea makes an assumption, viz that the articles give the preference stockholders the right in a winding up to share in surplus assets, which I for the moment accept but will later examine. Making that assumption, I yet see no validity in the plea. The company has at a stroke been deprived of the enterprise and undertaking which it has built up over many years: it is irrelevant for this purpose that the stroke is delivered by an Act of Parliament which at the same time provides some compensation. Nor can it affect the rights of the parties that the only reason why there is money available for repayment of capital is that the company has no longer an undertaking to

14 [1904] 1 Ch 87 at 101.
15 [1894] AC 399.

carry on. Year by year the 7% preference dividend has been paid; of the balance of the profits some part has been distributed to the ordinary stock-holders, the rest has been conserved in the business. If I ask whether year by year the directors were content to recommend, the company in general meeting to vote, a dividend which has left a margin of resources, in order that the preference stockholders might in addition to repayment of the capital share also in surplus assets, I think that directors and company alike would give an emphatic negative. Anyway they would, I think, add that they have always had it in their power, and have it still, by making use of articles 139 or 141, to see that what they had saved for themselves they do not share with others[16] ... Reading these articles as a whole with such familiarity with the topic as the years have brought, I would not hesitate to say, first, that the last thing a preference stockholder would expect to get (I do not speak here of the legal rights) would be a share of surplus assets, and that such a share would be a windfall beyond his reasonable expectations and, secondly, that he had at all times the knowledge, enforced in this case by the unusual reference in article 139 to the payment off of the preference capital, that at least he ran the risk, if the company's circumstances admitted, of such a reduction as is now proposed being submitted for confirmation by the court. Whether a man lends money to a company at 7% or subscribes for its shares carrying a cumulative preferential dividend at that rate, I do not think that he can complain of unfairness if the company, being in a position lawfully to do so, proposes to pay him off. No doubt, if the company is content not to do so, he may get something that he can never have expected but, so long as the company can lawfully repay him, whether it be months or years before a contemplated liquidation, I see no ground for the court refusing its confirmation. [His Lordship later held (**215**) that the preference shareholders had in any case no right to participate in 'surplus assets' in a liquidation.]

VISCOUNT MAUGHAM and LORD NORMAND delivered concurring opinions.

LORD MORTON OF HENRYTON dissented.

In a reduction of capital, the prima facie rule is that money is to be repaid and losses are to be borne in the order in which the different classes of shares would rank, as regards repayment or loss of capital respectively, in a winding up.

179 Re Chatterley-Whitfield Collieries Ltd [1948] 2 All ER 593 (Court of Appeal)

[The facts appear from the judgment.]

LORD GREENE MR: The issued capital of the company is £400,000, divided into 40,000 shares of £10 each, one-half of which are 6% preference shares and one-half ordinary shares. The preference shares are entitled in a winding up to priority of capital and arrears of dividend but to no further participation in assets. The company is a private company which had for a number of years before the Nationalisation Act[17] carried on with success the business

16 [These articles dealt respectively with the paying off of the preference capital out of a reserve fund, and the distribution of capitalised profits, in the form of bonus shares, to the ordinary shareholders.]
17 [Coal Industry Nationalisation Act 1946.]

of coal mining. This was its principal undertaking, and on 1 January 1947 this undertaking passed out of the company and vested in the National Coal Board.

In spite of the loss of its principal business in this manner, the company does not propose to go into liquidation. It proposes to embark in certain new businesses, one of them that of coal mining in Eire and Northern Ireland if prospecting operations in which it is engaged turn out to be successful, and another (carried on through a subsidiary company) the business of digging for clay in Northern Ireland and manufacturing tiles, drain pipes, etc. Appreciation of the fact that the company is going to continue an active existence is essential for the proper understanding of this case. In respect of the loss of its coal mining business under nationalisation, the company will eventually become entitled to compensation fixed in accordance with the Nationalisation Act ... It may be expected ... that the company will not receive its compensation until after the expiration of a considerable time, running perhaps into several years. In the meanwhile the company is faced with the following situation. Its principal business has gone and it is proposing to embark on certain new activities which may or may not turn out to be successful. So long as it was possessed of its colliery it clearly required to keep all its issued capital in the business—there was no question of its having capital surplus to its business requirements. The reduced form of its activities is, however, such that it has a great deal more capital than it requires, and it is not unimportant to observe that it finds itself in this position quite apart from any compensation which it may receive when its share of the compensation is ultimately ascertained and paid. The repayment can be made without recourse to the compensation.

What is a company in that situation to do? The business answer to this question does not admit of doubt, particularly where a substantial part of its capital consists of preference shares bearing a higher rate of dividend than the company is reasonably likely to earn in the future. It will do what this company seeks to do, i e reduce its capital by paying off as much of its preference capital as it is able to pay off out of its surplus. A company which satisfies its capital requirements by issuing preference shares only does so where it is satisfied that the new capital will earn at least the promised rate of dividend. A company which has issued preference shares carrying a high rate of dividend and finds its business so curtailed that it has capital surplus to its requirements and sees the likelihood, or at any rate the possibility, that its preference capital will not, if I may use the expression, 'earn its keep', would be guilty of financial ineptitude if it did not take steps to reduce its capital by paying off preference capital so far as the law allowed it to do so. That is mere commonplace in company finance.

There has been a tendency, indeed more than a tendency, to represent a company confronted by this sort of practical question as though it were nothing but an uneasy and warring combination of hostile classes of shareholders. In a sense, no doubt, it is. But it is more than this. The position of the company itself as an economic entity must be considered, and nothing can be more destructive of a company's financial equilibrium than to have to carry the burden of capital which it does not need, bearing a high rate of dividend which it cannot earn. In a company so situated, the ordinary shareholders will be unfairly treated vis-à-vis the preference shareholders, and the company may well fall into the situation when its preference dividends will begin to fall into irretrievable arrears. It is a fallacy to suppose that because ordinary shareholders will benefit, the transaction ought to be vetoed as being unfair to the preference shareholders.

It is a clearly recognised principle that the court, in confirming a reduction by the payment off of capital surplus to a company's needs, will allow, or rather require, that the reduction shall be effected in the first instance by payment off of capital which is entitled to priority in a winding up. Apart from special cases where by agreement between classes the incidence of reduction is arranged in a different manner, this is and has for years been the normal and recognised practice of the courts, accepted by the courts and by businessmen as the fair and equitable method of carrying out a reduction by payment off of surplus capital. I know of no case where this method has, apart from agreement, been departed from ...

In the argument before us there seemed to me at times to be involved some idea that preference shareholders, so far from being entitled to be paid off first, ought to be regarded as being entitled *not* to be paid off first, i e that a company, having once issued preference shares, is bound either to keep them for ever, irrespective of the fact that it has surplus capital sufficient to pay them off, or at any rate is only entitled to reduce its capital by spreading the reduction rateably over its preference and its ordinary capital, with the result that the company will always be left with a certain amount of preference capital. The theory at the bottom of this idea appears to be that a preference shareholder subscribes his capital on the basis that he is to receive a preferential dividend of an agreed amount and that it is unfair to him to oust him from the company and thus deprive him of his contractual expectation of dividend. Apart from the fact that no such principle has ever been recognised by the court, it is, in my opinion, unsound for the reason that it ignores the facts (1) that the risk of a reduction of capital taking place is as much an element in the bargain as the right to a preferential dividend, and (2) that the well-known practice of the courts involves what (as I have endeavoured to point out) is really in accordance with sound business practice and, moreover, is based on the recognised analogy of priorities as to capital in a winding up, viz that, at any rate where preference shares are not entitled to participate in surplus assets, they are to be paid off first on a reduction, and references to the reasonable expectations of preference shareholders which are intended to suggest that there is something inequitable in this form of treatment, have, in my judgment, no support either in practice or on principle, and are unsound ...

In the result, I am of opinion that the present appeal should be allowed and the proposed reduction confirmed, the application being otherwise in order.

ASQUITH LJ delivered a concurring judgment.

EVERSHED LJ dissented.

[This decision was affirmed by the House of Lords: *Prudential Assurance Co Ltd v Chatterley-Whitfield Collieries Ltd* [1949] AC 512, [1949] 1 All ER 1094.]

No separate class meetings are necessary to approve a reduction of capital if priority is given to the different classes in accordance with the terms on which they were issued.

180 Re Saltdean Estate Co Ltd [1968] 1 WLR 1844, [1968] 3 All ER 829 (Chancery Division)

The company's preferred shareholders were entitled to participate in the 'balance of profits' in each year after a 10% preferred dividend and an equivalent sum in dividends on the ordinary shares had been paid; but in a winding up they had no right to participate in surplus capital. The ordinary shareholders controlled the voting. The court was asked to confirm a reduction of capital which was to be effected by paying off the preferred shares at 75p per 50p share. The reduction was approved by the court, which ruled that there was no 'variation' of the preferred shareholders' rights which would call for approval by a separate class meeting.

BUCKLEY J: [It] is said that the proposed cancellation of the preferred shares will constitute an abrogation of all the rights attached to those shares which cannot validly be effected without an extraordinary resolution of a class meeting of preferred shareholders under article 8 of the company's articles. In my judgment, that article has no application to a cancellation of shares on a reduction of capital which is in accord with the rights attached to the shares of the company. Unless this reduction can be shown to be unfair to the preferred shareholders on other grounds, it is in accordance with the right and liability to prior repayment of capital attached to their shares. The liability to prior repayment on a reduction of capital, corresponding to their right to prior return of capital in a winding up, is a liability of a kind of which Lord Greene MR [in the *Chatterley-Whitfield* case (**179**)] said that anyone has only himself to blame if he does not know it. It is part of the bargain between the shareholders and forms an integral part of the definition or delimitation of the bundle of rights which make up a preferred share. Giving effect to it does not involve the variation or abrogation of any right attached to such a share. Nor, in my judgment, has s 72 of the Companies Act 1948 [CA 1985, s 127], upon which the opponents place some reliance, any application to this case. That section relates to variation of rights attached to shares, not to cancellation of shares ...

The fact is that every holder of preferred shares of the company has always been at risk that his hope of participating in undrawn or future profits of the company might be frustrated at any time by a liquidation of the company or a reduction of its capital properly resolved upon by a sufficient majority of his fellow members. This vulnerability is, and always has been, a characteristic of the preferred shares. Now that the event has occurred, none of the preferred shareholders can, in my judgment, assert that the resulting state of affairs is unfair to him.

For these reasons the opposition to this petition, in my judgment, fails.

NOTE

In *House of Fraser plc v ACGE Investments Ltd* [1987] AC 387, [1987] BCLC 478, HL, the House of Lords endorsed the above decision, and approved the following passage from one of the judgments in the court below (1987 SLT 273 at 278):

In our opinion the proposed cancellation of the preference shares would involve fulfilment or satisfaction of the contractual rights of the shareholders, and would not involve any variation of their rights. Variation of a right presupposes the existence of the right, the variation of the right, and the subsequent continued existence of the right as varied. A different situation obtains where a right is fulfilled and satisfied and thereafter ceases to exist.

A shareholder voting at a class meeting held in connection with a reduction of capital must have regard to the interests of the class of shareholders as a whole.

181 Re Holders Investment Trust Ltd [1971] 1 WLR 583, [1971] 2 All ER 289 (Chancery Division)

The company petitioned for confirmation of a reduction of capital, under which it was proposed to cancel its redeemable preference shares and to allot to the holders an equivalent amount of unsecured loan stock.[18] The reduction was approved by both a special resolution of the company and an extra-ordinary resolution of a separate class meeting of the preference shareholders. At the latter meeting, some 90% of the votes cast were held by certain trustees (referred to in the judgment as 'the supporting trustees') who also held about 52% of the ordinary stock and shares, and in that respect stood to gain substantially from the reduction. Megarry J held that the vote at the class meeting was ineffectual, because the majority preference shareholders had considered their own interests, without regard to what was best for the preference shareholders as a class.

MEGARRY J: Unopposed petitions by a company for the confirmation of a reduction of capital are a commonplace of the Companies' Court; but an opposed petition such as the one I have before me is a comparative rarity . . .

Put briefly, Mr Drake's opposition to the confirmation of the reduction is twofold. First, he contends that the extraordinary resolution of the preference shareholders was not valid and effectual because the supporting trustees did not exercise their votes in the way that they ought to have done, namely, in the interests of the preference shareholders as a whole. Instead, being owners of much ordinary stock and many shares as well, they voted in such a way as to benefit the totality of the stocks and shares that they held. Secondly, Mr Drake contends that even if the extraordinary resolution was valid, the terms on which the reduction of capital is to be effected are not fair, in particular in that the increase in the rate of interest from 5% to 6% is not an adequate recompense for having the right of repayment or redemption postponed from 31 July 1971, until at earliest 31 October 1985, and at latest some unspecified date in 1990. I may say at the outset that it is common ground that the proposed reduction is not in accordance with the class rights of the preference shareholders . . .

[His Lordship referred to *Carruth v ICI Ltd*,[19] *British America Nickel Corpn Ltd v M J O'Brien Ltd* (**217**) and *Shuttleworth v Cox Bros & Co* (*Maidenhead*) *Ltd* (**58**) and continued:]

In the *British America* case, Viscount Haldane, in speaking for a strong Board of the Judicial Committee, referred to 'a general principle, which is applicable to all authorities conferred on majorities of classes enabling them

18 A company, in reducing its capital, is not bound to pay off its shareholders in cash: see
  Ex p Westburn Sugar Refineries Ltd [1951] AC 625, [1951] 1 All ER 881, HL.
19 [1937] AC 707, [1937] 2 All ER 422.

to bind minorities; namely, that the power given must be exercised for the purpose of benefiting the class as a whole, and not merely individual members only ...' The matter may, I think, be put in the way in which Scrutton LJ put it in the *Shuttleworth* case, where the question was the benefit of the company rather than of a particular class of members. Adapting his language ... I have to see whether the majority was honestly endeavouring to decide and act for the benefit of the class as a whole, rather than with a view to the interests of some of the class and against that of others ...

I pause here to point the obvious. Without guidance from those skilled in these matters, many members of a class may fail to realise what they should bear in mind when deciding how to vote at a class meeting. The beneficial owner of shares may well concentrate on his own personal interests: even though he regards the proposal per se as one to be rejected, collateral matters affecting other interests of his may lead him to vote in favour of the resolution. Trustees, too, are under a fiduciary duty to do the best they properly can for their beneficiaries. A proposal which, in isolation, is contrary to the interests of those owning the shares affected may nevertheless be beneficial to the beneficiaries by reason of the improved prospects that the proposal will confer on other shares in the company which the trustees hold on the same trusts: and that, in essence, is what is in issue here ...

[His Lordship referred to correspondence between the 'supporting trustees' and their professional advisers, and continued:] That exchange of letters seems to me to make it perfectly clear that the advice sought, the advice given, and the advice acted upon, was all on the basis of what was for the benefit of the trusts as a whole, having regard to their large holdings of the equity capital. From the point of view of equity, and disregarding company law, this is a perfectly proper basis; but that is not the question before me. I have to determine whether the supporting trustees voted for the reduction in the bona fide belief that they were acting in the interests of the general body of members of that class. From first to last I can see no evidence that the trustees ever applied their minds to what under company law was the right question, or that they ever had the bona fide belief that is requisite for an effectual sanction of the reduction. Accordingly, in my judgment there has been no effectual sanction for the modification of class rights ...

[His Lordship considered the evidence, and ruled that the reduction had not been shown to be fair to the preference shareholders. Accordingly, he refused to confirm the reduction.]

QUESTION

In this case, Megarry J appears to have expected from the majority preference shareholders a 'detached altruism' which the court in such cases as *Mills v Mills* (**138**) dismissed as unrealistic. What advice should they have been given?

NOTE

This case was decided at common law, before the enactment of the statutory provisions which are now to be found in CA 1985, ss 125 ff.

Other statutory provisions

Other statutory rules relating to capital include the following:

(a) Every *public company* must have a *minimum* subscribed capital of
£50,000—a figure which can be altered by the Secretary of State (CA
1985, ss 11, 118); and at least a quarter of this sum must have been paid
to the company in money or money's worth before it commences business
(s 117). There is no corresponding rule for private companies (and in this
respect our law differs from that of most European countries); but of
course the law does insist that whatever the capital figures are shall be
fully disclosed in the annual return and accounts.
(b) Where a public company has suffered a 'serious loss' of capital (i e where
its net assets are reduced to half or less of its called-up share capital), the
directors must convene an extraordinary general meeting for the purpose
of considering what steps might be taken to deal with the situation (CA
1985, s 142).

Note also the concern which has been expressed at times by the courts (e g
Re Halt Garage (*1964*) *Ltd* (**123**), *Aveling Barford Ltd v Perion Ltd* (**183**))
that a payment may amount to a disguised violation of the maintenance of
capital principle, even where the issue before the court might appear to be
something unrelated.

QUESTIONS

(1) The directors of Precarious plc call a meeting under CA 1985, s 142 to report a
serious loss of capital. What is it within the shareholders' constitutional power to
do at that meeting?
(2) What are the creditors of Precarious plc likely to do when they hear that the
directors have summoned the meeting under s 142?

B. Dividends

Before 1980, there were no general rules in the Companies Acts regulating
the distribution of dividends to the members of a company, although there
were specific bans on using the share premium account (CA 1985, s 130)
and the capital redemption reserve (s 170) for this purpose. The only legal
constraint was a broad prohibition established by the cases that dividends
should not be paid out of 'capital'. Most of these cases were decided in the
late Victorian period, and reflected concepts of bookkeeping which were
regarded as odd even then by some contemporary critics. In fact, for the
greater part of this century the standards of propriety in relation to distributions have been set by the accountancy profession and not by the law
at all; and these standards have risen progressively over the decades. It is
likely that this will continue to be so, even after we now have formally enacted
legal rules about the payment of dividends in ss 263 ff of the Act—rules which
implement in part the Second EEC Directive and also incorporate some
recommendations made by the Jenkins Committee in 1962.
   The Act makes separate rules for private companies, public companies and
investment companies (defined in s 266).

The first and primary rule, applicable to all companies, is that a company may not make a 'distribution' (i e a cash payment or a transfer of assets) to any of its members except out of profits which are available for the purpose (s 263(1)).

This rule may be thought to correspond in its effect to the common law principle laid down in *Re Exchange Banking Co, Flitcroft's Case* (**182**), that dividends could not be paid from 'capital'; but when taken with other sections of the Act its consequences are altogether different from the position at common law. This may be illustrated by the following common law cases:

Lee v Neuchatel Asphalte Co (1889) 41 Ch D 1: a company could pay dividends out of its current trading profits without making provision for the depreciation of its fixed assets;

Verner v General and Commercial Investment Trust [1894] 2 Ch 239: a dividend could be paid from current trading profits without making good earlier losses in fixed capital;

Ammonia Soda Co Ltd v Chamberlain [1918] 1 Ch 266: a company could pay dividends out of current trading profits without making good past revenue losses;

Dimbula Valley (Ceylon) Tea Co Ltd v Laurie [1961] Ch 353, [1961] 1 All ER 769: a surplus resulting from the increase in the overall book value of a company's assets could be treated as a distributable profit even though it had not been realised by sale.[20]

In short, at common law, the current year's profit and loss account only was looked at, and the profits for that particular year reckoned by taking it in isolation; money lost in earlier years of trading, and a fortiori capital losses, did not have to be brought into account. And it was not necessary for profits to be realised profits before they were regarded as distributable— although of course, as a practical matter, the company had to have available or be able to raise the cash necessary to pay the dividend when declared.

Under Pt VIII of the 1985 Act, however (re-enacting changes made in 1980), 'profits' available for distribution by a company are to be 'its accumulated, realised, profits, so far as not previously utilised by distribution or capitalisation, less its accumulated, realised losses, so far as not previously written off in a reduction or reorganisation of capital duly made' (s 263(3)).

The two major changes introduced by this formulation are:

(1) we must now look not at the current year's trading figures in isolation but at the net overall position of the company, taking into account its *accumulated* surpluses and losses over the years; and
(2) the figures used in the calculation of profits must be those for the company's *realised*[1] profits and losses: mere 'revaluation surpluses'—the 'paper profits' relied on in the *Dimbula Valley* case (above)—cannot be brought into account in reckoning profits.

As a result, we have gone over to what is sometimes called the 'balance sheet surplus' approach: the company's cumulative position, involving past years as well as the current year, has to be considered, and dividends can be paid only if justified by the picture as a whole.

Special rules apply to *public* companies and to *investment* companies:

20 This was never the law in Scotland: *Westburn Sugar Refineries Ltd v IRC* [1960] TR 105.
1 The term 'realised' is not defined in the Act, but it has a settled meaning in accountancy practice. For a discussion of this and other points arising from the statutory rules, see M Renshall, (1980) 1 Co Law 194.

A *public* company must allow for any excess of *unrealised* losses over unrealised profits on the capital account—i e provision must be made for any unrealised revaluation deficit (s 264).

An *investment* company (defined in s 266) may also make a distribution out of the surplus on revenue account only (i e not including even *realised* capital profits, but at the same time not being bound to take account of unrealised or realised capital losses), provided that its assets are not reduced to less than one and a half times its liabilities (s 265).

At common law, dividends may not be paid from capital. Directors who pay dividends out of capital are liable to compensate the company personally for the money so paid away.

182 Re Exchange Banking Co, Flitcroft's Case (1882) 21 Ch D 519 (Court of Appeal)

The directors had for several years made it appear that the company had made profits, when in fact it had not, by laying before the shareholders reports and balance sheets in which debts known to be bad were entered as assets. On the faith of these reports, the shareholders had passed resolutions declaring dividends, which the directors had paid. In the winding up of the company the liquidator successfully applied to have the directors who had been responsible on each occasion made accountable to the company for the sums wrongly paid away.

JESSEL MR: A limited company by its memorandum of association declares that its capital is to be applied for the purposes of the business. It cannot reduce its capital except in the manner and with the safeguards provided by statute, and looking at the Act ... it clearly is against the intention of the legislature that any portion of the capital should be returned to the shareholders without the statutory conditions being complied with. A limited company cannot in any other way make a return of capital, the sanction of a general meeting can give no validity to such a proceeding, and even the sanction of every shareholder cannot bring within the powers of the company an act which is not within its powers. If, therefore, the shareholders had all been present at the meetings, and had all known the facts, and had all concurred in declaring the dividends, the payment of the dividends would not be effectually sanctioned. One reason is this—there is a statement that the capital shall be applied for the purposes of the business, and on the faith of that statement, which is sometimes said to be an implied contract with creditors, people dealing with the company give it credit. The creditor has no debtor but that impalpable thing the corporation, which has no property except the assets of the business. The creditor, therefore, I may say, gives credit to that capital, gives credit to the company on faith of the representation that the capital shall be applied only for the purposes of the business, and he has therefore a right to say that the corporation shall keep its capital and not return it to the shareholders, though it may be a right which he cannot enforce otherwise than by a winding-up order. It follows then that if directors who are quasi trustees for the company improperly pay away the assets to the shareholders, they are liable to replace them. It is no answer to say that the shareholders could not compel them to do so. I am of opinion that the company could in its corporate capacity compel them to do so, even if there were no winding up . . .

COTTON LJ: It was contended that though the directors might be ordered to repay what they had themselves retained, they ought not to be ordered to refund what they had paid to the other shareholders. But directors are in the position of trustees, and are liable not only for what they put into their own pockets, but for what they in breach of trust pay to others . . .

BRETT LJ delivered a concurring judgment.

NOTES

A shareholder who received payment of a dividend which had been improperly paid, and who had knowledge of the facts, was held liable to repay the amount as a constructive trustee in *Precision Dippings Ltd v Precision Dippings Marketing Ltd* [1986] Ch 447, [1985] BCLC 385, CA.

There has been no English case in which a shareholder has succeeded in an action brought to compel a company to pay a dividend. Indeed, in *Burland v Earle* (**242**) the Privy Council made it clear that this was a matter where the court would not interfere. In contrast, in the well-known US case *Dodge v Ford Motor Co* 170 NW 668 (1919), Ford was ordered to pay a substantial dividend to its shareholders when the directors would have preferred to expend the company's trading surplus on increasing the wages and improving the work conditions of its employees, reducing prices to its customers and similar altruistic objects.

However, in *Re a Company* (1988) 4 BCC 506 Harman J did not rule out the possibility that it might in a particular case be a ground for ordering the winding up of a company on the just and equitable ground (below, pp 557 ff) if it had pursued a restrictive dividend policy and denied the shareholders a return on their investment which they were reasonably entitled to expect. In *Re Sam Weller & Sons Ltd* (**253**), Peter Gibson J, differing from Harman J, held that such a policy might also justify relief on the ground of 'unfairly prejudicial conduct' (CA 1985, s 459). Section 459 has since been amended so as to put it beyond doubt that the view of Gibson J will be followed (see below, p 496).

QUESTION

Was it material in the *Precision Dippings* case (above) that the shareholder had knowledge of the impropriety?

'Bonus shares' or 'capitalisation issues'[2]

A profitable company which does not distribute all its earnings as dividends will accumulate reserves. The shares will in consequence have a market value which is greater than their nominal value. There will be a similar situation when a company's fixed assets appreciate in value as a result of inflation or of a movement in their market value. Suppose, for example, that a company with a nominal capital of 10,000 £1 shares, all issued and fully paid, has accumulated profits of £90,000. Instead of paying out this surplus to its shareholders as dividends it may resolve to 'capitalise' these reserves by issuing a further 90,000 shares, so that nine new shares are allotted to the holder of each existing share, and treating the new shares as fully paid because

2 Other terms used are 'scrip issue' and (in the US) 'stock dividend'.

the £90,000 is appropriated to meet the issue price. No cash changes hands at all. The formal result will be that the reserve has become capital and ceases to be available for distribution as dividend, the company's issued share capital has risen from £10,000 to £100,000, each shareholder now has ten times as many shares as before, and the market value of each share will have fallen back from something like £10 to £1.[3] (Of course, other factors influence the market price of shares, apart from their 'asset backing', but this in simplified terms will be what happens.)

A capitalisation issue is not a 'distribution' of profits or assets for the purposes of the statutory restrictions in ss 263 ff of the Act. It follows that profits which are not distributable (e g because they are unrealised profits) may be capitalised and issued to members as bonus shares provided the articles are so worded as to permit this.[4]

QUESTIONS

(1) What might be the advantages to (i) the company, (ii) its shareholders, of making an issue of bonus shares?
(2) Are the shareholders better off in any real sense as a result? Is the expression 'bonus shares' misleading?

C. The dissipation of corporate assets[5]

The abolition of the doctrine of ultra vires by CA 1989 has deprived the courts of the most potent of their traditional weapons when dealing with allegations that corporate property has been misapplied. Of course, with the gradual erosion of the doctrine as a result of the ingenuity of the draftsmen of objects clauses and progressive capitulation of the courts to their inno-vations, the occasions on which the doctrine could be successfully invoked were destined to become rather fewer—particularly after the Court of Appeal's ruling in the *Rolled Steel* case (**70**); but it remained readily available to deal with the most blatant cases of misappropriation such as *International Sales and Agencies Ltd v Marcus* (**72**).

With the demise of the ultra vires doctrine, the courts must now have recourse to other rules and remedies in such cases. As *Rolled Steel* itself shows, it may be possible to show that directors have behaved unconstitutionally, exceeded their authority, abused their powers or acted in breach of their fiduciary duties, with the consequence that the relevant transaction may be declared void or voidable and both they and any third person who has received corporate assets with knowledge of the circumstances will be liable to reimburse the company (*Selangor United Rubber Estates Ltd v Cradock* (*No 3*) (**144**)). If the third party has dealt in good faith, for value and without

3 Bonus issues may also be financed out of the share premium account and the capital redemption reserve.
4 This confirms the position at common law declared by Buckley J in *Dimbula Valley (Ceylon) Tea Co Ltd v Laurie* [1961] Ch 353, [1961] 1 All ER 769, but the judge's reasoning (based on the view that such profits were distributable) has not survived the statutory changes of 1980.
5 See A Clark, 'Ultra Vires after *Rolled Steel Products*' (1985) 6 Co Law 155, and the perceptive note by F Dawson on the Australian case *ANZ Executors and Trustees Co Ltd v Quintex Ltd* (1990) 8 ACLC 980 (Qld Full Ct), (1991) 107 LQR 202.

notice of the irregularity, the company's remedy against him will, of course, be lost; but very often he will be an 'insider' or party to the wrongdoing and not able to plead this defence. There is also the possibility that a formal or informal ratification of the irregular act will be alleged to have occurred. But some breaches of directors' duty are not capable of ratification (*Cook v Deeks* (**131**), *Kinsela v Russell Kinsela Pty Ltd* (above, p 254)), and in other cases the power to ratify is restricted by statute (CA 1985, s 35(3)); and where the act involves illegality (e g a prohibited distribution (s 263) or a breach of the 'financial assistance' prohibition (s 151)), it will not be capable of ratification at all. So the courts are still relatively well equipped to deal with cases of wrongful depletion of corporate assets.

It is possible that a new principle may be in the process of emerging, linked with the 'maintenance of capital' doctrine. In *Re Halt Garage (1964) Ltd* (**123**) Oliver J struck down a payment of remuneration to an inactive director as 'not genuine' and a 'dressed-up return of capital' to her. While the basis of this reasoning is open to question (not least because as a shareholder she held only one £1 share), it has since been adopted and applied by Hoffman J in *Aveling Barford Ltd v Perion Ltd* (**183**), where again the 'dressed-up return of capital' argument was somewhat shaky because the beneficiary of the asset-stripping, although totally lacking in merit, was not strictly a shareholder.

Where the company is insolvent or approaching insolvency, there is now an abundance of statutory provisions which may be invoked when corporate assets have been plundered or imperilled in the run-up to liquidation. These include preferences (IA 1986, s 239), transactions at an undervalue (ss 238, 423), floating charges subject to avoidance (s 245), fraudulent and wrongful trading (ss 231, 214) and misfeasance proceedings (s 212). In the light of these statutory developments in the UK, it is not likely that a new jurisdiction will develop here (although it may in Australasia) based on a duty owed by directors to creditors (see above, p 254).

A sale at an undervalue made by a company to one of its shareholders (or to another company controlled by him) may be open to challenge on the ground that it is not a genuine sale but a disguised return of capital.

183 Aveling Barford Ltd v Perion Ltd [1989] BCLC 626 (Chancery Division)

Aveling Barford and Perion were both owned and controlled by Lee. Aveling Barford, which was not at the material time insolvent but was not in a position to make any distribution to its shareholders, owned a sports ground which had planning permission for residential development. In October 1986 its directors resolved to sell this property to Perion for £350,000 when they knew that it had recently been valued at £650,000, but no binding contract was entered into at that stage. A later valuation put it at £1.15m and Perion was subsequently offered £1.4m. There was some evidence of an agreement reached in January 1987 that a further payment of £400,000 was to be paid to Aveling Barford by Perion if it resold the property within a year for more than £800,000. The property was conveyed to Perion for £350,000 in February 1987 and resold by it for £1.52m the following August. Aveling Barford was subsequently put into liquidation and successfully sued in this action to have Perion declared a constructive trustee of the proceeds of the sale.

HOFFMANN J: Counsel for the defendants said that even if the 10 January contract was a rewriting of history in the summer of 1987, when it was plain that Perion would be reselling for more than £800,000, it was reasonable for the parties retrospectively to affirm the sale at £750,000, which would have been a proper sum to fix as the value in February 1987. I do not agree. If the February sale was, as I think, a breach of duty and liable to be set aside at the time, Dr Lee or Mr Chapman [solicitor to all the parties] on his behalf had no right to confirm it retrospectively as a sale at £750,000 at a time when they knew the value to be over £1,400,000. It was the duty of the directors to set aside the February sale and obtain the full value of the land for Aveling Barford. On any view, therefore, the sale was a breach of fiduciary duty by Dr Lee. Perion, through Dr Lee and Mr Chapman, knew all the facts which made it a breach of duty and was therefore accountable as a constructive trustee.

In the alternative, counsel for the defendant submitted that whether or not the sale to Perion was a breach of fiduciary duty by Dr Lee, it cannot be challenged by the company because it was unanimously approved by the shareholders. This approval was both informal and formal. Informal approval was given at the time of sale by virtue of the fact that Dr Lee owned or controlled the entire issued share capital. Formally, a sale at £750,000 was approved when the 1987 accounts were adopted at the company's annual general meeting. For the purposes of this motion I shall assume that shareholder consent was given in both these ways.

The general rule is that any act which falls within the express or implied powers of a company conferred by its memorandum of association, whether or not a breach of duty on the part of the directors, will be binding on the company if it is approved or subsequently ratified by the shareholders: see *Rolled Steel Products (Holdings) Ltd v British Steel Corpn* (**105**). But this rule is subject to exceptions created by the general law and one such exception is that a company cannot without the leave of the court or the adoption of a special procedure return its capital to its shareholders. It follows that a transaction which amounts to an unauthorised return of capital is ultra vires and cannot be validated by shareholder ratification or approval. Whether or not the transaction is a distribution to shareholders does not depend exclusively on what the parties choose to call it. The court looks at the substance rather than the outward appearance. Thus in *Ridge Securities Ltd v IRC*[6] Pennycuick J was concerned with a tax avoidance scheme by a solvent company which involved the grant of a debenture to its parent under which very large and uncommercial sums were payable, purportedly as interest. He said that the 'interest' payments were ultra vires because they were dressed up gifts of capital to the parent company:

> A company can only lawfully deal with its assets in furtherance of its objects. The corporators may take assets out of the company by way of dividend, or, with the leave of the court, by way of reduction of capital, or in a winding up. They may of course acquire them for full consideration. They cannot take assets out of the company by way of

6 [1964] 1 All ER 275 at 288, [1964] 1 WLR 479 at 495.

voluntary disposition, however described, and if they attempt to do so, the disposition is ultra vires the company.

That case was followed by Oliver J in *Re Halt Garage* (*1964*) *Ltd* (**123**). In that case the liquidator of the company challenged payments of £30 a week purporting to be director's remuneration to a director and shareholder who had rendered no services to the company. Oliver J decided that so far as the payments exceeded £10 a week, which he considered to be the maximum remuneration reasonably payable to someone who merely held the office of director, they were dressed-up returns of capital to a shareholder and therefore ultra vires. The test, said the learned judge, was—

> whether the transaction in question was a genuine exercise of the power [to pay remuneration]. The motive is more important than the label. Those who deal with a limited company do so on the basis that its affairs will be conducted in accordance with its constitution, one of the express incidents of which is that the directors are entitled to be paid remuneration. Subject to that, they are entitled to have the capital kept intact. They have to accept the shareholders' assessment of the scale of that remuneration but they are entitled to assume that, whether liberal or illiberal, what is paid is genuinely remuneration and that the power is not used as a cloak for making payments out of capital to the shareholders as such . . .

So it seems to me in this case that looking at the matter objectively, the sale to Perion was not a genuine exercise of the company's power under its memorandum to sell its assets. It was a sale at a gross undervalue for the purpose of enabling a profit to be realised by an entity controlled and put forward by its sole beneficial shareholder. This was as much a dressed-up distribution as the payment of excessive interest in *Ridge Securities* or excessive remuneration in *Halt Garage*. The company had at the time no distributable reserves and the sale was therefore ultra vires and incapable of validation by the approval or ratification of the shareholder. The fact that the distribution was to Perion rather than to Dr Lee or his other entities which actually held the shares in Aveling Barford is in my judgment irrelevant . . .

Counsel for the defendants says that this was an act within the terms of the memorandum. It may have been a sale at an undervalue, but it was certainly a sale: a conveyance in exchange for a payment in money. It was not a sham. The terms of the transaction were in no way different from those appearing on the face of the documents. The purpose for which it was done was therefore irrelevant. Counsel submits that the test for the genuineness of the transaction proposed by Oliver J in *Re Halt Garage* admits by the back door all the questions about the motives, state of mind and knowledge of the company's directors which the Court of Appeal appeared to have expelled by the front door in the *Rolled Steel* case.

It is clear however that Slade LJ [in *Rolled Steel*] excepted from his general principle cases which he described as involving a 'fraud on creditors'. As an example of such a case, he cited *Re Halt Garage*. Counsel for the defendants said that frauds on creditors meant transactions entered into when the company was insolvent. In this case Aveling Barford was not at the relevant time insolvent. But I do not think that the phrase was intended to have such a narrow meaning. The rule that capital may not be returned to shareholders is a rule for the protection of creditors and the evasion of the rule falls within what I think Slade LJ had in mind when he spoke of a fraud on creditors. There is certainly nothing in his judgment to suggest that he disapproved of the actual decisions in *Re Halt Garage* or *Ridge Securities*. As for the transaction not being a sham, I accept that it was in law a sale. The false dressing it wore was that of a sale at arms' length or at market value. It was the fact that it was known and intended to be a sale at an undervalue which made it an unlawful distribution.

It follows that in my judgment even on the view of the facts most favourable to Perion, it has no arguable defence . . .

NOTES

(1) Although Hoffmann J several times described the transaction as ultra vires (and accordingly unratifiable), his remarks will continue to be valid and relevant despite the abolition of the ultra vires doctrine because of his ruling that the transaction was illegal as an unauthorised return of capital.
(2) In declining to make a distinction between Lee and his company Perion, Hoffmann J was 'lifting the veil', in circumstances somewhat similar to cases like *Jones v Lipman* (above, p 58).

CHAPTER 8

Borrowing, Debentures and Charges

A. Borrowing[1]

Like any other legal person, a company may borrow money, subject to any restrictions in its memorandum and articles of association.[2] There are, however, some special features of corporate borrowing which are worth noting.

(1) To raise very large sums of money, a company may wish to attract funds on the investment market, ie to borrow from very many lenders at once, or in sequence, all on the same terms. The mechanics of such a procedure are not greatly different from those involved in making an issue of shares, although in the result the investors will become a class of *creditors* rather than *members* of the company. The theoretical differences between being a creditor of a company and being a member are considerable, from a legal point of view, but (at least in the case of a solvent and prosperous company) the practical consequences for investors, apart sometimes from tax considerations, may be very similar.

(2) Where numerous investors advance money to a company in this way, it is usual for their rights to be regulated by a *trust deed,* under which trustees are appointed to represent the investors as a class vis-à-vis the company, and provision is made by the deed for their collective views to be ascertained by votes taken at meetings, with the usual apparatus of proxies, etc. Two basic arrangements are common. In the first, each investor lends to the company directly, and simultaneously agrees to be bound by the terms of the trust deed in his dealings with the company. In the second (which is the more usual form in modern practice), all the loans are funded and the aggregate sum is advanced to the company by the trustees, who alone stand in a contractual relationship with the company: each investor then subscribes for so much 'debenture stock' or 'loan stock' out of the fund. For an illustration of the former, see p 634.

(3) Where a company *charges* property to secure an obligation (not necessarily, of course, a borrowing obligation), the Companies Act requires that particulars of the charge be registered under the provisions of Pt XII, failing which the security will be for many (but not all) purposes void.

(4) A company has the ability, not enjoyed by an individual in English law, to create a 'floating charge' over assets such as stock-in-trade and book

---

1 RR Pennington, 'Loans to Companies: the Development of the Law' in *Company Law in Change* (1987), p 91.
2 A lender may, however, be protected from the effect of such restrictions by the internal management rule (above, pp 203 ff), by CA 1985, ss 35–35B, or by a provision in the articles.

debts, which may fluctuate from time to time, on terms that the company remains free to deal with them in the ordinary course of business.

(5) When a company makes default in any of its obligations under the document creating a charge, or when the security it has created is in jeopardy, the obligation is normally enforced by the appointment of a *receiver* to look after the creditor's interests.

(6) Borrowing transactions, and especially those secured by a floating charge, may raise special questions in a winding up.

NOTES

(1) It is apparent from the above discussion that an investment in debentures or debenture stock is very similar to an investment in shares: both are 'securities' in the corporate sector of the economy offering different kinds of risk and different kinds of return. Many companies have their debentures or debenture stock listed for dealing on The Stock Exchange. And these securities are transferred in the same way as shares, with companies maintaining registers of debentureholders alongside their registers of members.

(2) A company does not, however, have to issue documents in the nature of debentures—'securities' which can be bought and sold—when it raises money by borrowing. It may simply invite people to lend money to it on *deposit,* rather like a building society or savings bank does. A depositor is nothing more than an unsecured creditor, and has no real protection under the Companies Acts—e g an invitation to place money on deposit is not a prospectus within the statutory definition—and so special legislation had to be introduced, originally by the Protection of Depositors Act 1963 and more recently by the Banking Acts of 1979 and 1987, to regulate deposit-taking. There is now a system of licensing and control run by the Bank of England for this purpose.[3]

QUESTIONS

(1) List some of the points of similarity and difference between shareholders and debentureholders which follow from the fact that a shareholder is a *member*, while a debentureholder is a *creditor*, of the company. Think of:
   (a) the right to income;
   (b) application of the 'maintenance of capital' rules;
   (c) the right to return of capital during the lifetime of the company;
   (d) the right to return of capital in a liquidation;
   (e) taxation;
   (f) voting.
(2) Some of these points may be varied by the terms of issue of the share or debenture, e g a share *may* carry no vote, a debentureholder *may* be given a vote in some circumstances. Which of the points listed above may be varied in this way?

3 The Banking Act is primarily concerned with the protection of the general public. There are also 'wholesale markets' in which larger sums may be placed by banks and other institutions on both short-term and long-term deposit. These markets are separately supervised by the Bank of England under a system commonly referred to as the 'Grey Paper' regime.

B. Debentures[4]

Definition

Companies Act 1985
744   In this Act, unless the contrary intention appears, ... 'debenture' includes debenture stock, bonds and any other securities of a company, whether constituting a charge on the assets of the company or not.

185 Levy v Abercorris Slate and Slab Co (1887) 37 Ch D 260 (Chancery Division)

[The facts are immaterial.]

CHITTY J: In my opinion a debenture means a document which either creates a debt or acknowledges it, and any document which fulfils either of these conditions is a 'debenture'. I cannot find any precise legal definition of the term, it is not either in law or commerce a strictly technical term, or what is called a term of art.

An instrument may be a debenture although it is not under seal and gives no security for the company's obligation.

186 British India Steam Navigation Co v IRC (1881) 7 QBD 165 (Queen's Bench Division)

The company had issued instruments described on their face as 'debentures', by which the company undertook to pay the holder £100 on 30 November 1882, and to pay interest half-yearly at 5% per annum. It was argued unsuccessfully that the instruments, not being under seal, came within the definition of a promissory note and so did not attract the higher rate of stamp duty ordinarily payable on debentures.

LINDLEY J: Now, what the correct meaning of 'debenture' is I do not know. I do not find anywhere any precise definition of it. We know that there are various kinds of instruments commonly called debentures. You may have mortgage debentures, which are charges of some kind on property. You may have debentures which are bonds; and, if this instrument were under seal, it would be a debenture of that kind. You may have a debenture which is nothing more than an acknowledgement of indebtedness. And you may have a thing like this, which is something more; it is a statement by two directors that the company will pay a certain sum of money on a given day, and will also pay interest half-yearly at certain times and at a certain place, upon production of certain coupons by the holder of the instrument. I think any of these things which I have referred to may be debentures within the Act.

[His Lordship accordingly held that the instrument was a debenture and liable to be stamped as such.]

4 See generally W J Gough, *Company Charges* (London, 1978).

NOTE

It is established by these definitions that the term 'debenture' is capable in law of having a very wide meaning—simply a document evidencing a debt of any kind. But both in commercial usage and in the layman's understanding, it is commonly understood that the expression refers to a document evidencing some *secured* obligation, and so the rules of The Stock Exchange require that any issue of unsecured debentures be denominated 'unsecured', and indeed it is more common for the word to be avoided altogether in this situation and a term such as 'loan stock' or 'loan notes' used instead.

Debentures and debenture stock may be issued in bearer form, and may also be created on terms which make them negotiable instruments: *Bechuanaland Exploration Co v London Trading Bank* [1898] 2 QB 658. As regards convertible debentures, see above, p 347.

A mortgage of land granted by a company may be made irredeemable by virtue of s 193 of the Act.

187 Knightsbridge Estates Trust Ltd v Byrne [1940] AC 613, [1940] 2 All ER 401 (House of Lords)

The appellant company had mortgaged certain freehold properties to the Royal Liver Friendly Society to secure a loan of £310,000, which was to be repaid with interest by eighty half-yearly instalments. The House of Lords held that the combined effect of ss 74 and 380 of the Act of 1929 (corresponding to CA 1985, ss 193 and 744 [title 'debenture']) was to remove the application of the equitable doctrine of 'clogging' from mortgages given by companies; and so the appellant was not entitled to redeem the mortgage otherwise than by the agreed half-yearly instalments.

VISCOUNT MAUGHAM: My Lords, loans made to limited companies on the security of their assets are in general very different from loans made to individuals. Companies may be wound up, in which event their debts have, if possible, to be paid, but they do not die. To the knowledge of both the company and the lender the loan is intended in most cases to be of the nature of a permanent investment. The former can only in the rarest of circumstances be at the mercy of the latter. There is no likelihood of oppression being exerted against the company. Considerations such as these make it manifest that clauses in debentures issued by companies making them irredeemable or redeemable only after long periods of time or on contingencies ought to be given validity. It may be conceded that the ground for excluding the rule in equity is stronger in the case of a series of debentures issued in one of the usual forms than in the case of mortgages of land to an individual; but some of the reasons still remain. It is difficult to see any real unfairness in a normal commercial agreement between a company and (for example) an insurance society for a loan to the former on the security of its real estate for a very prolonged term of years. Both parties may be equally desirous that the mortgage may have the quality of permanence. There is a great deal to be said in such a case for freedom of contract.

LORD ROMER delivered a concurring opinion.

LORDS ATKIN, WRIGHT and PORTER concurred.

C. The floating charge

The floating charge allows a company to give security over its fluctuating assets, including property acquired after the creation of the charge, and to do so on terms that the assets may be dealt with by the company in the ordinary course of its business, free from any interference on the part of the charge-holder. It is an invention of the equity draftsmen in the latter part of last century.

It is not possible in English law[5] for individual borrowers to give a floating charge over their assets, because to do so would infringe the Bills of Sale Acts of 1878 and 1882 (and in particular it would be impossible to meet the requirement that the goods affected be specifically described in a schedule to the instrument)[6]. But these Acts do not apply to a company, and so the way was clear for the draftsmen to work out the details of the floating charge, but only for the corporate borrower.

In many businesses, fluctuating assets such as stock-in-trade, raw materials and book debts may be quite a significant part of the property of the concern, and be the only worthwhile security available for an advance. The proprietors of an unincorporated business which is in need of finance may find themselves advised that they have to form a company if they are to raise the loans they are seeking: hence the ability to give a floating charge can be an important consideration in deciding whether or not to trade in the corporate form. Banks, in particular, have wide experience of the floating charge and encourage its use by their clients.

The essential characteristics (if not a complete definition[7]) of the floating charge appear from the cases which follow. For an example of a debenture creating a floating charge, see below, p 635.

188 Governments Stock and Other Securities Investment Co v Manila Rly Co
[1897] AC 81 (House of Lords)

[The facts are immaterial.]

LORD MACNAGHTEN: A floating security is an equitable charge on the assets for the time being of a going concern. It attaches to the subject charged in the varying condition in which it happens to be from time to time. It is of the essence of such a charge that it remains dormant until the undertaking charged ceases to be a going concern, or until the person in whose favour the charge is created intervenes. His right to intervene may of course be suspended by agreement. But if there is no agreement for suspension, he may exercise his right whenever he pleases after default ...

---

5 An individual trader may create a floating charge in New Zealand; and the Cork Committee recommended that it should be made possible here: see Cmnd 8558 (1982), para 1569.
6 There was formerly also the possibility that the security might prove to be ineffective under the Bankruptcy Act 1914, s 38(1)(c), the 'reputed ownership' provision, which applied in the bankruptcy of individuals but not the insolvency of companies. The 'reputed ownership' provision was repealed by the Insolvency Act 1985.
7 The statutory definition in CA 1985, ss 744 and 462, throws light only on the position in Scots law. For the purposes of IA 1986, see the definition cited and discussed below, p 403.

189 Illingworth v Houldsworth [1904] AC 355 (House of Lords)

[The facts are immaterial.]

LORD MACNAGHTEN: With regard to the criticism which Vaughan Williams LJ passed, not I think unkindly, on some words of mine in the *Manila* case (**188**), I only wish to observe that what I said was intended as a description, not as a definition, of a floating security. I should have thought there was not much difficulty in defining what a floating charge is in contrast to what is called a specific charge. A specific charge, I think, is one that without more fastens on ascertained and definite property or property capable of being ascertained and defined; a floating charge, on the other hand, is ambulatory and shifting in its nature, hovering over and so to speak floating with the property which it is intended to affect until some event occurs or some act is done which causes it to settle and fasten on the subject of the charge within its reach and grasp . . .

[Parts of the judgments of the members of the Court of Appeal in this case, reported sub nom *Re Yorkshire Woolcombers Association Ltd* [1903] 2 Ch 284, are cited by Slade J in *Re Bond Worth Ltd* (**190**).]

190 Re Bond Worth Ltd [1980] Ch 228, [1979] 3 All ER 919 (Chancery Division)

This case concerned an attempt to draft a 'retention of title' (or *Romalpa*) clause (see below, (**200**)) which proved to be unsuccessful. 'Acrilan' fibre was supplied by Monsanto to Bond Worth for use in the manufacture of carpets. The sale agreement provided that 'equitable and beneficial ownership' of the fibre should remain with the sellers until payment of the price was received 'or until prior resale, in which case our beneficial ownership shall attach to the proceeds of resale'. Another clause stipulated that the suppliers should have 'the equitable and beneficial ownership' in any products made out of the fibre. Slade J held that the document created a floating charge, and that as such it was void for non-registration. (On this topic, see below, p 409.)

SLADE J: I turn to consider the relevant contracts. In my judgment at least the following points are fairly clear:

(1) They were absolute contracts for the sale of goods within the meaning of s 1(2) of the Sale of Goods Act [1979], though this is not to say that they did not comprise other features in addition.

(2) The legal title or property in the Acrilan fibre comprised in any one of the contracts passed to Bond Worth when the fibre was delivered to Bond Worth: see s 18, r 1 of the Sale of Goods Act [1979]. In using the term 'property' in this context I refer to the general property in the goods (which is the definition given to the word in s 62(1) of that Act) and not merely a special property, such as that possessed by a bailee.

(3) The risk in the goods likewise passed to Bond Worth on delivery. This followed not only from s 20 of the Sale of Goods Act [1979], but also from the opening words of sub-clause (a) of the retention of title clause. Thus if, after delivery, the goods had been stolen or destroyed before Bond Worth had had the opportunity to use them in any way, Bond Worth would nevertheless have had to pay the full purchase price for them.

(4) Though sub-clause (a) of the retention of title clause provided that 'equitable and beneficial ownership' in the goods would remain with Monsanto until full payment for the whole amount of the relevant order had been received or until prior resale, it was manifestly not the intention to confer on or reserve to Monsanto all the rights which would normally be enjoyed by a sui juris person, having the sole beneficial title to property, as against the trustee holding the legal title. Mr Sears, on behalf of Monsanto, expressly conceded and affirmed that Monsanto would not, by virtue of its so called 'equitable and beneficial ownership', have had the right to call for re-delivery of the goods, at any rate so long as Bond Worth was not in default under its payments. Bond Worth, on the other hand, was to have far-reaching rights even before payment to deal with the goods, which would not normally be possessed by a trustee holding the legal title therein on behalf of one sole, sui juris beneficiary.

(5) Even during the period before full payment had been received by Monsanto and notwithstanding the provisions relating to 'equitable and beneficial ownership', Bond Worth were to be at liberty to sell all or any part of the goods and to transfer the property therein to a purchaser. The words 'until prior resale', in sub-clause (a) of the retention of title clause, render the implication of such authority to resell inevitable. They go far beyond the provisions of s 25(1) of the Sale of Goods Act [1979] which empower a buyer of goods in possession after sale in some circumstances, even without the authority of his vendor, to resell and pass a good title to a purchaser on a resale, but confer no authority on him to effect such resale, as between him and his vendor.

(6) The parties nevertheless intended that if Bond Worth were to resell all or any part of the goods at a time when Monsanto had not yet been paid the full price due under the order, Monsanto's 'equitable and beneficial ownership', whatever that meant, would attach to the proceeds of sale or to the claim for such proceeds.

(7) Even during the period before full payment had been received by Monsanto and notwithstanding the provisions relating to 'equitable and beneficial ownership', Bond Worth were to be at liberty to use the goods for the purposes of manufacture ...

(8) The parties nevertheless intended that if, by virtue of such last-mentioned use, the goods should become constituents of or be converted into other products, the retention of title clause should attach to such other products as if they had been the original subject-matter of the sale ...

Thus far, the position would seem to me reasonably clear. The real difficulty arises concerning the meaning and legal effect, if any, of the provisions in the retention of title clause concerning 'equitable and beneficial ownership'. If the contracts embody something more than a mere sale, what is this additional feature? What is the nature of the relationship beyond a mere vendor-purchaser relationship between Monsanto and Bond Worth that comes into existence by virtue of the provisions relating to 'equitable and beneficial ownership'?

In *Aluminium Industrie Vaassen BV v Romalpa Aluminium Ltd* (**200**), to which I shall have to refer in greater detail later, it was expressly admitted that the retention of title clause had the effect of making the defendants *bailees* of the relevant goods while in their possession until all money owing had been paid. On the different facts of the present case, however, there can be no question of a bailor-bailee relationship, since it is common ground that the property in the Acrilan fibre passed to Bond Worth at latest when it was delivered, while it is of the essence of a bailment that the general property in the goods concerned remains in the bailor, while only a special property passes to the bailee, which entitles him to exercise certain possessory remedies. Nor can the relationship be one of agency, since the documents contain no suggestion that Bond Worth is to be regarded as an agent and the rights which by necessary implication are given it to deal with the goods on its own behalf are quite inconsistent with a principal-agent relationship.

In these circumstances, I think it plain that, if the retention of title clause operated to create any effective rights at all for the benefit of Monsanto, such rights can only have been rights either (i) by way of a trust under which Monsanto was the sole beneficiary or (ii) by way of a trust under which Monsanto had a charge in equity over the relevant assets to secure payment of the unpaid purchase price. No possible third alternative has occurred to me.

[His Lordship examined the authorities and continued:]

The implicit authority and freedom of Bond Worth to employ the relevant raw materials, products and other moneys as it pleased and for its own purposes during the subsistence of the operation of the retention of title clause were in my judgment quite incompatible with the existence of a relationship of Bond Worth as trustee and Monsanto as beneficiary solely and absolutely entitled to such assets, which is the relationship asserted.

I have, however, already indicated that this is not my own view of the effect, if any, of the retention of title clause when properly construed, but that such effect, if any, is a declaration of trust by Bond Worth in respect of the relevant assets by way of equitable charge to secure repayment of the moneys from time to time owing in respect of the relevant order. Does the authority and freedom of Bond Worth, to which I have last referred, by itself negative the existence of a valid trust by way of equitable charge? In my judgment, in so far as it might be suggested that the clause operated to create in this manner an immediate *specific* charge, the answer to this question must be 'yes'. It is in my judgment quite incompatible with the existence of an effective trust by way of specific charge in equity over specific assets that the alleged trustee should be free to use them as he pleases for his own benefit in the course of his own business.

There is, however, one type of charge (and I think one type only) which, by its very nature, leaves a company at liberty to deal with the assets charged in the ordinary course of its business, without regard to the charge, until stopped by a winding up or by the appointment of a receiver or the happening of some other agreed event. I refer to what is commonly known as a 'floating charge' ... Such a charge remains unattached to any particular property and leaves the company with a licence to deal with, and even sell, the assets falling within its ambit in the ordinary course of business, as if the charge had not been given, until it is stopped by one or other of the events to which I have referred, when it is said to 'crystallise'; it then becomes effectively fixed to the assets within its scope.

Romer LJ in *Re Yorkshire Woolcombers Association Ltd*[8] gave the following description of a floating charge:

8 [1903] 2 Ch 284 at 295 (affd sub nom *Illingworth v Houldsworth* (**189**)).

I certainly do not intend to attempt to give an exact definition of the term 'floating charge' nor am I prepared to say that there will not be a floating charge within the meaning of the Act, which does not contain all of the three characteristics that I am about to mention, but I certainly think that if a charge has the three characteristics that I am about to mention, it is a floating charge. (1) If it is a charge on a class of assets of a company present and future; (2) if that class is one which, in the ordinary course of the business of the company, would be changing from time to time; and (3) if you find that by the charge it is contemplated that, until some future step is taken by or on behalf of those interested in the charge, the company may carry on its business in the ordinary way as far as concerns the particular class of assets I am dealing with.

This description of a floating charge shows that it need not extend to all the assets of the company. It may cover assets merely of a specified category or categories. The third characteristic mentioned by Romer LJ is clearly present in relation to each of the four categories of charged assets in the present case; it was clearly contemplated that until some future step was taken by or on behalf of Monsanto, Bond Worth might carry on its business in the ordinary way in relation to each of these four categories. The second characteristic mentioned by him is likewise clearly present at least in relation to each of the second, third and fourth categories of charged assets; these are ex hypothesi classes of assets which in the ordinary course of business will be changing from time to time.

This much could be said against the existence of floating charges in the present case. As regards the first characteristic mentioned by Romer LJ, the charge on the first category of charged assets is exclusively a charge on present assets of the company, while the charges on the other three categories of charged assets are exclusively charges on future assets of the company. If the charges are looked at separately, they do not comprise classes of mixed present and future assets. Furthermore, the second characteristic mentioned by him is present in relation to the first category of charged assets (the raw fibre) only in the sense that the assets comprised in this category may diminish by being used for the purposes of manufacture or sale; they cannot be increased. I do not, however, think that these points of possible distinction prevent all or any of the four relevant charges from being floating charges within the ordinary meaning of legal terminology. Romer LJ himself disclaimed any intention of saying that there could not be a floating charge within the meaning of the Companies Acts which did not contain all the three characteristics that he mentioned.

The critical distinction in my judgment is that between a specific charge on the one hand and a floating charge on the other. Vaughan Williams LJ pointed out in the *Woolcombers* case that it is quite inconsistent with the nature of a specific charge, though not of a floating charge, that the mortagor is at liberty to deal with the relevant property as he pleases. He said, at p 294:

> I do not think that for a 'specific security' you need have a security of a subject matter which is then in existence. I mean by 'then' at the time of the execution of the security; but what you do require to make a specific security is that the security whenever it has once come into existence, and been identified or appropriated as a security, shall never thereafter at the will of the mortgagor cease to be a security. If at the will of the mortgagor he can dispose of it and prevent its being any

longer a security, although something else may be substituted more or less for it, that is not a 'specific security'.

When that case went on appeal to the House of Lords, under the name *Illingworth v Houldsworth* Lord Macnaghten drew the distinction between a specific charge and a floating charge in the following terms:

[His Lordship quoted the passage cited above (**189**), and continued]:

In the present case, in my judgment, the respective charges on each of the four categories of charged assets were ambulatory and shifting in their nature, and were intended to hover over them until the happening of an event which caused them to crystallise. The assets comprised in each of the four categories were of a fluctuating class, albeit in the case of the first category liable to fluctuate only by diminution. Until a crystallising event occurred, it was clearly not intended that any restriction should be placed on Bond Worth to deal with them in the ordinary course of its business.

Accordingly in the end I answer [the] question by saying that in my judgment the effect of the retention of title clause was to create floating equitable charges over the four categories of charged assets, for the purpose of securing payment of the purchase prices due under the relevant orders, and to constitute Bond Worth a trustee of such assets for the purpose of such security ...

A fixed charge may be created over future book debts.

191 Siebe Gorman & Co Ltd v Barclays Bank Ltd [1979] 2 Lloyd's Rep 142 (Chancery Division)

In 1971, R H McDonald Ltd executed a debenture in favour of Barclays Bank, secured by charges over various categories of property listed in clause 3 of the debenture. Clause 3 read:

The Company as beneficial owner hereby charges with the payment or discharge of all monies and liabilities hereby covenanted to be paid or discharged by the Company: . . . (d) by way of first fixed charge all book debts and other debts now and from time to time due or owing to the Company.

Clause 5 provided: . . . During the continuance of this security the Company . . . (c) shall pay into the Company's account with the Bank all monies which it may receive in respect of the book debts and other debts hereby charged and shall not without the prior consent of the Bank in writing purport to charge or assign the same in favour of any other person and shall if called upon to do so by the Bank execute a legal assignment of such book debts and other debts to the Bank.

Slade J held that a fixed charge had been created.

SLADE J: [If] I had accepted the premise that R H McDonald Ltd would have had the unrestricted right to deal with the proceeds of any of the relevant book debts paid into its account, so long as that account remained in credit, I would have been inclined to accept the conclusion that the charge on such book debts could be no more than a floating charge. I refer to the respective definitions of a floating charge and a specific charge given by Lord Macnaghten in *Illingworth v Holdsworth* (**189**) ...

If the debenture on its true construction had given the bank no rights whatsoever, at a time when the account of R H McDonald Ltd was in credit, to prevent the company from spending in the ordinary course of business all or any of the proceeds of book debts paid into its account, I would have been inclined to regard the charge, for all the wording of the debenture, as doing no more than 'hovering over and so to speak floating with' the book debts, within the words of Lord Macnaghten. Such, I would conceive, is the effect of a charge on future book debts in the form more usually employed. Commonly it is intended, by both creditor and debtor, that the debtor shall have the free disposal of the proceeds of future book debts which may come into his hands, so long as the creditor takes no steps to enforce his security, or the charge has not otherwise crystallised.

In my judgment, however, it is perfectly possible in law for a mortgagor, by way of continuing security for future advances, to grant to a mortgagee a charge on future book debts in a form which creates in equity a specific charge on the proceeds of such debts as soon as they are received and consequently prevents the mortgagor from disposing of an unencumbered title to the subject-matter of such charge without the mortgagee's consent, even before the mortgagee has taken steps to enforce its security ... This in my judgment was the effect of the debenture in the present case. I see no reason why the court should not give effect to the intention of the parties, as stated in cl 3(d), that the charge should be a first fixed charge on book debts. I do not accept the argument that the provisions of cl 5(c) negative the existence of a specific charge. All that they do, in my judgment, is to reinforce the specific charge given by cl 3. The mere fact that there may exist certain forms of dealing with book debts which are not specifically prohibited by cl 5(c) does not in my judgment turn the specific charge into a floating charge.

NOTE

In the Irish case *Re Armagh Shoes Ltd* [1984] BCLC 405, Hutton J held that the fact that a document by its express words purports to create a fixed or specific charge does not prevent the court from construing the charge as a floating one. The learned judge in that case was also prepared to infer from the terms of the charge as a whole that the company had a licence to deal with the assets charged in the ordinary course of its business, even though this was not stated.

Conversely, in *Re Brightlife Ltd* [1987] Ch 200, [1986] 3 All ER 673, Hoffmann J held that a charge over book debts which was expressed to be a fixed charge was in reality a floating charge. He said (at 209, 676–677):

> Although clause 3(A)(ii)(a) speaks of a 'first specific charge' over the book debts and other debts, the rights over the debts created by the debenture were in my judgment such as to be categorised in law as a floating charge ...
>
> It is true that clause 5(ii) does not allow Brightlife to sell, factor or discount debts without the written consent of Norandex [the debenture-holder]. But a floating charge is consistent with some restriction upon the company's freedom to deal with its assets. For example, floating charges commonly contain a prohibition upon the creation of other charges ranking prior to or pari passu with the floating charge. Such dealings would otherwise be open to a company in the ordinary course of its business. In this debenture, the significant feature is that Brightlife was free to collect its debts and pay the proceeds into its bank account. Once in the account, they would be outside the charge over debts and at the free disposal of the company. In my judgment a right to deal in this way with the charged assets for its own account is a badge of a floating charge and is inconsistent with a fixed charge.

QUESTION

In the light of the judgments in *Bond Worth* and *Siebe Gorman,* do the passages cited
from the judgments of Lord Macnaghten in *Governments Stock* (**188**) and *Illingworth*
(**189**) accurately state the modern law?

*A company may lawfully give security over its 'undertaking', charging all its
property both present and future.*

192 Re Panama, New Zealand and Australian Royal Mail Co (1870) 5 Ch
App 318 (Court of Appeal in Chancery)

By this decision, the validity of the floating charge was established. The
question was whether the debentures given by the company were effective to
give the holders a charge upon the proceeds of sale of the company's ships
and other assets, in priority to the claims of its general creditors, in the
winding up. The court held that they were.

The debentures were in the following form:

'The Panama, New Zealand, and Australian Mail Company, Ltd
Mortgage Debenture.

No 404   £100
    By virtue of the powers contained in our articles of association we,
the Panama, New Zealand, and Australian Royal Mail Company,
Limited, in consideration of the sum of £100 paid to us by J E Naylor,
of, etc, and the Rev T H Stokoe of, etc, are held firmly bound, and
do hereby for ourselves, our successors and assigns, charge the said
undertaking, and all sums of money arising therefrom, and all the estate,
right, title, and interest of the company therein, with the payment to the
said J E Naylor and T H Stokoe, their executors, administrators, or
assigns, of the said sum of £100, together with interest for the same at
the rate of £6 per cent by the year, the principal sum to be repaid on the
2nd January 1870, and the interest to be payable in the meantime half-
yearly, on the 1st of January and the 1st of July each year, until the
repayment thereof. Given under our common seal.'

GIFFARD LJ: This is an appeal from an order of Vice-Chancellor Malins by
which he has declared that the mortgage debentures issued under the seal of
the company are a charge upon the proceeds of the sale of the vessels and
other property of the company ...
    What I have to decide in the present case is simply this: What are the rights
of the debentureholders, the state of things being that the concern is being
wound up, and that the whole of its property is being realised? I confess that
I can have no doubt whatever as to what the effect of the debenture is. In
the first place, as regards the powers that were given to the company, there
was a power given to mortgage, and a power given to raise money by
debentures; but, of course, they might include in one and the same instrument
a mortgage and a debenture, that is to say, a mortgage and a bond. Accordingly they did issue what they called a mortgage debenture, which was, in
substance, a bond, and a charge upon their property for the sum borrowed
on bond. The form of the instrument is not an assignment but a charge; the
company charge the undertaking, and all sums of money arising therefrom,

and all estate, right, title and interest of the company therein, with payment of the principal sum and interest. I asked in the course of the argument what could be the subject-matter of that charge, and the answer given was, that there were valuable contracts, and that all that the charge was meant to cover was the income arising from the business being carried on, and that it would not extend to property, such as the ships and other property of that nature, which were absolutely essential to the carrying on of the concern. I cannot accede to any such proposition as that. I have no hesitation in saying that in this particular case, and having regard to the state of this particular company, the word 'undertaking' had reference to all the property of the company, not only which existed at the date of the debenture, but which might afterwards become the property of the company. And I take the object and meaning of the debenture to be this, that the word 'undertaking' necessarily infers that the company will go on, and that the debentureholder could not interfere until either the interest which was due was unpaid, or until the period had arrived for the payment of his principal, and that principal was unpaid. I think the meaning and object of the security was this, that the company might go on during that interval, and, furthermore, that during the interval the debentureholder would not be entitled to any account of mesne profits, or of any dealing with the property of the company in the ordinary course of carrying on their business. I do not refer to such things as sales or mortgages of property, but to the ordinary application of funds which came into the hands of the company in the usual course of business. I see no difficulty or inconvenience in giving that effect to this instrument. But the moment the company comes to be wound up, and the property has to be realised, that moment the rights of these parties, beyond all question, attach. My opinion is, that even if the company had not stopped the debentureholders might have filed a bill to realise their security. I hold that under these debentures they have a charge upon all property of the company, past and future, by the term 'undertaking', and that they stand in a position superior to that of the general creditors, who can touch nothing until they are paid. The appeal, therefore, must be dismissed with costs.

NOTE

It is clear from the cases above that a vital feature of the floating charge is that it authorises the company to deal with those assets in the ordinary course of business. It follows that the company may not only sell and buy such property during the currency of a floating charge, but—at least where the charge is expressed in conventional terms—may also create mortgages and charges, ranking in priority to the floating charge itself. Even where, by what is commonly termed a 'negative pledge clause', the creation of later charges is forbidden by the terms of the original charge, the claim of a subsequent debentureholder will prevail if he took the charge without notice of the earlier security. A floating charge is also vulnerable to set-offs and other claims arising in favour of unsecured creditors while the company's power to trade continues.

As Lord Macnaghten explains in the passages cited above (**188**) (**189**), in certain events—which are examined more particularly below, pp 395 ff—a floating charge will 'crystallise'. (We must ignore the mixed metaphor, which has been hallowed by a century's use.) On crystallisation, the charge becomes a fixed charge attaching to the company's assets at that point of time, and the company's freedom to trade and to incur cross-claims ceases; but until then, the security is subject to all the risks to which the assets may be exposed in the ordinary course of business.

A fixed charge may be created having priority over an earlier floating charge.

193 Re Castell & Brown Ltd [1898] 1 Ch 315 (Chancery Division)

In 1885, the company issued a series of debentures secured by a floating charge. The title deeds of various properties, which had been left in the possession of the company, were later deposited with the company's bank to secure an overdraft. The bank's charge was held to have priority over the earlier debentures.[9]

ROMER J: In the first place, I cannot hold that there was any negligence on the part of the bank. When making its advances to Castell & Brown Ltd (which I will hereafter call the company), it found the company in possession of the deeds in question, and apparently able, as unincumbered owner, to charge the property. The company purported as such unincumbered owner to give a charge to the bank, and I think the bank was, under the circumstances, entitled to rely upon obtaining a charge free from incumbrance. It is suggested on behalf of the debentureholders that the bank ought to have made some special inquiries of the company. But it is not suggested that the bank wilfully abstained from making inquiries, and as the bank had no reason to suppose that the company was not fully able to give a valid first charge, and found the company in possession of the deeds, which showed no incumbrance, I think the bank was not bound to make any special inquiry ...

And I now look to see how it was that the company retained possession of the deeds notwithstanding the issue of the debentures. The reason appears to me obvious. The debentures were only intended to give what is called a floating charge, that is to say, it was intended, notwithstanding the debentures, that the company should have power, so long as it was a going concern, to deal with its property as absolute owner. And I infer it was on this account that the company was allowed to, and did, retain possession of the deeds. In other words, the debentureholders, notwithstanding their charge, and indeed by its very terms, authorised their mortgagor, the company, to deal with its property as if it had not been incumbered, and left with their mortgagor the deeds in order to enable the company to act as owner.

A floating charge does not operate as an assignment to the debentureholder of the company's book-debts and other choses in action. Until the charge has crystallised, the company's unsecured creditors may set off debts due by the company against sums which they owe to it.

194 Biggerstaff v Rowatt's Wharf Ltd [1896] 2 Ch 93 (Court of Appeal)

[For another part of the decision in this case, see (**111**).]

The respondent company had, to the knowledge of Harvey Brand & Co, issued debentures secured by a floating charge. A receiver was appointed in

---

9 The debentures in this case contained a provision that the company was not to be at liberty to create any mortgage or charge having priority to the floating charge, but the bank had no knowledge or notice of this 'negative pledge' provision, and so was held not to have been affected by it. Under Pt XII of CA 1985 (as amended) the position would now be different, since the 'prescribed particulars' of which the bank would be deemed to have notice (s 416) include particulars of such a clause (s 415(2)(a)).

a debentureholders' action on 30 October 1894. On this date Harvey Brand & Co owed the respondent a liquidated sum for rent, while Harvey Brand & Co had a cross-claim against it for the price of 4,000 barrels at 3s 6d [17½p] each. Harvey Brand & Co were held entitled to set off their claim, on the ground that there had been no assignment of the respondent company's property to the debentureholders prior to the appointment of the receiver, so that Harvey Brand & Co had the earlier equity.

LOPES LJ: In the present case I think that Harvey, Brand & Co could sue for money had and received ... There is a total failure of consideration as regards the barrels not delivered, and the demand is a liquidated demand which can be set off against the rent.

But it is said that there is no right of set-off against an assignee of a chose in action where the person claiming the set-off had notice of the assignment when the debt due to him was contracted. That is quite true in ordinary cases; but a debenture differs from an ordinary assignment. If this doctrine were applied to debentures, no creditor of a company could ever get the benefit of a set-off where debentures had been issued. Now, it is the essence of a floating security that it allows the company to carry on business in its ordinary way until a receiver is appointed; and it would paralyse the business of companies to give to the issuing of debentures the effect now contended for. I am of opinion, therefore, that the set-off must be allowed ...

KAY LJ: It is true that as against an assignee there can be no set-off of a debt accrued after the person claiming set-off has notice of the assignment. But does that apply to debentures such as these? Counsel hesitated to go so far as that, but said that there was no right of set-off, as no action had been brought in which it could have been asserted before 30 October 1894. I think that is not so. I think that if at the time of the assignment there was an inchoate right to set-off it can be asserted after the assignment, for the assignment is subject to the rights then in existence. The question is whether the assignment took place at the issue of the debentures or at the appointment of a receiver. The debentures contain provisions the effect of which is that the company is at liberty to go on with its business as if the debentures did not exist, until possession is taken under them. From that time the company cannot deal with its assets as against the title of the debentureholders; up to that time it can deal with them in every legitimate way of business. Therefore the date to be regarded is the time of taking possession. A conclusion that set-off could not arise during the period before taking possession would be injurious to debentureholders, for it would hamper the company in carrying on its business, and so injure the debentureholders, whose interest is that the company should carry on a prosperous business. There was an inchoate right of set-off at the time when the receiver was appointed; and that, and not the time of issuing the debentures, is the time to be looked to. The debentures must be regarded as incomplete assignments which do not become complete until the time when the receiver is appointed ...

LINDLEY LJ delivered a concurring judgment.

Crystallisation of a floating charge

A floating charge will crystallise, and become a fixed charge attaching to the assets of the company at that time, (i) when a receiver is appointed; (ii) when the company goes into liquidation (since the licence to deal with the assets in the ordinary course of business will then necessarily terminate); (iii) when the company ceases to carry on business (**195**); (iv) in the case where the debenture empowers the charge-holder to convert the floating charge into a fixed charge by giving the company 'notice of conversion', and such a notice is given (**195**); and (v) where an event occurs which under the terms of the debenture causes 'automatic' crystallisation. This depends upon there being a provision in the document creating the charge which states that the charge will crystallise on the happening of some particular event—e g if a creditor of the company levies execution against its property, or if the company gives security over assets covered by the charge to a third party without the charge-holder's consent. There has been much controversy over automatic crystallisation clauses, both as to their legality and as to whether, as a matter of policy, their use should be prohibited or subjected to restrictions by law. Of course, it is reasonable to provide that the charge-holder shall have the right to *appoint a receiver* in such an event, since this is an overt act of which everyone can be aware; but the position is different where crystallisation is automatic, since this can take place without any act on the part of anyone. There are two schools of thought on the question. One takes the view that the floating charge is not an established phenomenon having fixed characteristics, but is simply the creature of the draftsman and that a creditor is free to strengthen his security in this way if he wants to. The other looks at the effect of such an arrangement on third parties and contends that it must be against public policy to have a charge crystallise in circumstances which may be unknown (and perhaps even unknowable) at the time, so that a company could not give a buyer a good title even though everyone was acting in good faith. (This is, however, pressing the argument too far, for the company would have ostensible authority to continue to deal with its property in such circumstances.[10]) There is clear authority upholding the effectiveness of an automatic crystallisation clause in New Zealand: *Re Manurewa Transport Ltd* [1971] NZLR 909. In the Australian decision *Stein v Saywell* (1969) 121 CLR 529, [1969] ALR 481, the High Court was divided in its opinion. In Canada, opposition to automatic crystallisation clauses can be found in *R v Consolidated Churchill Copper Corpn Ltd* [1978] 5 WWR 652. In *Re Woodroffes* (*Musical Instruments*) *Ltd* (**195**), Nourse J expressed the view, obiter, that 'the general body of informed opinion is of the view that automatic crystallisation is undesirable'. This may be contrasted with the remarks, also obiter, of Hoffmann J in *Re Brightlife Ltd* [1987] Ch 200 at 214–215, [1986] 3 All ER 673 at 680–681.[11] He said:

> [Counsel] said that public policy required restrictions upon what the parties could stipulate as crystallising events. A winding up or the appointment of a receiver would have to be noted on the register. But a notice [of conversion] need not be registered and a provision for automatic crystallisation might take effect without the knowledge of either the company or the debentureholder. The result might be prejudicial to third parties who gave credit to the company. Considerations of this kind impressed Berger J in the Canadian case of *R v Consolidated*

---

10 Goode, *Commercial Law* (London, 1982) at 799.
11 Hoffmann J reasserted this view in *Re Permanent Houses* (*Holdings*) *Ltd* [1988] BCLC 563 at 567: 'provided the language of the debentures was sufficiently clear, there was no conceptual reason why the parties should not agree that any specified event should cause the charge to crystallise'.

Churchill Copper Corpn Ltd[12] where the concept of 'self-generating crystallisation' was rejected.

I do not think that it is open to the courts to restrict the contractual freedom of parties to a floating charge on such grounds. The floating charge was invented by Victorian lawyers to enable manufacturing and trading companies to raise loan capital on debentures. It could offer the security of a charge over the whole of the company's undertaking without inhibiting its ability to trade. But the mirror image of these advantages was the potential prejudice to the general body of creditors, who might know nothing of the floating charge but find that all the company's assets, including the very goods which they had just delivered on credit, had been swept up by the debentureholder. The public interest requires a balancing of the advantages to the economy of facilitating the borrowing of money against the possibility of injustice to unsecured creditors. These arguments for and against the floating charge are matters for Parliament rather than the courts and have been the subject of public debate in and out of Parliament for more than a century.

Parliament has responded, first, by restricting the rights of the holder of a floating charge and secondly, by requiring public notice of the existence and enforcement of the charge. For example, priority was given to preferential debts in 1897 and the Companies Act 1907 invalidated floating charges created within three months before the commencement of the winding up. This period has since been extended and is now one year. The registration of floating and other charges was introduced by the Companies Act 1900. The Companies Act 1907 required registration of the appointment of a receiver and the Companies Act 1929 required notice of such appointment to be given on the company's letters and invoices.

These limited and pragmatic interventions by the legislature make it in my judgment wholly inappropriate for the courts to impose additional restrictive rules on grounds of public policy. It is certainly not for a judge of first instance to proclaim a new head of public policy which no appellate court has even hinted at before. I would therefore respectfully prefer the decision of the New Zealand Supreme Court in *Re Manurewa Transport Ltd*,[13] recognising the validity of a provision for automatic crystallisation, to the contrary dicta in the Canadian case I have cited.

The Cork Committee (1982, Cmnd 8558, paras 1578–79) considered that automatic crystallisation was 'not merely inconvenient', but that there was 'no place for it in a modern insolvency law'. The Committee recommended that the circumstances in which a floating charge crystallised should be defined by statute, and that all other ways (including automatic crystallisation) should be banned. But Parliament appears to have decided that automatic crystallisation should be allowed to stay, subject to safeguards which should remove any risks flowing from the possibility that it may occur without the knowledge of one or more of the parties concerned. Under s 410(3) of CA 1985, as amended, the Secretary of State is empowered to make regulations requiring registration of an event causing a floating charge to crystallise, and it is contemplated that the regulations will declare ineffective such a crystallising event until registration has been effected.

12 [1978] 5 WWR 652.
13 [1971] NZLR 909.

charge was unknown in Scots common law, as was the eceivership. Legislation making both possible was passed in (see now Pt XVIII of the CA 1985 and IA 1986, ss 50–71). y provisions do not allow for automatic crystallisation in

A floating charge crystallises when the company ceases to carry on business.

195 Re Woodroffes (Musical Instruments) Ltd [1986] Ch 366, [1985] 2 All ER 908 (Chancery Division)

The company had given a first floating charge to its bank and a second floating charge to Mrs Woodroffe. A provision in the latter instrument empowered Mrs Woodroffe by giving notice to the company to convert the charge into a fixed charge, and this she did on 27 August 1982. The bank appointed receivers on 1 September 1982. In this action, which was brought to establish the priorities as between the two debentureholders and the company's other creditors, Nourse J held that Mrs Woodroffe's notice did not have the effect of crystallising the bank's charge, as well as her own, on 27 August. He also ruled that the bank's charge would have crystallised if the company had ceased to carry on business at any time between 27 August and 1 September, but that there was no sufficient evidence that this had happened.

NOURSE J: On what date did the bank's floating charge crystallise? Mr Jarvis, for the bank, supported by Mr Marks, for Mrs Woodroffe, arguing in favour of 27 August, submit in the first instance that the effect of Mrs Woodroffe's notice of conversion was to crystallise not only her own charge, but also the bank's. They say that the notice, by determining Mrs Woodroffe's licence to the company to employ the assets subject to the charge in the ordinary course of its business, rendered any further use of those assets unlawful and impracticable, with the result that the company's business must be taken to have ceased at that time. Consequently, they submit that there was a crystallisation of both charges.

I find myself quite unable to accept that submission, which appears to me to run contrary to fundamental principles of the law of contract. I do not see how the determination of Mrs Woodroffe's licence can in some way work a determination of the bank's, or produce the effect that the bank has had its charge crystallised over its head and possibly contrary to its own wishes. The relationship between the company and the bank was governed by the [bank's] debenture, which, although it contained a prohibition against creating any subsequent charge without consent—see clause 5—did not provide for the bank's floating charge to crystallise either on the creation or crystallisation of a subsequent charge.

On analysis it appears to me that the arguments of Mr Jarvis on this point are founded, and can only be founded, on an implied term in the [bank's] debenture ... It does not seem to me to be at all clear that a term to the effect contended for by Mr Jarvis must be implied. Why should it be assumed that the bank and the company, in particular the bank, intended that the crystallisation of a subsequent charge should in all circumstances cause a crystallisation of the bank's? No doubt it might suit the bank's interests in the great majority of circumstances, but that does not mean that it can be assumed in all. For example, the bank might have taken the view that it was in its own interests that the business of the company should continue. Unless Mrs Woodroffe had either appointed her own receiver, or had applied for an injunction restraining it from dealing with its assets in contravention of her own fixed charge, I can see no reason why the company could not have continued to carry on its business. True it could only have done so in breach of its contract with Mrs Woodroffe, but the bank might have been prepared to indemnify it against that liability or even to pay off Mrs Woodroffe. I can see no ground for any species of implication to the effect contended for ...

The question whether the cessation of the company's business causes an automatic crystallisation of a floating charge is one of general importance upon which there appears to be no decision directly in point. Such authorities as there are disclose a uniform assumption in favour of crystallisation. There is a valuable discussion of them in *Picarda on The Law Relating to Receivers and Managers,* pp 16–18. One of the questions there raised is whether there is any distinction for this purpose between a company ceasing to carry on business on the one hand and ceasing to be a going concern on the other. My own impression is that these phrases are used interchangeably in the authorities ... but whether that be right or wrong, I think it clear that the material event is a cessation of business and not, if that is something different, ceasing to be a going concern.

[His Lordship referred to a number of authorities, and continued:] It is unnecessary for me to examine any of those cases in detail, or to quote extracts from the judgments of the many judges who decided them. They all, to a greater or lesser extent, assume that crystallisation takes place on a cessation of business ...

Although the general body of informed opinion is of the view that automatic crystallisation is undesirable (see in particular the Report of the Review Committee on Insolvency Law and Practice (Cmnd 8558) 30 April 1981, paras 1570–1582) I have not been referred to any case in which the assumption in favour of automatic crystallisation on cessation of business has been questioned. On that state of the authorities it would be very difficult for me to question it, even if I could see a good ground for doing so. On the contrary, it seems to me that it is in accordance with the essential nature of a floating charge. The thinking behind the creation of such charges has always been a recognition that a fixed charge on the whole undertaking and assets of the company would paralyse it and prevent it from carrying on its business: see, e g *Re Florence Land and Public Works Co, ex p Moor.*[14] On the other hand it is a mistake to think that the chargee has no remedy while the charge is still floating. He can always intervene and obtain an injunction to prevent the company from dealing with its assets otherwise than in the ordinary course of its business. That no doubt is one reason why it is preferable to describe the charge as 'hovering', a word which can bear an undertone of menace, rather than as 'dormant'. A cessation of business necessarily puts an end to the company's dealings with its assets. That which kept the charge hovering has now been released and the force of gravity causes it to settle and fasten on the subject of the charge within its reach and grasp. The paralysis, while it may still be unwelcome, can no longer be resisted ...

---

14 (1878) 10 Ch D 530 at 541, per Sir George Jessel MR.

[His Lordship then held that the evidence did not support the view that the company had ceased business before 1 September.]

Each debt accruing due to a company *after a floating charge which affects its future property has crystallised becomes immediately fixed with an equity in favour of the debentureholder. No debt becoming due* by a company *after crystallisation may be set off by a creditor so as to give him priority over the debentureholder.*

196 N W Robbie & Co Ltd v Witney Warehouse Co Ltd [1963] 1 WLR 1324, [1963] 3 All ER 613 (Court of Appeal)

The plaintiff company had given a debenture, secured by a floating charge, to the Bank of Ireland. The bank put in a receiver, who continued to carry on the company's business. The company sold goods to the defendants worth in all £1,346, and in this action the receiver claimed payment of the price. The defendants had meantime taken an assignment of a debt of £852 due by the company to English Spinners Ltd, and claimed to be entitled to set off this sum against the £1,346 sued for. It was held that the claim failed, because the debentureholder's equity had priority.

RUSSELL LJ: The facts giving rise to the present problem may be shortly stated. First: the mortgage created a floating charge which ceased to float, or crystallised, when the receiver and manager was appointed on 6 July 1961, under the power contained in the debenture dated 26 January 1960. Secondly: with the exception of £95 worth (as to which no special point is taken) the debts for goods delivered totalling £1,346 now sued upon arose as choses in action after the appointment of the receiver and manager, and the goods sold were all in stock when he was appointed. Thirdly: the debt of £852 due from the company which the defendants as assignees thereof seek to set off, arose before the appointment of the receiver and manager, was unsecured, and was assigned to the defendants after the last of the debts constituting the total of £1,346 came into existence.

The first question for consideration is whether on the true construction of the debenture the debt owed by the defendants as it arose became a chose in action of the company subject to an equitable charge in favour of the debentureholders. I consider that it did.

The relevant clauses and conditions of the debenture have already been referred to ... There is under clause 3 a charge on all future assets of the company without restriction: that amounts to an agreement for valuable consideration to charge all such future assets, which agreement enables equity to fasten a charge on those future assets when they arise: and every such equitable charge as it arises operates as an equitable assignment to the debentureholders of that asset: see, for example, *Durham Bros v Robertson,* per Chitty LJ,[15] and the references to assignment in *Biggerstaff v Rowatt's Wharf Ltd* (**194**). The fact that this charge is a floating charge cannot, it seems to me, operate to exclude assets from the agreement to charge. That particular quality of the charge (or agreement to charge) only means that its full operation is, so to speak, in suspense until certain events occur, and when

15 [1898] 1 QB 765 at 769.

such an event occurs the charge (or agreement to charge) loses that suspended quality. That in no way justifies the conclusion that the field of the charge is in any way restricted: it only means that after this particular quality disappears equity will fasten the charge directly upon all assets thereafter coming into existence as soon as they do so . . .

If that be a correct view of the construction of the debenture, then the choses in action consisting of the debts now sued upon became as they arose subject to an equitable charge—an equitable assignment—to the debentureholders . . .

Thus far, in my judgment, by force of the debenture charge an equitable charge attached in favour of the debentureholders not only on the £95 debt existing at the date of the appointment of the receiver and manager, but also upon the other debts constituting the total of £1,346 as they came into existence on delivery of goods to the defendants after such appointment. These choses in action belonging to the company became thus assigned in equity to the debentureholders, at times when the defendants had no crossclaim of any kind against the company and consequently no right of set-off. Before the defendants acquired by assignment this cross-claim the defendants must be fixed with knowledge of this equitable assignment to the debentureholders (by way of charge) of the debt owed by the defendants to the company. A debtor cannot set off his claim against X against a claim by X against him which the debtor knows has been assigned by X to Y before the debtor's claims arose. Just as an assignee of a chose in action takes subject to an already existing right of set-off, so a debtor with no existing right of set-off cannot assert set-off of a cross-claim which he first acquires after he has notice of the assignment of the claim against him: here, for instance, no part of the £852 could have been set off against the £95.

Applying these considerations to the present case, at the time when the defendants first acquired the claim for £852, the choses in action sought to be enforced against the defendants had been assigned to the debentureholders by way of charge, but the £852 claim in no way involved the debentureholders . . .

I conclude, therefore, that there is in this particular case no right of set-off because there is no 'mutuality' in beneficial interest. The claimants are primarily the debentureholders: the cross-claim is against the company alone, and is indeed one which in its origin could not be met and was not entitled to be met until the debentureholders had been paid off in full . . .

SELLERS LJ delivered a concurring judgment.

DONOVAN LJ dissented.

NOTE

This decision should be contrasted with the later case which is next cited, where the debt which it was sought to set off was an obligation that arose before crystallisation.

197 Rother Iron Works Ltd v Canterbury Precision Engineers Ltd [1974] QB 1, [1973] 1 All ER 394 (Court of Appeal)

The plaintiff company agreed to sell goods to the defendant company for £159, at a time when it already owed the defendant £124 under a previous contract. A receiver was appointed by the plaintiff's bank some two weeks later, under a power contained in a floating charge, and the goods were delivered to the defendant after a further two weeks. The Court of Appeal, affirming the county court judge, upheld the defendant's right to set off the earlier debt.

The judgment of the court (RUSSELL, CAIRNS and STAMP LJJ) was delivered by RUSSELL LJ: The argument for the plaintiff may be shortly stated. It proceeds thus: When the goods were delivered on 3 November the obligation to pay first arose as an asset of the plaintiff; simultaneously, it became subject to the charge in favour of the bank; the debt of £124 owed by the plaintiff to the defendant was no concern of the debentureholder, whereas the debt of £159 owed by the defendant, being caught by the debenture charge, was every concern of the debentureholder. There was therefore lacking the quality of mutuality required for set off.

The opposing contentions are these. The crystallisation of the floating charge on the appointment of the receiver operated to charge the plaintiff's rights under the existing contract for the purchase by the defendant of goods from the plaintiff. This was an equitable assignment (by way of charge) of those rights. Those rights were always subject to a right in the defendant to assert that since the plaintiff owed £124 to the defendant a payment of £35 would settle the account; and the debentureholder as equitable assignee could not be in a different or better position in that regard than the plaintiff.

Now, we are not concerned in the present case with a situation in which the cross-claim sought to be set off either arose, or first came to the hands of the defendant, after the crystallisation of the charge. Nor are we concerned with a claim made by a receiver against the defendant arising out of a contract made by the receiver subsequent to his appointment: for it is clear that the delivery of the goods was pursuant to the contract made by the plaintiff before the appointment. Nor are there here any special considerations that might arise from a winding up of the plaintiff company. The facts are simply as stated.

In our judgment, the argument for the defendant is to be preferred. It is true that the right of the plaintiff to sue for the debt due from the defendant was embraced, when it arose, by the debenture charge. But if this was because the chose in action consisting of the rights under the contract became subject to the charge on the appointment of the receiver, then the debentureholder could not be in a better position to assert those rights than had been the assignor plaintiff. And if the obligation of the defendant to pay £159 be regarded as a chose in action on its own it never, in our view, came into existence except subject to a right to set off the £124 as, in effect, payment in advance. That which became subject to the debenture charge was not £159, but the net claim sustainable by the plaintiff of £35 ...

Enforcement of floating charge; liquidation

It will be seen from the above cases that a floating charge can be a vulnerable form of security. There are, further, a number of statutory provisions which cut down the effectiveness of the floating charge. In the first place, IA 1986, ss 40, 386 and Sch 6 combine to ensure that, in the enforcement of a floating charge, the claims of those unsecured creditors who would have priority over other creditors in a winding up also fall to be satisfied before the holder of the floating charge. Further, under s 15 of the same Act, if an administration order has been made against a company, the administrator may dispose of or otherwise exercise his powers in relation to any property which is subject to a floating charge as if the property were unencumbered; but certain rights akin to tracing rights are preserved in favour of the charge-holder (s 15(4)). Again, IA 1986, s 245 declares that, subject to certain qualifications, a floating charge that is created within twelve months of a liquidation or an administration shall be invalid except to the extent that the charge-holder advances 'new money' or supplies goods or services to the company. This rule does not apply, at least in the normal case, if it is shown that the company immediately after the creation of the charge was solvent. But stricter conditions are applicable where the floating charge is given in favour of a person who is 'connected' with the company (e g a director or major shareholder, or a close relative of either, or an associated company). In this case the twelve-month period is extended to two years, and the exemption on the ground of solvency is not available.

Note that these statutory provisions apply only to *floating* charges. The debentureholder may therefore improve his security by taking a collateral *fixed* charge over any assets which the company is not expected to deal with in the course of its business.

Prior to 1986, it was sometimes possible for the holder of a floating charge to evade these statutory rules by showing that the charge had crystallised (and thereby become a fixed charge) before the commencement of the liquidation or other relevant statutory date. Thus in *Re Brightlife Ltd* [1987] Ch 200, [1986] 3 All ER 673, the debentureholder had given the company a notice converting the floating charge into a fixed charge a week before a resolution for voluntary winding up was passed. The court held that the preferential creditors no longer had any right to be paid in priority to the charge. To remedy this anomaly, a new statutory definition was introduced (IA 1986, s 251) which provides that 'floating charge' means 'a charge which, *as created,* was a floating charge'.

A floating charge which has already been redeemed cannot be attacked under IA 1986, s 245; but it may be open to challenge as a preference.

198 Re Parkes Garage (Swadlincote) Ltd [1929] 1 Ch 139 (Chancery Divisional Court)

The company, which was insolvent, on 15 June executed a floating charge to secure debts owed to a group of its creditors. On 27 July the company received a sum of money from the purchaser of a part of its business, and this sum was used to pay off the group of creditors, who endorsed a memorandum of discharge on the debenture. On 14 September a winding-up order was made on the petition of another creditor. It was held that the section equivalent to the present IA 1986, s 245 could not be invoked to compel repayment of the moneys after the debenture had been redeemed; but the court indicated that it was open to the liquidator to challenge the transaction as a fraudulent preference.

EVE J: Having regard to the facts which I have stated, about which there is no dispute, it is quite obvious that the learned county court judge had no option but to declare the charge to be invalid, and he so did. That part of his judgment, however, was not of much practical importance, because the charge had been satisfied by the payments which had been made, and it was then argued that the declaration of invalidity involved the further question: whether the debenture was still subsisting for any purpose, and if so were the simple contract debts, to secure which it had been issued, merged in the covenant contained in the debenture. An argument on those lines was addressed to the learned judge, at the conclusion of which he held that the simple contract debts were merged, and forgetting for the moment the limited extent to which he had declared the debenture invalid, he referred to the whole debenture as invalid, and held that the simple contract debts having been merged, and the debenture being invalid, the creditors were not entitled to retain the money paid to them through their trustee on 27 July.

At the first hearing the learned judge had not declared, nor could he declare, the debenture invalid; all he could declare invalid was the charge therein contained. The rest of the document, the covenants to pay principal and interest, survived and was valid, for nothing in s 212 [IA 1986, s 245] affects them. The position therefore was that the simple contract creditors, by their trustee, who was the covenantee, were entitled to the benefit of the covenants to pay principal and interest, and on 27 July, when the company was in sufficient funds to pay the principal and interest, they had no alternative but to pay the same, and the trustee cannot on this summons be ordered to repay. But having regard to what has been disclosed in these proceedings, that the company was hopelessly insolvent from the beginning of March down to the date of the winding-up order, and that the effect of the payments to these half-dozen creditors on 27 July was to apply the whole available assets of the company to the payment of their debts in full and to leave other creditors whose debts largely exceeded the aggregate amount paid to the half-dozen unprovided for, raises a doubt whether the whole transaction, which culminated in the payments on 27 July, was not in the nature of a fraudulent preference. We desire therefore to give the liquidator an opportunity of considering the position from this standpoint, and in allowing this appeal to state that the order is without prejudice to any application to set aside the payments or to question the validity of the debenture on the ground of its being a fraudulent preference[16] or on any other grounds which the liquidator may think fit to advance ...

MAUGHAM J concurred.

[*Re Parkes Garage* was followed in *Mace Builders* (*Glasgow*) *Ltd v Lunn* [1987] Ch 191, [1987] BCLC 55, where the debentureholder had put in a receiver to enforce the charge and the receiver had sold the charged assets before the commencement of the winding up. Although the charge had been created within twelve months of the liquidation, and at a time when the company was insolvent, it was held that the provision corresponding to IA 1986, s 245 (CA 1948, s 322) was inapplicable: transactions completed before the liquidation were not affected by the section.]

The phrase 'money[17] paid to the company' in IA 1986, s 245(2)(a) includes cheques met by a bank on the company's behalf.

16 [Now termed simply a 'preference': see IA 1986, s 239.]
17 Prior to IA 1986, the legislation used the phrase 'cash paid to the company'; but it would appear that the decision in *Re Yeovil Glove Co Ltd* is not affected by the change of wording.

199 Re Yeovil Glove Co Ltd [1965] Ch 148, [1964] 2 All ER 849 (Court of Appeal)

The company had gone into liquidation having unsecured debts totalling £94,000 and an overdraft with the National Provincial Bank Ltd amounting to £67,000. This overdraft was secured by a floating charge given less than twelve months previously. During the currency of the charge the bank had met cheques drawn by the company amounting to £110,000, and received some £111,000 for payment into the company's account. (There were in fact four accounts, but this is not important.) The unsecured creditors attacked the security under CA 1948, s 322 (broadly comparable with IA 1986, s 245), alleging that no 'cash' had been 'paid to the company' by the bank within the meaning of that section; but the court treated the bank's acts in meeting the company's cheques as equivalent. It followed that, by virtue of the rule in *Clayton*'s case,[18] the bank could claim that the whole of the £67,000 was cash advanced subsequently to the creation of the charge, so that the security was valid for this sum.

HARMAN LJ: [The] only question which arises is whether there was cash paid to the company at the time of or subsequently to the creation of, and in consideration for, the charge. It was admittedly created within twelve months of the winding up at a time when the company was insolvent. It is further agreed that so far as the overdraft was incurred before the date of the floating charge, the charge would not be a valid security for it. The liquidator's claim is a simple one, namely, that as neither cash nor a covenant to pay cash was made at the time of the execution of the document, there was no consideration for it in the legal sense of that term except the bank's immediate forbearance. This seemed to me, I confess, an attractive argument ...

It was argued that consideration in law is a well-known term and ought to receive its ordinary meaning, and that subsequent payments provided by the bank to defray the company's day-to-day outgoings or wages or salaries or indebtedness to its suppliers by cheque would not be consideration in law for the execution of a charge bearing an earlier date unless those payments were made in pursuance of a promise contained in, or made at or before the date of, the charge itself. It was, however, pointed out that such subsequent payments would in fact not be made in consideration for the charge, but in consideration for the promise.

Now it is apparent on the face of the section that cash subsequently paid to the company may be within the exception if so paid in consideration for the anterior charge, and the argument is that the words 'in consideration for' in this section cannot, therefore, be used in the technical sense, but mean 'by reason of' or 'having regard to the existence of' the charge. Oddly enough, there is no reported decision on these words, nor are they discussed in any of the well-known textbooks. There has, however, come to light a decision of Lord Romer, when a judge of first instance, in *Re Thomas Mortimer Ltd*,[19] in 1925, a decision on the corresponding section of the Companies (Consolidation) Act 1908, which was in the same terms as the present section except that the period was three instead of twelve months. A transcript of

18 (1816) 1 Mer 572, under which the earliest payments into an account are set off against the earliest payments out, and vice versa.
19 (1925), reported [1965] Ch 186n.

this judgment was before us. The facts of that case were, I think, indistinguishable from those of the present, and Romer J held that payments by the bank after the date of the charge were made in consideration for the charge . . .

That decision, if right, is enough to cover the present question, and Plowman J [at first instance] so held . . .

In the instant case some £111,000, representing its trading receipts, was paid into the no 1 account by the company between the date of the charge and the appointment of the receiver, and the bank paid out during the same period about £110,000. Those payments were either made directly to or to the order of the company, or were transfers to the no 3 and no 4 accounts against advances previously made to the company to defray wages or salaries. All the company's accounts were at all times overdrawn, so that every payment was a provision of new money by means of which, on the figures, it is overwhelmingly probable that all the creditors existing at the date of the charge were in fact paid off.

There arises at this point the consideration which has given me most trouble in this case, namely, that as the no 1 account was carried on after as well as before the charge in precisely the same way, the bank would be entitled in accordance with the rule in *Clayton*'s case, to treat payments in as being in satisfaction of the earliest advances made. The result is startling, for thus the bank pays itself out of moneys received subsequent to the charge for the whole of the company's indebtedness to it prior to the charge, and which was admittedly not covered by it. The result is that the whole of the pre-charge indebtedness is treated as paid off, and the bank is left bound to set off against its post-charge advances only the excess received after satisfying the company's pre-charge indebtedness. This would seem largely to nullify the effect of the section in the case of a company having at the date of the charge a largely overdrawn account with its bank, and which continues to trade subsequently. Of course, if at the date of the charge a line were drawn in the bank's books and a new account opened, then the company could successfully argue that payments out by the bank subsequent to the charge were, within a few hundred pounds, wholly repaid by the company from its trading receipts, with the result that no substantial sum would be due on the charge. It was, however, held by Romer J in *Re Thomas Mortimer Ltd* that *Clayton*'s case applied with the result stated, and I can see no escape from it, nor in spite of frequent pressing by the court did the appellant's counsel put forward any alternative . . . [It] follows, if the decision in *Re Thomas Mortimer Ltd* be right, that there is admittedly nothing left for the unsecured creditors. In my judgment Romer J's decision was right, and was rightly followed by Plowman J in the present case.

The fallacy in the appellant's argument lies, in my opinion, in the theory that, because the company's payments into the bank after the date of the charge were more or less equal to the payments out by the bank during the same period, no 'new money' was provided by the bank. This is not the fact. Every such payment was in fact new money having regard to the state of the company's accounts, and it was in fact used to pay the company's creditors. That the indebtedness remained approximately at the same level was due to the fact that this was the limit set by the bank to the company's overdraft. I can find no reason to compel the bank to treat all payments in after the charge as devoted to post-charge indebtedness. The law is in fact the other way . . .

WILLMER and RUSSELL LJJ delivered concurring judgments.

QUESTIONS

(1) What do you think are the policy reasons behind the enactment of IA 1986, s 245?
(2) What do you think are the policy reasons behind the enactment of IA 1986, s 40?

D. Retention of title clauses

Most trading companies use bank overdrafts to meet their short-term financial needs, and commonly also rely on bank loans for longer-term credit.
Almost invariably, such advances will be secured by floating charges over all
the company's assets, and possibly by an array of fixed charges as well. In
the event of insolvency, the bank and those creditors, such as the Revenue,
who are entitled to a statutory preference (see below, p 589) are very likely
between them to claim all that the company has, leaving ordinary trade
creditors with nothing. Many commentators consider that this situation is
unfair—see, for example, the Cork Committee's report (1982, Cmnd 8558)
and the remarks of Templeman J in *Business Computers Ltd v Anglo-African
Leasing Ltd* [1977] 2 All ER 741 at 742–743, [1977] 1 WLR 578 at 580:

> The question whether in this day and age it is necessary or desirable to
> permit the Crown and the holders of future floating charges the totality
> of the priorities which can be exercised under the existing law is not the
> subject of debate in this court, though I am inclined to think that it is
> at least debatable elsewhere.

There is particular unfairness in the case of those who supply the company
with goods on credit—perhaps the raw materials needed for its manufacturing
processes. The goods which they deliver become subject immediately to the
floating charge (if, as is usual, it affects future property), but it is the seller
and not the bank who is giving the credit. So suppliers have endeavoured to
protect themselves by 'retention of title' clauses. There is nothing novel about
this: the familiar hire-purchase agreement serves the same purpose. A Dutch
supplier succeeded in defeating the claims of a receiver in this way in the
celebrated *Romalpa* case in 1976.

200 Aluminium Industrie Vaassen BV v Romalpa Aluminium Ltd [1976] 1
WLR 676, [1976] 2 All ER 552 (Chancery Division and Court of Appeal)

Aluminium foil was supplied for processing by the plaintiffs, a Dutch
company, to the defendants. It was stipulated in the contract of sale that
ownership in the foil should not be transferred to the purchasing company
until the price had been paid in full; that products made from the foil should
be kept by the buyers as bailees (the contract, which was a translation from
a Dutch draft, used the un-English expression 'fiduciary owners') separately
from other stock, on the suppliers' behalf, as 'surety' for the outstanding
price; but that the buyers should have power to sell the manufactured articles
in the ordinary course of business, such sales to be made by them as the
suppliers' agents. Mocatta J, whose judgment was affirmed by the Court of
Appeal, held that the suppliers could trace the price due to them into the

proceeds of sales of the finished goods made by the buyers, ahead of the latter's secured and unsecured creditors.

MOCATTA J: The preservation of ownership clause contains unusual and fairly elaborate provisions departing substantially from the debtor/creditor relationship and shows, in my view, the intention to create a fiduciary relationship to which the [tracing] principle stated in *Re Hallett's Estate*[20] applies. A further point made by Mr Pickering was that if the plaintiffs were to succeed in their tracing claim this would, in effect, be a method available against a liquidator to a creditor of avoiding the provisions establishing the need to register charges on book debts: see s 95(1)(2)(e) of the Companies Act 1948 [CA 1985, s 396(1)(c)(iii)]. He used this only as an argument against the effect of clause 13 contended for by Mr Lincoln. As to this, I think Mr Lincoln's answer was well founded, namely, that if property in the foil never passed to the defendants with the result that the proceeds of sub-sales belonged in equity to the plaintiffs, s 95(1) had no application.

The plaintiffs accordingly succeed and are entitled to the reliefs sought.

[The decision of Mocatta J was affirmed by the Court of Appeal.]

NOTE

Since this decision, draftsmen of suppliers' contracts have endeavoured to adopt and improve upon '*Romalpa* clauses' with varying success. In those cases where the goods sold are still in the hands of the company and identifiable, the supplier has usually been successful. But in other cases the danger is that the court will hold that a charge has been created, which may be void in a subsequent insolvency for non-registration under CA 1985, ss 395ff and will, in any event, probably rank after the bank. *Re Bond Worth Ltd* (**190**) established that an attempt to reserve a mere equitable title (at least in a case where the buyer was free to resell) created a charge in the nature of a floating charge, which was void unless registered; and later cases have held that the same result follows where the manufacturing process is such as to destroy the identity of the raw material which was originally supplied: *Borden (UK) Ltd v Scottish Timber Products Ltd* [1981] Ch 25, [1979] 3 All ER 961 (resin used in making chipboard); *Re Peachdart Ltd* [1984] Ch 131, [1983] 3 All ER 204 (leather used for handbags). In regard to claims against the proceeds of sale, suppliers have not been successful unless the clause has created a duty to keep the moneys separate from other funds: *Hendy Lennox (Industrial Engines) Ltd v Grahame Puttick Ltd* [1984] 2 All ER 152, [1984] 1 WLR 485. Even then, the natural inference is that a charge has been created, since almost invariably the amount of the price owing to the supplier will be part only of the proceeds of resale: *E Pfeiffer Weinkellerei-Weineinkauf GmbH & Co v Arbuthnot Factors Ltd* [1988] 1 WLR 150, [1987] BCLC 522; *Compaq Computer Ltd v Abercorn Group Ltd* [1991] BCC 484.

There have been pleas for reform of the law so as to make all contracts containing retention of title clauses (and presumably also hire-purchase and leasing contracts) registrable as charges. The Diamond Report (HMSO, 1989), paras 17.8ff, 23.6.10, proposes that a distinction should be drawn between 'simple' clauses, which do no more than retain title to the goods sold, while they remain in their original state in the buyer's possession (with or without a claim to be entitled to the proceeds of sale of such goods) and more complex clauses, such as those which purport to assert title to the manufactured product. Professor Diamond recommends that the law should be clarified by a statutory provision which declares the latter category to be registrable as charges and the former to be exempt.

20 (1880) 13 Ch D 696.

The Insolvency Act 1986, s 15 empowers an administrator, with the leave of the court, to sell property affected by such contracts free from the supplier's interest on terms that the net proceeds are paid in discharge of the debt due to the supplier.

E. Registration of charges[1]

Sections 395ff of CA 1985 contain important provisions about the registration of charges created by a company over its property. Particulars, in a prescribed statutory form, of most kinds of charge created by a company (but not all: for the list of transactions to which the Act applies, see s 396) must be delivered to the registrar within 21 days. Failing registration, s 399 declares that the security is void against (a) an administrator or liquidator of the company, and (b) any person who for value acquires an interest in or right over property subject to the charge (unless the acquisition is expressly subject to the charge: s 405(1)). There are also criminal penalties for non-compliance.

The nature of this sanction of 'partial voidness' is curious. First, it should be noted that it is the *security* that is avoided, and not the obligation, which remains good as an unsecured debt.[2] Secondly, the charge is void only as against the persons mentioned and not, for instance, inter partes, nor against an execution creditor. And the chargee may dispose of the property in exercise of a power of sale and give a good title to the purchaser, even though the charge is 'void'; but there are statutory rules which postpone the claims of the charge-holder in the proceeds of sale to the holders of prior encumbrances, and nullify them altogether in an administration or liquidation (s 406).

As between the holders of successive charges over the same property, the position is complex. If particulars of both charges are duly registered within the respective 21-day periods, the ordinary rules of law apply and nothing turns on the time of registration: thus, broadly speaking, a legal charge will have priority over an equitable charge, a fixed charge over a floating charge and, as between two equitable charges, the earlier in time will prevail. Similar rules will apply if *neither* charge is registered. But if particulars (even defective particulars) of the later charge are registered either within the statutory 21 days or before *complete and accurate* particulars of the earlier charge are registered, the later charge will gain priority (s 404). Section 404(2) deals with the possibility that both sets of particulars may be incomplete or inaccurate— in effect it provides that, to the extent that the omission or inaccuracy is material, the first to have that vital element recorded prevails.

As between a charge-holder and an administrator or liquidator, omissions and errors in the registered particulars, if not corrected in time, will render a charge void to the extent that rights which ought to have been disclosed are not revealed; but the court has a discretion to order otherwise (s 402).

The *late delivery* of particulars does not render a charge void against an administrator or liquidator unless the company is insolvent at the date when particulars are delivered *and* the administration or liquidation proceedings begin within a specified period (varying from six months to two years) of that date: six months for a fixed charge, two years for a floating charge given to a person 'connected with' the company (as defined by IA 1986, s 249), and one year for any other floating charge (s 400).

1 The discussion in this section assumes that Pt IV of CA 1989 is in force.
2 Indeed, s 407 strengthens the position of the creditor by providing that the money secured by a charge which is rendered void becomes immediately payable.

The obligation to register particulars is placed by statute on the company, but any person interested in the charge may do so instead (s 398(1)). The registrar, after registration, sends a copy of the particulars to both the company and the chargee, with a note of the date when they were delivered (s 398(5)). This is a departure from the previous practice, under which it was necessary to send to the registrar the charge document itself along with the particulars and the registrar, after checking the particulars against the document, returned it to the person who had lodged it, together with a certificate of due registration which was conclusive evidence that the requirements of the Act had been complied with. This new regime, which relieves the registrar and his staff of the burdensome task of checking every charge document, streamlines the procedure but plainly gives the charge-holder far less protection.

Section 401 makes provision for the delivery of further particulars, in order to supplement or vary the registered particulars (e g where the sum secured by the charge has been increased), or even to correct them where those originally lodged were inaccurate; and s 403 allows for the registration of a memorandum that a charge has ceased to affect the company's property—a procedure which is purely optional and is not binding on an administrator or liquidator although, since the memorandum must be signed by both the company and the chargee, it would give rise to an estoppel in favour of a person who subsequently acquired an interest in the property in reliance on it.

The Act also provides for the registration of similar particulars when a company buys property which is already subject to a charge; but in this case the only sanction for non-registration is a fine, and the security itself is not struck down.

The *registered particulars* are those prescribed by regulation pursuant to s 415. Traditionally, the particulars have included the names and descriptions of the parties, the date and description of the instrument creating the charge, the amount due or owing on the charge, short particulars of all the property mortgaged or charged, and particulars of any commission or discount. But under the new legislation, significantly, s 415(2)(a) expressly authorises the inclusion in the prescribed particulars of a statement 'whether the company has undertaken not to create other charges ranking in priority to or pari passu with the charge', so that any 'negative pledge' clause will be disclosed, and a person wishing to take a subsequent charge will be deemed to have notice of it.

There is an obligation to give notice to the registrar of the appointment of a receiver (s 409), and power to extend this requirement by regulation (s 410) so as to include other events which operate to crystallise a floating charge (e g a 'notice of conversion' or the fact that the company has ceased to carry on business: see above, pp 395 ff). More specifically, in relation to an 'automatic crystallisation' clause, the regulations may provide that the crystallisation will be ineffective until notice of the event has been registered (s 410(3)).

The new statutory regime for the registration of charges does not go so far as Professor Diamond's report recommends. Ideally, he would have us adopt a comprehensive code dealing with all security interests in property other than land, on the model of the US Uniform Commercial Code and the Personal Property Security Acts in force in many Canadian jurisdictions. But, pending such a wholesale reform, the changes introduced by the 1989 Act go a long way to removing the imperfections of the earlier law. It goes without saying that decisions of the courts relating to the former system of registration should not be regarded as throwing any light on the new legislation, and for that reason they are no longer reproduced in this book.

The *company itself* is required also to keep a register of charges at its own office, together with a copy of every instrument creating or evidencing a charge over its property (s 411). Since this provision covers every kind of charge, and not only those of which particulars must be filed with the registrar, its obligations are potentially very burdensome indeed. But neither the validity of the charge nor any question relating to priority is affected by a failure to observe the requirements of this section, and in practice the criminal sanctions prescribed are never invoked.

Both the particulars of charges held by the registrar and the register of charges and copy charge instruments held by the company are open to public inspection (ss 709, 411). But whereas a person is not taken to have notice of the information at the company's own office (s 711A), the doctrine of constructive notice has been expressly preserved, *as against a person taking a charge on the company's property*, by s 416(1). Other persons, such as a purchaser of property from the company, are not deemed to have notice, even where such a person has 'failed to search the register in the course of making such inquiries as ought reasonably to have been made' (s 416(2)). A purchaser could, however, be affected with notice of particulars of a charge held by the registrar by reason of some other statutory provision (s 416(3))— e g of a floating charge affecting a company's land, by virtue of the Law of Property Act 1925, s 198.

Foreign companies which have charges over property situated in this country are obliged to register particulars with the registrar under similar rules as apply to local companies (ss 703 ff).

F. Debentureholders' remedies

A creditor whose debt is unsatisfied may, of course, sue to recover payment, and he may also seek to have the company wound up if it fails to meet a statutory demand for payment (IA 1986, ss 122(1)(f), 123(1)(a)). But a secured creditor will naturally wish to have recourse to his security. Where the charge affects specific property, powers of sale and of entry into possession may be exercised by the creditor of a company in the same way as against an individual, but (especially in the case of a floating charge) the remedy normally invoked will be to appoint a *receiver*. This may always be done by court order; but almost invariably the need to go to court (and the expense and the cumbersome procedure associated with it) will be obviated by the inclusion in the instrument creating the charge of a clause empowering the creditor (or the trustees, where there is a trust deed) to appoint a receiver himself in the event of default. If the charge is a floating charge secured over the whole or substantially the whole of the company's property, a receiver appointed by the debentureholder under such a power is given new statutory recognition by IA 1986 under the title of *administrative receiver*. As such, he has a number of powers and duties vested in him by the Act, including power to manage the company's business. He may choose to do this in the hope that the company will be able to trade itself back into profitability, or at the very least with a view to selling off its assets as a going concern rather than on a break-up basis so that they may fetch more. An administrative receiver must be a qualified insolvency practitioner.

The subject of receivers, including administrative receivers, is discussed further below, at pp 547 ff.

CHAPTER 9
Shares

A. Definition and nature[1]

A share in a partnership reflects the partner's proprietary interest in the partnership assets: the assets are jointly owned by the partners. In the case of a company, it is not the shareholders but the company that owns the corporate assets, and the concept of a share serves somewhat different functions. In the first place, it is a fraction of the capital, denoting the holder's proportionate *financial stake* in the company. Secondly, it is a measure of the holder's interest in the company *as an association* and the basis of his right to become a member and to enjoy the rights of voting, etc so conferred (CA 1985, s 22). And, thirdly, it is a *species of property* in its own right, a rather complex form of chose in action, which the holder can buy, sell, charge, etc, and in which there can be both legal and beneficial interests.

The terms 'shareholder' and 'member' are commonly regarded as interchangeable, but this is not always the case. A company limited by guarantee has members, but it cannot have shareholders, for it has no shares. On the other hand, the holders of bearer shares (CA 1985, s 188) do not become members, since entry in the register of members is necessary for this purpose (s 22).

Entry in the register of members is essential also to confer a legal title to the shares. Until this has been done the person entitled to the shares is neither a member nor their legal owner (**225**).

210 Borland's Trustee v Steel Bros & Co Ltd [1901] 1 Ch 279 (Chancery Division)

The company's articles provided that the shares of a member should in certain events, including bankruptcy, be transferable compulsorily to designated persons at a fair price not exceeding the par value. On the bankruptcy of Borland, who held 73 £100 shares, the company gave notice to his trustee in bankruptcy requiring him to transfer the shares in accordance with the articles. The trustee objected that this provision in the articles was void, either on the ground that it was repugnant to absolute ownership, or as tending to perpetuity. The court rejected both contentions.

FARWELL J: It is said, first of all, that such provisions are repugnant to absolute ownership. It is said, further, that they tend to perpetuity. They are likened to the case of a settlor or testator who settles or gives a sum of money subject to executory limitations which are to arise in the future, interpreting the articles as if they provided that if at any time hereafter, during centuries

---

1 RR Pennington, 'Can Shares in Companies be Defined?' (1989) 10 Co Law 140.

to come, the company should desire the shares of a particular person ... he must sell them. To my mind that is applying to the company law a principle which is wholly inapplicable thereto. It is the first time that any such suggestion has been made, and it rests, I think, on a misconception of what a share in a company really is. A share, according to the plaintiff's argument, is a sum of money which is dealt with in a particular manner by what are called for the purpose of argument executory limitations. To my mind it is nothing of the sort. A share is the interest of a shareholder in the company measured by a sum of money, for the purpose of liability in the first place, and of interest in the second, but also consisting of a series of mutual covenants entered into by all the shareholders inter se in accordance with s 16 of the Companies Act 1862 [CA 1985, s 14]. The contract contained in the articles of association is one of the original incidents of the share. A share is not a sum of money settled in the way suggested, but is an interest measured by a sum of money and made up of various rights contained in the contract, including the right to a sum of money of a more or less amount ... [His Lordship then held that the rule against perpetuities had no application to personal contracts such as this, and ruled that the article was valid and enforceable.]

B. Classes of shares

The shares in a company may be divided into different classes, either by the memorandum or articles or by some other means, such as the terms of an ordinary resolution to increase capital under s 121. Some classes of shares may fall into a well-known category such as 'preference shares', but even so there is no fixed formula defining such shares: it is a matter of construction of the terms of issue in each case what the rights of the particular class are. In broad terms, however, we may describe some well-known types of shares as follows.

Ordinary shares.   This is the basic or residual category. If all the company's shares are issued without differentiation, they will be ordinary shares. If the shares are divided into classes, and the special rights of other classes are set out, the remaining shares will be ordinary shares. Where the other class or classes are preference shares, then the ordinary shares are commonly called 'equity' shares; but in the Companies Act this term has a more elaborate definition (see s 744).

Preference shares.   These shares will usually be entitled to have dividends paid, at a predetermined rate (e g at a rate of 10% on their nominal value), in priority to any dividend on the ordinary shares. Of course, it is first necessary for the company to have distributable profits, and for a dividend to be declared; but if these conditions are met, the first claim on the corporate income in any year will be that of the preference shareholders. The right to a preference dividend may be *cumulative* (in which case arrears of preference dividends not declared in earlier years must be paid, as well as that for the current year, before any dividend is paid to the ordinary shareholders) or *non-cumulative* (when only the current year's preference dividend is payable). Where the preference shares are *participating*, they will be entitled to a further distribution after the ordinary shareholders have received a dividend equivalent to their own 10% (or whatever the rate is).

Preference shareholders very commonly also have a right to priority over the ordinary shareholders when capital is returned to the members in a winding up. It is quite usual for preference shareholders to have no voting rights at shareholders' meetings, or alternatively to have a vote only if the preference dividend is in arrear.

Deferred shares.   These are sometimes called 'founders' shares'. They are not common today except as part of tax-saving schemes. As the name implies, deferred shares normally enjoy rights to income or to return of capital ranking *after* the claims of the preference shareholders (if any) and the ordinary shareholders.

Redeemable shares.   These are created on terms that they shall be (or, at the option of the company or of the member, may be) bought back by the company at a future date. The rules governing such shares and their redemption are set out in CA 1985, ss 159 ff. Prior to 1981, only preference shares could be issued as redeemable, but it was never made clear in what respect this preference had to be. A company must always have *some* non-redeemable shares (s 159(2)).

Non-voting shares.   These may be issued where it is sought to restrict control of the company to the holders of the remaining shares. This is quite commonly desired when a family-controlled company looks to outside investors for additional capital (though it may, of course, find that the latter are not prepared to put up their money on those terms). A capital structure which includes non-voting shares may also be imposed on a company by an outside body, e g as a condition of obtaining a broadcasting licence (see *Heron International Ltd v Lord Grade* (**127**)). The Stock Exchange does not encourage listed companies to create non-voting shares, although it does not ban them altogether; they must, however, be clearly designated.

Shares with limited voting rights or enhanced voting rights.   These may also be created, even to the extent of giving one shareholder a right of veto in specified circumstances. We have seen examples in *Quin & Axtens Ltd v Salmon* (**95**) and *Bushell v Faith* (**120**).[2]

Employees' shares.   Many companies issue shares to their employees, commonly under an 'employees' share scheme' (defined in CA 1985, s 743), which carries certain tax advantages. Employees' shares are not usually designated as a separate class of shares by the memorandum or articles of association, but are issued simply as ordinary shares (or, as the case may be, preference shares, etc) ranking *pari passu* with the other shares of this class. Normally, however, they are subject to special restrictions (e g as to the holder's right of disposal) and would undoubtedly be regarded as a separate class of shares for some legal purposes. Various sections of the Companies Act make special provision for employees' shares: e g CA 1985, s 89(5) excludes shares that are to be held under an employees' share scheme from the restrictions (but not the benefits) of the usual pre-emptive rights rules.

---

2 In *Investment Trust Corpn Ltd v Singapore Traction Co Ltd* [1935] Ch 615, one 'management share' could outvote the remaining 399,999! A device of this kind (normally termed a 'golden share') is commonly employed to retain government control when a nationalised industry is privatised.

In addition, of course, classes of shares may be created for other reasons. Thus a 'quasi-partnership' company with three founding shareholders might well have a capital of £300 divided into £100 in 'A' shares, £100 in 'B' shares and £100 in 'C' shares, the shares to rank equally in all respects except that each class should have the right to appoint one of the directors of the three-man board. In this way, the right of each founder to participate in management could be entrenched.

Some common law rules about classes of shares and about the construction of the terms of issue of shares are illustrated by the cases which follow. The question of variation of class rights is discussed in the next section.

A company may alter its articles so as to take power to issue shares ranking in preference to its existing shares. There is no implied condition that all the shares in a company shall be equal.

211   Andrews v Gas Meter Co [1897] 1 Ch 361 (Court of Appeal)

[The facts appear from the judgment.]

The judgment of the court (LINDLEY, AL SMITH AND RIGBY LJJ) was delivered by LINDLEY LJ: The question raised by this appeal is whether certain preference shares issued by a limited company as long ago as 1865 were validly issued or not ... The company's original capital as stated in its memorandum of association was '£60,000, divided into 600 shares of £100 each, every share being sub-divisible into fifths, with power to increase the capital as provided by the articles of association'. By the articles of association which accompanied the memorandum of association, and were registered with it, power was given to the company to increase the capital (article 27), and it was provided that any new capital should be considered as part of the original capital (article 28). The issue of preference shares was not contemplated or authorised. In 1865 the company desired to acquire additional works, and passed a special resolution ... altering the articles and authorising the issue of 100 shares of £100 each, fully paid, and bearing a preferential dividend of £5 per cent per annum. Those shares were accordingly issued to the vendors of the works referred to, and are the shares the validity of which is now in question ... The learned judge has held that the creation of the preference shares was ultra vires, and that their holders never became and are not now shareholders in the company, and that they have none of the rights of shareholders, whether preference or ordinary ... The judgment against the validity of the preference shares is based upon the well-known case of *Hutton v Scarborough Cliff Hotel Co Ltd*,[3] which came twice before Kindersley V-C in 1865, and which Kekewich J very naturally held to be binding on him. Kindersley V-C's first decision was that a limited company which had not issued the whole of its original capital could not issue the unallotted shares as preference shares unless authorised so to do by its memorandum of association or by its articles of association. This decision was affirmed on appeal, and was obviously correct; and would have been correct even if the whole of the original capital had been issued and the preference shares had been new and additional capital. The company, however, afterwards passed

3 (1865) 2 Drew & Sm 514 at 521.

a special resolution altering the articles and authorising an issue of preference shares. This raised an entirely different question, and led to the second decision. The Vice-Chancellor granted an injunction restraining the issue of the preference shares, and he held distinctly that the resolution altering the articles was ultra vires. He did so upon the ground, as we understand his judgment, that there was in the memorandum of association a condition that all the shareholders should stand on an equal footing as to the receipt of dividends, and that this condition was one which could not be got rid of by a special resolution altering the articles of association under the powers conferred by ss 50 and 51 of the Act [CA 1985, ss 9 and 378(2)]. The judgment of the Vice-Chancellor is a little obscure, because he treats the condition as a condition of the constitution of the company, and he may have meant by that expression either the constitution as fixed by the memorandum of association or the constitution as fixed by the memorandum of association and the original articles. But unless he had meant the constitution of the company as fixed by the memorandum of association his decision is unintelligible; for, so far as the constitution depended on the articles, it clearly could be altered by special resolution under the powers conferred by ss 50 and 51 of the Act . . .

[His Lordship examined a number of cases, and continued:] These decisions turned upon the principle that although by s 8 of the Act [CA 1985, s 2] the memorandum is to state the amount of the original capital and the number of shares into which it is to be divided, yet in other respects the rights of the shareholders in respect of their shares and the terms on which additional capital may be raised are matters to be regulated by the articles of association rather than by the memorandum, and are, therefore, matters which . . . may be determined by the company from time to time by special resolution pursuant to s 50 of the Act. This view, however, clearly negatives the doctrine that there is a condition in the memorandum of association that all shareholders are to be on an equality unless the memorandum itself shows the contrary. That proposition is, in our opinion, unsound . . .

NOTE

Although this case established that there is no implied condition in the constitution of a company that all its shares should rank equally, there is nevertheless a presumption (as is shown by the cases which follow) that all shares do enjoy equal rights unless the terms of issue make some express provision to the contrary.

In many jurisdictions of the United States, the principle of equality as between shares was developed much further by the courts, so that shareholders commonly have pre-emptive rights as regards any new shares issued. This has been achieved in the UK only by legislation; see above, p 338.

Where the terms of issue make no express distinction between the rights of different categories of shareholders in respect of (a) dividend, (b) the return of capital (and participation in 'surplus assets' in a winding up), or (c) voting, the rule of construction in each case is that, prima facie, all shareholders rank equally. The fact that a preference in respect of any one of these matters is conferred does not imply any right to preference in some other respect: the presumption of equality is undisturbed.

212 Birch v Cropper (1889) 14 App Cas 525 (House of Lords)

The articles of the Bridgewater Navigation Co Ltd provided that dividends should be paid in proportion to the amounts paid up on the shares. There was no express provision governing the distribution of assets in a winding up. The company had issued 5% preference shares at £10 each which were paid up in full, and ordinary shares of £10 on which £3.50 had been paid. The House of Lords, reversing the Court of Appeal and varying the order of North J, held that in distributing the surplus assets available in the company's liquidation after the return of capital, the paid-up and partly paid shares were to be treated alike; and that the preference shareholders were to participate rateably with the ordinary shareholders in proportion to the nominal amounts of the shares held.

LORD MACNAGHTEN: The question before your Lordships is this: In the liquidation of a company limited by shares, what is the proper mode of distributing assets not required for payment of debts and liabilities, or for the costs of the winding up, or for the adjustment of the rights of the contributories amongst themselves? As incidental to that question, your Lordships have to consider whether the mode of distribution can be affected by one or more of the following circumstances: (1) That the shares of the company were paid up unequally, some being fully paid up, others being paid up only in part. (2) That the fully paid-up shares were issued separately as preference shares, carring a preferential dividend of 5%, without any further right to participate in the profits of the business. (3) That by the regulations of the company dividends on the company's shares were payable in proportion to the amounts paid up thereon.

The answer, as it seems to me, must depend on the principles applicable to companies limited by shares, and on the provisions contained in the Companies Act 1862 ...

Every person who becomes a member of a company limited by shares of equal amount becomes entitled to a proportionate part in the capital of the company, and, unless it be otherwise provided by the regulations of the company, entitled, as a necessary consequence, to the same proportionate part in all the property of the company, including its uncalled capital. He is liable in respect of all moneys unpaid on his shares to pay up every call that is duly made upon him. But he does not by such payment acquire any further or other interest in the capital of the company. His share in the capital is just what it was before. His liability to the company is diminished by the amount paid. His contribution is merged in the common fund. And that is all.

When the company is wound up, new rights and liabilities arise. The power of the directors to make calls is at an end; but every present member, so far as his shares are unpaid, is liable to contribute to the assets of the company to an amount sufficient for the payment of its debts and liabilities, the costs of winding up, and such sums as may be required for the adjustment of the rights of the contributories amongst themselves ...

Amongst the rights to be adjusted, the most important are those which arise when there is a difference between shareholders in the amount of calls paid in respect of their shares. Before winding up no such rights exist; whatever has been paid by the shareholders of one issue in excess of the contributions of their fellow shareholders of a different issue, must have been paid in pursuance of calls duly made or in accordance with the conditions under which the shares were held. While the company is a going concern no capital can be returned to the shareholders, except under the statutory provisions in that behalf. There is therefore during that period no ground for complaint; no room for equities arising out of unequal contributions. In the case of winding up everything is changed. The assets have to be distributed. The rights arising from unequal contributions on shares of equal amounts must be adjusted, and the property of the company, including its uncalled capital not required to satisfy prior claims, must be applied for that purpose. But when those rights are adjusted, when the capital is equalised, what equity founded on inequality of contribution can possibly remain? The rights and interests of the contributories in the company must then be simply in proportion to their shares ...

It now only remains to deal with the various claims put forward in the course of the argument.

The ordinary shareholders say that the preference shareholders are entitled to a return of their capital, with 5% interest up to the day of payment, and to nothing more. That is treating them as if they were debentureholders, liable to be paid off at a moment's notice. Then they say that at the utmost the preference shareholders are only entitled to the capital value of a perpetual annuity of 5% upon the amounts paid up by them. That is treating them as if they were holders of irredeemable debentures. But they are not debentureholders at all. For some reason or other the company invited them to come in as shareholders, and they must be treated as having all the rights of shareholders, except so far as they renounced those rights on their admission to the company. There was an express bargain made as to their rights in respect of profits arising from the business of the company. But there was no bargain—no provision of any sort—affecting their rights as shareholders in the capital of the company.

Then the preference shareholders say to the ordinary shareholders, 'We have paid up the whole of the amount due on our shares; you have paid but a fraction on yours. The prosperity of a company results from its paid-up capital; distribution must be in proportion to contribution. The surplus assets must be divided in proportion to the amounts paid up on the shares.' That seems to me to be ignoring altogether the elementary principles applicable to joint-stock companies of this description. I think it rather leads to confusion to speak of the assets which are the subject of this application as 'surplus assets' as if they were an accretion or addition to the capital of the company capable of being distinguished from it and open to different considerations. They are part and parcel of the property of the company— part and parcel of the joint stock or common fund—which at the date of the winding up represented the capital of the company. It is through their shares in the capital, and through their shares alone, that members of a company limited by shares become entitled to participate in the property of the company. The shares in this company were all of the same amount. Every contributory who held a preference share at the date of the winding up must have taken that share and must have held it on the terms of paying up all calls duly made upon him in respect thereof. In paying up his share in full he has done no more than he contracted to do; why should he have more than he bargained for? Every contributory who was the holder of an ordinary share at the date of the winding up took his share and held it on similar terms. He has done all he contracted to do; why should he have less than his bargain? When the preference shareholders and the ordinary shareholders are once placed on exactly the same footing in regard to the amounts paid up upon their shares, what is there to alter rights which were the subject of express contract? ...

Then it is said on behalf of the preference shareholders that the provision for payment of dividends in proportion to the amounts paid up on the shares leads to an inference that the distribution of surplus assets was to be made in the same proportion. I do not think that it leads to any inference of the kind. It is a very common provision nowadays, though it is not what you find in Table A. And it is a very reasonable provision, because during the continuance of the company, and while it is a going concern, it prevents any sense of dissatisfaction on the part of those who have paid more on their shares than their fellow shareholders of a different issue. But when it has come to an end I cannot see how it can be used to regulate or disturb rights with which it had nothing to do even while it was in force ...

LORDS HERSCHELL and FITZGERALD delivered concurring opinions.

NOTE

It will be observed that in this case the 'surplus assets' were in effect treated as capital. Later decisions in a variety of contexts have gone a long way towards establishing it as a general principle that no distinction is made between capital and income in a winding up. Unfortunately, however, the law is still in an unsettled state as a result of further proceedings which followed upon the decision in *Birch v Cropper*. In these proceedings, reported as *Re Bridgewater Navigation Co* [1891] 2 Ch 317, the ordinary shareholders were allowed to claim that three reserve funds representing undrawn profits, which might have been distributed to them as dividends before the liquidation, 'belonged' to them to the exclusion of the preference shareholders. A similar decision was reached as regards sums representing the difference between the realised value of certain assets and their book-value as shown in the company's accounts. By this ruling, the order of the House of Lords was modified to the point of virtual contradiction. Later cases have, in general, paid lip-service to the decision in *Re Bridgewater Navigation Co*, but at the same time managed to distinguish it as turning on the special wording of that company's articles.

Where the terms of issue do make express provision as to the rights of a class of shareholders in respect of (a) dividend, (b) the return of capital (and participation in 'surplus assets') or (c) voting, then that provision is presumed to be an exhaustive statement of the rights of the class in that particular respect.

213 Will v United Lankat Plantations Co Ltd [1914] AC 11 (House of Lords)

The articles of the company empowered it to issue new shares upon such terms, including preference, as the company in general meeting might direct. On 13 July 1891, at an extraordinary general meeting, resolutions were passed (1) that the capital of the company be increased by the creation of 50,000 new shares at £1 each, and (2) 'that the new shares be called preference shares and that the holders thereof be entitled to a cumulative preferential dividend at the rate of 10% per annum on the amount for the time being paid upon such shares: and that such preference shares rank, both as regards capital and dividend, in priority to the other shares'. The question before the court was whether the preference shareholders were entitled to a dividend of 10% and no more, or to share rateably with the ordinary shareholders in the profits remaining after the ordinary shareholders had also received 10%. The House of Lords upheld the first construction.

VISCOUNT HALDANE LC: My Lords, the action was brought by the appellant to obtain a declaration—and this is the only substantial point before the House—that the preferential shares which have been issued were entitled to rank for dividend pari passu with the ordinary shares of the company as against any profits of the company available for distribution as dividend after providing for a cumulative preferential dividend of 10% on the preference shares and a dividend of 10% on the ordinary shares. That was the claim and that was the point of controversy between the parties.

Now, my Lords, to see how the question so raised ought to be answered, it is necessary to turn to the documents which constituted the company. [His Lordship referred to the articles and resolutions and continued:] Your Lordships will observe that the second resolution gave the authority to make the bargain and defined the terms which the bargain was to contain. A shareholder comes to the company and says, 'I wish to contract with you for a share in your capital and so to become a shareholder.' He advances his money and the terms are contained in the bargain that is made between him and the company on the issue of the share to him, and that bargain is that he is to receive a cumulative preferential dividend at the rate of 10% on the amount paid up on his share and that his preference share is to rank both as regards capital and dividend in priority to other shares.

My Lords, I should have thought that if we were dealing with an ordinary case of two individuals coming together, and if a document were produced saying 'You are to have a cumulative preferential dividend of 10%' or whatever might be the equivalent in the circumstances of the bargain, it would by naturally concluded that that was the whole of the bargain between the parties on that point. You do not look outside a document of this kind in order to see what the bargain is; you look for it as contained within the four corners of the document. And, although it is quite true that in article 115 the phrase is 'Subject to any priorities that may be given upon the issue of any new shares, the profits of the company available for distribution (having regard to the provisions hereinbefore contained as to a reserve fund) shall be distributed as dividend among the members in accordance with the amounts paid on the shares held by them respectively', the real question is whether the documents have been silent as to the terms of distribution. If I am right the resolution was passed under the powers contained in article 43, and that defined the whole terms of the bargain between the shareholders and the company; and there is no room for saying that the general provisions of article 115 operate in a fashion in which they can only operate if the matter is not covered by express provision.

My Lords, I think that Farwell LJ called attention to what is really a cardinal consideration in this matter. Shares are not issued in the abstract and priorities then attached to them: the issue of shares and the attachment of priorities proceed uno flatu; and when you turn to the terms on which the shares are issued you expect to find all the rights as regards dividends specified in the terms of the issue. And when you do find these things prescribed it certainly appears to me unnatural to go beyond them and to look to the general provisions of an article which is only to apply if nothing different is said ...

EARL LOREBURN and LORD ATKINSON delivered concurring opinions.

LORD KINNEAR concurred.

214 Re National Telephone Co [1914] 1 Ch 755 (Chancery Division)

[The facts are immaterial.]

SARGANT J: [It] appears to me that the weight of authority is in favour of the view that, either with regard to dividend or with regard to the rights in a winding up, the express gift or attachment of preferential rights to preference shares, on their creation, is, prima facie, a definition of the whole of their rights in that respect, and negatives any further or other right to which, but for the specified rights, they would have been entitled ...

NOTE

Despite the view expressed in this case by Sargant J, the Court of Appeal in *Re William Metcalfe & Sons Ltd* [1933] Ch 142 ruled that the principle of construction as regards dividend rights in *Will*'s case (above) did not apply in relation to capital rights. It was not until 1949, in the case next cited, that the House of Lords upheld the opinion of Sargant J.

215 Scottish Insurance Corpn Ltd v Wilsons & Clyde Coal Co Ltd [1949] AC 462, [1949] 1 All ER 1068 (House of Lords)

[For the facts and another part of the decision, see above, (**178**).]

The rights of the preference shareholders were, so far as is material, defined by articles 159 and 160 of the articles of association as follows:

> 159. In the event of the company being wound up, the preference shares (first issue) shall rank before the other shares of the company on the property of the company, to the extent of repayment of the amounts called up and paid thereon.
> 160. In the event of the company being wound up, the preference shares (second issue) shall rank before the ordinary shares but after the said preference shares (first issue) on the property of the company to the extent of repayment of the amounts called up and paid thereon.

LORD SIMONDS: It is clear from the authorities, and would be clear without them, that, subject to any relevant provision of the general law, the rights inter se of preference and ordinary shareholders must depend on the terms of the instrument which contains the bargain that they have made with the company and each other. This means that there is a question of construction to be determined, and undesirable though it may be that fine distinctions should be drawn in commercial documents such as articles of association of a company, your Lordships cannot decide that the articles here under review have a particular meaning, because to somewhat similar articles in such cases as *Re William Metcalfe & Sons Ltd*[4] that meaning has been judicially attributed. Reading the relevant articles, as a whole, I come to the conclusion that articles 159 and 160 are exhaustive of the rights of the preference stockholders in a winding up. The whole tenor of the articles, as I have already pointed out, is to leave the ordinary stockholders masters of the situation. If there are 'surplus assets' it is because the ordinary stockholders have contrived that it should be so, and, though this is not decisive, in determining what the parties meant by their bargain, it is of some weight that it should be in the power of one class so to act that there will or will not be surplus assets...

But, apart from those more general considerations, the words of the specifically relevant articles, 'rank before the other shares ... on the property of the company to the extent of repayment of the amounts called up and paid thereon', appears to me apt to define exhaustively the rights of the preference stockholders in a winding up. Similar words, in *Will v United Lankat Plantations Co Ltd* (213) 'rank, both as regards capital and dividend, in priority to the other shares', were held to define exhaustively the rights of preference shareholders to dividend, and I do not find in the speeches of Viscount Haldane LC or Earl Loreburn in that case any suggestion that a different result would have followed if the dispute had been in regard to capital. I do not ignore that in the same case in the Court of Appeal[5] the distinction between dividend and capital was expressly made by both Cozens-Hardy MR and Farwell LJ, and that in *Re William Metcalfe & Sons Ltd*, Romer LJ reasserted it. But I share the difficulty, which Lord Keith has expressed in this case, in reconciling the reasoning that lies behind the judgments in *Will's* case and *Re William Metcalfe & Sons Ltd* respectively. [His Lordship accordingly held that the latter decision should be overruled.]

VISCOUNT MAUGHAM and LORD NORMAND delivered concurring opinions.

LORD MORTON OF HENRYTON dissented.

NOTE

The conclusion reached in the *Scottish Insurance* case naturally made preference shares a less secure form of investment. It was also thought at the time to be harsh on the holders of such shares, for the overruling of *Metcalfe*'s case inevitably depressed the value of shares carrying a high rate of return. To offset the effect of the *Scottish Insurance* decision, many listed companies thereafter adopted the 'Spens formula', under which the sum repaid to preference shareholders on a reduction of capital is geared to the recent market price of the shares. For an example, see below, p 633.

C. Class rights

If the share capital of a company has been divided into classes, statutory provisions come into play which restrict the ability of the company to alter the rights attached to a class of shares. Section 125(2) of CA 1985 requires the written consent of three-quarters in value of the shares of the class, or the sanction of an extraordinary resolution passed at a separate meeting of

4 [1933] Ch 142.
5 [1912] 2 Ch 571.

the holders of such shares, before any variation of the rights of that class can be made. (The company may make the rights even more secure by adding procedural hurdles which are more severe—though it cannot, at least for some purposes, make them easier (see s 125(3))—and it may entrench them still further by writing them into its *memorandum*.) Students should be warned that many readings will be necessary to master the intricacies of s 125: it is not for faint hearts.

These statutory provisions are reinforced by a rule of common law established in the *British American Nickel* case (**217**), that members voting at a class meeting must act 'in the interest of the class as a whole': a rule which obviously has some links with the 'bona fide for the benefit of the company as a whole' principle of *Allen v Gold Reefs of West Africa Ltd* (**55**), but which seems to have been carried beyond that in some later cases (e g *Re Holders Investment Trust Ltd* (**181**)). If taken literally, the rule as so interpreted would not allow a class to subordinate its own interests to those of the company as a whole, and class rights could never be varied except to the holders' advantage. This cannot surely have been intended.

Paradoxically, the judges have not shown themselves anything like so solicitous for the interests of class members in the cases concerned with the interpretation of the term 'variation', so that in many cases it may be possible to make class rights less effective without any 'variation' of the rights in a technical sense: this is illustrated by *White v Bristol Aeroplane Co* (**218**) and *Greenhalgh v Arderne Cinemas Ltd* (**219**).

There is much speculation in some textbooks over the meaning and scope of the term 'class right'. If the preference shareholders have a right under the articles to a 10% preference dividend, that is obviously a 'class right', but if the articles say nothing about the dividend rights of ordinary shareholders in the same company, is their dividend right a 'class right' too? And if nothing is said about voting in regard to either class of shares in their terms of issue, are their voting rights 'class rights'? In the example on p 416 above, where the only expressed right is that of appointing a director, are the dividend rights of each class 'class rights'? This can only be a matter of speculation. The only light thrown on this point by the Act itself is in s 125(7), which states that to meddle with (or, curiously, to insert) a 'variation of rights' provision in the articles is itself a variation of rights, and in s 125(8), which deals with the extinction of rights (but not with the extinction of the share itself: *Re Saltdean Estate Co Ltd* (**180**)).

In the *Cumbrian Newspapers* case (**216**), Scott J was called on to give the first judicial consideration to the meaning of the terms 'class of shares' and 'class rights'. His conclusion was that they might extend to include cases where rights are enjoyed by a particular member or category of members but no specific shares are designated to which those rights are referable. This is a surprisingly wide interpretation, but has the merit of ensuring that the protection conferred by s 125 will be applied fairly comprehensively.

Section 127 gives dissenting members of a class who hold at least 15% of the shares of that class the right to challenge the variation in court. They are thus given access to the court free from the hazards of *Foss v Harbottle* (**232**), but the requirement of 15% and the need to act within 21 days may lead to difficulties, especially in a large company.

Rights enjoyed by a member may be 'class rights' although they are not referable to particular shares.

216   Cumbrian Newspapers Group Ltd v Cumberland and Westmorland Herald Newspaper and Printing Co Ltd [1987] Ch 1, [1986] 2 All ER 816 (Chancery Division)

The plaintiff had acquired 10.67% of the ordinary shares in the defendant company ('Cumberland') in 1968 as part of an arrangement designed to concentrate the local newspaper publishing business under one title and to make it difficult for an outsider to acquire control of this paper. The articles of Cumberland were altered so that the plaintiff had (i) rights of pre-emption over the company's other ordinary shares (arts 7 and 9), (ii) rights in respect of unissued shares (art 5), and (iii) the right to appoint a director, so long as it held at least 10% of the shares (art 12). Scott J held that these were class rights enjoyed by the plaintiff which could only be altered pursuant to CA 1985, s 125.

SCOTT J: I turn to the critical question: are the plaintiff's rights under articles 5, 7, 9 and 12, rights attached to a class of shares?

Rights or benefits which may be contained in articles can be divided into three different categories. First, there are rights or benefits which are annexed to particular shares. Classic examples of rights of this character are dividend rights and rights to participate in surplus assets on a winding up. If articles provide that particular shares carry particular rights not enjoyed by the holders of other shares, it is easy to conclude that the rights are attached to a class of shares, for the purpose both of s 125 of the Act of 1985 and of article 4 of Table A [1948]. It is common ground that rights falling into this category are rights attached to a class of shares for those purposes. Mr Howarth submitted at first that this category should be restricted to rights that were capable of being enjoyed by the holders for the time being of the shares in question. Such a restriction would exclude rights expressly attached to particular shares issued to some named individual, but expressed to determine upon transfer of the shares by the named individual. *Palmer's Company Precedents*, 17th ed (1956), Pt I, p 818, contains a form for the creation of a life governor's share in a company. Mr Howarth accepted that the rights attached to a share in accordance with this precedent would be rights attached to a class of shares. He accepted, rightly in my judgment, that a provision for defeasance of rights on alienation of the share to which the rights were attached, would not of itself prevent the rights, pre-alienation, from being properly described as rights attached to a class of shares. The plaintiff's rights under articles 5, 7, 9 and 12 cannot, however, be brought within this first category. The rights were not attached to any particular shares. In articles 5, 7 and 9, there is no reference to any current shareholding held by the plaintiff. The rights conferred on the plaintiff under article 12 are dependent on the plaintiff holding at least 10% of the issued ordinary shares in the defendant. But the rights are not attached to any particular shares. Any ordinary shares in the defendant, if sufficient in number and held by the plaintiff, would entitle the plaintiff to exercise the rights.

A second category of rights or benefits which may be contained in articles (although it may be that neither 'rights' nor 'benefits' is an apt description), would cover rights or benefits conferred on individuals not in the capacity of members or shareholders of the company but, for ulterior reasons, connected with the administration of the company's affairs or the conduct of its business. *Eley v Positive Government Security Life Assurance Co Ltd* (**42**) was a case where the articles of the defendant company had included a provision that the plaintiff should be the company solicitor. The plaintiff sought to enforce that provision as a contract between himself and the company. He failed. The reasons why he failed are not here relevant, and I cite the case only to draw attention to an article which, on its terms, conferred a benefit on an individual but not in the capacity of member or shareholder of the company. It is, perhaps, obvious that rights or benefits in this category cannot be class rights. They cannot be described as rights attached to a class of shares. The plaintiff in *Eley v Positive Government Security Life Assurance Co Ltd* was not a shareholder at the time the articles were adopted. He became a shareholder some time thereafter. It is easy, therefore, to conclude that the article in question did not confer on him any right or benefit in his capacity as a member of the company. In a case where the individual had been issued with shares in the company at the same time and as part of the same broad arrangement under which the article in question had been adopted, the conclusion might not be so easy. But if, in all the circumstances, the right conclusion was still that the rights or benefits concurred by the article were not conferred on the beneficiary in the capacity of member or shareholder of the company, then the rights could not, in my view, be regarded as class rights. They would not be rights attached to any class of shares ...

In my judgment, the plaintiff's rights under those articles do not fall within this second category.

That leaves the third category. This category would cover rights or benefits that, although not attached to any particular shares, were nonetheless conferred on the beneficiary in the capacity of member or shareholder of the company. The rights of the plaintiff under articles 5, 7, 9 and 12 fall, in my judgment, into this category. Other examples can be found in reported cases.

In *Bushell v Faith* (**120**), articles of association included a provision that on a resolution at a general meeting for the removal of any director from office, any shares held by that director should carry the right to three votes. The purpose of this provision was to prevent directors being removed from office by a simple majority of the members of the company. The validity of the article was upheld by the Court of Appeal and by the House of Lords; the reasons do not, for present purposes, matter. But the rights conferred by the article in question fall, in my view, firmly in this third category. They were not attached to any particular shares. On the other hand, they were conferred on the director/beneficiaries in their capacity as shareholders. The article created, in effect, two classes of shareholders—namely, shareholders who were for the time being directors, on the one hand, and shareholders who were not for the time being directors, on the other hand.

The present case is, and *Bushell v Faith* was, concerned with rights conferred by articles. The other side of the coin is demonstrated by *Rayfield v Hands* (**44**). That case was concerned with obligations imposed on members by the articles. The articles of the company included an article entitling every member to sell his shares to the directors of the company at a fair valuation. In effect, the members enjoyed 'put' options exercisable against the directors. Vaisey J held that the obligations imposed by the article on the directors for the time being were enforceable against them. He held that the obligations were imposed on the directors in their capacity as members of the company. It follows from his judgment that, as in *Bushell v Faith*, there were in effect two classes of shareholders in the company. There were shareholders who were not for the time being directors, and shareholders who were for the time being directors: the former had rights against the latter which the latter did not enjoy against the former. The two classes were identifiable not by reference to their respective ownership of particular shares, but by reference to the office held by the latter. But the rights of the former, and the obligations of the latter, required their respective ownership of shares in the company. Accordingly, as a matter of classification, the rights in question fall, in my view, into the third category.

In the present case, the rights conferred on the plaintiff under articles 5, 7, 9 and 12 were, as I have held, conferred on the plaintiff as a member or shareholder of the defendant. The rights would not be enforceable by the plaintiff otherwise than as the owner of ordinary shares in the defendants. If the plaintiff were to divest itself of all its ordinary shares in the defendant, it would not then, in my view, be in a position to enforce the rights in the articles. But the rights were not attached to any particular share or shares. Enforcement by the plaintiff of the rights granted under articles 5, 7 and 9, would require no more than ownership by the plaintiff of at least some shares in the defendant. Enforcement by the plaintiff of the rights granted under article 12 require the plaintiff to hold at least 10% of the issued shares in the defendant. But any shares would do. It follows, in my judgment, that the plaintiff's rights under the articles in question fall squarely within this third category.

The question for decision is whether rights in this third category are within the meaning of the phrase in s 125 of the Companies Act 1985 and in article 4 of Table A, rights attached to a class of shares. [His Lordship examined the language and the background of the section and concluded that this was the case.]

A vote on a resolution to modify class rights must be exercised for the purpose, or dominant purpose, of benefiting the class as a whole.

217 British America Nickel Corpn Ltd v O'Brien [1927] AC 369 (Privy Council)

The company had issued mortgage bonds, secured by a trust deed which provided (inter alia) that a majority of the bondholders, representing not less than three-fourths in value, might sanction any modification of the rights of the bondholders. A scheme for the reconstruction of the company, which involved a modification of the bondholders' rights, was approved by the requisite majority; but it was objected that one of the bondholders, without whose vote the proposal would not have been carried, had been induced to give his support by a promise of a large block of ordinary stock. The Privy Council, affirming the decision of the Ontario courts, held that the vote was invalid.

The opinion of their Lordships was delivered by VISCOUNT HALDANE: To give a power to modify the terms on which debentures in a company are secured is not uncommon in practice. The business interests of the company may render such a power expedient, even in the interests of the class of debentureholders as a whole. The provision is usually made in the form of a power, conferred by the instrument constituting the debenture security, upon the majority of the class of holders. It often enables them to modify, by resolution properly passed, the security itself. The provision of such a power to a majority bears some analogy to such a power as that ... which enables a majority of the shareholders by special resolution to alter the articles of association. There is, however, a restriction of such powers, when conferred on a majority of a special class in order to enable that majority to bind a minority. They must be exercised subject to a general principle, which is applicable to all authorities conferred on majorities of classes enabling them to bind minorities; namely, that the power given must be exercised for the purpose of benefiting the class as a whole, and not merely individual members only. Subject to this, the power may be unrestricted. It may be free from the general principle in question when the power arises not in connection with a class, but only under a general title which confers the vote as a right of property attaching to a share. The distinction does not arise in this case, and it is not necessary to express an opinion as to its ground. What does arise is the question whether there is such a restriction on the right to vote of a creditor or member of an analogous class on whom is conferred a power to vote for the alteration of the title of a minority of the class to which he himself belongs ...

[His Lordship referred to *North-West Transportation Co Ltd v Beatty* (**129**) and *Burland v Earle* (**242**), and continued:] It has been suggested that the decisions in these two cases on the last point is difficult to reconcile with the restriction already referred to, where the power is conferred, not on shareholders generally, but on a special class, say, of debentureholders, where a majority, in exercising a power to modify the rights of a minority, must exercise that power in the interests of the class as a whole. This is a principle which goes beyond that applied in *Menier v Hooper's Telegraph Works* (**243**), inasmuch as it does not depend on misappropriation or fraud being proved. But their Lordships do not think that there is any real difficulty in combining the principle that while usually a holder of shares or debentures may vote as his interest directs, he is subject to the further principle that where his vote is conferred on him as a member of a class he must conform to the interest of the class itself when seeking to exercise the power conferred on him in his capacity of being a member. The second principle is a negative one, one which puts a restriction on the completeness of freedom under the first, without excluding such freedom wholly.

The distinction, which may prove a fine one, is well illustrated in the carefully worded judgment of Parker J in *Goodfellow v Nelson Line*.[6] It was there held that while the power conferred by a trust deed on a majority of debentureholders to bind a minority must be exercised bona fide, and while the court has power to prevent some sorts at least of unfairness or oppression, a debentureholder may, subject to this, vote in accordance with his individual interests, though these may be peculiar to himself and not shared by the other members of the class. It was true that a secret bargain to secure his vote by special treatment might be treated as bribery, but where the scheme to be voted upon itself provides, as it did in that case, openly for special treatment of a debentureholder with a special interest, he may vote, inasmuch as the other members of the class had themselves known from the first of the scheme. Their Lordships think that Parker J accurately applied in his judgment the law on this point ...

6 [1912] 2 Ch 324.

Their Lordships are of opinion that judgment was rightly given for the respondents in this appeal ... [It] is plain, even from his own letters, that before Mr JR Booth would agree to the scheme of 1921 his vote had to be secured by the promise of $2,000,000 ordinary stock of the Nickel Corporation. No doubt he was entitled in giving his vote to consider his own interests. But as that vote had come to him as a member of a class he was bound to exercise it with the interests of the class itself kept in view as dominant. It may be that, as Ferguson JA thought, he and those with whom he was negotiating considered the scheme the best way out of the difficulties with which the corporation was beset. But they had something else to consider in the first place. Their duty was to look to the difficulties of the bondholders as a class, and not to give any one of these bondholders a special personal advantage, not forming part of the scheme to be voted for, in order to induce him to assent ...

QUESTIONS

(1) You are asked to advise a preference shareholder about a class meeting which is to be held to consider a scheme to replace the preference shares with debentures. There is evidence suggesting that this will be to the disadvantage of the preference shareholders as a class, but that the scheme as a whole will benefit the company. Should he have regard to the interests of the class, or of the company, in deciding how to cast his vote; or is he free to weigh the relative merits of each? (See *Re Holders Investment Trust Ltd* (**181**) and *Re Hellenic and General Trust Ltd* (**259**), and contrast *Re Chatterley-Whitfield Collieries Ltd* (**179**).)

(2) If all the members of a class are to take account of the same considerations when voting, will a resolution invariably be carried (or lost) by 100% to nil?

The rights of a class of shareholders are not altered, or even 'affected', by a change in the company's structure (or in the rights attached to other shares) which affects merely the enjoyment of such rights.

218 White v Bristol Aeroplane Co [1953] Ch 65, [1953] 1 All ER 40 (Court of Appeal)

Article 68 of the defendant company's articles provided that the rights attached to any class of shares might be 'affected, modified, varied, dealt with, or abrogated in any manner' with the sanction of an extraordinary resolution passed at a separate meeting of the members of that class. The plaintiff, on behalf of the preference shareholders, claimed that a proposal to increase the capital of the company by a bonus issue of new shares (both preference and ordinary) to the existing shareholders 'affected' the voting rights attached to their shares, and therefore came within the terms of the article cited. The company's view, which was upheld by the Court of Appeal, was that the rights themselves (as distinct from the enjoyment or the effectiveness of those rights) were not 'affected' by the proposal, so that no class meeting was required.

ROMER LJ: The rights attaching to the preference stockholders are those which are conferred by articles 62 and 83; and the only relevant article for present purposes is article 83. Under that article it is provided ... that on a poll every member present in person or by proxy shall have one vote for every share held by him, or in the case of the preference stock, one vote for every £1 of preference stock held by him. It is suggested that, as a result of the proposed increase of capital, that right of the preference stockholders will in some way be 'affected'; but I cannot see that it will be affected in any way whatever. The position then will be precisely the same as now—namely, that the holder of preference stock will have on a poll one vote for every £1 of preference stock held by him. It is quite true that the block vote, if one may so describe the total voting power of the class, will, or may, have less force behind it, because it will pro tanto be watered down by reason of the increased total voting power of the members of the company; but no particular weight is attached to the vote, by the constitution of the company, as distinct from the right to exercise the vote, and certainly no right is conferred on the preference stockholders to preserve anything in the nature of an equilibrium between their class and the ordinary stockholders or any other class.

During the course of the discussion I asked Mr Gray whether it would not be true to say that the logical result of his argument would be that the rights of ordinary shareholders would be affected by the issue of new ordinary capital on the ground that every one of the considerations on which he was relying would be present in such a case. The votes of the existing shareholders would be diminished in power; and they would have other people with whom to share the profits, and, on a winding up, to share the capital assets. In answer to that he was constrained, I think rightly, to say that was so. But in my opinion it cannot be said that the rights of ordinary shareholders would be affected by the issue of further ordinary capital; their rights would remain just as they were before, and the only result would be that the class of persons entitled to exercise those rights would be enlarged; and for my part I cannot help thinking that a certain amount of confusion has crept into this case between rights on the one hand, and the result of exercising those rights on the other hand. The rights, as such, are conferred by resolution or by the articles, and they cannot be affected except with the sanction of the members on whom those rights are conferred; but the results of exercising those rights are not the subject of any assurance or guarantee under the constitution of the company, and are not protected in any way. It is the rights and those alone, which are protected, and ... the rights of the preference stockholders will not, in my judgment, be affected by the proposed resolutions ...

EVERSHED MR delivered a concurring judgment.

DENNING LJ concurred.

219 Greenhalgh v Arderne Cinemas Ltd[7] [1946] 1 All ER 512 (Court of Appeal)

The company had issued ordinary shares of 10s [50p] each and other ordinary shares of 2s [10p] each (created in 1941), ranking pari passu for all purposes. On a poll, every member had one vote for each share held by him, which meant that Greenhalgh, who held the bulk of the 2s shares, could control about 40% of the votes and so block a special resolution. The holders of the 10s shares procured the passing of an ordinary resolution subdividing the

7 For later litigation between the same parties, see above (60).

10*s* shares into five 2*s* shares, each ranking pari passu with the 1941 2*s* shares. Greenhalgh objected unsuccessfully that the rights attaching to his 2*s* shares were 'varied' by this manoeuvre.

LORD GREENE MR: Looking at the position of the original 2*s* ordinary shares, one asks oneself: What are the rights in respect of voting attached to that class within the meaning of article 3 of Table A[8] which are to be unalterable save with the necessary consents of the holders? The only right of voting which is attached in terms to the shares of that class is the right to have one vote per share pari passu with the other ordinary shares of the company for the time being issued. That right has not been taken away. Of course, if it had been attempted to reduce that voting right, e g by providing or attempting to provide that there should be one vote for every five of such shares, that would have been an interference with the voting rights attached to that class of shares. But nothing of the kind has been done; the right to have one vote per share is left undisturbed ... I agree, the effect of this resolution is, of course, to alter the position of the 1941 2*s* shareholders. Instead of Greenhalgh finding himself in a position of control, he finds himself in a position where the control has gone, and to that extent the rights of the 1941 2*s* shareholders are affected, as a matter of business. As a matter of law, I am quite unable to hold that, as a result of the transaction, the rights are varied; they remain what they always were—a right to have one vote per share pari passu with the ordinary shares for the time being issued which include the new 2*s* ordinary shares resulting from the subdivision.

In the result, the appeal must be dismissed with costs.

MORTON LJ delivered a concurring judgment.

SOMERVELL LJ concurred.

NOTE

See also *Re Saltdean Estate Co Ltd* (**180**) and *House of Fraser plc v ACGE Investments Ltd* (above, p 369), where it was held that no variation of rights was involved in the *cancellation* of a class of shares on a reduction of capital, this being consistent with the terms of issue of the shares in question.

Reference may also be made to *Re Hellenic and General Trust Ltd* (**259**), where Templeman J ruled that, for the purposes of a scheme of arrangement under ss 425–427A of the Act, ordinary shares owned by the intending purchaser's subsidiary constituted a different 'class' from ordinary shares owned by outsiders, although the terms of issue of all these shares were identical. This approach, taking account (as it does) of matters peculiar to the holder rather than to the shares themselves, is in strong contrast with that in the two cases last cited; but it may be justified by reference to the wording of s 425, which refers to classes of *members* rather than classes of *shares*.

8 [Of the 1929 Act; there is no equivalent article in the current Table A in view of the enactment of CA 1985, s 125.]

D. Transfer of shares

In this section we discuss the transfer of shares, but most of the remarks apply also to dealings in other company securities, such as debentures and debenture stock.

Shares in a company are in principle freely transferable, subject to any restrictions imposed by the company's articles of association.

Although a share is a species of chose in action, the transfer of shares is not governed by the ordinary rules of assignment. The legal title to shares is transferred only by registration of the new holder's name in the company's register of members.[9] Oddly, it is not possible to find any categorical statement to this effect in the Companies Act, although it is perhaps implicit from a reading of ss 182 ff. The true explanation of the rule is that it goes back to the days when shares normally had a substantial element of unpaid liability, and the act of registration established beyond argument the contractual bond of the new member to the company, so that his liability for calls could be enforced. (There was also probably some analogy with the transfer of Government stock, where the requirement of registration is statutory.)

Subject to these points, the transfer of shares and other company securities is governed—or rather, was until 1963, governed—by the articles of the company and the very limited statutory provisions corresponding to CA 1985, ss 182 ff. The signatures of both parties were invariably required. The Stock Transfer Act 1963 modified the former practice, in the case of fully paid securities, providing for the use of a simplified form of transfer signed only by the transferor; and, where the transaction takes place on a stock exchange, for a broker to name the transferee either in the original transfer document or in a separate instrument referred to as a 'brokers transfer'. The completed transfer, together with the share certificate to which it relates, is normally handed to the transferee in exchange for the purchase price, and he lodges these documents with the company for registration. The transfer is recorded by the company in the register of members and a new certificate, made out in the transferee's name, is issued to him.

Listed shares are now dealt with through a computerised settlement system for the transfer of shares and other securities. The Stock Exchange (Completion of Bargains) Act 1976 authorises the temporary vesting of shares in a Stock Exchange nominee (a company known as SEPON), which in due course re-transfers them to the purchaser.[10] The Act also provides for the keeping of a company's own records (such as its register of members) by computer, and for a company's share certificates to be authenticated by a special 'securities' seal, without any supporting signatures.

A further development is planned to take place in 1993—the introduction of paperless share dealing, sometimes referred to as 'dematerialisation' or TAURUS (transfer and automated registration of uncertificated stock). Statutory provision empowering the Secretary of State to make regulations 'for enabling title to securities to be evidenced and transferred without a written instrument' is made by CA 1989, s 207. Companies will then be able

---

9 Bearer shares are an exception: these are transferable by delivery. In Canada, the transfer of shares is governed by a modern code which comes close to making all share certificates negotiable instruments.

10 On the Act, see C Abrams, 'Talisman: a Legal Analysis' (1980) 1 Co Law 17.

to keep their records of shareholdings entirely on computer, and there will be no obligation to issue share certificates or to use a written form of transfer.

In smaller companies, the articles will almost invariably contain some restriction on a member's freedom to transfer his shares. In this way the relationship of confidence (and, in many cases, the family ties) which form the basis of so many small concerns can be safeguarded. It was, indeed, a statutory *requirement* until 1980 that the articles of a private company should contain such a restriction. The two provisions most commonly found are (i) an article giving the directors a discretion to refuse to register any transfer and (ii) some form of pre-emptive right for existing members.

Where the articles confer on the directors a discretion to refuse to register a transfer of shares, they must exercise their power bona fide; but, subject to this qualification, they may be given an absolute discretion.

220 Re Smith and Fawcett Ltd [1942] Ch 304, [1942] 1 All ER 542 (Court of Appeal)

Article 10 of the company's articles provided that the directors might in their absolute and uncontrolled discretion refuse to register any transfer of shares. There were only two directors and shareholders, Smith and Fawcett, who held 4,001 shares each. After Fawcett's death, Smith and a co-opted director refused to register a transfer of his shares into the names of his executors, or one of them; but Smith offered instead to register 2,001 shares and to buy the remaining 2,000 shares at a price fixed by himself. The court refused to intervene in the exercise of this discretion without evidence of mala fides.

LORD GREENE MR: The principles to be applied in cases where the articles of a company confer a discretion on directors with regard to the acceptance of transfer of shares are, for the present purposes, free from doubt. They must exercise their discretion bona fide in what they consider—not what a court may consider—is in the interests of the company, and not for any collateral purpose. They must have regard to those considerations, and those considerations only, which the articles on their true construction permit them to take into consideration, and in construing the relevant provisions in the articles it is to be borne in mind that one of the normal rights of a shareholder is the right to deal freely with his property and to transfer it to whomsoever he pleases. When it is said, as it has been said more than once, that regard must be had to this last consideration, it means, I apprehend, nothing more than that the shareholder has such a prima facie right, and that right is not to be cut down by uncertain language or doubtful implications. The right, if it is to be cut down, must be cut down with satisfactory clarity. It certainly does not mean that articles, if appropriately framed, cannot be allowed to cut down the right of transfer to any extent which the articles on their true construction permit. Another consideration which must be borne in mind is that this type of article is one which is for the most part confined to private companies. Private companies are in law separate entities just as much as are public companies, but from the business and personal point of view they are much more analogous to partnerships than to public corporations. Accordingly, it is to be expected that in the articles of such a company the control of the directors over the membership may be very strict indeed. There are, or may be, very good business reasons why those who bring such companies into existence should give them a constitution which confers on the directors powers of the widest description.

The language of the article in the present case does not point out any particular matter as being the only matter to which the directors are to pay attention in deciding whether or not they will allow the transfer to be registered. The article does not, for instance, say, as is to be found in some articles, that they may refuse to register any transfer of shares to a person not already a member of the company or to a transferee of whom they do not approve. Where articles are framed with some such limitation on the discretionary power of refusal as I have mentioned in those two examples, it follows on plain principle that if the directors go outside the matters which the articles say are to be the matters and the only matters to which they are to have regard, the directors will have exceeded their powers.

Mr Spens, in his argument for the plaintiff, maintained that whatever language was used in the articles, the power of the directors to refuse to register a transfer must always be limited to matters personal to the transferee and that there can be no personal objection to the plaintiff becoming a member of the company because the directors are prepared to accept him as the holder of 2,000 of the shares which have come to him as legal personal representative of his father. Mr Spens relies for his proposition on the observations in several authorities, but on examination of those cases it becomes clear that the form of article then before the court by its express language confined the directors to the consideration of the desirability of admitting the proposed transferee to membership on grounds personal to him ...

There is nothing, in my opinion, in principle or in authority to make it impossible to draft such a wide and comprehensive power to directors to refuse to transfer as to enable them to take into account any matter which they conceive to be in the interests of the company, and thereby to admit or not to admit a particular person and to allow or not to allow a particular transfer for reasons not personal to the transferee but bearing on the general interests of the company as a whole—such matters, for instance, as whether by their passing a particular transfer the transferee would obtain too great a weight in the councils of the company or might even perhaps obtain control. The question, therefore, simply is whether on the true construction of the particular article the directors are limited by anything except their bona fide view as to the interests of the company. In the present case the article is drafted in the widest possible terms, and I decline to write into that clear language any limitation other than a limitation, which is implicit by law, that a fiduciary power of this kind must be exercised bona fide in the interests of the company. Subject to that qualification, an article in this form appears to me to give the directors what it says, namely, an absolute and uncontrolled discretion ...

LUXMOORE LJ and ASQUITH J concurred.

NOTE

Re Smith and Fawcett Ltd is also a leading case on the general subject of directors' powers and duties. For this topic, see above, pp 284 ff.

In *Re Swaledale Cleaners Ltd* [1968] 3 All ER 619, [1968] 1 WLR 1710 it was held that the discretionary power of directors to refuse registration of a transfer must be affirmatively exercised: the directors must consider the matter and make a decision not to register within a reasonable time after the transfer has been submitted, failing which the transferee is entitled to registration. In the light of CA 1985, s 183(5), a reasonable time for this purpose is prima facie two months.

E. Share certificates and the certification of transfers

A share certificate is prima facie evidence that the person named thereon as shareholder is owner of the shares.[11] *The company is estopped from denying as against a bona fide purchaser of the shares that the person named is entitled to the shares referred to.*

221 Re Bahia and San Francisco Rly Co (1868) LR 3 QB 584 (Court of Queen's Bench)

Five shares in the company were owned by Miss Amelia Trittin. Without her knowledge Stocken and Goldner procured a forged transfer of the shares to themselves, and lodged the transfer and Miss Trittin's share certificate with the company for registration. The secretary in due course entered their names on the share register in place of Miss Trittin's, and issued a new share certificate in their names. Relying on this certificate, Burton and Mrs Goodburn, acting in good faith, bought the five shares on the stock exchange. After they had been registered as holders of the shares and issued with share certificates, the company was obliged to restore Miss Trittin's name to the share register. This action was brought by Burton and Mrs Goodburn, who claimed to be entitled to equivalent shares in the company, or damages. The court awarded them damages, holding the company estopped by the share certificate from denying the title of Stocken and Goldner.

COCKBURN CJ: I am of opinion that our judgment must be for the claimants. If the facts are rightly understood, the case falls within the principle of *Pickard v Sears*[12] and *Freeman v Cooke*.[13] The company are bound to keep a register of shareholders, and have power to issue certificates certifying that each individual shareholder named therein is a registered shareholder of the particular shares specified. This power of granting certificates is to give the shareholders the opportunity of more easily dealing with their shares in the market, and to afford facilities to them of selling their shares by at once showing a marketable title, and the effect of this facility is to make the shares of greater value. The power of giving certificates is, therefore, for the benefit of the company in general; and it is a declaration by the company to all the world that the person in whose name the certificate is made out, and to whom it is given, is a shareholder in the company, and it is given by the company with the intention that it shall be so used by the person to whom it is given, and acted upon in the sale and transfer of shares. It is stated in this case that the claimants acted bona fide, and did all that is required of purchasers of shares; they paid the value of the shares in money on having a transfer of the shares executed to them, and on the production of the certificates which

11 Compare CA 1985, s 186.
12 (1837) 6 Ad & El 469.
13 (1848) 2 Exch 654.

were handed to them. It turned out that the transferors had in fact no shares, and that the company ought not to have registered them as shareholders or given them certificates, the transfer to them being a forgery. That brings the case within the principle of the decision in *Pickard v Sears,* as explained by the case of *Freeman v Cooke,* that, if you make a representation with the intention that it shall be acted upon by another, and he does so, you are estopped from denying the truth of what you represent to be the fact.

The only remaining question is, what is the redress to which the claimants are entitled. In whatever form of action they might shape their claim, and there can be no doubt that an action is maintainable, the measure of damages would be the same. They are entitled to be placed in the same position as if the shares, which they purchased owing to the company's representation, had in fact been good shares, and had been transferred to them, and the company had refused to put them on the register, and the measure of damages would be the market price of the shares at that time; if no market price at that time, then a jury would have to say what was a reasonable compensation for the loss of the shares.

BLACKBURN, MELLOR and LUSH JJ delivered concurring judgments.

NOTE

A similar estoppel operates as regards the amount stated in the certificate to be paid up on the shares: see *Burkinshaw v Nicolls* (1878) 3 App Cas 1004.

It was particularly important at the time when this case was decided to establish liability on the basis of an estoppel, since there is no privity as between the company and the transferee which would give a remedy in contract, and the notion of a duty of care which would allow a claim to be based in negligence was then a century away. But now that liability in negligence for misrepresentations is well established (*Hedley Byrne & Co Ltd v Heller & Partners Ltd* [1964] AC 465, [1963] 2 All ER 575 and, perhaps most pertinently, *Ministry of Housing and Local Government v Sharp* [1970] 2 QB 223, [1970] 1 All ER 1009), a transferee would fairly clearly have a remedy on this ground, although of course he would need to be able to prove negligence.

QUESTION

Is the protection given by CA 1985, s 112(3) to transferees of shares which are not fully paid more extensive or less than that which they would get under *Burkinshaw v Nicolls* (above)?

In an appropriate case, the certificate holder may himself rely on an estoppel.

222　Balkis Consolidated Co v Tomkinson [1893] AC 396 (House of Lords)

Tomkinson, who held a share certificate stating that he was the owner of 1,000 shares in the company, sold the shares on the market to various purchasers. The company refused to register the transfers, on the ground that Powter, who had transferred the shares to Tomkinson, had had no title at the time, and that Powter had procured the issue of Tomkinson's certificate by fraud. Tomkinson bought shares on the market to honour the contracts with his transferees, and sued the company in damages to recoup this expenditure. The House of Lords, affirming the courts below, upheld his claim.

LORD HERSCHELL LC: After carefully considering the able arguments at the Bar, I have no hesitation in expressing my concurrence in the law laid down by the Court of Queen's Bench in *Re Bahia and San Francisco Rly Co* (**221**) ... The appellants argued, however, and correctly, that the present case is distinguishable from that in the Queen's Bench, inasmuch as it is not the purchasers who are seeking to render the company liable by way of estoppel, but the vendor of the shares, who himself received the certificate from the company. Does that, in the circumstances which your Lordships have to consider, make any difference? If the company must have known, as was said in the *Bahia and San Francisco Rly* case, that persons wanting to purchase shares might act upon the statement of fact contained in the certificate, it must equally have been within the contemplation of the company that a person receiving the certificate from them might on the faith of it enter into a contract to sell the shares. The plaintiff did enter into such a contract, and thereby altered his position by rendering himself liable to the persons with whom he contracted to sell the shares. All the elements necessary to create an estoppel would appear, therefore, to be present ...

LORDS MACNAGHTEN and FIELD delivered concurring opinions.

Where a certificate is issued which is based on the registration of a forged transfer, no estoppel arises against the company in favour of the person who submitted the transfer for registration.

223 Simm v Anglo-American Telegraph Co (1879) 5 QBD 188 (Court of Appeal)

Burge & Co bought stock in the telegraph company and had it registered in the names of their nominees. The transfer to them was a forgery, but none of the parties was aware of this: the stock in fact belonged to Coates, and had been sold by the fraud of his clerk. Burge & Co had their nominees execute a transfer to Simm and Ingelow to secure an advance from their bank, and the company in due course issued a certificate in the names of Simm and Ingelow. The forgery was discovered, and shortly afterwards the loan was repaid, so that Simm and Ingelow held as trustees for Burge & Co. The company refused to recognise the title which Burge & Co now claimed through Simm and Ingelow; and the court held that it was not bound by virtue of the certificate to do so.

COTTON LJ: When the real facts are ascertained, it is clear that independently of the question of estoppel, the action cannot be maintained; for the title of Simm and Ingelow has its origin in a forged transfer from one Coates. The stock which they claim is still at law and in equity vested in Coates, and he alone is entitled to be registered as the holder of it. But it has been urged that by the doctrine of estoppel the plaintiffs are to be deemed the owners of it, and the question has been argued as if Burge & Co were the only plaintiffs; I will, therefore, deal with the case upon that footing. I will first consider what is the meaning of the words 'title by estoppel' or if that phrase be objected to, 'right by estoppel'. As I understand, it means that where one person makes to another a statement which is afterwards acted upon, in any action afterwards brought upon the faith of that statement by the person to whom it was made, the person making it is not allowed to deny that the facts were what he represented them to be, although in truth they were different. It has been contended that upon this doctrine Burge & Co had a right of action against the company, and reliance has been placed upon *Re Bahia and San Francisco Rly Co* (**221**), and *Hart v Frontino Gold Mining Co*,[14] but they were in truth very different. In the present case certain persons on behalf of Burge & Co took to the company a transfer purporting to be executed by Coates: he was in fact a stockholder, but the transfer was a forgery, and the question is whether the company by issuing a certificate of registration to Simm and Ingelow, the nominees of Burge & Co, in any way made a representation, which prevents them from now saying that Simm and Ingelow are not the owners of the stock. I need only refer to the first of the two cases which I have mentioned, in order to show how different they are from this: there the persons making the application were not in the position of Burge & Co, but were in the position of a person who might have bought the stock in open market from the nominees of Burge & Co, and might have paid the price upon the faith of the certificate of registration issued by the company. To a buyer who did not know the real facts, the certificate would amount to a representation that the sellers were entitled to the stock, and under the doctrine of estoppel the buyer might maintain an action against the company, not as the real owner of the stock, but as a person whom the company were bound to treat as the real owner, because they had stated to him that the sellers to him were the real owners and that the transfer to the sellers was valid. But the facts here are very different. Burge & Co are driven to admit that Coates was the registered owner, and that he did not execute a transfer of the stock to them; but they contend that the company is estopped from denying that Coates did transfer the stock to them. Why ought the company to be estopped? All that occurred was that a transfer purporting to be executed by Coates was brought to the company's office; Burge & Co and the company had at least equal means of knowing whether the transfer was genuine ... There being in my opinion no duty between Burge & Co and the company to make inquiries, I think that there was no representation by the company to Burge & Co that the transfer was genuine: as it seems to me, the action cannot be maintained upon that ground. It is unnecessary to determine whether, if any representation had been made, Burge & Co could be considered to have acted upon it ...

[His Lordship then ruled that the fact that Simm and Ingelow might themselves have relied on an estoppel did not avail Burge & Co when they were once again owners of the stock.]

BRAMWELL and BRETT LJJ delivered concurring judgments.

NOTE

A person who presents a transfer to a company for registration, whether it is in favour of himself or someone else (e g a broker presenting a transfer on behalf of his client) impliedly warrants that it is genuine and, if it is not, may be liable to indemnify the company if it suffers loss by acting on it: *Sheffield Corpn v Barclay* [1905] AC 392;

14 (1870) LR 5 Exch 111.

Yeung Kei Yung v Hong Kong & Shanghai Banking Corpn [1981] AC 787, [1980] 2 All ER 599.

A forged share certificate is a nullity and does not bind the company.[15]

224 Ruben v Great Fingall Consolidated [1906] AC 439 (House of Lords)

[Another part of the decision is cited above (**108**).]

The plaintiffs Ruben and Ladenburg, who were stockbrokers, had procured a loan for one Rowe (the secretary of the defendant company) on the security of a share certificate for 5,000 shares in the defendant company, to which Rowe had affixed his own signature and the company's seal and had forged the signatures of two directors. The plaintiffs, having reimbursed the mortgagees, claimed damages from the company for failure to register them as owners of the shares. It was held that the company was not estopped by the certificate.

LORD MACNAGHTEN: My Lords, this case was argued at some length and with much ingenuity by the learned counsel for the appellants. In my opinion there is nothing in it.

Ruben and Ladenburg are the victims of a wicked fraud. No fault has been found with their conduct. But their claim against the respondent company is, I think, simply absurd.

The thing put forward as the foundation of their claim is a piece of paper which purports to be a certificate of shares in the company. This paper is false and fraudulent from beginning to end. The representation of the company's seal which appears upon it, though made by the impression of the real seal of the company, is counterfeit, and no better than a forgery. The signatures of the two directors which purport to authenticate the sealing are forgeries pure and simple. Every statement in the document is a lie. The only thing real about it is the signature of the secretary of the company, who was the sole author and perpetrator of the fraud. No one would suggest that this fraudulent certificate could of itself give rise to any right or bind or affect the company in any way. It is not the company's deed, and there is nothing to prevent the company from saying so.

Then how can the company be bound or affected by it? The directors have never said or done anything to represent or lead to the belief that this thing was the company's deed. Without such a representation there can be no estoppel.

The fact that this fraudulent certificate was concocted in the company's office and was uttered and sent forth by its author from the place of its origin cannot give it an efficacy which it does not intrinsically possess. The secretary of the company, who is a mere servant, may be the proper hand to deliver out certificates which the company issues in due course, but he can have no authority to guarantee the genuineness or validity of a document which is not the deed of the company.

I could have understood a claim on the part of the appellants if it were incumbent on the company to lock up their seal and guard it as a dangerous beast and if it were culpable carelessness on the part of the directors to

15 See, however, the comment at p 440, below.

commit the care of the seal to their secretary or any other official. That is a view which once commended itself to a jury, but it has been disposed of for good and all by the case of *Bank of Ireland v Evans' Charities Trustees*[16] in this House ...

LORD LOREBURN LC and LORDS DAVEY and JAMES OF HEREFORD delivered concurring opinions.

LORDS ROBERTSON and ATKINSON concurred.

NOTE

Ruben's case can be defended only upon the narrowest possible ratio decidendi, as set out at the head of this citation. As has already been observed (above, p 213), the company ought to be bound in such circumstances if a person who may be assumed to have authority to do so has put forward the share certificate as genuine. Now that it is recognised that the secretary of a company is not a 'mere servant', but a responsible officer having an important role in administrative matters (see the *Panorama* case (**148**)), it cannot be argued that he has no authority to guarantee the genuineness of a document such as a share certificate.

Even less supportable nowadays is the decision in *South London Greyhound Racecourses Ltd v Wake* [1931] 1 Ch 496, where the share certificate which was issued to Wake bore genuine signatures and a true impression of the company's seal, and the only irregularity was that the latter had been affixed without authority. Clauson J considered himself bound by the decision in *Ruben's* case to hold that the certificate was a 'forgery', upon which Wake could not base any claim.

A similar issue has arisen in a number of cases concerning the 'certification' of share transfers. Where part only of the shares to which a share certificate relates are transferred, it is customary for the transferor to lodge the certificate either with the company itself or with the stock exchange, instead of handing it to the purchaser. A 'certification' is then endorsed on the transfer form by the secretary of the company (or by an official of the stock exchange), confirming that the share certificate has been lodged. When the transfer is later presented to the company for registration, separate share certificates are issued which 'split' the original holding between those now entitled as separate owners. On the ordinary principles of vicarious liability, as recognised ever since *Lloyd v Grace Smith & Co* [1912] AC 716, the secretary's certification ought to be binding on the company (and that of the official binding on the stock exchange), even if he has acted fraudulently. However, in two decisions of the House of Lords, *George Whitechurch Ltd v Cavanagh* [1902] AC 117 and *Kleinwort v Associated Automatic Machine Corpn Ltd* (1934) 50 TLR 244, it was ruled that a secretary had no apparent authority to act for a company in the matter of the certification of transfers, so that where no certificate had in fact been lodged, the certification of a dishonest secretary was not binding on the company in favour of an innocent purchaser of the shares. These cases are seen by most commentators as an anomalous exception to the principle of *Lloyd v Grace Smith & Co*; but in the light of the new status accorded to the company secretary by the *Panorama* case (**148**), there is really no ground upon which they can be supported. It is, of course, now open to the House of Lords to disown its earlier rulings, in view of the relaxation of the strict doctrine of precedent. It is also possible that s 184 of the Act of 1985 modifies the effect of these cases, but the repeated use of the word 'authorised' in s 184(3) leaves room for doubt, since a court might well hold that this means 'having *actual* authority'.

16 (1855) 5 HL Cas 389.

QUESTION

Section 36A(6) of CA 1985 reads as follows:

> (6) In favour of a purchaser a document shall be deemed to have been duly executed by a company if it purports to be signed by a director and the secretary of the company, or by two directors of the company, and, where it makes it clear on its face that it is intended by the person or persons making it to be a deed, to have been delivered upon its being executed.
>
> A 'purchaser' means a purchaser in good faith for valuable consideration and includes a lessee, mortgagee or other person who for valuable consideration acquires an interest in property.

Would *South London Greyhound Racecourses Ltd v Wake* (above) be decided differently today in the light of this provision?

F. Competing claims to shares

A legal title to shares will prevail over an earlier equitable title; but a transfer of the legal title is not perfected until registration of the transferee as holder of the shares.[17]

225 Shropshire Union Railways and Canal Co v R (1875) LR 7 HL 496 (House of Lords)

Mrs Robson sought a writ of mandamus to compel the directors of the company to register a transfer of stock to her from George Holyoake, in whose name it stood. (Holyoake had given the transfer as security for a loan made by her late husband.) She failed because Holyoake had only a bare legal title (the beneficial interest being in the defendants themselves) and nothing which had happened had displaced the defendants' earlier equity.

LORD CAIRNS LC: [Undoubtedly] the position of matters was, that the defendants had the whole beneficial interest in the stock ... Theirs was the equitable title. Holyoake was a person who held merely the legal title and the right to transfer the stock. He was able, if not interfered with, to transfer the stock to any other person, and to give a valid receipt for the purchase-money to any person who had not notice of the beneficial interest of the defendants. On the other hand, any person with whom Holyoake might deal by virtue of his title upon the register, had, or ought to have had, these considerations present to his mind. He ought to have known that although Holyoake's name appeared upon the register as the owner of these shares, and although Holyoake could present to him the certificates of this ownership, still it was perfectly possible either that these shares were the beneficial property of Holyoake himself, or that they were the property of some other person. If he dealt merely by equitable transfer, or equitable assignment with Holyoake,

17 The requirement of registration had some justification in an earlier period when it was common for shares to be only partly paid up, but it makes less sense in the case of the fully-paid, listed security of the present day, where the responsibilities of a shareholder are negligible, the directors have no discretion to refuse registration, and the mechanics of transfer are a matter of pure routine. It is not obvious, for example, why the law should continue to refuse to recognise the possibility of a transfer of the title to such shares by (say) a deed of gift.

and if it turned out that the beneficial ownership of Holyoake was co-incident and co-extensive with his legal title, well and good; his right would be accordingly, so far as Holyoake was concerned, complete. But, if, on the other hand, it should turn out that Holyoake's beneficial interest was either nil, or was not co-extensive with the whole of his apparent legal title, then I say any person dealing with Holyoake, by way of equitable bargain or contract, should have known that he could only obtain a title which was imperfect, and would not bind the real beneficial owner. And, my Lords, he also might have known, and should have known, this, that if he desired to perfect his title, and make it entirely secure, he had the most simple means open to him—he had only to take Holyoake at his word. If Holyoake represented that he was the real owner of these shares, the proposed transferee had only to go with Holyoake, or to go with the authority of Holyoake in his possession, to the company, and to require a transfer of those shares from the name of Holyoake into his own name. If he had obtained that transfer, and the company had made it, no question could have arisen, and no litigation could subsequently have taken place ...

LORDS HATHERLEY and O'HAGAN delivered concurring opinions.

Where the equities as between successive transferees of shares are equal, the first in time prevails.

226 Peat v Clayton [1906] 1 Ch 659 (Chancery Division)

Clayton assigned all his property, including the blocks of shares in question, to trustees for the benefit of his creditors, but failed to hand over the share certificates when requested to do so. The trustees then gave notice of the assignment to the company, but took no further steps. [It should be appreciated that the company was not bound to receive this notice: see s 360 of the Act.] Clayton later sold the shares through Cohen & Co, brokers, on the stock exchange, handing over the certificates and transfers duly executed. When the company refused registration, Cohen & Co provided their purchaser with other shares in the company, and then in these proceedings sought to resist a claim brought by the trustees as plaintiffs for a declaration that they were entitled to the shares. It was held, however, that the trustees' interest prevailed, being prior in time.

JOYCE J: As I understand the law, where there are several claimants to shares registered in the name of a third person, the equitable title which is prior in time prevails, unless the claimant under a subsequent equitable title proves that, as between him and the company, he had acquired an absolute and unconditional right to be registered as the owner of the shares before the company received notice of the other claim.[18] In my opinion, therefore, the plaintiffs appear to be entitled to these forty shares in the Randfontein company. But Messrs Cohen claim a lien upon them. If they have any lien, however, it is only equitable, and can only be upon Clayton's interest, which is subject to the right of the plaintiffs under the deed of assignment. Then it

18 [In spite of assertions to this effect both here and in other cases, it is generally accepted that nothing short of the registration of the subsequent transferee as legal owner will defeat the prior equity.]

was said that the plaintiffs had disentitled themselves by negligence. I see no negligence on the part of the plaintiffs, unless it be, as Messrs Cohen allege, in not adopting the procedure now substituted by Ord 46, r 4, for the old procedure by distringas.[19] I cannot accede to the contention that by reason of the omission to adopt this course the plaintiffs must be postponed. If they had proceeded by distringas the result would have been just the same. It would only have prevented the company from registering the transfer to the purchaser, which in fact they did refuse to do by reason of the notice given to them on 8 November on behalf of the plaintiffs . . .

The result is that the plaintiffs are entitled to a declaration in their favour, and to an order . . . to register them as the holders of the shares.

[See also *Hawks v McArthur* (**228**).]

Although a company is not ordinarily bound by notice of a trust or other equitable interest affecting its shares, this rule does not apply when the company itself asserts an interest in the shares in competition with the person who gave notice.

227 Mackereth v Wigan Coal & Iron Co Ltd [1916] 2 Ch 293 (Chancery Division)

Shares in the defendant company which had formerly belonged to James Hodgson, deceased, were registered in the name of the trustees of his estate, one of whom was the son of the deceased, James Hodgson, junior. The company had notice that the registered shareholders held only as trustees. Later James Hodgson, junior, became indebted to the company and the company, purporting to exercise a lien conferred upon it by the articles, impounded certain dividends due on the shares and subsequently sold the shares to reduce the amount of the debt. It was held that this was an infringement of the rights of the beneficiaries of the estate, and that neither s 27 of CA 1908 [CA 1985, s 360] nor an article in similar terms applied in a case such as this, where the company was itself involved in the transaction.

PETERSON J: For the company it was argued that under s 27 of the Act of 1908, and the articles of association, no notice of any equitable interest or trust can affect the company in any way, and that, as the notice of the trust in the present case, which the company in fact received, must be treated as non-existent, or at least ineffectual, the lien which is conferred by the articles is operative. The argument leads far; for it would follow that, if a trustee of shares in a company informed the company that he held the shares for the benefit of other persons, and that he had not as against his cestui que trust any power of mortgaging them for his own benefit, he could yet effectually charge them to the company as security for money lent to him by the company . . . In several cases it has been stated in broad terms that a company 'need not take notice in any way of trusts': per Brett MR in *Société Générale de Paris v Tramways Union Co;*[20] or that any notice is absolutely inoperative to affect a company with any notice: per Lord Selborne in the same case in the

19 [Now RSC, Ord 50, rr 11–15: see below, p 444.]
20 (1884) 14 QBD 424 at 439.

House of Lords—*Société Générale de Paris v Walker*.[1] These observations had, however, reference to the obligation of the company to register transfers of shares. So too in *Re Perkins*[2] Lord Coleridge CJ said that companies have nothing whatever to do with the relations between trustees and a cestui que trust in respect of the shares of the company; but the question there was whether a cestui que trust of shares was a person entitled thereto as against the company, and it was held that the company had not a lien on the shares for the debt of the cestui que trust. If the passages in the judgments to which I have referred were intended to be of universal application, they are not in accordance with the judgments of the House of Lords in *Bradford Banking Co v Briggs & Co*.[3] The effect of this decision is briefly stated by Stirling LJ in *Rainford v Keith and Blackman Co*,[4] in these words: 'Where the company in which the shares are held sees fit to deal with the shares for its own benefit, then that company is liable to be affected with notice of the interest of a third party.'

I am therefore of opinion that s 27 of the Act of 1908 and article 9 of the articles of association do not protect a company which, in the face of notice that the shareholder is not the beneficial owner of the shares, makes advances or gives credit to the shareholder ... The result is that the company in the present case was wrong in asserting a lien against the beneficiaries, and must account for the proceeds of sale of the shares, and for the dividends which it has applied towards the satisfaction of the indebtedness of James Hodgson, junior.

NOTE

Although s 360 provides that no notice of any trust affecting shares shall be receivable by the company, it is possible by using the procedure prescribed by RSC, Ord 50, rr 11–14, to give an unregistered interest some protection with a 'stop notice'.

Rules of the Supreme Court, Ord 50

11 *Securities not in court: stop notice*

(1) Any person claiming to be beneficially entitled to an interest in any securities ..., other than securities in Court, who wishes to be notified of any proposed transfer or payment of those securities may avail himself of the provisions of this rule.

(2) A person claiming to be so entitled must file in the Chancery Chambers or in a District Registry—

(a) an affidavit identifying the securities in question and describing his interest therein by reference to the document under which it arises, and

(b) a notice in Form No 80 in Appendix A (a stop notice) signed by the deponent to the affidavit, and annexed to it, addressed to the Bank of England or, as the case may be, the body, state, territory or unit trust concerned,

1 (1885) 11 App Cas 20 at 30.
2 (1890) 24 QBD 613 at 616.
3 (1886) 12 App Cas 29.
4 [1905] 2 Ch 147 at 161.

and must serve an office copy of the affiadvit, and a copy of the notice sealed with the seal of Chancery Chambers or the District Registry, on the Bank or other person or body ...

12 *Effect of stop notice*

Where a stop notice has been served in accordance with rule 11, then, so long as the stop notice is in force, the Bank of England or other person or body on which it is served shall not register a transfer of the securities or take any other steps restrained by the stop notice until 14 days after sending notice thereof, by ordinary first class post, to the person on whose behalf the stop notice was filed, but shall not by reason only of that notice refuse to register a transfer, or to take any other step, after the expiry of that period ...

14 *Withdrawal, etc of stop notice*

(1) The person on whose behalf a stop notice was filed may withdraw it by serving a request for its withdrawal on the Bank of England or other person or body on whom the notice was served ...

QUESTION

To what extent does a stop notice give a person with an equitable interest in shares effective protection?

A transfer of shares for valuable consideration, even if it is irregular under the company's articles, is effective to transfer an equitable interest to the purchaser which will prevail over another equitable right accruing at a later date, e g a charging order nisi.

228 Hawks v McArthur [1951] 1 All ER 22 (Chancery Division)

[The facts appear from the judgment.]

VAISEY J: The plaintiff is the holder of a charging order affecting five hundred ordinary shares of £1 each in a private company called W Lucas & Sons Ltd, which stand in the name of, and were originally the property of, the first defendant, Mr Theodore Hunter McArthur, who has not entered an appearance in these proceedings. He claims that that charging order operates on Mr McArthur's interest in those shares, which, he says, is a complete interest, both legal and equitable. The second and third defendants, Mr Roberts and Mr Fraser, claim that the beneficial interest in the shares in question has passed to them as a result of transfers executed in their favour by Mr McArthur in pursuance of certain agreements entered into between themselves and Mr McArthur prior to the execution of those transfers, and they allege that Mr McArthur had no interest in the shares at the date of the charging order on which the charge could operate ...

There is, undoubtedly, a basic principle that a charging order only operates to charge the beneficial interest of the person against whom the order is made, and that it is not possible, for instance, to obtain an effective charging order over shares where the person against whom the order is made holds them as a bare trustee. The charging order affects only such interest, and so much of the property affected, as the person whose property is purported to be affected could himself validly charge ... [His Lordship then observed that the transfers of the shares had been made in total disregard of the requirements of the articles of association, which obliged an intending transferor to give notice to the company so that the other members could exercise rights of pre-emption. He continued:]

The real question in this case, I think, is whether the alleged agreements ... operated so as to amount in equity to a transfer of the shares held by Mr McArthur, as to 200 of them to Mr Roberts, and as to 300 of them to Mr Fraser, or whether the failure or neglect to follow the code laid down by articles 11, 12 and 13 completely vitiates the whole transaction, so that the transfers are worthless and there has been a total failure of consideration for the moneys which were admittedly paid over by Mr Roberts and Mr Fraser to Mr McArthur. It is suggested on behalf of Mr Roberts and Mr Fraser that, notwithstanding the complete failure to comply with the articles, the transfers and the antecedent agreements which must have been made—for one does not execute a transfer without a previous intention to do so—did, in fact, operate as a sale by Mr McArthur to Mr Roberts and Mr Fraser of, at any rate, the beneficial interest in the shares—otherwise the result would be that Mr Roberts and Mr Fraser paid their money and got nothing for it ...

Admittedly, Mr McArthur is still the legal owner of the shares. Admittedly, the plaintiff's rights under this charging order are in the nature of equitable rights. And admittedly, the rights of Mr Roberts and Mr Fraser, if they have any rights, are also equitable rights. As I have come to the conclusion that Mr Roberts and Mr Fraser have some rights and that what they did was not a complete nullity, the question is whose rights should prevail. A not irrelevant circumstance is that the equitable rights of Mr Roberts and Mr Fraser precede the equities or quasi-equitable rights under the charging order. In my opinion, the rights of Mr Roberts and Mr Fraser had already accrued at the time the charging order was obtained, and I think, as between the merits (not moral merits, but legal merits) of the plaintiff and the defendants, the rights of the second and third defendants, Mr Roberts and Mr Fraser, must prevail over the claims of the plaintiff ...

NOTE

A gratuitous transfer of shares may sometimes also be effective to transfer an equitable title to the shares. In two cases, each coincidentally named *Re Rose,* reported in [1949] Ch 78, [1948] 2 All ER 971 and [1952] Ch 499, [1952] 1 All ER 1217, it has been held that where a donor of shares has done everything in his power to divest himself in favour of the donee (e g by delivering to the donee, or to the company, an executed transfer and the relevant share certificate), the gift is complete in equity despite the absence of registration. This rule applies even where the directors have a discretion to refuse registration of the transfer. These decisions make all the more anomalous the old ruling in *Milroy v Lord* (1862) 4 De GF & J 264 that a gift of shares by deed is ineffective: equity now seems willing to assist some volunteers, but not others.

Note also *Tett v Phoenix Property and Investment Co Ltd* [1984] BCLC 599, where it was held at first instance that a transfer of shares made in breach of a pre-emption provision in a company's articles may be effective to confer an equitable title on a purchaser.

G. Disclosure of interests in shares

Substantial interests

Under provisions introduced for the first time in 1967, and significantly extended by the Acts of 1981 and 1989, *public* companies are required to maintain a register of what may conveniently be called 'substantial interests' in shares, and shareholders whose interests are 'substantial' in this sense are put under an obligation to notify the company of their shareholdings and of changes in the percentage of shares that they hold. The relevant provisions are now contained in CA 1985, ss 198–220 (as amended)—among the least intelligible parts of our legislation!

The rules now being discussed are additional to those which impose on *directors* an obligation to notify their companies of their shareholdings and of any changes therein and require companies to keep a similar register of directors' interests (ss 324 ff); but, as with those provisions, the interests of close relatives and of companies in which a person has a significant degree of control are aggregated with the person's own interests for the purposes of the statute. The object of these statutory measures is to enable directors and shareholders to know who has a controlling interest, or may be in a position to acquire such an interest, in their company. More particularly, they enable a close eye to be kept on those who might otherwise obtain control without adhering to the principles laid down in the City Code on Take-overs (below, pp 519 ff). It is an important feature of the provisions that beneficial as well as legal interests must be brought into the reckoning, so that the practice of secretly acquiring a large block of shares by placing them in the names of nominees ('warehousing') is thwarted; and options and rights convertible into shares are also covered.

Since the sections are concerned with questions of control, it is only voting shares which are affected. The percentage at present fixed as 'substantial' is 3%. A person comes under an obligation to notify the company within two days of his interest when he becomes aware that:

(a) it amounts to 3% or more;
(b) it is no longer 3% or more; or
(c) it is over 3% and has changed by a whole percentage point, e g from 8% to 9% or 7%.

Where the shares are held in someone else's name, the identity of such shares and their registered holders must be notified.

Concert parties

Where two or more people agree to act together to acquire shares in a particular company, or to use shares which they propose to acquire (e g as regards voting) in a particular way, they form what is commonly described as a 'concert party' and are obliged to notify the company of 'substantial interests' in the same way as if all the shares in question were held by each member of the party in his own right. In order to ensure that the members are aware that their combined interest is notifiable, they are placed by statute under an obligation to keep each other informed of changes in their individual shareholdings and of other relevant facts.

Register of interests in shares

As stated above, the information notified to a company under these statutory obligations must be kept in a register, where it is open to inspection (ss 211, 219).

Company investigations into share ownership

Under CA 1985, s 212, a company is empowered to require a person to inform it whether he has, or has had at any time within three years past, an interest in its voting shares and, if so, to supply information about that interest. The information so obtained must be recorded on the company's register of interests in shares. These powers apply to anyone, and not just to a member. And shareholders who themselves hold 10% or more of the voting shares may requisition the exercise of these powers by the company (s 214).[5]

Orders imposing restrictions on shares

Sections 454–457 provide for a special sanction which may be invoked for a failure to give a company information about share ownership under the statutory measure described above, or for giving false information: the court (s 216) or the Secretary of State (ss 210, 445) may impose restrictions on the shares in question, in effect freezing the right to transfer the shares and to receive dividends, vote and take advantage of rights offers. This can also be done by the company itself, if power to do so has been included in its memorandum or articles. The restriction order can be a particularly effective sanction in the case where holdings of shares are being built up secretly through nominees based overseas, who are not easily made amenable to our local jurisdiction and who may be able to shelter behind laws in their own country which protect the confidentiality of nominee arrangements. The weakness of the sections is, however, that the company must know which of its shares are being affected by the scheme which it supposes to exist.

H. Valuation of shares[6]

In the valuation of shares, the valuer is entitled to consider the realities of the company's situation, and may, e g decline to value the company's assets as a going concern if there is no expectation that the business will make profits.

229 Dean v Prince [1954] Ch 409 (Court of Appeal)

Dean (now deceased), Prince and Cowen had formed a private company in 1938, taking respectively 140, 30 and 30 shares. All three were 'working directors'. The company's articles provided that on the death of a director his shares should be bought by the surviving directors at a price to be certified as fair by the auditor. On Dean's death in 1951, his holding was valued for the purpose of this article at £7 per share. His widow challenged the valuation

---

5 There are also powers given to the Secretary of State under CA 1985, ss 442 ff to investigate questions of share ownership. These powers apply to all companies and not (like those of ss 198–220) just to public companies.

6 See generally N Eastway and H Booth, *Practical Share Valuation*, 2nd edn (London, 1991).

in these proceedings, but the Court of Appeal, reversing Harman J, held that the correct principles had been followed by the auditor and upheld his valuation.

DENNING LJ: In this case Harman J has upset the valuation on the ground that the auditor failed to take into account some factors and proceeded on wrong principles. I will take the points in order:

1 *The right to control the company.* Harman J said that the auditor should have taken into account the fact that the 140 shares were a majority holding and would give a purchaser the right to control the company. I do not think that the auditor was bound to take that factor into account. Test it this way: suppose it had been Prince who had died, leaving only 30 shares. Those 30 shares, being a minority holding, would fetch nothing in the open market. But does that mean that the other directors would be entitled to take his shares for nothing? Surely not. No matter which director it was who happened to die, his widow should be entitled to the same price per share, irrespective of whether her husband's holding was large or small. It seems to me that the fair thing to do would be to take the whole 200 shares of the company and see what they were worth, and then pay the widow a sum appropriate to her husband's holding. At any rate if the auditor was of opinion that that was a fair method, no one can say that he was wrong. The right way to see what the whole 200 shares were worth, would be to see what the business itself was worth: and that is what the auditor proceeded to do.

2 *Valuation of the business 'as a going concern'.* Harman J seems to have thought that the auditor should have valued the business as a going concern. I do not think that the auditor was bound to do any such thing. The business was a losing concern which had no goodwill: and it is fairly obvious that, as soon as Mrs Dean had sold the 140 shares to the other two directors—as she was bound to do—she would in all probability call in the moneys owing to herself and to her husband amounting to over £2,000. The judge said that she was not likely to press for the moneys because that would be 'killing the goose that laid the eggs', but he was wrong about this; because as soon as she sold the shares, she would have got rid of the goose and there was no reason why she should not press for the moneys. She was an executrix and the company's position was none too good. It had only £1,200 in the bank to meet a demand for £2,200. In these circumstances the auditor was of opinion that there was a strong probability of the company having to be wound up: and he rejected the going-concern basis. For myself, I should have thought he was clearly right, but at any rate no one can say that his opinion was wrong.

3 *Valuation of the assets of the business.* Once the going-concern basis is rejected, the only possible way of valuing the business is to find out the value of the tangible assets. Harman J thought that the assets should have been valued as a whole in situ. It was quite likely, he said, that 'some one could have been found who would make a bid for the whole thing, lock, stock and barrel'. But the judge seems to have forgotten that no one would buy the assets in situ in this way unless he could also buy the premises; and the company had no saleable interest in the premises. In respect of part of the premises the company had only a monthly tenancy: in respect of the rest the company had only a contract for the purchase of the premises on paying £200 a year for twenty-five years. It had no right to assign this contract;

and its interest was liable to be forfeited if it went into liquidation, either compulsory or voluntary; and the probability was, of course, that, if it sold all the assets, it would go into liquidation, and hence lose the premises. The company could, therefore, only sell the assets without the premises. That is how the auditor valued them and no one can say that he was wrong in so doing.

4 *Valuation on a 'break-up' basis.* The auditor instructed the valuer, Colonel Riddle, to value the plant and machinery at the break-up value as loose chattels on a sale by auction. Harman J thought that that was a wrong basis because it was equivalent to a forced sale. I would have agreed with the judge if the business had been a profitable concern. The value of the tangible assets would then have been somewhere in the region of £4,000 or £5,000, being either the balance sheet figure of £4,070 or Pressley's figure of £4,835. But the business was not a profitable concern. It was a losing concern: and it is a well-known fact that a losing concern cannot realise the book value of its assets. There is an element to be taken into account which is sometimes spoken of as 'negative goodwill'. It comes about in this way: if a business is making a loss, that shows that its assets, regarded as an entity, are not a good investment. A purchaser will decline, therefore, to buy on that basis. He will only buy on a piecemeal basis, according to what the various assets taken individually are worth: and it is obvious that on a sale of assets piecemeal, the vendor will suffer heavy losses as compared with the book figures. The auditor was therefore quite justified in asking the valuer to value the assets as loose chattels sold at an auction. At any rate, if he honestly formed that opinion, no one can say that he was wrong.

5 *The special purchaser.* Harman J thought that someone could have been found to buy the 140 shares who would use his majority holding to turn out the two directors, and reorganise the factory and put in his own business. In other words, that the shares would have a special attraction for some person (namely, the next-door neighbour) who wanted to put his own business into these premises. I am prepared to concede that the shares might realise an enhanced value on that account: but I do not think that it would be a fair price to ask the directors to pay. They were buying these shares—under a compulsory sale and purchase—on the assumption that they would continue in the business as working directors. It would be unfair to make them pay a price based on the assumption that they would be turned out. If the auditor never took that possibility into account, he cannot be blamed; for he was only asked to certify the fair value of the shares. The only fair value would be to take a hypothetical purchaser who was prepared to carry on the business if it was worth while so to do, or otherwise to put it into liquidation. At any rate if that was the auditor's opinion, no one can say that he was wrong.

I have covered, I think, all the grounds on which Harman J upset the valuation. I do not think they were good grounds. I would, therefore, allow the appeal and uphold the valuation.

EVERSHED MR and WYNN-PARRY J delivered concurring judgments.

NOTE

In holding that it was proper for the auditor not to take into account the fact that the block of shares carried with it control of the company, Denning LJ was no doubt correct on the particular facts of this case; but his remarks should not be accepted as laying down a general rule. In the court below, Harman J had held that the control factor was of paramount importance. In the Court of Appeal, Evershed MR said that he 'should not himself quarrel' with a rateable apportionment of an assets valuation among all the shares, but his judgment turned essentially on other points; while Wynn-Parry J held that no extra value should be placed on the controlling shares because (a) the article in question referred to the current worth of *the company*'s shares, not the deceased director's shares, and (b) whereas the seller might be parting with control, none of the surviving directors was necessarily *buying* it, since they were more than one in number.

It was established by *Short v Treasury Comrs* [1948] AC 534, [1948] 2 All ER 509 that where one purchaser is buying control but none of the vendors is himself selling a controlling interest, the extra value should be disregarded. But there are dicta in that case which strongly support the view that where a majority shareholding is sold by a single seller to a single buyer, it is proper to value the holding more highly. The same point is made obiter in *Re Grierson, Oldham & Adams Ltd* (**261**) and *Gold Coast Selection Trust Ltd v Humphrey* [1948] AC 459 at 473, [1948] 2 All ER 379 at 384.

An indication of the value of 'control' in practice can be gained from the following figures put by an expert on the value of different holdings in a small private company.[7]

Value of 100% shareholding: £100,000

,,	51%	,,	48,000
,,	50%	,,	35,000
,,	20%	,,	5,000
,,	10%	,,	1,000

Special considerations arise when the price of a minority holding of shares has to be fixed when the court orders it to be bought by the majority shareholders pursuant to an order under the 'unfairly prejudicial conduct' section (CA 1985, s 459): see below, pp 495 ff.

---

7 R M Walters, [1977] Brit Tax Rev 34, 44.

CHAPTER 10

Majority Rule and the Protection of Minorities[1]

A. The principle of majority rule

All powers within a company rest ultimately with one or other of its two organs, the shareholders in general meeting and the board of directors; and each of these bodies makes its decisions by majority vote. We have seen that the law normally allows a shareholder to treat his right to vote as an incident of property which he may prima facie exercise for his own advantage (*Peter's American Delicacy Co Ltd v Heath* (**59**)), and that even the strict fiduciary duties of directors do not go so far as to prohibit them altogether from acting in matters where their own personal interests are affected by what they do as directors (*Mills v Mills* (**138**)), still less from voting as they like in their capacity as shareholders (*North-West Transportation Co Ltd v Beatty* (**129**)). The three cases just referred to, and many others, also illustrate the traditional unwillingness of the courts to undertake to review matters of commercial judgment or policy or of internal administration. 'This Court,' said Lord Eldon, 'is not to be required on every Occasion to take the Management of every Playhouse and Brewhouse in the Kingdom.'[2]

The time-honoured and democratic principle of majority rule, backed by these other factors, necessarily means that quite substantial power is placed in the hands of those who control more than half of the votes on the board or at a shareholders' meeting—and, indeed, where shares are widely dispersed among a large number of members, comparable power can be wielded with command of a good deal less than 51% of the votes.[3] Minority members must, in principle, accept the decisions of the majority and must also acknowledge that the power lawfully enjoyed by their more numerous brethren is a fact of business life. In theory it is, of course, open to them to seek to bring about change by the normal democratic processes of persuasion, lobbying, publicity and so on; and it may sometimes be appropriate to argue that a shareholder who does not agree with the policy of those in control should sell his shares and invest his money elsewhere. In reality, however, neither of

---

1 For further reading, see A J Boyle, 'The Minority Shareholder in the Nineteenth Century' (1965) 28 MLR; Lord Wedderburn, 'Shareholders' Rights and the Rule in *Foss v Harbottle*' [1957] CLJ 194; [1958] CLJ 93; S M Beck, 'Shareholders' Derivative Action' (1974) 52 Can B Rev 159; A J Boyle, 'Minority Shareholders' Suits for Breach of Directors' Duties' (1980) 1 Co Law 3 and 'The Judicial Review of the Special Litigation Committee: the Implications for the English Derivative Action after *Smith v Croft* (1990) 11 Co Law 2; L S Sealy, 'Problems of Standing , Pleading and Proof in Corporate Litigation' in *Company Law in Change* (1987), p 1.

2 *Carlen v Drury* (1812) 1 Ves & B 154 at 158.

3 This is because the controllers can usually count on a high degree of apathy and inertia on the part of the small 'armchair' investor. In addition, various devices such as 'pyramid', circular and cross-holdings of shares between companies can be used to concentrate power: see the classic analysis of Berle & Means, *The Modern Corporation and Private Property* (New York, 1932) and M A Pickering, 'Shareholders' Voting Rights and Company Control' (1965) 81 LQR 248.

these courses may offer him a practical solution. He may not have the resources and will lack access to the necessary information to mount a successful campaign against those in the seat of power. And in a smaller company there will almost always be no market for his shares: the only available buyers (assuming that they are interested) will probably be the very majority shareholders with whom he is in disagreement, and they are likely to offer him only a derisory price.

In such circumstances, a frustrated minority shareholder may turn to the law for help; and it is obvious that the law must provide some remedies to meet those cases in which majority power has been abused. There cannot be power—including the power of control over other people's investments—without corresponding responsibility. But the law has to strike a delicate balance. If it too readily supports the majority and is prepared to condone unfair and wrongful acts and decisions on their part, the minority will be prejudiced and, in a small company, 'locked in' with an unrealisable investment which the majority can exploit to their own advantage. If, on the other hand, too great indulgence is shown to complaining minorities, they will be able to obstruct the company's legitimate business with tiresome requisitions and objections, and exploit their nuisance value.

Both the legislature and the judiciary have made attempts to reconcile the opposing needs and interests of controllers and minorities.

Statutory protection is given to minorities by formalities of various kinds, e g:

(a) requiring a special resolution rather than a simple majority vote in important matters, such as constitutional alterations;
(b) requiring the court's sanction, in matters like a reduction of capital or scheme of arrangement;
(c) giving dissentients a right to apply to the court to have a resolution cancelled, e g in an alteration of the memorandum or a variation of class rights, and sometimes empowering the court to order, alternatively, that they be bought out.

To balance this, some checks are imposed on the use of these measures by safeguards such as the requirement that dissentients applying to the court must have at least 15% support from their fellows.

Other statutory provisions give shareholders direct access to the courts. Foremost among these are the right to petition to have the company compulsorily wound up (IA 1986, s 124 (see below, pp 552 ff)) and the right to seek relief for 'unfairly prejudicial' conduct (s 459) (see below, pp 495 ff).

The judges for their part have allowed some rules to develop which are aimed at curbing the abuse of power by those with control. The directors, for example, are restrained by their fiduciary duties and by the 'bona fide' and 'proper purposes' principles. Majority shareholders, at least in the context of an alteration of articles and a variation of class rights, are also constrained to act bona fide in the common interest. But apart from these well-recognised (though not necessarily well-defined) limitations, the courts have by and large allowed laissez-faire principles to reign and majority rule to operate unchecked. They have thus avoided putting themselves into the position which so alarmed Lord Eldon.

The main judicial instrument by which this policy of non-intervention has been maintained is a rule not of substance but of procedure, which all company lawyers know as the rule in *Foss v Harbottle* (**232**). A minority shareholder who complains of a wrong or irregularity may well find this a formidable, and perhaps an insurmountable, barrier to his quest for justice, even where he has a real and well-founded grievance. The rule has attracted criticism from across the Atlantic both because of its complexity[4] and because it is considered unjust to recognise a substantive right but deny a remedy on procedural grounds.[5] But it has quite recently been defended with enthusiasm by the Court of Appeal in the *Prudential* case (**247**).

B. The rule in *Foss v Harbottle*

The court will not ordinarily intervene in a matter which it is competent for the company to settle itself or, in the case of an irregularity, to ratify or condone by its own internal procedure. Where it is alleged that a wrong has been done to a company, prima facie the only proper plaintiff is the company itself.

232 Foss v Harbottle (1843) 2 Hare 461 (Court of Chancery (Vice-Chancellor))

The bill in this case was brought by two shareholders in the Victoria Park Co (incorporated by statute) against the company's five directors and others, alleging that the property of the company had been misapplied and wasted and certain mortgages improperly given over the company's property. It asked that the defendants should be held accountable to the company, and also sought the appointment of a receiver. The Vice-Chancellor ruled, however, that it was incompetent for the plaintiffs to bring such proceedings, the sole right to do so being that of the company in its corporate character.

WIGRAM V-C: The Victoria Park Company is an incorporated body, and the conduct with which the defendants are charged in this suit is an injury not to the plaintiffs exclusively; it is an injury to the whole corporation by individuals whom the corporation entrusted with powers to be exercised only for the good of the corporation. And from the case of *A-G v Wilson*[6] (without going further) it may be stated as undoubted law that a bill or information by a corporation will lie to be relieved in respect of injuries which the corporation has suffered at the hands of persons standing in the situation of the directors upon this record. This bill, however, differs from that in *A-G v Wilson* in this—that, instead of the corporation being formally represented as plaintiffs, the bill in this case is brought by two individual corporators, professedly on behalf of themselves and all the other members of the corporation, except those who committed the injuries complained of—the plaintiffs assuming to themselves the right and power in that manner to sue on behalf of and represent the corporation itself.

It was not, nor could it successfully be, argued that it was a matter of course for any individual members of a corporation thus to assume to themselves the right of suing in the name of the corporation. In law the corporation and the aggregate members of the corporation are not the same

---

4 Dickerson, Howard and Getz, in *Proposals for a New Business Corporations Law for Canada* (Ottawa, 1971), §482, called it an 'infamous doctrine' which they recommended should be 'relegated to legal limbo without compunction'.

5 Hornstein, [1967] JBL 282.

6 (1840) Cr & Ph 1.

thing for purposes like this; and the only question can be whether the facts alleged in this case justify a departure from the rule which, prima facie, would require that the corporation should sue in its own name and in its corporate character or in the name of someone whom the law has appointed to be its representative ...

The first objection taken in the argument for the defendants was that the individual members of the corporation cannot in any case sue in the form in which this bill is framed. During the argument I intimated an opinion, to which, upon further consideration, I fully adhere, that the rule was much too broadly stated on the part of the defendants. I think there are cases in which a suit might properly be so framed. Corporations like this, of a private nature, are in truth little more than private partnerships; and in cases which may easily be suggested it would be too much to hold that a society of private persons associated together in undertakings, which, though certainly beneficial to the public, are nevertheless matters of private property, are to be deprived of their civil rights, inter se, because, in order to make their common objects more attainable, the Crown or the legislature may have conferred upon them the benefit of a corporate character. If a case should arise of injury to a corporation by some of its members, for which no adequate remedy remained, except that of a suit by individual corporators in their private characters, and asking in such character the protection of those rights to which in their corporate character they were entitled, I cannot but think that ... the claims of justice would be found superior to any difficulties arising out of technical rules respecting the mode in which corporations are required to sue.

But, on the other hand, it must not be without reasons of a very urgent character that established rules of law and practice are to be departed from, rules which, though in a sense technical, are founded on general principles of justice and convenience; and the question is whether a case is stated in this bill entitling the plaintiffs to sue in their private characters ...

Now, that my opinion upon this case may be clearly understood, I will consider separately the two principal grounds of complaint to which I have adverted, with reference to a very marked distinction between them. The first ground of complaint is one which, though it might prima facie entitle the corporation to rescind the transactions complained of, does not absolutely and of necessity fall under the description of a void transaction. The corporation might elect to adopt those transactions, and hold the directors bound by them. In other words, the transactions admit of confirmation at the option of the corporation. The second ground of complaint may stand in a different position; I allude to the mortgaging in a manner not authorised by the powers of the Act. This, being beyond the powers of the corporation, may admit of no confirmation whilst any one dissenting voice is raised against it[7] ...

On the first point it is only necessary to refer to the clauses of the Act to show that, whilst the supreme governing body, the proprietors at a special general meeting assembled, retain the power of exercising the functions conferred upon them by the Act of Incorporation, it cannot be competent to individual corporators to sue in the manner proposed by the plaintiffs on the present record. This in effect purports to be a suit by cestui que trusts complaining of a fraud committed or alleged to have been committed by

7 [It had not at this time been settled that an ultra vires transaction was incapable of ratification.]

persons in a fiduciary character. The complaint is that those trustees have sold lands to themselves, ostensibly for the benefit of the cestui que trusts. The proposition I have advanced is that, although the act should prove to be voidable, the cestui que trusts may elect to confirm it. Now, who are the cestui que trusts in this case? The corporation, in a sense, is undoubtedly the cestui que trust; but the majority of the proprietors at a special general meeting assembled, independently of any general rules of law upon the subject, by the very terms of the incorporation in the present case, has power to bind the whole body, and every individual corporator must be taken to have come into the corporation upon the terms of being liable to be so bound. How then can this court act in a suit constituted as this is, if it is to be assumed, for the purposes of the argument, that the powers of the body of the proprietors are still in existence, and may lawfully be exercised for a purpose like that I have suggested? Whilst the court may be declaring the acts complained of to be void at the suit of the present plaintiffs, who in fact may be the only proprietors who disapprove of them, the governing body of proprietors may defeat the decree by lawfully resolving upon the confirmation of the very acts which are the subject of the suit. The very fact that the governing body of proprietors assembled at the special general meeting may so bind even a reluctant minority is decisive to show that the frame of this suit cannot be sustained whilst that body retains its functions . . .

The second point which relates to the charges and incumbrances alleged to have been illegally made on the property of the company is open to the reasoning which I have applied to the first point, upon the question whether, in the present case, individual members are at liberty to complain in the form adopted by this bill; for why should this anomalous form of suit be resorted to, if the powers of the corporation may be called into exercise? But this part of the case is of greater difficulty upon the merits. I follow, with entire assent, the opinion expressed by the Vice-Chancellor in *Preston v The Grand Collier Dock Co*,[8] that if a transaction be void, and not merely voidable, the corporation cannot confirm it, so as to bind a dissenting minority of its members. But that will not dispose of this question. The case made with regard to these mortgages or incumbrances is, that they were executed in violation of the provisions of the Act. The mortgagees are not defendants to the bill, nor does the bill seek to avoid the security itself, if it could be avoided, on which I give no opinion. The bill prays inquiries with a view to proceedings being taken aliunde to set aside these transactions against the mortgagees. The object of this bill against the defendants is to make them individually and personally responsible to the extent of the injury alleged to have been received by the corporation from the making of the mortgages. Whatever the case might be, if the object of the suit was to rescind these transactions, and the allegations in the bill showed that justice could not be done to the shareholders without allowing two to sue on behalf of themselves and others, very different considerations arise in a case like the present, in which the consequences only of the alleged illegal acts are sought to be visited personally upon the directors. The money forming the consideration for the mortgages was received, and was expended in, or partly in, the transactions which are the subject of the first ground of complaint. Upon this, one question appears to me to be, whether the company could confirm the former transactions, take the benefit of the money that has been raised, and yet, as against the directors personally,

8 (1840) 11 Sim 327.

complain of the acts which they have done, by means whereof the company obtains that benefit which I suppose to have been admitted and adopted by such confirmation. I think it would not be open to the company to do this; and my opinion already expressed on the first point is that the transactions which constitute the first ground of complaint may possibly be beneficial to the company, and may be so regarded by the proprietors, and admit of confirmation. I am of opinion that this question—the question of confirmation or avoidance—cannot properly be litigated upon this record, regard being had to the existing state and powers of the corporation, and that therefore that part of the bill which seeks to visit the directors personally with the consequences of the impeached mortgages and charges, the benefit of which the company enjoys, is in the same predicament as that which relates to the other subjects of complaint. Both questions stand on the same ground, and, for the reasons which I stated in considering the former point, these demurrers must be allowed.

233 Mozley v Alston (1847) 1 Ph 790 (Court of Chancery (Lord Chancellor))

[The facts appear from the judgment.]

LORD COTTENHAM LC: This is a case in which two persons, not alleging distinctly that they are shareholders in a railway company, but so describing themselves, file a bill in which they allege that, owing to circumstances which I do not particularly enter into, twelve persons, who were originally appointed directors, ought, at a day now past, to have balloted out four of their number in order that four others might be elected in their stead; that they omitted to do so, and that, consequently, there is not now a body of directors constituted according to the Act; and, therefore, praying an injunction to the effect that these twelve persons may be restrained from voting or acting as directors of the company . . .

Now, it is not my intention to give any opinion upon the construction of the Act, because I see quite enough to make it my duty to allow these demurrers, without going into that question; and, indeed, one of the grounds on which I have come to this conclusion is, that it is not within the jurisdiction of this court to entertain that question at all, and I therefore abstain from expressing any opinion upon it.

The bill, as I stated, is a bill by two shareholders in their individual characters only, praying relief, in which all the other shareholders are interested. It is quite clear that some years ago no one would have entertained any doubt that such a bill was demurrable. It is true that the rule which requires all persons interested to be parties has been relaxed to meet the exigencies of modern times, it being found that too strict an adherence to it would operate in many cases as a denial of justice, and leave parties who had a real grievance without a remedy. And, therefore, where the grievance complained of is common to a body of persons too numerous to be all made parties, the court has permitted one or more of them to sue on behalf of all, subject, however, to this restriction, that the relief which is prayed must be one in which the parties whom the plaintiff professes to represent, have all of them an interest identical with his own . . .

The complaint against the defendants is, that they are illegally exercising the powers of directors, and illegally retaining the seal and property of the company. That, if it be an injury at all, it is an injury not to the plaintiffs personally, but to the corporation of which they are members—a usurpation of the office of directors, and, therefore, an invasion of the rights of the corporation; and yet no reason is assigned by the bill why the corporation does not put itself in motion to seek a remedy.

A case occurred some time ago before Vice-Chancellor Wigram, which is identical in principle with the present, I mean the case of *Foss v Harbottle* (**232**). An attempt, indeed, was made to distinguish them, but it entirely failed. In one respect, that was a stronger case for the interposition of this court than the present, for the bill stated a case of malversation in the corporate officers which was properly a subject of equitable relief. The plaintiffs sued, not as here in their individual characters only, but on behalf of themselves and all the other shareholders, except a few who were made defendants; but the Vice-Chancellor, after examining all the authorities, decided that such a bill could not be supported; and, as one of the reasons for coming to that conclusion, he said that, for anything that appeared to the contrary, there existed in the company the means of rectifying what was complained of, by a suit in the name of the corporation. And the same observation applies with still greater force to the present case, for not only does it not appear that the plaintiffs have not the means of putting the corporation in motion, but the bill expressly alleges that a large majority of the shareholders are of the same opinion with them; and, if that be so, there is obviously nothing to prevent the company from filing a bill in its corporate character to remedy the evil complained of. Such a bill would be free from the objections to which I have referred as existing in this case, for it would be a bill by a body legally authorised to represent the interests of the shareholders generally; but to allow, under such circumstances, a bill to be filed by some shareholders on behalf of themselves and others, would be to admit a form of pleading which was originally introduced on the ground of necessity alone, to a case in which it is obvious that no such necessity exists . . .

NOTE

Lord Cottenham's references to the novel form of pleading, modifying 'the rule which requires all persons interested to be parties . . . a form of pleading which was originally introduced on the ground of necessity alone' are an allusion to the representative action (below, p 464), which had been devised not long before.

QUESTION

Was the Lord Chancellor right in saying that the acts complained of were not 'an injury to the plaintiffs personally'? (Cf *Pulbrook v Richmond Consolidated Mining Co* (**93**).)

234 Gray v Lewis (1873) 8 Ch App 1035 (Court of Appeal in Chancery)

Gray brought a representative action[9] in equity on behalf of all the shareholders in C Lafitte & Co Ltd against the National Bank, alleging that the bank had applied certain moneys belonging to the company in breach of

---

9 See below, p 464.

trust. The claim was disallowed by the Court of Appeal on the merits, as it arose out of a series of illegal transactions (designed fraudulently to obtain a 'settling day' on the stock exchange); but it was also held that Gray had no right to sue.

JAMES LJ: I am of opinion that this bill was demurrable upon almost every ground on which a bill can be demurrable. I am of opinion that there is a wrong plaintiff, that there is a wrong forum, and that there is no cause of suit by a right plaintiff in a right forum. The bill should not have been filed by a shareholder on behalf of himself and all the other shareholders. It is very important, in order to avoid oppressive litigation, to adhere to the rule laid down in *Mozley v Alston* (**233**) and *Foss v Harbottle* (**232**), which cases have always been considered as settling the law of this court, that where there is a corporate body capable of filing a bill for itself to recover property either from its directors or officers, or from any other person, that corporate body is the proper plaintiff, and the only proper plaintiff. One object of incorporating bodies of this kind was, in my opinion, to avoid the multiplicity of suits which might have arisen where one shareholder was allowed to file a bill on behalf of himself and a great number of other shareholders. The shareholder who first filed a bill might dismiss it, and if he was a poor man the defendant would be unable to obtain his costs, then another shareholder might file a bill, and so on. It was also stated to us in the course of the argument that even after the plaintiff had dismissed his bill against a particular defendant a fresh bill might be filed against the defendants so dismissed. Therefore there might be as many bills as there are shareholders multiplied into the number of the defendants. The result would be fearful, and I think the defendant has a right to have the case made against him by the real body who are entitled to complain of what he has done.

Now in this case I am of opinion that the only person—if you may call it a person—having a right to complain was the incorporated society called Charles Lafitte & Co. In its corporate character it was liable to be sued, and was entitled to sue; and if the company sued in its corporate character, the defendant might allege a release or a compromise by the company in its corporate character—a defence which would not be open in a suit where a plaintiff is suing on behalf of himself and other shareholders. I think it is of the utmost importance to maintain the rule laid down in *Mozley v Alston* and *Foss v Harbottle,* to which, as I understand, the only exception is where the corporate body has got into the hands of directors and of the majority, which directors and majority are using their power for the purpose of doing something fraudulent against the minority, who are overwhelmed by them, as in *Atwool v Merryweather* (**241**), where Vice-Chancellor Wood, under those circumstances, sustained a bill by a shareholder on behalf of himself and others, and there it was after an attempt had been made to obtain a proper authority from the corporate body itself in public meeting assembled . . .

QUESTIONS

(1) Was it correct for James LJ to use the argument about avoiding a multiplicity of suits when Gray was suing in a representative capacity?
(2) Was the judge right to say that a defence alleging a release or compromise by the

company would not be open to a defendant who was being sued in a shareholders' representative action?

235 MacDougall v Gardiner (1875) 1 Ch D 13 (Court of Appeal)

[For other proceedings between the same parties, see (**238**).]

Gardiner, the chairman of the Emma Silver Mining Co, had adjourned a general meeting of the company without acceding to the request of a shareholder, MacDougall, and others, that a poll be held on the question of the adjournment. MacDougall now claimed a declaration that the chairman's action was improper, and an injunction restraining the directors from taking further action. The Court of Appeal held that this was a matter of internal management in which it should not interfere.

MELLISH LJ: In my opinion, if the thing complained of is a thing which in substance the majority of the company are entitled to do, or if something has been done irregularly which the majority of the company are entitled to do regularly, or if something has been done illegally which the majority of the company are entitled to do legally, there can be no use in having a litigation about it, the ultimate end of which is only that a meeting has to be called, and then ultimately the majority gets its wishes. Is it not better that the rule should be adhered to that if it is a thing which the majority are the masters of, the majority in substance shall be entitled to have their will followed? If it is a matter of that nature, it only comes to this, that the majority are the only persons who can complain that a thing which they are entitled to do had been done irregularly; and that, as I understand it, is what has been decided by the cases of *Mozley v Alston* (**233**) and *Foss v Harbottle* (**232**). In my opinion that is the rule that is to be maintained. Of course if the majority are abusing their powers, and are depriving the minority of their rights, that is an entirely different thing, and there the minority are entitled to come before this court to maintain their rights; but if what is complained of is simply that something which the majority are entitled to do has been done or undone irregularly, then I think it is quite right that nobody should have a right to set that aside, or to institute a suit in Chancery about it, except the company itself.

NOTE

For a comment on this case, and a suggested reconciliation with the apparently contrary ruling in *Pender v Lushington* (**240**), see C Baxter, 'Irregular Company Meetings' [1976] JBL 323, and the same author's 'The Role of the Judge in Enforcing Shareholder Rights' [1983] CLJ 96. His view is that 'the court will not interfere in the affairs of a company unless it is necessary to do so and that interference is always unnecessary when it has no practical consequence'. In the context of irregularities in company meetings, references to *Foss v Harbottle* are often gratuitous and irrelevant.

QUESTIONS

(1) The company's articles of association gave any five or more members the right to demand a poll, and MacDougall had the necessary support. Was there not a

wrong done here to MacDougall, a denial of his rights as a member? If so, how do you think he might have enforced them?

(2) Is the ratio decidendi of this case the same as that of the court in *Foss v Harbottle*?

236 Bamford v Bamford [1970] Ch 212, [1969] 1 All ER 969 (Court of Appeal)

[For the facts and another part of the decision, see (100).]

RUSSELL LJ: It is true that the point before us is not an objection to the proceedings on *Foss v Harbottle* (232) grounds. But it seems to me to march in step with the principles that underlie the rule in that case. None of the factors that admit exceptions to that rule appear to exist here. The harm done by the assumed improperly motivated allotment is a harm done to the company, of which only the company can complain. It would be for the company by ordinary resolution to decide whether or not to proceed against the directors for compensation for misfeasance. Equally, assuming that the allottee could not rely upon *Royal British Bank v Turquand* (102) it would be for the company to decide whether to institute proceedings to avoid the voidable allotment: and again this decision would be one for the company in general meeting to decide by ordinary resolution. To litigate or not to litigate, apart from very special circumstances, is for decision by such a resolution. If, as I consider, the company could validly decide by ordinary resolution not to institute proceedings to avoid the voidable allotment—a resolution which could not possibly be said to contradict or alter the articles— it seems to me to support entirely the view that an ordinary resolution in the terms posed in the point of law[10] would be effective, having as it would in substance the same purpose and effect as a resolution not to bring proceedings to avoid the allotment ...

HARMAN LJ delivered a concurring judgment.

KARMINSKI LJ concurred.

QUESTIONS

(1) Was Russell LJ right to say that the harm done by an improperly motivated allotment was a harm to the company of which only the company could complain? In *Re a Company* [1987] BCLC 82 at 84 Hoffmann J said:

Although the alleged breach of fiduciary duty by the board is in theory a breach of its duty to the company, the wrong to the company is not the substance of the complaint. The company is not particularly concerned with who its share-holders are. The true basis of the action is an alleged infringement of the petitioner's individual rights as a shareholder. The allotment is alleged to be an improper and unlawful exercise of the powers granted to the board by the articles of association, which constitute a contract between the company and its members. These are fiduciary powers, not to be exercised for an improper purpose, and it is generally speaking improper 'for the directors to use their fiduciary powers over the shares in the company purely for the purpose of destroying an existing majority, or creating a new majority which did not previously exist'. (See *Howard Smith Ltd v Ampol Petroleum Ltd* (141).) An abuse of these powers is an infringement of a member's contractual rights under the articles.

Are these views reconcilable?

10 [I e a resolution to ratify the allotment made irregularly by the directors.]

(2) Is it of any concern to a company who has control of it?

NOTE

In *Residues Treatment & Trading Co Ltd v Southern Resources Ltd (No 4)* (1988) 14 ACLR 569, the Supreme Court of South Australia held that an action to challenge an allotment of shares on the ground that the directors had acted for an improper purpose came within the 'personal rights' exception to the rule in *Foss v Harbottle* (**232**) (as well as being a breach of duty to the company for which the company itself could have sued), since such an allotment brought about an impermissible dilution of the plaintiff member's voting rights. King CJ said, at p 575: 'A member's voting rights and the rights of participation which they provide in the decision-making of the company are a fundamental attribute of membership and are rights which the member should be able to protect by legal action against improper diminution.' (He also expressed doubts whether *Bamford v Bamford* (**236**) was correct in treating such an act on the part of the directors as ratifiable; but it is submitted that *Bamford v Bamford* may be defended on this point for the reasons given above, p 156.)

Corporate litigation

In the passage cited above, Russell LJ says that 'to litigate or not to litigate' is for the company in general meeting to decide by ordinary resolution. But this is not a staightforward question. Where the articles confer the power to manage the company's business on the directors, and the question whether to sue (a debtor, say) *is* a matter of business, then plainly it is something within the directors' exclusive powers—and this will be so whether the intended defendant is an outsider, a member (*John Shaw & Sons (Salford) Ltd v Shaw* (**96**)) or an officer or former officer (*Regal (Hastings) Ltd v Gulliver* (**132**)). In a case brought while the company is in receivership, the receiver is the appropriate person to make the decision (but see *Newhart Developments v Co-operative Commercial Bank* (below, p 548), where exceptionally the directors were held to be competent) and, in a winding up, the liquidator.

But Russell LJ made his remarks in the context of a dispute which was not simply a 'business' matter: the question was whether the directors had exceeded or abused their powers. Where the directors are themselves implicated in the irregularity which is being complained of, it is of course consistent with such cases as *Foster v Foster* (above, p 198) that the shareholders should have the power to decide whether the company should sue or not, and this question will in many cases overlap with the question whether or not the irregularity should be ratified, with the result that the procedural and the substantive issues become confused. Most of the cases which are cited in this chapter are concerned with intra-corporate disputes relating to irregularities of this kind, and it was this sort of matter that Russell LJ had in mind.

The procedure adopted by the plaintiffs in *Foss v Harbottle* (**232**), and referred to (but not used) in *Mozley v Alston* (**233**), by which one or two persons are allowed to appear as plaintiffs or defendants on behalf of a number of persons having an identical interest in the proceedings, is known as a representative action. It was developed by the courts of Chancery in the early part of the nineteenth century, mainly to deal with the problems caused by the deed of settlement companies and other large unincorporated associations. Provision is made for representative actions in modern procedure by the Rules of the Supreme Court, Ord 15, r 12, part of which is cited below.

It is important to distinguish between three possible types of proceedings which may be brought in circumstances which are, at least in some degree, similar to those in *Foss v Harbottle*.

(1) A shareholder may sue to enforce some individual right of his own: for instance, in *Pender v Lushington* (**240**) the right to have a vote recorded or a proxy recognised. *Rayfield v Hands* (**44**) shows that the company is not a necessary party to such proceedings—unless, of course, it is claimed that the company is a party to the wrongdoing.

(2) A shareholder may claim that a right has been infringed which, although affecting him as an individual member, also affects in a similar way all or a number of the other shareholders. Those cases in which a shareholder has succeeded in a claim to have those in charge of the company observe the requirements of the Act or the constitution of the company itself are illustrations of this kind of action. The appropriate procedure here is a representative action: the company will usually be joined as a defendant in order that it will be bound by the court's decision.

(3) The right which has been infringed may, however, be purely one belonging to the company in its corporate capacity (eg the misapplication of its property, as in *Foss v Harbottle* itself). The only proper plaintiff in this case is the company itself. No problem arises if the action is brought in the company's name on the instruction of the board of directors or other appropriate organ. If anyone else begins an action in the name of the company, he does so at his peril, for the defendant may challenge his right to use the company's name, and if he cannot show that he had proper authorisation, both he and his solicitor will be personally liable to pay the costs. It is usual in such a case for the court to adjourn the proceedings and direct that a general meeting be held to confirm that the litigation has its support (see *Danish Mercantile Co Ltd v Beaumont,* (**237**)). This rule of practice is anachronistic, for it ignores the likelihood that in modern law the board of directors will have exclusive competence to make such a decision. However, it is apparent from the *Danish Mercantile* case itself that ratification by any duly constituted organ (in that case, the liquidator) will be effective.[11]

An alternative mode of procedure for the redress of a corporate wrong tacitly ignores the strict distinction between the company and the shareholders. It is usually referred to as a 'derivative' action (after the better-developed procedure of that name which has long been in use in the United States). This, which may be the only course open to a member in the case of a 'fraud on the minority' (see below, p 472), is to bring a *representative* action against the alleged wrongdoers, and to make the company a party by joining it as an additional defendant.[12] In contrast with the position in para (2) above,

11 See also the similar decision of the House of Lords in *Alexander Ward & Co Ltd v Samyang Navigation Co Ltd* [1975] 2 All ER 424, [1975] 1 WLR 673, where ratification by a liquidator of proceedings instituted without authority was held to operate retrospectively, so as to validate every step taken in the proceedings, including the arrest of a ship, which had occurred before the liquidator's appointment.

12 Note, however, that in *Wallersteiner v Moir (No 2)* (below, p 494), Lord Denning considered it to be in order for a shareholder to sue in his own name, on behalf of the company (which was added as defendant), without using the representative procedure. This is open to the objection that the other shareholders would not necessarily be bound by anything decided in Moir's proceedings; and Wallersteiner might very reasonably have objected that it exposed him to the risk of a multiplicity of suits.

where the relief sought may in fact be *against* the company, the primary beneficiary of the proceedings here will always be the company itself. The shareholder who initiates the action must show that the alleged wrongdoers are in control of the company, so that it is impossible for the company to bring a properly constituted action in its own name. In this way, an individual member can, exceptionally, sue to redress a corporate wrong.

Although it has long been established that a minority shareholder has *locus standi* to sue, using the derivative form, in order to redress certain types of corporate wrong, the recent cases of *Prudential Assce Co Ltd v Newman Industries Ltd (No 2)* (**247**) and *Smith v Croft (No 2)* (**249**) show that the courts are now adopting a restrictive attitude towards such suits: the shareholder will not be regarded as having a *right* to use the procedure unless he has the backing of a majority of his fellow shareholders, excluding the defendants. This new development is examined in more detail below, pp 491 ff.

Rules of the Supreme Court, Ord 15

12 *Representative proceedings*

(1) Where numerous persons have the same interest in any proceedings ... the proceedings may be begun, and, unless the Court otherwise orders, continued, by or against any one or more of them as representing all or as representing all except one or more of them ...

(3) A judgment or order given in proceedings under this rule shall be binding on all the persons as representing whom the plaintiffs sue or, as the case may be, the defendants are sued, but shall not be enforced against any person not a party to the proceedings except with the leave of the Court ...

The court may adjourn proceedings which have been brought without proper authority so that a meeting of the shareholders may be called to consider whether the proceedings should continue in the company's name.

237 Danish Mercantile Co Ltd v Beaumont [1951] Ch 680, [1951] 1 All ER 925 (Court of Appeal)

The defendants applied in interlocutory proceedings to strike out the name of the plaintiff company on the ground that the action had been commenced by the plaintiff's managing director without authority. Roxburgh J held that whether this was so or not, the action had since been ratified by the company (or rather by its liquidator, it being now in liquidation). The Court of Appeal affirmed his decision.

JENKINS LJ: I would refer to the passage in Buckley on the *Companies Acts* (12th ed), p 169, where the relevant law is, in my view, correctly summarised. The passage occurs in the course of a discussion on the circumstances in which a company's name can be used as plaintiff in an action and the exceptions to the general rule that a company is the only proper plaintiff in respect of a wrong done to the company, a discussion, in short, of the aspect of company law related to what is commonly called the rule in *Foss v Harbottle* (**232**).

The relevant passage (in Buckley) for the present purpose is in these terms:

'(6) If the case be one in which the company ought to be plaintiff, the fact that the seal is in the possession of the adverse party will not necessarily preclude the intending plaintiffs from using the company's name. Neither will it be necessary to obtain the resolution of a general meeting in favour of the action before the writ is issued. In many cases the delay might amount to a denial of justice. In a case of urgency, the intending plaintiffs may use the company's name at their peril, and subject to their being able to show that they have the support of the majority. In an action so constituted, the court may give interlocutory relief, taking care that a meeting be called at the earliest possible date to determine whether the action really has the support of the majority or not.'

That passage, where it refers to the calling of a meeting, accords with the well-settled practice of the court in cases in which, in proceedings brought by a company, a dispute arises as to the authority with which the company's name has been used as plaintiff. It is common practice in such cases to adjourn any motion brought to strike out the company's name, with a view to a meeting being called to see whether the company desires the action to be brought or not ...

I think that the true position is simply that a solicitor who starts proceedings in the name of a company without verifying whether he has proper authority so to do, or under an erroneous assumption as to the authority, does so at his own peril, and that, so long as the matter rests there, the action is not properly constituted. [It] can be stayed at any time, provided that the aggrieved defendant does not unduly delay his application; but it is open at any time to the purported plaintiff to ratify the act of the solicitor who started the action to adopt the proceedings, to approve all that has been done in the past, and to instruct the solicitor to continue the action. When that has been done, then, in accordance with the ordinary law of principal and agent and in accordance with the ordinary doctrine of ratification, in my view the defect in the proceedings as originally constituted is cured; and it is no longer open to the defendant to object on the ground that the proceedings thus ratified and adopted were, in the first instance, brought without proper authority.

For these reasons I am of the opinion that Roxburgh J came to a right conclusion, and that this appeal fails ...

HODSON LJ delivered a concurring judgment.

NOTE

In *Breckland Group Holdings Ltd v London & Suffolk Properties Ltd* [1989] BCLC 100, an action against A and others had been commenced in the name of L Ltd. The solicitors had acted on the instructions of H. H and A indirectly controlled respectively 51% and 49% of the votes at a general meeting of L Ltd, but under the terms of a shareholder agreement no decision on various matters, including the institution of legal proceedings, could be taken by the board of L Ltd without the affirmative support of two directors, each representing one of the major shareholders. Harman J held that this procedure could not be by-passed: without such a decision the action would not be properly constituted, and a general meeting (at which, of course, H's votes would carry the day) had no competence to interfere in the matter. The learned judge's ruling was based in part on the terms of the shareholder agreement and in part on the wording of an article which was similar in terms to Table A, art 70 (see above, p 187).

From this decision it would appear to follow that the practice referred to in *Danish*

Mercantile Co Ltd v Beaumont is out of line with modern views on the division of powers between a company's two principal organs, and that where there is a board capable of acting (and a fortiori where the articles or the terms of a shareholder agreement require some special procedure), a reference to the general meeting would be wrong.

The court will not intervene in a company's affairs by directing a meeting of shareholders to be called where those who are constitutionally empowered to summon or requisition a meeting bona fide decline to do so.

238 MacDougall v Gardiner (1875) 10 Ch App 606 (Court of Appeal in Chancery)

The plaintiff in a representative action sought a declaration that certain resolutions had been validly passed at a general meeting, or alternatively an order that a meeting of shareholders be summoned for the purpose of putting the resolutions to it afresh. Malins V-C ordered a meeting to be held, but on appeal it was held that the court had no power to do so.

[For other proceedings between the same parties, see (**235**).]

JAMES LJ:　[The] court has no jurisdiction whatever to do that which it is for the company itself to do according to the provisions of the articles. If a general meeting is wanted for any purpose, then the directors, if they think it for the interests of the company, have power to call a general meeting; but I do not think that the court has any jurisdiction to compel the directors to call the meeting, when they may honestly think it not for the interests of the company to do so. Then if the directors do not call the meeting, it is left to the shareholders to call it, with these restrictions, that before the company can be called together, and before they can be put to any such inconvenience, one-fifth[13] of the shareholders must give in a requisition to the directors, and if one-fifth do not join in it, then there is no power to call the meeting.

　Now, what power have we to say that a general meeting is to be called, if the directors do not think it right, and if one-fifth of the shareholders will not sign a requisition for the purpose? We have no authority, and there is, as it appears to me, no reason why we could interfere to do that which the shareholders have a right to do for themselves. The great principle laid down in the two cases of *Mozley v Alston* (**233**) and *Foss v Harbottle* (**232**) was, that whatever should be done by the company itself through its own internal organisation, ought to be left to the company, and ought not to be interfered with by this court ...

MELLISH LJ delivered a concurring judgment.

NOTE

This was not a case involving a dispute about the right to use the company's name in litigation: all that the judge was doing was enunciating the principle of majority rule, and drawing attention to the good sense that lies behind the normal constitutional provisions which allow a meeting to be requisitioned only when a significant percentage of supporters can be mustered. Curiously, this point does not seem to have

13 Now one-tenth: see CA 1985, s 368.

been considered in cases like *Danish Mercantile Co Ltd v Beaumont* (**237**), where there *is* a dispute about the use of the company's name in litigation: it seems to be assumed in those cases that a meeting will be held at the court's suggestion even though the self-appointed initiator of the litigation could not have requisitioned a meeting on his own and nobody else may wish to call one. It is doubtful whether for this purpose the court could invoke its powers under CA 1985, s 371. The Court of Appeal in *Prudential Assurance Co Ltd v Newman Industries Ltd (No 2)* (**247**) has ruled that the court must decide, *before* the substantive issues of the case are heard, the question whether a derivative action is properly constituted. For notes on other procedural aspects of the derivative suit, see below, p 494.

'Exceptions' to the rule in Foss v Harbottle

The exceptions to the rule in *Foss v Harbottle* are usually grouped under four heads. The rule is said to have no application:[14]

(1) Where the act complained of is ultra vires or illegal.
(2) Where the matter is one which could validly be done or sanctioned only by some special majority of members.
(3) Where the personal and individual rights of the plaintiff as a member have been invaded.
(4) Where what has been done amounts to a 'fraud on the minority'[15] and the wrongdoers are themselves in control of the company.

Whether these are properly regarded as exceptions depends upon the form in which the rule is stated. If the rule is expressed simply—that the only proper plaintiff in the case of a wrong affecting a company is the company itself—then all four may be seen as exceptions, for in each case an individual shareholder is allowed to sue. But if we think of acts which are strictly (and exclusively) wrongs to the company as a corporate body, then only the fourth is a true exception. Of course, not all wrongs that a shareholder complains of will be exclusively one thing or the other: an unconstitutional act by those in control may violate *both* his individual membership rights *and* those of the company, as has been recognised on many occasions: see, e g *Pulbrook v Richmond Consolidated Mining Co* (**93**) and *Pender v Lushington* (**240**). It ought to be possible in such a case for an action to be brought in the name of either the member or the company, but unfortunately the courts have not always appreciated this. We find them giving an individual complainant short shrift and showing him the door of the court on the basis of a somewhat peremptory ruling that the wrong person has been named as plaintiff. For an example, see *Lee v Chou Wen Hsien* (below, p 472); and contrast the views of Hoffmann J in *Re a Company* (above, p 461) with those expressed in *Bamford v Bamford* (**236**). If there really is a covert policy to discourage minority shareholders from engaging in litigation, it could hardly be better illustrated!

Exception (1) above now neeeds to be re-stated in consequence of the abolition of the ultra vires doctrine. A member now has a statutory right under CA 1985, s 35(2) to bring proceedings to restrain the doing of an act

---

14 These are the heads used as a basis for discussion by Wedderburn, 'Shareholders' Rights and the Rule in *Foss v Harbottle*' [1957] CLJ 194 at 203, to whom grateful acknowledgement is made. The same exceptions are listed (in a different order) by Jenkins LJ in *Edwards v Halliwell* (below).

15 More properly described in most cases as a fraud on the *company*: see the discussion below, p 476.

which would, but for the 1989 reforms, have been beyond the company's capacity (except an act to be done in fulfilment of an existing legal obligation). The position will thus be much the same, except that, whereas an ultra vires act was not capable of ratification at all at common law, this can now be done by special resolution (s 35(3)). But exception (1) will continue to apply to acts which are illegal, e g the support of an unlawful strike (*Taylor v National Union of Mineworkers* (*Derbyshire Area*) (below, p 494), or a transaction which violates the capital maintenance or financial assistance provisions of the Companies Acts (*Smith v Croft* (*No 2*) (**249**)). These two cases tend to confirm the view that in regard to illegal acts, the rules worked out with reference to ultra vires transactions will apply, namely that an individual member has a right to sue to restrain a *threatened* unlawful act (*Simpson v Westminster Palace Hotel Co* (1860) 8 HL Cas 712, HL) and to bring a derivative action to have an unlawful act set aside—which may involve restitutionary relief against a third party (*Russell v Wakefield Waterworks Co* (1875) LR 20 Eq 474); but that a claim to have directors and possibly others made personally liable for loss suffered by the company as a result of such a transaction will be treated in the same way as a fraud on the minority (below, p 476), and may not proceed without the support of a majority of disinterested shareholders. And, of course, illegal acts, like those under the former ultra vires doctrine, will continue to be unratifiable.

The rule in Foss v Harbottle *has no application where the articles require a special majority or procedure and the proceedings are brought to challenge a decision which has disregarded such a requirement.*

239 Edwards v Halliwell [1950] 2 All ER 1064 (Court of Appeal)

The plaintiffs as members of a trade union sued the union and the members of its executive committee claiming a declaration that a decision to increase the union dues payable by members was invalid on the ground that the union's rules, requiring a two-thirds vote on a ballot of members, had not been observed. Vaisey J granted the declaration, and his decision was affirmed by the Court of Appeal.

JENKINS LJ: The rule in *Foss v Harbottle* (**232**), as I understand it, comes to no more than this. First, the proper plaintiff in an action in respect of a wrong alleged to be done to a company or association of persons is prima facie the company or the association of persons itself. Secondly, where the alleged wrong is a transaction which might be made binding on the company or association and on all its members by a simple majority of the members, no individual member of the company is allowed to maintain an action in respect of that matter for the simple reason that, if a mere majority of the members of the company or association is in favour of what has been done, then cadit quaestio. No wrong has been done to the company or association and there is nothing in respect of which anyone can sue. If, on the other hand, a simple majority of members of the company or association is against what has been done, then there is no valid reason why the company or association itself should not sue. In my judgment, it is implicit in the rule that the matter relied on as constituting the cause of action should be a cause of action properly belonging to the general body of corporators or members of the company or association as opposed to a cause of action which some individual member can assert in his own right.

The cases falling within the general ambit of the rule are subject to certain exceptions. It has been noted in the course of argument that in cases where the act complained of is wholly ultra vires the company or association the rule has no application because there is no question of the transaction being confirmed by any majority. It has been further pointed out that where what has been done amounts to what is generally called in these cases a fraud on the minority and the wrongdoers are themselves in control of the company, the rule is relaxed in favour of the aggrieved minority who are allowed to bring what is known as a minority shareholders' action on behalf of themselves and all others. The reason for this is that, if they were denied that right, their grievance could never reach the court because the wrongdoers themselves, being in control, would not allow the company to sue. Those exceptions are not directly in point in this case, but they show, especially the last one, that the rule is not an inflexible rule and it will be relaxed where necessary in the interests of justice.

There is a further exception which seems to me to touch this case directly. That is the exception noted by Romer J in *Cotter v National Union of Seamen*.[16] He pointed out that the rule did not prevent an individual member from suing if the matter in respect of which he was suing was one which could validly be done or sanctioned, not by a simple majority of the members of the company or association, but only by some special majority, as, for instance, in the case of a limited company under the Companies Act, a special resolution duly passed as such. As Romer J pointed out, the reason for that exception is clear, because otherwise, if the rule were applied in its full rigour, a company which, by its directors, had broken its own regulations by doing something without a special resolution which could only be done validly by a special resolution could assert that it alone was the proper plaintiff in any consequent action and the effect would be to allow a company acting in breach of its articles to do de facto by ordinary resolution that which according to its own regulations could only be done by special resolution. That exception exactly fits the present case inasmuch as here the act complained of is something which could only have been validly done, not by a simple majority, but by a two-thirds majority obtained on a ballot vote. In my judgment, therefore, the reliance on the rule in *Foss v Harbottle* in the present case may be regarded as misconceived on that ground alone.

I would go further. In my judgment, this is a case of a kind which is not even within the general ambit of the rule. It is not a case where what is complained of is a wrong done to the union, a matter in respect of which the cause of action would primarily and properly belong to the union. It is a case in which certain members of a trade union complain that the union, acting through the delegate meeting and the executive council in breach of the rules by which the union and every member of the union are bound, has invaded the individual rights of the complainant members, who are entitled to maintain themselves in full membership with all the rights and privileges appertaining to that status so long as they pay contributions in accordance with the tables of contributions as they stood before the purported alterations of 1943, unless and until the scale of contributions is validly altered by the prescribed majority obtained on a ballot vote. Those rights, these members claim, have

16 [1929] 2 Ch 58.

been invaded. The gist of the case is that the personal and individual rights of membership of each of them have been invaded by a purported, but invalid, alteration of the tables of contributions. In those circumstances, it seems to me the rule in *Foss v Harbottle* has no application at all, for the individual members who are suing sue, not in the right of the union, but in their own right to protect from invasion their own individual rights as members . . .

EVERSHED MR and ASQUITH LJ delivered concurring judgments.

Where the rights of an individual member have been infringed, he may sue in the company's name notwithstanding the rule in Foss v Harbottle, *but he may also sue in his own name.*

240 Pender v Lushington (1877) 6 ChD 70 (Court of Chancery (Master of the Rolls))

Pender had split his shareholding among nominees in order to defeat a provision in the articles which fixed a maximum number of votes to which any one shareholder was entitled. The chairman refused to accept the nominees' votes and accordingly declared lost a resolution proposed by Pender, which would otherwise have been carried. The Master of the Rolls granted Pender (who brought a representative action on behalf of himself and the other shareholders, and also of the company) an injunction restraining the directors from acting on the basis that the nominees' votes had been bad. He also held that Pender had a right to sue in the company's name, at least until a general meeting resolved otherwise, and a further right to sue in his own name.

JESSEL MR: In all cases of this kind, where men exercise their rights of property, they exercise their rights from some motive adequate or inadequate, and I have always considered the law to be that those who have the rights of property are entitled to exercise them, whatever their motives may be for such exercise. [His Lordship then held that the registered shareholders were 'members' entitled under the articles to vote as they (or Pender) wished. He continued:]

I now come to the subordinated question, not very material in the view I take of the case, namely, whether you have the right plaintiffs here. The plaintiffs may be described as three, though they are really two. There is, first, Mr Pender himself, on behalf of himself; next, as the representative of the class of shareholders who voted with him, whose votes I hold to have been improperly rejected; and, next, there is the Direct United States Cable Company. It is said that the company ought not to have been made plaintiffs.

The reasons given were reasons of some singularity, but there is no doubt of this, that under the articles the directors are the custodians of the seal of the company, and the directors, who in fact are defendants, have certainly not given any authority to the solicitor for the plaintiffs on this record to institute this suit in the name of the company as plaintiffs. It is equally clear, if I am right in the conclusion to which I have come as to the impropriety of the decision of the chairman in rejecting these votes, that it is a case in which the company might properly sue as plaintiffs to restrain the directors from carrying out a resolution which had not been properly carried, and then comes the question whether I ought or ought not to allow the company now to remain as plaintiffs.

The first point to be considered is this: Supposing there was no objection to the right of a general meeting to direct an action to be brought, could I, even in that case, allow the company to sue? I think I could. In that case the general meeting, having a right to direct an action to be brought, would act by the majority of the members. The majority wish their rights to be protected. A meeting could be called, and, if the court was satisfied that the majority would direct an action to be brought, the company's name would not be taken away ...

But what is the court to do in the meantime, if it is satisfied that a real majority [would decide] in favour of bringing an action? Surely it must do something in the meantime, and it follows, I think, from that portion of the judgment, that in the meantime the court ought to grant the injunction to keep things in statu quo ... I think I ought not on this summons to take away the name of the company, but to let the summons stand over, leaving either party to call a meeting to decide whether the company's name is to be used or not. In the meantime, whether this is an action in the name of the shareholders or in the name of the company, in either case I think there should be an injunction ...

But there is another ground on which the action may be maintained. This is an action by Mr Pender for himself. He is a member of the company, and whether he votes with the majority or the minority he is entitled to have his vote recorded—an individual right in respect of which he has a right to sue. That has nothing to do with the question like that raised in *Foss v Harbottle* and that line of cases. He has a right to say, 'Whether I vote in the majority or minority, you shall record my vote, as that is a right of property belonging to my interest in this company, and if you refuse to record my vote I will institute legal proceedings against you to compel you.' What is the answer to such an action? It seems to me it can be maintained as a matter of substance, and that there is no technical difficulty in maintaining it ...

NOTE

The 'personal and individual rights' exception to *Foss v Harbottle* is well recognised, as the cases above show, but its limits cannot be defined with any confidence. The proposition is certainly true of some basic constitutional rights, such as the right to vote or to exercise a pre-emptive power over a retiring members' share, and *Edwards v Halliwell* illustrates it in operation in a trade union context, protecting a member against having his dues raised without proper procedure and from unjustifiable expulsion. But all these 'constitutional' rights have an element of property linked with them, and we can understand the readiness of the courts to come to the aid of a victimised plaintiff.

Where the complaint is about some mere matter of procedure, however, the courts seem much less willing to recognise what may be described as a 'right to have the company observe the terms of its own constitution' which an individual member can invoke to claim standing to sue. One difficulty about such a supposed right is that it is balanced by an obligation to abide by majority decisions, and there are some constitutional irregularities which it is within the competence of the members themselves to waive by a majority vote or even, on the reasoning of *MacDougall v Gardiner* (**235**), to acquiesce in. Certainly, dicta in cases such as *Re H R Harmer Ltd* (**251**) to the effect that members have a right to have their company conduct its affairs in accordance with its articles cannot be understood to apply without some such qualification.

Another difficulty concerns rights purportedly conferred on a member by the articles, but not in his character as member. Cases like *Eley v Positive Life Assurance Co* (**42**) are accepted as laying down a rule that 'outsider-rights' of this kind are not enforceable on a contractual basis by the member against the company, and it would be indeed odd if he could obtain indirectly what he could not get directly by bringing an action qua member to compel the company to comply with its 'constitutional' obligation to recognise his right. Note, however, *Pulbrook v Richmond Consolidated Mining Co* (**93**), where a director who had been excluded from board meetings was held to have suffered an individual wrong for redress of which he could sue in his own name, and also *Quin and Axtens Ltd v Salmon* (**95**).

QUESTIONS

(1) If a general meeting had been called and had voted against continuing the action, what would have happened to Pender's claim?

(2) In *Devlin v Slough Estates Ltd* [1983] BCLC 497 a shareholder sought a declaration that the directors had acted in breach of duty. He alleged that they had prepared accounts which failed to conform with the requirements of the Companies Acts, and also that they had failed to distribute accounts properly prepared in accordance with the Acts to the shareholders in advance of the annual general meeting as required by the company's articles. Dillon J held that Devlin did not have standing to bring either a derivative action on the company's behalf or an action in his own right complaining that his personal rights as a shareholder had been infringed. Is the decision of Dillon J consistent with the cases cited above?

(3) In *Lee v Chou Wen Hsien* [1984] 1 WLR 1202, [1985] BCLC 45, the plaintiff sued in his own name complaining that he had been improperly removed as a director by his fellow directors, who had purportedly acted under a power conferred by the articles. The Privy Council took the view that if a wrong had been done, it was done to the company, and that the rule in *Foss v Harbottle* precluded any action by the director in his own name. Do you agree?

(4) Gower, in the supplement to the 4th edn of *Modern Company Law*, p 579, suggests: 'The trade unions have, no doubt, been advised to buy a few shares in the companies in which their members are employed so that they can sue *qua* members on behalf of the company' to enforce the directors' duty to employees under CA 1985, s 309. Consider this recommendation.

Minority shareholders may bring an action on behalf of the company where it is alleged that a fraud has been committed against the company by those in control.

241 Atwool v Merryweather (1867) LR 5 Eq 464n (Court of Chancery (Vice-Chancellor))

Atwool brought this action on behalf of himself and all the other shareholders in the East Pant Du Lead Mining Co Ltd against Merryweather, Whitworth and the company, claiming rescission of a contract for the sale of certain mines by Merryweather and Whitworth to the company, and the return of money paid and shares allotted to them as consideration for the sale, on the ground that they had made a concealed profit. An earlier action, in which Atwool had filed a bill in the name of the company as plaintiff, had been declared incompetent because a majority of the shareholders, including

Merryweather and Whitworth, had opposed it. Page Wood V-C held that the plaintiff was entitled to bring an action in the present form (i e a derivative action) since, disregarding the votes of the alleged wrongdoers, a majority of the shareholders supported the plaintiff.

PAGE WOOD V-C: I think that, upon principle, a contract of this kind cannot stand, and that there is not such a defect in the constitution of the suit as would be fatal according to the authority of *Foss v Harbottle* (**232**).

Looking at the facts as they come out, I am clearly of opinion that this arrangement, by which Merryweather was to have £4,000 and Whitworth £3,000, was concealed from everybody, and that Merryweather assisted in that concealment by allowing his name to appear as the sole vendor, and taking the purchase-money.

Upon such a transaction the court will hold that the whole contract is a complete fraud ...

With regard to the frame of the suit, a question of some nicety arises how far such relief can be given at the instance of a shareholder on behalf of himself and other shareholders on the ground that the transaction might be confirmed by the whole body if they thought fit, and that the case would fall within *Foss v Harbottle,* according to which the suit must be by the whole company. On the previous occasion, when it was desired to take proceedings to set aside this transaction, a gentleman took upon himself to file a bill in the name of the company. A motion was made to take that bill off the file, as the person filing the bill was not the solicitor of the company, and was not authorised to file the bill, and I ordered the bill to be taken off the file. There was a majority against setting aside this transaction. The number of votes for rescinding the transaction was 324, and 344 the other way. But Merryweather, in respect of the shares obtained by this sale, which I have held cannot stand, had 78 votes, and Whitworth 28, making altogether 106 out of the 344. If I were to hold that no bill could be filed by shareholders to get rid of the transaction on the ground of the doctrine of *Foss v Harbottle,* it would be simply impossible to set aside a fraud committed by a director under such circumstances, as the director obtaining so many shares by fraud would always be able to outvote everybody else. I held on a former occasion, and I adhere to that decision, that the court must first be satisfied that the plaintiffs were authorised to call themselves the company, the solicitor who put the bill upon the file having no retainer under the corporate seal.

This bill being filed by the plaintiff on behalf of himself and the other shareholders, it is suggested that the proper course would be to file a bill on behalf of himself and the other shareholders for leave to use the name of the company, in order to set aside that contract. I do not think that circuitous course is necessary under any circumstances. It is quite clear that it is not necessary here, because in this case the purchase of the mines is the only thing for which this company was incorporated. It appears to me that it would not be competent for a majority of the shareholders against a minority to say that they insist upon a matter of that kind where the whole inception of the company is simply a motion by a fraudulent agent, qua director, to confirm a purchase as made for £7,000, which was made for £4,000. The whole thing was obtained by fraud, and the persons who may possibly form a majority of the shareholders, could not in any way sanction a transaction of that kind.

I think in this particular case it is hardly necessary to rely upon that, because, having it plainly before me that I have a majority of the shareholders, independent of those implicated in the fraud, supporting the bill, it would be idle to go through the circuitous course of saying that leave must be obtained to file a bill for the company, and pro forma have a totally different litigation. The only course now to take is to set aside the contract for sale and purchase of the mines, and cancel the agreement for such sale ...

242 Burland v Earle [1902] AC 83 (Privy Council)

The respondents, as shareholders, sued (inter alia) to compel the directors to declare a dividend, and to obtain an account from Burland, a director, of a profit made by him out of the purchase and resale to the company of certain plant and materials. The Privy Council rejected both claims. The question here discussed concerns the right of minority shareholders to sue when the alleged wrongdoers are in control.

The opinion of their Lordships was delivered by LORD DAVEY: It is an elementary principle of the law relating to joint stock companies that the court will not interfere with the internal management of companies acting within their powers, and in fact has no jurisdiction to do so. Again, it is clear law that in order to redress a wrong done to the company or to recover moneys or damages alleged to be due to the company, the action should prima facie be brought by the company itself. These cardinal principles are laid down in the well-known cases of *Foss v Harbottle* (232) and *Mozley v Alston* (233), and in numerous later cases which it is unnecessary to cite. But an exception is made to the second rule, where the persons against whom the relief is sought themselves hold and control the majority of the shares in the company, and will not permit an action to be brought in the name of the company. In that case the courts allow the shareholders complaining to bring an action in their own names. This, however, is mere matter of procedure in order to give a remedy for a wrong which would otherwise escape redress, and it is obvious that in such an action the plaintiffs cannot have a larger right to relief than the company itself would have if it were plaintiff, and cannot complain of acts which are valid if done with the approval of the majority of the shareholders, or are capable of being confirmed by the majority. The cases in which the minority can maintain such an action are, therefore, confined to those in which the acts complained of are of a fraudulent character or beyond the powers of the company. A familiar example is where the majority are endeavouring directly or indirectly to appropriate to themselves money, property or advantages which belong to the company, or in which the other shareholders are entitled to participate, as was alleged in the case of *Menier v Hooper's Telegraph Works* (243). It should be added that no mere informality or irregularity which can be remedied by the majority will entitle the minority to sue, if the act when done regularly would be within the powers of the company and the intention of the majority of the shareholders is clear. This may be illustrated by the judgment of Mellish LJ in *MacDougall v Gardiner* (235).

There is yet a third principle which is important for the decision of this case. Unless otherwise provided by the regulations of the company, a shareholder is not debarred from voting or using his voting power to carry a resolution by the circumstance of his having a particular interest in the subject-matter of the vote. This is shown by the case before this Board of the *North-West*

Transportation Co Ltd v Beatty (**129**).[17] In that case the resolution of a general meeting to purchase a vessel at the vendor's price was held to be valid, notwithstanding that the vendor himself held the majority of the shares in the company, and the resolution was carried by his votes against the minority who complained ...

QUESTION

Is the ratio decidendi of this case the same as that of Page Wood V-C in *Atwool v Merryweather* (**241**)?

A minority shareholder may bring an action where the majority shareholders are dealing with the assets of the company so as to benefit themselves at the expense of the minority.

243 Menier v Hooper's Telegraph Works (1874) 9 Ch App 350 (Court of Appeal in Chancery)

Hooper's company was a substantial shareholder in the European Telegraph Co, and had contracted with it to make and lay a cable to South America under certain concessions granted to the European company by the foreign governments concerned. Menier, a minority shareholder in the European company, claimed that Hooper's company had used its votes to procure the diversion of this business to a third company, to cause the abandonment of proceedings brought by the European company to assert its right to the concessions, and to have the European company wound up. The court, affirming Bacon V-C, held that a minority shareholder's action was properly brought in these circumstances.

JAMES LJ: The defendants, who have a majority of shares in the company, have made an arrangement by which they have dealt with matters affecting the whole company, the interest in which belongs to the minority as well as to the majority. They have dealt with them in consideration of their obtaining for themselves certain advantages. Hooper's company have obtained certain advantages by dealing with something which was the property of the whole company. The minority of the shareholders say in effect that the majority has divided the assets of the company, more or less, between themselves, to the exclusion of the minority. I think it would be a shocking thing if that could be done, because if so the majority might divide the whole assets of the company, and pass a resolution that everything must be given to them, and that the minority should having nothing to do with it. Assuming the case to be as alleged by the bill, then the majority have put something into their pockets at the expense of the minority. If so, it appears to me that the minority have a right to have their share of the benefits ascertained for them in the best way in which the court can do it, and given to them.

It is said, however, that this is not the right form of suit, because, according to the principles laid down in *Foss v Harbottle* (**232**), and other similar cases, the court ought to be very slow indeed in allowing a shareholder to file a bill,

17 [But note that even in that case the view was expressed that the minority ought to be allowed to sue, in order to try to establish that there *had* been impropriety: see above, p 259.]

where the company is the proper plaintiff. This particular case seems to me precisely one of the exceptions referred to by Vice-Chancellor Wood in *Atwool v Merryweather* (**241**), a case in which the majority were the defendants, the wrongdoers, who were alleged to have put the minority's property into their pockets. In this case it is right and proper for a bill to be filed by one shareholder on behalf of himself and all the other shareholders.

Therefore the demurrer ought to be overruled.

MELLISH LJ: I am entirely of the same opinion.

It so happens that Hooper's company are the majority in this company, and a suit by this company was pending which might or might not turn out advantageous to this company. The plaintiff says that Hooper's company being the majority, have procured that suit to be settled upon terms favourable to themselves, they getting a consideration for settling it in the shape of a profitable bargain for the laying of a cable. I am of opinion that although it may be quite true that the shareholders of a company may vote as they please, and for the purpose of their own interests, yet that the majority of shareholders cannot sell the assets of the company and keep the consideration, but must allow the minority to have their share of any consideration which may come to them. I also entirely agree that, under the circumstances, the suit is properly brought in the name of the plaintiff on behalf of himself and all the other shareholders.

The appeal will be dismissed with costs.

QUESTION

Was it important to the reasoning in this case that a winding up was imminent? Should this fact have made any difference?

NOTE

The cases of *Atwool v Merryweather* (**241**) and *Menier v Hooper's Telegraph Works* (**243**) are classic instances of the exception to the rule in *Foss v Harbottle* which is commonly known as 'fraud on the minority'—the fourth of the exceptions listed on p 467 above. It is in this situation that a derivative action is allowed to be brought by a shareholder even though the wrong that is being complained of is a corporate wrong and not one to him as an individual. 'Fraud on the minority' is plainly a misnomer in these cases, since the primary victim is the company itself; and a good deal of confusion would be avoided if the concept were renamed 'fraud on the company'. It is true that the minority shareholders suffer loss indirectly, since their investment is damaged or destroyed, but it would be wrong to attach much weight to this fact, since the Court of Appeal in the *Prudential* case (**247**) has ruled that such an indirect loss may not be relied on by a shareholder suing in his own right, even in an action of conspiracy or deceit. There are other cases in which a minority shareholder is allowed to sue to complain that he has been discriminated against or disadvantaged by the action of the majority shareholders (e g *Edwards v Halliwell* (**239**), *Alexander v Automatic Telephone Co* (**244**) and *Estmanco (Kilner House) Ltd v GLC* (**248**), and these may perhaps be termed 'fraud on the minority' in a true sense. The scope of the concept is not clearly settled: there is a difference of opinion, for instance, whether the cases in which an alteration of articles has been challenged (above, pp 111 ff) should be included. The cases which follow offer further illustration, even if it is only of the confused state of the law!

244 Alexander v Automatic Telephone Co [1900] 2 Ch 56 (Court of Appeal)

All the subscribers to the memorandum of association of the defendant company paid 6*d* [2½p] per share on subscription. The five directors of the company held a meeting at which it was resolved that a further 2*s* 6*d* [12½p] per share should be made, payable upon allotment by all the shareholders except the three directors who had the largest shareholdings (about 75% of the issued shares). The remaining two directors (who had in fact supported the resolution) then brought a representative action against the three directors and the company, claiming a declaration that *all* the shareholders were bound to pay the 2*s* 6*d*. The Court of Appeal, reversing Cozens-Hardy J, granted the relief asked.

LINDLEY MR: The fact ... that [other] subscribers of the memorandum paid 3*s* on their shares whilst the defendants did not, is difficult to reconcile with the existence of any understanding that all the subscribers should stand on their legal rights. The defendants rely on clause 5 of the articles as entitling the directors to issue shares on any terms they think expedient, and to make differences between some shareholders and others. But this, I am satisfied, is an afterthought. The defendants were not in fact acting on this article at all. But, even if they were, this article would not, in my opinion, justify them in making a difference in their own favour without disclosing the fact to the other shareholders and obtaining their consent to the arrangement. The Court of Chancery has always exacted from directors the observance of good faith towards their shareholders and towards those who take shares from the company and become co-adventurers with themselves and others who may join them. The maxim 'Caveat emptor' has no application to such cases, and directors who so use their powers as to obtain benefits for themselves at the expense of the shareholders, without informing them of the fact, cannot retain those benefits and must account for them to the company, so that all the shareholders may participate in them ...

In the present case there is no question but that, by obtaining 3*s* a share from the other shareholders and paying nothing themselves, the defendants threw upon the other shareholders a burden which they did not share themselves. It is true that by clause 121 of the articles dividends were only payable in proportion to the amounts paid up on the shares; and as regards dividends, had there been any, the defendants would have been at a disadvantage. But the advantage they obtained at the expense of the other shareholders was that of deferring their own contributions to the funds of the company at the expense of the other shareholders. This, in my opinion, was a clear breach of duty, unless the other shareholders knew of it and sanctioned it ...

Upon the merits of the case I come to the conclusion that a breach of duty by the directors to the company and the other shareholders in it has been established.

It is necessary, however, to consider the form of the action, and the relief which can be given. The breach of duty to the company consists in depriving it of the use of the money which the directors ought to have paid up sooner than they did. I cannot regard the case as one of mere internal management which, according to *Foss v Harbottle* (**232**) and numerous other cases, the court leaves the shareholders to settle amongst themselves. It was ascertained and admitted at the trial that, when this action was commenced, the defendants held such a preponderance of shares that they could not be controlled by the other shareholders. Under these circumstances an action by some shareholders on behalf of themselves and the others against the defendants is in accordance with the authorities, and is unobjectionable in form: see *Menier v Hooper's Telegraph Works* **(243)**. An action in this form is far preferable to an action in the name of the company, and then a fight as to the right to use its name. But this last mode of procedure is the only other open to a minority of shareholders in cases like the present . . .

RIGBY and VAUGHAN WILLIAMS LJJ delivered concurring judgments.

QUESTION

Should the two plaintiffs have been allowed to sue (and to do so in representative form) when they had themselves voted for the resolution?

NOTE

There seems to have been some confusion in this case whether the defendant directors had broken a duty to the company or to their fellow shareholders, or to both. The relief which was sought and granted certainly achieved the desired equality of treatment as between shareholders; but it also had the perhaps unwanted consequence that the company was obliged to receive, and the shareholders as a whole to pay, nearly four times the additional capital which appears to have been needed at the time of allotment. This could not have been returned without a formal reduction.

An individual plaintiff may not sue when the claim is based only on negligence.

245 Pavlides v Jensen [1956] Ch 565, [1956] 2 All ER 518 (Chancery Division)

The plaintiff, a minority shareholder in Tunnel Asbestos Cement Co Ltd, brought a representative action against the defendants, its directors, alleging that they had sold an asbestos mine in Cyprus to an associated company at a gross undervalue and had thereby been guilty of negligence. The defendants objected that he had no right to sue, and the court agreed.

DANCKWERTS J: It is contended on behalf of the defendants that the matters in respect of which the plaintiff complains, and in particular the question whether proceedings should be taken against the directors, is a matter of internal management of the company with which, on the principle stated in *Foss v Harbottle* **(232)**, the court normally will not interfere. It is contended further on behalf of the defendants that the present case—based on negligence of directors—is not within the few recognised exceptions to the above-mentioned rule, namely, cases of ultra vires, illegality, or fraud (including fraudulent oppression of a minority by the majority of the shareholders). Further, it is said, the case is not a case where the control of the voting power is in the hands of the directors of the company whose actions are impugned; for they are not the shareholders; the shares are held by another company of which the defendant directors merely happen also to be among the directors.

For the plaintiff, it is contended that the above-mentioned exceptions are not exhaustive, and the court will grant relief wherever justice requires on any ground, and particularly where an otherwise helpless minority shareholder is in need of assistance by the court. As regards control, it is contended that, except for an immaterial period, the defendant directors, being a majority of the directors of Portland Tunnel Cement Co Ltd (the holders of the vast bulk of the shares of the company) were in a position to stifle any attempt to institute proceedings in the name of the company against them. [His Lordship considered the authorities and continued:]

On the facts of the present case the sale of the company's mine was not beyond the powers of the company, and it is not alleged to be ultra vires. There is no allegation of fraud on the part of the directors or appropriation of assets of the company by the majority shareholders in fraud of the minority. It was open to the company, on the resolution of a majority of the shareholders, to sell the mine at a price decided by the company in that manner, and it was open to the company by a vote of the majority to decide that, if the directors by their negligence or error of judgment had sold the company's mine at an undervalue, proceedings should not be taken by the company against the directors. Applying, therefore, the principles as stated by Lord Davey,[18] it is impossible to see how the present action can be maintained.

I have examined again all of the large number of authorities which were cited to me in the course of the arguments. Though there are to be found, in one or two instances, observations which at first sight might justify a more liberal view of the extent of minority shareholders' rights, when taken out of their context, I do not think any of the authorities justify any conclusion other than that which I have reached.

That really disposes of the matter, and it is not really necessary to consider whether, on the allegations contained in the re-amended statement of claim, the defendant directors can be said to have such control of the company as to require (in any appropriate case) the allowance of an action by a minority shareholder. The defendant directors are not in fact the holders of the shares, the voting power of which would settle the company's decision. I think that it must be admissible in certain cases to go behind the apparent ownership of shares in order to discover whether a company is in fact controlled by wrongdoers—as, for instance, in the case where the shares were held by mere nominees, bound to vote as the owners required them to vote. In the present case, the shares are held by a company of which the defendant directors were, for the greater part of the material period, not only directors, but sufficient in number to outvote the other directors, of the shareholding company. In this manner, it is said they could prevent the shareholding company passing any resolution which might result in proceedings being taken in the name of the company which is alleged to have been injured against them. I suppose the shareholders of the shareholding company could in general meeting decide differently and disagree with the decision of the directors of that company. I am not satisfied that the defendant directors are in such control of the company as is necessary to justify an action by a minority shareholder, but I need not decide this question.

In the result, I reach the conclusion that on the facts alleged in the re-amended statement of claim the action is not maintainable by the plaintiff...

Negligence may, however, amount to 'fraud on the minority' if it is alleged that

18 [In *Burland v Earle* (**242**).]

the breach of duty by the wrongdoers has resulted in a benefit to them at the company's expense.

246 Daniels v Daniels [1978] Ch 406 (Chancery Division)

Three minority shareholders brought an action against Mr and Mrs Daniels, the two directors of the company, alleging that they had caused the company to sell a piece of land to Mrs Daniels at a fraction of its true value. In preliminary proceedings, Templeman J held that the plaintiffs had standing to sue, notwithstanding *Foss v Harbottle.*

TEMPLEMAN J: Mr Richards, for the first two defendants who bring this application to strike out, says there is no cause of action shown because the statement of claim does not allege fraud, and in the absence of fraud, minority shareholders are unable to maintain a claim on behalf of the company against a majority ... Mr Blackburne, for the plaintiffs, says of course he is not alleging fraud because the plaintiffs do not really know what happened: all they know is what is set out in the statement of claim. There has been a sale at an undervalue and the second defendant has made a substantial profit; therefore, fraud is not pleaded. But, says Mr Blackburne, when the authorities are considered, the rights of a minority are not limited to cases of fraud; they extend to any breach of duty. In the present case if the defendants sold at an undervalue then that was a breach of duty. As the plaintiffs cannot remedy the breach, save by a minority shareholders' action, they should be entitled to bring the action ...

In *Pavlides v Jensen* (**245**) it was alleged that directors had been guilty of gross negligence in selling a valuable asset of the company at a price greatly below its true market value, and it was alleged that the directors knew or well ought to have known that it was below market value. Danckwerts J struck out the statement of claim as disclosing no cause of action because no fraud was pleaded ... Mr Richards relies very strongly on this decision as showing that, whatever the exceptions to *Foss v Harbottle* (**232**) may be, mere gross negligence is not actionable, and he says all that is pleaded in the present case is gross negligence at the most. But in *Pavlides v Jensen* no benefits accrued to the directors ...

The authorities which deal with simple fraud on the one hand and gross negligence on the other do not cover the situation which arises where, without fraud, the directors and majority shareholders are guilty of a breach of duty which they owe to the company, and that breach of duty not only harms the company but benefits the directors. In that case it seems to me that different considerations apply. If minority shareholders can sue if there is fraud, I see no reason why they cannot sue where the action of the majority and the directors, though without fraud, confers some benefit on those directors and majority shareholders themselves. It would seem to me quite monstrous— particularly as fraud is so hard to plead and difficult to prove—if the confines of the exception to *Foss v Harbottle* were drawn so narrowly that directors could make a profit out of their negligence. Lord Hatherley LC in *Turquand v Marshall*,[19] opined that shareholders must put up with foolish or unwise directors. Danckwerts J in *Pavlides v Jensen* accepted that the forbearance of shareholders extends to directors who are 'an amiable set of lunatics'. Examples, ancient and modern, abound. To put up with foolish directors is

19 (1869) 4 Ch App 376 at 386.

one thing; to put up with directors who are so foolish that they make a profit of £115,000 odd at the expense of the company is something entirely different. The principle which may be gleaned from *Alexander v Automatic Telephone Co* (**244**) (directors benefiting themselves), from *Cook v Deeks* (**131**) (directors diverting business in their own favour) and from dicta in *Pavlides v Jensen* (directors appropriating assets of the company) is that a minority shareholder who has no other remedy may sue where directors use their powers, intentionally or unintentionally, fraudulently or negligently, in a manner which benefits themselves at the expense of the company.

NOTE

All the participants in this case seem to have been unnecessarily alarmed about the word 'fraud', Fraud in the sense of deceit *is* a concept that is rightly treated with caution: it is, as everyone knows, notoriously hard to prove; the rules of court require that particularised details of any alleged fraud be given in advance (something which it may be difficult to do in a jurisdiction such as ours which has no adequate procedure for pre-trial discovery); and a lawyer who pleads fraud without good reason is liable to be disciplined by the profession. But 'fraud' in equity may mean something quite different, as in 'fraud on a power', for example; and so in the phrase 'fraud on the minority', which was all that was in issue here.

Undoubtedly the most significant decision on *Foss v Harbottle* and the 'fraud on the minority' exception in recent times is *Prudential Assurance Co Ltd v Newman Industries Ltd (No 2)* [1982] Ch 204, [1982] 1 All ER 354 (**247**). It is, however, difficult to say just what this case has decided: its importance lies mainly in the fact that the Court of Appeal very firmly declined to give any encouragement to the notion that the rule in *Foss v Harbottle* might be due for some relaxation in the broad interests of justice. The circumstances of the case were unusual. At first instance, Vinelott J had deferred a ruling on the question of the plaintiff's standing to sue (under *Foss v Harbottle*), because he considered himself bound to hear all the evidence in any event for the purpose of a claim in conspiracy which the plaintiff had brought on the same facts; and when, at the end of a long hearing, he found fraud proved, it seemed plain in the interests of justice that the procedural obstacle of *Foss v Harbottle* should not be allowed to stand in the plaintiff's way. But when the case came before the Court of Appeal, it was not faced with the issue of *Foss v Harbottle* because the company itself (in whose favour the judgment of the lower court had been entered) had 'adopted' the plaintiff's case and the benefit of its victory. A very large sum had been run up in costs on all sides, and the Court of Appeal declined to increase the expense further by hearing argument on the question of the plaintiff's standing, which was by then academic. Even so, it did offer some observations on the subject of *Foss v Harbottle* generally. Among these we may note:

(a) A shareholder cannot bring a personal claim against a wrongdoer, even in a claim based on fraud or deceit, when the loss which he claims that he has suffered is the diminution in the value of his investment in the company as a consequence of the effect of the fraud on the company.[20] The company alone can sue for such a wrong.

---

20 Later courts seem to have skated deftly round this ruling. In *R P Howard Ltd v Woodman Matthew & Co* [1983] BCLC 117, Staughton J allowed a shareholder to sue because his shares had become 'less easily saleable', and in *Heron International Ltd v Lord Grade* (**131**) it was said that the shareholders were 'deprived of the opportunity of realising their shares to greater advantage'. It is far from clear that there is any real difference in these formulations. The Court of Appeal's views on diminution in value of the member's investment may also be contrasted with those of King CJ in *Residues Treatment & Trading Co Ltd v Southern Resources Ltd* (above, p 462).

(b) A judge must always give his ruling on a motion to strike out an action because of the plaintiff's want of standing *before* proceeding to hear the substantive case.[1]
(c) There is no broad exception to *Foss v Harbottle* based on 'the interests of justice'.

At first instance, Vinelott J had examined with some care the concepts of 'fraud' and 'control' which lie at the heart of a shareholder's right to bring a derivative suit. The extracts from his judgment which are cited below must be read with the caveat that it is by no means certain that the Court of Appeal would have endorsed them if the issue had been argued on appeal.

247 Prudential Assurance Co Ltd v Newman Industries Ltd (No 2) [1981] Ch 257, [1980] 2 All ER 841; [1982] Ch 204, [1982] 1 All ER 354 (Chancery Division and Court of Appeal)

The plaintiff, a large institutional investor, held 3% of the shares in Newman. It sought to bring a derivative action against Bartlett and Laughton, two directors of Newman who, it alleged, had defrauded Newman of over £400,000. The directors did not have a majority of the shares in Newman and so did not formally have 'control' of it. The transaction by which Newman had been allegedly defrauded had been approved by the shareholders in general meeting, but it was claimed that the shareholders had been misled into doing so. Vinelott J, after hearing all the evidence, found the case proved and held that there had been a 'fraud' by those in 'control' (in the sense that the wrongdoers had de facto control). The Court of Appeal allowed the appeal in part, and expressed the view that the plaintiffs should not have been allowed to bring a derivative suit.

VINELOTT J: . . .

Fraud

[The] authorities show that the exception [to the rule in *Foss v Harbottle* (**232**)] applies not only where the allegation is that directors who control a company have improperly appropriated to themselves money, property or advantages which belong to the company or, in breach of their duty to the company, have diverted business to themselves which ought to have been given to the company, but more generally where it is alleged that directors though acting 'in the belief that they were doing nothing wrong' (per Lindley MR in *Alexander v Automatic Telephone Co* (**244**)) are guilty of a breach of duty to the company, including their duty to exercise proper care, and as a result of that breach obtain some benefit. In the latter case it must be unnecessary to allege and prove that the directors in breaking their duty to the company acted with a view to benefiting themselves at the expense of the company; for such an allegation would be an allegation of misappropriation of the company's property. On the other hand, the exception does not apply if all that is alleged is that directors who control a company are liable to the company for damages for negligence, it not being shown that the transaction was one in which they were interested or that they have in fact obtained any benefit from it. It is not easy to see precisely where the line between these

---

1 In Australia, this ruling has been rejected as too inflexible: *Hurley v BGH Nominees Pty Ltd* (1982) 6 ACLR 791. It appears to be totally at odds with the reasoning of the House of Lords in the well-known 'judicial review' case in administrative law, *IRC v National Federation of Self-Employed & Small Businesses Ltd* [1982] AC 617, [1981] 2 All ER 93, decided just a few months before *Prudential*.

cases is to be drawn. For instance, is an action to be allowed to proceed if the allegation is that the controlling director is liable to the company for damages for negligence and that as a result of his negligence a benefit has been obtained by his wife or a friend or by a company in which he has a substantial shareholding? In *Pavlides v Jensen* (**245**) would it have been enough if, in addition to the allegation of negligence, it had been alleged that Portland Tunnel had a substantial shareholding in the Cyprus company and therefore benefited indirectly? It is also not easy to see what principle underlies the distinction. Whether the claim is for property improperly withheld or for damages for negligence or breach of fiduciary duty and, in the latter case, whether those controlling the company have or have not obtained some benefit the reason for the exception is the same, namely that the claim is brought against persons whose interests conflict with the interest of the company. It may be said, in a perfectly intelligible sense, to be a fraud on the minority that those against whom the claim would be brought are in a position to procure, and, if the derivative claim is not brought, will procure, that the company's claim, however strong it may appear to be, will not be enforced. Mr Scott, very frankly, admitted that he could not put forward any valid ground of distinction between a case where the claim by the company is of a proprietary nature and one where it is for damages only, nor between a claim for damages for negligence where the loss to the company is matched by a benefit to those in control and a claim for damages for negligence where the loss to the company is either not matched by any benefit to anybody or is not matched by a benefit to those in control. However, Mr Scott also conceded that the claim by Prudential is a claim founded on acts of a 'fraudulent character', whatever meaning is attributed to those words. I have endeavoured to state the principle which underlies the first limb of the exception, because the second limb cannot be construed in isolation from it, but it is unnecessary for me to decide precisely where the boundary limiting the category of cases which permit of a minority shareholders' action is to be drawn and it would be wrong for me to attempt to do so.

Control

The central issue in this case is whether a derivative action can be brought against defendants who do not have voting control of the company on whose behalf the derivative claim is brought and, if it can, in precisely what circumstances such a claim will be allowed to proceed.

At an early stage in these proceedings, ... Mr Scott ... indicated that it would be his submission that the court has no jurisdiction to entertain a derivative action at the suit of a minority shareholder unless the persons against whom relief is sought on behalf of the company are able to control a majority of votes capable of being cast in general meeting.

The rule and the exception have sometimes been expressed in terms of jurisdiction. In *Heyting v Dupont*[2] Plowman J, of his own motion, raised and decided the question whether the court could entertain the action. In the Canadian case of *Burrows v Becker*,[3] Norris JA said: '... once the rule is applied, any judgment or order that the learned trial judge may purport to give must be void and of no effect', and he cited with approval an observation

2 [1963] 3 All ER 97, [1963] 1 WLR 1192.
3 (1967) 63 DLR (2d) 100 at 121.

of Taschereau J in *Re Sproule*,[4] that proceedings brought in breach of the rule were 'a complete nullity, a nullity of non esse'. However, it became clear as Mr Scott's argument later developed that his initial simple and rigid formulation of the rule and of the exception to it is inconsistent with early authorities, in particular *Atwool v Merryweather* (**241**). [His Lordship discussed the facts and judgment in that case, and continued:]

The second ground of the decision in *Atwool v Merryweather* is inconsistent with the proposition that the exception to the rule in *Foss v Harbottle* is limited to cases where the persons against whom relief is sought control a majority of the votes in general meeting. It is also inconsistent, as I see it, with the proposition that the rule, and the exception to it, are founded upon any limitation in the court's jurisdiction, if by that is meant jurisdiction in the strict sense of the power of the court to enter upon and determine a dispute ... *Atwool v Merryweather* shows that the court has jurisdiction to entertain a claim by a minority shareholder and to make an order in favour of the defendant company even where the other defendants, alone or together with the plaintiff, do not have a majority of votes in general meeting and where the other shareholders are not parties. If that is so, then as I see it, the exception can only be founded on a general jurisdiction of the court to make an order for recovery of property or damages in favour of a defendant company against co-defendants where the jurisdiction is invoked by a minority shareholder. The question is then whether, in any given case, the jurisdiction is properly invoked. But that is a question not of jurisdiction but of the circumstances in which the court will allow the action to proceed and will make an order for the recovery of property or damages by the company...

Burrows v Becker shows that the exception applies—at least in Canada—where the persons alleged to have wronged the company do not control the company in general meeting, and are not a majority of the board of directors, and where it is not shown, as in *Atwool v Merryweather,* that a resolution has been passed by the use of the votes of the wrongdoers that no proceedings should be brought by the company but where it is otherwise shown that it would be 'futile' to call a general meeting because of the influence exercised by the wrongdoers over the board of directors, and directly or indirectly, through the use of proxy votes, over the votes capable of being cast in general meeting.

If the rule and the exception cannot be confined within the rigid formulation expressed in terms of voting control by the persons against whom relief is sought on behalf of the company, then the question whether a given case falls within the exception can only be answered by reference to the principle which underlies the rule and the exception to it. Mr Scott submitted, I think rightly, that the principle which underlies the rule is that it would be wrong to allow a minority shareholder to bring proceedings joining the company as defendant and claiming against other defendants relief on behalf of the company for a wrong alleged to have been done to it if the majority of the members of the company take the view that it is not in the interests of the company that the proceedings should be pursued. Indeed, it would be so plainly wrong that it might be said that, in a broad sense, the court would have no jurisdiction to allow the wishes of the minority to override the wishes of the majority in that way. The principle which underlies the exception to

4 (1886) 12 SCR 140 at 242.

the rule is that in ascertaining the view of the majority whether it is in the interests of the company that the claim be pursued, the court will disregard votes cast or capable of being cast by shareholders who have an interest which directly conflicts with the interest of the company. Those are general principles of substantive law and are not mere rules of procedure. But in any derivative action the plaintiff must allege in his statement of claim some ground which, if established at the trial, would bring the case within the exception and justify an order that the company recover damages or property from the other defendants: see *Birch v Sullivan*.[5] Thus the question whether an action falls within the exception will normally be tested at an early stage. So, if the defendants against whom relief is sought on behalf of the company control the majority of votes, the action will be allowed to proceed whether a resolution that no action should be brought by the company has been passed or not; so also, if the persons against whom relief is sought do not control a majority of the votes but it is shown that a resolution has been passed and passed only by the use of their votes ...

But there are an infinite variety of possible circumstances ... If shareholders having a majority of votes in general meeting are nominees, the court will look behind the register to the beneficial owners to see whether they are the persons against whom relief is sought: see *Pavlides v Jensen* (**245**). There seems no good reason why the court should not have regard to any other circumstances which show that the majority cannot be relied upon to determine in a disinterested way whether it is truly in the interests of the company that proceedings should be brought. For instance, some shareholders able to exercise decisive votes may have been offered an inducement to vote in favour of the wrongdoers ... Moreover, today it would be uncommon for any large number of shareholders to attend and vote in person at a general meeting of a large public company, and—an instance suggested by Mr Scott—directors alleged to be liable to the company might be able to determine the outcome of a resolution in general meeting in their own favour by the use of proxy votes. Similarly, most modern articles confide to the directors, the management of the business of the company (see e g, article [70] of Table A) and it is possible that an article in these terms vests in the directors a discretion whether proceedings should be commenced by the company which cannot be overridden by resolution in general meeting; see *Buckley on the Companies Acts,* 13th ed (1957), p 860 and *John Shaw & Sons (Salford) Ltd v Shaw* (**96**). If directors who have an interest direct or indirect in the question whether proceedings should be commenced refuse to submit that question to the shareholders in general meeting, the majority could in theory remove the directors, but might only be able to ensure that the question whether proceedings should be commenced is properly considered by a disinterested board by taking that extreme step, which, in turn, they might consider would involve damage to the company greater than any benefits to be derived from the action against the directors. Mr Scott at the end of his very clear and helpful argument summarised the principle that underlies the exception to the rule in these terms: it applies wherever the persons against whom the action is sought to be brought on behalf of the company are shown to be able 'by any means of manipulation of their position in the company' to ensure that the action is not brought by the company. That broad formulation

5 [1958] 1 All ER 56, [1957] 1 WLR 1247.

I accept, provided that the means of manipulation of the defendant's position in the company are not too narrowly defined ...

[The judgment of the Court of Appeal (CUMMING-BRUCE, TEMPLEMAN and BRIGHTMAN LJJ) included the following passages:]

It is commonly said that an exception to the rule in *Foss v Harbottle* arises if the corporation is 'controlled' by persons implicated in the fraud complained of, who will not permit the name of the company to be used as plaintiffs in the suit ... But this proposition leaves two questions at large, first, what is meant by 'control', which embraces a broad spectrum extending from an overall absolute majority of votes at one end, to a majority of votes at the other end made up of those likely to be cast by the delinquent himself plus those voting with him as a result of influence or apathy. Secondly, what course is to be taken by the court if, as happened in *Foss v Harbottle,* in the *East Pant Du* case[6] and in the instant case, but did *not* happen in *Atwool v Merryweather* (**241**), the court is confronted by a motion on the part of the delinquent or by the company, seeking to strike out the action? For at the time of the application the existence of the fraud is unproved. It is at this point that a dilemma emerges. If, upon such an application, the plaintiff can require the court to assume as a fact every allegation in the statement of claim, as in a true demurrer, the plaintiff will frequently be able to outmanoeuvre the primary purpose of the rule in *Foss v Harbottle* by alleging fraud and 'control' by the fraudster. If on the other hand the plaintiff has to prove fraud and 'control' before he can establish his title to prosecute his action, then the action may need to be fought to a conclusion before the court can decide whether or not the plaintiff should be permitted to prosecute it. In the latter case the purpose of the rule in *Foss v Harbottle* disappears. Either the fraud has not been proved, so cadit quaestio; or the fraud has been proved and the delinquent is accountable unless there is a valid decision of the board or a valid decision of the company in general meeting, reached without impropriety or unfairness, to condone the fraud.

We think that this brief look at the authorities is sufficient for present purposes. For it so happens that this court cannot properly on this appeal decide the scope of the exception to the rule in *Foss v Harbottle*. The reason is this ...

Newman by its counsel, acting (as we must assume) upon due authority conferred by the company, stated before us that if the finding of fraud stood it would accept the benefit of the order made in its favour. That is the end of *Foss v Harbottle* so far as this appeal is concerned.

It was in the light of these considerations that we declined to hear any argument from Mr Caplan and Mr Curry on the topic of *Foss v Harbottle*. However desirable it might be in the public interest that we should express our conclusions on Vinelott J's analysis of the rule in *Foss v Harbottle* and what he saw as the exception to it, it was necessary for us to bear in mind that the rule had ceased to be of the slightest relevance to the case. It would have been a grave injustice to all parties to increase the already horrendous costs of this litigation by allowing time for argument on an interesting but irrelevant point. Such consideration of the law as appears in this judgment is, apart from a few submissions made by Mr Bartlett, merely a reflection of our own thoughts without the benefit of sustained argument.

In the result it would be improper for us to express any concluded view

6 (1864) 2 Hem & M 254.

on the proper scope of the exception or exceptions to the rule in *Foss v Harbottle*. We desire, however, to say two things. First, as we have already said, we have no doubt whatever that Vinelott J erred in dismissing the summons of May 10 1979. He ought to have determined as a preliminary issue whether the plaintiffs were entitled to sue on behalf of Newman by bringing a derivative action. It cannot have been right to have subjected the company to a 30-day action (as it was then estimated to be) in order to enable him to decide whether the plaintiffs were entitled in law to subject the company to a 30-day action. Such an approach defeats the whole purpose of the rule in *Foss v Harbottle* and sanctions the very mischief that the rule is designed to prevent. By the time a derivative action is concluded, the rule in *Foss v Harbottle* can have little, if any, role to play. Either the wrong is proved, thereby establishing conclusively the rights of the company; or the wrong is not proved, so cadit quaestio. In the present case a board, of which all the directors save one were disinterested, ... had reached the conclusion before the start of the action that the prosecution of the action was likely to do more harm than good. That might prove a sound or unsound assessment, but it was the commercial assessment of an apparently independent board. Obviously the board would not have expected at that stage to be as well informed about the affairs of the company as it might be after 36 days of evidence in court and an intense examination of some 60 files of documents. But the board clearly doubted whether there were sufficient reasons for supposing that the company would at the end of the day be in a position to count its blessings; and clearly feared, as counsel said, that it might be killed by kindness. Whether in the events which have happened Newman (more exactly the disinterested body of shareholders) will feel that it has all been well worth while, or must lick its wounds and render no thanks to those who have interfered in its affairs, is not a question which we can answer. But we think it is within the bounds of possibility that if the preliminary issue had been argued, a judge might have reached the considered view that the prosecution of this great action should be left to the decision of the board or of a specially convened meeting of the shareholders, albeit less well informed than a judge after a 72-day action.

So much for the summons of May 10. The second observation which we wish to make is merely a comment on Vinelott J's decision that there is an exception to the rule in *Foss v Harbottle* whenever the justice of the case so requires. We are not convinced that this is a practical test, particularly if it involves a full-dress trial before the test is applied. On the other hand we do not think that the right to bring a derivative action should be decided as a preliminary issue upon the hypothesis that all the allegations in the statement of claim of 'fraud' and 'control' are facts, as they would be on the trial of a preliminary point of law. In our view, whatever may be the properly defined boundaries of the exception to the rule, the plaintiff ought at least to be required before proceeding with his action to establish a prima facie case (i) that the company is entitled to the relief claimed, and (ii) that the action falls within the proper boundaries of the exception to the rule in *Foss v Harbottle*. On the latter issue it may well be right for the judge trying the preliminary issue to grant a sufficient adjournment to enable a meeting of shareholders to be convened by the board, so that he can reach a conclusion in the light of the conduct of, and proceedings at, that meeting ...

The rule in *Foss v Harbottle* is founded on principle but it also operates fairly by preserving the rights of the majority. We were invited to give judicial approval to the public spirit of the plaintiffs who, it was said, are pioneering a method of controlling companies in the public interest without involving regulation by a statutory body. In our view the voluntary regulation of companies is a matter for the City. The compulsory regulation of companies is a matter for Parliament. We decline to draw general conclusions from the exceptional circumstances of the present case. But the results of the present action give food for thought. Vinelott J thought it possible that Newman had suffered damage amounting to £445,000 by the fraud of Mr Bartlett and Mr Laughton. Counsel for Newman submitted in the court below that damage to Newman by the prosecution of the action exceeded the benefits liable to be derived from the action. The costs of the proceedings at the end of the trial were said in newspaper reports to be in the region of £750,000 ...

If this appeal succeeds the burden of the costs on the plaintiffs will be enormous. The innocent shareholders of Newman ... and [of] the plaintiffs may well wonder, whether this appeal succeeds or not, if there is not something to be said after all for the old-fashioned rule in *Foss v Harbottle*.

[The Court of Appeal allowed the appeal in part, reducing the damages payable to £45,000.]

QUESTIONS

(1) Does the ruling of the Court of Appeal that the issue of standing must be settled as a preliminary matter mean that it will not be possible to go into questions of de facto control in the way that Vinelott J did?

(2) The six directors of a company negligently sell a piece of the company's land at an undervalue to X, one of their number. When their negligence is exposed by S, a minority shareholder, they put before a shareholders' meeting a resolution 'ratifying' the sale. The resolution is carried by the votes of the six directors, but those of X alone were not sufficient to have affected the result. Can S challenge the directors' acts in court?

It may be a 'fraud on the minority' to stultify the purposes for which the company was formed, against the wishes of some members.

248   Estmanco (Kilner House) Ltd v Greater London Council [1982] 1 WLR 2, [1982] 1 All ER 437 (Chancery Division)

The Council, when under Conservative control, had formed the Estmanco company to regulate the management of a block of sixty flats which it had rehabilitated and had begun to sell off to owner-occupiers. As each flat was sold, one of the sixty shares in the company was transferred by the Council to the buyer, but the right to vote in respect of each share was retained by the Council until all sixty flats had been sold. The Council had entered into an agreement with the company by which it covenanted to use its best endeavours to sell all the flats. After 12 flats had been sold, there were local elections and control of the Council changed. The new members resolved upon a new housing policy and decided to break the terms of the agreement and use the unsold flats to accommodate the needy. A shareholder, one of the flatowners, sought leave to prosecute a derivative action on the company's behalf against the Council to enforce the covenant, in the face of opposition from the Council itself as the sole voting shareholder. Megarry V-C held that a derivative action would lie.

MEGARRY V-C: If the rule in *Foss v Harbottle* (232) had remained unqualified, the way would have been open for the majority to stultify any proceedings which were for the benefit of the minority and to the disadvantage of the majority. Accordingly a number of exceptions from the rule have been established; and it is here that the difficulties begin. For convenience, I use the word 'exceptions' to embrace cases which are outside the true scope of the rule. It is far from clear just what the exceptions are, or what is the ambit of some of them. I do not think that it can simply be said that there is an exception from the rule whenever the justice of the case requires it. There are some dicta which support such a view (see, e g *Edwards v Halliwell* (239)), and this seems to have been part to the ratio [of Vinelott J] in *Prudential Assurance Co Ltd v Newman Industries Ltd (No 2)* (247). But in the Court of Appeal in the latter case, the court ... observed that this was 'not a practical test'; and I would respectfully concur. If it were the test, I feel no doubt that in this case the applicant would succeed.

Although the concept of injustice is not the test, I think that it is nevertheless a reason, and an important reason, for making exceptions from the rule; yet the reasons for an exception must not be confused with the exception itself. If the test were simply justice or injustice, this would mean different things to different men; and the courts have in fact proceeded by way of formulating, not always with great clarity, a number of individual exceptions. The subject has, indeed, been gradually developing; and unless the remedy introduced by s 75 of the Companies Act 1980 [CA 1985, s 459] inhibits that development, no doubt one day the courts will distil from the exceptions some guiding principle that is wide enough to comprehend them all and yet narrow enough to be practicable and workable. It may be that the test may come to be whether an ordinary resolution of the shareholders could validly carry out or ratify the act in question; but I do not think that a motion in the Long Vacation is the time or place for a judge to attempt any far-reaching analysis of the exceptions, or any distillation of a guiding principle to be found in them ...

Plainly there must be some limit to the power of the majority to pass resolutions which they believe to be in the best interests of the company and yet remain immune from interference by the court. It may be in the best interests of the company to deprive the minority of some of their rights or some of their property, yet I do not think that this gives the majority an unrestricted right to do this, however unjust it may be, and however much it may harm shareholders whose rights as a class differ from those of the majority. If a case falls within one of the exceptions from *Foss v Harbottle*, I cannot see why the right of the minority to sue under that exception should be taken away from them merely because the majority of the company reasonably believe it to be in the best interests of the company that this should be done. This is particularly so if the exception from the rule falls under the rubric of 'fraud on a minority'.

It was on the firmly established exception of 'fraud on a minority' that Mr Steinfeld mainly relied. It does not seem to have yet become very clear exactly what the word 'fraud' means in this context; but I think it is plainly wider than fraud at common law, in the sense of *Derry v Peek*.[7] On a valuable

---

7 (1889) 14 App Cas 337.

survey of the authorities, Templeman J recently came to the conclusion that this head permitted the minority to sue even though there had not been even an allegation of fraud: *Daniels v Daniels* (**246**) ... The principle which he derived from the cases was that

> ... a minority shareholder who has no other remedy may sue where directors use their powers, intentionally or unintentionally, fraudulently or negligently, in a manner which benefits themselves at the expense of the company.

Apart from the benefits to themselves at the company's expense, the essence of the matter seems to be an abuse or misuse of power. 'Fraud' in the phrase 'fraud on a minority' seems to be being used as comprising not only fraud at common law but also fraud in the wider equitable sense of that term, as in the equitable concept of a fraud on a power.

Now of course *Daniels v Daniels* was a case on acts by directors as such, rather than by shareholders, and I do not forget this. At the same time it seems to me to be useful as preventing 'fraud' from being read too narrowly. Suppose, too, the decision to sell the land had been made not by the husband and wife qua directors, but by a resolution of the company carried by their votes: could it then be said that the minority could not sue? Is this exception from the rule in *Foss v Harbottle* open to easy evasion by directors who hold the majority of votes in general meeting if they take care to reach their decisions not by voting as directors but by voting as shareholders? I think not.

In considering whether there is a fraud on a minority in this case in the sense which this phrase has acquired ... certain matters seem plain enough. First, I do not think that it can reasonably be said to have been established that it is, or could reasonably be thought to be, for the benefit of the company that [this] action should be discontinued. This is not a case of a trading company, seeking to make a profit. The company is a non-profit-making company, and so the test cannot be the financial benefit of the company. The company was formed for a particular purpose, namely to manage the block of flats under the control of the purchasers of the flats; and the covenant by the council with the company was part of the mechanism for securing this result. On the face of it I do not think that it can readily be said to be for the benefit of a company to stultify a substantial part of the purpose for which it was formed ...

Second, it is very far from clear that the council, or any properly authorised organ of the council, ever adequately considered and decided what was for the company's benefit before voting at the extraordinary general meeting ...

Third, the council does not appear to have considered the effect of its vote on the rights of purchasers qua shareholders. Mr Brodie emphasised more than once that the applicant's real complaint was not as a shareholder but as a purchaser of a flat. Instead of having as her neighbours the occupants of 59 other flats which had all been purchased on long leases, she would have only 11 flats occupied thus, and 48 occupied by tenants who would not have the stake in the block of flats which the purchase of long leases would have bought. That, of course, is so; but it is not all. What she bought, inter alia, was a share which had no voting rights, but would have voting rights at a future point of time, namely, when all the other flats had been sold ... Furthermore, when she obtained her voting rights, she and all the other purchasers of flats would be in control of the company, which would not only manage the block of flats as they collectively wished, but would also, as landlord, be able to enforce the terms of the leases against all the purchasers. The council's conclusion that it is in the best interests of the company that clause 3(1) of the agreement should not be enforced is a conclusion that it is in the best interests of the company (including the applicant as one of the corporators) that this state of affairs, so plainly intended by the documents, should never be reached; and there is not a shred of evidence to suggest that this was ever considered by the council ...

As I have indicated, I do not consider that this is a suitable occasion on which to probe the intricacies of the rule in *Foss v Harbottle* and its exceptions, or to attempt to discover and expound the principles to be found in the exceptions. All that I need say is that in my judgment the exception usually known as 'fraud on a minority' is wide enough to cover the present case, and that if it is not, it should now be made wide enough. There can be no doubt about the 12 voteless purchasers being a minority; there can be no doubt about the advantage to the council of having the action discontinued; there can be no doubt about the injury to the applicant and the rest of the minority, both as shareholders and as purchasers, of that discontinuance; and I feel little doubt that the council has used its voting power not in order to promote the best interests of the company but in order to bring advantage to itself and disadvantage to the minority. Furthermore, that disadvantage is no trivial matter, but represents a radical alteration in the basis on which the council sold the flats to the minority. It seems to me that the sum total represents a fraud on the minority in the sense in which 'fraud' is used in that phrase, or alternatively represents such an abuse of power as to have the same effect.

I appreciate, of course, that there is a difference between the applicant's rights as a shareholder and her rights as a purchaser of a flat; but I think, first, that the injury to her rights as a shareholder suffices in itself, and, second, that her rights as a shareholder form such an integral part of the scheme as a whole as to make it unreal to consider those rights independently of her rights as a purchaser. No right of a shareholder to vote in his own selfish interests or to ignore the interests of the company entitle him with impunity to injure his voteless fellow shareholders by depriving the company of a cause of action and stultifying the purpose for which the company was formed ...

A minority shareholder who has standing to sue on behalf of the company, under an established exception to the rule in Foss v Harbottle, may be debarred from proceedings if a majority of the members, independent of the defendants, is opposed to the litigation.

249 Smith v Croft (No 2) [1988] Ch 114, [1987] 3 All ER 909 (Chancery Division)

The plaintiffs were minority shareholders claiming (inter alia) to recover, on behalf of their company, sums which had been paid away in transactions which were both ultra vires and in breach of the statutory prohibition on financial assistance (above, pp 353 ff). With their supporters, the plaintiffs had 14% of the voting rights in the company and the defendants 63%; and there were other shareholders commanding 21% of the votes who did not wish the litigation to proceed. Knox J held that (i) a prima facie case of ultra

vires and illegality had been made out, for which the company was entitled
to relief; (ii) the plaintiffs accordingly had standing to bring a derivative
action; but that (iii) the plaintiffs nevertheless had no right to sue if a majority
of the shareholders, who were independent of the defendants, did not want
the action to continue.

KNOX J: The questions of law can be formulated as follows.

(1) Is a minority shareholder always entitled as of right to bring and
prosecute an action for the company to recover money paid away in the course
of a transaction which was ultra vires the company or is the prosecution of
such an action susceptible of coming within the rule in *Foss v Harbottle* so
that there can be circumstances in which the court will not allow it to
continue?

(2) If the latter view is the correct one in relation to those categories of
claims based on ultra vires transactions, and also in all cases of minority
shareholders' actions to recover money for the company in respect of acts
which constitute a fraud on the minority, will the court pay regard to the
views of the majority of shareholders who are independent of the defendants
to the action on the question whether the action should proceed? . . .

Another way of putting the question is to ask whether if a minority has been
the victim of a fraud entitling the company in which they are shareholders to
financial redress, the majority within that minority can prevent the minority
within that minority from prosecuting the action for redress. The usual reason
in practice for wanting to abandon such an action is that there is far more
to lose financially by prosecuting the right to redress than by abandoning or
not pursuing it, and that view will be reinforced in the minds of those who
wish to abandon the claim if their opinion is that it is a bad claim anyway.

The third question which arises is whether in this case Wren Trust [a
minority shareholder alleged to be connected with the defendants] should be
treated as independent, if the views of an independent majority are relevant?
That is a question of fact . . .

Upon the first question of law which arises, in my judgment the solution
is to be found by a correct analysis of the rights which the minority shareholder is seeking to exercise or enforce in relation to the result of an ultra
vires transaction. There was no dispute before me but that any individual
shareholder, be he in a minority or not, has a personal right to apply to the
court to restrain a threatened action which if carried out would be ultra vires.
Neither the right to object to such an action nor the shareholder's locus
standi to bring proceedings admits of any doubt. The rule in *Foss v Harbottle*
poses no obstacle, because neither of the two bases for the rule is applicable,
that is to say the matter is not, by definition, a mere question of internal
management nor is the transaction capable of ratification by or on behalf of
the company . . .

The difficulty arises in this case when one considers not the restraint of an
illegal or ultra vires transaction but the recovery on behalf of the company
of money or property which the company is entitled to claim as the result of
the ultra vires transaction . . .

Treating the matter as a question of principle for the moment, when a
minority shareholder seeks to enforce a right of the company to claim
compensation for a past ultra vires transaction there are two quite separate
rights involved. First, there is the minority shareholder's right to bring
proceedings at all and secondly, there is the right of recovery which belongs

to the company but is permitted to be asserted on its behalf by the minority shareholder.

But as Lord Davey said in *Burland v Earle* (**242**) the plaintiffs cannot have a larger right to relief than the company itself would have if it were plaintiff. And from that it follows in my judgment that if there is a valid reason why the company should not sue it will equally prevent the minority shareholder from suing on its behalf. He is therefore liable to be defeated on two points, first by any ground preventing him from exercising his procedural remedy, and secondly by any ground preventing the company from exercising its substantive right ...

Where ultra vires transactions are involved the number of grounds upon which the company can be debarred from suing is limited. In particular it was not argued that ratification of the ultra vires transaction, by however large a majority of shareholders, could prevent the company from suing. There is, however, a clear difference in principle between ratifying what has been invalidly done in the past and abandoning, compromising or not pursuing rights of action arising out of a past ultra vires transaction, and I see no reason in principle why in appropriate circumstances the latter should not intervene to prevent the prosecution of a suit on behalf of the company in relation to such rights of action ...

I turn now to the question whether it is right for the court to have regard to the views of the majority inside a minority which is, I assume for this purpose, in a position to bring an action to recover on behalf of the company in respect of breaches of duty by persons with overall control.

The ... defendants claim that it is, the plaintiffs claim that it is not. On their view of the matter all that the court is concerned with, in cases where the exception to the rule in *Foss v Harbottle* based on frauds on the minority applies, is the single question whether the defendants have control ...

Mr Potts submitted that no reported authority held that in a case falling within the fraud on a minority exception to the rule in *Foss v Harbottle* the court should go beyond seeing whether the wrongdoers are in control and count heads to see what the other shareholders, i e those other than the plaintiffs and the wrongdoers, think should be done. I accept that in many reported cases the court has not gone on to the second stage.

[His Lordship examined the authorities and continued:] In my judgment the word 'control' was deliberately placed in inverted commas by the Court of Appeal in *Prudential Assurance Co Ltd v Newman Industries Ltd (No 2)* (**247**) because it was recognised that voting control by the defendants was not necessarily the sole subject of investigation. Ultimately the question which has to be answered in order to determine whether the rule in *Foss v Harbottle* applies to prevent a minority shareholder seeking relief as plaintiff for the benefit of the company is 'Is the plaintiff being improperly prevented from bringing these proceedings on behalf of the company?' If it is an expression of the corporate will of the company by an appropriate independent organ that is preventing the plaintiff from prosecuting the action he is not improperly but properly prevented and so the answer to the question is 'No'. The appropriate independent organ will vary according to the constitution of the company concerned and the identity of the defendants who will in most cases be disqualified from participating by voting in expressing the corporate will.

Finally on this aspect of the matter I remain unconvinced that a just result is achieved by a single minority shareholder having the right to involve a company in an action for recovery of compensation for the company if all the other minority shareholders are for disinterested reasons satisfied that the proceedings will be productive of more harm that good. If Mr Potts' argument is well founded once control by the defendants is established the views of the rest of the minority as to the advisability of the prosecution of the suit are necessarily irrelevant. I find that hard to square with the concept of a form of pleading originally introduced on the ground of necessity alone in order to prevent a wrong going without redress.

I therefore conclude that it is proper to have regard to the views of independent shareholders. In this case it is common ground that there would be no useful purpose served by adjourning to enable a general meeting to be called. For all practical purposes it is quite clear how the votes would be cast...

[His Lordship then held that a majority of shareholders, excluding the defendants but including the Wren Trust (which he ruled was 'independent') were opposed to continuing the action, and ordered that it should be struck out.]

NOTE

The Vice-Chancellor's suggestion in *Estmanco* that the test for making exceptions to the rule 'may come to be whether an ordinary resolution of the shareholders could validly carry out or ratify the act in question' echoes the theme of the important article by Lord Wedderburn, 'Shareholders' Rights and the Rule in *Foss v Harbottle*', [1957] CLJ 194, [1958] CLJ 93. But, as the case last cited shows, it is plainly an over-simplification to run together all the questions of authorisation, ratification, affirmation of a transaction otherwise voidable, release and condonation of wrong-doers and wrongdoing, etc, and to try to match them up with the issue of a plaintiff's right to sue.[8] See also *Taylor v National Union of Mineworkers* (*Derbyshire Area*) [1985] BCLC 237, where Vinelott J held that individual members of a union were entitled to sue for orders restraining its officers from making ultra vires payments but that an action to make the officers personally liable to make restitution of moneys wrongly paid away might be barred if the members voted by a majority not to pursue the claim: this shows how mistaken it may be to try to bring everything within one formula. Certainly the 'ratifiability' test cannot easily be squared with some decided cases: *Alexander v Automatic Telephone Co* (**244**), *Hogg v Cramphorn Ltd* (**140**) and *Devlin v Slough Estates Ltd* (above, p 472) to name but three.

Other cases on procedural aspects of the rule in *Foss v Harbottle* may be mentioned.

Birch v Sullivan [1958] 1 All ER 56, [1957] 1 WLR 1247, where Harman J held that when an individual plaintiff institutes a derivative action to enforce a right belonging to the company, he must specifically allege in his pleadings, and be prepared to prove, that those in control of the company would prevent the company from suing in its own name.

Heyting v Dupont [1963] 3 All ER 97, [1963] 1 WLR 1192 (affd [1964] 2 All ER 273, [1964] 1 WLR 843), where Plowman J declared that the issue of standing under the rule in *Foss v Harbottle* was a matter going to jurisdiction, which the court could, and should, raise on its own initiative and which the parties had no power to waive.[9]

Wallersteiner v Moir (*No 2*) [1975] QB 373, [1975] 1 All ER 849, in which the Court of Appeal considered the question of the plaintiff shareholder's costs. The court ruled that it was proper in a minority shareholder's action to order that the company should

8 On this question, see R J C Partridge, 'Ratification and the Release of Directors from Personal Liability' [1987] CLJ 122.
9 Vinelott J in the *Prudential* case (**247**) expressed doubts whether this view was consistent with *Atwool v Merryweather* (**241**).

indemnify the plaintiff against the costs of the action—even if the action should fail, provided that it was brought on reasonable grounds; and that a plaintiff might apply ex parte to the Master at an early stage in the proceedings for an order approving their continuance, at the company's eventual expense, until close of pleadings, or until after discovery, or until trial.[10]

In *Nurcombe v Nurcombe* [1985] 1 All ER 65, [1985] 1 WLR 370 the Court of Appeal declared that a plaintiff shareholder seeking to bring a derivative suit must 'come with clean hands': a defendant was entitled to raise against the plaintiff any defence which could have been raised against him in an action that had been brought by him personally.

Fargo Ltd v Godfroy [1986] 3 All ER 279, [1986] 1 WLR 1134. A minority shareholder may not bring a derivative action when a company has gone into liquidation: only the liquidator is competent to represent the company in a winding up.

C. Minority shareholders' remedy under s 459[11]

The Cohen Committee (Cmnd 6659, 1945) considered that the law ought to be amended to provide a remedy for a minority shareholder who was the victim of 'oppression', and who did not wish to take the drastic step of petitioning to have the company wound up—a step which would all too often be in nobody's interest, killing the goose that laid the golden eggs. As a result, s 210 of the Companies Act 1948 was enacted, providing a discretionary remedy which was expressed to be available only where the facts would justify a winding-up order on the 'just and equitable' ground (see below, pp 557 ff).

Although the new remedy got off to an encouraging start, with the *Scottish Co-operative* (**250**) and *Harmer* (**251**) decisions, it rapidly ran into procedural obstacles (some attributable to the drafting of the section and some of the judges' own devising) with the result that there were no further successful cases reported in the ensuing decades. The Jenkins Committee (Cmnd 1749, 1962) recommended that the section be recast so as to remove some of the barriers which stood in minority shareholders' way, and after a long delay the remedy was enacted in its new form as s 75 of the Companies Act 1980 (now CA 1985, s 459).

Among the changes which s 459 has made from the old s 210 are the following:

(a) It is no longer necessary to show that the facts would justify the making of a winding-up order.

(b) The petitioner has now to show conduct that is '*unfairly prejudicial* to the interests of its members generally[12] or of some part of its members (including himself)'; under s 210 the phrase was '*oppressive* to some part of the members (including himself)'—an expression which the courts had interpreted as meaning 'burdensome, harsh or wrongful', or at least as involving 'want of probity'.

(c) It is plain that the new section covers isolated acts and omissions; the

---

10 For a recent survey, see D D Prentice, '*Wallersteiner v Moir*: a Decade Later' [1987] Conv 167.

11 For further reading, see A J Boyle, 'The Judicial Interpretation of Part XVII of the Companies Act 1985' in *Company Law in Change* (1987) p 23; D D Prentice, 'The Theory of the Firm: Minority Shareholder Oppression' (1988) 8 OJLS 55; Brenda Hannigan, 'S 459 of the Companies Act 1985:—a Code of Conduct for the Quasi-Partnership?' [1988] LMCLQ 60.

12 The words 'of its members generally' were added by CA 1989, Sch 19: see below, p 497.

old section had been construed as requiring a continuing course of conduct.

(d) Section 459(2) makes it clear that the personal representatives of a deceased member and other persons upon whom shares have devolved by operation of law shall have the same remedy as a member. This was not expressed to be so under the former section, but the courts had construed the section in the same sense anyway.

(e) Among the possible remedies which the Act now suggests that a court may invoke in response to a s 459 petition is an order that someone be authorised to sue the wrongdoers in the company's name. Great hopes are held by some for this power to circumvent *Foss v Harbottle* (**232**), but of course it will mean that two full-scale hearings have to be held before the malefactors are brought to justice.

Although there have been a very large number of petitions presented under the new section, a large number have been settled without going to trial. Many of the decisions which have been reported have dealt with isolated issues (often on a preliminary point of law, which explains why so many are recorded anonymously as *Re a Company*); and so it may still be helpful by way of background to study the two leading cases decided under the repealed s 210, *Scottish Co-operative Wholesale Society Ltd v Meyer* (**250**) and *Re H R Harmer Ltd* (**251**)—always bearing in mind that the scope and wording of the new section is significantly different.

The relief most commonly sought by a petitioner under the section is that the majority shareholders should be ordered to buy the petitioner's shares at a fair price. Some reported cases have considered the questions (i) at what date should the shares be valued, and (ii) how far should the conduct of either party be considered relevant when this remedy is decreed—an issue with unfortunate echoes of matrimonial property litigation!

Various other points have been raised by commentators:

(a) The language of s 210 of the old Act was construed as being confined to oppression of the petitioner *qua member*: will the new section be subject to a similar restriction?

(b) What does 'unfairly prejudicial' mean? *Gore-Browne*, a leading practitioners' handbook, has suggested that the member must show that the value of his shareholding has been seriously impaired. This may be sufficient, but is it necessary?

(c) Mere mismanagement, however damaging, did not amount to 'oppression' under the former section (*Re Five Minute Car Wash Service Ltd* [1966] 1 All ER 242, [1966] 1 WLR 745): will it be held 'unfairly prejudicial'? (It is perhaps worth noting that in the *Five Minute Car Wash* case, Buckley J pointed out that there was nothing 'unfair' to the petitioner in the way the company had been managed, or rather mismanaged.)

One contentious point has been resolved by statutory amendment. Both CA 1948, s 210 and CA 1985, s 459 used the phrase '*some part of the members (including at least himself)*'. This wording appeared to rule out recourse to the section where the conduct complained of was injurious to the whole body of shareholders; and in the main the judges agreed. Thus in *Re Carrington Viyella plc* (1983) 1 BCC 98,951 one ground of complaint was that the company had entered into a disadvantageous service agreement with its chief executive. Vinelott J declined to grant a remedy because the conduct, even if prejudicial, would have affected all the shareholders equally. (It was, however, possible in some cases to argue that conduct which had the same *legal* effect for all shareholders was *in fact* more injurious to some than to others: for example, in *Re a Company* [1985] BCLC 80 Harman J considered that it might be unfairly prejudicial conduct for majority shareholders to propose a rights issue in the knowledge that the minority could not afford to take it up: cf *Scottish Co-operative Wholesale Soc Ltd v Meyer* (**250**).) The controversy has now been put to rest by CA 1989, Sch 19, which has amended s 459 so that it reads: 'unfairly prejudicial to the interests of its members generally or of some part of its members (including at least himself)'. This welcome amendment has also removed an anomaly created by s 461(2)(c), which lists among the possible remedies for unfairly prejudicial conduct a power for the court to 'authorise civil proceedings to be brought in the name and on behalf of the company'—something which would have been inappropriate when the conduct had to be prejudicial to 'some *part* of the members'.

Cases on CA 1948, s 210

250 Scottish Co-operative Wholesale Society Ltd v Meyer [1959] AC 324, [1958] 3 All ER 66 (House of Lords)

This was a case decided under the old s 210. Scottish Textile & Manufacturing Co Ltd was a private company formed in 1946 by the appellant society and the respondents, Meyer and Lucas, to manufacture rayon cloth at a time when this product was subject to a system of state licensing. The society held the majority of the issued shares and had appointed three of its own directors to the board; the respondents, who held the rest of the shares, were joint managing directors and as such filled the remaining seats on the board. The society had formed this subsidiary because it could not have secured a licence to produce rayon cloth without experienced managers, and the respondents had the necessary experience. After licensing ceased in 1952, the society, by transferring the company's business to another branch of its organisation and cutting off the supply of raw materials on which the company was dependent, caused its activities to come to a standstill, with the result that it made no profits and the value of its shares fell greatly. The respondents petitioned for relief under s 210, and the House of Lords, confirming the decision of the Court of Session, ordered the society to purchase their shares at a fair price.

LORD DENNING discussed the facts, and continued:
   Such being 'the matters complained of' by Dr Meyer and Mr Lucas, it is said: 'Those are all complaints about the conduct of the co-operative society. How do they touch the real issue—the manner in which the affairs of the textile company were being conducted?' The answer is, I think, by their impact on the nominee directors. It must be remembered that we are here concerned with the manner in which the affairs of the textile company were being conducted. That is, with the conduct of those in control of its affairs. They may be some of the directors themselves, or, behind them, a group of shareholders who nominate those directors or whose interests those directors serve. If those persons—the nominee directors or the shareholders behind them—conduct the affairs of the company in a manner oppressive to the other shareholders, the court can intervene to bring an end to the oppression.
   What, then, is the position of the nominee directors here? Under the articles

of association of the textile company the co-operative society was entitled to nominate three out of the five directors, and it did so. It nominated three of its own directors and they held office, as the articles said, 'as nominees' of the co-operative society. These three were therefore at one and the same time directors of the co-operative society—being three out of twelve of that company—and also directors of the textile company—three out of five there. So long as the interests of all concerned were in harmony, there was no difficulty. The nominee directors could do their duty by both companies without embarrassment. But, so soon as the interests of the two companies were in conflict, the nominee directors were placed in an impossible position. It is plain that, in the circumstances, these three gentlemen could not do their duty by both companies, and they did not do so. They put their duty to the co-operative society above their duty to the textile company in this sense, at least, that they did nothing to defend the interests of the textile company against the conduct of the co-operative society. They probably thought that 'as nominees' of the co-operative society their first duty was to the co-operative society. In this they were wrong. By subordinating the interests of the textile company to those of the co-operative society, they conducted the affairs of the textile company in a manner oppressive to the other shareholders.

It is said that these three directors were at most only guilty of inaction—of doing nothing to protect the textile company. But the affairs of a company can, in my opinion, be conducted oppressively by the directors doing nothing to defend its interests when they ought to do something—just as they can conduct its affairs oppressively by doing something injurious to its interests when they ought not to do it . . .

Your Lordships were referred to *Bell v Lever Bros Ltd* (**137**), where Lord Blanesburgh said that a director of one company was at liberty to become a director also of a rival company. That may have been so at that time. But it is at the risk now of an application under s 210 if he subordinates the interests of the one company to those of the other.

So I would hold that the affairs of the textile company were being conducted in a manner oppressive to Dr Meyer and Mr Lucas . . .

One of the most useful orders mentioned in the section—which will enable the court to do justice to the injured shareholders—is to order the oppressor to buy their shares at a fair price: and a fair price would be, I think, the value which the shares would have had at the date of the petition, if there had been no oppression . . .

VISCOUNT SIMONDS and LORDS MORTON OF HENRYTON and KEITH OF AVONHOLM delivered concurring opinions.

251 Re H R Harmer Ltd [1959] 1 WLR 62, [1958] 3 All ER 689 (Court of Appeal)

In 1947 Harmer senior ('the father') formed a private company to take over the stamp-dealing business which he had founded many years earlier; and although as a result of a succession of gifts and purchases the majority of the shares in the company were now held by his sons, the father retained voting control. The father and sons were appointed life directors by the articles of association, which also constituted the father 'governing director'—an office not defined as carrying any special or distinctive powers.

The sons petitioned for relief under CA 1948, s 210 [CA 1985, s 459], alleging that the father (by now aged upwards of 88) ran the business of the company as if it were entirely his own, ignoring the wishes of his co-directors, the resolutions of the board, and the interests of the shareholders. (He had, inter alia, founded a branch of the business in Australia, against the wishes of the other directors, which proved unprofitable; purportedly dismissed an old servant and fellow director on his own initiative; procured the appointment of his own 'yes-men' to the board; drawn unauthorised expenses for himself and his wife; engaged a detective to watch the staff; countermanded resolutions of the board; and endeavoured to sell off the company's American business, severely damaging its goodwill.) Roxburgh J granted the sons relief, ordering, inter alia, 'that the company should contract for the services of the father as philatelic consultant at a named salary, that the father should not interfere in the affairs of the company otherwise than in accordance with the valid decision of the board of directors, and that he should be appointed president of the company for life, but that this office should not impose any duties or rights or powers'.

The order was upheld by the Court of Appeal.

JENKINS LJ referred to the evidence and continued: The question remains whether, on these facts, the petitioners were rightly granted the relief which Roxburgh J thought fit to grant under s 210. Upon this issue Mr Harold Brown, for the father, made in effect these submissions ... First, he said that the sons should not be heard to complain since they acquired their shares through the generosity of their father, who having built up the business, proceeded to turn it into a company and to hand over a major part of the beneficial interest in the form of shares to his sons virtually by way of gift. As to this, the sons did at all events pay for their preference shares, and if they had not paid anything, two of them at all events had long been working in the business, while the third gave up his career in the Colonial Office in order to take up employment in the business. Moreover, the question of consideration appears to me to be irrelevant, a mere matter of prejudice. Suppose the transaction was a mere matter of gift, the gift, if valid (and there is no suggestion it was not) must surely have conferred the same rights as if the transaction had been for full consideration.

Mr Harold Brown's second point was that the sons knew full well when the company was formed that the father was to retain control by means of his predominant holding of 'B' shares so long as he lived. I agree, but I cannot concur with Mr Brown in adducing from this that the sons must be taken to have assumed that the father would exercise his control irregularly by doing what he thought fit without reference to the board or in defiance of the board's decisions.

Then the third submission of Mr Harold Brown was that what was done by the father was not oppressive of the rights of the sons as members, but merely oppressive of their rights as directors. I cannot accept this. It appears to me that the sons as members and not merely as directors were oppressed by the singular conduct of the father. The oppression must no doubt be oppression of members as such, but it does not follow that the fact that the oppressed members are also directors is a disqualifying circumstance when the question of relief under s 210 arises. I think there may well be oppression from the point of view of member-directors where a majority shareholder (that is to say, a shareholder with a preponderance of voting power) proceeds, on the strength of his control, to act contrary to the decisions of, or without the authority of, the duly constituted board of directors of the company.

Fourthly, Mr Harold Brown said that the acts complained of might have been restrained by injunction in so far as they were acts done without the authority of the board. As to this, I do not think a wrongdoer in this field can well complain that the person wronged might have chosen another remedy ...

Finally, he submitted that the father got no pecuniary benefit out of what he did. That is not literally true, but even if it was, I do not think it is essential to a case of oppression that the alleged oppressor is oppressing in order to obtain pecuniary benefit. If there is oppression, it remains oppression even though the oppression is due simply to the controlling shareholder's over-whelming desire for power and control, and not with a view to his own advantage in the pecuniary sense. It seems to me the result rather than the motive is the material thing.

Then on the other side, Mr Milner Holland's submissions were to this effect:

(1) The question is whether the course of conduct complained of was 'bur-densome, harsh or wrongful' to shareholders, that is to say, a part of the shareholders, including the petitioners.

(2) If a person, relying on majority control in point of voting power, dispenses with the proper procedure for producing the result he desires to achieve, and simply insists on this or that being done or omitted, his conduct is oppressive because it deprives the minority of shareholders of their right as members of the company to have its affairs conducted in accordance with its articles of association.

(3) It is not shown that if the father had acted strictly in accordance with the articles of association, he could have achieved his object. The proper procedure cannot be put on one side as mere machinery. It is the duty of the board to consider any proposal. If a majority shareholder desires to override the board, there must be a proper meeting, whether of the board or the company, and at least an opportunity of discussion. Moreover, if a majority shareholder sets about asserting his power in accordance with the articles and succeeds in point of numbers, he may be faced with questions as to fraud on the minority and so forth, which are burked by the expedient of simply doing what he chooses without ceremony on the ground that if it came to a vote he could outvote anyone.

In his judgment, Roxburgh J, after saying that he adopted the reasoning of the Lord President, Lord Cooper in *Meyer v Scottish Co-operative Wholesale Society Ltd*,[13] said: 'That being so, for my part the section seems to admit of no ambiguity. The word "oppression" is a word in common use and understanding in the English language. But I would just observe in passing that it does not say "who complains of acts of oppression"; it says "that the affairs of the company are being conducted in a manner oppressive". In other words, I think it invites attention not to events considered in isolation, but to events considered as part of a consecutive story; and it is because I take that view that I have not dealt (and do not propose to deal) with each of the items which I have enumerated one by one ... I do not know that it has any particular bearing on the case, but this case is curious in that it is not a

13 1954 SC 381 at 392; on appeal (**250**).

minority beneficial interest that is being oppressed, and that would be the normal case; it is a majority beneficial interest which is being oppressed because the voting control is placed in the hands of a minority beneficial interest. In my judgment, I reach the opinion—because that is what I have to do—that at the date of the presentation of this petition the affairs of the company were being conducted in a manner oppressive to the petitioners.'

Having given the best consideration I can to this not altogether easy case, I have come to the same conclusion ...

ROMER and WILLMER LJJ delivered concurring judgments.

Cases on CA 1980, s 75 and CA 1985, s 459

It is not necessary that a petitioner seeking relief under CA 1985, s 459 should 'come with clean hands', but his conduct may be relevant in deciding whether relief should be granted and what the nature of such relief should be.

252 Re London School of Electronics Ltd [1986] Ch 211, [1985] BCLC 273 (Chancery Division)

LSE was a company which ran courses in electronics. The petitioner, Lytton, a teacher, held 25% of the shares and a company, CTC (which ran a tutorial college), held the remainder. The directors (other than Lytton) were dissatisfied with various aspects of Lytton's conduct. They agreed to transfer most of LSE's students to courses run by CTC and to remove Lytton as a director. Lytton terminated his association with LSE and set up a rival teaching institution, LCEE, taking with him some of the students enrolled with LSE. When Lytton petitioned for relief under CA 1980, s 75 (CA 1985, s 459), Nourse J held that the fact that his own conduct was open to criticism did not disqualify him from seeking relief under the section, although it could be taken into account in determining whether he was entitled to relief and what that relief should be.

NOURSE J: Mr Oliver [counsel for the respondents] submitted that a petitioner under section 75 must come to the court with clean hands ... I do not share Mr Oliver's view of s 75. I agree with Mr Instone, for the petitioner, that that section must be construed as it stands. The combined effect of subsections (1) and (3) is to empower the court to make such order as it thinks fit for giving relief, if it is first satisfied that the affairs of the company are being or have been conducted in a manner which is unfairly prejudicial to the interests of some part of the members. The conduct of the petitioner may be material in a number of ways, of which the two most obvious are these. First, it may render the conduct on the other side, even if it is prejudicial, not unfair: cf *Re R A Noble & Sons (Clothing) Ltd*.[14] Secondly, even if the conduct on the other side is both prejudicial and unfair, the petitioner's conduct may nevertheless affect the relief which the court thinks fit to grant under subs (3). In my view there is no independent or overriding requirement that it should be just and equitable to grant relief or that the petitioner should come to the court with clean hands.

In the circumstances I hold that the petitioner is entitled to an order under

14 [1983] BCLC 273.

s 75 requiring CTC to purchase his shares. That makes it necessary for me to go on and consider three further questions. First, at what date ought the shares to be valued? Secondly, ought the valuation to be made on the footing that the students which the petitioner removed to LCEE remained with the company or ought they to be left out of account? Thirdly, ought the price to be fixed pro rata according to the value of shares as a whole or ought it to be discounted on the ground that the petitioner's shares constitute a minority in number?

Both counsel urged me to hold that there is a general rule as to the date on which shares which are ordered to be purchased pursuant to s 75 ought to be valued. Mr Instone submitted that the valuation ought usually to be made at the date of the order as being the only fair method of compensating an unwilling vendor of the equivalent of a partnership share. Mr Oliver, although I think with less enthusiasm for a general rule, submitted that the valuation ought usually to be made at the date of presentation of the petition or perhaps at the date when the unfair prejudice occurred. He said that the petition date is a natural starting point, because that is when the petitioner formally elects to buy or to be bought out ...

If there were to be such a thing as a general rule, I myself would think that the date of the order or the actual valuation would be more appropriate than the date of the presentation of the petition or the unfair prejudice. Prima facie an interest in a going concern ought to be valued at the date on which it is ordered to be purchased. But whatever the general rule might be it seems very probable that the overriding requirement that the valuation should be fair on the facts of the particular case would, by exceptions, reduce it to no rule at all.

[His Lordship decided that there was no general rule and, in his discretion, that the date of the presentation of the petition was the appropriate valuation date. He continued:] I am also in no doubt that the valuation ought to be made on the footing that the students which the petitioner removed to LCEE remained with the company. Mr Oliver's primary submission here was that the petitioner's continuing status as a director rendered him accountable to the company in a fiduciary capacity for any profits earned by LCEE in respect of those students. I do not dissent from that submission, but it seems to me that it would in any event be fair to treat those students as having remained with the company, since the whole object of the exercise is that the petitioner should be bought out on the footing that the unfair prejudice had never occurred, in which event both he and the students would have remained with the company.

Finally, it is clear that the price must be fixed pro rata according to the value of the shares as a whole and not discounted: see *Re Bird Precision Bellows Ltd*.[15] Mr Oliver argued that this was a case where the petitioner had made a constructive election to sever his connection with the company and thus to sell his shares, but that argument falls with the findings of fact which I have already made.

253 Re Sam Weller & Sons Ltd [1990] Ch 682, [1990] BCLC 80 (Chancery Division)

The principal complaint of the petitioners, who together held approximately

---

15 [1984] Ch 419, [1984] 3 All ER 444; affd [1986] Ch 658, [1985] 3 All ER 523, CA.

42.5% of the shares in a family company controlled by their uncle, Mr Sam Weller, was that the company had not increased its dividend in 37 years, despite having been prosperous in recent years: in 1985, out of net profits of over £36,000, it had paid out only £2,520 in dividends. Peter Gibson J in these proceedings ruled that the non-payment of dividends was capable of being unfairly prejudicial conduct.

PETER GIBSON J: [It] is asserted by the petitioners that the sole director is conducting the affairs of the company for the exclusive benefit of himself and his family, and that while he and his sons are taking an income from the company, he is causing the company to pay inadequate dividends to the shareholders. The facts are striking because of the absence of any increase in the dividend for so many years and because of the amount of accumulated profits and the amount of cash in hand. I ask myself why the payment of low dividends in such circumstances is incapable of amounting to conduct unfairly prejudicial to the interests of those members, like the petitioners, who do not receive directors' fees or remuneration from the company. I am unable to see any sufficient reason. It may be in the interests of Mr Sam Weller and his sons that larger dividends should not be paid out and that the major part of the profits of the company should be retained in order to enhance the capital value of their holdings. Their interests are not necessarily identical with those of other shareholders. It may well be in the interests of the other shareholders, including the petitioners, that a more immediate benefit should accrue to them in the form of larger dividends. As their only income from the company is by way of dividend, their interests may be not only prejudiced by the policy of low dividend payments, but unfairly prejudiced.

I do not intend to suggest that a shareholder who does not receive an income from the company except by way of dividend is always entitled to complain whenever the company is controlled by persons who do derive an income from the company and when profits are not fully distributed by way of dividend. I have no doubt that the court will view with great caution allegations of unfair prejudice on this ground. Nevertheless, concerned as I am with an application to strike out, I must be satisfied, if I am to accede to the application, that the allegations in the petition relating to the payment of dividends are incapable of amounting to unfair prejudice to the interests of some part of the members, including the petitioners. For the reasons that I have given, I cannot be so satisfied. . . .

254 Re Elgindata Ltd [1991] BCLC 959 (Chancery Division)

Rowland, the petitioner, had invested in a company controlled by Mr and Mrs Purslow. The remarks of Warner J quoted here relate to the question whether mismanagement is capable of constituting unfairly prejudicial conduct.

WARNER J referred to *Re Five Minute Car Wash Service Ltd* (above, p 496) and continued:

I was referred, on this point also, to the judgment of Peter Gibson J in *Re Sam Weller & Sons Ltd* (**253**) at the end of which he said that he had no doubt that the court would ordinarily be very reluctant to accept that managerial decisions could amount to unfairly prejudicial conduct. . . .

I do not doubt that in an appropriate case it is open to the court to find that serious mismanagement of a company's business constitutes conduct that is unfairly prejudicial to the interests of minority shareholders. But I share Peter Gibson J's view that the court will normally be very reluctant to accept that managerial decisions can amount to unfairly prejudicial conduct.

Two considerations seem to me to be relevant. First, there will be cases where there is disagreement between petitioners and respondents as to whether a particular managerial decision was, as a matter of commercial judgment, the right one to make, or as to whether a particular proposal relating to the conduct of the company's business is commercially sound. ... In my view, it is not for the court to resolve such disagreements on a petition under s 459. Not only is a judge ill-qualified to do so, but there can be no unfairness to the petitioners in those in control of the company's affairs taking a different view from theirs on such matters.

Secondly, as was persuasively argued by Mr Chivers, a shareholder acquires shares in a company knowing that their value will depend in some measure on the competence of the management. He takes the risk that that management may prove not to be of the highest quality. Short of a breach by a director of his duty of skill and care (and no such breach on the part of either Mr Purslow or Mrs Purslow was alleged) there is prima facie no unfairness to a shareholder in the quality of the management turning out to be poor. It occurred to me during the argument that one example of a case where the court might none the less find that there was unfair prejudice to minority shareholders would be one where the majority shareholders, for reasons of their own, persisted in retaining in charge of the management of the company's business a member of their family who was demonstrably incompetent. That of course would be a very different case from this. Mr Rowland deliberately invested in a company controlled and managed by Mr Purslow, whom he had known for five years or so. Indeed, he did so, despite Mr Purslow's reluctance to have him as a shareholder in his company. Mr Nurse submitted that Mr Rowland had a right to expect a reasonable standard of general management from Mr Purslow. In my view, he had no such right. He took the risk that Mr Purslow's management of the company might not be up to the standard that he, Mr Rowland, had hoped and expected. ...

Other reported decisions on CA 1980, s 75 and CA 1985, s 459 include the following:

Re a Company [1983] Ch 178, [1983] 2 All ER 36. A minority shareholding in a small but profitable company was held by executors of an estate; the beneficiaries were two infant children. The executors wanted the company to put forward a scheme of arrangement or a proposal to repurchase the estate's shares, so that the full value of the shares could be realised for the benefit of the children; but the directors declined to do so. Lord Grantchester QC (sitting as a deputy judge of the Chancery Division) held that there was no obligation on the part of the directors to take either step and that their failure to do so was not 'unfairly prejudicial' conduct. He expressed the view (obiter) that the section, like the old s 210, was confined to conduct affecting a member qua member, and cited without any particular comment the views of Gore-Browne (above, p 496) on the relevance of diminution in share value to 'unfair prejudice'.

Re a Company [1983] 2 All ER 854, [1983] 1 WLR 927 was a winding-up case. Vinelott J said obiter: 'It seems to me unlikely that the legislature could have intended to exclude from the scope of s 75 of the 1980 Act a shareholder in the position of Mr Ebrahimi in the *Westbourne Galleries* case **(284)**'— i e a shareholder in a 'quasi-partnership' company who is excluded from involvement in management. This view was confirmed by Hoffmann J in *Re a Company* [1986] BCLC 376, who said: 'In the case of a small private company in which two or three members have ventured their capital by subscribing for shares on the footing that dividends are unlikely but that each will earn his living by working for the company as a director ... [the] member's interests as a member may include a legitimate expectation that he will continue to be employed as a director and his dismissal from that office and exclusion from the management of the company may therefore be unfairly prejudicial to his interests as a member.'

Re R A Noble & Sons (Clothing) Ltd [1983] BCLC 273. A small company formed on the basis of mutual confidence between its two founding members was ordered to be wound up on the grounds that that confidence had broken down (on this point, see below, pp 561 ff); but Nourse J declined to make an order on a petition for alternative relief under CA 1980, s 75, since the petitioner was himself substantially to blame through his own disinterest for the other member's decision to exclude him from participation. Nourse J said:

Although the authorities on s 210 of the 1948 Act are, and will continue to be, of importance in cases where relief is sought under s 75 of the 1980 Act, it is unnecessary for me to refer to any of them in this case. I merely desire respectfully to adopt the following observation of Slade J in *Re Bovey Hotel Ventures Ltd*.[16]

For my own part, while I can think of many hypothetical cases that might fall within s 75 but would not fall within s 210, I can think of no hypothetical cases which, though giving rise to the court's jurisdiction under s 210, would not give rise to such jurisdiction under s 75. ...

In the *Bovey* case, Slade J said this in regard to unfairly prejudicial conduct:

I do not think it necessary or appropriate in this judgment to attempt any comprehensive exposition of the situations which may give rise to the court's jurisdiction under s 75. Broadly, however, I would say this. Without prejudice to the generality of the wording of the section, which may cover many other situations, a member of a company will be able to bring himself within the section if he can show that the value of his shareholding in the company has been seriously diminished or at least seriously jeopardised by reason of a course of conduct on the part of those persons who have had de facto control of the company, which has been unfair to the member concerned. The test of unfairness must, I think, be an objective, not a subjective, one. In other words it is not necessary for the petitioner to show that the persons who have had de facto control of the company have acted as they did in the conscious knowledge that this was unfair to the petitioner or that they were

16 (31 July 1981, unreported).

acting in bad faith; the test, I think, is whether a reasonable bystander observing the consequences of their conduct, would regard it as having unfairly prejudiced the petitioner's interests. . . .

Re Bird Precision Bellows Ltd [1986] Ch 658, [1985] 3 All ER 523, CA, affirming the decision of Nourse J [1984] Ch 419, [1984] 3 All ER 444. The only issue before the court was the issue of valuing shares when (in this case pursuant to an order made by consent) the petitioner's shares were to be purchased by the majority under s 75. Nourse J, at first instance, held that the conduct of the parties could be relevant in determining whether the interests of the respective parties in the company were to be valued pro rata or whether the minority's interest should be discounted. (On this topic, see above, pp 448 ff.) He said:

> Broadly speaking, shares in a small private company are acquired either by allotment on its incorporation or by transfer or devolution at some later date. In the first category it is a matter of common occurrence for a company to be incorporated in order to acquire an existing business or to start a new one, and in either event for it to be a vehicle for the conduct of a business carried on by two or more shareholders which they could, had they wished, have carried on in partnership together. Although it has been pointed out . . . that the description may be confusing, it is often convenient and it is certainly usual to describe that kind of company as a quasi-partnership. In the second category, irrespective of the nature of the company, it is a matter of common occurrence for a shareholder to acquire shares from another at a price which is discounted because they represent a minority holding. It seems to me that some general observations can usefully be made in regard to each of these examples . . .
>
> I would expect that in a majority of cases where purchase orders are made under s 75 in relation to quasi-partnerships the vendor is unwilling in the sense that the sale has been forced upon him. Usually he will be a minority shareholder whose interests have been unfairly prejudiced by the manner in which the affairs of the company have been conducted by the majority. On the assumption that the unfair prejudice has made it no longer tolerable for him to retain his interest in the company, a sale of his shares will invariably be his only practical way out short of a winding up. In that kind of case it seems to me that it would not merely not be fair, but most unfair, that he should be bought out on the fictional basis applicable to a free election to sell his shares in accordance with the company's articles of association, or indeed on any other basis which involved a discounted price. In my judgment the correct course would be to fix the price pro rata according to the value of the shares as a whole and without any discount, as being the only fair method of compensating an unwilling vendor of the equivalent of a partnership share. Equally, if the order provided . . . for the purchase of the shares of the delinquent majority, it would not merely not be fair, but most unfair, that they should receive a price which involved an element of premium.
>
> Of the other, I would expect more rare, cases in which the court might make a purchase order in relation to a quasi-partnership, the arguments

of Mr Jacob require me to mention one. Suppose the case of a minority shareholder whose interests had been unfairly prejudiced by the conduct of the majority, but who had nevertheless so acted as to deserve his exclusion from the company. It is difficult to see how such a case could arise in practice, because one would expect acts and deserts of that kind to be inconsistent with the existence of the supposed conduct of the majority. Be that as it may the consideration of that possibility has been forced upon me by the agreement for the price to be determined by the court without any admission of unfairly prejudicial conduct on the part of the respondents. As will appear, Mr Jacob submitted that the petitioners did act in such a way as to deserve their exclusion from the company. He further submitted that it would therefore be fair for them to be bought out on the basis which would have been applicable if they had made a free election to sell their shares pursuant to the articles, ie at a discount. Assuming, at present, that the respondents can establish the necessary factual basis, I think that Mr Jacob's further submission is correct. A shareholder who deserves his exclusion has, if you like, made a constructive election to sever his connection with the company and thus to sell his shares.

On appeal, the Court of Appeal declined to interfere with the judge's approach, which was a matter for his discretion.

Re O C (Transport) Services Ltd [1984] BCLC 251: on another question concerning valuation, Mervyn Davies J held that it was proper to back-date a valuation to the commencement of the 'unfairly prejudicial' conduct, so that the value of the shares would not be affected by the changes which that conduct had brought about. In this, he was following the approach of the Court of Appeal under the old s 210 in the *Scottish Co-operative* case (**250**).

Re a Company [1985] BCLC 80 (Harman J): it may be unfairly prejudicial conduct for majority shareholders to propose a rights issue in the knowledge that the minority will not be able to afford to take it up (cf *Pennell Securities Ltd v Venida Investments Ltd* (above, p 287)).

Re a Company [1986] BCLC 382 (Hoffmann J): a failure by directors to advise shareholders impartially in regard to two competing take-over bids (in one of which they were themselves personally interested) is capable of constituting unfairly prejudicial conduct.

Re a Company [1987] BCLC 94, [1987] 1 WLR 102 (Hoffmann J): the majority had followed a procedure laid down by the company's articles to deal with a situation of deadlock: it was held not to be unfairly prejudicial conduct to have done so.

Re a Company, ex p Schwarcz (No 2) [1989] BCLC 427 (Peter Gibson J): the following extract from the judgment (at p 437) is of interest, particularly in regard to the position where alternative relief is available to the petitioner:

> Four points on the wording of the section are to be noted: (1) the relevant conduct (of commission or omission) must relate to the affairs of the company of which the petitioners are members; (2) the conduct must be both prejudicial (in the sense of causing prejudice or harm) to the

relevant interests and also unfairly so: conduct may be unfair without being prejudicial or prejudicial without being unfair and in neither case would the section be satisfied; (3) the test is of unfair prejudice, not of unlawfulness, and conduct may be lawful but unfairly prejudicial; (4) the relevant interests are the interests of members (including the petitioners) as members, but such interests are not necessarily limited to strict legal rights under the company's constitution, and the court may take into account wider equitable considerations such as any legitimate expectation which a member has which go beyond his legal rights. The developing jurisprudence on s 459 petitions has established that the court, even on a striking-out application, will consider whether the relief sought by a petitioner is inappropriate and whether it is unreasonable to pursue a petition when, for example, it is clear that the petitioner must leave the company and a fair offer has been made for the petitioner's shares (see, for example, *Re a Company (No 003843 of 1986)*[17] [or] when a petitioner seeking an order for the sale of his shares might have achieved that result by invoking the transfer machinery available in the articles but failed to do so (see *Re a Company (No 007623 of 1986)*[18] and *Re a Company (No 004377 of 1986)*[19]). If the court is of the view that the relief sought is wholly inappropriate and the petitioner is acting unreasonably in pursuing the petition, it may stay or strike out the petition as being an abuse of the process.

NOTE

IA 1986, s 27—a provision which is plainly modelled on CA 1985, s 459—gives a remedy to a creditor or other interested party where an administrator has conducted a company's affairs in a manner which is 'unfairly prejudicial' to the interests of its creditors or members generally, or to some part of its creditors or members. The following remarks of Millett J in *Re Charnley Davies Ltd* (No 2) [1990] BCC 605, a case brought under s 27, throw light on the meaning of the phrase 'unfairly prejudicial' and are of relevance, it is submitted, in the context of s 459.

> Mr Crystal submitted (1) that to constitute management 'in a manner which is unfairly prejudicial' the administrator's conduct must be 'inequitable, dishonest or partial': (2) that while there need not be a conscious intent to act unfairly or to the prejudice of the petitioners, the conduct complained of must be deliberate and not merely negligent or inadvertent; (3) that the unfairly prejudicial management must still be continuing at the date of the petition; and (4) that conduct which injures the company itself and all the members and creditors in accordance with their respective interests cannot constitute unfairly prejudicial conduct.
> I would be reluctant to accept any of those submissions. As to (1), it would be wrong to substitute different language for that chosen by Parliament; if the substituted language means the same it is not helpful, and if it means something different it distorts the intention of Parliament. As to (2) it is difficult to envisage a case where conduct which was negligent or inadvertent could fall within the section, but it would be unwise to dismiss the possibility altogether. As to (3) the tenses employed in the section are not easy to give effect to, but the submission is contrary to decided cases under s 459 of the Companies Act 1985 and its predecessor where the tenses are the same. As to (4) I would not wish to rule

17 [1987] BCLC 562.
18 [1986] BCLC 362.
19 [1987] BCLC 94, [1987] 1 WLR 102.

outside the section a case where a company's affairs were managed by an administrator in a manner which unfairly subordinated the interests of its creditors to those of the creditors of another company in the group of which he was also appointed administrator.

I equally reject Mr Oliver's submissions, which effectively equated 'prejudice' with 'detriment' and 'unfair' with 'tortious', and which ignored the fact that s 27, like s 459 from which it is obviously derived, does not speak of 'unfair prejudice' but of management of the company's affairs 'in a manner which is unfairly prejudicial to the interests' of creditors or members. It is directed to the manner in which the administrator has managed the company's affairs, not to specific breaches of duty giving rise to financial loss, save in so far as these may be evidence or instances of the unfairly prejudicial manner in which he has managed its affairs.

In *Re Sam Weller & Sons Ltd* (253) Peter Gibson J observed that the word 'interests' is wider than a term such as 'rights'. It is plainly wider than 'legal rights'. . . . An allegation that the acts complained of are unlawful or infringe the petitioner's legal rights is not a necessary averment in a s 27 petition. In my judgment it is not a sufficient averment either. The petitioner must allege and prove that they are evidence or instances of the management of the company's affairs by the administrator in a manner which is unfairly prejudicial to the petitioner's interests. Unlawful conduct may be relied upon for this purpose, and its unlawfulness may have a significant probative value, but it is not the essential factor on which the petitioner's cause of action depends.

Mr Oliver asked: 'If misconduct in the management of the company's affairs does not without more constitute unfairly prejudicial management, what extra ingredient is required?' In my judgment the distinction between misconduct and unfairly prejudicial management does not lie in the particular acts or omissions of which complaint is made, but in the nature of the complaint and the remedy necessary to meet it. It is a matter of perspective. The metaphor is not a supermarket trolley but a hologram. If the whole gist of the complaint lies in the unlawfulness of the acts or omissions complained of, so that it may be adequately redressed by the remedy provided by law for the wrong, the complaint is one of misconduct simpliciter. There is no need to assume the burden of alleging and proving that the acts or omissions complained of evidence or constitute unfairly prejudicial management of the company's affairs. It is otherwise if the unlawfulness of the acts or omissions complained of is not the whole gist of the complaint, so that it would not be adequately redressed by the remedy provided by law for the wrong. In such a case it is necessary to assume that burden, but it is no longer necessary to establish that the acts or omissions in question were unlawful, and a much wider remedy may be sought.

A good illustration of the distinction is provided by *Re a Company*.[20] In that case the petitioners, who were minority shareholders, alleged that the respondent, who was the majority shareholder, had disposed of the company's assets in breach of his fiduciary duty to the company and in a manner which was unfairly prejudicial to the interests of the petitioner. Hoffmann J refused to strike out the petition, holding that the fact that the petitioners could have brought a derivative action did not prevent them seeking relief under s 459.

I respectfully agree. The very same facts may well found either a derivative action or a s 459 petition. But that should not disguise the fact that the nature of the complaint and the appropriate relief is different in the two cases. Had the petitioners' true complaint been of the unlawfulness of the respondent's conduct, so that it would be met by an order for restitution, then a derivative action would have been appropriate and a s 459 petition would not. But that was not the true nature of the petitioners' complaint. They did not rely on the unlawfulness of the respondent's conduct to found their cause of action; and they would not have been content with an order that the respondent make restitution to the company. They relied on the respondent's unlawful conduct as evidence of the manner in which he had conducted the company's affairs for his own benefit and in disregard of their interests as minority shareholders; and they wanted to be bought out. They wanted relief from mismanagement, not a remedy for misconduct.

When the petitioners launched the present proceedings, they wrongly believed that Mr Richmond was managing the affairs of the company in a manner which disregarded their interests and those of the creditors generally. That was a perfectly proper complaint to bring under s 27. Long before the case came to trial, however, it had become a simple action for professional negligence and nothing more. That, if established, would amount to misconduct; but it would neither constitute nor evidence unfairly prejudicial management. In my judgment it would be a misuse of language to describe an administrator who has managed the company's affairs fairly and impartially and with a proper regard for the interests of all the creditors (and members where necessary), conscientiously endeavouring to do his best for them, but who has through oversight or inadvertence fallen below the standards of a reasonably competent insolvency practitioner in the carrying out of some particular transaction, as having managed the affairs of the company in a manner which is unfairly prejudicial to the creditors. ...

D. Other remedies

Another remedy available to a minority member is to petition the court for a compulsory winding-up order on the 'just and equitable' ground: see below, pp 557 ff.

There is, at least in theory, the possibility of invoking the powers of the Department of Trade and Industry under CA 1985, Pt XIV, to have the affairs of the company investigated (see below, pp 531 ff). In practice, the Department's powers are most commonly invoked in cases of insolvency, fraudulent trading and financial scandal—that is, in matters of interest to the investing public and to creditors— while minority shareholders who seek aid are sent away empty-handed. Mr Moir (see *Wallersteiner v Moir (No 2)* above, p 494) is reported to have made fifteen unsuccessful requests to the Department (Economist, 8 February 1975).

CHAPTER 11

Reconstructions, Arrangements and Take-overs[1]

The terms used in this chapter are commonly used without any great precision. By the term 'reconstruction' is usually meant the transfer of the undertaking and business of a company (or, sometimes, several companies) to a new company specially formed for the purpose. The old company is put into liquidation and its shareholders, instead of being repaid their capital by the liquidator in cash, agree to take equivalent shares in the new company. In the result, the same shareholders carry on the same enterprise through the medium of a new company. The statutory provisions governing this procedure are contained in IA 1986, ss 110–111. The sanction of the court is not required, but a dissentient shareholder may always require that he be paid out in cash rather than take the new shares. Creditors who do not agree to look to the new company for payment of their debts may prove in the liquidation of the old company.

A 'merger' or 'amalgamation' takes place when the undertakings of more than one company are brought under the ownership and control of a single company, which may be one of the companies involved or a new one. The result is that the shareholders who were members of the several amalgamating companies now together own and control the same enterprises as one venture. In a straightforward case, the procedure laid down by s 110 may be used. Much the same consequences may follow from a 'take-over', which is a general term used to describe the acquisition by one company[2] of control over another, usually by buying all or a majority of its shares. In the ordinary case, the company taken over is the smaller; in a 'reverse take-over', a smaller company gains control of a larger one. An offer addressed to all the shareholders of a company to buy the shares of each member at a stated price is known as a 'take-over bid'. It is usually expressed to be conditional upon a designated percentage of shares being accepted by a given date. This is commonly set at 90%, because CA 1985, s 429 permits a company which has acquired 90% or more of a company's shares by a 'take-over bid' to buy the remaining shares compulsorily, and conversely s 430A empowers the minority shareholders in such a situation to insist on being bought out.

Where the company making a take-over bid offers to exchange its own shares for those in the company being acquired, rather than make a bid for cash, the result is to all intents and purposes an amalgamation of the two companies as described above.

A 'scheme of arrangement' under CA 1985, ss 425–427A enables a company to alter the rights of its members *or its creditors,* with the sanction of the court. The section is sufficiently wide to accommodate schemes of considerable

---

1 For further reading, see Rabinowicz (ed), *Weinberg and Blank on Take-overs and Mergers,* 5th edn (London, 1989).
2 A take-over bid may also be made by one or more individuals, or by a group of companies. The restrictive wording which formerly confined the scope of ss 428 ff to a bid made by a single company has been removed by amendments made by the Financial Services Act 1986.

complexity, which may involve more than one company. The more elaborate kinds of merger will usually need to be dealt with under these sections, and so will any scheme of reconstruction which is intended to affect creditors (and especially debentureholders) as well as shareholders. Unless the court orders otherwise or refuses its sanction altogether, the members or creditors who dissent are bound to accept the terms of the scheme. In contrast with IA 1986, s 110, there is no liquidation of the company or companies involved.

Corporate businesses may, of course, be split up as well as aggregated. The most common procedure by which part of a company's undertaking is sold off is usually referred to as 'hiving down'. The company forms a subsidiary and vests the assets in question in its name, or transfers the assets to an existing subsidiary, and sells the shareholding in that subsidiary to new owners. These may include the managers of that part of the business who have hitherto been employees of the vendor (a 'management buy-out'). Alternatively, there may be a simple sale of the assets, either for cash or in consideration of the allotment of shares in the purchasing company to the vendor, or to the shareholders of the vendor if it is a company. This last type of transaction, which is not common in this country, is known as a 'demerger' or 'scission'.

A merger achieved by a transfer of assets in consideration of the allotment of shares in the transferee company to the former shareholders of the trans-feror, and a demerger as described above, must observe the requirements of CA 1985, Sch 15A as well as ss 425–427A. This schedule was incorporated into the Act to implement the Third and Sixth EEC Company Law Directives. The innovation will have little effect in practice, however, since the standard procedures here of take-over and hiving down involve the purchase and sale of shares and not of assets.

A. Schemes of reconstruction under IA 1986, ss 110–111

A company cannot by a provision in its memorandum and articles authorise a scheme of reconstruction which disregards the rights of dissentients under s 111.

255 Bisgood v Henderson's Transvaal Estates Ltd [1908] 1 Ch 743 (Court of Appeal)

The company in general meeting resolved to carry out a scheme whereby each fully paid £1 share was to be exchanged for one £1 share in a new company, to be credited as paid up to an amount of $87\frac{1}{2}$p. Under the scheme, the 'new' shares of those who dissented were to be sold en bloc for what they would fetch, and the proceeds distributed pro rata amongst them. The company's memorandum and articles purported to authorise such a trans-action; but it was held to be unlawful.

The judgment of the court (COZENS-HARDY MR and FLETCHER MOULTON and BUCKLEY LJJ) was delivered by BUCKLEY LJ: The question involved is whether by clauses even in the memorandum of association of a company limited by shares the limit upon the shareholder's liability can be raised—whether the constitution of the company can provide that the majority may impose upon the minority a scheme under which the member must either come under an increased liability or accept such compensation as the scheme offers him.

Section 161 of the Companies Act 1862 [IA 1986, s 111] protects the dissentient member by securing him the value of his interest to be determined by arbitration or agreement. The purpose of schemes such as that here in question is to evade or escape the provisions of that section. Their object is to impose upon the shareholders what is generally called an assessment—to require that in a limited company after the shares are fully paid the shareholder must either come under liability to make further contributions to capital or submit to take, not the value of his interest to be determined by arbitration or agreement, but such satisfaction as the scheme offers him. That satisfaction commonly means, and in substance means in this case, the surrender of his interest in the company . . .

The question is whether the reorganisation scheme contained in the agreement and resolutions is intra vires. The argument is that it is because it is justified by clauses in the memorandum of association . . .

The purpose of the memorandum and articles . . . is not confined to defining and limiting the purposes of the corporation; it extends also within proper limits to defining and ascertaining the rights of the corporators. I have no doubt that within proper limits the memorandum and articles may provide how, as between the corporators, the corporate assets shall be dealt with after liquidation. But in this, as in many matters, there are limits imposed by the statutes. There are matters in respect of which the constitution of the company cannot provide that the corporator shall not enjoy rights and immunities which the statute gives him. For instance, s 82 of the Companies Act 1862 [IA 1986, s 124] empowers a contributory to present a winding-up petition. His right in that respect cannot be excluded by the articles: *Re Peveril Gold Mines* (**275**) . . . Upon a like principle the articles cannot exclude a shareholder from his right of dissent under s 161 of the Companies Act 1862 . . . It is, therefore, not necessarily true that, because there are found in the memorandum and articles clauses such as those upon which the question here arises, the corporators as individuals are contractually bound by them. The question is not whether each individual corporator can bind himself in respect of his distributive share in the assets. The question is whether, consistently with the statutes, the constitution of the corporation can be such that every corporator shall in the matter of distribution—or a fortiori of distribution and further liability—be bound by the vote of the majority . . .

In the matter of liability upon his shares the statute provides in plain terms by s 38(4) [IA 1986, s 74(2)(d)], that in the case of a company limited by shares no contribution shall be required from any member exceeding the amount unpaid on his shares. In my opinion, any attempt so to define the constitution of the company as that the member shall in any event be liable for a larger sum is in breach of the statute and is ultra vires. Any clauses which can be used to maintain a scheme which imposes upon the member the alternative of accepting liability for a larger sum or of being dispossessed of his status as shareholder upon terms which he is not bound to accept are, I think, ultra vires . . .

The company, it is true, have issued the allotment letters in such form as that the shareholder could sell his right to an allotment and put forward the name of a purchaser if he found one. And the old company could within the language of the agreement sell the shares which are not applied for, and under the fifth resolution the proceeds would be distributable among the non-assenting members. Shortly stated, the scheme is one under which the shareholder is told that he may take the share in the new company with its liability or sell the share in the new company with its liability, but he shall have nothing but the share in the new company or its proceeds; that he must be assessed or find some one who will take the new share with the assessment or take his chance that the liquidator may find some one who will do so, but that he shall have nothing else. In my opinion this is ultra vires. The plaintiff is, in my judgment, entitled to an injunction to restrain the defendants from carrying out the reorganisation scheme.

In a reconstruction under IA 1986, ss 110–111, the general meeting has no power to decide that the consideration received shall be distributed among the members otherwise than in accordance with their rights in a winding up.

256 Griffith v Paget (1877) 5 Ch D 894 (Chancery Division)

The capital of the Argentine Tramways Co Ltd was divided into preferred shares and deferred shares each of a nominal value of £10, the former being entitled to a cumulative 12% preferential dividend. There was no provision as to the relative rights of the classes in a winding up. The preferred dividend had not been paid in full for many years. A scheme of reconstruction was proposed under which the shares in the existing company should be exchanged for shares, all of one class, in a new company, on a basis which gave the preferred shareholders approximately the par value of their existing holdings, but the deferred shareholders only about 15% of such value. The plaintiff, a preferred shareholder, who considered that this scheme gave the deferred shareholders more than the market value of their shares, objected that the general meeting had no power to fix the mode of distribution of the new shares; and the court upheld his view.

JESSEL MR: The question which is now raised, as far as I know for the first time, is this, whether in the case of a limited liability company, when there are two or more classes of shareholders having different rights inter se, and the powers conferred by the Companies Act 1862, s 161 [IA 1986, s 110], are exercised, the company can do more than decide on the nature of the consideration to be accepted, or whether it can, at the same time, by the statutory majority, decide as to the mode of distribution of the consideration so accepted between the two classes of shareholders. In my opinion it cannot do the latter at all.

I think the meaning of s 161, stated broadly, was this, that instead of disposing of the assets of the company, wound up under a voluntary winding up, for money, you may dispose of them for shares in any other company, or policies, or any like interest, or future profits or other benefit from the purchasing company, but that whatever the benefit was, in whatever shape it was taken, it was to be given, or paid, or handed over to the liquidators for the benefit of the contributories, if I may call them so, of the company wound up—of course subject to the payment of their debts; and that there was no authority conferred by the Act of Parliament on the general meeting, or rather the statutory majority, to direct a distribution as between those contributories otherwise than according to their rights inter se. I think that is tolerably plain from the nature of the case.

First, what is to become of the assets of the company when wound up voluntarily in the ordinary way? In that case we find, by s 133 [IA 1986, s 107], the property, after being applied in satisfaction of the liabilities, is to 'be distributed among the members according to their rights and interests in the company'. Therefore, if the liquidator sells the assets for money, there is no power given to a general meeting to alter the rights of the contributories inter se. They are to share according to their rights and interests ...

NOTE

There is an obvious advantage to a company in proceeding under CA 1985, ss 425–427A rather than s 110, in that dissentient shareholders cannot be forced to accept a scheme under the latter section, but may insist on their right under s 111 to be paid out in cash. In the case next cited, an attempt was made to formulate rules governing the freedom of a company to choose between the two forms of procedure.

257 Re Anglo-Continental Supply Co Ltd [1922] 2 Ch 723 (Chancery Division)

[The facts are immaterial.]

ASTBURY J: As a result of his researches, Mr Maugham [counsel for the company] has formulated three propositions which, when expressed as follows, are in my judgment sound: (1) When a so-called scheme is really and truly a sale, etc under s 192 [IA 1986, s 110] simpliciter, that section must be complied with and cannot be evaded by calling it a scheme of arrangement under s 120 [CA 1985, s 425]: see per Warrington LJ in *Re Guardian Assurance Co.*[3] (2) Where a scheme of arrangement cannot be carried through under s 192, though it involves (inter alia) a sale to a company within that section for 'shares, policies and other like interests', and for liquidation and distribution of the proceeds, the court can sanction it under s 120 if it is fair and reasonable in accordance with the principles upon which the court acts in these cases, and it may, but only if it thinks fit, insist as a term of its sanction on the dissentient shareholders being protected in manner similar to that provided for in s 192. (3) Where a scheme of arrangement is one outside s 192 entirely, the court can also and a fortiori act as in proposition (2), subject to the conditions therein mentioned ...

B. Schemes of arrangement under ss 425–427A

258 Re Alabama, New Orleans, Texas and Pacific Junction Rly Co [1891] 1 Ch 213 (Court of Appeal)

[The following passage describes the function of the court in considering whether to sanction a scheme under ss 425–427A.]

LINDLEY LJ: [What] the court has to do is to see, first of all, that the provisions of that statute have been complied with; and, secondly, that the majority has been acting bona fide. The court also has to see that the minority is not being overridden by a majority having interests of its own clashing with those of the minority whom they seek to coerce. Further than that, the court has to look at the scheme and see whether it is one as to which persons acting honestly, and viewing the scheme laid before them in the interests of

3 [1917] 1 Ch 431.

those whom they represent, take a view which can be reasonably taken by businessmen ...

[Note also the observations of Maugham J in *Re Dorman Long & Co* (**90**). A further illustration follows.]

259 Re Hellenic & General Trust Ltd [1976] 1 WLR 123, [1975] 3 All ER 382 (Chancery Division)

Hambros Ltd, through a wholly owned subsidiary (referred to in the judgment as 'MIT') held 53% of the ordinary shares of the company, Hellenic & General Trust Ltd. A scheme of arrangement was proposed under which Hambros would acquire all the ordinary shares for a cash consideration of 48p per share. At a meeting of ordinary shareholders, over 80% approved the scheme: MIT voted in support, but the National Bank of Greece, a minority shareholder holding some 14% of the shares, opposed the scheme because it would be liable to pay heavy taxes under Greek law. Templeman J refused to sanction the scheme, first, because he ruled that there should have been a separate 'class' meeting of those ordinary shareholders who were not already a wholly owned subsidiary of Hambros, and secondly because, although the scheme was objectively fair, it was as a matter of discretion not fair to allow the use of CA 1948, s 206 (CA 1985, s 425) to achieve the compulsory purchase of shares which could not be acquired by the use of the procedure now contained in CA 1985, ss 428 ff.

TEMPLEMAN J: The first objection put forward is that the necessary agreement by the appropriate class of members has not been obtained. The shareholders who were summoned to the meeting consisted, it is submitted, of two classes. First there were the outside shareholders, that is to say the shareholders other than MIT: and secondly MIT, a subsidiary of Hambros. MIT were a separate class and should have been excluded from the meeting of outside shareholders. Although s 206 provides that the court may order meetings, it is the responsibility of the petitioners to see that the class meetings are properly constituted, and if they fail then the necessary agreement is not obtained and the court has no jurisdiction to sanction the arrangement ...
   The question therefore is whether MIT, a wholly owned subsidiary of Hambros, formed part of the same class as the other ordinary shareholders. What is an appropriate class must depend upon the circumstances but some general principles are to be found in the authorities. In *Sovereign Life Assurance Co v Dodd*,[4] the Court of Appeal held that for the purposes of an arrangement affecting the policyholders of an assurance company the holders of policies which had matured were creditors and were a different class from policyholders whose policies had not matured. Bowen LJ said: 'It seems plain that we must give such a meaning to the term "class" as will prevent the section being so worked as to result in confiscation and injustice, and that it must be confined to those persons whose rights are not so dissimilar as to make it impossible for them to consult together with a view to their common interest.' Vendors consulting together with a view to their common interest in an offer made by a purchaser would look askance at the presence among them of a wholly owned subsidiary of the purchaser ... Mr Heyman, on behalf of the petitioners, submitted that since the parent and subsidiary were

4 [1892] 2 QB 573.

separate corporations with separate directors, and since MIT were ordinary shareholders in the company, it followed that MIT had the same interests as the other shareholders. The directors of MIT were under a duty to consider whether the arrangement was beneficial to the whole class of ordinary shareholders, and they were capable of forming an independent and unbiased judgment, irrespective of the interests of the parent company. This seems to me to be unreal. Hambros are purchasers making an offer. When the vendors meet to discuss and vote whether or not to accept the offer, it is incongruous that the loudest voice in theory and the most significant vote in practice should come from the wholly owned subsidiary of the purchaser. No one can be both a vendor and a purchaser and in my judgment, for the purpose of the class meetings in the present case, MIT were in the camp of the purchaser. Of course this does not mean that MIT should not have considered at a separate class meeting whether to accept the arrangement. But their consideration will be different from the considerations given to the matter by the other shareholders. Only MIT could say, within limits, that what was good for Hambros must be good for MIT ...

Accordingly I uphold the first objection, which is fatal to the arrangement. But in view of the careful arguments put forward by both sides I will consider the other objections which are raised by Mr Wright and which are material if the class meeting in the present case, contrary to my view, was properly constituted.

The second objection is founded on the analysis of the arrangement as an offer by Hambros to acquire the ordinary shares for 48p. Section 209 [CA 1985, ss 428 ff] provides safeguards for minority shareholders in the event of a takeover bid and in a proper case provides machinery for a small minority of shareholders to be obliged to accept a takeover against their wishes ... If the present arrangement had been carried out under s 209, MIT as a subsidiary of Hambros would have been expressly forbidden to join in any approval for the purposes of s 209,[5] and in any event the objectors could not have been obliged to sell because they hold 10% of the ordinary shares of the company.

The fact that an arrangement under s 206 [CA 1985, s 425] produces a result which is the same as a takeover under s 209 is not necessarily fatal. [His Lordship referred to a number of cases (including *Re Bugle Press Ltd* (**260**)), and continued:]

Whereas in *Bugle Press* the motives of the applicants for the scheme were not particularly praiseworthy I hasten to say that in the present case the motives of the petitioners are entirely different, as will appear when I come to consider the details of the scheme. The petitioners are anxious that the ordinary shareholders should be offered the full net asset value of their shares which exceed the value of those shares on the open market. They are persisting with the scheme because they do not consider that it is fair to those shareholders who wish to accept the scheme that they should be frustrated by the opposition of the objectors. But the decision in *Bugle Press Ltd* fortifies me in thinking that where one has what is in effect a s 209 scheme then, putting it at its lowest, there must be a very high standard of proof on the part of the petitioner to justify obtaining by s 206 what could not be obtained by s 209, especially when there is the added element that s 206 itself only works with the help of a wholly owned subsidiary of the petitioners.

5 [See now the more detailed provisions contained in CA 1985, s 430E.]

The third alternative objection raised by Mr Wright is that the arrangement is unfair to all the ordinary shareholders. [His Lordship discussed the evidence, and continued:] I am quite satisfied that the scheme is fair or more than fair to the ordinary shareholders as a class.

Mr Heyman says, that being so, I ought to ignore the earlier indications of unfairness, namely, the effect of the s 209 machinery, and the exploitation of the s 206 machinery; and it may be that in some extraordinary case that would be true. But I cannot bring myself to believe that it would be right to exercise a discretion in favour of the petitioners in the present case ... Substantially the objectors' view is coloured by the fact that they will, as the evidence states, although I am not given details, become liable to a swingeing capital gains tax in Greece. Mr Heyman says the tax must be ignored because in considering their votes at a meeting under s 206 each shareholder must put himself in the impossible position of deciding what is in the best interests of the class. That appears from the judgment of Megarry J in *Re Holders Investment Trust Ltd* (**181**), and in particular the passage where Megarry J refers to a general principle that a power conferred on a majority of a class to bind minorities, must be exercised for the purpose of benefiting the class as a whole and not merely individual members only. Similarly in *Re Grierson, Oldham & Adams Ltd* (**261**), under s 209 it was held the test was one of fairness to the body of shareholders and not to individuals and the burden was on the applicants to prove unfairness and not merely that the scheme was open to criticism. Although under s 206 the onus is the other way round it is submitted that the test of fairness is exactly the same.

In a good many cases so it would be, but in the present case it seems to me that the individual loss which the objectors will suffer from the scheme is one which should be borne in mind. When one adds together the three objections of Mr Wright, ... it seems to me that it is unfair to deprive the objectors of shares which they were entitled to assume were safe from compulsory purchase and with the effect of putting on the objectors a swingeing fiscal impost which, if the matter had proceeded under s 209, they could have avoided simply and quite properly by refusing to join in approving the scheme under that section.

Accordingly in the result, both as a matter of jurisdiction and as a matter of discretion, I am not prepared to make any order approving this scheme.

QUESTION

You are consulted in advance of the meeting by the National Bank of Greece, and asked to advise it whether it would be proper for the Bank to consider its tax position in deciding how to cast its vote at the class meeting. What would your advice be? (See *Re Holders Investment Trust Ltd* (**181**).)

NOTE

In *Re National Farmers' Union Development Trust Ltd* [1973] 1 All ER 135, [1972] 1 WLR 1548 a non-profit-making company wished to write down its capital and reduce the number of its members from 94,000 to 7 in order to reduce its administrative expenses. The proposal had the support of an 85% majority vote. But Brightman J held that he had no power to sanction the scheme under what is now s 425, since the statutory terms 'compromise' and 'arrangement' implied some element of accommodation on each side and were not appropriate to describe a scheme under which some members surrendered their rights altogether.

The Cork Committee on Insolvency made the following observations about the present procedure under ss 425–427A and its utility in corporate involvencies (1982, Cmnd 8558, paras 406 ff):

> Because of the long and involved procedure, it is virtually impossible to shorten the period of time between initial formulation of a scheme of arrangement and its becoming effective by Court Order below eight weeks. During those eight weeks each individual creditor can exercise all the rights and remedies available to him against the company debtor ...
>
> The insolvent company's inability—particularly if it is a trading company— to hold the position (that is to prevent winding up or the random seizure of assets by individual creditors) during the period necessary for the devising and processing of a scheme, makes it extremely difficult for even the most uncomplicated scheme of arrangement to be launched. A straightforward moratorium on the payment of debts to unsecured creditors for a limited period, or such a moratorium coupled with a composition, say the reduction of all debts by 25%, may be the plainest good sense for all concerned, but it often cannot be done ...
>
> The Court is heavily involved in the procedure under section [425]. There are two distinct phases. First, the convening of the necessary meetings of creditors and contributories and, secondly, the petition to the Court for the sanctioning of the scheme as approved by the appropriate majorities at the meetings ...
>
> [We] believe that the Court procedure could be substantially streamlined and greatly improved. We cannot believe that there is the need for quite so many applications to, or attendances on, the Court. We doubt whether painstaking perusal of documents by Court officials with little or no experience of commerce or finance provides any real protection for creditors or contributories.

There has been no reform of ss 425–427A to meet the Committee's criticisms. However, the insolvency legislation of 1985–86 has introduced two new procedures designed to enable a corporate rescue package to be put together in a situation of imminent insolvency— the voluntary arrangement (IA 1986, Pt I) and the administration order (Pt II): see below, p 542. Early experience of the new legislation suggests that these two procedures, particularly if used in conjunction, may go a long way to meet the need to which the Committee drew attention.

C. Take-overs[6]

Where a company acquires control over another by buying all or a majority holding of its shares, this is termed a 'take-over'. A general offer to buy addressed to all the shareholders of a company is called a 'take-over bid'. This is by far the commonest method used in this country for merging one corporate business with another. The two companies are usually referred to respectively as the 'offeror' company and the 'target' or 'offeree' company.

The law has very few special rules for take-overs. The most important are to be found in CA 1985, ss 428 ff, which confer on a bidder who has succeeded

---

6 For further reading, see Sir A Johnson *The City Take-over Code* (Oxford, 1980); E Stamp and C Marley *Accounting Principles and the City Code: The Case for Reform* (1970); Rice, 'Good and Bad Take-over Bids' [1960] JBL 308; A J Boyle, 'The Sale of Controlling Shares' (1964) 13 ICLQ 185; R R Pennington, 'Take-over Bids in the United Kingdom' [1969] Am J Comp L 159; D D Prentice, 'Take-over Bids—the City Code on Take-overs and Mergers' (1972) 18 McGill LJ 385; Lord Alexander of Weedon, 'Take-overs: the Regulatory Scene' [1990] JBL 203; D Calcutt, 'The Work of the Take-over Panel' (1990) 11 Co Law 203.

in gaining acceptances for 90% or more of the target company's shares the right to buy out the outstanding minority on the same terms, and conversely entitle any member of such a minority to demand that he be bought out.

There is an emerging, if somewhat inconclusive, body of case-law concerned with the legal duties of the directors of a target company when faced with a bid: see below, pp 523 ff.

However, much of the regulation of take-overs is not a matter for the law at all: it comes under the supervisory powers of the City Panel on Take-overs and Mergers, administering the 'City Code'. The Code was prepared and issued by representatives of various City bodies, including the Bank of England, The Stock Exchange, and the Issuing Houses Association, as a statement of the principles of commercial morality which those taking part in a take-over are expected to follow. Its rules carry no direct legal sanction but are backed by the disciplinary powers of the professional institutions and the City's Self-Regulatory Organisations over their own members, and by the fact that the constituent bodies of the Panel control access to the share-market. The function of the Panel is to give advice and rulings on the due observation of the principles of the Code. The Panel has been judicially recognised as discharging a public function, and its decisions are in principle subject to judicial review, but interlocutory remedies will not ordinarily be granted against it (the *Datafin* case (**264**)). The Panel may also, in an appropriate case, request the Department of Trade and Industry to investigate the affairs of a company under Part XIV of CA 1985.

Extracts from the City Code appear in the Appendix (below, p 642). Specimen documents used in a recent take-over bid are reproduced below, pp 624 ff.

There is, of course, also a political dimension to take-overs and, indeed, the question of mergers generally, if as a result of an acquisition there is likely to be an infringement of the monopolies legislation. For this topic, see below, p 539.

Section 429 may not be used by majority shareholders to expropriate a minority.

260 Re Bugle Press Ltd [1961] Ch 270, [1960] 3 All ER 791 (Court of Appeal)

The £10,000 issued share capital of Bugle Press Ltd was held as to 4,500 £1 shares each by Shaw and Jackson ('the majority shareholders') and as to the remaining 1,000 shares by Treby. The majority shareholders formed a £100 company, Jackson & Shaw (Holdings) Ltd, which they caused to make an offer, addressed to the shareholders in Bugle Press Ltd, to purchase their holdings at £10 per share. After Shaw and Jackson had accepted this offer, and Treby had refused it on the ground that the price was too low, the offeror company gave Treby notice of its intention to purchase his holding compulsorily under CA 1948, s 209 [CA 1985, s 429]. The Court of Appeal, affirming Buckley J, exercising the discretion conferred by the section, declared that the scheme was not binding on Treby.

LORD EVERSHED MR: Mr Instone [Counsel for the offeror company] freely accepts that the mechanism of the section has here been invoked by means of the incorporation of this holding company, Jackson & Shaw (Holdings) Ltd, especially for the purpose, and in order to enable the two persons, Shaw and Jackson, to expropriate the shares of their minority colleague, Treby. He says that although that is undoubtedly true, nevertheless, in the result, the case does fall within the strict language of the section and falling within it the consequences must follow. If that argument is right, it would enable by a device of this kind the 90% majority of the shareholders always to get rid of a minority shareholder whom they did not happen to like. And that, as a matter of principle, would appear to be contrary to a fundamental principle of our law that prima facie, if a man has a legal right which is an absolute right, then he can do with it or not do with it what he will ...

[It] is, I think, relevant ... to note that by the terms of the section itself one must have regard to what lies behind the invocation of the section. ... [I]t seems to me plain that what the section is directed to is a case where there is a scheme or contract for the acquisition of a company, its amalgamation, reorganisation or the like, and where the offeror is independent of the shareholders in the transferor company or at least independent of that part of fraction of them from which the 90% is to be derived. Even, therefore, though the present case does fall strictly within the terms of s 209, the fact that the offeror, the transferee company, is for all practical purposes entirely equivalent to the nine-tenths of the shareholders who have accepted the offer, makes it in my judgment a case in which, for the purposes of exercising the court's discretion, the circumstances are special ... It is no doubt true to say that it is still for the minority shareholder to establish that the discretion should be exercised in the way he seeks. That, I think ... follows from the language of the section which uses the formula which I have already more than once read 'unless on an application made by the dissenting shareholder the court thinks fit to order otherwise'. But if the minority shareholder does show, as he shows here, that the offeror and the 90% of the transferor company's shareholders are the same, then as it seems to me he has, prima facie, shown that the court ought otherwise to order, since if it should not so do the result would be ... that the section has been used not for the purpose of any scheme or contract properly so called or contemplated by the section but for the quite different purpose of enabling majority shareholders to expropriate or evict the minority; and that, as it seems to me, is something for the purposes of which, prima facie, the court ought not to allow the section to be invoked—unless at any rate it were shown that there was some good reason in the interests of the company for so doing, for example, that the minority shareholder was in some way acting in a manner destructive or highly damaging to the interests of the company from some motives entirely of his own ...

HARMAN LJ delivered a concurring judgment.

DONOVAN LJ concurred.

[The approach of the courts in considering an application under s 430C was discussed in the following case.]

261 Re Grierson Oldham and Adams Ltd [1968] Ch 17, [1967] 1 All ER 192 (Chancery Division)

The company, which dealt in wines and spirits, had been the subject of a successful take-over bid by John Holt & Co (Liverpool) Ltd. The offer made by Holts of 6s [30p] per 2s [10p] ordinary share had been accepted by 99.9%

of the shareholders, and notice had been given of Holt's intention to acquire the remaining shares compulsorily at the same price pursuant to CA 1948, s 209 [CA 1985, s 429]. The applicants, who had paid between 6s 7½d [33p] and 6s 9d [34p] per share for their holdings, objected on the ground that the price offered was unfair to them; but the court declined to intervene.

PLOWMAN J: The contentions which are put forward by the applicants fall under two main heads. In the first place it is said that the price of 6s a share is unfair, taking into account the assets and future prospects of the company and the advantages which will accrue to Holts by the take-over; and secondly, that it is unfair to the applicants that they should be compelled to sell their shares at a loss. Before considering those contentions in more detail, there are two or three general observations which I should make and which I think are justified by the authorities on this section to which I have been referred.

The first general observation is that the onus of proof here is fairly and squarely on the applicants, and indeed they accepted that that is so. The onus of proof is on them to establish, if they can, that the offer was unfair ...

The second general observation which seems to me to be relevant is this: that since this is not a case of a purchase of assets, but of a purchase of shares, the market price on the stock exchange of those shares is cogent evidence of their true value; not conclusive evidence, of course, but cogent evidence ... And in this case it is a formidable onus that the applicants have set out to discharge, bearing in mind that not only was the offer price above the stock exchange price, but that over 99% of the ordinary shareholders accepted the offer.

The third general observation which arises out of the arguments that have been put forward concerns the question whether the test of the fairness of the offer is fairness to the individual shareholder or fairness to the body of shareholders as a whole. In my judgment, the test of fairness is whether the offer is fair to the offerees as a body and not whether it is fair to a particular shareholder in the peculiar circumstances of his own case ... It would quite obviously be impossible, at any rate in most cases, for the offeror to know the circumstances of every individual shareholder and, therefore, to frame an offer which would necessarily be fair to every individual shareholder in the peculiar circumstances of his case.

The other general observation, which arises from the *Sussex Brick* case,[7] is that the fact that the applicants may be able to demonstrate that the scheme is open to criticism, or is capable of improvement, is not enough to discharge the onus of proof which lies upon them. Vaisey J said:

> I agree that certain criticisms set out in the applicant's affidavit show that a good case could be made out for the formulation of a better scheme, of a fairer scheme, of one which would be more attractive to the shareholders if they could have understood the implications of the criticisms. I have no doubt at all that a better scheme could have been evolved, but is that enough? ...
>
> A scheme must be obviously unfair, patently unfair, unfair to the meanest intelligence. It cannot be said that no scheme can be effective to bind a dissenting shareholder unless it complies to the extent of 100 per cent with the highest possible standards of fairness, equity and reason ...   It must be affirmatively established that, notwithstanding the view

7 [1961] Ch 289n, [1960] 1 All ER 772n.

of the majority, the scheme is unfair, and that is a different thing from saying that it must be established that the scheme is not a very fair one or not a fair one: a scheme has to be shown affirmatively, patently, obviously and convincingly to be unfair.

With those general observations, let me refer in a little more detail to some of the points which have been put forward on the part of the applicants. They have complained that the market price was substantially higher than 6*s* a share for a number of years [His Lordship cited prices ranging up to 9*s* 9*d* [49p]]; equally, as Mr Gurney-Champion said, in each of those years the lowest price for the shares was under 6*s*. But however that may be, it seems to me that the real point is, was 6*s* a fair price at the time when the offer was made, namely, in September 1965?

[His Lordship referred to the company's balance sheet and continued:] Then it is said that the price of 6*s* a share does not reflect the advantages accruing to Holts by their obtaining complete control of the company. I agree with Mr Instone that that might possibly be used as an argument to justify paying a shareholder with a controlling interest a larger price for the shares than the price paid to minority holders. But, in my judgment, it is not unfair to offer a minority shareholder the value of what he possesses, i e a minority shareholding ...

Then Mr Gurney-Champion submitted that it was unfair that he should be compelled to sell these shares at a loss, particularly having regard to the fact that the loss would be one which was not available for capital gains tax purposes, for the reason that he had bought the shares before 6 April 1965, and on that day the price of the shares was less than the purchase price. If I am right in thinking that the question of unfairness has to be judged without reference to the particular circumstances of the applicant, then it seems to me that this argument is irrelevant, and I am bound to reject it because I have already indicated the view that the particular circumstances of the applicant is not a matter with which the court is concerned. What the court is concerned with is the fairness of the offer as a whole ...

QUESTION

Was Plowman J right to think that the question of unfairness has to be judged without reference to the particular circumstances of the applicant? Can this view be reconciled with *Re Hellenic & General Trust Ltd* (**259**)?

Directors' role in a take-over

The position of the directors of the target company in a take-over has been the subject of judicial consideration in some cases. It is well established that they may not use their powers (e g to issue further shares) as a defensive tactic to thwart a take-over bid (see *Hogg v Cramphorn Ltd* (**140**) and the other cases cited above, pp 288 ff). It is also obvious that, in giving information relevant to the bid to their shareholders—as they are required to do by the Take-over Code—they must act in an honest way and not seek to mislead them. This was confirmed in *Gething v Kilner* [1972] 1 All ER 1166, [1972] 1 WLR 337. The ruling in *Heron International Ltd v Lord Grade* (**127**) that the directors in that case were under fiduciary duties towards their company's shareholders cannot be taken to be of general application, since it turned upon the special article which gave the board control over the transfer of the voting shares. The extracts which follow throw some light on the question, but each must be read in the light of the facts of the particular case.

262 Re a Company [1986] BCLC 383 (Chancery Division)

Rival take-over bids had been made for the shares in a private company, one (referred to in the judgment as 'the N bid') by a company controlled by the target company's own directors and another, higher, bid by a trade competitor. The chairman had sent a circular to the shareholders urging them to accept the N bid and explaining, with reasons, why the higher bid could not succeed. In these proceedings it was claimed that the directors had been in breach of duty in not recommending the higher offer and in not taking steps to facilitate the chances of that offer being successful.

HOFFMANN J: I cannot accept the proposition that the board must inevitably be under a positive duty to recommend and take all steps within their power to facilitate whichever is the highest offer. In a case such as the present, where the directors propose to exercise their undoubted right as shareholders to accept the lower offer in respect of their own shares and, for understandable and fully disclosed reasons, hope in their personal capacities that a majority of other shareholders will accept it as well, it seems to me that it would be artificial to say that they were under a positive duty to advise shareholders to accept the higher offer. The fact that they would get more money by taking the higher offer is hardly something which needs to be pointed out. I do not think that fairness can require more of the directors than to give the shareholders sufficient information and advice to enable them to reach a properly informed decision and to refrain from giving misleading advice or exercising their fiduciary powers in a way which would prevent or inhibit shareholders from choosing to take the better price. Thus I doubt whether it would have been unfair if the directors, on receipt of the rival bid, had issued a statement saying something along the following lines:

> Shareholders will have received both bids. We think that they contain sufficient information to enable shareholders to reach a properly informed decision and there is nothing which the board wish to add. As individual shareholders, your directors propose to accept the N bid and hope that other shareholders who have no contrary fiduciary duties will have sufficient family loyalty to do so also.

263 Dawson International plc v Coats Patons plc (1988) 4 BCC 305 (Court of Session (Outer House))

[The facts are immaterial.]

LORD CULLEN: At the outset I do not accept as a general proposition that a company can have no interest in the change of identity of its shareholders upon a take-over. It appears to me that there will be cases in which its agents, the directors, will see the take-over of its shares by a particular bidder as beneficial to the company. For example, it may provide the opportunity for integrating operations or obtaining additional resources. In other cases the directors will see a particular bid as not in the best interests of the company...

I next consider the proposition that in regard to the disposal of their shares on a take-over the directors were under a fiduciary duty to the shareholders and accordingly obliged to act in such a way as to further their best interests. It is well recognised that directors owe fiduciary duties to the company. Thus the directors have the duty of fiduciaries with respect to the property and funds of the company...

In contrast I see no good reason why it should be supposed that directors are, in general, under a fiduciary duty to shareholders, and in particular current shareholders with respect to the disposal of their shares in the most advantageous way. The directors are not normally the agents of the current shareholders. They are not normally entrusted with the management of their shares. The cases and other authorities to which I was referred do not seem to me to establish any such fiduciary duty. It is contrary to statements in the standard textbooks ... The absence of such a duty is demonstrated by the remarkable case of *Percival v Wright* (**125**). I think it is important to emphasise that what I am being asked to consider is the alleged fiduciary duty of directors to current shareholders as sellers of their shares. This must not be confused with their duty to consider the interests of shareholders in the discharge of their duty to the company. What is in the interests of current shareholders as sellers of their shares may not necessarily coincide with what is in the interests of the company. The creation of parallel duties could lead to conflict. Directors have but one master, the company. Further it does not seem to me to be relevant to the present question to build an argument upon the rights, some of them very important rights, which shareholders have to take steps with a view to seeing that directors act in accordance with the constitution of the company and that their own interests are not unfairly prejudiced.

If on the other hand directors take it upon themselves to give advice to current shareholders, the cases cited to me show clearly that they have a duty to advise in good faith and not fraudulently, and not to mislead whether deliberately or carelessly. If they fail to do so the affected shareholders may have a remedy, including the recovery of what is truly the personal loss sustained by them as a result. However, these cases do not, in my view, demonstrate a pre-existing fiduciary duty to the shareholders but a potential liability arising out of their words or actions which can be based on ordinary principles of law. This, I may say, appears to be a more satisfactory way of expressing the position of directors in this context than by talking of a so-called secondary fiduciary duty to the shareholders.

Decisions of the City Panel are in principle subject to judicial review. However, the court will not normally intervene while the Panel is actively dealing with a matter, but only grant relief of a declaratory nature after the event.

264 R v Panel on Take-overs and Mergers, ex p Datafin plc [1987] QB 815, [1987] 1 All ER 564 (Court of Appeal)[8]

[The facts are immaterial.]

8 See Lord Alexander of Weedon, 'Judicial Review and City Regulators' (1989) 52 MLR 640.

SIR JOHN DONALDSON MR: The Panel on Take-overs and Mergers is a truly remarkable body. Perched on the 20th floor of the Stock Exchange building in the City of London, both literally and metaphorically it oversees and regulates a very important part of the United Kingdom financial market. Yet it performs this function without visible means of legal support.

The panel is an unincorporated association without legal personality ... It has no statutory, prerogative or common law powers and it is not in contractual relationship with the financial market or with those who deal in that market.

[His Lordship read extracts from the City Code (below, pp 642 ff), and continued:] 'Self-regulation' is an emotive term. It is also ambiguous. An individual who voluntarily regulates his life in accordance with stated principles, because he believes that this is morally right and also, perhaps, in his own long-term interests, or a group of individuals who do so, are practising self-regulation. But it can mean something quite different. It can connote a system whereby a group of people, acting in concert, use their collective power to force themselves and others to comply with a code of conduct of their own devising. This is not necessarily morally wrong or contrary to the public interest, unlawful or even undesirable. But it is very different.

The panel is a self-regulating body in the latter sense. Lacking any authority de jure, it exercises immense power de facto by devising, promulgating, amending and interpreting the City Code on Take-overs and Mergers, by waiving or modifying the application of the code in particular circumstances, by investigating and reporting upon alleged breaches of the code and by the application or threat of sanctions. These sanctions are no less effective because they are applied indirectly and lack a legally enforceable base.

The principal issue in this appeal, and only issue which may matter in the longer term, is whether this remarkable body is above the law. Its respectability is beyond question. So is its bona fides. I do not doubt for one moment that it is intended to, and does, operate in the public interest and that the enormously wide discretion which it arrogates to itself is necessary if it is to function efficiently and effectively. Whilst not wishing to become involved in the political controversy on the relative merits of self-regulation and governmental or statutory regulation, I am content to assume for the purposes of this appeal that self-regulation is preferable in the public interest. But that said, what is to happen if the panel goes off the rails? Suppose, perish the thought, that it were to use its powers in a way which was manifestly unfair. What then? ...

[His Lordship outlined the facts of the case and continued:] It will be seen that there are three principal issues, viz: (a) Are the decisions of the panel susceptible to judicial review? This is the 'jurisdictional' issue. (b) If so, how in principle is that jurisdiction to be exercised given the nature of the panel's activities and the fact that it is an essential part of the machinery of a market in which time is money in a very real sense? This might be described as the 'practical' issue. (c) If the jurisdictional issue is answered favourably to the applicants, is this a case in which relief should be granted and, if so, in what form? ...

The jurisdictional issue

As I have said, the panel is a truly remarkable body, performing its function without visible means of legal support. But the operative word is 'visible', although perhaps I should have used the word 'direct'. Invisible or indirect support there is in abundance. Not only is a breach of the code, so found by the panel, ipso facto an act of misconduct by a member of the Stock Exchange, and the same may be true of other bodies represented on the panel, but the admission of shares to the Official List may be withheld in the event of such a breach. This is interesting and significant for listing of securities is a statutory function performed by the Stock Exchange in pursuance of the Stock Exchange (Listing) Regulations 1984 (SI 1984/716), enacted in implementation of EEC directives. And the matter does not stop there, because in December 1983 the Department of Trade and Industry made a statement explaining why the Licensed Dealers (Conduct of Business) Rules 1983 (SI 1983/585) contained no detailed provisions about take-overs.[9]

[His Lordship read extracts from the statement and continued:] The picture which emerges is clear. As an act of government it was decided that, in relation to take-overs, there should be a central self-regulatory body which would be supported and sustained by a periphery of statutory powers and penalties wherever non-statutory powers and penalties were insufficient or non-existent or where EEC requirements called for statutory provisions ...

The issue is thus whether the historic supervisory jurisdiction of the Queen's courts extends to such a body discharging such functions, including some which are quasi-judicial in their nature, as part of such a system. Mr Alexander, for the panel, submits that it does not. He says that this jurisdiction only extends to bodies whose power is derived from legislation or the exercise of the prerogative. Mr Lever for the applicants, submits that this is too narrow a view and that regard has to be had not only to the source of the body's power, but also to whether it operates as an integral part of a system which has a public law character, is supported by public law in that public law sanctions are applied if its edicts are ignored and performs what might be described as public law functions.

[His Lordship referred to the analogous position of the Criminal Injuries Compensation Board, which had been considered by the Divisional Court in *R v Criminal Injuries Compensation Board, ex p Lain,*[10] and continued:] In fact, given its novelty, the panel fits surprisingly well into the format which this court had in mind in the *Criminal Injuries Compensation Board* case. It is without doubt performing a public duty and an important one. This is clear from the expressed willingness of the Secretary of State for Trade and Industry to limit legislation in the field of take-overs and mergers and to use the panel as the centrepiece of his regulation of that market. The rights of citizens are indirectly affected by its decisions ... At least in its determination of whether there has been a breach of the code, it has a duty to act judicially and it asserts that its raison d'être is to do equity between one shareholder and another. Its source of power is only partly based upon moral persuasion and the assent of institutions and their members, the bottom line being the statutory powers exercised by the Department of Trade and Industry and the Bank of England. In this context I should be very disappointed if the courts could not recognise the realities of executive power and allowed their vision to be clouded by the subtlety and sometimes complexity of the way in which it can be exerted ...

In reaching my conclusion that the court has jurisdiction to entertain

9 [SI 1984/716 has now been incorporated in FSA 1986 (see below, p 538), and the same Act has superseded the Licensed Dealers Rules.]
10 [1967] 2 QB 864, [1967] 2 All ER 770.

applications for the judicial review of decisions of the panel, I have said nothing about the substantial arguments of Mr Alexander based upon the practical problems which are involved. These, in my judgment, go not to the existence of the jurisdiction, but to how it should be exercised and to that I now turn.

The practical issue

... In many cases of judicial review where the time scale is far more extended than in the financial markets, the decision-maker who learns that someone is seeking leave to challenge his decision may well seek to preserve the status quo meanwhile and, in particular, may not seek to enforce his decision pending a consideration of the matter by the court. If leave is granted, the court has the necessary authority to make orders designed to achieve this result, but usually the decision-maker will give undertakings in lieu. All this is but good administrative practice. However, against the background of the time scales of the financial market, the courts would not expect the panel or those who should comply with its decisions to act similarly. In that context the panel and those affected should treat its decisions as valid and binding, unless and until they are set aside. Above all they should ignore any application for leave to apply of which they become aware, since to do otherwise would enable such applications to be used as a mere ploy in take-over battles which would be a serious abuse of the process of the court and could not be adequately penalised by awards of costs.

[His Lordship referred to the various functions of the panel and expressed the opinion that it was unlikely that the courts would often have occasion to intervene. He continued:] Nothing that I have said can fetter or is intended to or should be construed as fettering the discretion of any court to which application is made for leave to apply for judicial review of a decision of the panel or which, leave having been granted, is charged with the duty of considering such an application. Nevertheless, I wish to make it clear beyond a peradventure that in the light of the special nature of the panel, its functions, the market in which it is operating, the time scales which are inherent in that market and the need to safeguard the position of third parties, who may be numbered in thousands, all of whom are entitled to continue to trade upon an assumption of the validity of the panel's rules and decisions, unless and until they are quashed by the court, I should expect the relationship between the panel and the court to be historic rather than contemporaneous. I should expect the court to allow contemporary decisions to take their course, considering the complaint and intervening, if at all, later and in retrospect by declaratory orders which would enable the panel not to repeat any error and would relieve individuals of the disciplinary consequences of any erroneous finding of breach of the rules. This would provide a workable and valuable partnership between the courts and the panel in the public interest and would avoid all of the perils to which Mr Alexander alluded.

[His Lordship then ruled that a case for intervention in the present instance had not been made out.]

LLOYD and NICHOLLS LJJ delivered concurring judgments.

CHAPTER 12

Company Administration and Regulation

A. The Companies Registry and the disclosure philosophy

The Registrar of Companies

Section 704 of CA 1985 confirms the role of the Registrar of Companies, whose duties and functions date back to 1844.

There are two Companies Registries: that for England and Wales is situated in Cardiff, with an ancillary office in the City of London, and the Scottish counterpart is in Edinburgh. The registrar maintains a file for every company and adds to it all documents relating to that company as they are lodged with him for registration over the years. Files are open to public search, using a microfiche system.

The 'disclosure' principle[1]

From the very earliest days it has been recognised that the 'price' which companies should pay for the privileges of incorporation and limited liability should be a fair degree of openness and publicity about their affairs. The Companies Acts have been largely based on this philosophy. Even the termination 'Limited' is intended to achieve the same purpose, warning those dealing with a company that its resources are finite. The Act secures this publicity primarily by the system of registration: all the company's most important documents relating to its constitution and its history subsequent to its incorporation, together with information about its membership, finances and management must be notified to the registrar with, as history shows, each successive Act stepping up the reporting obligations.

A person searching the records of a company at the registry will find the following documents available: the memorandum and articles of association, notices giving the situation of its registered office and details of its directors and secretary, particulars of charges over its property and trust deeds covering issues of debentures, copies of any prospectus or listing particulars that may have been issued, returns of allotments and lists of current members. In addition, there must be filed once a year an *annual return* giving all the information specified in the Fifteenth Schedule, and copies of the company's annual accounts, together with the auditors' report (s 236) and directors' report (s 235). Other events in the life of a company, both major ones such as alterations of its constitution (ss 4, 9) or the appointment of a receiver (s 405(1)), and relatively minor ones like the issue of shares for a non-cash consideration (s 103) may trigger filing obligations (s 111): today's company secretary needs the aid of very extensive checklists.

The registration system is first and foremost an information service: not

1 See further L S Sealy, 'The Disclosure Philosophy and Company Law Reform' (1981) 2 Co Law 51.

many legal consequences are made to turn on the fact that a document has or has not been filed—of these, the most important for the student are (i) what remains of the constructive notice doctrine (above, pp 200 ff), (ii) the sanction of partial voidness which follows from the non-registration of charges, and (iii) official notification.

Official notification

Under the EEC-inspired provisions of s 42 of the Act, the registrar is obliged to give publicity in the *Gazette* to various events affecting a company's administration or status—an alteration of its constitution or change in its directorate, for instance. This is really only token publicity, for very few copies of the special Companies Supplement to the *Gazette* are sold. But, in contrast to the indigenous registration laws above, some legal consequences, at least so far as concern the company's relations with third parties, do depend upon the question whether a matter has been officially notified: see above, p 232.

Publicity at the company's own registered office

Many of the statutory provisions requiring registration of matters at the Companies Registry are duplicated or supplemented by an obligation to maintain copies of documents or some other information at the company's own office and to have facilities there for searching these records. Normally, this means public search; but sometimes the right is restricted to members of the company or to members and creditors. Little use is made in practice of these search facilities, people preferring the anonymity of the registrar's public office even if it may mean getting less up-to-date or less detailed information.

Information for members

Most of the material which the Act requires a company to send to its members is linked to the annual general meeting: with the notice summoning the meeting there will be sent copies of the accounts for the past year and the auditors' report and directors' report. The confidentiality which one might associate with these essentially domestic reports is, however, destroyed by the statutory requirement that they be filed also with the registrar and made available at his office for public inspection. The *directors' report*, in particular, has in recent times become a vehicle for giving publicity to matters of general interest, such as the company's policy to regard to employment of the disabled. The Seventh Schedule lists those items currently required to be covered.

There are other scattered sections of the Act which make it obligatory to provide information to shareholders or to keep documents available for them to inspect, e g directors' service contracts (s 318) and contracts relating to share repurchase (s 169(4)).

The Stock Exchange

Those companies whose shares are listed for dealing on The Stock Exchange (including the Unlisted Securities Market) are required, as one of the conditions for the admission of their securities to listing, to undertake to make regular disclosure of various matters about their financial and other affairs to the Quotations Department and to the investing public. These obligations go beyond the statutory pattern laid down by the Companies Acts, under which specified information must be notified at stated intervals or on particular occasions: there is a 'continuing disclosure' obligation whereby the company must at times on its own initiative ensure that publicity is given promptly to matters which might affect its securities and their price in the market.

B. Administrative control of companies

This century has seen a continuing increase in the involvement of government, through one agency or another, in the affairs of companies. A succession of legislative developments has seen the setting up of the Restrictive Practices Court, the Office of Fair Trading, the National Enterprise Board, and so on. Important as these agencies are to the functioning of companies in practice, their concern is primarily with the regulation of industry and commerce in general, rather than of intervention in the company affairs as such. The regulation of take-overs and mergers is, in contrast, directly concerned with companies; but since a detailed study of this legislation does not form part of most company law courses, no material under this head is included in the present work.[2]

The powers of the Secretary of State to appoint inspectors to investigate the affairs of companies under Pt XIV of CA 1985 may seem of relatively small significance in comparison with those of the other government agencies mentioned above. While this is undoubtedly true as a matter of economics or even of politics, it is again the dictates of the company law syllabus which justify their discussion here.

In reaching a decision whether to appoint inspectors to investigate the affairs of a company, the Secretary of State is not bound by the rules of natural justice.

266 Norwest Holst Ltd v Secretary of State for Trade [1978] Ch 201, [1978] 3 All ER 280 (Court of Appeal)

[The facts appear from the judgments.]

LORD DENNING MR: Ever since 1948 there has been a valuable provision of the Companies Act by which the Board of Trade can appoint inspectors to investigate the affairs of a company. Many investigations have been held by inspectors, usually one of Queen's Counsel, and the other an accountant. In a case we had fairly recently, *Re Pergamon Press Ltd* (**267**), we had to consider the position of the inspectors under such an inquiry. It was held by this court that the inspectors were under a duty to act fairly in the conduct of their inquiry.

Now we have to consider a different point. It is said that the minister

---

2 For an outline of the subject in general, see T Hadden, *Company Law and Capitalism* (2nd edn, 1977), Chapter 14; and the same author's 'Fraud in the City: Enforcing the Rules' (1980) 1 Co Law 9; and on the regulation of mergers, Paul Davies, *The Regulation of Take-Overs and Mergers* (1976).

himself has done wrong. His conduct is challenged. It is said that the minister has acted beyond his powers in appointing inspectors. He ought, it is said, to have warned the company beforehand and given them a chance of being heard. Furthermore, it is said that the minister exercised his discretion erroneously. He ought to have had sufficient reasons, and he had none in this case. It is said further that he is acting on the information of informers, which is inadmissible as being against the public interest.

On these grounds the company has brought an action to try to stop the inspectors proceeding with the inquiry. The minister applied to strike it out. Foster J struck it out. The company appeal to this court...

On 11 March 1977, the Secretary of State ordered the inquiry now in question. He did it under s 165(b)(ii) of the Companies Act 1948 [CA 1985, s 432(2)].

On 25 March 1977, the secretary of the group wrote:

> I am authorised to say that it does not appear to my board that there are any circumstances which would justify the exercise of your discretionary power under the section to appoint inspectors.

He asked: What were the circumstances? Would they be disclosed? The Secretary of State declined to give that information...

As the minister gave no information, the company started this action. They delivered a statement of claim, which they afterwards amended. The burden of the statement of claim is that the company know of no wrongdoing which has been done by them or any of their people; and therefore it was wrong that the minister should appoint inspectors without, as they say, any proper justification. They put it in these words in their final amended pleadings:

> ... It is implicit in the provisions of s 165(b)(ii) of the said Act that the discretionary power to appoint inspectors is to be exercised fairly and/or in accordance with the principles of natural justice.

They ask for a declaration that the appointment or purported appointment was ultra vires and invalid.

It is important to know the background of the legislation. It sometimes happens that public companies are conducted in a way which is beyond the control of the ordinary shareholders. The majority of the shares are in the hands of two or three individuals. These have control of the company's affairs. The other shareholders know little and are told little. They receive the glossy annual reports. Most of them throw them into the wastepaper basket. There is an annual general meeting but few of the shareholders attend. The whole management and control is in the hands of the directors. They are a self-perpetuating oligarchy: and are virtually unaccountable. Seeing that the directors are the guardians of the company, the question is asked: Quis custodiet ipsos custodes—Who will guard the guards themselves?

It is because companies are beyond the reach of ordinary individuals that this legislation has been passed so as to enable the Department of Trade to appoint inspectors to investigate the affairs of a company. Mr Brodie, who appears for Norwest Holst Ltd, drew our attention to the practice of the Board of Trade from 1948 to 1962. It was given in evidence to Lord Jenkins' Company Law Committee (1962) (Cmnd 1749). The Board of Trade said (at p 79) that it was very necessary to hear both sides before deciding whether or not an inspector should be appointed. By so doing it is often possible in cases where no fraud is alleged to bring the parties together or for them to reach a mutually satisfactory arrangement so that an investigation is not necessary.

That was the practice before 1962. Mr Brodie submitted that that practice was required by the common law. He said that the principles of natural justice are to be applied; and, accordingly, both sides should be heard before an inspector is appointed.

That may have been the practice of the Board of Trade in those years: but I do not think that it was required by the common law. There are many cases where an inquiry is held—not as a judicial or quasi-judicial inquiry—but simply as a matter of good administration. In these circumstances there is no need to give preliminary notice of any charge, or anything of that sort. Take the case where a police office is suspected of misconduct. The practice is to suspend him pending inquiries. He is not given notice of any charge at that stage, nor any opportunity of being heard. The rules of natural justice do not apply unless and until it is decided to take proceedings. Other instances can be given in other fields. For instance, the Stock Exchange may suspend dealings in a company's shares. They go by what they know, without warning the company beforehand.

Equally, so far as s 109 [CA 1985, s 447] is concerned, when the officers of the Department of Trade are appointed to examine the books, there is no need for the rules of natural justice to be applied. If the company was forewarned and told that the officers were coming, what is to happen to the books? In a wicked world, it is not unknown for books or papers to be destroyed or lost.

So also with the appointment of inspectors, under s 165(b)(ii). The inspectors are not to decide rights or wrongs. They are to investigate and report. This inquiry is a good administrative arrangement for the good conduct of companies and their affairs. It is not a case to which the rules of natural justice apply. There is no need for them to be given notice of a charge, or a fair opportunity of meeting it. I would say that, so long as the minister acts in good faith, it is not incumbent upon him to disclose the material he has before him, or the reasons for the inquiry.

ORMROD and GEOFFREY LANE LJJ delivered concurring judgments.

Inspectors appointed by the Secretary of State must act fairly, but their function is not judicial or quasi-judicial.

267 Re Pergamon Press Ltd[3] [1971] Ch 388, [1970] 3 All ER 535 (Court of Appeal)

Maxwell and others, the directors of a company which was the subject of an investigation ordered under s 165(b) of the Act of 1948 [CA 1985, s 432(2)] had declined to answer questions unless they were first given assurances that, in effect, the proceeding would be conducted as if it were a judicial inquiry. The inspectors, acting under CA 1948, s 167(3) [CA 1985, s 436(2),(3)] referred

---

3 See B J Davies, 'An Affair of the City' (1973) 36 MLR 457.

this refusal to the court. The Court of Appeal, affirming Plowman J, held that the directors were not entitled to the assurances.

LORD DENNING MR: [Counsel for the directors] claimed that they had a right to see the transcripts of the evidence of the witnesses adverse to them ... [and] to cross-examine the witnesses [and] that they ought to see any proposed finding against them before it was included finally in the report. In short, the directors claimed that the inspectors should conduct the inquiry much as if it were a judicial inquiry in a court of law in which Mr Maxwell and his colleagues were being charged with an offence.

It seems to me that this claim on their part went too far. This inquiry was not a court of law. It was an investigation in the public interest, in which all should surely co-operate, as they promised to do. But if the directors went too far on their side, I am afraid that Mr Fay, for the inspectors, went too far on the other. He did it very tactfully, but he did suggest that in point of law the inspectors were not bound by the rules of natural justice. He said that in all the cases where natural justice had been applied hitherto, the tribunal was under a duty to come to a determination or decision of some kind or other. He submitted that when there was no determination or decision but only an investigation or inquiry, the rules of natural justice did not apply ...

I cannot accept Mr Fay's submission. It is true, of course, that the inspectors are not a court of law. Their proceedings are not judicial proceedings ... They are not even quasi-judicial, for they decide nothing; they determine nothing. They only investigate and report. They sit in private and are not entitled to admit the public to their meetings ... They do not even decide whether there is a prima facie case ...

But this should not lead us to minimise the significance of their task. They have to make a report which may have wide repercussions. They may, if they think fit, make findings of fact which are very damaging to those whom they name. They may accuse some; they may condemn others; they may ruin reputations or careers. Their report may lead to judicial proceedings. It may expose persons to criminal prosecutions or to civil actions. It may bring about the winding up of the company, and be used itself as material for the winding up ... When they do make their report, the Board are bound to send a copy of it to the company; and the Board may, in their discretion, publish it, if they think fit, to the public at large. Seeing that their work and their report may lead to such consequences, I am clearly of the opinion that the inspectors must act fairly. This is a duty which rests on them, as on many other bodies, even though they are not judicial, nor quasi-judicial, but only administrative: see *R v Gaming Board for Great Britain, ex p Benaim and Khaida*.[4] The inspectors can obtain information in any way they think best, but before they condemn or criticise a man, they must give him a fair opportunity for correcting or contradicting what is said against him. They need not quote chapter and verse. An outline of the charge will usually suffice.

That is what the inspectors here propose to do, but the directors of the company want more. They want to see the transcripts of the witnesses who speak adversely of them, and to see any documents which may be used against them. They, or some of them, even claim to cross-examine the witnesses.

In all this the directors go too far. This investigation is ordered in the

4 [1970] 2 QB 417, [1970] 2 All ER 528.

public interest. It should not be impeded by measures of this kind. Witnesses should be encouraged to come forward and not hold back. Remember, this not being a judicial proceeding, the witnesses are not protected by an absolute privilege, but only by a qualified privilege ... It is easy to imagine a situation in which, if the name of a witness were disclosed, he might have an action brought against him, and this might deter him from telling all he knew. No one likes to have an action brought against him, however unfounded. Every witness must, therefore, be protected. He must be encouraged to be frank. This is done by giving every witness an assurance that his evidence will be regarded as confidential and will not be used except for the purpose of the report. This assurance must be honoured. It does not mean that his name and his evidence will *never* be disclosed to anyone. It will often *have* to be used for the purpose of the report, not only in the report itself, but also by putting it in general terms to other witnesses for their comments. But it *does* mean that the inspectors will exercise a wise discretion in the use of it so as to safeguard the witness himself and any others affected by it. His evidence may sometimes, though rarely, be so confidential that it cannot be put to those affected by it, even in general terms. If so, it should be ignored so far as they are concerned. For I take it to be axiomatic that the inspectors must not use the evidence of a witness so as to make it the basis of an adverse finding unless they give the party affected sufficient information to enable him to deal with it.

It was suggested before us that whenever the inspectors thought of deciding a conflict of evidence or of making adverse criticism of someone, they should draft the proposed passage of their report and put it before the party for his comments before including it. But I think this also is going too far. This sort of thing should be left to the discretion of the inspectors. They must be masters of their own procedure. They should be subject to no rules save this: they must be fair. This being done, they should make their report with courage and frankness, keeping nothing back. The public interest demands it. They need have no fear because their report, so far as I can judge, is protected by an absolute privilege ...

SACHS and BUCKLEY LJJ delivered concurring judgments.

NOTE

In later proceedings (reported as *Maxwell v Department of Trade and Industry* [1974] QB 523, [1974] 2 All ER 122), Mr Maxwell claimed that the inspectors had not acted fairly in that, before making their report, they had not first formulated their criticisms of him in tentative form and given him an opportunity of meeting them. The Court of Appeal, affirming Wien J, held that this procedure was unnecessary: it was sufficient that, in the course of the inquiry, all the matters which appeared to call for an explanation or an answer by a witness should have been put to him; and in substance this had been done.

In *R v Secretary of State for Trade, ex p Perestrello* [1981] QB 19, [1980] 3 All ER 28, Woolf J held that there was a similar obligation to act fairly, but, again, no requirement to observe the rules of natural justice, in exercising the power to demand production of a company's books and papers under CA 1967, s 109 [CA 1985, s 447].

The fact that a journalist wishes to protect his sources of information does not of itself provide a reasonable excuse for failing to answer questions put to him by inspectors investigating suspected insider dealing.

268 Re an Inquiry under the Company Securities (Insider Dealing) Act 1985
[1988] AC 660, [1988] 1 All ER 203 (House of Lords)

Warner, a financial journalist, had published two articles which appeared to be based on first-hand information about confidential decisions within a government department. Inspectors, who had been appointed to investigate suspected insider dealing based on the same information, required Warner to reveal his sources so that they could trace the Crown servant responsible for the leaks; but he refused, claiming that as a journalist it was necessary for him to treat his sources as confidential. The inspectors referred the matter to the court, asking that Warner be dealt with as if he had been in contempt of court (Financial Services Act 1986, s 178). The House of Lords ruled that Warner was bound to answer the inspectors' questions. [Subsequently he was fined £20,000 for contempt, having persisted in his refusal. The fine was paid by the newspaper for which he worked.]

LORD GRIFFITHS delivered an opinion in favour of the inspectors.

LORD OLIVER OF AYLMERTON: My Lords, I have had the advantage of reading in draft the speech delivered by my noble and learned friend, Lord Griffiths. I entirely agree that, for the reasons which he has given, s 10 of the Contempt of Court Act 1981 is not directly applicable to a reference to the court under s 178 of the Financial Services Act 1986. I also agree, however, that, even though not directly applicable, s 10 is indicative of a general policy which should, on such a reference, be applied by way of analogy. Thus the essential question raised by this appeal is whether, it being accepted that unless the information sought can be brought within one or other of the exceptions mentioned in s 10 Mr Warner has a reasonable excuse for declining to disclose it, it is information which is 'necessary . . . for the prevention of . . . crime'.
    Like my noble and learned friend, I have found myself unable to accept that the expression 'prevention of . . . crime' in s 10 of the Act of 1981 is to be construed in the narrow sense for which Mr Kentridge has contended. Clearly, in enacting s 10, Parliament was enunciating a public policy for the protection of a journalist's or author's sources of information. Equally clearly, in providing for exceptional circumstances in which that protection should be overridden, it did so on the footing that those exceptions would have some practical application. The narrow construction contended for would, as it seems to me, largely deprive the exception of any useful content at all, for it is difficult to imagine circumstances in which a court or tribunal would be concerned to investigate a particular anticipated crime. The words must bear a wider meaning than that and must, I think, at least embrace the detection and prosecution of crimes which are shown to have been committed and where detection and prosecution could sensibly be said to act as a practical deterrent to future criminal conduct of a similar type. I do not, therefore, for my part doubt that a disclosure required to enable persons shown to have been engaged in a criminal activity to be identified and prosecuted is a disclosure required for 'the prevention of . . . crime'. At the same time it has to be borne in mind that the protection against disclosure is not lightly to be cast aside and that the conditions required for its removal have to be positively established to the satisfaction of the court. If there is a

danger that the exception may be deprived of any useful content by too narrow an interpretation of the requirements for its application, there is equally a danger of the protection itself being attenuated to an unacceptable degree if the need for positive establishment of those requirements is too lightly regarded. What has chiefly concerned me in the instant appeal is whether this onus has been sufficiently discharged by the evidence filed on behalf of the inspectors. I have to confess to having entertained doubts on this score during the course of the hearing, although a careful examination of that evidence in the context of the inquiry which the inspectors were required to undertake has finally convinced me that the onus has been discharged. In my judgment, however, it has only narrowly been discharged and I am concerned that it should not be thought that the protection afforded by the Act can be overcome merely by a ritualistic assertion on affidavit that particular information is required for the prevention of crime. Obviously the court will pay a proper regard to the views of those constituting the inquiring body who, in the nature of things, know better than anyone else the stage which their inquiries have reached and what is needful for their successful prosecution. But it cannot, in my judgment, and must not be thought to be sufficient simply to say that the inquiry upon which the body is engaged is one which has as its object the detection and prevention of crime and that, because a deponent says that certain information is required for the purpose of the inquiry, it therefore follows inexorably that the information is necessary for 'the prevention of . . . crime'. The court must, in my judgment, be presented at least with sufficient material to enable it to exercise an independent judgment on the extent of the need.

If the evidence filed on behalf of the inspectors is open to the criticism that it could have been more specific about the results so far of the inquiries undertaken, one can, at the same time, see very good reasons why the inspectors, in an inquiry whose avowed purpose is to identify and report on criminal activity, should not wish to reveal in greater detail than is strictly requisite the course which their inquiries are taking. What the evidence does disclose is, first, that there is a ring of people who have dealt on the Stock Exchange using price-sensitive information derived from at least one servant of the Crown. Secondly, it is demonstrated that the dealings have been on a considerable scale. Thirdly, it is an irresistible inference that the Crown servant or servants responsible for providing the price-sensitive information has or have been acting in breach of a duty of confidence. Fourthly, the inference is well-nigh irresistible that unless both the source of the information and the persons engaged in the ring can be identified and stopped the course of criminal conduct involved in such dealings is likely to continue. Fifthly, it is beyond dispute that Mr Warner, without any suggestion of impropriety on his part, is the author of two articles in which unpublished information has been deployed with an accuracy which cannot reasonably be attributed to mere coincidence. That information clearly was, before its publication by Mr Warner, price-sensitive information and it can, initially, only have come from a Crown servant. Now obviously the precise purpose which will be served by the disclosure of the source of Mr Warner's information is not capable of being predicated with complete accuracy until the disclosure takes place, but I cannot for my part think that the evidence can properly be criticised as insufficient simply on that score. It may be that it will lead, whether by way of original inquiry or by way of confirmation, directly to the identification of a member of the ring or of the Crown servants involved. It may be that it will lead to the identification of someone not at present even suspected as a member of the dealing ring or to the revelation of a second and at present unidentified ring of dealers. It may be entirely inconclusive or serve only for the purpose of elimination. None of these results appears to me, on analysis, to disqualify it as information 'necessary ... for the prevention of ... crime', for, if the exception in s 10 is to have any sensible operation, it cannot, in my judgment, be an essential characteristic of such information that the result to which it will lead should be capable of being predicated with precision before it is even known what the information is. For these reasons and for the reasons contained in the speech of my noble and learned friend, Lord Griffiths, I agree that the appeal should be dismissed.

LORDS KEITH OF KINKEL, ROSKILL and GOFF OF CHIEVELEY concurred.

C. The regulation of investment business

Most of the world's developed countries have a Securities Regulation Act of some kind. Uniquely, the control of securities dealing in the United Kingdom has traditionally not been a matter for the law at all. It has largely been left in the hands of 'self-regulatory' agencies such as The Stock Exchange and the Issuing Houses Association, with some informal backing from institutions like the Bank of England. For the enforcement of their rules these bodies had to rely almost entirely on extra-legal sanctions, such as the disciplinary powers which they could exercise over their own members (e g stockbrokers) who acted as intermediaries in securities dealings, and the power to suspend or withdraw the listing of a particular company's securities. These sanctions were, on the whole, remarkably effective, but only because the self-regulatory bodies had virtual monopoly control of access to the securities markets.

Supplementing this informal regime was a modest array of legislation, principally the Prevention of Fraud (Investments) Act 1958, which imposed limitations on the distribution of circulars and other inducements to invest, and also controls on dealers in securities who were not members of The Stock Exchange or otherwise exempted.

The enactment of the Financial Services Act 1986, following the report on investor protection of Professor Gower in 1984,[5] marked a new departure for investment business in this country. This Act imposes a new and comprehensive scheme of regulation, requiring all investment businesses to be registered with a 'self-regulatory organisation' (SRO) or 'recognised professional body' (RPB), which is in turn supervised by a regulatory body known as the Securities and Investment Board (SIB). SIB is responsible to government but largely independent of it, and independently financed. But SIB, unlike The Stock Exchange in former times,[6] has statutory backing and breaches of its rules carry legal sanctions. We have thus a system of 'self-regulation within a statutory framework', which is designed to combine the flexibility, expertise and independence of a self-regulatory regime and the authority and accountability associated with control by a statutory body.

5 *Review of Investor Protection*, Cmnd 9125, 1984.
6 In fact, The Stock Exchange was accorded partial statutory backing for its rules shortly before FSA 1986 by The Stock Exchange (Listing) Regulations 1984 (SI 1984/716), implementing the three EEC Directives on listing particulars and reporting obligations: see above, pp 4, 329. These regulations have now been superseded by FSA itself.

There have as yet been no significant cases dealing with the Financial Services Act or the bodies set up under it, but the decision in the *Datafin* case (**264**) makes it clear that these bodies, discharging as they do functions of public importance, will be amenable to proceedings by way of judicial review. For further reading on the Act, reference should be made to specialist works[7] and the appropriate chapters in company law textbooks.

As we have seen (above, pp 327 ff), the Financial Services Act 1986 has also now superseded the Companies Act as the statute providing controls over the contents and distribution of prospectuses and listing particulars.

One self-regulatory body, the City Panel on Take-overs and Mergers, continues to function on a non-statutory basis and remains largely unaffected by the Act of 1986. The Panel has existed since 1968. After a somewhat shaky beginning, it has established itself successfully as a City 'watchdog' to monitor the conduct of take-overs and impose its Code, ensuring that fair and proper tactics are employed both by those who are making bids and those who are resisting them. It has its own executives and staff and is financed independently of government. (The *merits* of a bid are not the concern of the Panel, nor is its justification in the public interest—although both the Monopolies and Mergers Commission and the EEC Commission may have to rule on the latter question.)

Extracts from the City Code[8] are cited in the Appendix (below, pp 642 ff).

D. Insider dealing

There has been much interest in the past decade or two in the topic of 'insider dealing' or 'insider trading'. These terms are used to describe the use (or, rather, the misuse) of confidential information by people who, as company officers or employees or as civil servants, avail themselves of knowledge which they acquire in the course of their work or by reason of their office to deal to their own profit in a company's securities. Most people regard this practice as unfair in itself and damaging to the confidence of investors in the integrity of the share market.

Until 1980, the only constraints available to deal with insider trading were those imposed extra-legally by the self-regulatory agencies of the City, and in particular by the Take-over Panel, and the possibility that there might be civil liability in at least some cases. It seemed that decisions like *Regal (Hastings) Ltd v Gulliver* (**132**) and *Boardman v Phipps* (above, p 275) might be used as authority for making directors and others similarly placed liable to account *to their company* for any profit that they made, and indeed that is very much what happened in *Regal*. There was also the possibility of some form of liability for breach of confidence as an equitable remedy in its own right (*Seager v Copydex Ltd* [1967] 2 All ER 415, [1967] 1 WLR 923). But all these possible claims were open to the criticism that in most insider dealing cases the company is not the real loser, and might have no incentive to pursue the wrongdoer. *Percival v Wright* (**125**) seemed to bar the development of a claim based on breach of duty between the director (or other 'insider') and the person to whom he had sold or from whom he had brought the shares.

---

7 E g B A K Rider, C Abrams and E Ferran *Guide to the Financial Services Act 1986* (2nd edn, 1989).

8 On the Code, see TP Lee, 'The New Take-over Code: a Clarification' (1981) 2 Co Law 99.

However, there have been hints in cases such as *Coleman v Myers* (above, p 251) that there could potentially be developed here a civil remedy for victims of insider trading similar to that which has evolved in the United States through such cases as *SEC v Texas Gulf Sulphur Co* 401 F 2d 833 (1968) and *Diamond v Oreamuno* 24 NY 2d 494 (1969) (though the authority of the latter is questionable, since it was not followed in the company's home State, Florida: see *Schein v Chasen* 313 So 2d 739 (1975)).

All these question centring on possible civil liability for insider dealing remain live issues, but they have had less of the limelight since the Act of 1980 introduced provisions establishing criminal penalties for those guilty of the offences of insider dealing as there defined. These sections have not been consolidated into the Act of 1985 but have been re-enacted separately in the Company Securities (Insider Dealing) Act 1985. They are of limited scope, being confined to dealings on a stock exchange or investment exchange, and to listed or advertised securities. Only individuals and not corporate offenders can be liable; and there is no civil liability based on infringements of the Act. The Act covers both 'primary' insider dealing and also those who give or receive 'tips' on dealing.

There have been a few prosecutions under the statutory provisions since 1980, but no decisions worthy of citation at length, and so the student should rely primarily on the text of the Act, as explained in the books and articles on the subject.[9] However, mention should be made of the ruling in *A-G's Reference (No 1 of 1988)* [1989] AC 971, [1989] 2 All ER 1, HL, an appeal on a question of law from the acquittal of the defendant in *R v Fisher* (1988) 4 BCC 360. Fisher, who had been attempting to buy a controlling interest in T plc, a listed public company, was told by the merchant bank advising that company that the deal was off because the shareholding was to be sold to other buyers. This information was given to Fisher in confidence, ahead of the press announcement about the sale. He bought 6000 shares in T plc the same day, and later sold them at a considerable profit. In the Crown Court, Judge Butler acquitted Fisher of insider dealing as a tippee (Company Securities (Insider Dealing) Act 1985, s 1(3), 1(4)(a)), taking the view that a tippee should not be regarded as having 'obtained' information unless he had actively sought it; it was not sufficient that he was a mere passive recipient. The House of Lords, affirming the Court of Appeal, held that he was wrong: Parliament intended to penalise a recipient of inside information who deals in securities, whether he procures the information from the primary insider by purpose and effort or comes by it without any purpose and action on his part. 'The crucial element is the dealing. The obtaining on its own is of no import.'

Note also *Re an Inquiry under the Companies (Insider Dealing) Act 1985* (the *Jeremy Warner* case) (**268**).

---

9   B A K Rider and H L Ffrench *The Regulation of Insider Trading* (London, 1979); B A K Rider *Insider Trading* (Bristol, 1983); B M Hannigan. *Insider Dealing* (1988); on civil liability, D Sugarman in Rider (ed) *The Regulation of the British Securities Industry* (London, 1979), pp 51 ff.

CHAPTER 13

Insolvency and Winding up[1]

A. Introduction

There is no necessary connection between insolvency and winding up: a very large number of companies are wound up whose balance sheets are in healthy surplus. However, the two topics are now dealt with together in the Insolvency Act 1986 and it is therefore convenient to do so in this book. For the purposes of this chapter, we shall also follow that Act in treating the subject of receivership as an insolvency procedure, even though the company concerned may not be in any technical sense insolvent at the time.

The Insolvency Act 1986 is a consolidation of IA 1985 and those parts of CA 1985 which dealt with receivership and winding up. The insolvency legislation of 1985 introduced comprehensive reforms to both the law of corporate insolvency and that of individual bankruptcy—the first major overhaul of either subject for over a hundred years. It was largely based on the report of the Cork Committee (*Report of the Review Committee on Insolvency Law and Practice* (Cmnd 8558, 1982)).

There are many ways of defining insolvency. It is sufficient for present purposes to note three.

(1) *'Commercial' insolvency.* A company may be described as insolvent if it is unable to pay its debts as they fall due. In other words, even though its overall asset position may not appear to be in deficit, it has cash-flow problems which prevent it from paying its way. This is the commonest reason for the making of a compulsory winding-up order (IA 1986, s 122(1)(f)). There is a statutory definition of this type of insolvency (and also certain rules and presumptions relating to proof) in IA 1986, s 123 (1).

(2) *'Balance-sheet' insolvency.* A company may also be said to be insolvent if the value of its assets is less than the amount of its liabilities. While the company is a going concern, an assessment of insolvency in this sense will depend upon the business judgment of those concerned. It is proper to take account for this purpose of the company's contingent and prospective liabilities (see IA 1986, s 123(2)), although the value of these will necessarily be very difficult to estimate. A company which is insolvent in balance-sheet terms will not necessarily be commercially insolvent: it may, for instance, have a heavy potential liability in tort and yet for the time being have a perfectly satisfactory cash flow. And, of course, it may happen that if its assets are realised there is in fact a surplus at the end of the day.

(3) *'Ultimate' insolvency.* This definition of insolvency is based on the final

1 See D Milman and C Durrant, *Corporate Insolvency: Law and Practice* (1987); R R Pennington, *Corporate Insolvency Law* (1991).

position when the company's assets are sold up, e g by a liquidator, and there is not sufficient realised to pay its creditors in full. This unhappy result may occur even though the company had previously seemed solvent under definitions (1) and (2), for assets which are quite reasonably valued highly on a historic cost or going concern basis may fetch very little in a forced sale.

B. Insolvency procedures

The Insolvency Act 1986 deals with four 'insolvency' procedures (although we should bear in mind that some of these procedures may be invoked when the company concerned is not insolvent in any of the senses described above, or that the insolvency may only be temporary or technical). These are:

(1) *Company voluntary arrangements.* This is an informal procedure, provided for by IA 1986, ss 1–7, under which a company may seek to achieve an accommodation with its creditors under the supervision of a qualified insolvency practitioner. The arrangement, if approved by the requisite majority (over 75%) of the creditors and members, is binding on the minorities as well. But the weaknesses of this procedure are (i) that it cannot be made binding on secured or preferential creditors without their consent, and (ii) that there is no statutory provision for a moratorium while the quite lengthy formalities are gone through: thus one impatient creditor can thwart the whole scheme. This latter difficulty can be avoided (but only at the cost of making the procedure more elaborate and expensive) by combining a proposal for a voluntary arrangement with one for the appointment of an administrator under (2) below.

The new procedure had a lukewarm reception: only 21 arrangements were recorded in the first year of its operation. But the number has since increased to over 100 a year, possibly because in a growing number of cases an arrangement is used in conjunction with an administration order.

(2) *Administration orders.*[2]   Part II of IA 1986, following a recommendation of the Cork Committee, establishes a second new insolvency procedure, the administration order. A company may be put into administration only by order of the court, which must be satisfied that the company is, or will be, insolvent (i e unable to pay its debts). An order may be sought to achieve any of four purposes: (i) the survival of the company or its undertaking as a going concern, (ii) the approval of a voluntary arrangement (see (1) above), (iii) the sanctioning of a scheme of arrangement under CA 1985, ss 425 ff (see above, pp 511 ff), and (iv) a more advantageous realisation of the company's assets than would be effected on a winding up (IA 1986, s 8(3)). The administration procedure thus allows an ailing company an alternative to liquidation where there is a chance that it may be rehabilitated, and an option similar to being placed in receivership where there is no secured creditor willing or able to appoint a receiver and no way of having a receiver appointed by the court. It also (if made for purpose (iv) above) allows the company a breathing space, even where liquidation is inevitable, so that its assets can be realised to better advantage, e g by selling the business as a going concern.

---

2   See G Stewart, *Administrative Receivers and Administrators* (1987).

Again, this procedure involves putting the company's affairs in the hands of a qualified insolvency practitioner while proposals are worked out and put to the creditors (but not, in this case, the members) for approval. However, in contrast with a voluntary arrangement, an application for an administration order effectively imposes a moratorium that is binding on all creditors, and while an order is in force there is a ban on putting the company into liquidation.

An administration order cannot be made when the company is in receivership, unless either the debentureholder who has appointed the receiver consents to vacate the receivership (IA 1986, s 9(3), 11(1)), or the floating charge under which the receiver has been appointed is invalidated under IA 1985, ss 238 ff or 245 (see above, pp 403 ff). Even if there is no receiver in office, a floating charge-holder can block the making of an administration order by appointing a receiver himself instead.

An administrator has wide powers to deal with the company's property, including certain powers to deal with charged property (IA 1986, ss 14–15, Sch 1).

There are no preferential debts in administration.

An administration order will be discharged either when the purpose of the order has been achieved (e g the rehabilitation of the company, when control will be handed back to the company's own organs), or if the administrator decides that this is impossible and that there is no alternative to liquidation.

The new procedure has got off to a good start: 131 orders were made during the first year of operation of the new legislation, and the number is now over 200 per annum. This reflects a perhaps surprising willingness on the part of banks and other secured creditors to stand aside and allow a court-appointed administrator to act, rather than a receiver of their own choosing. In the cases which have been reported so far, the courts, too, appear to have been ready to give a broad interpretation to the statutory provisions so that the administration procedure is not unduly fettered by technicalities. The cases cited below **(270)**–**(272)**, which illustrate the working of the new regime in practice, give some indication of this approach.

(3) *Receivership.*   This is discussed under heading C, below.

(4) *Winding up.*   This is discussed under heading D, below.

270 Re Harris Simons Construction Ltd [1989] 1 WLR 368, [1989] BCLC 202 (Chancery Division)

[The facts appear from the judgment.]

HOFFMANN J: ... The company carries on business as builders. Over the past four years there has been a spectacular increase in turnover, from £830,000 in the year to April 1985 to £17m in the year to April 1987 and £27m in the year to April 1988. Almost all of this increased turnover has come from one client, a property developer called Berkley House plc, with which the directors had a close relationship. Recently the relationship has turned sour. There are disputes over a number of contracts and Berkley House has purported to dismiss the company and require its employees to leave their sites. It is also withholding sums running into several million pounds which the company says are due and in respect of which Berkley House says it has cross-claims. The effect on the company's cash flow has been that it is unable to pay its debts as they fall due and several writs and a statutory demand have been served. If no administration order is made, the company cannot carry on trading. There is no debentureholder who can be invited to appoint a receiver. The company will have to go into liquidation more or less immediately. The workforce will have to be dismissed and the contracts and work in progress will become a tangle of disputes and probably litigation. The report of the proposed administrator says that in those circumstances it would be extremely difficult to sell any part of the business.

If an administration order is made, the company will have what is usually called a breathing space but unless some source of funding can be found, will continue to have serious respiratory problems with its cash flow. It has however been able to negotiate at least an armistice with Berkley House by which the latter will, conditionally upon an administration order being made, provide sufficient funding to enable the company to complete four current contracts on condition that it quietly removes itself from the other sites in dispute. It is hoped that the four remaining contracts will produce a profit and that it may thereby be possible to stabilise and preserve a business which can either survive or be sold to a third party. In the meanwhile, it may be possible to arrive at a negotiated settlement of the underlying dispute with Berkley House. The administration order is therefore proposed to achieve two of the purposes specified in section 8(3) of the Act: '(*a*) the survival of the company, and the whole or any part of its undertaking, as a going concern;' and '(*d*) a more advantageous realisation of the company's assets than would be effected on a winding up' ...

Section 8(1) gives the court jurisdiction to make an administration order if it '(*a*) is satisfied that a company is or is likely to become unable to pay its debts' and it '(*b*) considers that the making of an order ... would be likely to achieve' one or more of the purposes specified in section 8(3). I am satisfied on the evidence that the company is unable to pay its debts. Whether the order would be likely to achieve one of the specified objects is not so easy to answer. When the statute says that I must consider it likely, what degree of probability does this involve? In *Re Consumer and Industrial Press Ltd,*[3] Peter Gibson J said:

> As I read section 8 the court must be satisfied on the evidence put before it that at least one of the purposes in section 8(3) is likely to be achieved if it is to make an administration order. That does not mean that it is merely possible that such purpose will be achieved; the evidence must go further than that to enable the court to hold that the purpose in question will more probably than not be achieved.

He therefore required that on a scale of probability of 0 (impossibility) to 1 (absolute certainty) the likelihood of success should be more than 0.5. I naturally hesitate to disagree with Peter Gibson J, particularly since he had the benefit of adversarial argument. But this is a new statute on which the judges of the Companies Court are still feeling their way to a settled practice and I therefore think I should say that in my view he set the standard of probability too high. My reasons are as follows. First, 'likely' connotes probability but the particular degree of probability intended must be gathered

3 [1988] BCLC 177, 178.

from qualifying words (very likely, quite likely, more likely than not) or context. It cannot be a misuse of language to say that something is likely without intending to suggest that the probability of its happening exceeds 0.5, as in 'I think that the favourite, Golden Spurs at 5–1, is likely to win the Derby.' Secondly, the section requires the court to be 'satisfied' of the company's actual or likely insolvency but only to 'consider' that the order would be likely to achieve one of the stated purposes. There must have been a reason for this change of language and I think it was to indicate that a lower threshold of persuasion was needed in the latter case than the former. The first of the sentences I have quoted from the judgment of Peter Gibson J suggests that he did not take this variation into account. Thirdly, some of the stated purposes are mutually exclusive and the probability of any one of them being achieved may be less than 0.5 but the probability of one or other of them being achieved may be more than 0.5. I doubt whether Parliament intended the courts to embark on such calculations of cumulative probabilities. Fourthly, as Peter Gibson J said, section 8(1) only sets out the conditions to be satisfied before the court has jurisdiction. It still retains a discretion as to whether or not to make the order. It is therefore not likely that the legislature intended to set a modest threshold of probabilty to found jurisdiction and to rely on the court's discretion not to make orders in cases in which, weighing all the circumstances, it seemed inappropriate to do so. Fifthly, the Report of the Review Committee on Insolvency Law and Practice (1982). (Cmnd 8558), para 508, which recommended the introduction of administratorship, said that the new procedure was likely to be beneficial

> only in cases where there is a business of sufficient substance to justify the expense of an administration, and where there is a real prospect of returning profitability or selling as a going concern.

Elsewhere the report speaks of an order being made if there is a 'reasonable possibility' of a scheme of reconstruction. I think that this kind of phraseology was intended to be reflected in the statutory phrase 'considers that [it] would be likely' in section 8(1)(*b*).

For my part, therefore, I would hold that the requirements of section 8(1)(*b*) are satisfied if the court considers that there is a real prospect that one or more of the stated purposes may be achieved. It may be said that phrases like 'real prospect' lack precision compared with 0.5 on the scale of probability. But the courts are used to dealing in other contexts with such indications of the degrees of persuasion they must feel. 'Prima facie case' and 'good arguable case' are well known examples. Such phrases are like tempo markings in music; although there is inevitably a degree of subjectivity in the way they are interpreted, they are nevertheless meaningful and useful.

On the facts as they appear from the evidence before me, I think there is a real prospect that an administration order, coupled with the agreement with Berkley House, will enable the whole or part of the company's undertaking to survive or at least enable the administrator to effect a more advantageous realisation of the assets than would be effected in a winding up. Certainly the prospects for the company, its employees and creditors look bleak if no administration order is made and there has to be a winding up. Consequently, although I cannot say that it is more probable than not that one of the specified purposes will be achieved, I accept the opinion of the prospective administrator that 'the making of an administration order offers the best prospect for preserving the company's future and maximising the realisation of the company's assets for the benefit of its creditors.' I therefore make the order.

NOTE

Other judges, including Peter Gibson J, have since followed the views expressed in this case.

271 Bristol Airport plc v Powdrill [1990] Ch 744, [1990] 2 All ER 493 (Court of Appeal)

[The facts are immaterial.]

BROWNE-WILKINSON V-C: ... [I]t may be helpful to state what, in my opinion, is the correct approach to the construction of the provisions dealing with administrators contained in Part II of the Act. The judge was very much influenced in his construction by the manifest statutory purpose of Part II of the Act. I agree with this approach. The provisions of Part II themselves, coupled with the mischief identified in the Cork Report, show that the statutory purpose is to install an administrator, as an officer of the court, to carry on the business of the company as a going concern with a view to achieving one or other of the statutory objectives mentioned in section 8(3). It is of the essence of administration under Part II of the Act that the business will continue to be carried on by the administrator. Such continuation of the business by the administrator requires that there should be available to him the right to use the property of the company, free from interference by creditors and others during the, usually short, period during which such administration continues. Hence the restrictions on the rights of creditors and others introduced by sections 10 and 11 of the Act. In my judgment in construing Part II of the Act it is legitimate and necessary to bear in mind the statutory objective with a view to ensuring, if the words permit, that the administrator has the powers necessary to carry out the statutory objectives, including the power to use the company's property ...

WOOLF and STAUGHTON LJJ delivered concurring judgments.

272 Re Charnley Davies Ltd (No 2) [1990] BCLC 760 (Chancery Division)

[The facts are immaterial.]

MILLETT J: ... It was common ground that an administrator owes a duty to a company over which he is appointed to take reasonable steps to obtain a proper price for its assets. That is an obligation which the law imposes on anyone with a power, whether contractual or statutory, to sell property which does not belong to him. A mortgagee is bound to have regard to the interests of the mortgagor, but he is entitled to give priority to his own interests, and may insist on an immediate sale whether or not that is calculated to realise the best price; he must 'take reasonable care to obtain the true value of the property at the moment he chooses to sell it': see *Cuckmere Brick Co Ltd v Mutual Finance Ltd.*[4] An administrator, by contrast, like a liquidator, has no interest of his own to which he may give priority, and must take reasonable

4 [1971] Ch 949, [1971] 2 All ER 633.

care in choosing the time at which to sell the property. His duty is 'to take reasonable care to obtain the best price that the circumstances permit': see *Standard Chartered Bank Ltd v Walker.*[5]

It is to be observed that it is not an absolute duty to obtain the best price that circumstances permit, but only to take reasonable care to do so; and in my judgment that means the best price that circumstances *as he reasonably perceives them to be* permit. He is not to be made liable because his perception is wrong, unless it is unreasonable.

An administrator must be a professional insolvency practitioner. A complaint that he has failed to take reasonable care in the sale of the company's assets is, therefore, a complaint of professional negligence and in my judgment the established principles applicable to cases of professional negligence are equally applicable in such a case. It follows that the administrator is to be judged, not by the standards of the most meticulous and conscientious member of his profession, but by those of an ordinary, skilled practitioner. In order to succeed the claimant must establish that the administrator has made an error which a reasonably skilled and careful insolvency practitioner would not have made ...

C. Receivership[6]

Any secured creditor may enforce his security by the appointment of a receiver (see above, p 411). So, e g, if a company has given a creditor a fixed charge over its book-debts, the appointment of a receiver will enable the debts to be collected and applied in satisfaction of the company's obligation. Until the reforming insolvency legislation of 1985–86, the subject of receivership was largely a matter for the common law. There are now a number of provisions in IA 1986, Pt III which apply generally to receiverships: for example, there is a prohibition on the appointment of a body corporate or an undischarged bankrupt (ss 30–31); there must be notification on the company's stationery of the appointment of a receiver (s 39); and it is declared that normally a receiver is personally liable on any contracts he makes, but subject to a right of indemnity out of the assets under his control (ss 37(1), 44). A receiver appointed by the court is an officer of the court and accountable to it, and is not subject to direction or dictation by the creditor in whose interests he has been appointed. A receiver appointed independently may in theory be the agent either of the company or of the creditor who appointed him: in practice, he is always expressly made the former.

The primary duty of a receiver is to get in and, as necessary, realise sufficient of the company's assets to satisfy the outstanding debt of the creditor on whose behalf he has been appointed. He does not owe duties of a fiduciary nature (in the fullest sense) to the company or the other creditors, although he may be liable to them if he acts negligently (*Standard Chartered Bank Ltd v Walker* [1982] 3 All ER 938, [1982] 1 WLR 1410), and he is under an obligation to keep and produce to the company proper accounts (*Smiths Ltd v Middleton* [1979] 3 All ER 842).

---

5 [1982] 3 All ER 938, [1982] 1 WLR 1410.
6 See G Lightman and G Moss, *The Law of Receivers of Companies* (1986), G Stewart, *Administrative Receivers and Administrators* (1987), H Picarda, *The Law Relating to Receivers, Managers and Administrators* (2nd edn, 1990).

It is very common for an appointment to be made, not simply of a receiver, but of a *receiver and manager*—a twin office under which the appointee is empowered to manage the business and not just get in and sell off its assets. This is done in the hope either that the company may be able to trade its way back into profitability, or at the very least that its business can be sold as a going concern rather than on a break-up basis and in that way fetch more. Of course, a power to manage 'the business' of a company can be given to a receiver only if the charge is over the whole of the company's undertaking—which means that it must be a floating charge.

The appointment of a receiver and manager puts an end to the directors' powers to manage the business, though they will revert once he has discharged his functions, so long as the business or part of it has survived. But the directors do retain their *office,* and their other powers and functions: in *Newhart Developments v Co-operative Commercial Bank* [1978] QB 814, [1978] 2 All ER 896 it was held that they had power to issue a writ claiming damages for breach of contract against the very creditor who had appointed the receiver![7]

A company which is in receivership may be put into liquidation. The liquidator has then, in principle, to allow the receiver to continue to act until the claims of his debentureholder are met out of the security. Conversely, a receiver may be appointed after a company has gone into liquidation; and, as we have seen, the fact of liquidation is itself effective to crystallise a floating charge. But a receivership cannot co-exist with an administration.

Where a receiver is appointed to enforce a floating charge, the claims of certain preferential creditors (e g the Revenue, for PAYE and social security contributions) must be paid ahead of the debenture-holder: see IA 1986, s 40 and above, p 402.

The main innovation made by the insolvency legislation of 1985–86 is the introduction of a separate category of receiver, the *administrative receiver.* An administrative receiver is defined by IA 1986, s 29(2): essentially, he is a receiver and manager of the whole, or substantially the whole, of the property of a company appointed by or on behalf of the holders of a debenture of the company secured by a floating charge.[8] The Act of 1986 stipulates that an administrative receiver must be a qualified insolvency practitioner (ss 45(2), 388–389), and confers on him a number of statutory powers (ss 42–43). It also declares that he is deemed to be the company's agent, unless the company is in liquidation (s 44); this confirms as a rule of law what was already the standard practice under the usual terms of floating charge debentures before the Act. The Act requires the directors to provide an administrative receiver with information about the company by submitting to him a statement of affairs (s 47), but in turn requires the administrative receiver to keep the company's unsecured creditors informed about the progress of the receivership.

The holder of a charge owes no duty of care to the chargor in deciding whether

---

7 In *Tudor Grange Holdings Ltd v Citibank NA* [1992] Ch 53, [1991] 4 All ER 1 Browne-Wilkinson V-C expressed doubts whether the *Newhart* case was rightly decided. He ruled that in any event the directors could not sue on a cause of action which it was competent for the receiver to bring.
8 Or a person who would be such a receiver but for the fact that there is someone else already in office as the receiver of part of the company's property under a prior-ranking charge.

to exercise the right to appoint a receiver. He and the receiver owe a limited duty of care in exercising a power to sell the charged property, but this duty is subordinated to the interests of the charge-holder.

273 Shamji v Johnson Matthey Bankers Ltd [1986] BCLC 278 (Chancery Division and Court of Appeal)

In this case it was alleged, unsuccessfully, that the charge-holders, JMB, had acted in breach of a duty of care in appointing a receiver at a time when negotiations to refinance the debtor company's borrowing were still being conducted.

HOFFMANN J ... Counsel for the defendants said under the terms of the security documents as pleaded in the statement of claim, JMB had a contractual right to appoint a receiver at any time after demanding payment. In the absence of bad faith, the bank could not owe the mortgagors or guarantors a duty of care in deciding whether to exercise that right. It might owe some duty in the way in which the right was exercised (e g it might owe a duty to take reasonable care not to appoint an incompetent) but not as to whether it was exercised or not. Counsel for the plaintiffs relied on *Cuckmere Brick Co Ltd v Mutual Finance Ltd*,[9] *Standard Chartered Bank Ltd v Walker*[10] and *Tse Kwong Lam v Wong Chit Sen*[11]. These cases demonstrate that a mortgagee or receiver exercising a power to sell the mortgaged property owes a duty to the mortgagor or the guarantor to take reasonable care to obtain the fair value. It is important however to observe that in this matter there can be no real conflict of interest between mortgagor and mortgagee. As Lord Denning MR said in the *Standard Chartered Bank* case:

> He owes this duty not only to himself, to clear off as much of the debt as he can, but also to the mortgagor so as to reduce the balance owing as much as possible, and also to the guarantor so that he is made liable for as little as possible on the guarantee.

Lord Moulton in *McHugh v Union Bank of Canada*[12], in a passage quoted in the *Tse Kwong Lam* case described the duty as—

> to behave in conducting such realisation as a reasonable man would behave in the realisation of his own property.

It is clear, however, that in the case of a conflict between the interests of the mortgagor and mortgagee, any duty of care which the mortgagee owes to the mortgagor is subordinated to his right to act in the protection of his own interests. As Salmon LJ said in the *Cuckmere Brick Co* case:

> If the mortgagee's interests, as he sees them, conflict with those of the mortgagor, the mortgagee can give preference to his own interests ...

The appointment of a receiver seems to me to involve an inherent conflict of interest. The purpose of the power is to enable the mortgagee to take the management of the company's property out of the hands of the directors and entrust it to a person of the mortgagee's choice. That power is granted to the

9 [1971] Ch 949, [1971] 2 All ER 633, CA.
10 [1982] 3 All ER 938, [1982] 1 WLR 1410, CA.
11 [1983] 3 All ER 54, [1983] 1 WLR 1349, PC.
12 [1913] AC 299, 311, PC.

mortgagee by the security documents in completely unqualified terms. It seems to me that a decision by the mortgagee to exercise the power cannot be challenged except perhaps on grounds of bad faith. There is no room for the implication of a term that the mortgagee shall be under a duty to the mortgagor to 'consider all relevant matters' before exercising the power. If no such qualification can be read into the security documents, I do not think that a wider duty can exist in tort ...

[The decision of HOFFMANN J was affirmed by the Court of Appeal, [1991] BCLC 36.]

274 Re Atlantic Computer Systems [1991] BCLC 606 (Court of Appeal)

[The facts are immaterial. This extract describes the role of an administrative receiver and his relationship to the company and its property.]

NICHOLLS LJ: ... Typically, when lending money to a company, a bank will take as security a charge over all or most of the assets of the company, present and future, the charge being a fixed charge on land and certain other assets, and a floating charge over the remaining assets. The deed authorises the bank to appoint a receiver and manager of the company's undertaking, with power to carry on the company's business. Such a receiver is referred to in the 1986 Act as an 'administrative receiver'.

Normally the deed creating the floating charge and authorising his appointment provides that an administrative receiver shall be the agent of the company. Now the 1986 Act, in s 44(1), provides that this shall always be so, unless and until the company goes into liquidation. For many years the position regarding a receiver appointed as agent of the company was that in general he was not personally liable for contracts entered into by him for and on behalf of the company. He was no more personally liable than was a director who entered into a contract for and on behalf of his company. This position was changed by s 87(2) of the Companies Act 1947. The position now, with regard to administrative receivers, is set out in s 44(1) and (2) of the 1986 Act. Under that section an administrative receiver is personally liable on (a) any contract entered into by him in the carrying out of his functions, except in so far as the contract otherwise provides, and (b) on any contract of employment 'adopted' by him in the carrying out of those functions. In the latter regard the administrative receiver has, in effect, a period of 14 day's grace after his appointment. Head (b) represents a statutory overruling of the effect of the decision in *Nicoll v Cutts*.[13] In cases where he is personally liable an administrative receiver is entitled to an indemnity out of the assets of the company (s 44(1)(*c*)). But even today an administrative receiver is not, in general, personally liable, and hence the statutory indemnity out of the assets of the company does not arise, in respect of contracts adopted by him in the course of managing the company's business, other than contracts of employment. With that one special exception, personal liability is confined, in general, to new contracts made by him. Thus he is not personally liable for the rent payable under an existing lease, or for the hire charges payable under an existing hire-purchase agreement. This is not a surprising conclusion. It does not offend against basic conceptions of justice or fairness. The rent and hire charges were a liabilty undertaken by the

13 [1985] BCLC 322.

company at the inception of the lease or hire-purchase agreement. The land or goods are being used by the company even when an administrative receiver is in office. It is to the company that, along with other creditors, the lessor and the owner of the goods must look for payment.

Nor is a lessor or owner of goods in such a case entitled to be paid his rent or hire instalments as an 'expense' of the administrative receivership, even though the administrative receiver has retained and used the land or goods for the purpose of the receivership. The reason is not far to seek. The appointment of an administrative receiver does not trigger a statutory prohibition on the lessor or owner of goods such as that found in s 130 in the case of a winding-up order. If the rent or hire is not paid by the administrative receiver the lessor or owner of the goods is at liberty, as much after the appointment of the administrative receiver as before, to exercise the rights and remedies available to him under his lease or hire-purchase agreement. Faced with the prospect of proceedings, an administrative receiver may choose to pay the rent or hire charges in order to retain the land or goods. But if he decides not to do so, the lessor or owner of goods has his remedies. There is no occasion, assuming that there is jurisdiction, for the court to intervene and order the administrative receiver to pay these outgoings ...

D. Winding up[14]

In the winding up (or liquidation—the terms are synonymous) of a company it gives up its business, sells off its assets, pays its debts (or, if it is insolvent, does so to the extent that its funds allow) and distributes whatever surplus remains amongst its shareholders or otherwise as its memorandum and articles of association may provide.

The conduct of the winding up is placed by law in the hands of a *liquidator*; and on his appointment the directors' power to manage the business of the company lapses.

The company continues in being throughout the process of winding up: there is still a corporate personality; and all corporate acts in the course of the liquidation, such as the transfer of property and the institution of legal proceedings, are done in its name rather than by the liquidator in his own name. The company ceases to exist only by the formal act of *dissolution* (IA 1986, ss 201 ff) after the whole of the winding up procedure has been completed.[15]

A company may be wound up *compulsorily,* ie by court order, or *voluntarily,* as a consequence of an extraordinary resolution passed by the shareholders. In a compulsory winding up the liquidator is appointed by the

---

14 See B H McPherson, *The Law of Company Liquidation* (3rd edn, Australia), 1987; R R Pennington, *Company Liquidations, the Substantive Law* (1987); H Rajak, *Company Liquidations* (1988).

15 In practice, the largest number of companies is dissolved by the simple administrative procedure of 'striking off the register'. CA 1985, s 652 empowers the registrar to do this, after advertisement, if his inquiries show or suggest that the company has ceased to carry on business. This is a useful sanction in the case of a company which has failed to file accounts or annual returns. It is quite common for the registrar to be invited by the company itself to exercise these powers, and in this way the expense of a formal liquidation is avoided. There is provision in s 653 for the reinstatement by court order of a company which has been struck off.

court and is in law regarded as an officer of the court acting under its direction and control. In a voluntary winding up, the liquidator is appointed by the shareholders if the directors are able to declare that the company is solvent (a 'members' voluntary winding up'); if not, the company's creditors have the power of appointment and exercise general control over the conduct of the liquidation (a 'creditors' voluntary winding up').

In contrast with most of the topics covered in earlier chapters, where the cases are often quite as important a source of law (and even of principle) as the statute, in this section of the subject the Act is unquestionably the primary basis of the law and the cases, though numerous, deal mainly with detailed points of construction. Only a few cases which can be said to contain something of substance are to be found. The selection which follows, there-fore, deals with isolated points only: the main subject of study should be the Act itself.

1. Compulsory winding up: petitioners

Section 124 of IA 1986 provides that a petition for the compulsory winding up of a company may be presented to the court by any of the following:[16]
(a) the company itself;
(b) its directors;
(c) any creditor (including a contingent or prospective creditor);
(d) any 'contributory' (a term which includes a present member and a former holder of partly-paid shares who has transferred them within the past year (s 79): such a person may in some circumstances remain liable for unpaid calls on the shares);
(e) if the company is already being wound up voluntarily, the Official Receiver;
(f) the Secretary of State (ss 124(4), 124A).

Every contributory has a statutory right to petition for a winding up, which cannot be excluded or limited by any provision in the articles.

275 Re Peveril Gold Mines Ltd [1898] 1 Ch 122 (Court of Appeal)

The company's articles provided that no member should petition for the winding up of the company unless (a) two directors had consented in writing, or (b) a general meeting had so resolved, or (c) the petitioner held at least 20% of the issued capital. A shareholder presented a petition without satisfying any of these conditions. It was held that the articles were ineffective to prevent him from doing so.

LINDLEY MR: Anyone who is familiar with the Companies Acts knows perfectly well that these registered limited companies are incorporated on certain conditions; they continue to exist on certain conditions; and they are liable to be dissolved on certain conditions. The important sections of the

16 This is not an exhaustive list. For example, a charitable company may be wound up on the petition of the Attorney-General (Charities Act 1960, s 30). Under IA 1986, the supervisor of a voluntary arrangement (s 7(4)(b)) and an administrator or administrative receiver (Sch 1, para 21) have power to apply to the court for a winding-up order.

Act of 1862, with regard to dissolution, are ss 79 and 82 [IA 1986, ss 122, 124]. Section 79 states the circumstances under which such a company may be dissolved by the court, and s 82 states the persons who may petition for a dissolution. Any article contrary to these sections—any article which says that the company is formed on the condition that its life shall not be terminated when any of the circumstances mentioned in s 79 exist, or which limits the right of a contributory under s 82 to petition for a winding up, would be an attempt to enforce on all the shareholders that which is at variance with the statutory conditions, and is invalid. It is no answer to say that the right to petition may be waived by any contributory personally. I do not intend to decide whether a valid contract may or may not be made between the company and an individual shareholder that he shall not petition for the winding up of the company. That point does not arise now. But to say that a company is formed on the condition that its existence shall not be terminated under the circumstances, or on the application of the persons, mentioned in the Act is to say that it is formed contrary to the provisions of the Act, and upon conditions which the court is bound to ignore. The view taken by Byrne J was right, and the appeal must be dismissed.

CHITTY LJ delivered a concurring judgment.

VAUGHAN WILLIAMS LJ concurred.

A holder of fully-paid shares has no standing to petition for a winding-up order unless he can show that there will be assets available for the return of capital to members.

276 Re Rica Gold Washing Co (1879) 11 Ch D 36 (Court of Appeal)

[The facts appear from the judgment.]

JESSEL MR: This is an appeal from the decision of Vice-Chancellor Hall dismissing a petition to wind up the company, on the ground that it was not a bona fide petition, and that the petitioner, as I read the judgment, had not sufficient interest to support it ...

Now I will say a word or two on the law as regards the position of a petitioner holding fully paid-up shares. He is not liable to contribute anything towards the assets of the company, and if he has any interest at all, it must be that after full payment of all the debts and liabilities of the company there will remain a surplus divisible among the shareholders of sufficient value to authorise him to present a petition. That being his position, and the rule being that the petitioner must succeed upon allegations which are proved, of course the petitioner must show the court by sufficient allegation that he has a sufficient interest to entitle him to ask for the winding up of the company. I say 'a sufficient interest', for the mere allegation of a surplus or of a probable surplus will not be sufficient. He must show what I may call a tangible interest. I am not going to lay down any rule as to what that must be, but if he showed only that there was such a surplus as, on being fairly divided, irrespective of the costs of the winding up, would give him £5, I should say that would not be sufficient to induce the court to interfere in his behalf ...

I have to add one word more about the amount of the petitioner's claim. I am sorry to say I have had a very lengthened experience in winding-up cases, both at the Bar and on the Bench, and I cannot believe that a shareholder who has 75 £1 paid-up shares can imagine that he has sufficient interest to make it worth his while to present a winding-up petition ... I have no doubt that, as the Vice-Chancellor says, this is not a bona fide petition, but a petition presented with a very different object than that of obtaining for the petitioner, the £75, or any part of it. In my opinion it is either presented for the purpose of obtaining costs, or for the purpose of annoyance to some other person or persons; and I entirely agree with the Vice-Chancellor that it is not a bona fide petition. Therefore I think we must dismiss this appeal.

BRETT LJ delivered a concurring judgment.

BRAMWELL LJ concurred.

NOTE

The Jenkins Committee (1962, Cmnd 1749, para 503(h)), recommended the reversal of this rule by statute. In *Re Chesterfield Catering Co Ltd* [1977] Ch 373, [1976] 3 All ER 294, the decision was affirmed as being still good law, notwithstanding an argument by counsel that in the light of *Ebrahimi v Westbourne Galleries Ltd* (**284**) the principle of *Rica Gold* should be regarded not as a strict rule admitting of no exceptions, but merely as one of the considerations for the court to take into account in assessing whether it was just and equitable to order a winding up.

QUESTIONS

(1) What would you say was the ratio decidendi of this case?
(2) If a petition for winding up is presented by a holder of a small parcel of fully-paid shares on facts similar to *Re German Date Coffee Co* (**279**) or *Re Thomas Edward Brinsmead & Sons* (**281**), should the court apply the *Rica Gold* rule?
(3) It costs a filing fee of over £300 to lodge a winding-up petition, and that is in addition to whatever the petitioner is charged by his lawyers—a sum running into four figures for a contested case. A petition which is not well founded may be dismissed with an order that the petitioner pay the company's costs, and in some cases it may be struck out in limine as vexatious (see *Charles Forte Investments Ltd v Amanda* (**286**)). Does the law need the rule in *Rica Gold*?

An unpaid creditor who establishes that the company is insolvent is ordinarily entitled to a winding-up order as of right, subject to the wishes of the creditors as a class. An order will not be refused on the ground that there are no assets unless it is shown that to make an order would be pointless.

277 Re Crigglestone Coal Co Ltd [1906] 2 Ch 327 (Chancery Division and Court of Appeal)

The petitioner asked for a winding-up order based on a debt of £716 for electrical cables supplied. The debt and the company's insolvency were not disputed. The petition was not opposed by either the company or any of the other unsecured creditors, but the debentureholders objected on the grounds that there were no assets available for unsecured creditors, and that their security might be affected by a winding-up order since the company's lessors would then have power to re-enter. Buckley J nevertheless granted an order; and his decision was affirmed by the Court of Appeal.

BUCKLEY J: I will state shortly what I take to be the law. First, as between the creditor and the company, who are his debtors, the unpaid creditor who shows insolvency is entitled ex debito justitiae (as it is generally termed) to a winding-up order—that is to say, to an order by virtue of which the creditor, by the hands of a liquidator, is entitled to seize the assets of his debtor and administer them for the payment of himself and other creditors . . .

But then comes another consideration, viz that the order which the petitioner seeks is not an order for his benefit, but an order for the benefit of a class of which he is a member. The right ex debito justitiae is not his individual right, but his representative right. If a majority of the class are opposed to his view, and consider that they have a better chance of getting payment by abstaining from seizing the assets, then, upon general grounds and upon s 91 of the Companies Act 1862 [IA 1986, s 195] the court gives effect to such right as the majority of the class desire to exercise. This is no exception. It is a recognition of the right, but affirms that it is the right not of the individual, but of the class: that it is for the majority to seek or to decline the order as best serves the interest of their class. It is a matter upon which the majority of the unsecured creditors are entitled to prevail, but on which the debtor has no voice . . .

The outcome of it, therefore, in my opinion, is that it is no answer, as between the petitioner and the company, that the debentureholders will or may sweep away all the assets. As between the creditors and the company, the former are entitled to seize and administer so as, if possible, to escape that result. Is it, then, an answer as between the petitioner and those who appear to oppose this petition? . . . As between the petitioners[17] and the debentureholders who . . . appear to oppose, the matter seems to me to stand in this position. The debentureholders are not members of the class on whose behalf the petitioners apply to the court. They are persons who claim to stand as mortgagees outside of and before the petitioners' class, and who say that the petitioners are without a remedy because they, the debentureholders, rank before them. They are for all purposes the petitioners' opponents, and not members of the class that they represent. In determining what the petitioners' rights are, the court ought, I think, to disregard the fact that a different course may be more advantageous for the mortgagees . . .

[The decision of Buckley J was affirmed by the Court of Appeal, [1906] 2 Ch 327 at 336.]

NOTE

See also IA 1986, s 125(1), which provides that the court shall not refuse to make a winding-up order on the ground only that the company has no assets, or that the assets are mortgaged for more than their value.

---

17 [The petitioner was incorporated: the singular and the plural appear to be used indifferently in the report.]

QUESTION

Is there any reason in principle for having this rule for a creditor and an opposite rule for a member (**276**)?

2. Compulsory winding-up: grounds

Compulsory winding-up orders may be sought on any of the grounds listed in IA 1986, s 122(1). In practice, they are most often sought by creditors who cannot get their debts paid (see ss 122(1)(f) and 123)—although the court strenuously insists that its jurisdiction is based on public policy and repels all suggestions that its procedures have anything to do with debt-collection. Only a few petitions are brought by members, mostly under s 122(1)(g)—the 'just and equitable' ground; and the Secretary of State may invoke the same subsection in the public interest in cases of notoriety, most often following an investigation of the company's affairs under CA 1985, Pt XIV (above, pp 531 ff).

A winding-up order will not be made on the basis of a debt which is bona fide disputed.

278 Re London and Paris Banking Corpn (1874) LR 19 Eq 444 (Master of the Rolls)

The petitioner, Zuccani, had charged the company £267 for furniture which he had supplied, but the directors considered this an excessive price and offered £155 and later, after having received the report of two valuers, £197. An action had been commenced in the Court of Exchequer to resolve the dispute, but Zuccani, who had earlier served a statutory demand, presented a winding-up petition. The Master of the Rolls refused to make an order.

JESSEL MR: It has been asserted on the part of the petitioner that there is a statutory right to a winding-up order given by the 80th section of the Companies Act 1862 (IA 1986, s 123) to any creditor who has given the statutory notice if non-payment has occurred by the company for a space of three weeks. Now, first of all, what does the statute say? It says that whenever a creditor to whom a company is indebted in a sum exceeding £50[18] has served on the company in a certain way a demand under his hand requiring the company to pay the sum so due, and the company has for the space of three weeks succeeding the service of such demand, neglected to pay such sum or to secure or compound for the same to the reasonable satisfaction of the creditor, then the company shall be deemed to be unable to pay its debts. It is very obvious, on reading that enactment, that the word 'neglected' is not necessarily equivalent to the word 'omitted'. Negligence is a term which is well known to the law. Negligence in paying a debt on demand, as I understand it, is omitting to pay without reasonable excuse. Mere omission by itself does not amount to negligence. Therefore I should hold, upon the words of the statute, that where a debt is bona fide disputed by the debtor, and the debtor alleges, for example, that the demand for goods sold and

---

18 Now £750: see IA 1986, s 123(1)(a).

delivered is excessive, and says that he, the debtor, is willing to pay such sum as he is either advised by competent valuers to pay, or as he himself considered a fair sum for the goods, then in that case he has not neglected to pay, and is not within the wording of the statute ...

[His Honour stated the facts and continued:]

That being the position of matters, on 11 November the petitioner thinks it right to present the petition. I cannot treat that as a bona fide attempt on the part of the petitioner to wind up the company. Obviously, if it had any meaning at all, it was to put pressure upon the company, perhaps by threat of the advertisements, or by some other means, to compel them to pay; in other words, to extort from them a sum larger than they bona fide believed to be due from them, and a sum which they had been advised by two valuers was excessive. I cannot encourage any such course of proceeding, and I therefore dismiss the petition with costs.

It is just and equitable to wind up a company when its 'substratum' or principal object has failed.[19]

279 Re German Date Coffee Co (1882) 20 Ch D 169 (Court of Appeal)

[The facts appear from the judgment.]

JESSEL MR: The company is stated to be registered for several objects. The first object is to acquire a German patent granted to one Henley for manufacturing from dates a substitute for coffee. The second is to make and use the same invention or any improvement of it. That refers to the German patent. The memorandum is tautologous, an observation which need not be confined to this memorandum— it is very common as regards all memorandums of association. The third object is to adopt and carry out an agreement dated 16 February 1881. When we come to look at that, it is an agreement for the sale of the German patent. Article 4 is to manufacture and sell the preparations which are the subject of the said invention. That is pure tautology. Nobody has been able to suggest that there is anything there which is not included in articles 1 and 2. Article 5 is to grant licences. Of course, if you have no patent you cannot grant licences. Article 6 is to apply for and obtain patents for improvements or extensions of the said invention, and so on. Article 7 is to acquire and purchase, or otherwise to use, exercise, and vend, any other inventions for the above-mentioned or cognate subject. All those are merely ancillary provisions. Then there is Article 8, which I read to be this, to import all descriptions of produce, in connection with the above-mentioned purpose, or otherwise for the purposes of the company. It never can mean to import and export food produce generally. That would be making it a company for an entirely new and distinct purpose. The other reading is, in my opinion, the more grammatical reading of the two; whether

---

19 On the 'just and equitable' ground generally, see F H Callaway, *Winding up on the Just and Equitable Ground* (1978); B H McPherson, 'Winding up on the Just and Equitable Ground' (1964) 27 MLR 282. The author suggests that the decided cases fall into three broad categories: (i) where it initially is, or later becomes, impossible to achieve the objects for which the company was formed; (ii) where it has become impossible for the company to carry on its business; (iii) where there has been serious fraud, misconduct or oppression in regard to the affairs of the company.

it is so or not, it is, I think, the correct reading, and is merely ancillary. That being so, it appears to me that this memorandum, when fairly read, and notwithstanding the rather loose use of general words, is simply to buy this patent, and to work it either with or without improvements. That is the substance of the whole thing.

Now what happened was this. I have no reason to doubt that the framers of the memorandum and articles believed that they would obtain the German patent, for they said, 'for which a patent has or will be granted by the Empire of Germany'. But they were a little too sanguine, and they cannot complain if, like other prophets, their prophecies are sometimes not verified by the result. It turned out that the German empire would not grant the patent. When that happened what ought they to have done? Surely they ought to have said, 'We cannot carry on business, and we must wind up'; and that is exactly what Mr Justice Kay ordered to be done ... Then it turns out that the company has, quite bona fide, in anticipation of the granting of the German patent, established at Hamburg a factory for the manufacture of this substance called date coffee, and they say they have sold a good deal of it and are doing a prosperous trade. They have also entered into an agreement with the parent company, an English company called the Date Coffee Company, by which that company has agreed not to compete with this company in Germany. I ought also to refer to the affidavit of Mr Gardiner, who says that he applied in September for a patent on behalf of Mr Henley, but he does not say that he obtained it, and I therefore assume that for some reason or other it was refused. This application, whatever the result may have been, appears to me no ground for varying the order which has been made. That being so, it seems to me, as the learned judge of the court below said, the whole substratum of the company is gone. Its business was not to make a substitute for coffee from dates, but to work a German patented invention in Germany; to work it under the monopoly granted by the German government to the patentee, and not to enter into any such business generally. Therefore the shareholders have a right to say, and the minority of the shareholders have a right to say, 'We did not enter into partnership on these terms' ... It was not a general partnership to make a substitute for coffee from dates, but to work a particular patent, and as that particular patent does not exist, and cannot now exist, they are entitled to say the company ought to be wound up.

It appears to me the learned judge in the court below has arrived at the right conclusion, and that this appeal ought to be dismissed. If the full effect of the general words is allowed they might carry on any business whatever.

BAGGALLAY and LINDLEY LJJ delivered concurring judgments.

NOTE

It is perhaps reasonable to observe that the memorandum in this case was both drafted and construed in a rather old-fashioned way. The case next cited shows a more modern approach in both respects.

280 Re Kitson & Co Ltd [1946] 1 All ER 435 (Court of Appeal)

The company was incorporated in 1899. The first three sub-clauses of the objects clause in its memorandum read as follows:

(1) To acquire and take over as a going concern the business now carried on at Airedale Foundry, Hunslet, in the city of Leeds, under the style or firm of 'Kitson & Co', and all or any of the assets and liabilities ...

(2) To carry on the business of locomotive engine manufacturers, iron-founders, mechanical engineers and manufacturers of agricultural implements and other machinery, tool makers, brass founders, metal workers, boiler makers ...

(3) To carry on any business relating to the winning and working of minerals, the production and working of metals, and the production, manufacture and preparation of any other materials which may be usefully or conveniently combined with the engineering or manu-facturing business of the company, or any contracts undertaken by the company ...

In July 1945 the company agreed to sell the goodwill and assets of the engineering business which was carried on at the Airedale foundry, and although there was some evidence that the directors had at that time proposed to go out of engineering altogether, the present directors stated that they intended to acquire the assets of a subsidiary ('Balmforth') and to continue an engineering business. It was held that the substratum had not gone.

LORD GREENE MR: [The] form of the memorandum is the common form where a business is being acquired. It sets out in the usual way the acquisition of the business as the first step which the company is going to undertake. We are not considering now whether failure in 1899 to acquire the business of Kitson & Co would have destroyed the substratum of the company. It might possibly have been thought that unless it got this business it was not really starting its career in the way in which the shareholders bargained it should be started; but the question we have to decide is whether, that business having been acquired, forty-six years ago, the disposal of it last year amounted to a destruction of the substratum. In my opinion, the main and paramount object of this company was to carry on an engineering business of a general kind. It was such a business that was carried on by Kitson & Co, and I cannot bring myself to construe this memorandum as limiting the paramount object and restricting the contemplated adventure of the shareholders to the carrying on of what could be called the business of Kitson & Co. The impossibility of applying such a construction seems to me to be manifest when one remembers that a business is a thing which changes. It grows or it contracts. It changes; it disposes of the whole of its plant; it moves its factory; it entirely changes its range of products, and so forth. It is more like an organic thing. Counsel for the respondents quoted to us a number of very well-known authorities on which it has been held that on particular facts the substratum of particular companies had gone. I do not propose to examine those authorities because they do not assist me in construing this particular memorandum. It must be remembered in these substratum cases that there is every difference between a company which on the true construction of its memorandum is formed for the paramount purpose of dealing with some specific subject-matter and a company which is formed with wider and more comprehensive objects. I will explain what I mean. With regard to a company which is formed to acquire and exploit a mine, when you come to construe its memorandum of association you must construe the language used in reference to the subject-matter, namely, a mine, and, accordingly, if the mine cannot be acquired or if the mine turns out to be no mine at all, the object of the company is frustrated, because the subject-matter which the company was formed to exploit has ceased to exist. It is exactly the same way with a patent, as in the well-known *German Date Coffee* case (**279**). A patent is a defined subject-matter, and, if the main object of a company is to acquire and work a patent and it fails to acquire that patent, to compel the shareholders to remain bound together in order to work some other patent or make some unpatented article is to force them into a different adventure to that which they contracted to engage in together; but, when you come to subject-matter of a totally different kind like the carrying on of a type of business, then, so long as the company can carry on that type of business, it seems to me that prima facie at any rate it is impossible to say that its substratum has gone. So far as this stage of the argument is concerned, it is to my mind quite impossible upon the true construction of this memorandum of association to limit the paramount object of this company to the specific business of Kitson & Co, so as to lead to the result that as soon as Kitson & Co's business was sold the substratum of the company had gone ...

MORTON and TUCKER LJJ delivered concurring judgments.

NOTE

In *Re Tivoli Freeholds Ltd* [1972] VR 445 (SC Vic) a winding-up petition was granted on the just and equitable ground. The main objects of the company had been to own and build theatres and to carry on theatrical and similar entertainment businesses. An outside group acquired control of the company and, having realised nearly all of its assets, used the funds so raised to mount corporate raids on other firms. (These activities were quite profitable and dividends were regularly paid on the strength of the profits, so an alternative petition based on alleged oppression of the minority shareholders (see above, pp 495 ff) was rejected by the judge.) Although it was not contended that the company could not, if it chose, have continued to pursue its original objects, the court accepted that the evidence showed that the business for which the company was formed had been conclusively abandoned, and granted relief on a basis analogous to a failure of substratum.

A company formed for a fraudulent purpose may be wound up on the 'just and equitable' ground.

281 Re Thomas Edward Brinsmead & Sons [1897] 1 Ch 406 (Court of Appeal)

Three men named Brinsmead, former employees of John Brinsmead & Sons, the well-known piano makers, formed the present company to make pianos which were to be passed off as the product of the older-established firm. An injunction had been obtained, restraining the company from this action; but meantime shares in the company worth many thousands of pounds had been subscribed for by the public in a promotion fraud instigated by the Consolidated Contract Corporation. On this evidence, it was held to be just and equitable to grant a winding-up order.

The judgment of the court (LINDLEY, AL SMITH and RIGBY LJJ) was read by AL SMITH LJ: In our judgment it has been proved that this company—i e Thomas Edward Brinsmead & Sons Limited—was initiated to carry out a fraud, and that, until restrained by injunction, it continued therein; and that a strong prima facie case has been made out that the Consolidated Contract Corporation are at the present moment dishonestly keeping the shareholders' money to which the shareholders, and not they, are entitled, and are resisting the petition to wind up in order to continue to do so. If the sums which they have improperly obtained from the company can be recovered from them, there will probably be something to distribute among the shareholders and, although the petitioner is a fully paid-up shareholder, he cannot be said to have no locus standi. The company is hopelessly embarrassed by the actions already brought against it, and there will, no doubt, be many more of the same sort if this petition is dismissed; and if it is not wound up the £35,000 obtained from it by its promoters will remain in their hands.

Although the words 'just and equitable' have had a narrow construction put upon them, they have never been construed so narrowly as to exclude such a case as this. If ever there was a case in which it was just and equitable that a company should be wound up by the court, we cannot doubt that the case is this case. For the reasons above, we dismiss this appeal with costs.

It is just and equitable to wind up a small company, if it is in effect an incorporated partnership, on the same grounds as would justify the court in decreeing the dissolution of a partnership, e g a deadlock between the members.[20]

282 Re Yenidje Tobacco Co Ltd [1916] 2 Ch 426 (Court of Appeal)

The company was formed by two tobacco manufacturers, Rothman and Weinberg, in order to amalgamate their businesses. They were the only shareholders, with equal voting rights, and the only directors. The parties had been for some time in a state of continuous quarrel. Rothman had brought an action against Weinberg alleging fraud; they had spent over £1,000 in litigation over the validity of the dismissal of a factory manager; they had argued over the terms of employment of a traveller; and they had been communicating with each other only through the secretary of the company. In this situation (despite the fact that the company was making larger profits than ever before), the court granted a winding-up order on Weinberg's petition.

LORD COZENS-HARDY MR: In those circumstances, supposing it had been a private partnership, an ordinary partnership between two people having equal shares, and there being no other provision to terminate it, what would have been the position? I think it is quite clear under the law of partnership, as has been asserted in this court for many years and is now laid down by the Partnership Act, that that state of things might be a ground for dissolution of the partnership for the reasons which are stated by Lord Lindley in his book on *Partnership* at p 657 in the passage which I will read, and, which, I think, is quite justified by the authorities to which he refers: 'Refusal to meet on matters of business, continued quarrelling, and such a state of animosity as precludes all reasonable hope of reconciliation and friendly co-operation

20 See further M R Chesterman, 'The "Just and Equitable" Winding up of Small Private Companies', (1973) 36 MLR 129; D D Prentice, 'Winding up on the Just and Equitable Ground—the Partnership Analogy' (1973) 89 LQR 107; B A K Rider, 'Partnership Law and its Impact on "Domestic Companies"' [1979] CLJ 148.

have been held sufficient to justify dissolution. It is not necessary, in order to induce the Court to interfere, to show personal rudeness on the part of one partner to the other, or even any gross misconduct as a partner. All that is necessary is to satisfy the Court that it is impossible for the partners to place that confidence in each other which each has a right to expect, and that such impossibility has not been caused by the person seeking to take advantage of it' ...

I ask myself the question: When one of the two partners has commenced, and has not discontinued, an action charging his co-partner with fraud in the inception of the partnership, is it likely, is it reasonable, is it common sense, to suppose those two partners can work together in the manner in which they ought to work in the conduct of the partnership business?

[His Lordship referred to other aspects of the dispute and continued:] Is it possible to say that it is not just and equitable that that state of things should not be allowed to continue, and that the court should not intervene and say this is not what the parties contemplated by the arrangement into which they entered? They assumed, and it is the foundation of the whole of the agreement that was made, that the two would act as reasonable men with reasonable courtesy and reasonable conduct in every way towards each other, and arbitration was only to be resorted to with regard to some particular dispute between the directors which could not be determined in any other way. Certainly, having regard to the fact that the only two directors will not speak to each other, and no business which deserves the name of business in the affairs of the company can be carried on, I think the company should not be allowed to continue. I have treated it as a partnership, and under the Partnership Act of course the application for a dissolution would take the form of an action; but this is not a partnership strictly, it is not a case in which it can be dissolved by action. But ought not precisely the same principles to apply to a case like this where in substance it is a partnership in the form of the guise of a private company? It is a private company, and there is no way to put an end to the state of things which now exists except by means of a compulsory order. It has been urged upon us that, although it is admitted that the 'just and equitable' clause is not to be limited to cases ejusdem generis, it has nevertheless been held, according to the authorities, not to apply except where the substratum of the company has gone or where there is a complete deadlock. Those are the two instances which are given, but I should be very sorry, so far as my individual opinion goes, to hold that they are strictly the limits of the 'just and equitable' clause as found in the Companies Act. I think that in a case like this we are bound to say that circumstances which would justify the winding up of a partnership between these two by action are circumstances which should induce the court to exercise its jurisdiction under the just and equitable clause and to wind up the company ... [His Lordship then ruled it irrelevant that the company was making large profits.]

WARRINGTON LJ delivered a concurring judgment.

PICKFORD LJ concurred.

It is just and equitable to wind up a company where there is a justifiable lack of confidence in the management of the company's affairs.

283 Loch v John Blackwood Ltd [1924] AC 783 (Privy Council)

The engineering business of John Blackwood had, after his death, been formed into a company and run by one of his trustees, McLaren, for the benefit of the three beneficiaries in his estate: McLaren's wife (who was to take one-half), Mrs Loch (one-quarter) and Rodger (since deceased, one quarter). The business had been run very profitably by McLaren, but (as is described in the judgment) he had run it in a manner which was oppressive to the beneficiaries other than his wife. They accordingly petitioned for the winding up of the company on the ground that it was just and equitable to do so. The Chief Justice of Barbados made an order, which was reversed by the West Indian Court of Appeal but restored by the Privy Council. [The remaining facts appear from the judgment.]

The opinion of the Privy Council was delivered by LORD SHAW OF DUN-FERMLINE: The board of directors now consists of Mr McLaren, his wife Mrs McLaren, who was appointed in 1913, and Mr Yearwood. Under this directorate the business of the company appears to have been energetically managed and to have amassed considerable profits.

The arrangement of the capital was this: the total amount was 40,000 in £1 shares; 20,000 of these were allotted to Mrs McLaren; of the remaining 20,000, 10,000 should have gone to Mrs Loch and 10,000 to Mr Rodger. Mrs Loch, however, was allotted 9,999; Mr Rodger, 9,998; and the three shares left over were allotted one to Mr McLaren and one each to Mr Yearwood and Mr King (Mrs McLaren's nominees; the first being Mr McLaren's clerk and the second his solicitor). This was quite a natural and proper arrangement; but, of course, in the event of a division of opinion in the family between what may be called the McLaren interest on the one hand, and the interest of the nephew and niece on the other, the preponderance of voting power lay with the former. It is thus seen that although taking the form of a public company the concern was practically a domestic and family concern. This consideration is important,[1] as also is the preponderance of voting power just alluded to.

In the petition for winding up eight different reasons are assigned therefor. The first is: that the statutory conditions as to general meetings have not been observed; the second that balance-sheets, profit and loss accounts and reports have not been submitted in terms of the articles of the company; and the third is that the conditions under the statute and articles as to audit have not been complied with. All these allegations are true, and it seems naturally to follow from the preponderance already alluded to, that there is at least considerable force in the fifth reason that it is impossible for the petitioners to obtain any relief by calling a general meeting of the company. There are further submissions—namely, that the company and the managing director, Mr McLaren, have refused to submit the value of the shares to arbitration, and that without winding up it is impossible for the petitioners to realise the true value of their shares. But the principal ground of the petitioner is that in the circumstances to be laid before the court it is just and equitable that the company should be ordered to be wound up. This last ground was affirmed by the Court of Common Pleas.

---

1 Although an important factor, it is probably not vital. In some jurisdictions overseas it has been held that the principle is not confined to domestic companies: see *Re Wondoflex Textiles Pty Ltd* [1951] VLR 458; *Re R J Jowsey Mining Co Ltd* [1969] 2 OR 549.

With regard to the first three submissions made in the petition, it was strenuously argued on behalf of the company, which practically means the directorate or the McLaren interest, that however true it might be that owing to the informal way in which the books of the company had been kept it appeared as if both the statute and the articles of association had been violated in various particulars and that no general meetings of the company had been held, and no auditors properly appointed, and it was certain that no balance-sheets, profit and loss accounts and reports had been submitted for the critical years 1919 and 1920, still these were no grounds for winding up. Other applications, it was said, might competently be made to the court to compel the statute and articles to be properly complied with. It may be doubtful whether such a course of conduct lasting in several particulars since its inception until now, would be insufficient as a ground for winding the company up. But their Lordships think it unnecessary to give any separate decision upon such a point.

In their opinion, however, elements of that character in the history of the company, together with the fact that a calling of a meeting of shareholders would lead admittedly to failure and be unavailable as a remedy, cannot be excluded from the point of view of the court in a consideration of the justice and equity of pronouncing an order for winding up. Such a consideration, in their Lordships' view, ought to proceed upon a sound induction of all the facts of the case, and should not exclude, but should include circumstances which bear upon the problem of continuing or stopping courses of conduct which substantially impair those rights and protections to which shareholders, both under statute and contract, are entitled. It is undoubtedly true that at the foundation of applications for winding up, on the 'just and equitable' rule, there must lie a justifiable lack of confidence in the conduct and management of the company's affairs. But this lack of confidence must be grounded on conduct of the directors, not in regard to their private life or affairs, but in regard to the company's business. Furthermore the lack of confidence must spring not from dissatisfaction at being outvoted on the business affairs or on what is called the domestic policy of the company. On the other hand, wherever the lack of confidence is rested on a lack of probity in the conduct of the company's affairs, then the former is justified by the latter, and it is under the statute just and equitable that the company be wound up.

The judgment of the court below appears to have proceeded upon the view that this statutory prescription for winding up under the sixth subsection—namely, when the court is of opinion that it is just and equitable that this should be done—is restricted to cases ejusdem generis with those enumerated in the other sub-ss 1–5 of s 127 of the Barbados Companies Act.[2]

The Board, having fully considered the authorities, the judgments and the arguments, are of opinion that this is not the law ...

Their Lordships ... are of opinion that the learned Greaves CJ is correct when he says that: 'The directors in control since the death of Blackwood Rodger have, I think, laid themselves open to the suspicion that by omitting to hold general meetings, submit accounts and recommend a dividend, their object was to keep the petitioners in ignorance of the truth and acquire their shares at an under value.'

The Board agrees with these views. In the opinion which they have formed,

2 [IA 1986, s 122(1)(a)–(f) are approximately equivalent.]

Mr McLaren, for reasons not unnatural, had come to be of opinion that the business owed much of its value and prosperity to himself. But he appears to have proceeded to the further stage of feeling that in these circumstances he could manage the business as if it were his own. Had Mrs Loch and Mr Rodger, or after his death Mr Rodger's executor, obtained a dividend which year by year represented in any reasonable measure a just declaration out of the undoubted profits of the concern, they might no doubt have been content to allow this state of matters to go on; but although on one or two occasions, Mr McLaren paid trifling and fragmentary sums to Mrs Loch, neither she nor the Rodger family have ever obtained any dividend at all. And it is not to be wondered at that in the transaction now about to be mentioned they completely lost confidence in Mr McLaren, and had only too great justification for doing so ...

[His Lordship then referred to a decision of the directors to pay McLaren an increased salary and to transfer to him £12,500 War Loan stock, and continued:] No notice was given to the respondents, as shareholders, of this piece of business being contemplated, and no notice was given of what had been done. Four days after this extraordinary transaction, Mr McLaren wrote to Mrs Loch's husband a letter dated 5 May 1920 proposing to her that £10,000 should be given by him as the cumulative value of Mrs Loch's shares and Mr J B Rodger's executor's shares. These shares in all amounted to one-half of the capital of the company—namely, £20,000—and, as already mentioned, it is evident that the true value of assets much exceeded this amount. The proposal was to buy Mrs Loch and the Rodger family out for £10,000. But a further suggestion, which in some ways seems to have been mixed up with the umbrage felt by Mr McLaren in regard to the contents of Mr Rodger's will, was made, and that was that Mr Loch should be a participant in a scheme whereby the £10,000 to be paid should be distributed—£8,000 to herself and only £2,000 to the Rodgers family.

Their Lordships do not desire to characterise these suggestions in the language which perhaps they fully deserve. The Rodger family, entitled to one-fourth of the holding in the company, nominally £10,000, but in reality of a much higher value, were to be bought off for £2,000, and Mrs Loch was to be the agent in this scheme. No confidence in the directorate could survive such a proposal. To crown all this, as was afterwards discovered, the £10,000 could be comfortably paid by Mr McLaren out of the £12,500 which, four days before, he and his wife and clerk had voted to himself out of the funds of the company. Their Lordships express no surprise at the instant repudiation of Mr McLaren's proposals by Mrs Loch—a repudiation which is creditable to her—and at the application for a winding up of the company being made. Upon the principles already set forth in this judgment that application must succeed. The broad ground is that confidence in its management was, and is, and that most justifiably, at an end ...

NOTE

In *Re R A Noble & Sons (Clothing) Ltd* [1983] BCLC 273, Nourse J held that, so long as the conduct of those in control has been 'the substantial cause' of the destruction of the mutual confidence between the parties, it is unnecessary to show either that that conduct has been in some way underhand or that the petitioner's own conduct has been above reproach. The Privy Council took a similar view in *Vujnovich v*

Vujnovich [1990] BCLC 227. But note that the court has a discretion under IA 1986, s 125(2) to refuse an order on the 'just and equitable' ground if the petitioner is acting unreasonably in seeking to have the company wound up instead of pursuing some other remedy. In *Re a Company* [1983] 2 All ER 854, [1983] 1 WLR 927, Vinelott J held that a petitioner had acted unreasonably in refusing an offer made by the majority shareholders to buy his shares, following a breakdown of confidence, and refused him a winding-up order.[3] In this context the conduct of the petitioner himself may well be relevant.

It may be just and equitable to wind up a company even though the controllers have acted within their strict legal rights.

284 Ebrahimi v Westbourne Galleries Ltd [1973] AC 360, [1972] 2 All ER 492 (House of Lords)

The company was formed in 1958 to take over a business which Nazar and Ebrahimi had run in partnership for over a decade. At first, the two were equal shareholders and the only directors, but soon afterwards Nazar's son joined the company as a director and shareholder, so that Ebrahimi found himself in a minority position both on the board of directors and at a general meeting. In 1969, after some disagreement between the parties, an ordinary resolution was passed under s 184 of the Act of 1948 [CA 1985, s 303], removing Ebrahimi as director. Ebrahimi sought relief under s 210, or, alternatively, s 222(f) of the 1948 Act [respectively CA 1985, s 459 and IA 1986, s 122(1)(g)]. Plowman J declined to make an order under s 210 because (inter alia) Ebrahimi's complaint was in his capacity as director rather than as member (see above, p 496); but he did make a winding-up order. The Court of Appeal reversed the latter ruling, holding that the exercise by a majority of its constitutional and statutory rights, unless shown to be mala fide, was not a ground for 'just and equitable' relief under s 222(f). The House of Lords restored the decision of the trial judge.

LORD WILBERFORCE: My Lords, the petition was brought under s 222(f) of the Companies Act 1948 [IA 1986, s 122(1)(g)], which enables a winding-up order to be made if 'the court is of the opinion that it is just and equitable that the company should be wound up'. This power has existed in our company law in unaltered form since the first major Act, the Companies Act 1862. Indeed, it antedates that statute since it existed in the Joint Stock Companies Winding Up Act 1848. For some fifty years, following a pronouncement by Lord Cottenham LC in 1849, the words 'just and equitable' were interpreted so as only to include matters ejusdem generis as the preceding clauses of the section, but there is now ample authority for discarding this limitation. There are two other restrictive interpretations which I mention to reject. First, there has been a tendency to create categories or headings under which cases must be brought if the clause is to apply. This is wrong. Illustrations may be used, but general words should remain general and not be reduced to the sum of particular instances. Secondly, it has been suggested, and urged upon us, that (assuming the petitioner is a shareholder and not a creditor) the words must be confined to such circumstances as affect him in

3 *Re a Company* may be contrasted with *Virdi v Abbey Leisure Ltd* [1990] BCLC 342, CA, where the court exercised its discretion in the petitioner's favour on a similar issue.

his capacity as shareholder. I see no warrant for this either. No doubt, in order to present a petition, he must qualify as a shareholder, but I see no reason for preventing him from relying upon any circumstances of justice or equity which affect him in his relations with the company, or, in a case such as the present, with the other shareholders.

One other signpost is significant. The same words 'just and equitable' appear in the Partnership Act 1890, s 35, as a ground for dissolution of a partnership and no doubt the considerations which they reflect formed part of the common law of partnership before its codification. The importance of this is to provide a bridge between cases under s 222(f) of the Act of 1948 and the principles of equity developed in relation to partnerships.

The winding-up order was made following a doctrine which has developed in the courts since the beginning of this century. As presented by the appellant, and in substance accepted by the learned judge, this was that in a case such as this the members of the company are in substance partners, or quasi-partners, and that a winding up may be ordered if such facts are shown as could justify a dissolution of partnership between them. The common use of the words 'just and equitable' in the company and partnership law supports this approach. Your Lordships were invited by the respondents' counsel to restate the principle on which this provision ought to be used; it has not previously been considered by this House. The main line of his submission was to suggest that too great a use of the partnership analogy had been made; that a limited company, however small, essentially differs from a partnership; that in the case of a company, the rights of its members are governed by the articles of association which have contractual force; that the court has no power or at least ought not to dispense parties from observing their contracts; that, in particular, when one member has been excluded from the directorate, or management, under powers expressly conferred by the Companies Act and the articles, an order for winding up, whether on the partnership analogy or under the just and equitable provision, should not be made. Alternatively, it was argued that before the making of such an order could be considered the petitioner must show and prove that the exclusion was not made bona fide in the interests of the company.

[His Lordship discussed a number of earlier cases and continued:]

My Lords, in my opinion these authorities represent a sound and rational development of the law which should be endorsed. The foundation of it all lies in the words 'just and equitable' and, if there is any respect in which some of the cases may be open to criticism, it is that the courts may sometimes have been too timorous in giving them full force. The words are a recognition of the fact that a limited company is more than a mere legal entity, with a personality in law of its own: that there is room in company law for recognition of the fact that behind it, or amongst it, there are individuals, with rights, expectations and obligations inter se which are not necessarily submerged in the company structure. That structure is defined by the Companies Act and by the articles of association by which shareholders agree to be bound. In most companies and in most contexts, this definition is sufficient and exhaustive, equally so whether the company is large or small. The 'just and equitable' provision does not, as the respondents suggest, entitle one party to disregard the obligation he assumed by entering a company, nor the court to dispense him from it. It does, as equity always does, enable the court to subject the exercise of legal rights to equitable considerations; considerations, that is, of a personal character arising between one individual and another, which may make it unjust, or inequitable, to insist on legal rights, or to exercise them in a particular way.

It would be impossible, and wholly undesirable, to define the circumstances in which these considerations may arise. Certainly the fact that a company is a small one, or a private company, is not enough. There are very many of these where the association is a purely commercial one, of which it can safely be said that the basis of association is adequately and exhaustively laid down in the articles. The superimposition of equitable considerations requires something more, which typically may include one, or probably more, of the following elements: (i) an association formed or continued on the basis of a personal relationship, involving mutual confidence—this element will often be found where a pre-existing partnership has been converted into a limited company; (ii) an agreement, or understanding, that all, or some (for there may be 'sleeping' members), of the shareholders shall participate in the conduct of the business; (iii) restriction upon the transfer of the members' interest in the company—so that if confidence is lost, or one member is removed from management, he cannot take out his stake and go elsewhere.

It is these, and analogous, factors which may bring into play the just and equitable clause, and they do so directly, through the force of the words themselves. To refer, as so many of the cases do, to 'quasi-partnerships' or 'in substance partnerships' may be convenient but may also be confusing. It may be convenient because it is the law of partnership which has developed the conceptions of probity, good faith and mutual confidence, and the remedies where these are absent, which become relevant once such factors as I have mentioned are found to exist: the words 'just and equitable' sum these up in the law of partnership itself. And in many, but not necessarily all, cases there has been a pre-existing partnership the obligations of which it is reasonable to suppose continue to underlie the new company structure. But the expressions may be confusing if they obscure, or deny, the fact that the parties (possibly former partners) are now co-members in a company, who have accepted, in law, new obligations. A company, however small, however domestic, is a company, not a partnership or even a quasi-partnership and it is through the just and equitable clause that obligations, common to partnership relations, may come in.

My Lords, this is an expulsion case, and I must briefly justify the application in such cases of the just and equitable clause. The question is, as always, whether it is equitable to allow one (or two) to make use of his legal rights to the prejudice of his associate(s). The law of companies recognises the right, in many ways, to remove a director from the board. Section 184 of the Companies Act 1948 [CA 1985, s 303] confers this right upon the company in general meeting whatever the articles may say. Some articles may prescribe other methods: for example, a governing director may have the power to remove (compare *Re Wondoflex Textiles Pty Ltd*).[4] And quite apart from removal powers, there are normally provisions for retirement of directors by rotation so that their re-election can be opposed and defeated by a majority, or even by a casting vote. In all these ways a particular director-member may find himself no longer a director, through removal, or non-re-election: this situation he must normally accept, unless he undertakes the burden of proving fraud or mala fides. The just and equitable provision nevertheless comes to his assistance if he can point to, and prove, some

4 [1951] VLR 458.

special underlying obligation of his fellow member(s) in good faith, or confidence, that so long as the business continues he shall be entitled to management participation, an obligation so basic that, if broken, the conclusion must be that the association must be dissolved ...

I come to the facts of this case. It is apparent enough that a potential basis for a winding-up order under the just and equitable clause existed. The appellant after a long association in partnership, during which he had an equal share in the management, joined in the formation of the company. The inference must be indisputable that he, and Mr Nazar, did so on the basis that the character of the association would, as a matter of personal relation and good faith, remain the same. He was removed from his directorship under a power valid in law. Did he establish a case which, if he had remained in a partnership with a term providing for expulsion, would have justified an order for dissolution? This was the essential question for the judge. Plowman J dealt with the issue in a brief paragraph in which he said: '... while no doubt the petitioner was lawfully removed, in the sense that he ceased in law to be a director, it does not follow that in removing him the respondents did not do him a wrong. In my judgment, they did do him a wrong, in the sense that it was an abuse of power and a breach of the good faith which partners owe to each other to exclude one of them from all participation in the business upon which they have embarked on the basis that all should participate in its management. The main justification put forward for removing him was that he was perpetually complaining, but the faults were not all on one side and, in my judgment, this is not sufficient justification. For these reasons, in my judgment, the petitioner, therefore, has made out a case for a winding-up order.' Reading this in the context of the judgment as a whole, which had dealt with the specific complaints of one side against the other, I take it as a finding that the respondents were not entitled, in justice and equity, to make use of their legal powers of expulsion and that, in accordance with the principles of such cases as *Blisset v Daniel*[5] the only just and equitable course was to dissolve the association ...

LORD CROSS OF CHELSEA delivered a concurring opinion.

VISCOUNT DILHORNE, LORD PEARSON and LORD SALMON concurred.

NOTE

In a number of cases decided prior to *Ebrahimi v Westbourne Galleries Ltd* it had been held that the provisions of the articles or memorandum were of importance in determining whether it was just and equitable to make a winding-up order and, in particular, that the bona fide exercise by directors or majority shareholders of powers expressly conferred on them by the corporate constitution or by the Act was something of which a minority shareholder could not complain. In the best known of these cases, *Re Cuthbert Cooper & Sons Ltd* [1937] Ch 392, [1937] 2 All ER 466, Simonds J had declined to order a winding up where the directors of a family company had used the powers conferred upon them by the articles to prevent their younger brothers from becoming registered as holders of the shares left to them by their father in his will. This decision was overruled by the House of Lords in the *Westbourne Galleries* case.

In other cases, it has been held proper in exercising the 'just and equitable' jurisdiction to have regard to 'the settled and accepted course of conduct between the parties, whether or not cast into the mould of a contract', as well as to the articles

5 (1853) 10 Hare 493.

themselves. These words come from the judgment of Megarry J in *Re Fildes Bros Ltd* [1970] 1 All ER 923, [1970] 1 WLR 592. The two brothers concerned had followed a practice of sharing the profits made by the two butchery companies which were jointly owned, but separately controlled, by them. It was held that the 'settled and accepted course of conduct' between the brothers did not go so far as to require the one brother to find employment in his company for the other after the latter's business had failed, and that it was not 'just and equitable' grounds for a winding-up order to refuse to look after the unsuccessful brother in this way. (We may compare this case with the similar ruling of Lord Grantchester QC in *Re a Company* (above, p 504) in relation to a s 459 petition.)

Paradoxically, in one case decided since the *Westbourne Galleries* decision, *Re A & BC Chewing Gum Ltd* [1975] 1 All ER 1017, [1975] 1 WLR 579, the judge claimed to be applying the 'equitable considerations' which were stressed in *Westbourne,* when he was in reality enforcing the strict *legal* rights of the petitioner, as set out in a shareholders' agreement. This agreement provided that the petitioner, an outside corporate investor who had put up one-third of the share capital, should enjoy a fifty-fifty say in management despite its minority shareholding. The decision has attracted criticism (see, e g Mrs Womack in [1975] CLJ 209) on the ground that a direct remedy to enforce the contract by injunction was available, and this would not have had the same catastrophic consequences for the business as a winding-up order.

In *Bentley-Stevens v Jones* [1974] 2 All ER 653, [1974] 1 WLR 638 the shareholders had voted to remove the plaintiff from the board, which meant in effect that he was to be excluded from participation in management. He sought an injunction claiming that he was a quasi-partner and that, on the authority of *Ebrahimi v Westbourne Galleries Ltd,* the majority had no right to exclude him. But Plowman J said: 'there is nothing in that case which suggests that the plaintiff is entitled to an injunction to interfere with the defendant company's right to remove him from its board. What it does decide is that if the plaintiff is removed under a power valid in law then he may, in appropriate circumstances, be entitled to a winding-up order on the just and equitable ground.' This suggests that the 'equitable' principle of *Ebrahimi* should be confined to the statutory context of s 122. However, in *Clemens v Clemens Bros Ltd* (**88**) and in *Pennell Securities Ltd v Venida Investments Ltd* (above, p 287) courts of first instance have applied Lord Wilberforce's judgment to decisions made while a company was a going concern, without discussing the question of its appropriateness.

Re Zinotty Properties Ltd [1984] 3 All ER 754, [1984] 1 WLR 1249 is a recent illustration of a successful petition based on the breakdown of mutual trust and confidence. A property company had been formed between Brown and Perry to develop a particular site. The running of the company had been left largely in the hands of Perry and a business associate of his. Brown complained that (i) he had never been appointed a director as he had expected, (ii) the company had not been dissolved on completion of the development, as he had assumed it would be, but had lent cash, interest-free and without security, to other ventures in which Brown had no interest, (iii) the company had not kept proper accounts or held meetings, and (iv) certain unexplained payments needed investigation. Mervyn Davies J ruled that it was appropriate to make a compulsory winding-up order.

Many of the earlier cases in which a winding-up order was made on the 'just and equitable' ground (e g *Loch v John Blackwood Ltd* (**283**)) would now be more appropriately made the subject of proceedings under s 459 (discussed above, pp 495 ff). But ironically, since this remedy is available only where the petitioner can show that he has suffered unfair prejudice qua member—a limitation which does not apply in the case of s 122(1)(g)—the more versatile solution offered by s 459 may not be available to a large number of complainants in quasi-partnership situations. (See, however, the remarks of Vinelott J in *Re a Company,* quoted above, pp 504–505.)

A winding-up order will be refused if a petition is brought for an extraneous or improper purpose.

285 Re Surrey Garden Village Trust Ltd [1965] 1 WLR 974, [1964] 3 All ER 962 (Chancery Division)

Petitions were brought for the winding up of two Industrial and Provident Societies which had been formed to further the interests of their members as owners and occupiers of what were originally agricultural smallholdings near Croydon, and to preserve the rural character of the area. The petitioners were members, not commanding a majority vote, who wished to sell their land at a considerable profit for development by commercial builders ('Wates'). They claimed that it was just and equitable to wind the societies up, alleging, inter alia, that there was a justifiable lack of confidence in the management, and that the societies' objectives were no longer being carried out. The court refused an order because the petitioners' real purpose, as stated above, was extraneous to the interests of the members as such.

PLOWMAN J: It is obvious to me that the real object of the petitions was to remove an additional obstacle to the sales to Wates. I am not, of course, concerned with any question of planning permission or of the modification or removal of the restrictive covenants which affect the land; but the continued existence of the societies threatens the success of Wates' applications in regard to those matters, in that the management committee of both societies feel it their duty, in the interests of the societies, to oppose those applications.

This disappearance would therefore facilitate Wates' plans by destroying a source of opposition and, incidentally, by destroying the very covenantees themselves.

The Wates faction [i e the members who wished to sell their properties to Wates] shaped its policy accordingly. At no time has it been able to command a sufficient majority to enable it to appeal with any chance of success to the domestic forum of either society in order to obtain an alteration of the rules, or the dismissal of the management committee, or the passing of a resolution for winding up, or the necessary number of signatures to an instrument of dissolution. It has, therefore, adopted a different strategy. Being unable to win a pitched battle, it has sought to infiltrate the enemy lines. [His Lordship stated the facts relating to the struggles of the 'Wates faction' to gain control of the societies and continued:] In my judgment both these petitions have been brought simply and solely for the purpose of removing an obstacle in the way of the petitioners and others disposing of their holdings at inflated prices, and not for any purpose which is relevant to the interests of the members of the societies as members. It is natural and understandable that the petitioners should wish to exploit the gold mine in the possession of which they find themselves, but I see no reason why the court should assist them to achieve that object at the expense of their fellow members to whom the continued existence of the societies represents an advantage which they are unwilling to give up. I go further and say that in my judgment it is oppressive and an abuse of the process of the court for shareholders to make use of a winding-up petition for the purpose of seeking to facilitate the achievement of a purely sectional and extraneous object which, as I say, has no relevance to the interests of the members as such ...

NOTE

In *Re J E Cade & Son Ltd* [1991] BCC 360, a minority shareholder owned the freehold of a farm which had been occupied under licence by the company for some years. He sought a winding-up order on the 'just and equitable' ground or, alternatively, relief under CA 1985, s 459; but the court struck out his petition because his real object in bringing the proceedings was not to protect his interests as a member but to secure possession of the farm.

The court has inherent jurisdiction to strike out a petition for winding up which is bound to fail, and to grant an injunction restraining the presentation of such a petition.

286 Charles Forte Investments Ltd v Amanda [1964] Ch 240, [1963] 2 All ER 940 (Court of Appeal)

The directors of the plaintiff company had under the articles an absolute discretion to decline to register any transfer of shares without giving reasons. The respondent Amanda, who had formerly been employed by the company, submitted to the board three transfers covering his holding of 10,000 shares in the company, but registration was refused. He then wrote threatening that unless a transfer of his shares was registered he would present a winding-up petition on the ground that the directors' refusal constituted an abuse of their fiduciary powers. The company countered by moving for an injunction to restrain him from presenting the threatened petition, and the court, reversing Pennycuick J, held that this was justified.

WILLMER LJ: The plaintiffs' case can, I think, be summarised under three heads. First, it is said that the defendant's petition is not sought to be presented for any proper purpose, but merely as a means of bringing pressure to bear on the directors to reverse the decision at which the board arrived. As such, it is claimed that such a petition would be an abuse of the process of the court. Secondly, it is said that there is no evidence of any facts sufficient to substantiate the allegation made against the directors, which is virtually an allegation of lack of bona fides. On that ground it has been contended that the petition is a petition which is bound to fail, and is therefore an abuse of the process of the court which should be halted in limine. Perhaps that is not quite the correct expression, because I suppose what is really said is that it should never reach the threshold at all. Thirdly, it is said that even if there were evidence to support the allegations put forward, a winding-up petition is not the proper remedy. The proper remedy, if the defendant has any legitimate grievance, would be an action for rectification of the register or a proceeding by way of motion under s 116 of the Companies Act 1948 [CA 1985, s 359]. It is pointed out that if what the defendant wants to do is to have the transfer registered, a winding-up petition will not give him the relief which he seeks. On the other hand, if he brought an action, and assuming he was able to prove his facts, he could possibly get what he seeks, or, alternatively, he could obtain damages for the refusal to register the transfers.

The plaintiffs here invoke the inherent jurisdiction of the court to stay proceedings which are vexatious or an abuse of the process of the court. They do not rely on any of the Rules of the Supreme Court, but solely upon the inherent jurisdiction ...

[In] the present case, as I think, there is good reason to think that the presentation of a winding-up petition, with the consequent necessity for advertisement, might cause irreparable damage. There can, I think, be no doubt that the allegations in the proposed petition amount to a very grave attack upon the directors of the plaintiff company, who are the same people as the directors of Forte's (Holdings) Ltd. The publicising of this attack could therefore, have a damaging effect on Forte's (Holdings) Ltd, with the possibility of damage (possibly irreparable) to quite innocent shareholders in that company.

In those circumstances, I do not doubt that this would be a proper case for the exercise of the inherent jurisdiction of the court, if the plaintiffs can otherwise make good their claim that this is a petition which is bound to fail and amounts in the circumstances to an abuse of the process of the court.

[His Lordship examined the evidence and held that it was inadequate to discharge the heavy onus of showing that the directors' refusal to act was not bona fide. He continued:]

But even if I am wrong about that, it seems to me that there is another ground on which it can be said that this petition is bound to fail; for it seems to me that this is a case in which a winding up petition is not the proper remedy. I say that on the assumption that I am wrong in everything else I have said so far, and on the assumption that there is sufficient evidence before the court to justify some at least of the allegations made by the defendant. Even assuming that, I venture to think that a winding up petition is not a proper remedy ... It is to be observed that by bringing an action the defendant, if he has a good case, could not only more easily obtain what he is really after, but he could do so without incurring the risk of inflicting damage, possibly irreparable damage, on the company, and possibly also on other innocent shareholders.

In those circumstances, it seems to me that that is an additional reason for holding that the injunction which is sought ought to be granted ...

DANCKWERTS LJ and CROSS J delivered concurring judgments.

3. *Position of the liquidator*

The rules governing the functions, powers and duties of a liquidator are partly set out in the Insolvency Act 1986 and Insolvency Rules 1986, and partly established by the case-law. The Act now makes it obligatory for a liquidator to be a qualified insolvency practitioner (s 230(3)). A liquidator acts in the name of the company (which continues to have a separate corporate personality) and not in his own name, although sometimes, exceptionally, an order of the court is sought vesting all or part of the corporate property in the liquidator's name (IA 1986, s 145): this might be necessary, for example, to deal with the local assets of a foreign company which had already been dissolved in its home jurisdiction. Certain statutory powers of a liquidator are conferred by IA 1986, ss 165 ff and Sch 4. These, or rather the circumstances in which they may be exercised, vary slightly depending on the type of winding up. Other powers (e g to make calls upon the contributories) are given by the Act in the first place to the court but are then delegated to the liquidator by the rules, pursuant to s 160.

Although a liquidator acts in the company's name and not in his own name, he can sometimes incur personal liability, e g where he institutes proceedings and the costs exceed the amount of the company's assets: *Re Wilson Lovatt & Sons Ltd* [1977] 1 All ER 274. A liquidator may also be liable to the company in misfeasance proceedings under IA 1986, s 212, e g where he wrongly admits a claim by an alleged creditor: *Re Home and Colonial Insurance Co* [1930] 1 Ch 102; and he may be sued for breach of statutory duty, after the dissolution of the company, if he has not distributed the company's assets properly among the persons entitled: *Pulsford v Devenish* [1903] 2 Ch 625.

A liquidator is not in the position of a trustee for the individual creditors or contributories.

287 Knowles v Scott [1891] 1 Ch 717 (Chancery Division)

[The facts appear from the judgment.]

ROMER J: In my judgment this action fails. It is an action brought against the liquidator of a company which was being wound up voluntarily for damages arising from delay in delivering up to the plaintiff, as a shareholder, his proportion of cash and shares forming part of the company's assets, this delay being attributed to the negligence of the liquidator.

It is admitted that there is no mala fides on the part of the liquidator; that it is not a case of dishonesty or fraud, or of the liquidator knowingly and wilfully, in other words mala fide, declining to give to the plaintiff his proportion of the assets. At most it is only a case of a liquidator making an honest mistake in judgment ... The action is certainly novel; it is admitted that there is no precedent for it. The ground on which it is based is, that at law the defendant is a trustee for the plaintiff of his proportion of the assets in the liquidator's hands, and that the liquidator is liable in his capacity of trustee for negligence. In my judgment the liquidator is not a trustee in the strict sense, with such a liability affecting his position as has been contended for by the plaintiff. The consequences would be very serious if such a doctrine were to be upheld. If a liquidator were held to be a trustee for each creditor or contributory of the company, his liability would indeed be onerous, and would render the position of a liquidator one which few persons would care to occupy.

In support of the plaintiffs' contention reference has been made to the dicta of distinguished judges in various cases, which describe a liquidator as a trustee—or as holding assets of his company in trust. No doubt in a sense and for certain purposes a liquidator may fairly enough be described as a trustee; but he is not in my judgment, in the strict sense in which the plaintiff must use the term to enable him to succeed in this action, a trustee ...

In my view a voluntary liquidator is more rightly described as the agent of the company—an agent who has, no doubt, cast upon him by statute and otherwise special duties, amongst which may be mentioned the duty of applying the company's assets in paying creditors and distributing the surplus among the shareholders. Lord Justice James referred to this as being his true position in the case of *Re Anglo-Moravian Hungarian Junction Rly Co.*[6] If this be the true position of a liquidator, and I think at any rate agency more

6 (1875) 1 Ch D 130 at 133.

nearly defines his true position than trusteeship, it is clear that he could not as agent be sued by a third party for negligence apart from misfeasance or personal misconduct.

QUESTION

Would it be more in keeping with modern usage to describe the liquidator as an 'organ' of the company rather than an agent?

A liquidator is not as such personally liable on contracts made by him on the company's behalf.

288 Stead, Hazel & Co v Cooper [1933] 1 KB 840 (King's Bench Division)

The plaintiffs had agreed to sell cotton to Trent Mill (1920) Ltd, to be delivered by monthly instalments. During the currency of the contract, the company went into liquidation; the liquidator did not disclaim the contract but confirmed it on varied terms. When the company failed to accept delivery of the final instalment, the plaintiffs brought this action against the liquidator personally. It was held that on the ordinary principles of agency he was not liable.

LAWRENCE J: It is contended on behalf of the plaintiffs that the liquidator is personally liable, first, because he wrote the letter of 20 June 1930 by which it is said he undertook personal liability, and secondly, because he had the right to disclaim the contract under s 267 of the Companies Act 1929 [IA 1986, ss 178 ff], and is therefore personally liable on any contract which he has not disclaimed.

In my opinion, neither of these contentions is sound, and I hold that the defendant is not personally liable.

Mr Winstanley, a partner in the plaintiff firm, was the only witness called, but his evidence did not carry the case any further than the correspondence, since he never saw the defendant; and it is evident from the documents, and was admitted by Mr Winstanley, that until 14 March 1932 no claim against the defendant personally was ever suggested, and that all the delivery notes, invoices, and receipts were sent to the company or to the defendant as liquidator. I see nothing in the letter of 20 June 1930 to suggest that the defendant intended to undertake a personal liability, and even if that letter and its acceptance by the plaintiffs constituted a new contract it was, in my judgment, a contract which purported to be a contract by the liquidator as agent for the company.

But it is contended that a liquidator appointed by the court is in exactly the same position as a receiver and manager appointed by the court, and that there is a presumption that when he performs a contract without disclaimer, or makes a new contract, he does so in his personal capacity, and that this presumption is not rebutted by his describing himself as liquidator. Reliance was principally placed upon *Burt, Boulton & Haywood v Bull*,[7] where it was held on the facts that a receiver and manager appointed by the court who had given an order for goods in his own name, but describing himself

7 [1895] 1 QB 276.

as receiver and manager, was personally liable, because a receiver and manager of a company is not the agent of the company,[8] and the words 'receiver and manager' would therefore not suggest that the receiver was contracting as agent for the company.

In my view, the position of a liquidator appointed by the court is not the same as that of a receiver and manager appointed by the court. A liquidator is the agent of the company: *Re Anglo-Moravian Hungarian Junction Rly Co, ex p Watkin*,[9] a receiver is not: *Burt, Boulton & Hayward v Bull*. It is true that both are appointed and can be dismissed by the court, and both control the assets of the company and may have to carry out the contracts of the company, but the liquidator acts for and in the interests of the company; whereas the receiver and manager acts for and in the interests of the debenture holders and not for the company. I think, therefore, that the description 'liquidator' has not the same significance as the description 'receiver and manager', and I find that the defendant did not purport to contract on his own behalf, nor did the plaintiffs give him credit on his own behalf . . .

4. Conduct of the liquidation

The way in which a liquidation is conducted can be described in general terms, but there are differences in detail between compulsory and voluntary liquidations and between a members' and a creditors' voluntary winding up which can be discovered only from a study of the 1986 Act and the Insolvency Rules.

For many statutory purposes,[10] a winding up takes effect from its 'commencement', which may involve some back-dating. Section 86 of IA 1986 provides that a voluntary winding up is deemed to commence at the time of the passing of the resolution for winding up. In the case of a compulsory winding up, the liquidation is deemed to commence at the time of the presentation of the petition (and not the making of the order itself), but if the company is already in voluntary liquidation when the petition is presented, the relevant time is when the winding-up resolution was passed (s 129). These provisions have important consequences, for from the date of commencement:

(a) dispositions of property by the company (in a compulsory winding up) are avoided, unless the court otherwise orders (s 127);
(b) attachments, distress and execution (in a compulsory winding up) which have not been completed are void (s 128);[11]
(c) transfers of shares are avoided (ss 88, 127);
(d) some categories of creditor are given preferential rights in regard to debts

---

8 The reference is to a receiver and manager appointed by the court. A receiver appointed out of court is normally declared to be the agent of the company by the terms of the debenture under which he is appointed; and such an agency is expressly deemed to exist by statute in the case of an administrative receiver: IA 1986, s 44: see above, p 547.

9 (1875) 1 Ch D 130 at 133–134.

10 But not all: for example, the value of a debt is reckoned for the purpose of proof at the date when the company goes into liquidation: *Re Lines Bros Ltd* [1983] Ch 1, [1982] 2 All ER 183, CA; and the periods of time prescribed by the Limitation Act 1980 cease to run against the company's creditors (other than the petitioning creditor himself) on the making of the winding-up order: *Re Cases of Taff's Well Ltd* [1992] Ch 179, [1991] 3 WLR 731.

11 In any case, the rights of creditors in levying execution, etc are restricted by ss 183–184 in every type of winding up.

incurred within prescribed periods before that date, e g up to twelve months' taxes and four months' salaries and wages (ss 175, 386 and Sch 6);[12]

(e) transactions entered into within prescribed periods before that date may be invalidated as having been 'at an undervalue' or 'preferences' (ss 238–241: see *Re M C Bacon Ltd* (**290**), below);

(f) a floating charge created within twelve months (or, in some cases, two years) of that date may be invalidated (s 245: see above, p 403).[13]

It is not easy to reconcile these 'back-dating' provisions with those of CA 1985, s 42, which aims to protect third parties without actual notice until 15 days after the 'official notification' of the making of a winding-up order or, in a voluntary liquidation, of the appointment of a liquidator.[14] It is plain that the full implications of this statutory misfit (which are the result of implementing the First EEC Directive) have not been fully thought through by our legislators. One suggestion, made by *Gore-Browne,* is that when the back-dating provisions operate 'the company' is not 'relying' on the making of a winding-up order or on the appointment of a liquidator.

The effect of the statutory provisions referred to in paras (a), (b), (e) and (f) above is to allow the liquidator to 'claw back' property which has been transferred away by the company and to avoid some transactions which it has entered into in the period immediately preceding the winding up, thus increasing the assets available for distribution to the creditors generally. The Insolvency Act 1986 has in various ways extended the scope of these provisions by comparison with the previous law. First, references to fraud and dishonesty have been removed from the definitions, so that a wider range of activities are included: 'fraudulent conveyances' have become 'transactions at an undervalue' (s 238), and 'fraudulent preferences' have become 'preferences' (s 239). Secondly, the new rules operate more strictly where the other party to the transaction is a person 'connected with' the company (e g a director or a substantial shareholder, or a close relative of such a person, or another company in the same group: for the full definition, see ss 249, 435). Where a connected person is involved, the time limits may be extended (ss 240(1)(a), 245(3)(a)), the onus of proof may be reversed (ss 239(6), 249(2)), or a possible defence disallowed (s 245(4)). It goes without saying that a very careful reading of the Act is necessary to discover exactly which rules are applicable in a particular case.

The Insolvency Act 1986 (in addition to imposing criminal liability for various forms of misconduct which may be revealed in the course of a winding up) contains a number of provisions under which the directors of a company in liquidation and, in some cases, others may be made liable to account, pay compensation or contribute to the assets of the company in the hands of the liquidator:

(1) IA 1986, s 212 provides a summary remedy for establishing accountability or assessing damages against delinquent officers. This is a purely procedural provision, which creates no new liabilities but merely provides a simpler mechanism for the recovery of property or compensation in a winding up. The 1986 Act does, however, enlarge the scope of the section by including

---

12 See below, p 589.
13 See further D D Prentice, 'The Effect of Insolvency on Pre-Liquidation Transactions' in *Company Law in Change* (1987), p 69.
14 See above, p 232.

certain office-holders, e g an administrative receiver, who were not caught by the section as previously worded, and by extending liability to include a 'breach of any fiduciary or other duty', which is plainly wider than the former 'breach of trust'. Earlier decisions such as *Re B Johnson & Co (Builders) Ltd* [1955] Ch 634, [1955] 2 All ER 775, which held that the provision did not cover claims based on negligence, are probably now no longer authoritative.

(2) If, in the course of a winding up, it is found that any business of the company has been carried on with intent to defraud creditors or for any other fraudulent purpose ('fraudulent trading'), the court may order those who were knowingly parties to this misconduct to contribute to the company's assets (s 213). For the purposes of this provision, actual dishonesty must be proved (*Re Patrick & Lyon Ltd* [1933] Ch 786).

(3) A former director (or 'shadow director') of a company in liquidation may also be ordered to contribute personally to the assets in the hands of the liquidator if there have been circumstances constituting 'wrongful trading' (a phrase used in the side-note, but not the text, of the Act): s 214. The complex provisions of this section need careful study. Prerequisites for liability are that (i) the person has been a director (or 'shadow director') and (ii) the company has gone into insolvent liquidation. The person must have known, or should have concluded, that there was no reasonable prospect that the company would avoid going into insolvent liquidation; but he can avoid liability if the court is satisfied that he 'took every step with a view to minimising the potential loss to the company's creditors' that he ought to have taken. Although described as 'wrongful trading', as noted above, the possible scope of this section is very wide indeed. It can cover passive inactivity just as much as positive wrongdoing; there need be no actual 'trading', but conduct such as allowing the payment of unjustified remuneration or dividends could be caught; and (as s 214(4) makes clear, and the *Produce Marketing* case cited below (**291**) confirms) the director's behaviour is to be judged by objective as well as subjective standards.

Cases like *Re Patrick & Lyon Ltd,* which were decided before the 1986 legislation, will continue to be relevant to a charge of *fraudulent* trading (s 213); but the introduction of the concept of 'wrongful' trading, which can lead to the same consequences with a much lighter burden of proof, will surely mean that s 213 will be very rarely invoked in the future.

Money that is ordered to be paid under ss 213 and 214 goes into the general assets of the company in the hands of the liquidator and is not awardable directly to those affected by the fraudulent or wrongful trading. This avoids the danger that a particular creditor might bring pressure on the directors of a company that was close to insolvency in order to induce them to pay him off ahead of the other creditors.

The Company Directors Disqualification Act 1986 also authorises the court to make a disqualification order (above, p 310) against anyone held liable for fraudulent or wrongful trading.

The Cork Committee, on whose recommendation the concept of wrongful trading was introduced, were concerned also with another situation, popularly referred to as 'the phoenix syndrome', where a person who has been trading through the medium of a company allows it to go into insolvent liquidation and then forms a new company, sometimes with a similar name, and carries on trading much as before. He may even use assets in the new business which he has bought at a knock-down price in the liquidation of the old company, so that the old company's creditors subsidise his fresh start.

The Committee (1982, Cmnd 8558, para 1827) recommended that such a person should be personally liable for the second company's debts if it goes into insolvent liquidation within three years. However, instead of this, the Insolvency Act focuses on the re-use of the name of a defunct company by a person who was one of its directors. This is made a criminal offence (s 216) and the director, without the need of any court order, is made personally liable for the debts of the new business, whether or not it becomes insolvent.

Another problem discussed by Sir Kenneth Cork and his committee was that of 'group trading'—the 'runt of the litter' situation criticised by Templeman LJ in *Re Southard & Co Ltd* (above, p 62). Is it in keeping with commercial morality that a parent company can allow one of its subsidiaries to decline into insolvency while the rest of the group prospers? A fortiori, for the debts owed by the subsidiary to other members of the group to rank equally with those of outside creditors—or even, if secured, ahead of them? The Committee recommended (para 1963) that the law should be changed so that inter-company indebtedness could in some circumstances be postponed to the claims of outside creditors; but it hesitated to follow the bolder reform made in New Zealand, which empowers the court to order one company in a group to pay the debt of another in the insolvent winding up of the latter. The Insolvency Act may have met these problems in part by its 'wrongful trading' provisions and by its measures to extend the circumstances in which floating charges given to 'connected persons' can be invalidated (companies within the same group are 'connected persons').[15]

The cases which follow illustrate the operation in practice of some of the provisions of IA 1986 that are discussed above.

289 Re Gray's Inn Construction Co Ltd [1980] 1 All ER 814, [1980] 1 WLR 711 (Court of Appeal)

The company, which carried on a building business, was ordered to be wound up by the court. Between the time when the petition was presented and the date of the order its bank had allowed it to continue to operate its account. During this period it had traded unprofitably. The Court of Appeal held that both the amounts credited to the company's account and those debited to it constituted 'dispositions' of the company's property and, in the exercise of its discretion under IA 1986, s 127, declined to validate most of these banking transactions. In the course of his judgment, Buckley LJ enunciated some principles for the guidance of courts in relation to the jurisdiction under s 127.

BUCKLEY LJ: It is a basic concept of our law governing the liquidation of insolvent estates, whether in bankruptcy or under the Companies Acts, that the free assets of the insolvent at the commencement of the liquidation shall be distributed rateably amongst the insolvent's unsecured creditors as at that date. ... In a company's compulsory winding up [this] is achieved by section 227 [of CA 1948, equivalent to IA 1986, s 127]. There may be occasions, however, when it would be beneficial, not only for the company but also for its unsecured creditors, that the company should be enabled to dispose of some of its property during the period after the petition has been presented but before a winding-up order has been made. An obvious example is if the

15 See above, p 403.

company has an opportunity by acting speedily to dispose of some piece of property at an exceptionally good price. Many applications for validation under the section relate to specific transactions of this kind or analogous kinds. It may sometimes be beneficial to the company and its creditors that the company should be enabled to complete a particular contract or project, or to continue to carry on its business generally in its ordinary course with a view to a sale of the business as a going concern. In any such case the court has power under section 227 of the Companies Act 1948 to validate the particular transaction, or the completion of the particular contract or project, or the continuance of the company's business in its ordinary course, as the case may be. In considering whether to make a validating order the court must always, in my opinion, do its best to ensure that the interests of the unsecured creditors will not be prejudiced. Where the application relates to a specific transaction this may be susceptible of positive proof. In a case of completion of a contract or project the proof may perhaps be less positive but nevertheless be cogent enough to satisfy the court that in the interests of the creditors the company should be enabled to proceed, or at any rate that proceeding in the manner proposed would not prejudice them in any respect. The desirability of the company being enabled to carry on its business generally is likely to be more speculative and will be likely to depend on whether a sale of the business as a going concern will probably be more beneficial than a break-up realisation of the company's assets. In each case, I think, the court must necessarily carry out a balancing exercise ... Each case must depend upon its own particular facts.

Since the policy of the law is to procure so far as practicable rateable payments of the unsecured creditors' claims, it is, in my opinion, clear that the court should not validate any transaction or series of transactions which might result in one or more pre-liquidation creditors being paid in full at the expense of other creditors, who will only receive a dividend, in the absence of special circumstances making such a course desirable in the interests of the unsecured creditors as a body. If, for example, it were in the interests of the creditors generally that the company's business should be carried on, and this could only be achieved by paying for goods already supplied to the company when the petition is presented but not yet paid for, the court might think fit in the exercise of its discretion to validate payment for those goods. ...

It may not always be feasible, or desirable, that a validating order should be sought before the transaction in question is carried out. The parties may be unaware at the time when the transaction is entered into that a petition has been presented; or the need for speedy action may be such as to preclude an anticipatory application; or the beneficial character of the transaction may be so obvious that there is no real prospect of a liquidator seeking to set it aside, so that an application to the court would waste time, money and effort. But in any case in which the transaction is carried out without an anticipatory validating order the disponee is at risk of the court declining to validate the transaction. It follows, in my view, that the parties when entering into the transaction, if they are aware that it is liable to be invalidated by the section, should have in mind the sort of considerations which would influence the court's decision.

A disposition carried out in good faith in the ordinary course of business at a time when the parties are unaware that a petition has been presented may, it seems, normally be validated by the court ... unless there is any ground for thinking that the transaction may involve an attempt to prefer the disponee, in which case the transaction would probably not be validated. In a number of cases reference has been made to the relevance of the policy of ensuring rateable distribution of the assets ...

But although that policy might disincline the court to ratify any transaction which involved preferring a pre-liquidation creditor, it has no relevance to a transaction which is entirely post-liquidation, as for instance a sale of an asset at its full market value after presentation of a petition. Such a transaction involves no dissipation of the company's assets, for it does not reduce the value of those assets. It cannot harm the creditors and there would seem to be no reason why the court should not in the exercise of its discretion validate it. A fortiori, the court would be inclined to validate a transaction which would increase, or has increased, the value of the company's assets, or which would preserve, or has preserved, the value of the company's assets from harm which would result from the company's business being paralysed ...

GOFF LJ and SIR DAVID CAIRNS concurred.

290 Re MC Bacon Ltd [1990] BCLC 324 (Chancery Division)

The company, which carried on business as a bacon importer and wholesaler, had been profitable until it lost its principal customer. It continued trading on a reduced scale for a time, but eventually had to go into liquidation. This action was brought to challenge a debenture which had been given to its bank during this latter period, at a time when it was actually or virtually insolvent and could not have continued without the bank's support. Millett J held that the debenture was not liable to be struck down either (a) as a preference under IA 1986, s 239, since the directors in granting it had not been motivated by a desire to prefer the bank but only by a desire to avoid the calling in of the overdraft and their wish to continue trading, or (b) as a transaction at an undervalue under s 238 because the giving of the security had neither depleted the company's assets nor diminished their value.

MILLETT J ...

Voidable preference

So far as I am aware, this is the first case under the section and its meaning has been the subject of some debate before me. I shall therefore attempt to provide some guidance.

The section replaces s 44(1) of the Bankruptcy Act 1914, which in certain circumstances deemed fraudulent and avoided payments made and other transactions entered into in favour of a creditor 'with a view of giving such creditor ... a preference over the other creditors'. Section 44(1) and its predecessors had been construed by the courts as requiring the person seeking to avoid the payment or other transaction to establish that it had been made 'with the dominant intention to prefer' the creditor.

Section 44(1) has been replaced and its language has been entirely recast. Every single word of significance, whether in the form of statutory definition or in its judicial exposition, has been jettisoned. 'View', 'dominant', 'intention' and even 'to prefer' have all been discarded. These are replaced by 'influenced', 'desire', and 'to produce in relation to that person the effect mentioned in sub-s (4)(*b*)'.

I therefore emphatically protest against the citation of cases decided under the old law. They cannot be of any assistance when the language of the statute has been so completely and deliberately changed. It may be that many of the cases which will come before the courts in future will be decided in the same way that they would have been decided under the old law. That may be so, but the grounds of decision will be different. What the court has to do is to interpret the language of the statute and apply it. It will no longer inquire whether there was 'a dominant intention to prefer' the creditor, but whether the company's decision was 'influenced by a desire to produce the effect mentioned in sub-s (4)(*b*)'.

This is a completely different test. It involves at least two radical departures from the old law. It is no longer necessary to establish a *dominant* intention to prefer. It is sufficient that the decision was *influenced* by the requisite desire. That is the first change. The second is that it is no longer sufficient to establish an *intention* to prefer. There must be a *desire* to produce the effect mentioned in the subsection.

This second change is made necessary by the first, for without it it would be virtually impossible to uphold the validity of a security taken in exchange for the injection of fresh funds into a company in financial difficulties. A man is taken to intend the necessary consequences of his actions, so that an intention to grant a security to a creditor necessarily involves an intention to prefer that creditor in the event of insolvency. The need to establish that such intention was dominant was essential under the old law to prevent perfectly proper transactions from being struck down. With the abolition of that requirement intention could not remain the relevant test. Desire has been substituted. That is a very different matter. Intention is objective, desire is subjective. A man can choose the lesser of two evils without desiring either.

It is not, however, sufficient to establish a desire to make the payment or grant the security which it is sought to avoid. There must have been a desire to produce the effect mentioned in the subsection, that is to say, to improve the creditor's position in the event of an insolvent liquidation. A man is not to be taken as *desiring* all the necessary consequences of his actions. Some consequences may be of advantage to him and be desired by him; others may not affect him and be matters of indifference to him; while still others may be positively disadvantageous to him and not be desired by him, but be regarded by him as the unavoidable price of obtaining the desired advantages. It will still be possible to provide assistance to a company in financial difficulties provided that the company is actuated only by proper commercial considerations. Under the new regime a transaction will not be set aside as a voidable preference unless the company positively wished to improve the creditor's position in the event of its own insolvent liquidation.

There is, of course, no need for there to be direct evidence of the requisite desire. Its existence may be inferred from the circumstances of the case just as the dominant intention could be inferred under the old law. But the mere presence of the requisite desire will not be sufficient by itself. It must have influenced the decision to enter into the transaction. It was submitted on behalf of the bank that it must have been the factor which 'tipped the scales'. I disagree. That is not what sub-s (5) says; it requires only that the desire should have influenced the decision. That requirement is satisfied if it was one of the factors which operated on the minds of those who made the decision. It need not have been the only factor or even the decisive one. In my judgment, it is not necessary to prove that, if the requisite desire had not been present, the company would not have entered into the transaction. That would be too high a test.

It was also submitted that the relevant time was the time when the debenture was created. That cannot be right. The relevant time was the time when the decision to grant it was made. In the present case that is not known with certainty. ... But it does not matter. If the requisite desire was operating at all, it was operating throughout.

[His Lordship ruled that the directors had been motivated by the desire to continue trading and not by a desire to give the bank a preference in the event of a liquidation. He continued:]

Transactions at an undervalue

Section 238 of the 1986 Act is concerned with the depletion of a company's assets by transactions at an undervalue. [His Lordship read s 238(4) and continued:]

The granting of the debenture was not a gift, nor was it without consideration. The consideration consisted of the bank's forbearance from calling in the overdraft and its honouring of cheques and making of fresh advances to the company during the continuance of the facility. The applicant relies therefore on para (*b*).

To come within that paragraph the transaction must be (i) entered into by the company; (ii) for a consideration; (iii) the value of which measured in money or money's worth; (iv) is significantly less than the value; (v) also measured in money or money's worth; (vi) of the consideration provided by the company. It requires a comparison to be made between the value obtained by the company for the transaction and the value of consideration provided by the company. Both values must be measurable in money or money's worth and both must be considered from the company's point of view.

In my judgment, the applicant's claim to characterise the granting of the bank's debenture as a transaction at an undervalue is misconceived. The mere creation of a security over a company's assets does not deplete them and does not come within the paragraph. By charging its assets the company appropriates them to meet the liabilities due to the secured creditor and adversely affects the rights of other creditors in the event of insolvency. But it does not deplete its assets or diminish their value. It retains the right to redeem and the right to sell or remortgage the charged assets. All it loses is the ability to apply the proceeds otherwise than in satisfaction of the secured debt. That is not something capable of valuation in monetary terms and is not customarily disposed of for value.

In the present case the company did not suffer that loss by reason of the grant of the debenture. Once the bank had demanded a debenture the company could not have sold or charged its assets without applying the proceeds in reduction of the overdraft; had it attempted to do so, the bank would at once have called in the overdraft. By granting the debenture the company parted with nothing of value, and the value of the consideration which it received in return was incapable of being measured in money or money's worth.

Counsel for the applicant (Mr Vos) submitted that the consideration which the company received was, with hindsight, of no value. It merely gained time and with it the opportunity to lose more money. But he could not and did not claim that the company ought to have received a fee or other capital sum in return for the debenture. That gives the game away. The applicant's real complaint is not that the company entered into the transaction at an undervalue but that it entered into it at all.

In my judgment, the transaction does not fall within sub-s (4) . . .

291 Re Produce Marketing Consortium Ltd (No 2) [1989] BCLC 520 (Chancery Division)

This was the first reported case decided under IA 1986, s 214 ('wrongful trading'). The two directors, David and Murphy, had continued to run the company's fruit importing business when they ought to have known that there was no prospect of avoiding insolvent liquidation. Knox J, in holding them liable for wrongful trading, emphasised that their conduct was to be judged, in part, by the objective standards laid down by s 214—that is, by more exacting criteria then those of the common law (see above, pp 296ff).

KNOX J. . .

Section 214 of the 1986 Act, which re-enacts s 15 of the Insolvency Act 1985, reads, so far as is material, as follows:

> (1) Subject to subsection (3) below, if in the course of the winding up of a company it appears that subsection (2) of this section applies in relation to a person who is or has been a director of the company, the court, on the application of the liquidator, may declare that the person is to be liable to make such contribution (if any) to the company's assets as the court thinks proper.
>
> (2) This subsection applies in relation to a person if—(a) the company has gone into insolvent liquidation, (b) at some time before the commencement of the winding up of the company, that person knew or ought to have concluded that there was no reasonable prospect that the company would avoid going into insolvent liquidation, and (c) that person was a director of the company at that time; but the court shall not make a declaration under this section in any case where the time mentioned in paragraph (b) above was before 28 April 1986.
>
> (3) The court shall not make a declaration under this section with respect to any person if it is satisfied that after the condition specified in subsection (2) (b) was first satisfied in relation to him that person took every step with a view to minimising the potential loss to the company's creditors as (assuming him to have known that there was no reasonable prospect that the company would avoid going into insolvent liquidation) he ought to have taken.
>
> (4) For the purposes of subsections (2) and (3), the facts which a director of a company ought to know or ascertain, the conclusions which he ought to reach and the steps which he ought to take are those which would be known or ascertained, or reached or taken, by a reasonably diligent person having both—(a) the general knowledge, skill and experience that may reasonably be expected of a person carrying out the same functions as are carried out by that director in relation to the company, and (b) the general knowledge, skill and experience that that director has.
>
> (5) The reference in subsection (4) to the functions carried out in

relation to a company by a director of the company includes any functions which he does not carry out but which have been entrusted to him . . .

The first question is whether it appears that sub-s (2) applies to Mr David and Mr Murphy. There is no question but that they were directors at all material times and that PMC [the company] has gone into insolvent liquidation. The issue is whether at some time after 27 April 1986 and before 2 October 1987, when it went into insolvent liquidation, they knew or ought to have concluded that there was no reasonable prospect that PMC would avoid going into insolvent liquidation. It was inevitably conceded by counsel for the first respondent that this question has to be answered by the standards postulated by sub-s (4), so that the facts which Mr David and Mr Murphy ought to have known or ascertained and the conclusions that they ought to have reached are not limited to those which they themselves showing reasonable diligence and having the general knowledge, skill and experience which they respectively had, would have known, ascertained or reached but also those that a person with the general knowledge, skill and experience of someone carrying out their functions would have known, ascertained or reached. . . .

The 1986 Act now has two separate provisions; s 213 dealing with fraudulent trading, . . . and s 214 which deals with what the sidenote calls 'wrongful trading'. It is evident that Parliament intended to widen the scope of the legislation under which directors who trade on when the company is insolvent may, in appropriate circumstances, be required to make a contribution to the assets of the company which, in practical terms, means its creditors.

Two steps in particular were taken in the legislative enlargement of the court's jurisdiction. First, the requirement for an intent to defraud and fraudulent purpose was not retained as an essential, and with it goes what Maugham J[16] called 'the need for actual dishonesty involving real moral blame'.

I pause here to observe that at no stage before me has it been suggested that either Mr David or Mr Murphy fell into this category.

The second enlargement is that the test to be applied by the court has become one under which the director in question is to be judged by the standards of what can reasonably be expected of a person fulfilling his functions, and showing reasonable diligence in doing so. I accept the submission of counsel for the first respondent in this connection, that the requirement to have regard to the functions to be carried out by the director in question, in relation to the company in question, involves having regard to the particular company and its business. It follows that the general knowledge, skill and experience postulated will be much less extensive in a small company in a modest way of business, with simple accounting procedures and equipment, than it will be in a large company with sophisticated procedures.

Nevertheless, certain minimum standards are to be assumed to be attained. Notably there is an obligation laid on companies to cause accounting records to be kept which are such as to disclose with reasonable accuracy at any time the financial position of the company at that time: see the Companies Act 1985, s 221(1) and (2)(*a*). In addition directors are required to prepare a profit and loss account for each financial year and a balance sheet as at the end of it: Companies Act 1985, s 227(1) and (3). Directors are also required, in

---

16 [In *Re Patrick & Lyon Ltd* [1933] Ch 786, 790.]

respect of each financial year, to lay before the company in general meeting copies of the accounts of the company for that year and to deliver to the registrar of companies a copy of those accounts, in the case of a private company, within 10 months after the end of the relevant accounting reference period (see the Companies Act 1985, ss 241(1) and (3) and 242(1) and (2)).

As I have already mentioned, the liquidator gave evidence that the accounting records of PMC were adequate for the purposes of its business. The preparation of accounts was woefully late, more especially in relation to those dealing with the year ending 30 September 1985 which should have been laid and delivered by the end of July 1986.

The knowledge to be imputed in testing whether or not directors knew or ought to have concluded that there was no reasonable prospect of the company avoiding insolvent liquidation is not limited to the documentary material actually available at the given time. This appears from s 214(4) which includes a reference to facts which a director of a company ought not only to know but those which he ought to ascertain, a word which does not appear in sub-s (2)(*b*). In my judgment this indicates that there is to be included by way of factual information not only what was actually there but what, given reasonable diligence and an appropriate level of general knowledge, skill and experience, was ascertainable. This leads me to the conclusion in this case that I should assume, for the purposes of applying the test in s 214(2), that the financial results for the year ending 30 September 1985 were known at the end of July 1986 at least to the extent of the size of the deficiency of assets over liabilities.

Mr David and Mr Murphy, although they did not have the accounts in their hands until January 1987, did, I find, know that the previous trading year had been a very bad one. They had a close and intimate knowledge of the business and they had a shrewd idea whether the turnover was up or down. In fact it was badly down in that year to £526,459 and although I have no doubt that they did not know in July 1986 that it was that precise figure, I have no doubt that they had a good rough idea of what it was and in particular that it was well down on the previous year. A major drop in turnover meant almost as night follows day that there was a substantial loss incurred, as indeed there was. That in turn meant again, as surely as night follows day, a substantial increase in the deficit of assets over liabilities.

That deals with their actual knowledge but in addition I have to have regard to what they have to be treated as having known or ascertained and that includes the actual deficit of assets over liabilities of £132,870. ... It was a deficit that, for an indefinite period in the future could not be made good even if the optimistic prognostications of level of turnover entertained by Mr David and Mr Murphy were achieved. ...

Counsel for the first respondent was not able to advance any particular calculation as constituting a basis for concluding that there was a prospect of insolvent liquidation being avoided. He is not to be criticised for that for in my judgment there was none available. Once the loss in the year ending 30 September 1985 was incurred PMC was in irreversible decline, assuming (as I must) that the respondents had no plans for altering the company's business and proposed to go on drawing the level of reasonable remuneration that they were currently receiving. ...

The next question which arises is whether there is a case under s 214(3) for saying that after the end of July 1986 the respondents took every step with a view to minimising the potential loss to the creditors of PMC as, assuming them to have known that there was no reasonable prospect of PMC avoiding insolvent liquidation, they ought to have taken. This clearly has to be answered No, since they went on trading for another year. ...

I am therefore driven to the conclusion that the court's discretion arises under s 214(1). ...

In my judgment the jurisdiction under s 214 is primarily compensatory rather than penal. Prima facie the appropriate amount that a director is declared to be liable to contribute is the amount by which the company's assets can be discerned to have been depleted by the director's conduct which caused the discretion under sub-s (1) to arise. But Parliament has indeed chosen very wide words of discretion and it would be undesirable to seek to spell out limits on that discretion, more especially since this is, so far as counsel were aware, the first case to come to judgment under this section. ...

I take into account the following factors in addition to those set out above, which give rise to the existence of the court's discretion under s 214(1).

This was a case of failure to appreciate what should have been clear rather than a deliberate course of wrongdoing.

There were occasions when positive untruths were stated which cannot just be treated as unwarranted optimism. ...

The most solemn warning given by the auditor in early February 1987 was effectively ignored. ...

The affairs of PMC were conducted during the last seven months of trading in a way which reduced the indebtedness to the bank, to which Mr David had given a guarantee, at the expense of trade creditors. ... The bank is, if not fully, at least substantially secured. If this jurisdiction is to be exercised, as in my judgment it should be in this case, it needs to be exercised in a way which will benefit unsecured creditors. ...

Taking all these circumstances into account I propose to declare that Mr David and Mr Murphy are liable to make a contribution to the assets of PMC of £75,000. ...

NOTES

(1) Although Knox J expressed the opinion that the jurisdiction under s 214 should be exercised 'in a way which will benefit unsecured creditors', it appears that the primary beneficiary of his order was the company's bank, since the compensation which he ordered to be paid went in the first place to discharge the company's secured overdraft. The Cork committee appears similarly to have assumed that the wrongful trading remedy would improve the lot of the general creditors.

(2) In related proceedings (*Re Produce Marketing Consortium Ltd* [1989] 3 All ER 1, [1990] 1 WLR 745) it was held that a person held liable under s 214 for wrongful trading may not seek relief under CA 1985, s 727 on the ground that he 'acted honestly and reasonably and ought fairly to be excused'.

(3) In *Re DKG Contractors Ltd* [1990] BCC 903 the respondent was held liable to the company under IA 1986, s 212 (misfeasance), s 214 (wrongful trading) and s 239 (preference). The court ordered that these liabilities should not all be cumulative but that payments made under ss 212 and 239 should go towards satisfying the liability under s 214.

(4) A transaction at an undervalue may also be challenged under IA 1986, s 423 ('transactions defrauding creditors'), which replaces earlier legislation that can be traced back at least as far as 1571. Under this provision there are no time limits and the company need not be in liquidation or even insolvent; but it must be shown that the transaction was entered into *for the purpose* of putting assets

beyond the reach of a creditor or potential creditor or of prejudicing the interests of such a person. For an example, see *Arbuthnot Leasing International Ltd v Havelet Leasing Ltd (No 2)* [1990] BCC 636, where a company's business and assets had been transferred on legal advice to an off-the-shelf company shortly before it went into receivership, and the court ordered the reversal of the trans-action.

QUESTIONS

(1) What difference might the insolvency legislation of 1986 have made to the outcome of the following cases:
  (a) *Salomon v Salomon & Co Ltd* (**12**);
  (b) the *Multinational Gas* case (**143**);
  (c) *Re Horsley & Weight Ltd* (**68, 98**);
  (d) *Re Halt Garage (1964) Ltd* (**123**)?

(2) Would any of the persons concerned in the cases (a) to (d) above have been liable to disqualification or compensation orders, as directors or shadow directors?

5. *Application of assets*

The assets available to the liquidator in a winding up will include the following (or their proceeds after realisation):

(a) all property beneficially owned by the company at the commencement of the winding up, apart from any property that the liquidator elects to disclaim under IA 1986, ss 178 ff;
(b) unpaid calls recovered from contributories;
(c) moneys paid out of capital within the preceding twelve months for the repurchase of shares and recovered from past members and directors (s 76);
(d) money or property recouped as a result of a court order nullifying a 'transaction at an undervalue' entered into within the preceding two years (s 238);
(e) property and money paid away by the company within the preceding six months (or, if the recipient is a 'connected person', two years) and recovered by the liquidator as a preference (s 239);
(f) property disposed of after the commencement of the liquidation under transactions which are invalidated by s 127, unless the court orders other-wise;
(g) property not fully seized in execution or distress (s 183), or attached after the commencement of the winding up (s 128);
(h) property recovered and compensation ordered to be paid by court order made against directors and others on the grounds of misfeasance (s 212), fraudulent trading (s 213) and wrongful trading (s 214).

The liquidator will take the assets subject to any security validly created in favour of a debentureholder or other creditor prior to the commencement of the winding up unless it is:

(a) void against the liquidator for non-registration under CA 1985, s 399;
(b) void as a preference under s 239;
(c) a *floating* charge created within the preceding twelve months or, if the

chargee is a 'connected person', two years), except to the extent that it is valid under s 245.[17]

Property in the hands of the company will also be taken by the liquidator subject to any equities and set-offs enforceable against the company before it went into liquidation.

The claims of a secured creditor rank in principle ahead of any claim in the winding up—including even the costs of the liquidation. But a *floating* charge-holder must first meet the claims of the preferential creditors under s 175 and also—somewhat anomalously—the expenses of the winding up (unless the charge had already crystallised before the commencement of the liquidation): *Re Barleycorn Enterprises Ltd* [1970] Ch 465, [1970] 2 All ER 155, CA.

Assets will be applied, after the claims of secured creditors (other than holders of floating charges) have been satisfied, in the following order of priority:

(a) the costs of the liquidation;
(b) the debts declared to be preferential debts by s 386 and Sch 6: broadly speaking, this means twelve months' PAYE and social security payments, six months' VAT, and employees' accrued holiday pay and arrears of wages or salary earned during the preceding four months, subject in the latter case to a maximum of £800;[18]
(c) floating charge-holders;
(d) unsecured creditors—but note that some loans made to the company by shareholders, such as moneys paid in advance of calls and sums due by way of dividends, are postponed to outside creditors (s 74(2)(f));
(e) interest on all debts proved in the winding up (s 189);
(f) money due to a member under a contract to redeem or repurchase shares which has not been completed prior to the winding up (CA 1985, s 178);
(g) the debts due to members mentioned in (d) above;
(h) repayment of capital to preference shareholders;
(i) repayment of capital to ordinary shareholders.

Any 'surplus assets' then go to whoever is entitled under the memorandum and articles; normally, this will be the ordinary shareholders.

A contract under which creditors agree to vary the statutory rules governing the distribution of a company's assets in a liquidation is contrary to public policy and void.

292 British Eagle International Air Lines Ltd v Cie Nationale Air France
[1975] 1 WLR 758, [1975] 2 All ER 390 (House of Lords)

Many airlines set up a 'clearing house' scheme under which their mutual debts and credits were not set off one against another but were pooled with a third party, IATA. Under the agreement, participants could not claim against each other but only against IATA for any net balance due to the particular airline under the scheme. British Eagle went into liquidation at a

---

17 See above, p 403.
18 A bank or other creditor which has lent the company funds to pay these wages is entitled to the same priority.

time when it was a net debtor to the scheme in respect of its aggregated claims but, as between itself and Air France, it was a net creditor. The liquidator successfully challenged the legality of the clearing house arrangement.

LORD CROSS OF CHELSEA: [What] the respondents are saying here is that the parties to the 'clearing house' arrangements by agreeing that simple contract debts are to be satisfied in a particular way have succeeded in 'contracting out' of the provisions contained in [CA 1948], s 302 [IA 1986, s 107] for the payment of unsecured debts 'pari passu'. In such a context it is to my mind irrelevant that the parties to the 'clearing house' arrangements had good business reasons for entering into them and did not direct their minds to the question how the arrangements might be affected by the insolvency of one or more of the parties. Such a 'contracting out' must, to my mind, be contrary to public policy. The question is, in essence, whether what was called in argument the 'mini liquidation' flowing from the clearing house arrangements is to yield to or to prevail over the general liquidation. I cannot doubt that on principle the rules of the general liquidation should prevail ...

LORDS DIPLOCK and EDMUND-DAVIES concurred.

LORDS MORRIS OF BORTH-Y-GEST and SIMON OF GLAISDALE dissented.

NOTE

There are strong arguments for saying that it may often be in the interests of public policy to allow creditors to vary the statutory priorities by arrangement among themselves. One particular situation where this is so is when the existing creditors of a company that is in difficulties are willing to let a new creditor advance money in an attempt to save the company from liquidation, on the understanding that if the attempt is unsuccessful the claim of the 'rescuer' should not rank equally with their own. The *British Eagle* case indicates that a 'subordination agreement' of this kind is unlawful. The Cork Committee recommended that subordination should be permitted by law, but the Insolvency Act has done nothing to implement this proposal. However, it can in fact be achieved in practice by the use of more elaborate techniques than a simple contractual arrangement.

Special legislative provision has been made by Part VII of CA 1989 to allow 'netting' arrangements of the type rejected in the *British Eagle* case to be used by investment exchanges, clearing houses and money market institutions and in banking settlement arrangements.

It is sometimes possible to avoid the application of the *British Eagle* ruling by establishing a *trust,* so that the sum which would ordinarily be payable as a debt to a particular creditor is held by the company as a trustee on his behalf: see *Re Kayford Ltd* [1975] 1 All ER 604, [1975] 1 WLR 279; *Carreras Rothmans Ltd v Freeman Mathews Treasure Ltd* [1985] Ch 207, [1985] 1 All ER 155. The courts have, on occasion, been prepared to *infer* the existence of a trust in such circumstances: e g *Barclays Bank Ltd v Quistclose Investments Ltd* [1970] AC 567, [1968] 3 All ER 651, HL.

In the United States, the courts have developed an equitable jurisdiction in which they have a discretion to subordinate the claims of some creditors to others—e g to postpone the claims of creditors who are members of the same corporate group. It would require legislation to bring about any reform along these lines in this country.

6. Dissolution; reinstatement

The corporate entity created under the Companies Act ceases to exist by the formal act of *dissolution,* which takes place automatically three months after the registrar has been notified of the completion of the winding-up procedure (IA 1986, ss 94, 106, 172(8), 201, 205). It is, however, possible for a dissolved company to be reinstated by court order, subject to a two-year time-limit[19]— a step which may be necessary if, e g further assets are discovered, or someone wishes to bring a damages claim for which the former company was insured (CA 1985, s 651).

A company also ceases to exist when it is struck off the register (a purely administrative act performed by the registrar under CA 1985, s 652). Again, there is provision for restoration to the register by court order; but for this purpose the limitation period is twenty years. Restoration, unlike reinstatement, is retrospective in its effect, validating everything that has been done in the name of the company during the period when it was struck off.

The Insolvency Act 1986, ss 202–204 establishes a new procedure for the early dissolution of an insolvent company against which a compulsory winding-up order has been made: if the Official Receiver is satisfied that its assets are not sufficient to cover winding-up expenses and that its affairs require no further investigation, he may notify the Registrar of Companies and, unless some interested person intervenes meantime, the company is dissolved automatically three months later.

---

19 This time-limit is extended to 20 years where an application is made under CA 1985, s 651(5), for the purpose of bringing proceedings against the company for damages for personal injuries or damages under the Fatal Accidents Act 1976.

Appendix

[The forms and tables which follow are reproduced by permission of the persons and bodies mentioned on p xiii, to whom acknowledgment is again made.]

A. Forms

1. Certificate of incorporation
2. Memorandum of association
3. Prospectus (listing particulars)
4. Directors' annual report and accounts
5. Letter to shareholders containing rights offer
6. Provisional allotment letter
7. Take-over offer
8. Form of acceptance and authority
9. Share certificate (preference shares)
10. Debenture (with summary of trust deed)
11. Debenture (fixed and floating charge)

B. The City Code on Take-overs and Mergers

C. Tables

1. Summary of changes in the number of companies on the register, 1990–91
2. Public and private companies incorporated and on the register, 1990–91
3. New company registrations analysed by type, 1990–91
4. Number of new registrations of companies having a share capital: analysed by amount of nominal capital, 1990–91
5. Liquidations notified, 1990–91
6. Inspection of company records at Companies Registration Offices, 1990–91

A. Forms

1. Certificate of incorporation

No 561235

[Royal Arms]
Certificate of Incorporation
I Hereby Certify, That

VARSITY PUBLICATIONS LIMITED

is this day Incorporated under the Companies Act 1948, and that the Company is Limited.

Given under my hand at London this *Tenth* day of *February* One Thousand Nine Hundred and Fifty *six.*

WB Langford
Registrar of Companies

2. Memorandum of association[1]

The Companies Act 1948
COMPANY LIMITED BY SHARES
MEMORANDUM OF ASSOCIATION
of
VARSITY PUBLICATIONS LIMITED

1. The name of the Company is 'VARSITY PUBLICATIONS LIMITED'.
2. The registered office of the Company will be situate in England.
3. The objects for which the Company is established are—

(A) To acquire and take over as a going concern the business at present carried on by certain undergraduate members of the University of Cambridge in connection with the production and publication of the newspaper known as 'Varsity' and the handbook known as 'Hand Book' and the copyrights and other assets thereof and also the liabilities thereof.
(B) To carry on business as proprietors, printers and publishers of newspapers, journals, magazines, periodicals, books and other literary undertakings of any kind with a view to providing training and experience for graduate and undergraduate members of the University of Cambridge in as many branches of journalism as possible.

---

1 Table A may be taken as typical of a company's articles of association. It will be observed that Table B and Table F are not typical of the modern company's memorandum. (For these Tables, see SI 1985/805.)

(c) To carry on any other trade or business whatsoever which can, in the opinion of the Board of Directors, be advantageously carried on by the Company in connection with or as ancillary to any of the above businesses or the general business of the Company.

(D) To purchase, take on lease or in exchange, hire or otherwise acquire and hold for any estate or interest any lands, buildings, easements, rights, privileges, concessions, patents, patent rights, licences, secret processes, machinery, plant, stock-in-trade, and any real or personal property of any kind necessary or convenient for the purposes of or in connection with the Company's business or any branch or department thereof.

(E) To erect, construct, lay down, enlarge, alter and maintain any roads, railways, tramways, sidings, bridges, reservoirs, shops, stores, factories, buildings, works, plant and machinery necessary or convenient for the Company's business, and to contribute to or subsidise the erection, construction and maintenance of any of the above.

(F) To borrow or raise or secure payment of money for the purposes of or in connection with the Company's business...[2]

(G) To mortgage and charge the undertaking and all or any of the real and personal property and assets, present or future, and all or any of the uncalled capital for the time being of the Company...

(H) To issue and deposit any securities which the Company has power to issue by way of mortgage ... and also by way of security...

(I) To receive money on deposit or loan...

(J) To make advances to customers and others...

(K) To grant pensions, allowances, gratuities and bonuses ... and to support or subscribe to any charitable funds or institutions, the support of which may, in the opinion of the Directors, be calculated directly or indirectly to benefit the Company or its employees...

(L) To draw, make, accept, endorse, negotiate, discount and execute promissory notes, bills of exchange and other negotiable instruments.

(M) To invest and deal with the moneys of the Company...

(N) To pay for any property or rights acquired by the Company, either in cash or fully or partly paid-up shares...

(O) To accept payment for any property or rights sold [in any form]...

(P) To enter into any partnership...

(Q) To establish or promote or concur in establishing or promoting any other company...

(R) To purchase or otherwise acquire [other businesses]...

(S) To sell, improve, manage, develop, turn to account, exchange, let ... and in any other manner deal with or dispose of the undertaking and all or any of the property and assets for the time being of the Company for such consideration as the Company may think fit.

(T) To amalgamate with any other company...

(U) To distribute among the members in specie any property of the Company...

(V) To do all or any of the above things in any part of the world, and either as principals, agents, trustees, contractors or otherwise...

(W)To do all such other things as are incidental or conducive to the above objects or any of them.

4. The liability of the members is limited.

2 [This and the succeeding objects clauses have been greatly curtailed.]

5. The share capital of the Company is £100, divided into 100 shares of £1 each. The shares in the original or any increased capital may be divided into several classes, and there may be attached thereto respectively any preferential, deferred or other special rights, privileges, conditions or restrictions as to dividend, capital, voting or otherwise.

[The Memorandum is then signed, dated and attested as in Table B.]

3. Prospectus (listing particulars)[3]

[This prospectus has been much abbreviated.]

A copy of this document, which comprises listing particulars with regard to Micro Scope plc ('Micro Scope' or the 'Company') in accordance with The Stock Exchange (Listing) Regulations 1984,[4] has been delivered to the Registrar of Companies in England and Wales for registration in accordance with those Regulations.

Application has been made to the Council of The Stock Exchange for the ordinary share capital of the Company issued and now being issued to be admitted to the Official List. The listing particulars have been approved by the Council of The Stock Exchange.

The directors of the Company (the 'Directors'), whose names appear in this document, are the persons responsible for the information contained in this document. To the best of the knowledge and belief of the Directors (who have taken all reasonable care to ensure that such is the case) the information contained in this document is in accordance with the facts and does not omit anything likely to affect the import of such information. The Directors accept responsibility accordingly.

MICRO SCOPE plc

(Incorporated in England under the Companies Acts 1948 to 1976 – No. 1424455)

Offer for Sale

by

Kleinwort, Benson Limited

of 3,200,000 Ordinary Shares of 10p each
at a price of 120p per share payable in full on application

Applications for the Ordinary Shares now being offered for sale must be received by 10.00 a.m. on Tuesday, 18 June 1985. The application list will close as soon thereafter as Kleinwort, Benson Limited may determine. The procedure for application and an Application Form are set out at the end of this document.

SHARE CAPITAL

		Issued and fully paid following
Authorised		*this Offer for Sale*
£1,350,000	in Ordinary Shares of 10p each	£1,067,353

The Ordinary Shares now offered for sale rank in full for all dividends hereafter declared, made or paid.

3 The Financial Services Act 1986 makes a distinction between *Listing Particulars,* issued in respect of securities which have an official Stock Exchange listing, and a *prospectus,* for securities which do not. (See FSA 1986, Parts IV and V, respectively.) But the term 'prospectus' may be used in a generic sense to refer to both types of document.

4 [Now FSA 1986, Part IV.]

INDEBTEDNESS

At the close of business on 24 May 1985, the Company had outstanding secured loans amounting to £600,000, £250,000 unsecured loan stock and other unsecured loans amounting to £56,000. . . .

SUMMARY INFORMATION

The following information should be read in conjunction with the full text of this document, from which it is derived:

Business

Micro Scope supplies technical consultancy, design and development services for the application of microprocessor technology. It has become a leader in the field of interactive videotex communications. The Company's videotex products have been installed in both private and public videotex networks for customers in Europe and Australasia. The public telecommunications authorities of Belgium, New Zealand and Norway have selected the Company's products for their national videotex networks.

The founders' belief that profitable products would emerge from a consultancy-based business remains a central part of Micro Scope's corporate philosophy. Established in 1979, Micro Scope has developed a major product in each year from 1980 to 1984 and further products are being introduced in 1985. In addition to its range of videotex products, the Company has developed general data communications products and a range of software packages.

Over the last five years, turnover has increased over tenfold from £253,000 in the year ended 31 October 1980 to £2,596,000 in the year ended 31 October 1984. Profit before taxation has increased from £17,000 in the year ended 31 October 1981 to £594,000 in the year ended 31 October 1984 and is forecast to be not less than £1,000,000 in respect of the year ending 31 October 1985.

OFFER FOR SALE STATISTICS

Issued share capital

Ordinary Shares issued and now being issued   10,673,528

Offer for sale price

120p per Ordinary Share

Market capitalisation

£12.8 million

Forecast results for the year ending 31 October 1985

Turnover   £3,700,000

Profit before taxation   £1,000,000

Earnings per Ordinary Share
   —based on the anticipated 30 per cent tax charge   7.14p
   —based on a notional 35 per cent tax charge   6.63p

Price earnings multiple
   —based on the anticipated 30 per cent tax charge   16.8 times
   —based on a notional 35 per cent tax charge   18.1 times

Dividends

Net dividends per Ordinary Share which the Directors would
   have expected to recommend if the Company's shares had
   been listed throughout the year ending 31 October 1985   1.5p

Gross dividend yield based on the above indicated net dividends
   per Ordinary Share of 1.5p (equivalent to 2.14p with the
   related tax credit at the current rate)   1.79%

[There follow particulars of the company's directors, secretary and registered office, and its professional advisers for the issue. The 'summary information' given above is then elaborated in a detailed account extending over many pages. This includes descriptions of the company's history, business, current developments, markets, customers and marketing, manufacturing and supplies, management and employees, property, financial record, current trading and profit forecast, and dividends. The document continues:]

REASONS FOR THE ISSUE

The shares being offered for sale include 1,950,000 shares being sold by certain of the existing shareholders of the Company. The subscription of the balance of 1,250,000 shares will, after deducting the expenses of the Offer for Sale, raise approximately £1 million of new permanent capital for the Company.

The Directors regard the listing of Micro Scope's shares as a significant event in the Company's development as a vigorous and progressive business. The Directors believe that the listing will enhance the status of the Company with customers and suppliers and assist it to attract new personnel of the highest calibre

Immediately following the Offer for Sale, the £250,000 outstanding unsecured loan stock will be repaid. Part of the balance of the capital raised for the Company will be applied in financing the new premises, to the extent not covered by internally generated resources. The remaining capital will support an increasing level of trading and provide greater flexibility to take advantage of growth opportunities which may arise.

The Directors also recognise that the ability to offer listed securities may facilitate acquisitions. They have not as yet actively pursued an acquisition policy but will give consideration to any suitable opportunities.

PROSPECTS

The Directors believe that, with the development of new and increasingly complex technology and the continual growth of the information technology industry, the demand for broadly-based technical consultancy will continue to increase. Micro Scope's reputation for supplying well researched and designed solutions should ensure that the Company retains its position in this market.

The founders' belief that profitable products would emerge from a consultancy-based business remains a central part of Micro Scope's corporate philosophy. Early signs for the Company's products launched in late 1984 and 1985 are encouraging and further products will be introduced in the remainder of the year. . . .

The Company is continuously extending its product range in response to market conditions. For instance, a number of public telecommunications authorities are planning the introduction of high speed digital data communication lines. Micro Scope has already designed an enhanced version of Videogate, compatible with the existing model, to take advantage of the increased performance of these new lines.

Micro Scope has an established reputation in the fields of microprocessor applications and communications technology and also as a supplier of a range of quality products. The Directors are confident of the Company's continuing success both in the United Kingdom and overseas.

ACCOUNTANTS' REPORT

The Directors,
Micro Scope plc,

and

The Directors,
Kleinwort, Benson Limited.

11 June 1985

Gentlemen,

We have reviewed the audited financial statements of Micro Scope plc (the 'Company') for the five years ended 31 October 1984 and the six months ended 30 April 1985. We have acted as auditors to the Company throughout the period under review. . . .

The financial summaries set out . . . below are based on the audited financial statements of the Company prepared under the historical cost convention. No adjustments were necessary. In our opinion, for the purposes of the Offer for Sale document to be dated 12 June 1985, the financial summaries present a true and fair view under the historical cost convention of:

(i) the results and source and application of funds of the Company for the five years ended 31 October 1984 and the six months ended 30 April 1985; and

(ii) the state of affairs of the Company at 31 October in each of the years 1980 to 1984 and at 30 April 1985. . . .

[Profit and loss accounts for the periods in question, balance sheets and a statement of source and application of funds follow, set out over six pages.]

Yours faithfully,

Thornton Baker
Chartered Accountants

GENERAL INFORMATION

1. The Company and its share capital

(1) The Company was incorporated in England on 31 May 1979 as a private limited company (with registered number 1424455) under the Companies Acts 1948 to 1976 with the name Gendeve Limited. On 10 August 1979 the name of the Company was changed to Micro Scope Limited. The Company was re-registered as a public limited company on 25 February 1985 with the name Micro Scope plc.

(2) The Company is the holding company of the company referred to in paragraph 2 below. The principal objects of the Company as set out in Clause 4 of its Memorandum of Association are to carry on the business of a computer utility organisation. The Company's registered office and principal place of business are at Mill Lane, Taplow, Maidenhead, Berkshire SL6 0AA.

(3) (a) On 1 June 1982 the authorised share capital of the Company was £100 divided into 100 Ordinary Shares of £1 each, all of which had been issued fully paid or credited as fully paid. . . .

[There follows an account of a number of increases and other alterations in the company's share capital. On the occasion of the latest of these increases in share capital, the members had agreed to disapply the provisions of CA 1980, s 17 (CA 1985, s 89).]

    (g) Following completion of the Offer for Sale the authorised share capital of the Company will be £1,350,000 divided into 13,500,000 Ordinary Shares of 10p each of which 10,673,528 will be issued and fully paid or credited as fully paid and will as from 26 July 1985 be in registered form.

    (h) The provisions of section 17 of the Companies Act 1980 [CA 1985, s 89] (which, to the extent not disapplied, confer on shareholders rights of pre-emption in respect of the allotment of equity securities which are or are to be issued for cash) apply to the authorised but unissued Ordinary Shares which are not the subject of the disapplication referred to above. The statutory rights of pre-emption have been disapplied in order (i) to permit the Directors to allot the Ordinary Shares being subscribed under this Offer for Sale at a price per share considered appropriate by the Directors after consultation with Kleinwort Benson and (ii) to give the Directors flexibility in relation to rights issues and issues of Ordinary Shares for cash involving up to 5 per cent of the authorised share capital of the Company. Notwithstanding the disapplication, the continuing obligations for listed companies require that, in the absence of special Stock Exchange dispensation or the approval of shareholders in general meeting, equity securities to be issued for cash must be offered in the first place to existing holders of equity securities in proportion to their holdings.

(4) (a) Save as disclosed in paragraph 1(3) above and in paragraphs 3 and 6(2) below:

    (i) no share or loan capital of the Company or its subsidiary has within the three years preceding the date of this document been issued or is proposed to be issued fully or partly paid either for cash or for a consideration other than cash;

    (ii) no commissions, discounts, brokerages or other special terms have within the same three year period been granted by the Company or its subsidiary in connection with the issue or sale of any share or loan capital; and

    (iii) no share or loan capital of the Company or its subsidiary is under option or has been agreed conditionally or unconditionally to be put under option.

(b) 286,472 Ordinary Shares will remain authorised but unissued following completion of the Offer for Sale. No material issue of Ordinary Shares (except to shareholders pro rata to existing holdings) will be made within one year of the date of this document without the prior approval of the Company in general meeting. No issue of Ordinary Shares will be made which would effectively alter the control of the Company without the prior approval of the Company in general meeting.

2. Subsidiary company[Details omitted.]

3. Offer For Sale arrangements

By an agreement (the 'Offer for Sale Agreement') dated 12 June 1985 and made between the Directors (1) Weedrush and others (the 'Vendors') (2) P R Malton and others (the 'Convenantors') (3) Kleinwort Benson (4) and the Company (5):

(a) Kleinwort Benson has agreed, subject to the entire share capital of the Company issued and now being issued being admitted to the Official List by not later than 2 July 1985, to purchase from the Vendors 1,950,000 Ordinary Shares of 10p each at a price of 117.6p per share, to subscribe for 1,250,000 Ordinary Shares of 10p each at a price of 120p per share, and to offer all such shares for sale to the public at a price of 120p per share (the 'Offer for Sale price');

(b) The Company has agreed to pay to Kleinwort Benson a commission of 2 per cent on the total value of the shares for which it has agreed to subscribe at the Offer for Sale price, plus VAT thereon; Kleinwort Benson will pay an underwriting commission of $1\frac{1}{4}$ per cent on the aggregate value at the Offer for Sale price of the shares being offered for sale; all other costs, charges and expenses of the incidental to the Offer for Sale and the application for admission to the Official List will be borne by the Company;

(c) the Directors and the Company have given certain warranties and indemnities to Kleinwort Benson and the Covenantors have given certain indemnities to Kleinwort Benson and to the Company against liabilities to taxation; and

(d) certain of the vendors (the 'Major Vendors') have agreed not to dispose of any shares in the Company retained by them following the Offer for Sale prior to the conclusion of the Annual General Meeting at which the accounts of the Company for the year ending 31 October 1986 are laid before it without the prior written consent of Kleinwort Benson.

The Major Vendors include Weedrush [an investment company] (573,900 Ordinary Shares), P R Malton and certain of his family interests (425,000 Ordinary Shares), C J Sealy and certain of his family interests (425,000 Ordinary Shares), and P F Shimell and certain of his family interests (425,000 Ordinary Shares).

4. Directors' and other interests

(1) The interests (as defined in the Companies Act ...), all of which are beneficial, of the Directors in the Ordinary Shares of 10p each of the Company immediately following completion of the Offer for Sale will be as follows:

[Details omitted.]

5. Directors' service contracts

(1) The following is a summary of the Directors' service contracts:

[Details omitted.]

6. Employee Share Schemes

(1) *Micro Scope Profit Sharing Scheme*

The Company adopted a scheme on 15 May 1985 which contains the following principal features:

[Details omitted.]

7. Articles of Association

[Details omitted.]

8. Material contracts

The following contracts, not being contracts in the ordinary course of business, have been entered into within two years immediately preceding the date of this document and are or may be material:

[Details omitted.]

9. Property

The principal establishments of the Company are as follows:

[Details omitted.]

10. Taxation

(1) The Directors have been advised that, following completion of the Offer for Sale, the Company will be a close company within the meaning of the Income and Corporation Taxes Act 1970.

(2) The Company has received clearance under section 464 of the Income and Corporation Taxes Act 1970 in respect of the transactions involved in this Offer for Sale.

(3) When the Company pays a dividend, it must (subject to any set-off in respect of tax withheld on its franked investment income) remit to the Inland Revenue an amount of advance corporation tax at a rate which is related to the basic rate of income tax and is currently 3/7ths of the dividend paid.

11. Working capital

The Directors are of the opinion that, taking into account available bank facilities and the net proceeds of the Offer for Sale receivable by the Company, the Company has sufficient working capital for its present requirements.

12. General

(1) The total costs payable by the Company in connection with this Offer for Sale are estimated to amount to £450,000 (and VAT of approximately £65,000 attributable thereto). The estimated net cash proceeds accruing to the Company from the Offer for Sale are approximately £1 million and will be used as described in 'Reasons for the Issue'.

(2) The Ordinary Shares now offered for sale have a nominal value of 10p each and the issue premium is 110p per share.

(3) Neither the Company nor its subsidiary is, or has in the twelve months prior to the date hereof, been engaged in or threatened with any litigation or arbitration proceedings which may have or has had a significant effect on the financial position of the Company and no litigation or claim or threat thereof which may have such effect is known to the Directors.

(4) Save as disclosed herein, there has been no significant change in the financial or trading position of the Company and its subsidiary since 30 April 1985 being the date of the latest audited interim financial statement.

(5) Thornton Baker, Chartered Accountants, have given and have not withdrawn their written consent to the issue of this document with the inclusion herein of copies of their report and letter in the form and context in which they are respectively included.

(6)[5] The financial information concerning the Company and its subsidiary contained in this document does not amount to [statutory] accounts within the meaning of section [240] of the Companies Act [1985]. [Statutory] accounts relating to each financial year to which the financial information relates have been delivered to the registrar of companies. Thornton Baker have made a report under section [235] of the Companies Act [1985] in respect of each such set of accounts and each such report was an unqualified report within the meaning of section [240(3)(d)] of the Companies Act [1985].

13. Documents for inspection

Copies of the following documents may be inspected at the offices of Macfarlanes, 10 Norwich Street, London EC4A 1BD during usual business hours on any weekday (Saturdays and public holidays excepted) for a period of fourteen days from the date of publication of this document:

(1) the Memorandum and Articles of Association of the Company;
(2) the audited consolidated accounts of the Company and its subsidiary for the two years ended 31 October 1984 and the six months ended 30 April 1985;
(3) the Accountants' Report set out herein;
(4) the Directors' service contracts referred to in paragraph 5 above;
(5) the rules of the employee share schemes referred to in paragraph 6 above;
(6) the material contracts referred to in paragraph 8 above;
(7) the written consent referred to in paragraph 12 above; and
(8) the letters relating to the profit forecast set out herein.

Dated 12 June 1985.

PROCEDURE FOR APPLICATION

Application must be made on the Application Form provided and must be for a minimum of 100 Ordinary Shares or in one of the following multiples:

– for not more than 2,000 shares, in multiples of 100 shares.
– for more than 2,000 shares, but not more than 10,000 shares, in multiples of 500 shares.
– for more than 10,000 shares, but not more than 20,000 shares, in multiples of 1,000 shares
– for more than 20,000 shares, but not more than 50,000 shares, in multiples of 5,000 shares.
– for more than 50,000 shares, in multiples of 10,000 shares.

You must send the completed Application Form by post, or deliver it by hand to Lloyds Bank Plc, Registrar's Department, Issue Section, PO Box 1000, 61 Moorgate, London, EC2R 6BL, so as to arrive not later than 10 a.m. on Tuesday, 18 June 1985.

The right is reserved to present all cheques and bankers' drafts for payment on receipt by the receiving bankers.

5 [The text has been altered so that the language and references correspond with amendments made to the former law by CA 1989.]

DEALING ARRANGEMENTS

The basis on which applications have been accepted will be announced as soon as possible after the application list closes. It is expected that letters of acceptance will be posted to successful applicants on Monday, 24 June 1985 and that dealings in the Ordinary Shares will commence on Tuesday, 25 June 1985.

Arrangements will be made for registration by the Company of all the Ordinary Shares now offered for sale, free of stamp duty and registration fees, in the names of purchasers or persons in whose favour letters of acceptance are duly renounced provided that, in cases of renunciation, letters of acceptance (duly completed in accordance with the instructions contained therein) are lodged for registration by 3.00 pm on 25 July 1985. Share certificates will be despatched on 8 August 1985.

A total of 320,000 Ordinary Shares will be made available to meet applications from employees of the Company.

APPLICATION FORM

Micro Scope plc

Offer for Sale by Kleinwort, Benson Limited of 3,200,000 Ordinary Shares of 10p each at 120p per share

I/We offer to purchase from Kleinwort, Benson Limited ...... **Ordinary Shares** of 10p each in Micro Scope plc at 120p per share on the terms and subject to the conditions overleaf

and I/we attach a cheque or bankers' draft for the amount payable of £.....

Signature

Mr, Mrs, Miss or title   Forename(s) (in full)

. . . .
Surname

. . . .
Address (in full)

. . . .

. . . .
Postcode

TERMS AND CONDITIONS

(a) Acceptance of applications will be conditional upon the Ordinary Shares being admitted to the Official List of The Stock Exchange not later than 2 July 1985 (and on or before that date your remittance may be presented for payment and, if so, it will be kept by Lloyds Bank Plc in a separate bank account). If the Ordinary Shares are not so admitted your application money will be returned (without interest).

(b) Kleinwort, Benson Limited ('Kleinwort Benson') reserves the right to reject or scale down any application and, in particular, multiple or suspected multiple applications. If any application is not accepted or is scaled down, the application moneys, or the balance thereof, as the case may be, will be returned (without interest) by crossed cheque through the post at the risk of the person(s) entitled thereto.

(c) By completing and delivering an Application Form, you (as the applicant):

    (i) offer to purchase the number of Ordinary Shares specified in your Application Form (or such smaller number for which the application is accepted) on the terms of and subject to the conditions set out in the prospectus dated 12 June 1985 (the 'Prospectus') and subject to the Memorandum and Articles of Association of the Company;

    (ii) authorise Lloyds Bank Plc to send a letter of acceptance for the number of Ordinary Shares for which your application is accepted, and/or a cheque for any money returnable by post, at the risk of the person(s) entitled thereto to the address of the person (or the first-named person) named in the Application Form and to procure that your name (together with the names of any other joint applicants) is/are placed on the register of members of the Company in respect of such Ordinary Shares the entitlement to which has not been effectively renounced;

    (iii) agree that, in consideration of Kleinwort Benson's agreeing to consider applications upon the terms and subject to the conditions set out in the Prospectus, your application may not be revoked until after 2 July 1985 and that this paragraph shall constitute a collateral contract between you and Kleinwort Benson which will become binding upon receipt by Lloyds Bank Plc of your application;

    (iv) warrant that your remittance will be honoured on first presentation;

    (v) agree that all applications, acceptances of applications and contracts resulting therefrom under this Offer for Sale shall be governed by and construed in accordance with English law;

    (vi) warrant that, if you sign the Application Form on behalf of somebody else, you have due authority to do so;

    (vii) agree that any letter of acceptance and any moneys returnable may be retained by Lloyds Bank Plc pending clearance of your payment; and

    (viii) confirm that in making such application you are not relying on any information or representations in relation to the Company other than those contained in the Prospectus and accordingly agree that no person responsible for the Prospectus or any part of it shall have any liability for any such other information or representations.

QUESTION

Can you suggest why the company chose to market its shares with the low nominal value of 10p and to do so at a premium of 110p, rather than with a nominal value closer to the issue price?

4. Directors' annual report and accounts[6]

MICRO SCOPE plc

Report and Accounts

for the year ended 31 October 1986

REPORT OF THE DIRECTORS

The directors present their report together with the financial statements for the year ended 31 October 1986.

Principal activity

The company supplies technical consultancy, design and development services for the application of microprocessor technology and develops, assembles and distributes a range of communications and other products.

Results

The profit for the year after taxation amounted to £640,000. An interim dividend of £56,000 was paid in July 1986 and the directors recommend a final dividend absorbing £107,000, making a total of £163,000, leaving £477,000 retained and transferred to reserves.

Post balance sheet events

No events having a material effect on the financial position of the company have taken place since the balance sheet date.

Directors

The directors in office at the end of the year are listed below. All served on the board throughout the year. M C Stead and N R Toeman retire by rotation and being eligible, offer themselves for re-election at the Annual General Meeting to be held on 26 January 1987.

The unexpired period of the directors' service contracts at the balance sheet date was five months, apart from M C Stead who does not have a service contract with the company.

The beneficial and other interests of the directors and their families in the shares of the company at 1 November 1985 and at 31 October 1986, as recorded in the register maintained by the company in accordance with the provisions of the Companies Act 1985, were as follows:

[Details omitted.]

---

6 Including notice of annual general meeting.

In the period between 31 October 1986 and 10 December 1986, there were no changes in these holdings.

No director had, during or at the end of the year, any material interest in a contract which was significant in relation to the company's business.

Research and development

The company's policy is to write off research and development expenditure in the period in which it is incurred.

Employee share schemes

The employee profit sharing scheme was adopted by the company on 11 May 1985 and is open to eligible employees. The trustees of the scheme have been allocated £8,000 to purchase ordinary shares in the company. There is also an executive share option scheme as descibed in note 17.

Tax status

The directors are of the opinion that the company is a close company within the provisions of the Income and Corporation Taxes Act 1970.

Substantial shareholders

At 31 October 1986 the following, other than directors, had an interest in 5% or more of the issued share capital of the company having full voting rights:

[Details omitted.]

Auditors

Grant Thornton offer themselves for reappointment as auditors in accordance with section 384(1) of the Companies Act 1985.

ON BEHALF OF THE BOARD

P. F. SHIMELL
Secretary

10 December 1986

MICRO SCOPE plc

PROFIT AND LOSS ACCOUNT

for the year ended 31 October 1986

	1986	*1985*
	£'000	£'000
Turnover	4,896	3,873
Change in stock of finished goods and work in progress	74	38
Total operating output	4,970	3,911
Operating charges and other operating income	3,914	2,805
Operating profit	1,056	1,106
Interest payable	115	27
Profit on ordinary activities before taxation	941	1,079
Taxation	301	297
Profit on ordinary activities after taxation	640	782
Dividends	163	157
Profit retained	477	625
Statement of retained profits		
Retained profits at 1 November 1985	855	230
Retained profit for year to 31 October 1986	477	625
Retained profits at 31 October 1986	1,332	855
Earnings per ordinary share of 10p	6.0p	8.0p

MICRO SCOPE plc

BALANCE SHEET AT 31 OCTOBER 1986

	1986		1985	
	£'000	£'000	£'000	£'000
Fixed assets				
Tangible assets		2,840		2,331
Investment		— —		— —
Current assets				
Stocks	550		571	
Debtors	2,455		1,311	
Cash at bank and in hand	50		425	
	3,055		2,307	
Creditors: amounts falling due within one year	1,633		1,345	
Net current assets		1,422		962
Total assets less current liabilities		4,262		3,293
Creditors: amounts falling due after more than one year		1,040		528
Provision for liabilities and charges		74		94
		3,148		2,671
Capital and reserves				
Called up share capital		1,067		1,067
Share premium account		749		749
Profit and loss account		1,332		855
		3,148		2,671

The financial statements were approved by the Board of Directors on 10 December 1986.

P R MALTON

               Directors

C J SEALY

MICRO SCOPE plc

STATEMENT OF SOURCE AND APPLICATION OF FUNDS

for the year ended 31 October 1986

	1986		*1985*	
	£'000	£'000	£'000	£'000
Source of funds from operations				
Profit on ordinary activities before taxation		941		1,079
Adjustment for items not involving the movement of funds				
Depreciation		227		126
Total generated from operations		1,168		1,205
From other sources				
Proceeds of disposal of tangible fixed assets	5		9	
Bank loan (secured)	440		600	
Loan stock (unsecured)	— —		250	
Issue of shares	— —	445	2,100	2,959
		1,613		4,164
Application of funds				
Dividend paid	(163)		(50)	
Taxation paid	(92)		(258)	
Purchase of tangible fixed assets	(740)		(2,012)	
Short-term loan repaid	— —		(600)	
Unsecured loan stock repaid	— —		(250)	
Share issue expenses	— —		(434)	
Bank loan repayments	(8)		(48)	
		(1,003)		(3,652)
Net inflow of funds		610		512
Increase/(decrease) in working capital				
Stocks		(21)		385
Debtors		1144		53
Creditors: amounts falling due within one year		66		(167)
		1189		271
Net liquid funds				
Cash at bank and in hand	(375)		122	
Bank overdraft	(204)		119	
		(579)		241
Net increase in working capital		610		512

REPORT OF THE AUDITORS TO THE MEMBERS OF
MICRO SCOPE plc

We have audited the financial statements [above] in accordance with approved Auditing Standards.

In our opinion the financial statements, which have been prepared under the historical cost convention, give a true and fair view of the state of the company's affairs at 31 October 1986 and of its profit and source and application of funds for the year then ended and comply with the Companies Act 1985.

GRANT THORNTON

London
19 December 1986

NOTICE OF ANNUAL GENERAL MEETING

MICRO SCOPE PLC

NOTICE IS HEREBY GIVEN that the Annual General Meeting of the Company will be held at 9.00 am on 26 January 1987 at The Connaught Rooms, 61 Great Queen Street, London WC2 for the following purposes:

ORDINARY BUSINESS

1. To receive and, if approved, adopt the Report of the Directors and Financial Statements for the year ended 31 October 1986.
2. To declare a final dividend.
3. To re-elect Nicholas R Toeman as a Director of the Company.
4. To re-elect Martin C Stead as a Director of the Company.
5. To re-appoint the Company's Auditors until the next Annual General Meeting.
6. To authorise the Directors to fix the remuneration for the Auditors.

SPECIAL BUSINESS

To consider and, if thought fit, pass the following Resolution which will be proposed as a Special Resolution:

7. THAT the Board be and is hereby empowered pursuant to Section 95 of the Companies Act 1985 to allot equity securities (within the meaning of Section 94(2) of the said Act) for cash pursuant to the authority conferred by a Special Resolution of the Company passed on 10 June 1985 as if subsection (1) of Section 89 of the said Act did not apply to any such allotment provided that this power shall be limited to:

   (a) the allotment of equity securities in connection with a rights issue in favour of ordinary shareholders where the equity securities respectively attributable to the interests of all ordinary shareholders are proportionate (as nearly as may be) to the respective numbers of Ordinary Shares held by them subject to such exclusions or arrangements as the Directors may deem necessary or desirable to deal with fractional entitlements otherwise arising or legal or practical problems under the laws of, or the requirements of, any recognised regulatory authority in any territory; and

   (b) the allotment (otherwise than pursuant to sub-paragraph (a) above) of equity securities provided that the maximum number of Ordinary Shares so allotted does not exceed an aggregate nominal value of £67,500;

   and shall expire on the date of the next Annual General Meeting of the Company after the passing of this Resolution save that the Company may before such expiry make an offer or agreement which would not or might require equity securities to be allotted after such expiry and the Board may allot equity securities in pursuance of such offer or agreement as if the power conferred hereby had not expired.

BY ORDER OF THE BOARD
Paul F Shimell,

Dated 2 January 1987 *Secretary*

NOTES:

1. Any member who is entitled to attend and vote at this meeting is entitled to appoint a proxy to attend and vote instead of him. A proxy need not be a member of the Company.

The instrument appointing a proxy and the power of attorney or other authority (if any) under which it is signed or a notarially certified copy of such power or authority must be lodged at the offices of the Registrars of the Company, Lloyds Bank Plc, Registrar's Department, Goring-by-Sea, Worthing, West Sussex BN12 6DA not less than 48 hours before the meeting or adjourned meeting at which it is to be used and in default shall not be treated as valid. There is enclosed a form of proxy for use if required.

2. The Directors' contracts of service are available for inspection during normal business hours at the Registered Office of the Company until 26 January 1987 when the documents will be available for inspection 15 minutes prior to and during the course of the Annual General Meeting.

3. The dividend, if approved, will be paid on 29 January 1987 to members on the register at the close of business on 2 January 1987.

5. Letter to shareholders containing rights offer

This document is important and requires your immediate attention.

If you are in any doubt as to the action you should take, you should consult your stockbroker, bank manager, solicitor, accountant or other professional adviser immediately....

This document comprises, *inter alia*, listing particulars with regard to Tricentrol PLC in accordance with The Stock Exchange (Listing) Regulations 1984[7] and the requirements of the Council of The Stock Exchange. A copy of this document has been delivered for registration to the Registrar of Companies, as required by such Regulations.

The Council of The Stock Exchange has granted permission for the Convertible Unsecured Loan Stock now being issued to be admitted to the Official List.

TRICENTROL PLC

Rights Issue of £46,332,668 11 per cent Convertible Unsecured Loan Stock 1995/2005 at par.

TRICENTROL PLC

Registered Office
Capel House
New Broad Street
London EC2M 1JS

(Registered in England No 145954)

18 February 1985

To the holders of ordinary shares

Dear Shareholder,

RIGHTS ISSUE OF £46,332,668 CONVERTIBLE STOCK

It was announced on 14 February 1985 that Tricentrol is raising approximately £45.3 million (after estimated expenses of approximately £1 million) by the issue at par of £46,332,668 11 per cent Convertible Unsecured Loan Stock 1995/2005 by way of rights to shareholders in the proportion of £1 nominal of Convertible Stock for every 2 shares held. The issue has been underwritten by Morgan Grenfell & Co Limited; the brokers to the issue are de Zoete & Bevan.   I am now giving you the details of the issue and the reasons for the need for additional funds.

7 Now FSA 1986, Part IV.]

Description of the Group

The Group is engaged in the business of exploring for and producing oil and gas in the UK sector of the North Sea, onshore UK, in Canada, the United States and elsewhere. Subsidiary companies are engaged in trading crude petroleum and petroleum products. The Group's principal oil and gas producing properties are the Thistle and Buchan fields in the North Sea, the Wytch Farm oil field in Dorset, in Montana and the Gulf of Mexico in the United States and in Alberta, Canada.

Reasons for the issue

It is Tricentrol's policy to finance exploration and appraisal costs either from cash-flow generated from existing operations or from issues of equity or equity-related capital. Bank borrowing is used to finance development expenditure either on a project basis or secured against regional operating company credit.

Tricentrol intends to maintain a high level of exploration expenditure during the next two years which is, I believe, justified by recent successful programmes. During 1984 the activities of our Exploration Departments added 40 per cent to our proven and probable reserves. As a result of these and earlier exploration successes, appraisal programmes for Blocks 48/11b, 43/26 and 44/22 and the Amethyst field in the southern basin of the North Sea, the Don field in Block 211/18a and the Talisman oil discovery in Block WA 191P in Australia require substantial funding.

The proceeds of the proposed rights issue of Convertible Stock will finance the planned exploration and appraisal programmes. Your Directors consider that this issue, made by way of rights to the Company's shareholders, is the most appropriate method of raising funds in the present market conditions.

Details of the issue

The Convertible Stock offered by way of rights has been provisionally allotted to holders of Tricentrol ordinary shares on the register at the close of business on 8 February 1985, in the proportion of £1 nominal of Convertible Stock for every 2 Tricentrol ordinary shares then held and in the same proportion for any other number of Tricentrol ordinary shares. Fractions of £1 nominal of Convertible Stock have not been so allotted, but have been aggregated and may be sold in the market for the benefit of the Company.

The main details of the Convertible Stock are as follows:

Interest	11 per cent per annum (subject to deduction of income tax) payable half-yearly on 31 May and 30 November, commencing on 31 May 1985.
Conversion Price	The effective conversion price at the issue price of par is 200p per Tricentrol ordinary share, based on the conversion rate of 50 shares per £100 nominal of Convertible Stock. This compares with a price of 203p per share on 13 February 1985 (the latest practicable date prior to the printing of this document) being the

	middle market quotation derived from The Stock Exchange Daily Official List.
Conversion Periods	The month of June in each of the years 1988 to 1995 inclusive.

The first payment of interest on the Convertible Stock, in respect of the period from 11 March 1985 to 31 May 1985, will be made on 31 May 1985 and will amount to £2.47 (subject to deduction of income tax) per £100 nominal of Convertible Stock.

The Company has the right to repay at par any Convertible Stock in whole or in part on or at any time after the sixtieth day following the final conversion date. Any Convertible Stock outstanding on 30 November 2005 will be repaid at par on that date together with accrued interest. The Convertible Stock will be in registered form following the issue of Stock Certificates. Following the expiry of the Provisional Allotment Letters, which act as temporary documents of title, the Convertible Stock will be transferable by reference to the Register.

Profit estimate and dividend forecast

The Board of Tricentrol estimates that, on the basis referred to in paragraph 2 of Part II of this document, profit after taxation and before extraordinary charges for the year ended 31 December 1984 was approximately £30.0 million (1983: £24.2 million). The Board of Tricentrol intends, in the absence of unforeseen circumstances, to recommend a final dividend of 6p net per share payable on 31 May 1985, making a total dividend for the year ended 31 December 1984 of 10p net per share (1983: 10p net). Given the extensive exploration and appraisal programmes to be undertaken in 1985, the Board of Tricentol envisages that the level of dividends for the year ending 31 December 1985 will be maintained but not increased.

US and Canadian shareholders

The nominee for Morgan Guaranty Trust Company of New York, as depositary for holders of ADRs, has been provisionally allotted Convertible Stock in respect of the ADRs. The Convertible Stock has not been (nor will be) registered under US securities laws or qualified for sale or exchange under Canadian securities laws. Accordingly such provisionally alloted Convertible Stock will be sold outside the USA and Canada in the market nil paid, if a premium can be obtained. Any net proceeds will be distributed *pro rata* by cheque to the holders of ADRs as of a record date which is expected to be 4 March 1985.

The attention of holders of ordinary shares who have registered addresses in the United States or Canada is drawn to paragraph 11 of Part III of this document.

Procedure for acceptance

The enclosed Provisional Allotment Letter contains full instructions regarding acceptance, payment, renunciation and registration. If you wish to subscribe for the Convertible Stock to which you are entitled, the enclosed Provisional Allotment Letter, together with a remittance for the full amount payable on acceptance, must be lodged, in accordance with the instructions printed thereon, with Barclays Bank PLC, New Issues Department, PO Box 123, Fleetway House, 25 Farringdon Street, London EC4A 4HD, so as to be received not later than 3.00 pm on 11 March 1985. Cheques should be made payable to 'Barclays Bank PLC' and crossed 'Not Negotiable' and be drawn on a bank in the United Kingdom. If you wish to sell all or part of your rights, you should follow the instructions on the face of the enclosed Provisional Allotment Letter relating to renunciation and splitting and which are summarised in paragraph 12 of Part III of this document.

Any Convertible Stock not taken up by 3.00 pm on 11 March 1985 will be deemed to have been declined and will be sold in the market not later than the close of business on 13 March 1985 if it is possible to obtain a premium over the subscription price and expenses of sale. Any net proceeds (after deducting the subscription price and expenses) will be distributed *pro rata* by cheque among the provisional allottees originally entitled thereto whose rights have not been taken up, except that no payment will be made of any amount of less than £2, which will be retained for the benefit of the Company.

UK taxation

Summary information on UK taxation of capital gains and income which may arise in connection with the Convertible Stock is given in paragraph 9 of Part III of this document.

If you are in any doubt as to your tax position in the UK or elsewhere, you should consult your professional adviser.

Further information

Your attention is drawn to the further information which appears in Parts II, III and IV of this document.

Yours sincerely,

JGS LONGCROFT

Chairman

[Parts II, III and IV (which are omitted) give further details about the company and the group, profit estimate and prospects, and information about the stock offered and the stockholders' conversion rights.]

6. Provisional allotment letter

[This is the renounceable provisional allotment letter referred to in the letter of rights set out above.]

IMPORTANT

The securities represented hereby have not been registered under the United States Securities Act of 1933 and have not been qualified for sale or exchange under the Securities Laws of Canada or any Province or Territory of Canada and may not be offered or sold directly or indirectly in the United States or Canada or to US persons or to Canadian persons.[8] Expressions used in this paragraph are as defined in the circular letter enclosed herewith.

This document is of value and is negotiable. If you are in any doubt about it or if prior to receiving it you have sold (other than ex rights) all or part of your registered holding of ordinary shares in the company, you should consult your stockbroker, bank manager, solicitor, accountant or other professional adviser immediately. This offer expires at 3 pm on 11 March 1985.

List Particulars relating to Tricentrol PLC required by The Stock Exchange (Listing) Regulations 1984 have been published and are contained in the Circular Letter dated 18 February 1985 enclosed herewith additional copies of which may be obtained from or inspected at: the registered office of the Company; at Barclays Bank PLC, Registrars Department, Radbroke Hall, Knutsford, Cheshire WA 16 9EU; and at the Company Announcements Office, The Stock Exchange, Throgmorton Street, London EC2P 2BT.

The Council of The Stock Exchange has granted permission for the Convertible Stock now being issued to be admitted to the Official List.

TRICENTROL PLC

Registered Office
Capel House
New Broad Street
London EC2M 1JS

(Registered in England No 145954)

18 February 1985

RIGHTS ISSUE OF £46,332,668 11 PER CENT CONVERTIBLE
UNSECURED LOAN STOCK 1995/2005 AT PAR
Payable in full on acceptance not later than 3 pm on 11 March 1985

Provisional Allotment Letter

(1) Holding of ordinary shares as at 8 February 1985: . . . .
(2) Nominal Amount of Convertible Stock provisionally allotted to you:
(3) Amount payable on acceptance of the Convertible Stock provisionally allotted to you by 3 pm on 11 March 1985: . . . .

---

8 [See Note (2) below, p 632.]

Last dates (by 3 pm in each case) for:

Splitting (nil paid)	7 March 1985
Acceptance and payment	11 March 1985
Splitting (fully paid)	24 April 1985
Registration of Renunciation	26 April 1985

Stock certificates will be despatched on 24 May 1985

Dear Sir or Madam,

As explained in the accompanying Circular Letter dated 18 February 1985 your Directors have decided to issue £46,332,668 nominal of 11 per cent Convertible Unsecured Loan Stock 1995/2005 (the 'Convertible Stock') at par by way of rights and you have been provisionally allotted the nominal amount of Convertible Stock set out in box (2)[9] above. Allotments have been made to ordinary shareholders on the register at the close of business on 8 February 1985 in the proportion of £1 nominal of Convertible Stock for every 2 ordinary shares then held. Fractions of £1 nominal of Convertible Stock will not be allotted but will be aggregated and may be sold in the market nil paid if a premium in excess of the expenses of sale can be obtained for the benefit of the Company. Transfers of the Company's ordinary shares lodged with the Registrars for registration by 8 February 1985 were recorded on the register of members by that date.

Interest on the Convertible Stock will be payable half-yearly on 31 May and 30 November in each year. The first payment will be made on 31 May 1985 in respect of the period from 11 March 1985 to 31 May 1985 and will amount to £2.47 (subject to deduction of tax) per £100 nominal of Convertible Stock.

Acceptance and payment. If you wish to accept all the Convertible Stock provisionally allotted to you, this Letter must be lodged with BARCLAYS BANK PLC, NEW ISSUES DEPARTMENT, PO POX 123, FLEETWAY HOUSE, 25 FARRINGDON STREET, LONDON EC4A 4HD accompanied by a remittance for the full amount due (shown in box(3)[9] above) not later than 3 pm on 11 March 1985. Such remittance when received will constitute acceptance of this provisional allotment in accordance with the aforesaid terms and subject to the Trust Deed to constitute the Convertible Stock. This Letter, with the receipt at the foot hereof duly completed, will be returned to the person making payment who, unless named above, must complete the appropriate Paying Agent's box at the foot hereof. If this Letter is not lodged by 3 pm on 11 March 1985 the provisional allotment will be deemed to have been declined, and will lapse. Cheques must be made payable in pounds sterling to 'Barclays Bank PLC' and crossed 'Not Negotiable' and be drawn on a bank in the United Kingdom. No interest will be allowed on payments made before the due date.

Any Convertible Stock not taken up by 3 pm on 11 March 1985 may be sold in the market not later than the close of business on 13 March 1985 if it is possible to obtain a premium over the subscription price and expenses of sale. Any net proceeds (after deduction of the subscription price and expenses) will be distributed *pro rata* among the provisional allottees originally entitled thereto whose rights have not been taken up, except that no payment will be made of any amount of less than £2, which will be retained for the benefit of the Company.

9 [Boxes not shown.]

Renunciation, splitting and registration. See the instructions below which form an integral part of this Letter.

Stock certificates. In the case of persons originally entitled thereto who accept their provisional allotment, Stock Certificates will be despatched by post at the risk of the person(s) entitled thereto on 24 May 1985 to the registered holder or, in the case of joint holders, to the first-named registered holder, unless between 26 April 1985 and 17 May 1985 this Letter (with the stamp or, as the case may require, name and address of the person(s) lodging it impressed or inserted in the panel overleaf) is lodged with Barclays Bank PLC in which case the Stock Certificate will be despatched on 24 May 1985 to the person(s) lodging this Letter. In the case of renunciation Stock Certificates will be despatched on 24 May 1985 to the person(s) lodging the Letter for registration at the risk of the person(s) entitled thereto. After 24 May 1985 this Letter will cease to be valid for any purpose whatsoever.

Transfers. After 26 April, and pending the issue of Stock Certificates, instruments to transfer will be certified by the Company's Registrars against lodgment of fully paid Letters and/or against Form Z bearing the stamp of Barclays Bank PLC.

By Order of the Board,
HR HARLOW,
Secretary

Renunciation, splitting and registration

[There follow detailed instructions as to the procedure for 'splitting' the stock amongst several allottees, consolidating the stock comprised in more than one allotment letter, and renouncing the stock in favour of other persons.]

FORM X **FORM OF RENUNCIATION**
To the Directors of
Tricentrol PLC

I/We hereby renounce my/our right to the Convertible Stock specified in this Letter in favour of the person(s) named in the Registration Application Form, Form Y, below.

....

All Joint Allottees must sign. *Signature(s)*

....

In the case of a Corporation ....
the Common Seal must be affixed.
Dated .... **1985.** ....

Forms of Renunciation on Split Allotment Letters will be marked 'Original duly renounced'.

FORM Y **REGISTRATION APPLICATION FORM**
In the event of renunciation this Form must be completed by or on behalf of the person(s) in whose name(s) the Convertible Stock is to be registered.

FULL NAME(S) AND FULL POSTAL ADDRESS(ES)

Full name(s) (stating title, if any, or whether Mr, Mrs or Miss) and full postal address(es) (including postal code(s)) of the person(s) in whose name(s) the Convertible Stock is to be registered.

To the Directors of
Tricentrol PLC

I/We request registration in the above name(s) of the Convertible Stock specified in this Letter and in the Provisional Allotment Letters (if any) detailed in the Consolidation Listing Form totalling £   nominal Convertible Stock, subject to the Circular Letter and the Trust Deed to constitute the Convertible Stock.

I/We hereby declare that I am not/we are not a US Person or a Canadian Person and am/are not acquiring any of the Convertible Stock referred to herein for the account of any US Person or any Canadian Person or with a view to the offer or sale of any Convertible Stock or the ordinary shares issuable upon conversion thereof in the United States or Canada or to US Persons or Canadian Persons.

Dated   1985   Signature:

FORM Z   **TRICENTROL PLC**

In the event of renunciation this Form must be completed by the person lodging this Letter of registration.

Issue of £46,332,668 11 per cent Convertible Unsecured Loan Stock 1995/2005

LODGED for registration by (Name) ....
of (Address) ....
....

Provisional Allotment Letter(s) for £   Convertible Stock in the name(s) of
(name(s) as in Form Y)
A Stock Certificate will be despatched on 24 May 1985 to the person or agent by whom this Letter is lodged for registration. Until this time transfers will be certified by the Company's Registrar against surrender of this Form.

7. Take-over offer

GEC

Recommended Offer

by

de Zoete & Bevan Limited

on behalf of

The General Electric Company plc

to acquire the whole of the share capital of

MICRO SCOPE PLC

LETTER FROM THE CHAIRMAN OF MICRO SCOPE

27 May 1987

To Micro Scope shareholders and participants in the Micro Scope Executive Share Option Scheme.

Dear Sir or Madam,

Recommended Cash Offer on behalf of GEC

On 12 May 1987, I wrote to you setting out a press announcement which stated that agreement had been reached with GEC on the terms of an offer to be made for the whole of the share capital of Micro Scope. I am writing to you to explain the background to the Offer and why your Board unanimously recommends that you accept.

Over the last two years, Micro Scope has undergone a period of rapid and impressive growth. Turnover grew by some 89 per cent between 1984 and 1986 and exports have increased significantly. The number of staff at Micro Scope, in the same period, has more than doubled. However, these achievements were not reflected in increased profitability in 1986 and the Micro Scope share price has suffered as a result. It has become clear that a larger resource base is needed to ensure that Micro Scope is able to develop and exploit commercial opportunities as effectively as possible.

It was against this background that your Board decided, after careful consideration, to accept the approach made to it by GEC. In addition to GEC providing the resources of Britain's largest manufacturing business, the activities of its computer subsidiary, GEC Computers Limited, and those of Micro Scope are complementary in a number of product areas, notably in videotex, where Micro Scope is a market leader, and in data communications. Micro Scope's success has been due in large part to the skills and dedication of its staff. GEC has indicated that it recognises the importance of Micro Scope's staff to Micro Scope's future profitability.

Details of the Offer are set out in the letter from de Zoete & Bevan Limited [below].

The Offer of 150p in cash per Micro Scope share values Micro Scope at approximately £16.0 million and represents an increase of 61 per cent over the middle market quotation, as derived from The Stock Exchange Daily Official List, of 93p per Mirco Scope share on 8 May 1987, the last business day before the announcement of the Offer. The price represents a multiple of 25 times earnings for the year ended 31 October 1986, and a premium of 408 per cent to shareholders' funds as disclosed in the latest accounts. You will see that there is an alternative of 150p nominal of GEC Loan Notes per Micro Scope share, particulars of which are set out in Appendix 4.

The decision as to whether you choose to receive cash, GEC Loan Notes or a combination of each will depend, inter alia, upon your personal circumstances and your tax position. . . .

If you are in any doubt as to whether or not you should elect for GEC Loan Notes or as to your tax position, you should contact your professional adviser.

Directors of Micro Scope, together with certain other shareholders ... have irrevocably undertaken to accept, or procure acceptance of, the Offer in respect of 6,507,028 Micro Scope shares (representing approximately 61 per cent of the issued share capital of Micro Scope). The directors of Micro Scope intend to accept the Offer in respect of their own beneficial shareholdings.

Your Board and its advisers, Kleinwort Benson Limited, consider the terms of the Offer to be fair and reasonable and your Board unanimously recommends all shareholders to accept.

Yours faithfully,
Paul Malton,
Chairman.

DE ZOETE & BEVAN LIMITED

27 May 1987

To the shareholders of Micro Scope and participants in the Micro Scope Executive Share Option Scheme

Dear Sir or Madam,

Recommended Cash Offer on behalf of GEC

On 11 May 1987, the Boards of GEC and Micro Scope announced that they had reached agreement on the terms of an offer for the ordinary share capital of Micro Scope. This document contains the formal Offer which we are making on behalf of GEC.

You will see from the letter from your Chairman (which is set out [above] and forms part of this document) that **the directors of Micro Scope and their advisers, Kleinwort Benson Limited, consider the terms of the Offer to be fair and reasonable and the directors of Micro Scope unanimously recommend all shareholders to accept. . . .**

Instructions on how to accept the Offer are set out [below].

1. The Offer

On behalf of GEC, we hereby offer to acquire, on the terms and subject to the conditions set out in this document and in the Form of Acceptance, all the Micro Scope shares on the following basis:

For each Micro Scope share   **150p in cash**

2. The Loan Note Alternative

As alternative consideration under the Offer, a Micro Scope shareholder may elect to receive GEC Loan Notes instead of cash in respect of all or any of the Micro Scope shares in respect of which he accepts the Offer, on the following basis:

For each Micro Scope share   **150p nominal amount
of GEC Loan Notes**

The GEC Loan Notes will carry interest varying with six month London Inter-Bank Bid Rate, will be redeemable at the option of the holders at six month intervals commencing 1 October 1988 and will have a final redemption date in 1992. Particulars of the GEC Loan Notes are set out in Appendix 4 . . .

No application has been or is intended to be made to any stock exchange for the GEC Loan Notes to be listed or dealt in.

3. Terms and conditions

The Micro Scope shares will be acquired free from all charges, liens or encumbrances and together with all rights attaching thereto, including the right to all dividends and other distributions hereafter declared, made or paid.

The Offer is subject to the conditions and to the further terms set out in Appendix 1 of this document and in the Form of Acceptance.

4. Financial effects of acceptance

The following tables show the increases in capital value and income which a holder of one Micro Scope share would obtain as a result of acceptance of the Offer on the bases set out in the notes below:

(a) Capital value	p
Cash consideration or GEC Loan Notes	150
Value of one Micro Scope share	93
Increase	57
This represents an increase of	**61 per cent**
(b) Income	p
Gross income arising from cash consideration or from GEC Loan Notes	13.31
Gross dividends on one Micro Scope share	2.10
Increase	11.21
This represents an increase of	**534 per cent**

Notes:

The above comparisons are calculated on the following bases:

(i) the value of one Micro Scope share is taken as 93p, being the middle market quotation for a Micro Scope share as derived from The Stock Exchange Daily Official List for 8 May 1987, the last dealing day preceding the announcement of the Offer;

(ii) the value of the GEC Loan Notes is taken as par; in the opinion of de Zoete & Bevan, based on current market conditions, the value of the GEC Loan Notes would be approximately par;

(iii) dividend income on one Micro Scope share is based on a dividend of 1.53p per share, excluding the associated tax credit, being the total of the dividends per share paid in respect of the year ended 31 October 1986;

(iv) shareholders are taken to be entitled to a tax credit of 27/73rds of the dividend[10];

(v) the annual income arising from the cash consideration or from the GEC Loan Notes is taken to be $8\frac{7}{8}$ per cent, per annum (being the current six month London Inter-Bank Bid Rate); and

(vi) no account has been taken of any liability to taxation.

5. UK taxation of capital gains

Any liability of a Micro Scope shareholder to UK taxation of capital gains which might arise as a result of acceptance of the Offer will depend upon the individual circumstances of that shareholder and the form of consideration received.

The receipt of cash under the Offer will give rise to a disposal or part disposal for the purposes of UK taxation of capital gains and may give rise to a liability to taxation.

The directors of GEC have been advised that, in the event of an election for the Loan Note Alternative by a holder of Micro Scope shares who, together with persons connected with him, holds no more than 5 per cent of the Micro Scope shares currently in issue, the receipt of GEC Loan Notes by such a holder will not give rise to a disposal for the purposes of UK taxation of capital gains of the Micro Scope shares in respect of which the GEC Loan Notes are received.

Persons electing for the Loan Note Alternative and who, on the basis mentioned above, hold or are treated as holding more than 5 per cent of the Micro Scope shares currently in issue are informed that an application for clearance has been made to the Inland Revenue under section 88 of the Capital Gains Tax Act 1979. If such clearance is not given, the treatment of such persons might differ from that described in the preceding paragraph.

If you are in any doubt as to your tax position, you should consult your professional adviser.

6. Information regarding GEC

GEC is the UK's largest manufacturing business, employing approximately 160,000 people worldwide. It operates internationally in the fields of elec-

10 [At current tax rates, this would be 25/75ths.]

tronic systems and components, telecommunications and business systems, automation and control, medical equipment, power generation, electrical equipment, consumer products and other industrial products.

Included within GEC's telecommunications and business systems group is GEC Computers Limited ('GEC Computers'), a successful company engaged principally in the design, development and manufacture of real-time computers and software for commercial, industrial, research and defence applications. GEC Computers also supplies a comprehensive range of videotex products and is a leading supplier of public videotex systems.

For the year to 31 March 1986, GEC's sales to customers outside the GEC group and profits before tax were £5,253 million and £701 million respectively and net tangible assets at that date were £2,614 million. During the half year to 30 September 1986 sales and profits before tax were £2,511 million and £275 million respectively.

7. Information regarding Micro Scope

Micro Scope was formed in 1979 to provide consultancy, design and development services for the application of microprocessor technology.

In 1982, Micro Scope sold its first videotex product. Videotex is an interactive electronic information system which enables users to execute transactions, as well as to access information, by means of the public telephone systems and inexpensive terminals or modified television sets.

Micro Scope has developed and expanded its videotex and data communications ranges of products and its activities, which have grown to include substantial consultancy and after-sales services, are now carried on in fifteen countries including the United States and several in Western Europe. Overseas clients include the national PTTs of Denmark, Finland and New Zealand. In the UK, Micro Scope has also developed an impressive client list.

For the year to 31 October 1986, Micro Scope's sales and profits before tax were £4.9 million and £941,000 respectively. Earnings per share for the year were 6.0p and dividends per share 1.53p.

8. Reasons for the Offer

The Boards of GEC and Micro Scope believe that the proposed acquisition of Micro Scope will enhance business opportunities for both groups.

As part of a major international group, greater resources will be available to develop and promote aggressively Micro Scope's videotex and other products and services.

The acquisition of Micro Scope will help GEC in the development of its UK and international communications interests. Micro Scope offers GEC a leading position in an important niche market. Micro Scope brings to GEC an innovative product range in networking systems and technical expertise in data communications. GEC brings to Micro Scope access to research, international distribution and a customer base which will enhance the growth of both GEC Computers and Micro Scope.

9. Management and employees

The Micro Scope group will continue to operate under its existing management as part of GEC's computer and software services activities. GEC recognises that Micro Scope's strength derives from the commitment and expertise of its employees and has agreed that existing terms and conditions of employment of Micro Scope's employees will continue to apply and will not be subject to change without prior consultation.

10. Participants in the Micro Scope Share Option Scheme

The Offer extends to any Micro Scope shares issued while the Offer remains open for acceptance pursuant to the exercise of options granted under the Micro Scope Share Option Scheme. Holders of options under the Micro Scope Share Option Scheme should note that they may be liable to income tax on the exercise of their options or on any disposal of the Micro Scope shares acquired on exercise.

11. Procedure for acceptance

[Details omitted. The procedure is described again on the form of acceptance and authority set out below.]

12. Settlement

Cheques in respect of the cash consideration and/or definitive certificates for the appropriate nominal amount of GEC Loan Notes will be despatched to accepting Micro Scope shareholders not later than 14 days after the Offer becomes or is declared unconditional in all respects or 14 days after receipt of a complete and valid acceptance, whichever is the later.

13. Further information

Your attention is drawn to the further information contained in:

Appendix 1—Conditions and further terms of the Offer;
Appendix 2—Financial information relating to the GEC group;
Appendix 3—Financial information relating to the Micro Scope group;
Appendix 4—The GEC Loan Notes; and
Appendix 5—Additional information.

Yours faithfully,
for de ZOETE & BEVAN Limited.
D R Porter
Director.

[There follow five appendices, giving financial and other details about the two companies and further information about the bid.]

8. Form of acceptance and authority

[This form is for the acceptance of the take-over offer set out above.]

Recommended Offer

on behalf of

The General Electric Company plc

for

Micro Scope plc

Form of Acceptance and Authority

ACTION TO BE TAKEN

1. To accept the Offer you must complete and sign Part A (whether or not you wish to elect for the Loan Note Alternative).
2. If you wish to elect for the Loan Note Alternative in respect of some or all of your Micro Scope shares, you must also complete and sign Part B indicating therein the number of Micro Scope shares in respect of which you wish to receive GEC Loan Notes. Such number should not exceeed the number of Micro Scope shares in respect of which you have accepted the Offer in Part A.

AND THEN

3. You should send the completed form (accompanied by your share certificate(s) and/or other document(s) of title) to National Westminster Bank PLC, New Issues Department, PO Box No 79, 2 Princes Street, London EC2P 2BD, as soon as possible, but in any event so as to arrive **not later than 3.00 pm on Wednesday 17 June 1987.** A reply-paid envelope is enclosed for your convenience.

If your share certificate(s) and/or other document(s) of title is/are not readily available or is/are lost, the completed form should nevertheless be delivered as stated above and the document(s) of title forwarded as soon as possible thereafter.

PART A

FORM OF ACCEPTANCE AND AUTHORITY

To: de Zoete & Bevan Limited
      The General Electric Company plc
1. I/We, the person(s) executing this form, have received the recommended offer document dated 27 May 1987 (the 'offer document') from de Zoete & Bevan. The definitions used in the offer document apply in this form. I/We hereby irrevocably accept the Offer, on the terms and subject to the conditions set out in the offer document and this form, in respect of .... Micro Scope shares.

2. Subject to the Offer becoming unconditional in all respects, my/our execution of this form shall constitute my/our irrevocable authority and request:

(a) to GEC or its agents, to send by post at my/our risk a cheque in respect of the cash consideration to which I/we may become entitled to the person or agent whose name and address is set out at the foot of this page or, if none is set out, to the first-named holder at his/her registered address; and
(b) [to certain other persons authorised to execute particular documents on behalf of Micro Scope shareholders in certain circumstances set out in the offer document.]

3. Subject to and with effect from the Offer becoming unconditional in all respects, I/we hereby irrevocably appoint any director of GEC or any director of de Zoete & Bevan or any person nominated by any such director as my/our attorney in my/our or his name and on my/our behalf:

(a) to execute all or any form(s) of transfer and/or other document(s) in the attorney's discretion in relation to the Micro Scope shares in respect of which I/we have, or am/are deemed to have, accepted the Offer and to deliver such form(s) of transfer and/or other documents in the attorney's discretion together with the certificate(s) and other document(s) relating to such Micro Scope shares for registration and to do all such other acts and things as may in the opinion of such attorney be necessary or expedient for the purpose of, or in connection with, the acceptance of the Offer and, if applicable, election for the Loan Note Alternative and to vest in GEC, or its nominee, the Micro Scope shares in respect of which I/we have, or am/are deemed to have, accepted the Offer; and
(b) to sign any consent to short notice of a general meeting of Micro Scope on my/our behalf...

I/We agree to ratify each and every act or thing which may be done or effected by my/our attorney, or any proxy appointed pursuant to the foregoing, in the exercise of his power hereunder.

4. Subject to and with effect from the Offer becoming unconditional in all respects, I/we hereby irrevocably authorise and direct Micro Scope to send any notice, circular, warrant or other document or communication which I/we may be entitled to receive as a member of Micro Scope to me/us at the registered office of GEC.

5. I/We undertake to execute any further document(s) and give any further assurance(s) that may be required in connection with my/our acceptance of the Offer.

6. If the Offer lapses, I/we authorise and request GEC or its agents to return this form and the relative share certificate(s) and/or other document(s) of title (if any) by post at my/our risk to the person or agent whose name and address is set out at the foot of this page or, if none is set out, to the first-named holder at his/her registered address.

Please insert full name(s) and address(es) of holder(s).

....

....

SIGNED, SEALED AND DELIVERED BY THE SAID SHAREHOLDER(S)

....

....

Name and address of person to whom the consideration should be sent. If this space is left blank, the consideration will be sent to the first-named holder at his/her registered address.

Name ....

Address ....

PART B

FORM OF ELECTION FOR THE LOAN NOTE ALTERNATIVE

[Details omitted.]

NOTES

(1) The 'Form of acceptance and authority' is somewhat unusual. The more straight-forward way would have been to use a 'Form of acceptance and transfer', attaching a stock transfer form for the selling shareholder to sign and send in with his acceptance.

(2) The exclusion of US shareholders from the loan note alternative made it unnecessary for the bidding company to comply with the onerous SEC Regulations which govern applications inviting people in that country to invest in shares and other securities. The legitimacy of a discriminatory offer of this kind was upheld by Goulding J in *Mutual Life Insurance Co of New York v Rank Organisation Ltd* [1985] BCLC 11.

(3) Micro Scope plc became, as a consequence of this agreed take-over, a wholly owned subsidiary of GEC, in which character it continues to prosper.

9. Share certificate (preference shares)

Security Code   Number of Shares ....
   0–28654–3
   No. 0000

$5\frac{1}{2}$% Cumulative Preference
The Preference Shares confer the dividend and capital rights specified
on the reverse of this certificate
THE DUNLOP COMPANY LIMITED
Incorporated under the Companies Acts

This is to Certify that ....
is/are the registered proprietor(s) of ....
FIVE AND A HALF PER CENT CUMULATIVE PREFERENCE
SHARES OF £1 EACH. *fully paid, in* THE DUNLOP COMPANY
LIMITED, *subject to the Memorandum and Articles of Association of*
the Company.

GIVEN *under the Common Seal of the Company,*
this .... *day of* .... *19* ....

No transfer of any of the Shares represented by this Certificate will be
registered without this Certificate being surrendered to the Company's
Registrars: Midland Bank Limited, Registrar's Department, Beaufort
House, Gravel Lane, London, E1.

[The terms set out on the reverse of the certificate incorporate the 'Spens formula' (see above, p 423:]

The $5\frac{1}{2}$ per cent Cumulative Preference Shares confer the right to receive in priority to all other shares out of the profits of the Company which it shall be determined to distribute a cumulative preferential dividend at the rate of $5\frac{1}{2}$ per cent per annum on the capital paid up thereon and the prior right on a return of assets on liquidation or otherwise to payment of the prescribed sum in respect of every such Preference Share together with payment of all arrears and accruals of the preferential dividend down to the date of repayment of capital (whether earned or declared or not) but do not confer any further right to participate in profits or assets.

The prescribed sum shall be the greater of (a) [£1.10] or (b) the nominal amount paid up on such share together with a sum equal to the amount by which the average of the respective means of the daily nominal quotation of the said Preference Shares on The Stock Exchange, London, during the six months preceding the date of the notice of the meeting at which the Resolution for such liquidation or return of capital is passed exceeds the nominal amount paid up on such share (such average to be calculated and certified by the Auditors of the Company).

10. Debenture (with summary of trust deed)

NMA COMPANY OF NEW ZEALAND LIMITED
(Incorporated in England under the Companies Acts)

DEBENTURE

£..........*Stg*

Date Due ....
NMA Company of New Zealand Limited *hereby acknowledge that they owe to*

....
the sum of .... Pounds sterling for money lent and paid by [him] *to the Company. And they agree on delivery of this Debenture with the receipt endorsed thereon duly completed to pay that sum to* [him] *or to* [his] *..............*
executors administrators or assigns on the .... day of .... or upon such earlier date as the said sum shall become payable pursuant to the provisions of the Trust Deed hereinafter mentioned or upon such subsequent date as may hereafter be mutually agreed upon by minute to be endorsed hereon in London at the Registered Office of the Company for the time being. And they further agree in the meantime and until such payment to pay to the Registered Holder hereof for the time being interest on the said sum in sterling at the rate of .... per cent per annum by half-yearly payments on the .... day of ...... and the ...... day of .... in each year the first of such payments to be made on the .... day of .... next and to be calculated from the .... day of ....
And they further declare that the persons or corporations for the time being entitled to the Debentures now or hereafter to be issued by the Company under the Trust Deed hereinafter mentioned (including this Debenture) are and will be entitled pari passu to the benefit and subject to the provisions of a Trust Deed dated the 31st day of January 1969 and made between the Company of the first part [and others] whereunder (inter alia) the whole of the Company's undertaking and all its property and assets both present and future (including its uncalled capital) are charged by way of a first floating charge with the payment of the principal amount premium and interests and other moneys secured by the said Deed in respect of the Debentures therein referred to including this Debenture.

GIVEN *under the Common Seal of the Company,*
this .... day of .... 19 ....

[The Trust Deed referred to contains 52 clauses and four schedules. By it the company (i) appoints three trustees, two of them corporate; (ii) states that it will issue debentures ranking pari passu, up to prescribed limits; (iii) covenants to pay principal and interest, and to carry on its business efficiently; (iv) gives a floating charge over its undertaking and assets as security; (v) undertakes (subject to prescribed exceptions) not to create other charges ranking in priority or pari passu. It is further provided that (vi) the security shall become enforceable in certain events, with details as to the manner of exercise of the trustees' power of sale and the disposition of the proceeds; (vii) the trustees may appoint a receiver, or enter into possession and carry on the business, in certain events; (viii) the trustees shall be entitled to remuneration. Finally, there are elaborate provisions for the holding of debenture holders' meetings, which may be summoned by the trustees or the company, or requisitioned by the holders of one tenth of the amount currently outstanding.]

NOTE

The issue of debentures in a series in this form, secured under the provisions of a trust deed, is nowadays less common than the issue of *debenture stock.* For this purpose, the whole of the capital which the company intends to borrow is made the subject of a single, consolidated advance by the trustees of a trust deed, and the advance is secured by a single debenture to which the company and the trustees alone are parties. Each individual lender is then given a *debenture stock certificate* for the amount that he advances towards the composite loan. There is no direct contractual relationship between the debenture stock holders and the company (as there is under the debenture reproduced above), but only between the company and the trustees. *Unsecured* loan stock is issued in a similar way, but of course without any charge to secure repayment of the loan.

11. Debenture (fixed and floating charge)

3i PLC

DEBENTURE

dated the   day of   19

Payment Covenant
1. THE Company named in the Second Schedule hereto (hereinafter called 'the Company') HEREBY COVENANTS with 3i plc whose registered office is at 91 Waterloo Road London SE1 8XP (hereinafter called '3i') ... that it will on such date or dates as provided by Clause 2 hereof PAY or DISCHARGE to 3i all moneys and liabilities now or at any time or times hereafter due or owing or incurred by the Company to 3i in any manner whatever whether actually or contingently and whether as principal or surety including interest thereon at such rate as may be agreed in writing from time to time between the Company and 3i whether before or after the execution of this Debenture and together also with all commission charges costs and expenses payable in connection therewith.

Payment Date
2. ALL or any moneys and liabilities due or owing or incurred by the Company to 3i shall be repaid or discharged by the Company on demand unless otherwise agreed in writing from time to time between the Company and 3i whether before or after the execution of this Debenture (such agreement or agreements in writing being hereinafter together referred to as 'the Agreement').

Charging Clause
3. THE Company as beneficial owner HEREBY CHARGES with the payment and discharge to 3i of all moneys and liabilities ... hereby

covenanted to be paid and discharged by the Company and all other sums intended to be hereby secured:—

FIRST—THE property described in the Third Schedule hereto together with all buildings and fixtures (including trade fixtures) and fixed plant and machinery from time to time thereon and therein;

SECOND—ALL other freehold and leasehold property of the Company both present and future together with all buildings and fixtures (including trade fixtures) and fixed plant and machinery from time to time thereon and therein;

THIRD—ALL the plant machinery chattels or other equipment described in the Fourth Schedule hereto ...

FOURTH—THE goodwill and the uncalled capital of the Company both present and future;

FIFTH—THE book debts and other debts due or owing to the Company both present and future;

SIXTH—THE stock-in-trade work-in-progress pre-payments investments quoted on a recognised Stock Exchange and cash of the Company both present and future;

SEVENTH—ALL other the undertaking and all other property and assets of the Company both present and future.

Nature of Charges
4. THE charges on the property and assets FIRST SECOND THIRD FOURTH and FIFTH described are created as fixed charges and constitute charges by way of legal mortgage on the property FIRST and SECOND described which is now vested in the Company ...

The charges on the property and assets SIXTH and SEVENTH described (and also on such other property and assets of the Company both present and future as 3i may have agreed in writing to exclude from the fixed charge or are otherwise not charged hereunder by way of fixed charge) are created as floating charges until a demand has been made under Condition 8 set out in the First Schedule hereto or until the provisions of Condition 9 set out in the First Schedule hereto become operative when the floating charges shall crystallise and become fixed charges.

The charges created hereby shall be a continuing security and shall unless otherwise agreed in writing by 3i be first charges. The Company shall not without the previous written consent of 3i:—

   (i) create or continue any mortgage or charge upon the mortgaged chattels or any part thereof or allow any lien to arise on or affect the mortgaged chattels or any part thereof;

   (ii) create or continue any mortgage or charge upon any part of the other property or assets hereby charged which would rank either in priority to or pari passu with the charges hereby created;

   (iii) allow any lien to arise on or affect any part of the other property or asets hereby charged except in the case of a lien arising by operation of law in the ordinary course of business.

Warranty
5. THE Company HEREBY WARRANTS to 3i that it is the absolute beneficial owner free from all liens charges and encumbrances of all the mortgaged chattels.

Incorporation of Conditions
6. THIS Debenture is issued subject to and with the benefit of the conditions set out in the First Schedule hereto. The property and assets FIRST and SECOND above described are therein referred to as 'the specifically mortgaged property'. The specifically mortgaged property and the property and assets THIRD FOURTH FIFTH SIXTH and SEVENTH described are therein together referred to as 'the mortgaged property'. The bank specified in the Fifth Schedule hereto (or such other bank as 3i may agree to in writing) is therein referred to as 'the Bank'.

EXECUTED as a Deed by the Company the day and year first above written.

THE FIRST SCHEDULE hereinbefore referred to

CONDITIONS

Deposit of deeds and documents of title
1. Subject to the rights of any prior mortgagee the Company shall deposit with 3i and 3i shall during the continuance of this security be entitled to hold and retain all deeds and documents of title relating to the specifically mortgaged property and all invoices documents of title guarantees and maintenance agreements relating to the mortgaged chattels.

Further charges
2. The Company shall forthwith if and when called upon by 3i so to do execute in favour of 3i or as 3i shall direct such further legal or other mortgages or charges as 3i shall require ...

Leases
3. The Company shall pay the rents reserved by and perform and observe all the covenants agreements and stipulations on the part of the lessee contained in any lease or leases of the specifically mortgaged property ...

Payments
4. The Company shall as and when the same shall become payable pay all taxes rates duties charges assessments and outgoings whatsoever ... which shall be assessed charged or imposed upon or payable in respect of the specifically mortgaged property or any part thereof ...

After-acquired property
5. Upon the acquisition or purchase by the Company from time to time of any freehold or leasehold property the Company shall forthwith notify 3i in writing.

Use of premises
6. (A) The Company shall use the specifically mortgaged property only for such purpose or purposes as may for the time being be authorised as the

permitted use or user thereof under or by virtue of the Planning Acts (as hereinafter defined) . . .

Use of chattels
(B) The Company shall not use or permit the mortgaged chattels to be used in contravention of any legislation (as hereinafter defined) or otherwise in any way contrary to law . . .

Development
7. The Company shall not carry out any development within the meaning of the Planning Acts in or upon the specifically mortgaged property or any part thereof without first obtaining such permission as may be required under or by virtue of the Planning Acts . . .

Crystallisation of security subject to demand for repayment
8. In respect of any moneys or liabilities due owing or incurred by the Company to 3i which by virtue of the Agreement are to be discharged otherwise than on demand 3i shall nevertheless be entitled by notice to the Company to demand the immediate payment and discharge thereof (or any part thereof) together with all interest and any other sums forthwith (or otherwise as 3i may require) at any time after the happening of any of the following events:—

(A) if the Company makes default in the payment on due date of any money which may have become due hereunder or under the Agreement or under any deed or document supplemental hereto or thereto;

(B) if any distress execution sequestration or other process is threatened levied or enforced upon or sued out against all or any of the property of the Company or any company or individual who has guaranteed or become surety for repayment of all or any part of the moneys and liabilities hereby secured (hereinafter referred to as 'a Guarantor') or 3i is of the opinion that such property is otherwise in jeopardy;

(C) if the Company or a Guarantor is unable to pay its debts within the meaning of section 123 of the Insolvency Act 1986 or certifies that it is unable to pay its debts as and when they fall due;

(D) if the Company or a Guarantor fails to comply with any of the covenants conditions or provisions contained herein or in the Agreement or in any deed or document supplemental hereto or thereto or if any warranty given by the Company or a Guarantor or any Director (as defined in the Agreement or in any deed or document supplemental thereto) to 3i proves to be materially untrue;

(E) if the specifically mortgaged property or the mortgaged chattels (both as defined herein or in any deed or document supplemental hereto or to the Agreement) or any part thereof is compulsorily acquired by or by order of any local or other authority and as a result the business of the Company or a Guarantor is seriously affected;

(F) if a proposal is made to the Company or a Guarantor and its creditors for a voluntary arrangement pursuant to section 1 of the Insolvency Act 1986;

(G) if a meeting of the Company or a Guarantor is convened for the purpose of considering a resolution for the winding up of the Company or a Guarantor;

(H) if an application is made to the Court for an order for the winding up of the Company or a Guarantor.

If any of the aforementioned events occurs 3i shall be under no obligation to advance any moneys under the Agreement.

Upon any demand being made for payment of any moneys hereby secured such moneys shall become payable immediately and all rights of the Company to deal for any purpose whatever with the mortgaged property or any part thereof shall forthwith cease and any floating charge shall forthwith crystallise and become a fixed charge.

Crystallisation of security without demand
9. The moneys hereby secured shall become immediately payable and all rights of the Company to deal for any purpose whatever with the mortgaged property or any part thereof shall forthwith cease and the floating charges shall forthwith crystallise and become fixed charges on the happening of any of the following events:—

(A) if an order is made for the winding up of the Company or a Guarantor by the court or if an effective resolution is passed for the members' or creditors' voluntary winding up of the Company or a Guarantor;

(B) if a petition is presented for an administration order to be made in relation to the Company or a Guarantor pursuant to the Insolvency Act 1986;

(C) if the Company or a Guarantor stops payment or ceases to carry on its business or substantially the whole of its business or threatens to cease to carry on the same or substantially changes the nature of its business;

(D) if the Company without the previous consent of 3i shall sell transfer lease dispose of or deal with the mortgaged chattels or any part thereof or purport so to do;

(E) if any encumbrancer takes possession or a receiver (as hereinafter defined) is appointed of all or any part of the property and assets of the Company or a Guarantor;

(F) if a Guarantor (being an individual) makes application to the court for a voluntary arrangement pursuant to section 253 of the Insolvency Act 1986 or enters into some other scheme of arrangement with creditors or is unable to pay his debts within the meaning of section 268 of the Insolvency Act 1986 or presents a debtor's petition to the court pursuant to the Insolvency Act 1986.

If any of the aforementioned events occurs 3i shall be under no obligation to advance any moneys under the Agreement.

In this Debenture 'receiver' shall mean both a receiver or receiver and manager of part only of the mortgaged property and an administrative receiver as defined by the Insolvency Act 1986.

Receiver Appointment
10. (A) At any time after the moneys hereby secured shall have become payable or at the request of the Company 3i may without further notice appoint in writing under its hand any person or persons to be a receiver or receivers (hereinafter called a 'Receiver' which expression shall include any substituted receiver or receivers) of all or any parrt of the mortgaged property in like manner in every respect as if 3i had become entitled under the Law of Property Act 1925 to exercise the power of sale thereby conferred and every Receiver so appointed shall have and be entitled to exercise all powers conferred by the said Act as if such Receiver had been duly appointed thereunder and in particular by way of addition to but without hereby limiting any general powers hereinbefore referred to every such Receiver so appointed shall have the powers hereinafter referred to.

Removal
(B) 3i may from time to time by writing under its hand remove any Receiver appointed by it (but in the case of an administrative receiver such removal shall only be with the sanction of the court) and may whenever it may deem it expedient appoint a new Receiver in the place of any Receiver whose appointment may for any reason have terminated and may from time to time fix the remuneration of any Receiver appointed by it.

Powers
(C) At any time after the moneys hereby secured shall have become payable any Receiver appointed hereunder may without further notice exercise all or any of the following powers:—

    (i) take immediate possession of get in and collect the mortgaged property or any part thereof . . .;

    (ii) carry on the business of the Company . . .;

    (iii) make and effect all repairs and insurances and do all other acts which the Company might do in the ordinary conduct of its business as well for the protection as for the improvement of the mortgaged property;

    (iv) sell convert into money and realise all or any part of the mortgaged property . . .;

[Remaining powers omitted.]
In addition to the above powers an administrative receiver may exercise all the powers conferred upon him by Schedule 1 to the Insolvency Act 1986.

Sale
11. Section 103 of the Law of Property Act 1925 shall not apply to this Debenture . . .

Book Debts
12. During the continuance of this security the Company shall:—

(A) pay into a current account or a separate designated account (as 3i may require) of the Company with the Bank all moneys which it may receive in respect of the book debts and other debts hereby charged and (subject to any rights of the Bank in respect thereof) pay or otherwise deal with such moneys standing in such account in accordance with any directions from time to time given in writing by 3i . . .;

(B) if called upon to do so by 3i execute a legal assignment of such book debts and other debts to 3i in such terms as 3i may require and give notice thereof to the debtors from whom the debts are owing or incurred and take such other steps as 3i may require to perfect such legal assignment;

(C) deal with such book debts and other debts in accordance with any directions from time to time given in writing by 3i (subject to any rights of the Bank in respect thereof) and in default of and subject to any such directions deal with the same only in the ordinary course of getting in and realising the same (but not sell assign factor or discount the same in any way) ...

[Clauses 13–29, dealing with obligations of the company to repair, insure, etc are omitted.]

THE SECOND SCHEDULE hereinbefore referred to

Name Registered Office and Registered Number of the Company

THE THIRD SCHEDULE hereinbefore referred to

Description of Freehold or Leasehold property specifically charged

THE FOURTH SCHEDULE hereinbefore referred to

Description of Plant Machinery or Equipment mortgaged

THE FIFTH SCHEDULE hereinbefore referred to

Name and Address of Branch of the Bank

THE COMMON SEAL of THE COMPANY
was hereunto affixed in the
presence of:—

Director

Secretary

THE COMMON SEAL of 3i plc
was hereunto afffixed
in the presence of:—

Authorised Sealing Officer

B. The City Code on Take-overs and Mergers

General principles

INTRODUCTION

It is impracticable to devise rules in sufficient detail to cover all circumstances which can arise in offers. Accordingly, persons engaged in offers should be aware that the spirit as well as the precise wording of the General Principles and the ensuing Rules must be observed. Moreover, the General Principles and the spirit of the Code will apply in areas or circumstances not explicitly covered by any Rule.

While the boards of an offeror and the offeree company and their respective advisers have a duty to act in the best interests of their respective shareholders, these General Principles and the ensuing Rules will, inevitably, impinge on the freedom of action of boards and persons involved in offers; they must, therefore, accept that there are limitations in connection with offers on the manner in which the pursuit of those interests can be carried out...

GENERAL PRINCIPLES

1. All shareholders of the same class of an offeree company must be treated similarly by an offeror.
2. During the course of an offer, or when an offer is in contemplation, neither an offeror, nor the offeree company, nor any of their respective advisers may furnish information to some shareholders which is not made available to all shareholders. This principle does not apply to the furnishing of information in confidence by the offeree company to a bona fide potential offeror or vice versa.
3. An offeror should only announce an offer after the most careful and responsible consideration. Such an announcement should be made only when the offeror has every reason to believe that it can and will continue to be able to implement the offer: responsibility in this connection also rests on the financial adviser to the offeror.
4. Shareholders must be given sufficient information and advice to enable them to reach a properly informed decision and must have sufficient time to do so. No relevant information should be withheld from them.
5. Any document or advertisement addressed to shareholders containing information or advice from an offeror or the board of the offeree company or their respective advisers must, as is the case with a prospectus, be prepared with the highest standards of care and accuracy.
6. All parties to an offer must use every endeavour to prevent the creation of a false market in the securities of an offeror or the offeree company. Parties involved in offers must take care that statements are not made

which may mislead shareholders or the market.

7. At no time after a bona fide offer has been communicated to the board of the offeree company, or after the board of the offeree company has reason to believe that a bona fide offer might be imminent, may any action be taken by the board of the offeree company in relation to the affairs of the company, without the approval of the shareholders in general meeting, which could effectively result in any bona fide offer being frustrated or in the shareholders being denied an opportunity to decide on its merits.

8. Rights of control must be exercised in good faith and the oppression of a minority is wholly unacceptable.

9. Directors of an offeror and the offeree company must always, in advising their shareholders, act only in their capacity as directors and not have regard to their personal or family shareholdings or to their personal relationships with the companies. It is the shareholders' interests taken as a whole, together with those of employees and creditors, which should be considered when the directors are giving advice to shareholders. Directors of the offeree company should give careful consideration before they enter into any commitment with an offeror (or anyone else) which would restrict their freedom to advise their shareholders in the future. Such commitments may give rise to conflicts of interest or result in a breach of the directors' fiduciary duties.

10. Where control of a company is acquired by a person, or persons acting in concert, a general offer to all other shareholders is normally required; a similar obligation may arise if control is consolidated. Where an acquisition is contemplated as a result of which a person may incur such an obligation, he must, before making the acquisition, ensure that he can and will continue to be able to implement such an offer.

[The 'General Principles' are followed by more detailed 'Rules'. Those Rules of particular interest to students include the following:]

2.1 The vital importance of absolute secrecy before an announcement must be emphasised. All persons privy to confidential information, and particularly price-sensitive information, concerning an offer or contemplated offer must treat that information as secret and may only pass it to another person if it is necessary to do so and if that person is made aware of the need for secrecy. All such persons must conduct themselves so as to minimise the chances of an accidental leak of information.

9.1 Except with the consent of the Panel, when:

(a) any person acquires, whether by a series of transactions over a period of time or not, shares which (taken together with shares held or acquired by persons acting in concert with him) carry 30% or more of the voting rights of a company; or

(b) any person who, together with persons acting in concert with him, holds not less than 30% but not more than 50% of the voting rights and such person, or any person acting in concert with him, acquires in any period of 12 months additional shares carrying more than 2% of the voting rights, ...

such person shall extend offers, on the basis set out in Rules 9.3, 9.4 and 9.5, to the holders of any class of equity share capital whether voting or non-voting and also to the holders of any class of voting non-equity share capital in which such person or persons acting in concert with him hold shares. Offers for different classes of equity capital must be comparable; the Panel should be consulted in advance in such cases.

C. Tables[11]

1. Summary of changes in the number of companies on the register, 1990–91

	(000)
On register at start of period	1,115.0
New companies registered	108.7
Dissolved	99.8
Restored to the registers	1.3
On register at end of period	1,125.1
Change on previous year	*0.9%*
Of which: in liquidation	68.3
in course of removal	78.5
Effective numbers on register	
at end of period	978.3
Change on previous year	*2.1%*

2. Public and private companies incorporated and on the register, 1990–91[12]

	(000)
Public companies	
New incorporations	1.4
Conversions from private	1.8
Dissolved	1.1
In liquidation/course of removal	0.9
Effective number on register at end of period	11.7
Public companies as percentage of effective register	*1.1%*
Private companies	
New incorporations	114.0
Conversions from public	0.5
Dissolved	104.3
In liquidation/course of removal	154.0
Effective number on register at end of period	1,020.2
Of which: Unlimited	4.3

11 [Numbers relate to England and Wales, except as stated.]
12 [Including Scotland.]

3. New company registrations analysed by type, 1990–91

	(000)
Total companies incorporated	108.7
With share capital	106.5
Of which: Unlimited	0.1
Average nominal	
share capital (£000s)	*202.0*
Without share capital	2.2

4. Number of new registrations of companies having a share capital: analysed by amount of nominal capital, 1990–91

	(000)
Up to £100	37.2
Over £100 & under £1,000	0.4
£1,000 & under £5,000	55.9
£5,000 & under £10,000	0.6
£10,000 & under £20,000	4.6
£20,000 & under £50,000	0.6
£50,000 & under £100,000	1.8
£100,000 & under £200,000	3.4
£200,000 & under £500,000	0.5
£500,000 & under £1m	0.4
£1m & over	1.2
All companies	106.5
Total nominal share capital (£m)	21,504

5. Liquidations and receiverships notified, 1990–91[13]

	(000)
Compulsory liquidations	6,786
Creditors' voluntary	
liquidations	10,378
Total insolvencies	17,164
Members' voluntary	
liquidations	3,941
Total liquidations	21,105
Receiverships notified	5,327
Administrator appointments	222
Company voluntary	
arrangements	75

13 [In addition 88,600 companies were struck off the register under CA 1985, s 652 during the period.]

6. Inspection of company records at Companies Registration Offices, 1990–91[14]

In the period, some 3,438,000 files were inspected by the public, an average of 3.3 searches per live company.

14 [Including Scotland.]

Index